endorsed for
:BTEC

Pearson
BTEC National
Health and
Social Care

Student Book 1

Marilyn Billingham
Pamela Davenport
Elizabeth Haworth
Nicola Matthews
Beryl Stretch
Hilary Talman

ALWAYS LEARNING

PEARSON

Published by Pearson Education Limited, 80 Strand, London, WC2R 0RL.

www.pearsonschoolsandfecolleges.co.uk

Copies of official specifications for all Edexcel qualifications may be found on the website: www.edexcel.com

Text © Pearson Education Limited
Designed by Andy Magee
Typeset by Tech-Set Ltd
Original illustrations © Pearson Education Ltd
Illustrated by Tech-Set Ltd
Cover design by Vince Haig
Cover photo/illustration © Shutterstock.com: Natalia van D, Passion Images, roroto12p

First published 2016

19 18 17 16

10 9 8 7 6 5 4 3 2

British Library Cataloguing in Publication Data
A catalogue record for this book is available from the British Library

ISBN 978 129212 601 2

Acknowledgements
We would like to thank Andy Ashton for his invaluable help in reviewing this book.

The publisher would like to thank the following for their kind permission to reproduce their photographs:

(Key: b-bottom; c-centre; l-left; r-right; t-top)

123RF.com: Maxim Blinkov 379, rawpixel 349, sjenner13 431; Alamy Images: Ange 439, Arcaid Images 101, Arterra Picture Library 290, BSIP SA 456cr, Caminada Creative 372, Celia Mannings 40, Chris Howes / Wild Places Photography 341, GeoPic 130, Ian Francis stock 125, Ian Leonard 315b, Indigo Images 332, John Birdsall 91, Mark Morgan 447, MBI 77, Mint Images 283, Oleksiy Maksymenko Photography 64, Phanie 458, RichardBaker 450, Shotshop 44, Stocktrek 444; BananaStock: Alamy 456tl; Carers Trust: 244; Fotolia.com: De Visu 99, DeeMPhotography 353, George Wada 389, Joni Hofmann 21, kiattisakch 456tr, Kzenon 137, Lisa F. Young 238, lunamarina 166, Martinan 9, Monkey Business 115, 144, 184r, 258, 380, Pavla Zakova 391, photoniko 295, stocksolutions 89, Volker Witt 293; Getty Images: Hero Images 15, joloei 339; Imagemore Co., Ltd: 25t; Macmillan Cancer Support: 280; MIXA Co., Ltd: 340; Pearson Education Ltd: David Sanderson 338, Gareth Boden 27, 303, 348, Lord and Leverett 111, 269, 326, MindStudio 241, Richard Smith 328, Roddy Paine 24, Jules Selmes 25b, 71, 294, 310, 475; Photofusion Picture Library: John Birdsall 84; Science Photo Library Ltd: BSIP / Laurent 305, Mike Devlin 315t, National Cancer Institute 160; Shutterstock.com: Alsu 271t, beerkoff 288, Charles B. Ming Onn 337, Cheryl E.Davis 301, Djomas 432, EdBookStock 442, GVictoria 476, iko 229, 390, jstudio 23, Marcel Jancovic 233, Maridav 184l, Michaelpuche 85, Monkey Business Images 82, 366, 433, Orla 149, Paul Prescott 1, Poznyakov 249, Robert Kneschke 460, StockLite 358, Sue MacDonald 438, Tyler Olsen 463, v.s.anandhakrishna 347, Voronin 76 300; Widget Health: 271b

All other images © Pearson Education

This book contains information which is © Crown copyright. Contains public sector information licensed under the Open Government Licence v3.0.

The publisher would like to thank the following organisations for their kind permission to reproduce their materials:

p.11 Figure 1.2 Changes in life expectancy chart was found at the Office of National Statistics under a Click Use licence; **p.48** Figure 1.4 Average changes in household incomes bar chart is reproduced by permission of Poverty.org; **p.55** Figure 1.5 The Holmes-Rahe Life Stress Inventory - "This survey is used with special permission by The American Institute of Stress. To read more on this or other stress and health topics please visit www.stress.org"; **p.104** Table 2.3 Examples of types of waste and appropriate methods of disposal was adapted from Nolan, Y (1998) Care NVQ Level 2, p.78. Published by Pearson Education; p.**125** Information on Ofsted: Common inspection framework: education, skills and early years from September 2015 was taken from Ofsted. Used by the Government Open

Licence v.3.0; **p.126** Information on: Care and Social Services Inspectorate Wales is used by the Government Open Licence v. 3.0; **p.126** Information about the Healthcare Inspectorate Wales http://www.hiw.org.uk/about-us. Used with permission; **p.135** Text about MENCAP under heading Learning disability is used with permission of Mencap; **p.108** Text relating to Care Certificate guidelines is used by permission of the NHS Trust; **p.248** Table 5.2 NHS checklist for running a meeting to manage conflict is used under a Government Open Licence v.3.0; **p.243** Case study: Bournewood Hospital was found at: http://www.equalityhumanrights.com The Copyright and all other intellectual property right in the material to be reproduced are owned by, or licensed to, the Commission for Equality and Human Rights, known as the Equality and Human Rights Commission ('The EHRC'); **p.260** Table 5.5 The NHS Patient Experience Framework (2011) is Crown Copyright; **p.263** Table 6.8 Do you know what all the different terms written here mean? Was taken from: "Working Together to Safeguard Children" and used under Government Open Licence v.3.0; **p.271** Makaton signs and symbols (c) Makaton are used with kind permission of The Makaton Charity; **p.287** Figure 5.7 The NHS Confidentiality Model, outlining how patients are to be provided with a confidential service is used under the Government Open Licence v.3.0; **p.307** Case study: Baby P was taken from: https://www.gov.uk/government/uploads/system/uploads/attachment_data/file/182527/first_serious_case_review_overview_report_relating_to_peter_connelly_dated_november_2008.pdf. Used under Government Open Licence v. 3.0; **p.309** Figure 7.1 There are many different forms of abuse and neglect, the effects of which can be long-term and devastating is used with permission from the Advocacy Centre for the Elderly; **p.322** Case Study on Whistleblowing. Was taken from: https://www.england.nhs.uk/wp-content/uploads/2014/11/transforming-commissioning-services.pdf. Used under Government Open Licence. 3.0; **p.326** Assessment activity 7.2 was taken from: https://www.westsussex.gov.uk/media/5171/orchid-view-serious-case-review.pdf. Used under Creative Commons Licence; **p.329** Figure 7.2 The Care Act 2014 replaces previous legislation, consolidating it into one act was taken from: Calderdale.gov.uk. Used with permission; **p.335** Table 7.4 A simple care plan was taken from: http://www.stroke4carers.org/?p=3592. Used by permission of Chest Heart & Stroke Scotland; **p.337** Step-by-step: Hand washing technique was taken from: http://www.nhsprofessionals.nhs.uk. Used under the Government Open Licence v.3.0; **p.362** Figure 10.4 Proportion of employees with no or few qualification who are low paid was taken from: http://www.poverty.org.uk. Used by permission of Poverty.org; **p.381** Table 10.4 Age distribution of the UK population was taken from the Office of National Statistics. Used under the Click Use Licence; **p.382** Figures 10.5 Life expectancy at birth and 10.6 Infant mortality in the UK taken from the Office of National Statistics. Used under the Click Use Licence; **p.383** Figure 10.7 Percentage of UK households by household size pie chart was taken from the Office of National Statistics. Used under a Click Use licence; **p.386** Figure 10.8 Infant death bar chart was taken from: http://www.poverty.org.uk. Used by permission of Poverty.org; **p.418** Treatment of eating disorders was taken from: "Binge Eating: Nature assessment and Treatment" by Fairburn, Marcus and Wilson, published by Guilford Press. Used by permission of Guilford Press.

Websites
Pearson Education Limited is not responsible for the content of any external internet sites. It is essential for tutors to preview each website before using it in class so as to ensure that the URL is still accurate, relevant and appropriate. We suggest that tutors bookmark useful websites and consider enabling students to access them through the school/college intranet.

Contents

How to use this book

Welcome to your BTEC National Health and Social Care course.

You are joining a course that has a 30-year track record of learner success, with the BTEC National widely recognised within the industry and in higher education as the signature vocational qualification. Over 62 per cent of large companies recruit employees with BTEC qualifications and 100,000 BTEC learners apply to UK universities every year.

There are many roles available in the Health and Social Care sector, providing varied opportunities to make a difference to people's lives in a positive way – and the demand for skilled people is growing. Whether you are thinking of pursuing a career in nursing, healthcare science or social work, the BTEC National in Health and Social Care includes pathways that will help you to fulfil your ambition. Once you have completed your studies, whatever you choose to do you will be doing a job that is varied, rewarding and worthwhile.

You will be studying a range of units which will help you to gain skills that will be valuable in your chosen profession or future study. You will learn about the human body and how it changes over time. You will also learn about what it means to work in the sector and what skills and behaviours you will need to demonstrate. If you are studying the larger qualification sizes such as the Foundation Diploma or one of the Extended Diplomas, you will also learn about the principles of safe practice when working in the sector, and the importance of respecting the individual differences and needs of service users.

How your BTEC is structured

Your BTEC National is divided into **mandatory units** (the ones you must do) and **optional units** (the ones you can choose to do). The number of units you need to do and the units you can cover will depend on the type and size of qualification you are doing.

This book covers **units 1, 2, 3, 5, 7, 10, 11 and 14**. If you are doing the **Certificate or Extended Certificate in Health and Social Care**, you will find all the units you need in this book. If you are taking the **Foundation Diploma,** there are all the mandatory units and enough optional units here for you to choose from to complete your course. If you are studying the **Diploma or Extended Diploma**, this book is designed to be used together with the *Pearson BTEC National Health and Social Care Student Book 2*, which includes further mandatory and optional units for these larger sizes of qualification. The table below shows how each unit in this book maps to the BTEC National Health and Social Care qualifications.

Unit title	Mandatory	Optional
Unit 1 Human Lifespan Development	All sizes	
Unit 2 Working in Health and Social Care	All sizes except Certificate	
Unit 3 Anatomy and Physiology for Health and Social Care	Extended Diplomas only	
Unit 5 Meeting Individual Care and Support Needs	All sizes	
Unit 7 Principles of Safe Practice in Health and Social Care	All sizes except Certificate and Extended Certificate	
Unit 10 Sociological Perspectives		All sizes except Certificate and Extended Diploma for Health Studies pathway
Unit 11 Psychological Perspectives		All sizes except Certificate
Unit 14 Physiological Disorders and their Care		All sizes except Certificate

Your learning experience

You may not realise it but you are always learning. Your educational and life experiences are constantly shaping you, your ideas, your thinking, and how you view and engage with the world around you.

You are the person most responsible for your own learning experience so it is really important you understand what you are learning, why you are learning it and why it is important both to your course and your personal development.

Your learning can be seen as a journey which moves through four phases.

Phase 1	Phase 2	Phase 3	Phase 4
You are introduced to a topic or concept; you start to develop an awareness of what learning is required.	You explore the topic or concept through different methods (e.g. research, questioning, analysis, deep thinking, critical evaluation) and form your own understanding.	You apply your knowledge and skills to a task designed to test your understanding.	You reflect on your learning, evaluate your efforts, identify gaps in your knowledge and look for ways to improve.

During each phase, you will use different learning strategies. As you go through your course, these strategies will combine to help you secure the core knowledge and skills you need.

This student book has been written using similar learning principles, strategies and tools. It has been designed to support your learning journey, to give you control over your own learning and to equip you with the knowledge, understanding and tools to be successful in your future studies or career.

Features of this book

In this student book there are lots of different features. They are there to help you learn about the topics in your course in different ways and understand it from multiple perspectives. Together these features:

▶ explain what your learning is about

▶ help you to build your knowledge

▶ help you understand how to succeed in your assessment

▶ help you to reflect on and evaluate your learning

▶ help you to link your learning to the workplace.

In addition, each individual feature has a specific purpose, designed to support important learning strategies. For example, some features will:

▶ get you to question assumptions around what you are learning

▶ make you think beyond what you are reading about

▶ help you make connections across your learning and across units

▶ draw comparisons between your own learning and real-world workplace environments

▶ help you to develop some of the important skills you will need for the workplace, including team work, effective communication and problem solving.

Features that explain what your learning is about

Getting to know your unit

This section introduces the unit and explains how you will be assessed. It gives an overview of what will be covered and will help you to understand *why* you are doing the things you are asked to do in this unit.

Getting started

This appears at the start of every unit and is designed to get you thinking about the unit and what it involves. This feature will also help you to identify what you may already know about some of the topics in the unit and acts as a starting point for understanding the skills and knowledge you will need to develop to complete the unit.

Features that help you to build your knowledge

Research

This asks you to research a topic in greater depth. These features will help to expand your understanding of a topic and develop your research and investigation skills. All of this will be invaluable for your future progression, both professionally and academically.

Worked example

Our worked examples show the process you need to follow to solve a problem, such as a maths or science equation or the process for writing a letter or memo. This will also help you to develop your understanding and your numeracy and literacy skills.

Theory into practice

In this feature you are asked to consider the workplace or industry implications of a topic or concept from the unit. This will help you to understand the close links between what you are learning in the classroom and the affects it will have on a future career in your chosen sector.

Discussion

Discussion features encourage you to talk to other students about a topic in greater detail, working together to increase your understanding of the topic and to understand other people's perspectives on an issue. This will also help to build your teamworking skills, which will be invaluable in your future professional and academic career.

Safety tip

This provides advice around health and safety when working on the unit. It will help build your knowledge about best practice in the workplace, as well as make sure that you stay safe.

Key terms

Concise and simple definitions are provided for key words, phrases and concepts, allowing you to have, at a glance, a clear understanding of the key ideas in each unit.

Link

This shows any links between units or within the same unit, helping you to identify where the knowledge you have learned elsewhere will help you to achieve the requirements of the unit. Remember, although your BTEC National is made up of several units, there are common themes that are explored from different perspectives across the whole of your course.

Step by step:

This practical feature gives step-by-step descriptions of particular processes or tasks in the unit, including a photo or artwork for each step. This will help you to understand the key stages in the process and help you to carry out the process yourself.

Further reading and resources

This contains a list of other resources – such as books, journals, articles or websites –you can use to expand your knowledge of the unit content. This is a good opportunity for you to take responsibility for your own learning, as well as preparing you for research tasks you may need to do academically or professionally.

Features connected to your assessment

Your course is made up of a series of mandatory and optional units. There are two different types of mandatory unit:
▶ externally assessed
▶ internally assessed.

The features that support you in preparing for assessment are below. But first, what is the difference between these two different types of units?

Externally assessed units

These units give you the opportunity to present what you have learned in the unit in a different way. They can be challenging, but will really give you the opportunity to demonstrate your knowledge and understanding, or your skills in a direct way. For these units you will complete an assessment, set directly by Pearson, in controlled conditions. This could take the form of an exam or it could be a type of task. You may have the opportunity in advance to research and prepare notes around a topic, which can be used when completing the assessment.

Internally assessed units

Most of your units will be internally assessed. This involves you completing a series of assignments, set and marked by your teacher. The assignments you complete could allow you to demonstrate your learning in a number of different ways, from a written report to a presentation to a video recording and observation statements of you completing a practical task. Whatever the method, you will need to make sure you have clear evidence of what you have achieved and how you did it.

Assessment practice

These features give you the opportunity to practise some of the skills you will need when you are assessed on your unit. They do not fully reflect the actual assessment tasks, but will help you get ready for doing them.

Plan – Do – Review

You'll also find handy advice on how to plan, complete and evaluate your work after you have completed it. This is designed to get you thinking about the best way to complete your work and to build your skills and experience before doing the actual assessment. These prompt questions are designed to get you started with thinking about how the way you work, as well as understand why you do things.

Getting ready for assessment

For internally assessed units, this is a case study from a BTEC National student, talking about how they planned and carried out their assignment work and what they would do differently if they were to do it again. It will give you advice on preparing for the kind of work you will need to for your internal assessments, including 'Think about it' points for you to consider for your own development.

Getting ready for assessment

This section will help you to prepare for external assessment. It gives practical advice on preparing for and sitting exams or a set task. It provides a series of sample answers for the types of questions you will need to answer in your external assessments, including guidance on the good points of these answers and how these answers could be improved.

Features to help you reflect on and evaluate your learning

⏸ PAUSE POINT

Pause points appear after a section of each unit and give you the opportunity to review and reflect upon your own learning. The ability to reflect on your own performance is a key skill you'll need to develop and use throughout your life, and will be essential whatever your future plans are.

Hint

Extend

These also give you suggestions to help cement your knowledge and indicate other areas you can look at to expand it..

Reflect

This allows you to reflect on how the knowledge you have gained in this unit may impact your behaviour in a workplace situation. This will help not only to place the topic in a professional context, but also help you to review your own conduct and develop your employability skills.

Features which link your learning with the workplace

Case study

Case studies throughout the book will allow you to apply the learning and knowledge from the unit to a scenario from the workplace or industry. Case studies include questions to help you consider the wider context of a topic. They show how the course content is reflected in the real world and help you to build familiarity with issues you may find in a real-world workplace.

THINK ▶FUTURE

This is a special case study where someone working in the industry talks about the job role they do and the skills they need. This comes with a *Focusing your skills* section, which gives suggestions for how you can begin to develop the employability skills and experiences that are needed to be successful in a career in your chosen sector. This is an excellent opportunity to help you identify what you could do, inside and outside of your BTEC National studies, to build up your employability skills.

Human Lifespan Development 1

Getting to know your unit

Assessment
You will be assessed using an externally set written task worth 90 marks.

Understanding human lifespan development, the different influences on an individual's development and how this relates to their care needs is important when you are establishing your career in the health or social care professions. Health and social care professionals meet and work with a wide range of individuals who have diverse needs.

In this unit, you will be introduced to the biological, psychological and sociological theories associated with human lifespan development. You will explore the different aspects of physical, intellectual, emotional and social development across an individual's lifespan. You will examine factors affecting an individual's growth and development such as the environment or genetic inheritance, and consider the positive and negative influences these have on development, including the impact on an individual's concept of self. You will explore the physical effects of ageing and the theories that help to explain psychological changes.

How you will be assessed

You will be assessed by a paper-based examination, lasting for 1 hour 30 minutes, that is worth 90 marks. The examination will consist of short- and long-answer questions. The questions are intended to assess your understanding of growth and development throughout an individual's lifespan and how this may be affected by personal and environmental factors, health and the effects of ageing. You will be expected to make reasoned connections between theories and models of human growth and development to demonstrate your understanding. You will give your answers in response to the information you are given in case studies about members of one family.

This table contains the areas of essential content that learners must be familiar with prior to assessment.

Essential content	
A	Human growth and development through the life stages
B	Factors affecting human growth and development
C	Effects of ageing

Getting started

What do you already know about lifespan development? Using the life stages infancy, early childhood and adolescence, write a short description about your development so far. For early and late adulthood, predict how you think your development will progress. Reflect at the end of this unit to see whether you would change your description or predictions.

A Human growth and development through the life stages

A1 Physical development across the life stages

Physical growth and development continues throughout a person's life but you will have noticed that development is not always smooth. During puberty you may have suddenly grown a few centimetres in a short period of time and then stayed the same height for a while. You may have noticed a small child who suddenly goes from crawling to climbing the stairs. In this section you will look at the key features of physical growth and development across the life stages.

▶ **Table 1.1** Key features of growth and physical development at each life stage

Life stage	Age	Key features
Birth and infancy	0–2 years	Infants grow rapidly reaching approximately half their adult height by the time they are two years old. At around one year old infants can walk and by two years of age they can run.
Early childhood	3–8 years	Children continue to grow at a steady pace. They continue to develop strength and coordination.
Adolescence	9–18 years	Adolescents experience growth spurts. They develop sexual characteristics during puberty.
Early adulthood	19–45 years	Young adults reach the peak of their physical fitness.
Middle adulthood	46–65 years	The ageing process begins with some loss of strength and stamina. Women go through menopause.
Later adulthood	65 years onwards	The ageing process continues with gradual loss of mobility. Older adults will experience a loss of height of up to a few centimetres.

Growth and development are different concepts

Growth is an increase in a measurable quantity such as height or weight or other dimensions. **Development** is about the complex changes in skills and capabilities that an individual experiences as they grow.

During their lifespan, an individual will pass through the different stages shown in Table 1.1. Life stages are marked by physical, physiological and psychological changes.

Key terms

Growth – an increase in some measured quantity, such as height or weight.

Development – complex changes including an increase in skills, abilities and capabilities.

Skills and abilities such as gross and fine motor skills and thinking and language skills develop alongside the social roles and expectations associated with different stages of the lifespan. These are referred to as milestones.

Principles of growth

Growth describes an increase in quantity. For example, children grow taller as they get older. As height increases, so does weight – this is referred to as a process of growth. Although growth is continuous, the rate is not smooth. There can be periods of more rapid growth in infancy and again during puberty which means there can be quite a difference between the rates of growth of two people who are the same age. There are also differences in the growth rates of boys and girls. Growth rates also vary in different parts of the body, for example the head circumference grows more rapidly than other areas in the first months of life. When referring to growth it is important to consider two dimensions:

▶ weight
▶ length/height.

At birth and then between six to eight weeks, a baby's head circumference will be measured to check the size and growth of the brain.

Infants grow rapidly during the first six months of their lives. Healthy newborns double their birth weight by four to five months, and triple it by the time they reach a year old. By the age of two, a healthy infant will be approximately half their adult height. Not only can growth measurements help a health visitor to monitor a child's health and development, they can also identify other issues, for example if an infant is under- or overweight or growing too slowly. Infants will grow on average about 12 cm (4 inches) and gain about 2.5 kg (5 lbs) between one and two years of age. Between their second and third birthday, an infant will gain another 2 kg (4 lbs) and grow about 8 cm (3 inches) more. A health visitor will carry out the measurements and plot the results on a growth chart to ensure that an infant is meeting their milestones.

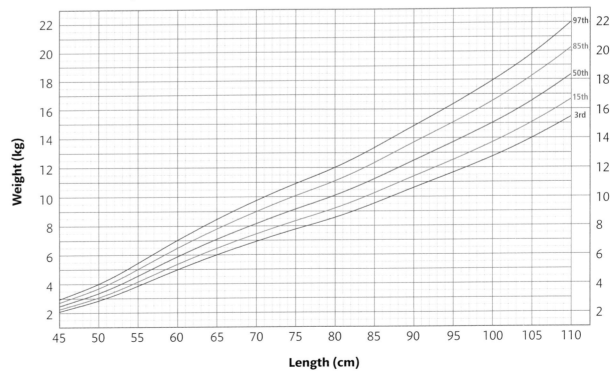

▶ **Figure 1.1** An example of a height–weight chart for girls

If an infant or child is growing as expected their weight will rise steadily following the **centile lines** marked on their growth chart. All information is recorded in a personal child health record. This ensures that if there is cause for concern about weight or height an early referral to a paediatrician can be made. An infant's head circumference will also be measured if there is any concern about development.

Principles of development

Development describes changes that might be complex and involve ability levels altering.

Development happens:

- from head to toe – an infant will first be able to control their head, then develop control over their body to enable them to sit and finally have control over their legs and feet to allow them to crawl and eventually walk

- from the inside to the outside – an infant learns to control movements in their body first then in their arms and legs until, finally, they can control the small muscles in their fingers

- in the same sequence but at different rates

- holistically – areas of development are dependent on and influence each other.

Development can be seen as a journey. As the journey progresses, children reach a number of key **milestones**. These are also referred to as **developmental norms** and describe the skills that infants, children and adolescents are expected to develop at particular ages or stages of their life. These norms include walking, talking or tying shoe laces. The four main areas of skills acquisition are:

1 physical – gross and fine motor skills
2 social development
3 emotional development
4 intellectual development and language skills.

Although children will pass through the same developmental stages, you should remember that every child is unique and develops at their own rate. Norms help professionals describe an average set of expectations. If a child develops faster than the norm it does not necessarily mean that the child is 'gifted'. Neither does it mean that there is something wrong if a child develops more slowly.

Very few people experience their life in 'compartments' labelled 'physical', 'intellectual', 'emotional' or 'social'. Most people experience physical, intellectual, emotional and social development holistically. For instance, the development of a child's social skills is dependent upon the development of their intellectual and language skills. One developmental aspect cannot be assessed without looking at the other aspects. Developmental milestones provide a useful guide for professionals and enable them to recognise, monitor and take appropriate action if development is delayed in one or more of the developmental areas.

Physical development in infancy and early childhood

Two aspects of physical development are **gross motor skills** and **fine motor skills**.

Development of gross motor skills

Gross motor skills are movements that involve using the large muscles of the body. These skills allow children to control those body movements that require the use of

---

Key term

Centile lines (percentiles) – lines on a graph used to show average measurements of height, weight and head circumference. The lines represent the values of the measurements taking into account age and sex.

Key terms

Development norms – a description of an average set of expectations with respect to a young child's development. For example, by the age of 12 months a child has the ability to stand alone.

Milestone – an ability achieved by most children by a certain age. It can involve physical, social, emotional, cognitive and communication skills, for example walking, sharing with others, expressing emotions, recognising familiar sounds and talking.

Gross motor skills – large movements that involve using the large muscles of the body which are required for mobility, for example rolling over.

Fine motor skills – involve smaller movements that require more precise direction (dexterity) and use smaller muscles, for example picking up a pencil.

large muscles in the legs, arms and the torso of the body. As soon as a baby is born, their gross motor skills begin to develop. Gross motor skills are essential for physical play for example playing 'tag', which involves running after friends, catching up with them, reaching out and touching someone. Everyday tasks like walking upstairs, running, jumping and throwing a ball, require the use of gross motor skills.

Development of fine motor skills

In contrast, fine motor skills are actions that require the use of smaller muscles in the hands, fingers and toes. These allow infants to pick things up using their finger and thumb, wriggle their toes in the sand and hold a crayon or small toy. Dressing and undressing, drawing, scribbling and stacking toys are other examples of fine motor skills.

Infancy (0–2 years)

Development milestones

Newborn babies are helpless when it comes to muscle coordination and control. They are unable to hold up their heads, roll over, sit up or use their hands to move objects deliberately. Developing both gross and motor skills allows increasing and more complex movement. By around the age of two, infants develop and use both gross and fine motor skills as they become more independent. For example, when playing with shape-sorting toys, they use gross motor skills to hold their body steady enough to grasp the shapes firmly and use fine motor skills to fit each shape in the correct slot. Table 1.2 shows some developmental milestones for gross and fine motor skills for infants aged from birth to two years.

▶ **Table 1.2** Gross and fine motor skills developmental milestones in infancy

Age	Gross motor skills	Fine motor skills
Newborn	Primitive reflexes such as grasp.	Holds their thumbs tucked into their hands.
1 month	Lifts chin, some control of head.	Opens hands to grasp a finger.
3 months	Can lift their head and chest when lying on front.	Can briefly grasp a rattle.
6 months	Rolls over, can sit up for a short time without support, kicks legs when held up.	Moves objects from hand to hand, can pick up dropped toys if they are in sight.
9–10 months	Crawls, begins to cruise (walking while holding on to objects).	Uses finger and thumb to hold a small object.
12–13 months	Stands alone, can walk without help.	Manipulates and places toys.
18 months	Climbs onto furniture.	Builds a short tower with blocks.
2 years	Propels a sit-on toy with their feet, throws a large ball.	Draws lines and circles, turns a page.
2 and a half years	Jumps from a low step, kicks a ball.	Uses a spoon and fork, builds a tower of 7–8 blocks.

Early childhood (3–8 years)

Development of gross motor skills

Children's practical abilities associated with gross motor skills continue to develop. By the age of three, most children will be able to use pedals to ride a tricycle, run and balance on one foot for one second. By the age of four, children may be able to kick and throw a large ball. At five years, they can hop using each foot separately. By the age of six or seven a child may be able to skip and ride a bicycle. At eight years old they will have good strength and body coordination so that they can take part in many sports and activities.

Research

Find more developmental milestones charts and create a table like Table 1.2.

See when most children would be able to:

- run forwards and backwards
- button and unbutton clothing
- write their own name
- use joined-up writing
- walk in a straight line
- turn the pages of a book.

For each of the points above, state whether this is an example of a gross motor skill or a fine motor skill.

Development of fine motor skills

Fine motor skills are the ability to control and coordinate smaller movements and muscles such as the movement of hands and fingers. By the age of three, children should be able to control their movements enough to use a pencil to copy letters or build a tower with cubes. By the age of five, most children should be able to dress and undress on their own, including tying their own shoelaces. At eight years of age, they will have good control of their small muscles and be able to draw detailed pictures.

Adolescence (9–18 years)

During **adolescence**, males and females will experience a number of physical and growth changes.

Development of primary and secondary sexual characteristics

Puberty takes place over several years. It is a period of rapid change and growth and is experienced by both females and males. Table 1.3 shows some primary and secondary sexual characteristics for both sexes. Primary sexual characteristics relate to the changes and development of reproductive organs, while secondary characteristics are outward signs of development from a child into a man or woman.

Key term

Adolescence – an important status change following the onset of puberty during which a young person develops from a child into an adult.

▶ **Table 1.3** Primary and secondary sexual characteristics

Primary sexual characteristics (present at birth and develop during puberty)		Secondary sexual characteristics (develop during puberty)	
Female	**Male**	**Female**	**Male**
The uterus enlarges and the vagina lengthens.	Enlargement of penis and testes.	Breasts develop and the areola (the area around the nipple) swells and darkens.	Changes in larynx (Adam's apple) causing voice to deepen.
The ovaries begin to release eggs.	Spontaneous erections caused by blood flowing into chambers in the penis may happen.	Hair grows in armpits and pubic area.	Hair grows in armpits and pubic area, facial hair.
The menstrual cycle commences.	The testicles begin to produce spermatozoa (sperm), beginning of ejaculation.	Redistribution of body fat causing hips to widen.	Redistribution of muscle tissue and fat.

Puberty – a period of rapid growth during which young people reach sexual maturity, and become biologically able to reproduce and secondary sexual characteristics develop.

Hormones – chemical substances produced in the body and transported in the blood stream that control or regulate body cells or body organs. For example, the sex hormones produced by the ovaries and testes are responsible for the development of secondary sexual characteristics in puberty.

Puberty in girls often starts between the ages of 11 and 13 although it may begin earlier. Boys generally start puberty later, often between 13 and 15 years of age. Puberty is a development stage that prepares the body for sexual reproduction. It is triggered by the action of **hormones** that control sexual development. Both boys and girls may experience a 'growth spurt' when they grow taller at a faster rate than before.

The role of hormones in sexual maturity

Sex hormones are responsible for the changes that occur in puberty. The pituitary gland controls the release of sex hormones in both females and males. The release of sex hormones controls the onset and rate of puberty, the physical changes such as pubic and axillary hair growth and egg and sperm production. It can prove to be a difficult time emotionally for young people as levels of hormones going up or down often cause mood swings.

The main female hormones are oestrogen and progesterone. The ovaries start to produce oestrogen and progesterone which are responsible for changes including ovulation and menstruation. The first period is a significant, notable change for young females as it indicates the onset of fertility.

The main male hormone is testosterone. The testes start to produce testosterone which stimulates sperm production, indicating the onset of fertility. Testosterone is also responsible for the development of secondary sexual characteristics such as a deeper pitch and tone of the voice.

Case study

Changes in adolescence

Jake is 13 and his parents have noticed that he has suddenly become very shy, locking the bathroom door and asking them to knock before they enter his bedroom. Jake has noticed that his penis has grown (primary sexual characteristic) and he knows that his testes can produce sperm. His mum has noticed that Jake's voice has begun to change and he has hair growing under his armpits (secondary sexual characteristics).

Sarah is 12 and she is embarrassed as her periods have started. Her mum has explained to Sarah that her uterus and vagina have grown (primary sexual characteristics). Sarah has noticed that her breasts have grown and her

mum has taken her shopping to buy a bra. Sarah has also noticed that she has armpit and pubic hair. Sarah has grown taller and put on weight (caused by increased fat layers under the skin). These are all secondary sexual characteristics. Sarah is getting anxious about changing for her PE lessons at school as she thinks other girls will laugh at her.

Check your knowledge

1 Thinking about Jake and Sarah, write a definition that explains the difference between primary and secondary sexual characteristics.

2 List the female and male sex hormones and write a brief description of their function in puberty.

Research

Physical development is not controlled purely by genetics. Berryman et al (1991) argue that records show that, in the 1860s, girls did not start puberty until aged 16. It seems that children now start puberty earlier. Consider what environmental influences might have an impact on physical development, for example improvements in diet and increased body weight.

Early adulthood (19–45 years)

Physical strength peaks

Young adults are usually at the peak of their physical performance between the ages of 19 and 28. By this age, young adults have reached their full height and strength, and reaction time and manual dexterity are also at their peak. After this age adults may gradually lose some strength and speed, although these changes are often unnoticed outside of competitive sport. Decline in physical capabilities may be exacerbated towards the end of this life stage if individuals have an unhealthy diet, do not take regular exercise and maintain an unhealthy lifestyle.

Exercise and a healthy diet can help to develop physical fitness and athletic skills into middle adulthood.

▶ What are the physical and psychological benefits of regular exercise in adulthood?

> **Reflect**
>
> As an individual moves from adolescence to adulthood, new life experiences and challenges will occur. Do you think that it is easy to identify when adolescence ends and adulthood begins?

Pregnancy and lactation

Pregnancy and lactation are key phases in an adult female's lifespan. During early pregnancy, women experience many physical and emotional changes in preparation for parenthood. Pregnancy hormones can cause mood swings.

Hormonal changes take place, with an increase in progesterone which maintains the pregnancy, while the increase in oestrogen may be responsible for the sickness some women suffer in early pregnancy. Hormones also affect the shape and appearance of their breasts, including darkened veins due to increased blood supply. Nipples and areolas darken and breasts become more sensitive and tender, preparing the breasts to produce milk (lactation) to feed the baby.

Perimenopause

By the time a woman is in her forties her ovaries gradually begin to make less oestrogen. This means that the ovaries stop producing an egg each month. This stage is generally referred to as the perimenopause transition. Perimenopause lasts until the **menopause** which is the point when the ovaries stop releasing eggs. On average perimenopause lasts four years. However, this can vary between lasting a few months or as long as 10 years. Perimenopause ends when a woman has not had a monthly period for 12 months. The reduction in oestrogen causes physical and emotional symptoms.

> **Key term**
>
> **Menopause** – the ending of female fertility, including the cessation of menstruation and reduction in production of female sex hormones.

Women in perimenopause generally experience some of these symptoms:
▶ hot flushes and night sweats
▶ breast tenderness
▶ loss of libido (lower sex drive)
▶ fatigue
▶ irregular or very heavy periods
▶ vaginal dryness, discomfort during sex
▶ mood swings
▶ trouble sleeping
▶ urine leakage when coughing or sneezing
▶ urinary urgency (an urgent need to urinate more frequently).

Middle adulthood (46-65 years)

The menopause

Women are most fertile (able to conceive children) in their late teens and early twenties. The risk of miscarriage and pregnancy complications rises with age. Between 45 and 55 years of age fertility reduces and then comes to an end in a process called the menopause. It can take several years to complete.

The menopause involves:
▶ gradual ending of menstruation (or stopping having periods) and a large reduction of fertile eggs in the ovaries
▶ an increase in the production of hormones called gonadotropins that try to stimulate egg production, which can cause irritability, hot flushes and night sweats
▶ a reduction in the sex hormones (oestrogen and progesterone) produced by a woman's ovaries, resulting in some shrinkage of sexual organs and sometimes a reduction in sexual interest
▶ associated problems such as osteoporosis, which can be caused by a reduction in the production of sex hormones.

For some women, the general hormonal changes, especially reduction in oestrogen levels experienced during the perimenopause and menopause, can lead to mood changes, depression and anxiety. This can make a woman feel that she is on an emotional roller coaster. Some women experience overwhelming sadness that they are no longer able to have children and this can affect their self-image of being a 'desirable' woman. Self-esteem and self-image can become low, which may impact on self-confidence and on quality of life during this transitional stage of the lifespan.

Effects of the ageing process

Often adults put on weight as they age. 'Middle aged spread' may happen because adults still eat the same amount of food as they did when they were younger although they have become much less active.

Along with a change in body shape – increased weight and waistline, loss of skin elasticity and loss of muscle tone and strength – people also begin show other signs of ageing, such as greying and thinning of hair and hair loss.

⏸ PAUSE POINT

Close your book and draw an outline of a female body. Note the symptoms of perimenopause around the body.

Hint

Think about what particular physical functions are changing and possible emotional changes.

Extend

Conduct a risk assessment of an athlete's training programme – how are they putting themselves at risk?

Later adulthood (65-plus years)

Predicting your life course becomes more difficult in the later life stages. Where 'old age' was once deemed to be from 65 years of age until the end of one's life, as **life expectancy** has risen, people's ideas of what is 'old' are also changing.

Key term

Life expectancy – an estimate of the number of years, on average, that a person can expect to live. Sometimes called longevity.

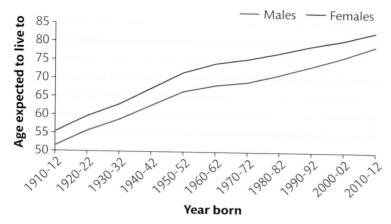

▶ **Figure 1.2** Changes in life expectancy for males and females over the last 100 years (based on Office for National Statistics data)

In round figures, 120 years is often accepted as the maximum lifespan for a human being. Britain's oldest living person in 2015 was Gladys Hooper from Ryde, Isle of Wight. Mrs Hooper celebrated her 113th birthday in January 2016.

Deterioration of health

In later adulthood, there are many changes associated with the ageing process. For example, there are changes in body systems and organs which could be the result of disease and that can impact on an individual's lifestyle. Although most body systems continue to function fairly well, the heart becomes more susceptible to disease. Individuals may begin to lose height in middle adulthood which continues into later life. By the age of 80, individuals may have lost as much as 5 cm in height. This is caused by changes in posture and compression of the spinal discs and joints. The ageing process also continues with further loss of strength and muscle loss, as well as a reduction in stamina. Mobility (gross motor skills) and dexterity (fine motor skills) become more difficult. There are small changes to the brain which include loss or shrinkage of nerve cells and a general slowing of movement and responses.

Visual and hearing problems may interfere with daily life. Older people can be more susceptible to accidents and falls due to lack of muscular strength and problems with balance or reaction time.

Older people can retain reasonable health, especially if they follow a lifestyle that includes a healthy diet and exercise. It can be a time when people take up new interests and hobbies that help to keep them physically mobile and their mind active.

Deterioration of intellectual abilities

Although many older people are in good mental health, major depressive disorders tend to be undiagnosed. Diseases and conditions that can affect health and wellbeing, for example Parkinson's disease and Alzheimer's disease, are more common in older people. As people are now living longer, Alzheimer's disease has become more prevalent. Mild **cognitive impairment** may be an early sign of the disease.

Key term

Cognitive impairment – when a person has trouble remembering, learning new skills, concentrating or making decisions that affect their everyday life.

Ageing can involve a loss of nerve cells in the brain and a reduction in the ability of nerves to transmit electrical signals. However, this does not mean that people lose their ability to think logically or to reason as they have a wealth of experience to draw on. Many older people experience cognitive impairment and report problems with memory recall. For example, finding themselves often asking 'Where did I put my glasses?' Older people may say that it takes longer to do things and they may feel they are slowing down. They may take longer to respond to questions. Reaction times might also be slower, but older people often compensate for these changes, for instance, driving more carefully. Although older people may worry, changes are a natural process of ageing and not necessarily symptoms of dementia.

A2 Intellectual development across the life stages

During their lifespan, an individual develops useful ways of thinking and learning. Intellectual and cognitive development refers to how individuals organise their ideas and make sense of the world in which they live. There are five important aspects associated with intellectual development.

1 Language development, which is essential for organising thoughts and to share and express ideas. It is also important for clarification.
2 Problem solving is an important skill that is required both to work things out and to make predictions about what might happen.
3 Memory is required for storing, recalling and retrieving information.
4 Moral development allows for reasoning and making choices, and informs the individual how to act in particular situations and how to act towards self and others.
5 Abstract thoughts and creative thinking are essential for thinking and discussing situations and events that cannot be observed.

Understanding how individuals learn, mature and adapt to their life stage is an essential aspect of human growth and development. As an individual progresses through the various development stages, their intellectual and cognitive ability increases. This is highlighted by studying the difference between adult and children's learning styles. The stages of intellectual development across the lifespan can be seen in Table 1.4.

▶ **Table 1.4** Stages of intellectual development across the lifespan

Stage	Development
Infancy and early childhood	Stages of rapid intellectual development.
Adolescence to early adulthood	Development of logical thought, problem solving and memory recall skills.
Middle adulthood	Can think through problems and make sound judgements using life experiences.
Later adulthood	Changes in the brain can cause short-term memory decline and slower thought processes and reaction times.

Intellectual and language skills in infancy and early childhood

The brain grows very rapidly during the first few years of life. During this time children learn all sorts of new skills and abilities. For example, in early infancy and childhood, there is a rapid growth in language and intellectual skills. Young children have an ability both to understand and to use language, for example a 12-month-old baby saying her first words, a two-year-old child naming parts of his body and a five-year-old constructing complex sentences.

Over an individual's lifespan, their brain grows at an amazing rate. At birth, a baby's brain is about 30 per cent of the size of an adult's brain. By the age of two, the child's brain has increased to approximately 80 per cent of the size of an adult's brain.

Speech and language are essential skills needed to communicate with others. Language development begins before birth and develops rapidly (see Table 1.5). From the age of two months, most babies will be 'cooing', and, by six months old, they will be responding by making 'babbling' noises. The fastest learning takes place for most children between the ages of two and five. By the time a child has reached the age of seven, they have learned the basics of vocabulary, grammar and sentence formation.

▶ **Table 1.5** The stages of language development

Age	Language development
Around 3 months	Infants begin to make babbling noises as they learn to control the muscles associated with speech.
Around 12 months	Infants begin to imitate sounds made by carers such as 'da da'. This develops into using single words.
Around 2 years	Infants begin to make two-word sentences, such as 'cat goed' (meaning the cat has gone away). The infant begins to build their vocabulary (knowledge of words).
Around 3 years	Children begin to make simple sentences, such as 'I want drink'. This develops into the ability to ask questions, 'when we go?'. Knowledge of words (vocabulary) grows very rapidly.
Around 4 years	Children begin to use clear sentences that can be understood by strangers. Children can be expected to make some mistakes with grammar, 'we met lots of peoples at the shops today'.
5 years	Children can speak using full adult grammar. Although vocabulary will continue to grow and formal grammar will continue to improve, most children can be expected to use language effectively by the age of five.

There are many different ways in which language development can be promoted. See Table 1.6 for some examples.

▶ **Table 1.6** Encouraging language development

Infants	Young children	Adolescence
• Blow bubbles. • Play with puppets. • Watch and listen to other children. • Join in with action rhymes and songs. • Look at picture books.	• Take part in circle time. • Take part in group activities. • Imaginary play in 'home corner'. • Share stories and rhymes. • Play word games and riddles.	• Read a wide range of books and journals. • Take part in group projects. • Discuss ideas. • Plan and deliver presentations.

Theory into practice

Visit a video-sharing website such as YouTube and search for 'Speech Journey'. Watch the video clip about the milestones that most children will achieve. Make notes of some examples of one- or two-word phrases that you hear.

If you have any placements with children, see if you can identify these speech milestones.

Discuss your examples with other learners. Can you identify a general pattern in the way children develop language? Compare and contrast ways in which individual children develop differently.

Key terms

Abstract logical thinking – the ability to solve problems using imagination without having to be involved practically. This is an advanced form of thinking that does not always need a practical context in order to take place.

Egocentric thinking – not being able to see a situation from another person's point of view. Piaget thought that a young child assumed that other people see, hear and feel exactly the same as the child does.

Concrete logical thinking – the ability to solve problems providing an individual can see or physically handle the issues involved.

Piaget's model

Cognitive development is a child's ability to learn and solve problems, for example, a two-month-old baby learning to explore the environment with their hands or eyes or a five-year-old learning how to solve simple mathematical problems. One theorist who provided insight into cognitive development was the Swiss developmental psychologist, Jean Piaget.

Stages of cognitive development

His research focused on how children acquire the ability to think. He came to the conclusion that children think differently to adults. He suggested that a four-year-old cannot use abstract logic (**abstract logical thinking**) because they are not mature enough (no matter how well they are taught). He observed that infants use **egocentric thinking**, which means they can only understand the world from their own perspective. Piaget believed that the ability to think logically does not happen until around the age of seven years old when children can use simple logic (**concrete logical thinking**) to solve problems, for example that the amount of water stays the same when poured into a different shaped container.

Piaget believed that there were four stages of intellectual development which mature or 'unfold' during the early stages of the lifespan (see Table 1.7).

▶ **Table 1.7** Piaget's stages of cognitive development

Stage	What occurs
Sensorimotor: birth–2 years	Infants think by interacting with the world using their eyes, ears, hands and mouth. As a result, the infant invents ways of solving problems such as pulling a lever to hear the sound of a music box, finding hidden toys and putting objects into and taking them out of containers. Piaget believed that a baby would not have a way of remembering and thinking about the world until they were about 18 months old.
Preoperational: 2–7 years	Children use symbols to represent their earlier sensorimotor discoveries. Development of language and make-believe play takes place. Piaget believed that children at this stage cannot properly understand how ideas like number, mass and volume really work. A child might be able to count to 100 but might not understand what a set of 10 really means. If 10 buttons are stretched out in a line and 10 buttons are placed in a pile, a child might say that there are more buttons in the line because it is longer!
Concrete operational: 7–11 years	Children's reasoning becomes logical providing the issues are concrete. In the concrete operational stage, children may be able to understand simple logical principles. For example, if the teacher asks, 'Jessica is taller than Joanne, but Jessica is smaller than Sally, who is the tallest?' A 7 or 8-year-old might find it difficult to imagine the information needed to answer the question. However, if the teacher shows a picture of Jessica, Joanne and Sally, the child might quickly point out who is the tallest.
Formal operational: 11–18 years	This is when the capacity for abstract thinking allows adolescents to reason through symbols that do not refer to objects in the real world, as is required in advanced mathematics. Young people can also think of possible outcomes of a scientific problem, not just the obvious ones. Abstract thinking enables individuals to think through complicated ideas in their heads without having to see the concrete image.

Piaget's theory explains cognitive developmental stages up to adolescence. Some psychologists suggest that there is a 'post-formal operational' stage of thinking in which adults become more skilled in their ability to make flexible judgements. It may be that many adults develop an ability that could be called 'wisdom' as they grow older. Thinking becomes pragmatic expert knowledge about the practical aspects of life, which permits using judgement about important matters.

The development of schemas

An important aspect of Piaget's cognitive development theory was the notion that children go through a series of stages of intellectual development. He referred to these stages as schemas. According to Piaget, a schema is a category of knowledge as well as the process of acquiring knowledge. A child develops concepts about the world around them (a state of **equilibrium**). As they experience situations where new information is presented, their schemas are upset and they reach a state of **disequilibrium**. As the new information is **accommodated**, the original schemas are modified or changed so they again reach a stage of equilibrium. For example, Jack is two years old and loves walking near the farm in his village to see the animals in the fields. Jack has developed a schema for a cow. He knows that a cow is large, has four legs and a tail. When Jack sees a horse for the first time he might initially call it a cow as it fits with his schema of a large animal. Once Jack has been told that the horse is a different animal, he will modify his existing schema for a cow and create a new schema for a horse.

What do you think will happen the first time that Jack sees a miniature horse? He could mistakenly identify it as a dog unless someone explains that the animal is actually a very small horse. He must modify his existing schema for a horse to include the fact that while some horses are very large animals, others can be very small.

Tests of conservation

In the operational stage (see Table 1.7), children understand the theory of conservation – that something's appearance may change but that its quantity will stay the same. By the age of seven, they have the ability to understand that when you move liquid from a wide container to a tall thin container it does not affect its volume. Younger children might not understand this and think that the amount of liquid has changed because the appearance of the container it is in has changed. This is illustrated by the following case study.

> **Key terms**
>
> **Equilibrium** – a state of cognitive balance when a child's experience is in line with what they understand.
>
> **Disequilibrium** – a state of cognitive imbalance between experience and what is understood.
>
> **Accommodation** – modifying schemas (concepts) in relation to new information and experiences.

Case study

Using play

Jack is five and a half years old. He is at Piaget's pre-operational stage. Jack loves water play and his mum is using a play activity to introduce him to the idea of the conservation concept. According to Piaget's theory, Jack will have little understanding of conservation involving liquid quantity until he is six or seven.

His mum takes two short fat plastic glasses and begins to fill them with coloured water. She asks Jack to say when the two glasses have the same amount of water in them. She pours a little of the water from one glass to the other until Jack agrees that the level of coloured water is the same. She next pours the coloured water from one of the short fat glasses into a tall thin plastic glass and asks Jack which glass has more coloured water in it. Jack, like most children under the age of six, points to the tall glass. Jack has not developed a concept or schema for the quantity of liquid remaining the same when it is poured into a different glass.

Egocentrism

Much of Piaget's preoperational stage focuses on what children are unable to do. Like the concept of conservation, the idea of egocentric behaviour centres on abilities that children have not yet developed. Egocentrism is best described as a young child's inability to see a situation from another person's point of view. They assume that other adults and children see, feel, and hear exactly the same as they do. At nursery, preoperational children engage in parallel play – they play alongside rather than together with other children. They are absorbed in their own world and speech is used to externalise their thinking rather than to communicate with other children.

Criticisms of Piaget

Although Piaget's theory remains influential in the early years sector, there are criticisms that he based his theory on observations of a small number of children. Critics of Piaget also suggest that the age/stages he describes may be more fluid than he thought and that he underestimated and/or overestimated children's cognitive abilities. Watching children playing at the age of five, for instance, often shows that they do understand other's feelings and are far less egocentric than Piaget suggested. Bruner did not agree with Piaget's notion of fixed stages and 'readiness' to learn. He believes that, with adult support, children can be helped to progress to higher level thinking skills. He, like others, thought that an individual's ability to use formal logical thought may depend on how much encouragement they have received to think logically. Other research suggests that children take longer than 11 years to become skilled at abstract logical thinking. Cognitive development might not be part of a maturation process, it could depend on a child's environment and the quality of their formal and informal education.

> **Research**
>
> Research Piaget's stages of cognitive development, the development of schemas and how he used his tests of conservation. You can watch examples of Piaget's conservation experiment on video-sharing websites. To what extent do you think his theory may be used in explaining childrens' thoughts and actions? What do critics say about Piaget's theories?

 **PAUSE POINT**   Close the book and draw a flow chart to show Piaget's theory on the development of schemas.

Hint   Schemas are ideas or concepts that children develop, eg based on experiences or things that they see in their environment.

Extend   Produce a case study that helps to explain your chart.

Chomsky's model of language acquisition

Noam Chomsky (1959) believed that the ability to develop a signed or spoken language is genetically programmed into individuals. This means that all individuals have the ability to understand and use language, regardless of other abilities, and to become fluent in their first language by the age of five or six.

Language acquisition device (LAD)

Chomsky states that individuals are born with a 'language acquisition device' (LAD) that enables children to recognise and develop the languages they experience. According to Chomsky's theory, children are 'preprogrammed' to acquire language and it evolves naturally in the same way that children have the ability to stand and to walk. The ability to use language develops because of maturation – it is the unfolding of an individual's biological potential. Chomsky believes that a child could not possibly learn a new language through imitation alone because the grammar and syntax of the language around them is often highly irregular. For example, an adult's speech is often broken up, and they use slang or jargon and ungrammatical sentence construction. Chomsky believes that babies need to experience other people using language but that they do not need to be trained in order to speak. He noted that even if adults around a child use correct grammar or even correct a child, they will continue to apply plural 'rules', for instance 'deers' or 'geeses', if they have reached that particular stage of language development. Chomsky applied his theory to all languages, not just English, as they all contain nouns, verbs, consonants and vowels.

Critics of Chomsky point out the lack of scientific evidence to support his theory. Social constructivists such as Bruner would argue that social interaction, particularly in the early stages of language development, is critical and has far more influence on children than Chomsky suggested. Others argue that Chomsky put too much emphasis on the grammar in sentence structure rather than how children construct meaning from their sentences. Chomsky did not take into consideration children who experience delayed language development for a variety of reasons, for example children who have a learning disability or hearing or speech impairments. Children with Down's syndrome are among those whose language is frequently delayed.

Sign	Sign note
Sleep	
Where?	

Discussion

Working in small groups, discuss how quickly you learnt to speak when you were young. Compare this with your experience of trying to learn a second language in school. Reflect on how far personal experiences can be explained in terms of a genetic basis for a person's first language.

Early to middle adulthood

In early adulthood, individuals apply the knowledge, skills and experience they have gained during their life. This helps them to think logically and find realistic answers. At this life stage, they are likely to be in job roles which require them to think through problems and make decisions, sometimes relating to complex situations. New brain cells will continue to develop even though, in middle adulthood, there may be a gradual decline in the speed of processing information.

The effects of age on the function of memory

Memory loss in later adulthood

It is assumed that memory loss is associated with the ageing process. However, the brain has an amazing capacity to produce new brain cells at any age. Just as exercise can protect muscular strength, lifestyle, health activities and daily activities have an impact on the brain. Age-related memory lapses can be frustrating but are not necessarily a sign of dementia. Physiological changes that can cause a temporary malfunction in the way the brain functions are part of the ageing process. It might take an older person longer to learn and recall information and this is often mistaken for memory loss. There is a difference between memory lapses and the type of memory loss associated with Alzheimer's disease and other forms of dementia.

Ⅱ PAUSE POINT
Remember the life stages and key physical and intellectual development milestones. Draw a life pathway labelling each stage along the route.

Hint
There are six life stages described in this unit. Make sure you know and can give age ranges for each life stage.

Extend
Note one example of physical and intellectual development for each life stage and then check your ideas against the milestones.

A3 Emotional development across the life stages

Emotional development is the way an individual begins to feel about and value themselves and other people. This forms the basis of **emotional literacy** and **empathy**. Emotional development begins with **attachments** which an infant forms to their main caregiver. If a child forms a strong attachment to their main caregiver, it can help to ensure a positive **self-image** and good **self-esteem**. Table 1.8 shows the key features of emotional development throughout the lifespan.

> **Key terms**
>
> **Emotional literacy** – the ability to recognise, understand and appropriately express emotions. Emotional literacy is essential for forming positive social relationships.
> **Empathy** – the ability to identify with or understand another's situation or feelings, 'walking a mile in someone else's shoes'.
> **Attachment** – a strong emotional connection between a child and caregiver.
> **Self-image** – the way an individual sees themselves, their mental image of themselves.
> **Self-esteem** – how a person feels about themselves, self-worth or pride.

▶ **Table 1.8** Key features of emotional development

Life stage	Emotional development
Infancy: 0–2 years	**Attachment** Bowlby (1953) argued that infants have an inbuilt need to form an attachment with a carer. The quality of this attachment may affect emotional development for the rest of the child's life. Salter Ainsworth et al (1978) and Marris (1996) argue that the quality of our early attachment influences the assumptions we make about ourself and others. Infants who are securely attached will grow up with the emotional resources needed to cope with uncertainty in life. Infants who are insecurely attached may have a reduced ability to cope with stress and major life events.

▶ **Table 1.8** – *continued*

Early childhood: 3–8 years	**Understanding self and others** Children use their imagination to begin to understand the social roles that other people play. Children begin to imagine a 'me', an idea of self or **self-concept**. Relationships with other family members may influence whether a child feels valued or has a sense of self-worth. The way a child gets on with teachers and friends may influence their self-confidence. The child might develop a permanent sense of confidence or a sense of failure and inferiority.
Adolescence: 9–18 years	**Identity** During adolescence, this sense of self continues to develop. An adolescent needs to develop a secure self-concept. A person needs a clear understanding of identity in order to feel secure when working with other people or in order to make a loving sexual attachment. This may be a stressful time as self-esteem may depend on developing identity.
Early and middle adulthood: 19–65 years	**Intimacy** In adulthood, an individual's self-esteem is influenced by lifestyle such as their job or marital status. Self-image is affected by personal appearance and how others see you. Individuals need to learn to cope with emotional attachment to a sexual partner. This may involve not being too self-centred or defensive and not becoming emotionally isolated.
Later adulthood: 65+ years	**Making sense of your life** Older people need a secure sense of self to enable them to cope with the physical changes associated with ageing and death. People who fail to make sense of their lives might experience emotional despair.

> **Key term**
>
> **Self-concept (sense of identity)** – an awareness formed in early childhood of being an individual, a unique person and different from everyone else.

Attachment to caregivers

A secure attachment to a main caregiver means that a child will feel secure, loved and have a sense of belonging. Caregivers are the secure base from which children explore the world around them. They are protectors and help the child to feel happy, secure and confident. It is important that parents ensure that children have the physical, mental and emotional nourishment to develop healthily. Secure attachments in childhood lead to happier and healthier attachments with others in the future. If there is a lack of a healthy attachment, then a mistrust of caregivers or adults in authority could develop. Insecure attachments can lead to behavioural issues, a lack of ability to receive affection or manipulative behaviour. Children may not develop the secure base necessary to cope with life events.

Theories of attachment

John Bowlby refers to attachment as a deep and enduring emotional bond that connects a child to their primary caregiver.

His attachment theory originated during the 1930s. While working as a child psychiatrist treating many emotionally disturbed children, Bowlby began to consider a child's relationship with their mother. Bowlby linked the importance of social, emotional and cognitive development to the relationship that the child had with their mother. He believed that children were biologically preprogrammed to form attachments and that infancy is a critical period for forming positive attachments. This led Bowlby to consider problems associated with early separation from the primary caregiver.

Working with James Robertson, Bowlby observed that children experienced **separation anxiety**, an intense distress, when separated from their mothers. The child's distress and anxiety did not disappear even when they were being fed by another carer. Bowlby suggested that attachment could be understood as evolving from the caregiver providing safety and security for the infant. According to Bowlby, infants have a universal need to seek close proximity with their caregiver when under stress or feeling threatened.

Critics argue that Bowlby oversimplified his theory. Rutter argues that maternal **deprivation** in itself may not result in long-term problems. He suggests that **privation** is far more damaging. Privation happens when children have not had the opportunity to form attachments or have poor quality attachments caused by a lack of social or intellectual stimulation. While Bowlby believed that attachment is a natural, biological process, others suggest that it is learned behaviour influenced by factors such as the environment, culture and/or the baby's temperament. You can read more about the nature/nurture argument later in this unit.

Research by Schaffer and Emerson suggests that babies are most likely to form attachments to caregivers who respond effectively to their signals. This is not necessarily the person they spend the most time with. This is referred to as sensitive responsiveness. The most important factor in forming attachments, therefore, is not the adult who feeds and changes the baby but the adult who plays and communicates with them.

Schaffer and Emerson (1964) identified a sequence in the development of attachment (see Table 1.9).

> **Key terms**
>
> **Deprivation** – being deprived of a caregiver to whom an attachment already exists.
>
> **Privation** – being deprived of the opportunity to form an attachment.
>
> **Separation anxiety** – the fear and apprehension that infants experience when separated from their primary caregiver.

▶ **Table 1.9** Schaffer and Emerson's sequence of attachment

Age range	Stage
Up to 3 months	Most babies respond indiscriminately to any caregiver.
3 months up to 7 months	Infants can distinguish the difference between their main caregiver and other people. The infant will accept care from other people.
7 months up to 9 months	This is when the infant looks to particular people for security, comfort and protection. The baby shows fear of strangers and unhappiness when separated from their main caregiver. Some infants are more likely to display fear of strangers and **stranger anxiety** than others.
9 months +	The baby starts to become more independent and forms several attachments, referred to as multiple attachments.

> **Key term**
>
> **Stranger anxiety** – when an infant becomes anxious and fearful around strangers.

Parenting is one of the most important factors affecting children's development. The way in which parents feel about their child and how they form a relationship with them is crucial. Babies need strong attachments in order to be emotionally and socially well developed. Children with good attachments are likely to have more confidence, higher self-esteem and are, therefore, less likely to show clinginess and demanding behaviour. However, there are several factors that can affect the attachment process and impact on a child's overall development.

Prematurity – if a premature baby is in an incubator, they cannot be picked up and held. This can affect the attachment process.

Disability – some parents find it harder to attach to a baby with a disability, and they may struggle with their feelings. Some babies with disabilities may experience difficulty forming attachments.

Post-natal depression (PND) – some mothers are depressed after birth, but PND lasts longer and may affect a mother's ability to bond with her baby.

Attachment may not go smoothly because of:

Emotional unavailability – may be due to parents having problems with alcohol or drug abuse, illness or generally struggling with their role.

Separation – separation of parents from their baby, eg due to illness, bereavement or the parents divorcing, can affect attachment. This can impact on a baby's sense of identity.

Foster care/adoption – 'looked after children', children within the care system, may experience inconsistency of caregivers, which can affect attachments and their sense of identity.

▶ **Figure 1.3** Examples of reasons for poor attachment

Case study

Ibrahim – early attachment

Ibrahim was born two months' prematurely and the midwife quickly realised that he had Down's syndrome. Ayesha, Ibrahim's mum, was 47 years old when he was born and had experienced a difficult pregnancy. After the birth, Ibrahim was taken to the maternity intensive care unit. Ayesha experienced a severe bout of post-natal depression. Ayesha's husband Farid worked long

hours as a senior pharmacist and her eldest daughter, Samira, was overseas on a gap year before going to university. Tariq, aged 15 had always been very close to his mum and he helped to look after the baby. Tariq was very good at talking and playing with Ibrahim as well as feeding and bathing him and changing his nappies. Ibrahim soon developed an attachment to Tariq and was very upset when his brother was not with him, refusing to take his feed and becoming very distressed.

Check your knowledge

1 Describe what attachment means and explain the importance of attachment in a child's development.

2 Explain three factors that have affected Ibrahim's attachment to his mother.

3 To what extent can Bowlby's theory justify Ibrahim's reaction to being separated from his brother?

The development and importance of self-concept

Definitions and factors involved in developing positive or negative self-esteem

Positive self-esteem is an important part of emotional wellbeing. Self-esteem involves both self-confidence and self-acceptance. In children, self-esteem is shaped by what they think and feel about themselves. Children who have high self-esteem have an easier time in relationships, resisting peer pressure, making friends and handling conflicts. Children with a positive self-esteem have a generally optimistic view of the world and their life in general. Babies and infants can achieve a growing sense of self and a positive self-esteem through the attachments which they develop with their main caregivers, as shown in Table 1.10.

▶ **Table 1.10** Development of self-esteem

Age	Developmental stage
0–18 months	During infancy, babies start to build self-esteem by having their basic needs met, for example closeness, love and comfort. Babies gradually become aware that they are loved as their primary caregivers provide comfort, care, support and attention. This shows the infant that they are important, as well as safe and secure.
18 months–2 years	Although infants have not yet developed a clear understanding of self-esteem, every time they learn a new skill they begin to realise what they can achieve and begin to learn about themselves, what they can do, what they look like and where they belong. If infants are shown love by their primary caregivers and treated as special, this impacts on their self-esteem. Infants who feel unloved find it more difficult to develop a sense of self-worth and to value themselves.

By the time a child reaches the age of four, positive self-esteem is reinforced by what the child can do successfully and independently, and also by the feedback they receive from their carers. Parents and carers can help to foster a child's self-esteem by teaching problem-solving skills. They should also include children in tasks that provide a sense of accomplishment, asking children for their opinions and introducing children to social settings. Parents can also encourage young children to accept failure as well as success, seeing it as a learning experience and not a negative process.

In contrast, children with low self-esteem can become passive, withdrawn and depressed. These children have difficulty dealing with problems, are very self-critical and speak negatively about themselves. A number of factors impact on children's self-esteem. They may be experiencing difficulties at school, for example completing schoolwork, being bullied or not having friends. There could be stress at home, sibling rivalry or parents arguing. Children facing these problems become pessimistic about themselves and life in general. They can become easily frustrated and see temporary problems as permanent issues.

The physical and emotional changes which occur during puberty and adolescence can present new challenges to young people. Fitting in with peer groups and gaining acceptance is very important. This is a period when young people can learn from their own mistakes and take responsibility for their own actions. Self-esteem can become fragile and may change from day to day. Many teenagers become overly concerned about their physical appearance and how they are viewed and accepted by their peers. Body image is an essential part of a young person's self-esteem. Young people who have a poor body image, who think they are fat, not pretty enough or not muscular enough, can experience low self-esteem.

There has been research into low self-esteem in young people and the problems which are associated with it. For example poor school achievement, behaviour problems, experiencing bullying, teenage pregnancy, smoking and using alcohol and drugs. Other factors include refusing to go to school, depression and thoughts of suicide.

Self-esteem is not fixed and may fluctuate through the life stages. In adulthood, the factors that impact on self-esteem may change. Career development and other personal achievements will increase a person's self-worth while stress and life events that are difficult to cope with can result in lack of confidence and negative self-esteem.

Definitions and factors involved in developing positive or negative self-image

Self-image is the mental picture, a personal view that an individual has of themselves. In other words it is like an internal dictionary which describes an individual's characteristics, for example intelligent, talented, kind, selfish, ugly, beautiful, fat or thin.

▶ What do you see when you look in the mirror?

Self-image is determined in early childhood by the quality of social interaction and the influence of parents or caregivers. A parent who makes positive comments about a child's appearance in a consistent way lays the foundations for a positive self-image. If a parent either ignores a child or constantly makes negative comments then this can impact on the way the child begins to see and think about themselves. Experiences with other people, teachers, family and friends can reinforce what we think and feel about ourselves. For example, if a young person is being made fun of and bullied because of the way they look, then this can lead to physical and psychological problems.

An individual's self-image can be a real or distorted view of who they actually are. It does not necessarily reflect reality. Feelings about image can become internalised and affect how an individual acts. During adolescence, physical appearance becomes particularly important because young people have to come to terms with changes in their body shape and sometimes unwanted physical characteristics, such as acne. The media often portray an ideal image of the female and male figure in advertisements. Self-image is more than what an individual looks like or how other people see the individual. It is also how a person thinks, feels and reacts to self-perceived physical attributes. A young person with anorexia or bulimia who is thin may have a self-image in which they see themselves as fat. A negative body image can lead to psychological problems including anxiety, eating disorders, depression and a negative feeling of self-worth.

Self-image can also be affected by life events and social roles. These influence how others see us and how we define ourselves. Roles such as learner, parent or member of a football team not only help others to recognise the status of an individual but also provide guidelines for behaviour. Life events, roles and status influence personal traits that can also be an important part of self-image. These lead to self-description that can include things like, 'I am impulsive', 'I am generous', 'I tend to worry a lot'.

Interestingly, younger people have a tendency to describe themselves in terms of personal traits whereas older people feel defined by their social status. For example, 'I am a wife', I am a mother', 'I am a midwife', 'I am a member of the badminton team'.

Understanding self-image is very important because it explains how an individual thinks about themselves and how they interact with other people and the world around them. A positive self-image can enhance physical, social, mental, emotional and spiritual wellbeing.

Theory into practice

Produce a leaflet with the definitions and factors involved in developing positive or negative self-esteem.

Also include the definitions and factors involved in developing positive or negative self-image.

A4 Social development across the life stages

When considering social development across the lifespan, it is important to be aware of the great difference between generations and the cultural variations in the way in which individuals will experience social relationships during the course of their lives.

Social development involves learning how to interact socially with other individuals in the family and society in general. Social development provides the opportunities and skills that enable people to develop relationships. Not all individuals will experience social relationships in the same way. Some of the different factors are listed in Table 1.12.

The stages of play, in infancy and early childhood

Children learn and practise basic social skills through play. They develop a sense of self, learn to interact with other children, how to make friends and how to role play.

Jean Piaget highlighted the importance of play for learning and development. When infants play independently it is known as solo play. It starts in infancy and is common at this life stage because they have limited social, cognitive, and physical skills. Solo play provides infants with a variety of learning opportunities, in particular the chance to explore the environment at their own pace. It can help infants to focus their attention, become self-reliant, learn by making mistakes and increase their self-esteem.

Parallel play

Between the ages of two and three, infants move from solo play to playing alongside other children. They have not yet developed the sharing and turn-taking skills required for group or co-operative play. Although infants are engaged in similar activities such as water or sand play, there will be little interaction as each infant will be engrossed in their own independent activity, which is not influenced or shared with others. However, although infants may appear not to interact with other infants and older children, they do show an interest in what other children are doing and still like to be in the presence of adults and other children.

Co-operative play

Between the ages of three and eight, children begin to widen their social network group and form relationships with their peers and other adults. By the age of three, a child has become more co-operative in their play, helped by their language development. For example, moving away from having temper tantrums if they cannot get their own way, playing together with other children, sharing toys and taking turns in games. By the age of seven, most children have established a number of important friendships and others may refer to one friend as their 'best friend'.

Play is essential for communication skills, negotiating roles and beginning to appreciate the feelings of other children. By responding to their peers' feelings, children learn to be more co-operative in their play.

▶ **Table 1.11** Ages and stages of play

Type of Play	Age	Description of Play
Solo play	0–1 year	Looks at adults closely, puts things into mouth and touches things with hands. Plays alone with toys. Gradually begins to play simple games, for example peek-a-boo and begins to explore toys alone.
Solo play	12–18 months	Begins to play and talk alone, repeats actions and starts to play with adults, notices other children.
Parallel play	18 months–2 years	Begins to enjoy repetitive actions, such as putting objects into and taking them out of boxes. Begins to copy other children and adults. Enjoys playing with adults as well as on own. Learns to complete tasks through trial and error.
Associative play	3–4 years	Begins to play co-operatively with other children and starts to show reasoning skills by asking questions, 'why' and 'how'. They join in pretend and fantasy games negotiating and taking on roles.
Co-operative play	4–6 years	Begins to use simple rules in games. Plays co-operatively towards a shared goal and takes turns when playing table top games with other children.
Co-operative play	6–8 years	Begins to enjoy playing in small groups, making up own games and rules. Enjoys understanding and using rules, but does not usually cope well with losing.

Ⅱ PAUSE POINT

Use Piaget's stages of cognitive development to show how the theory helps to explain the stages of play.

Hint

Consider the importance of senses for infants when they are absorbed in solo play (sensorimotor stage) and of symbolic play and language for children during co-operative play (pre-operational stage).

Extend

Go on to explain Chomsky's model of language development in terms of the development of play.

The importance of friendships and friendship groups

Social benefits of friendships

There are many different social benefits associated with friendship groups. On a practical level, friends can help an individual cope with traumatic life events, for example job loss, serious illness, bereavement or relationship breakdown. Close friendships can help support an individual to maintain a healthy lifestyle, for example by encouragement to avoid excessive drinking, or junk food and to take regular exercise. On an emotional level, friendship groups can help people avoid loneliness, provide a sense of belonging, a sense of self-worth and self-confidence. This can lead to reduction of stress and depression and a boost in happiness. As people get older, friendships may take a back seat due to changing interests or circumstances. Other priorities begin to emerge, career and home commitments, caring for children or vulnerable parents, and may lead to friendship groups growing apart.

Effects of peer pressure on social development

Between the ages of 9 and 18, young people enter puberty and adolescence, and there is a close link between their social and emotional development. During adolescence, young people become more independent, socialising outside the family and gaining more freedom. Peer groups play an important part in this stage of social development and begin to have a greater influence on values, views and opinions. Peer pressure can be challenging for teenagers and their families, for example encouraging risky behaviour such as drinking alcohol, taking drugs and engaging in unprotected sexual activities.

▶ Peer groups influence social development

Developing relationships with others

Friendship between young children is very different from friendship between older children, adolescents or adults. Young children tend to form relationships based on play. They quickly fall out with each other and just as quickly make up. Relationships for older children, adolescents and adults are more complex and may involve much more than friendship. This may require new skills. Just as children grow and develop in an observable sequence, the ability to develop relationships also tends to follow a pattern. As children mature and start to think beyond their own needs and are able to see the world from other people's viewpoints, they become able to develop meaningful relationships.

Relationships with others may be informal or formal. Informal relationships develop within families and significant people in individuals' lives. They start in infancy and develop into strong bonds as they are built on trust and understanding. Informal relationships promote a positive self-concept that prepares adolescents and adults for developing intimate relationships that show mutual respect.

Formal relationships develop in different contexts between people who are not related or friends, for instance between colleagues or between teacher and pupil. Formal relationships do not involve emotional attachments but are important to social development. They demand different skills, confidence and self-esteem. Children who have positive relationships with family and others are likely to be successful in developing effective formal relationships.

▶ **Table 1.12** The development of social relationships

Life stage	Social development
Infancy 0–2 years	**Interacting with carers** Infants appear to have an in-built tendency to interact with carers. By 2 months, they may start to smile at human faces. At 3 months, they will respond when adults talk. At 5 months, infants can distinguish between familiar and unfamiliar people. Infants make their first relationships as they form an emotional attachment to carers. In the later stages of infancy, infants will play alongside other children (parallel play).
Childhood 3–8 years	**First social learning** Young children are emotionally attached and dependent on the adults that care for them. Children begin to learn social roles and behaviour within their family context (first or primary socialisation). A family environment might provide a 'safe base' from which to explore social relationships with other children through play. Children will learn to co-operate with other children (co-operative play). As children grow older they become increasingly independent and begin to form friendships based on a sense of mutual trust. Friendships become increasingly important as children grow towards adolescence. Children may begin to form social networks or 'circles' of friends who like and who agree with each other.
Adolescence 9–18 years	**Secondary social learning** During adolescence a person's sense of self-worth may be more influenced by their peers than by their family. Adolescents copy the styles of dress, beliefs, cultural values and behaviours of their own network of friends. Historically, adolescence was seen as a time of 'storm and stress'. Adolescents have to cope with the development of their own sexuality (the impact of sex hormones at puberty) and the social transition to full independence from the family. Recent research suggests that many adolescents experience a smooth transition to adult roles without serious conflict with parents.
Adulthood 19–65 years	**Maturity** During early adulthood, friendship networks continue to be very important. For most people, early adulthood is dominated by forming intimate partnerships and by the need to find employment/establish a career. For many people, marriage and parenthood represent major social developments in their life. In middle adulthood individuals experience time pressures that may limit their social activity. Mature adults may have to split their time between work, caring for parents, other family commitments and wider social activities. Some mature adults report a reduction in the amount of social activity due to these pressures.
Older adulthood 65+ years	Following retirement, older adults have more free time to develop friendships through taking up new hobbies, pastimes and travel. Others may choose to increase their involvement with close friends and family rather than extend their network of social contacts.

The development of independence through the life stages

Infancy and childhood

In infancy, young children are totally dependent on others for their care but, towards the end of this life stage, they begin to assert their need to become independent and attempt to do more for themselves. This comes with increased skills and abilities in dressing and feeding themselves. In early childhood, although still very dependent on parents and carers, they are widening their experience – starting school and joining clubs and activities outside the home. Children gradually become less reliant on close family and start to make their own decisions. Initially, these may be limited to activities, food choices or which clothes to wear but, by the time they reach the end of this life stage, they will have developed clear likes and dislikes.

Peer influence in adolescence

In adolescence, young people begin to question their sense of identity, and who they are, and begin to see themselves as separate and independent from their family. Young people may begin to question their family's values and become influenced by peer group norms and values. Peer influence can lead a young person to question choices and decisions that have been made on their behalf. Young people can learn from real-life experiences about the consequences of making good or poor choices.

Starting employment

Between the ages of 16 and 18, many young people begin to make important decisions about their career options. Young people need to be realistic and empowered to make informed choices about their future career prospects. Starting employment is an important transition and is effectively the first step into an adult world as their status changes from learner to employed worker. It is important to adapt from the rules and routines of a school/college/university day to the policies and procedures of the workplace. The financial independence associated with starting employment is also a step towards full independence. Managing finances, from reading a wage slip, opening a bank account to developing budgeting skills are all important aspects of becoming independent.

Leaving home

There is a clear relationship between leaving home, independence and adulthood. Independence means different things to different people but moving out of the family home is an important step in the process. At some stage in their early twenties, many young people decide to leave their family home. Although many now stay at home longer, because they are studying, unable to work or cannot afford to live independently. Leaving the parental home represents a major transitional event, which is more complex than simply changing address. It could mean making certain sacrifices such as a lower standard of living. While this allows for a new level of independence and self-reliance, juggling household chores with work and managing household bills require young adults to develop a new set of skills.

Starting a family

The new status and responsibilities associated with starting a family may be an important aspect of developing independence. Developing parenting skills and becoming part of a new family unit can provide a sense of identity and a feeling of achievement. Becoming a parent is a major life change and the transition requires lifestyle changes and sometimes financial difficulties. New parents must put the needs of the new baby before their own, which can involve making sacrifices. For instance, a parent may choose to put their career on hold or change working patterns and this can impact on financial and emotional independence. Although family members may be able to offer support, the ultimate responsibility is with the new parents. Parenting can be hard work, making demands on both time and energy.

Discussion

In a small group, discuss what independence means to you.

Consider situations where you might lose some of your independence such as through accident and illness, and identify the effects it would have on your emotional development.

Share ideas with other groups.

Middle adulthood

By middle adulthood, people often have fewer family responsibilities and they can more easily pursue their hobbies and interests. It is in this life stage when individuals are more likely to reach the peak of their career and they may have more disposable income that gives them more independence, choice and freedom. It is during this life stage that individuals may begin to establish different social networks and be able to travel more. However, this is not true for everyone in this age group. Changes to the pension system may result in individuals working longer or taking on part-time work when retired. When retired, many parents at this life stage act as carers for their grandchildren or provide support for elderly parents. This can mean restrictions to an independent lifestyle.

Older adulthood

During the twenty-first century it has become apparent that Britain is an ageing society. According to a report by Age UK, the number of centenarians living in the UK has risen by 73 per cent in the last decade. Many people remain active in their eighties and nineties. For this reason, later adulthood is best viewed in two stages. After retirement between the ages of 65 and 75, many older people remain active with a busy social life, enjoying freedom from a career. Many older people take advantage of free bus passes and concessionary entrance costs. This means that independence can be maintained in later life. The internet and social media makes it easier to explore new interests and relationships. Many older people develop IT skills and make good use of social media that helps them to keep in touch. Although many people remain socially active, which is positive for all aspects of development, some older people begin to disengage from society, especially if spouses and friends have died. This can be a lonely and vulnerable stage which means they lose much of their independence and have to rely on others for their care.

> **Research**
>
> There are aids available that help people to maintain their independence, for example mobility aids or sensory aids.
>
> Find out what aids are available for older people and how they can be accessed.

Assessment practice 1.1

`A1` `A2` `A3` `A4`

Ayesha is 43. She has two children, Amina who is 14 years old and Saeed aged three.

Amina is experiencing puberty.

Ayesha has begun perimenopause.

Saeed's language is developing well. He is forming simple sentences and beginning to ask questions but sometimes gets his tenses and plural words wrong.

1   Explain, giving two examples, how puberty may affect Amina at her life stage.

2   Discuss the physical and emotional effects of perimenopause for Ayesha.

3   To what extent does Chomsky's language acquisition device help to explain Saeed's language development?

Plan
- What am I being asked to do?
- Do I need clarification about anything?

Do
- Have I considered all aspects of each question?

Review
- I can explain how I approached the task.
- Have I related the answer to the individuals in the case study?

B Factors affecting human growth and development

B1 The nature/nurture debate

There has been great debate about influences on human behaviour. Psychologists refer to this as the nature/nurture debate. **Nature** refers to genetic inheritance and other biological factors, whereas **nurture** refers to external influences on development such as the environment you grow up in or social influences.

Certain physical characteristics are biologically determined by genetic inheritance, for example the colour of eyes, straight or curly hair and skin pigmentation. Other physical characteristics appear to be strongly influenced by the genetic make-up of the birth parents, such as height, weight, life expectancy and vulnerability to specific diseases. However, there is still a debate as to whether psychological characteristics such as behavioural tendencies, personality traits and mental abilities are also 'wired in' before a child is born or whether they are influenced by their environment.

Bowlby's theory of attachment is a biological perspective of development (nature) as it explains the bond between mother and child as being an innate process. Chomsky's proposal that language is developed through the use of an innate language acquisition device also comes from a biological perspective. In contrast, Bandura's social learning theory (see below) is based on an understanding that the environment influences development (nurture) and that children learn through imitation and role modelling.

Characteristics and differences not observed at birth but which emerge later in life, are referred to as **maturation**. The 'nature' perspective is based on an assumption that all individuals have an inner 'biological clock' that determines when and at what rate physical development will progress.

Development as a result of genetic or inherited factors

Gesell's maturation theory

The psychologist and paediatrician Arnold Gesell was interested in children's biological maturation (that part of their growth determined by genetically determined physiological processes). In the 1940s – 1950s he developed a new methodology or 'normative approach' to researching child development which involved observing large numbers of children to find the skills and abilities that most children had in each age group. His findings were used to establish 'norms' or milestones for each developmental aspect. Gesell noted that each child moved through the sequence at their own pace. He came to the conclusion that development was predetermined and that the environment had little influence. If a child experiences delayed development, then the problem is heredity rather than the result of the child's environment and circumstances. Milestones are helpful for educators and parents today to measure children's development and to recognise developmental delay. It is important, however, to recognise individual differences in children that are influenced by environmental factors. Critics of Gesell suggest that maturation theory is not helpful in explaining individual or cultural differences or for children with learning difficulties.

> **Key terms**
>
> **Nature** – genetic inheritance and other biological factors.
>
> **Nurture** – the influence of external factors after conception such as social and environmental factors.

> **Key term**
>
> **Maturation** – a genetically programmed sequence of change, for example the onset of the menopause.

> **Discussion**
>
> In a small group, discuss the importance of milestones for professionals when observing and assessing the development of infants and children. Give reasons for how knowing a child's stage of development can improve developmental outcomes for children in the long term.

Development as a result of environmental factors

Bandura's social learning theory

Albert Bandura's social learning theory is based on his observations of learning occurring through observing the behaviour of others. You may have seen a young child modelling behaviours, for instance pretending they are on a mobile phone or copying dance moves. Unfortunately, children may copy unwanted behaviour such as hitting as well. Bandura suggested there were four stages of behavioural learning. Firstly, the child notices the behaviour of another person. This is likely to be someone close to them or who they admire, such as an older sibling. Secondly, the child 'internalises' the action by remembering what they have observed. Thirdly, although they may not copy straight away, they will reproduce the behaviour when the opportunity occurs. Lastly, depending on the outcome (**positive** or **negative reinforcement**) children will either repeat the behaviour or desist. Bandura (1961) based his theory on a famous experiment using a Bobo doll in which he demonstrated that children learn and copy aggressive behaviour by observing adults behaving aggressively. The importance of modelling appropriate behaviours is recognised by many teachers and parents.

Stress-diathesis model

The **stress-diathesis** psychological model helps to explain how stress caused by life events (nurture) can interact with an individual's genetic vulnerability (nature) to impact on their mental wellbeing. According to this theory, some individuals are born with certain biological or genetic predispositions to a mental illness, referred to as diathesis. A person who has a genetic predisposition to a psychological disorder might never develop the disorder if they do not experience stress in their life. High levels of stress, such as family conflict, abuse, trauma or problems at school, could trigger the onset for those with a predisposition.

> **Key terms**
>
> **Positive reinforcement** – the behaviour is repeated because of personal satisfaction (intrinsic reinforcement) or rewards (extrinsic reinforcement).
>
> **Negative reinforcement** – the behaviour is not repeated to avoid an adverse experience such as lack of satisfaction or to avoid being told off.

> **Key term**
>
> **Diathesis** – a predisposition or vulnerability to mental disorder through abnormality of the brain or neuro-transmitters.

> **Reflect**
>
> Form small groups to discuss what nature/nurture means to you. Draw overlapping circles on a large sheet of paper. Note the characteristics that you mainly associate with your genetic makeup (nature) in one circle and those you mainly associate with your environment (nurture) in the other. Place characteristics that are affected by both in the overlap.

While these theories are useful guidance they do not provide the answers as to whether development throughout the lifespan is down to nature or nurture. It is probably more useful to assume that hereditary and environmental factors (nature and nurture) interact to influence the type of person an individual becomes and the type of behaviour they display.

B2 Genetic factors that affect development

Each living cell in the human body has a nucleus containing 23 pairs of chromosomes. In each pair of chromosomes, one comes from the father and one from the mother. Each chromosome carries units of inheritance known as genes, and these genes interact to create a new set of instructions for making a new person. Genes, for example, determine the colour of your eyes and hair and whether you will be short or tall.

Genes are made of a substance called deoxyribonucleic acid (DNA). DNA contains the instructions for producing proteins. It is these proteins that regulate the development of a human being.

Genetic predispositions to particular conditions

A predisposition is the possibility that you will develop a certain condition. A **genetic predisposition** means that you inherit that possibility from one or both of your biological parents. However, a genetic predisposition does not mean that it is a certainty that you will develop that condition. Although the genetic make-up that predisposes these conditions cannot be altered, we can sometimes alter environmental factors and offer support and treatment to allow the individuals to develop and lead life as healthily as possible. There are some inherited conditions, some rarer than others, that have serious consequences for a child's growth and development.

> **Key term**
>
> **Genetic predisposition** – inherited genes that determine physical growth, development, health and appearance.

Cystic fibrosis

Cystic fibrosis is caused by a faulty gene thought to be carried by as many as 4 per cent of the UK population. The gene is recessive, which means that both parents must be carriers for their children to develop cystic fibrosis. When both parents carry the faulty gene, there is a one-in-four chance that their child will be born with cystic fibrosis.

Cystic fibrosis results in a defective protein being produced that can cause the lungs to become clogged with thick sticky mucus. People with cystic fibrosis may have problems absorbing nourishment from food and they may also suffer from respiratory and chest infections. In the past, children with cystic fibrosis often had a very short life expectancy, but contemporary medical treatments have succeeded in extending both quality of life and life expectancy. Physiotherapy helps people with cystic fibrosis to clear mucus from their lungs. Various drugs help control breathing and throat and lung infections, and a special diet and drugs help with food absorption. In the future, it may become possible to use genetic therapy to replace the faulty gene.

Brittle bone disease

Brittle bone disease may be passed from a person's parents, but it can also develop from a genetic mutation. Children born with brittle bone disease are at high risk of fracturing or breaking their bones easily because their bones develop without the right amount or type of a protein called collagen. There are different types of the disease and some types are more serious than others. Children with brittle bone disease can often be helped through physiotherapy, assistive equipment and drug treatments to help strengthen their bones.

Phenylketonuria (PKU)

PKU is a rare genetic disorder that prevents a child from breaking down phenylalanine, an amino acid (a building block for protein) found in many foods such as milk, meat and eggs. In PKU, if the child eats foods containing phenylalanine there is a build-up of harmful substances in the body that damages brain development. The condition cannot be cured. All babies in the UK are screened at birth by a heel-prick blood test. If a high phenylalanine level is detected, treatment will be started immediately with a special diet and medication to prevent the build-up of harmful substances. A baby born with undetected PKU would fail to meet developmental milestones and experience developmental delay as their brain became damaged. Untreated PKU would result in severe learning disability and the child's death.

Huntington's disease

Huntington's disease can develop at any age but often starts between the ages of 35 and 55. Huntington's disease is an inherited neurodegenerative genetic disorder that causes progressive damage to certain nerve cells in the brain. It can affect muscle coordination and cause mental decline and behavioural changes. The brain damage gets progressively worse over time, with perception, awareness, thinking and judgement (cognition) affected. Although the symptoms of the disease can vary between individuals, and even affected members of the same family, the progress of the disease is usually predictable.

The earliest signs are hardly noticeable and may be missed or mistaken for other conditions, for example subtle changes in personality and mood swings, irritability, altered behaviour and fidgety movements. As the disease progresses, the features of the disease can include psychiatric problems, problems associated with feeding, communication and erratic behaviour. During the later stages of the disease, movement, behaviour and cognitive abilities are affected and the individual becomes increasingly dependent on other people for care and support.

Klinefelter Syndrome

Klinefelter syndrome is not easy to identify in small children as the signs and symptoms are not always obvious. It is estimated that around one in 600 boys will be born with this condition, sometimes referred to as XXY. The extra X chromosome is acquired after the baby is conceived; it is not an inherited condition. Some of the signs include that the baby is slow in reaching milestones such as sitting up, crawling and walking. The baby may be born with undescended testicles. Poor muscle power, delayed communication and a passive personality may also be signs. Many boys with this condition also experience difficulty socialising and expressing their feelings which can impact on emotional development and lead to low self-confidence.

Some boys with this condition experience mild learning difficulties such as low attention span and difficulty with literacy skills, especially reading, writing and spelling. They also experience higher rates of dyslexia or dyspraxia. Other physical signs include low energy levels and extra growth spurts, particularly in the legs and widening of the hips. The onset of puberty is often not affected. However, the testes do not increase in size and there may be a lack of testosterone leading to a flabby body, low muscle tone, a reduction in calcium in the bones, small firm testicles, a small penis and lack of body or facial hair. There may be difficulties with sex drive (libido) and fertility. Treatment is available for low testosterone levels.

Most adult males with this syndrome are able to live independently and establish careers and relationships.

Down's Syndrome

Down's syndrome is a genetic condition that occurs as a result of an extra chromosome (chromosome 21). The condition can cause varying levels of learning disability, the characteristic physical features and associated medical issues. Each year, approximately 750 babies born in the UK will have Down's syndrome and recent research estimates that 60,000 people in the UK have the condition.

In the vast majority of cases, Down's syndrome is not inherited. It is simply the result of a one-off genetic 'mistake' in the sperm or egg. There is a higher risk of giving birth to a baby with Down's syndrome for women 45 years and older (about 1 in 50). In comparison, a 20-year-old woman has a risk of one in 1500.

The life expectancy of people who have Down's syndrome is generally between 50 and 60 years but with improvements in health care a small number of people with the condition live into their 70s.

According to research by NHS Scotland (2004), people with Down's syndrome experience a higher incidence of depression. Other health conditions that are more common are hearing, visual or heart problems.

Improved health and social care support and education has provided opportunities for young people who have Down's syndrome to leave home and live independently so that they are able to form new relationships and gain employment.

Colour blindness

True colour blindness is a very rare condition in which an individual has no colour perception at all. Colour vision deficiency, where individuals have difficulty in distinguishing between different colours, is commonly known as colour blindness. It affects approximately 2.7 million people in Britain, about 4.5 per cent of the population, mostly men. The condition can vary in severity and some people do not realise that they are colour blind, leading healthy lives without treatment.

For the majority of people, the condition is genetic. Inherited colour vision deficiency is a result of an abnormality in the retina (the light-sensitive layers of cells that line the back of the eye). Others will experience the condition as a result of other diseases such as diabetes and multiple sclerosis. The ageing process or side effects of certain types of medication can also affect colour recognition.

Although it is important to identify any colour blindness in young children so that their learning experience is not affected, for most people the condition does not lead to long-term health problems. It is important that health and social care providers take colour blindness into consideration when delivering services by using appropriate colour schemes when producing printed information.

Duchenne muscular dystrophy

The muscular dystrophies (MD) are a group of inherited genetic conditions that gradually weaken muscles leading to disability. It is a progressive condition and worsens over time. Muscular dystrophy is caused by changes in the genes responsible for the structure and functioning of a person's muscles. This causes changes in the muscle fibres that interfere with their ability to function. The most common and severe form of the muscular dystrophies is Duchenne muscular dystrophy. This condition is inherited on the female gene and is passed only to male offspring.

According to research by Muscular Dystrophy UK (2015), about 1 in 3500 boys in the UK are born with Duchenne muscular dystrophy. There are about 2500 boys living with the condition in the UK at any one time.

Duchenne muscular dystrophy is caused by genetic mutations on the X chromosome. This prevents the body from producing a vital muscle protein, dystrophin, which is essential for building and repairing muscles. The muscular weakness is not noticeable at birth but becomes more noticeable in early childhood and more prominent as the child grows older.

The condition is usually diagnosed by the age of five and, by the time an individual is 12, they may have to use a wheelchair. It is a serious condition with muscle weakness mainly in muscles near to the trunk of the body, around the hips and the shoulders. This means that fine motor skills such as using hands and fingers, are less affected than gross motor skills. Many young men with Duchenne muscular dystrophy face severe health problems, especially by their late teens, as the muscles of their heart and lungs weaken.

Although the condition is severely disabling, many young men with Duchenne muscular dystrophy are able to lead active lives. Survival beyond the age of 30 was rare, but research and medical advances are increasing this and life expectancy is beginning to improve. The right specialist health and social care can make a huge difference to both the quality and length of life.

Susceptibility to disease

According to the World Health Organization (WHO), most diseases involve environmental factors and the complex interaction of many genes. In other words, although an individual may not be born with a disease, their genetic make-up may make them susceptible to acquiring it later in life. Diseases and disorders that are more likely to happen in individuals with a **susceptibility** include certain types of cancer, diabetes and having high blood cholesterol.

Cancer

There are over 200 types of cancer. Cancer is a cell disease that results in them becoming abnormal and dividing to make even more abnormal cells. Most cancers are attributed to environmental and lifestyle factors. For example, lung cancer is closely linked with tobacco use and skin cancer to over exposure to ultraviolet (UV) light. It is estimated that over 40 per cent of cancers can be prevented by making different lifestyle choices such as diet, not smoking, reducing alcohol intake, exercising and avoiding environmental factors such as exposure to the sun or asbestos dust. Some people are more at risk because they have inherited gene faults that increase their risk. There are a number of cancers where a genetic link has been shown, including cancer of the breast, bowel, womb and kidney. For those with the faulty gene, getting cancer is not inevitable although an unhealthy lifestyle will increase the risk.

Diabetes

Diabetes is an increasingly common chronic condition affecting millions of people in the UK. Approximately 1 in 16 people (3.9 million) in the UK have diabetes and this figure has doubled since 1996. Although other factors, such as environment and lifestyle are more likely to play a role in Type 2 (later/mature onset) diabetes, there is a strong predisposition to developing both Type 1 (early onset, insulin-dependent) and Type 2 diabetes. The genetic risk of developing Type 1 diabetes is higher if either or both, biological parents have diabetes. The risk for developing Type 2 diabetes is almost 90 per cent if you have an identical twin who is diabetic.

High blood cholesterol

Lifestyle factors, such as unhealthy diet, smoking or lack of exercise increase the chance of having a high blood cholesterol level for most people. Cholesterol is a fatty substance that is carried around the body by proteins. Too much can cause a build-up in the artery walls. This can cause heart disease and other cardiovascular diseases.

Another reason for high cholesterol levels is an inherited condition that runs in families, known as familial hypercholesterolaemia. In the UK, approximately 1 in 600 people have this condition. It is caused by a gene alteration inherited from a parent. People with this type of high blood cholesterol are born with the condition and it can lead to early heart problems unless treated. There is a 50 per cent chance that a child or a sibling of someone diagnosed with familial hypercholesterolaemia will also have the condition.

Biological factors that affect development

The environment inside a mother's womb can have a dramatic influence on a child's development. If a woman smokes or drinks alcohol during pregnancy, foetal development may be affected. The nicotine inhaled in smoking contains carbon dioxide which gets into the blood stream restricting the amount of oxygen to the foetus. Children born to mothers who smoke tend to weigh less at birth and are more prone to infections and are twice as likely to die of cot death. It can affect a child's long-term development including their attention span and learning abilities. Taking drugs and getting some types of infection can also damage a child's development in the womb.

Foetal alcohol syndrome

Drinking alcohol during pregnancy carries a huge risk to a baby's health and development. Mothers may give birth to children with foetal alcohol syndrome. Children with this condition have developmental and physical defects which have life-long effects. They tend to be smaller and to have smaller heads than normal caused by poor brain development. These children may also have heart defects, learning difficulties and neurological problems.

Maternal infections during pregnancy

If a pregnant woman is exposed to, or acquires infections such as rubella (a type of measles) or cytomegalovirus (a herpes-type virus) the foetus may be adversely affected. Rubella is particularly dangerous during the first month of pregnancy. If a mother becomes infected in this period her baby may be born with impaired hearing or eyesight, or a damaged heart. Most women are vaccinated against rubella to prevent this risk. Cytomegalovirus (CMV) is a common virus belonging to the herpes family. It spreads via bodily fluids. Most people are infected with CMV at some stage of their life but the majority have no noticeable symptoms. If a pregnant woman has an active infection they can pass it to the foetus and this is referred to as congenital CMV. Around one or two babies in 200 are born with congenital CMV and around 13 per cent of those are born with symptoms such as deafness and learning difficulties and 14 per cent will develop problems later on.

Lifestyle/diet during pregnancy

Our biological life starts at conception, approximately nine months before we are born. Babies are affected by what their mothers eat during pregnancy and breast-feeding. Some recent animal research suggests that if a pregnant or breast-feeding woman has a diet high in sugar and fat it can result in an increased risk of high blood cholesterol and later heart disease for the child. Malnutrition or a lack of healthy food during pregnancy may result in a lifetime of poor health for the child. The Food Standards Agency (FSA) recommends that pregnant women should eat plenty of fresh fruit and vegetables, plenty of starchy foods such as bread and pasta and rice, foods rich in protein such as lean meat, chicken and fish, plenty of fibre and foods containing calcium such as milk and cheese. They also advise that women should avoid or limit alcohol and avoid too much caffeine, which may result in a low birth weight.

PAUSE POINT   Write a one-sentence definition for: Genetic predisposition, Susceptibility to disease and Biological factors.

> Hint   Complete this sentence. 'Genetic predisposition is an increased likelihood of developing the condition because ...'

> Extend   Write a short case study for each factor to expand your answer.

Congenital defects

Congenital defects are the most common cause of childhood chronic illness, disability and death. About 9 in every 1000 children in the UK are born with congenital defects. The most common and severe congenital disorders are heart defects, **neural tube defects** and Down's syndrome.

Congenital defects may be genetic but other factors can also be responsible, for example:

▶ **socio-economic factors** especially lack of access to sufficient nutritious food during pregnancy

> **Key terms**
>
> **Congenital** – present at birth.
>
> **Neural tube defects** – congenital defects of the brain, spine or spinal cord, such as spina bifida.

- **environmental factors** such as working or living in polluted areas, exposure to chemicals or pesticides, excessive use of tobacco, alcohol and drugs during pregnancy
- **infectious diseases (during pregnancy)** such as syphilis and rubella.

Sometimes it can be difficult to identify a specific cause.

Some congenital defects can be prevented by adequate antenatal care including screening, vaccination and adequate intake of nutrients such as minerals and vitamins, especially folic acid.

> **Theory into practice**
>
> Research and put together a presentation for other students about genetic factors that affect development. Make your presentation creative and colourful. Include the key words and definitions in the form of a glossary.

B3 Environmental factors that affect development

Exposure to pollution

Air and water pollution can influence development and be a major source of ill health. There is growing concern about the impact of air quality, both indoors and outdoors, and the contribution it makes to causing particular illnesses such as asthma and other respiratory problems. The environment may contain many chemicals from vehicle exhaust systems and industrial emissions. Household **pollutants** include mould and some cleaning products that emit poisonous gases.

Respiratory disorders

Tobacco smoke, combustion products and air pollution associated with various toxins and pollutants are among the major substances harmful to the respiratory system. These substances affect the nerves and muscles used for breathing and can also have a bad effect on the lining of the air passages. **Respiratory disorders** range from mild, for example a runny nose or sore throat to more severe conditions such as bacterial pneumonia, chronic obstructive pulmonary disease and lung cancer.

Cardiovascular problems

The risk factors associated with **cardiovascular problems** include smoking tobacco and air pollution. Recent studies suggest that environmental pollution is linked to increased illness and death. Tobacco smoke is linked to changes in the lining of the heart and blood vessels causing clots (thrombosis), which may lead to a heart attack. Exposure to other chemicals that cause air pollution has also been reported as increasing the risk of thrombosis and raised blood pressure. Exposure to pollution during pregnancy may be linked to the baby having congenital heart defects and cardiovascular disease in later life.

Allergies

Allergies are caused by irritants such as dust or pollen causing the immune system to overreact. Hay fever and asthma are examples of respiratory system allergic reactions. These conditions are usually chronic as they are a response to the environment in which the individual lives. Hay fever is a seasonal reaction to certain types of pollen. It can cause sneezing, watery eyes and a runny nose, lethargy and flu-like symptoms. Asthma can range from a mild reaction to a life-threatening condition. An asthma attack causes difficulty in breathing as the airways (bronchi and bronchioles) become inflamed and constricted (narrowed). This is usually a temporary

> **Key terms**
>
> **Pollutant** – a substance that contaminates something such as air or water and may make it unsafe.
>
> **Respiratory disorders** – conditions affecting the upper respiratory tract, trachea, bronchi, bronchioles, alveoli, pleura and pleural cavity.
>
> **Cardiovascular problems** – any disorder or disease of the heart or blood vessels.

reaction and can be relieved by using an inhaler to widen the airways, although it can cause distress to young children. Asthma UK has reported that the number of people living with this condition has plateaued, but on average three people a day die from asthma.

Motor vehicles produce a range of pollutants including carbon monoxide, nitrogen oxides, volatile organic compounds and particulate matter. People who live near busy roads may be particularly exposed to this pollution.

Power stations are burning less coal, which has contributed to a fall in sulphur dioxide pollution. Improved vehicle technology, such as catalytic converters, has also contributed to a reduction in air pollution. Evidence from *Social Trends Survey* (2009) reported that emissions of nitrogen oxides fell by 46 per cent between 1990 and 2006. Diesel vehicles, originally thought to be less polluting than petrol engines, emit four times more toxic pollution than a bus.

While official statistics report improvements in the levels of air pollution, there are concerns that it is still a serious problem. Research by King's College London (2015) identified that nearly 9500 people die prematurely in London each year as a result of long-term exposure to air pollution. The research identified that London, Birmingham and Leeds are the most polluted cities in the UK. London has been found to have air pollution twice the level permitted by WHO standards. People living in cities may be more at risk of developing cardiovascular problems and respiratory disorders.

Research

Just how serious is air pollution in your own area? Research the sources and level of risk of pollution. You could share and discuss your findings with other learners to help you decide how serious this issue is.

Reflect

According to the British Heart Foundation, people with coronary heart disease should avoid spending long periods of time in areas where traffic pollution is a high risk. In February 2015, the European Commission took legal action against the UK Government for failing to reduce nitrogen dioxide emissions quickly enough.

Levels of pollution appear to be falling, but are current levels acceptable? Think about the impact on young children and people who have heart or respiratory disorders.

Poor housing conditions

Poor quality housing is associated with poor health and quality of life. The WHO (2010) published a report that focused on the links between poor housing and the impact on the health and wellbeing of individuals. The English Housing Survey (2011) showed that there are approximately 4.5 million households in the UK experiencing fuel poverty. Evidence suggests that living in poor housing increases the risk of respiratory and cardiovascular disease, as well as anxiety and depression. A cold damp home with excessive mould and structural defects presents many different risks to health and wellbeing, including accidents and illness.

▶ How many health problems can you think of that would be associated with living in these type of conditions?

Overcrowded housing may limit people's access to washing, cooking and cleaning facilities. Indoor air pollution, drying clothes indoors and inadequate ventilation can be associated with respiratory disorders. Infection is more easily spread in overcrowded conditions with inadequate sanitary provision. There may also be issues with the lack of access to outdoor exercise and green spaces in some areas, particularly in low income areas, reducing opportunities for physical activity outdoors. The Child Poverty Action Group (2013) reported more play areas in deprived areas in the UK, but poorer quality spaces and equipment, and vandalism, playground misuse and danger of injury being deterrents to their use.

Respiratory disorders

Overcrowded housing, lack of heating and poor ventilation causing damp and mould in homes can lead to respiratory problems, especially asthma and other allergic responses. Babies, young children and older people are particularly vulnerable. Research has identified that more than a million children in England (English Household Survey, 2012) live in overcrowded households and that they are more at risk of getting meningitis and respiratory problems.

Cardiovascular problems

Children living for extended periods in overcrowded housing tend to have problems with their growth rate and an increased risk of heart disease in later life. Poor quality housing, especially for vulnerable adults and older people, can lead to stress which can affect an individual's blood pressure. High blood pressure can result in damage to artery walls and an increased risk of blood clots and strokes. Lack of exercise and poor diet can also lead to cardiovascular problems. Other factors that may be associated with poor living conditions are unhealthy lifestyles, including smoking, drinking and poor diet. Ready-made meals and heavily processed convenience food are often high in sugar, salt and saturated fats resulting in larger calorie intake leading to an increased risk of cardiovascular disease. There are also issues with the lack of green spaces in some areas, particularly in low income areas, preventing people taking part in physical activity outdoors.

Hypothermia

Cold homes and homelessness are major causes of hospital admission to treat **hypothermia.** The number of families living in fuel poverty is rising. Families with low incomes are unable to afford to heat their homes, especially in older properties. Age UK (2012) found a link between loneliness and the risk of hypothermia for elderly people living in poor conditions. Many people over the age of 65 spend more time at home and factors such as poor heating and lack of insulation have been linked to a rise in winter deaths. Older people on low incomes may worry about the cost of heating their homes, especially if they live in older, less well-insulated properties that incur higher heating bills. Research shows that older people are more likely to live in substandard housing.

Anxiety and depression

Poor quality housing may cause stress, anxiety, depression and mental health issues. Living in substandard housing with rising fuel bills can lead to disturbed sleep patterns, resulting in stress and anxiety. Many children living in overcrowded and poor standard housing experience anxiety and mental health issues.

> **Key term**
>
> **Hypothermia** – excessively low body temperature, below 35 °C (normal body temperature is 37 °C).

 PAUSE POINT   Close your book and list four features of poor housing.

 Hint   Think about the features affecting the home itself and the immediate environment.

Extend   For each point, give two possible effects on a person's health and development.

Access to health and social care services that affect development

According to National Institute for Health and Care Excellence, local authorities need to improve services for people who do not usually use health and social care services. Each local public health authority has to ensure multi-agency and partnership working within health and social care services to meet the needs of people who live in the local community.

In line with the Equality Act 2010, all health and social care services should be inclusive and have a positive impact on local people and communities. The local authority has a responsibility to identify barriers to accessing services. These could include transport, opening times, cultural and behaviour barriers. Additionally, new ways of supporting people who would not normally access services need to be identified.

Availability of transport

Travelling to appointments can be stressful. The Office for National Statistics (2006) reported that 11 per cent of households without access to a car have difficulty getting to their local GP's surgery compared to only 4 per cent of car users. Living in remote areas may mean that there is no public transport at all. Unreliable public transport services and stressful journeys can result in cancelled or missed appointments. This can have a negative impact on the health and wellbeing of frail and vulnerable people or families with young children. Missed appointments also have financial implications for health and social care services.

Using hospital car parks outsourced to private contractors can be expensive for people attending regular hospital appointments or visiting relatives in hospital.

Opening hours of services

The National Health Service provides health care for everyone. However, there are concerns that some groups of people may not have the same access to GP services and preventative health services as others. Recruitment of GPs and nurses may be difficult in deprived areas. Hospital and GP appointments during working hours may be inconvenient and there have been discussions that opening hours should better reflect the busy lifestyles of some service users. Several services have been introduced to improve access to primary care services such as NHS Walk-in Centres, the NHS 111 service and NHS Direct.

❚❚ PAUSE POINT

Identify the particular problems of accessing health and social care services that a person with a learning disability might face.

Hint   Think about factors such as communication and mobility.

Extend   Give examples of other groups or individuals who may have difficulty in accessing services.

Research

Using the internet and other sources, investigate the services offered by the NHS outside of normal working hours. What might be the barriers to accessing these services?

Needs and requirements of particular services

Local health and social care services aim to promote an early intervention policy to tackle disadvantage and poor access to services. They intend to improve the health and wellbeing of young children and their families. Improving health and reducing poverty is important for preventing long-term health problems and reducing the risk of premature death.

They emphasise the importance of focusing on the health and wellbeing of people who would not usually access services.

People who do not access services

Homeless people and vulnerable immigrants, who may be at risk of infectious diseases, such as tuberculosis, are particular groups who find it difficult to access services. Some families are difficult to reach, for example travelling families and families for whom English is not their first language. It is important to ensure that children in these families receive regular health checks and are fully immunised against childhood infections such as meningitis C and measles to prevent health and development problems.

According to a Department of Health report, 'Healthy Lives Healthy People' (2011), many people may be reluctant to register with a GP or not be registered. There are many reasons why people are unable to attend GP surgeries, for example because of caring commitments, working long hours or transport difficulties. According to the Office for National Statistics, cardiovascular disease mortality is high in deprived communities. This may be due to people not registering with a GP surgery, being reluctant to attend surgeries or having difficulty getting/attending an appointment.

Discussion

Working in small groups, discuss the following issues. Why might people require health or social care in their own home? What kind of support is available and who might deliver it? Share your findings with the whole group.

Working in pairs, research your local community.

1. Produce a demographic profile including age, social economic grouping, environmental factors, housing and ethnic groups.

2. Note the type of health and social care services that are available and any gaps in services.

B4 Social factors that affect development

A family is a social group of people, often related genetically, by marriage or by living together as a group. There are many different types of family. Being part of a family group can help you to develop in the following ways:

▶ forming your first emotional relationships and attachments

▶ providing your first experiences of social interaction

▶ influencing your view of what is expected of you in social settings, and what is normal or socially acceptable behaviour

▶ providing a setting that meets your physical needs for protection, food, shelter and warmth

▶ supporting each other emotionally and protecting family members from stress

▶ helping each other financially or practically, for example families may support older relatives.

Discussion

Working in pairs discuss: 'Which social factors affect human growth and development and how can they influence an individual's health, wellbeing and life opportunities?'

Produce a thought shower of all the points you have identified.

Family dysfunction

Some families are unable to conform to the social norms expected, which prevents the family performing its expected functions. A **dysfunctional family** is a family that does not provide some or all of the benefits listed above. There are many reasons why a family may become dysfunctional. Family members may become stressed because of health problems including mental health problems, poor housing and low income. Some adults have poor parenting skills. Some may try to control other family members in aggressive or manipulative ways. Others may be insufficiently involved with their children and neglect them. Some parents may be inconsistent in the way that they teach children to behave socially and some may have grown up within a dysfunctional family themselves and have little practical experience of providing appropriate relationships and support for other family members. Stressful family environments may disadvantage children. It may be hard to develop self-confidence if there are constant emotional tensions at home.

Parental divorce or separation

Increase in parental divorce and separation has been associated with particular consequences for children's growth and development. Parental divorce can be associated with negative outcomes and children/adolescents can experience emotional problems that may affect their self-esteem and self-confidence, leading

Key term

Dysfunctional family – a family that is not providing all of the support and benefits associated with being in a family.

to emotional distress, moodiness and depression. Children and adolescents may lack resilience, placing greater reliance on and being influenced by their peers. This could lead to risky behaviours such as smoking, taking drugs or using alcohol. Additionally, there is some evidence that children of divorced parents are more likely to experience poverty and underachievement in education.

Sibling rivalry

In his social learning theory, Bandura explored the impact of role modelling and imitating behaviour. Constant exposure to high levels of family conflict, especially in dysfunctional families, could lead to a child becoming aggressive and displaying bullying behaviour towards other children in the family. Research by the psychologists Rosenthal and Doherty (1984) suggests that children who are in rivalry with their siblings or involved in bullying behaviour have quite often been bullied by their primary carers. This can be a way of children trying to gain a sense of control and power in a household in which they feel helpless and powerless. Parents or primary carers may also be responsible for deliberately or inadvertently causing sibling conflict by encouraging competition, and sometimes conflict, between siblings.

▶ Do you have brothers and/or sisters? If so, do you always get on well together?

Parenting styles

The developmental psychologist Diana Baumrind (1960s) identified three different **parenting styles** that she felt could contribute to the overall development of children.

▶ **Authoritative** – parents are not overly strict; children are brought up to respect authority and develop appropriate values and boundaries. Children in these households are often more resilient and conform more easily to the social norms of society.

▶ **Authoritarian** – parents have very high expectations, often overwhelming their children with strict rules and regulations. Children in these households are often rebellious and may become problematic both in the family home and in wider social settings.

▶ **Permissive** – parents make few demands, and may be reluctant to implement rules or values into the lives of their children. Children in these households often lack a sense of self-control as they have no set boundaries or respect for personal space – children may later experience problems in managing relationships and adult responsibilities.

Key term

Parenting styles – a definition of the different strategies/ways that parents use to bring up their children.

A fourth style, uninvolved parenting, was identified through further research. This type is characterised by parents who are not involved in their children's lives. They make few demands of them and lack responsiveness.

Some parents are unaware of the power they hold over their children. Developmental theorists, such as Piaget and Erikson, believed that family dysfunction was a result of lack of education and inadequate role modelling. This leads to a parenting style that is detrimental to a child's growth and development. Some parents lack emotional intelligence and the skills required to raise their children to be resilient and prepared for the outside world. Parents experiencing mental health issues or substance dependency may struggle with their own mental health or emotional issues and find it difficult to meet all the needs of their children. In some cases, this can result in neglect and abuse of their children.

Bullying

Effects of bullying on self-esteem

There is no legal definition of bullying. It can be described as repetitive behaviour intended to hurt an individual emotionally and/or physically. Many children experience bullying at school but adults can also experience bullying behaviour. It can undermine self-esteem and lead to stress, depression and anxiety.

Individuals might be bullied for many reasons, for example their religion, race or particular group or culture they belong to. Bullying behaviour can take different forms – it can be non-physical such as teasing a person or name calling. More serious forms of bullying might involve making threats or physical violence. With the rising use of social media, in particular with the increased use of mobile phones, cyber bullying has increased. This type of bullying takes place online, via email, instant messenger and social networks.

Bullying can have long-term effects on self-esteem, lasting even into adulthood. The Department for Education provides advice and guidance to educational settings about how to deal with bullying behaviour. By law, all state schools must have a behaviour policy that includes measures to prevent bullying and that clearly outlines the steps that must be taken to support young people. The workplace should also have procedures to report and deal with bullying.

Self-harm

The effects of bullying can impact on a child's growth and development, especially on their emotional development. It might lead to a child feeling unsafe, lonely and isolated and losing self-confidence. They may become self-critical and believe that what is said about them is true or that it is their fault. For some people (children, young people and adults), self-harm is a way of releasing their feelings of guilt, self-loathing, distress and emotional pain. Hurting themselves makes them feel better. Self-harmers often hide their behaviour, for example by always wearing long sleeves to disguise cuts on their arms. Some children, adolescents and even adults can experience anxiety and severe depression which may result in suicidal thoughts or even suicide.

Culture, religion and beliefs

The UK is a religious and culturally diverse society. Health and social care providers may be working with service users whose culture or religious beliefs could influence treatment decisions. This can lead to complex situations and emotional distress that affects the relationship between the care provider and family members.

Medical intervention

Most faith groups emphasise the importance of prayer as part of the healing process and there is a general belief that prayer complements medical care. However, some religious groups believe that certain medical procedures should not be allowed and reject medical intervention. For example, Jehovah's Witnesses believe (based on commands in the Bible) that blood transfusions, even if needed to save a person's life, must not be accepted. In some cases, doctors have had to take legal proceedings to ensure that children can receive a life-saving blood transfusion. This affects many areas of care, for example pregnancy and childbirth, where women may require special care and counselling before delivery to minimise blood loss and deal with haemorrhage. Although Jehovah's Witnesses cannot accept blood, they do accept most other medical procedures. Most hospitals have a list of doctors who are prepared to treat patients without using a blood transfusion.

Some cultures do not believe in medical intervention and may use their own remedies for a long time before coming into the healthcare system only in a crisis. For example, many older Chinese people will use traditional or herbal remedies or diets. When they do come into the healthcare system, they may not disclose this as they fear the healthcare professional's disapproval of or disbelief in traditional medicine. This can cause problems if medication is required as there may be interactions with the herbs/remedies they are using.

Dietary restrictions

It is important to consider dietary differences linked to religion and culture when planning a balanced diet. The commonest dietary differences encountered in health care are vegetarianism, halal and kosher diets. Part of faith-based dietary practice includes the food itself, the way it is prepared and served and not being allowed specific items of food. For example, dairy and meat products should be kept separate in kosher diets, with different implements used for meat and dairy products when preparing and serving kosher meals, and when washing up afterwards. Jewish people do not eat pork or shellfish. Hindu and Sikh vegetarian diets require that both equipment and diets do not come into contact with any meat. Muslims do not eat pork or non-halal meats, and they do not consume alcohol.

Whatever the rules, it is important that a balanced diet is followed to reduce the effects on health and development. Vegetarianism, for example, may have positive or negative effects on a person's development. There are usually higher levels of fruit, vegetables and fibre and lower fats in the diets which lowers the risk of high cholesterol, heart disease and high blood pressure. However, there are also health risks of nutritional deficiency for those whose diet does not contain meat or fish. For instance, calcium deficiency can result in weakened bones and teeth. Iron and vitamin B12 deficiency may affect the production of red blood cells, and protein deficiency could impact on muscle and organ function, affect the elasticity of skin and weaken bones.

Link

For more information, see *Unit 19: Nutritional Health*, learning aim B.

Link

See *Unit 2: Working in Health and Social Care* for further details.

Poor housing

Clive and Mandy Taylor have three children. They live in a two bedroom flat in a deprived area of the city. They have complained to the landlord about the damp. There is a high crime rate in the area which has made Mandy fearful for herself and her family and she is reluctant to go out. Mandy has been self-harming but is now getting help and has been diagnosed with depression. This worries Clive, as Mandy's mother has suffered mental illness for a number of years.

Check your knowledge

1 Using the information about the family, evaluate the likely explanations for Mandy's current state of health.

B5 Economic factors that affect development

Personal development can be affected by a number of key money-related or economic factors.

Income and expenditure

Income is the amount of money that households receive. People with a low income and who experience poverty are most likely to suffer ill health and reduced opportunities for personal development.

A lack of income may mean a lack of resources and not being able to live in the minimum acceptable way of society. Household resources include clothing, food and housing. Those people without the means to pay for essential resources are deemed as living in absolute poverty. Some people can afford basic resources but not much else. This is known as relative poverty, as they are poor compared to the rest of the people in society. A lack of resources may mean a person finds it hard to take part in the community. This can lead to social exclusion and a family becoming marginalised. Children born into families experiencing poverty may find it difficult to escape and become trapped in a situation that has a powerful effect on their confidence and self-esteem.

Research by the Child Poverty Action Group has highlighted that poverty is associated with higher risks of illness and premature death. Poorer health has an impact on life expectancy. For example, professional people on higher incomes live on average 8 years longer than unskilled workers on low wages. Children born in the poorest areas of the UK weigh on average 200 grams less at birth than children who are born into wealthier families and have a higher risk of mortality at birth.

According to the Trussell Trust, there are 445 food banks in the UK. There has been a year-on-year increase in food bank use since 2009. However, there is concern about the nutritional value of the food provided. An article in *The Guardian* (March, 2015) reported on research by Birmingham City University about the impact on families of using food banks long-term. The report identified that many food banks provided processed food, including tinned soup, meat, puddings and pasta sauce rather than fresh products. This leads to an unbalanced diet. The long-term risks could be that children and families become deficient in fibre, calcium, iron and a variety of vitamins.

The economic resources that an individual or family has can have a major impact on their quality of life. A person's weekly income enables them to pay for their accommodation and to buy food and clothes. Income mainly comes from:

▶ wages from employment
▶ profits from your business if you are self-employed
▶ benefits paid by the government
▶ money from invested wealth, such as interest on bank accounts or bonds
▶ money raised through the sale or rent of property you own.

Income is not distributed equally in the UK. According to the Office for National Statistics and the Department of Work and Pensions, people in the bottom-earning 10 per cent of the population have an average net annual income of £8,468, resulting in them living in poverty. In comparison, the top earning 10 per cent have an average annual income of £79,100 – almost 10 times that of the lowest earners. Research shows that households with an income that is less than 60 per cent of the **median** income in the UK, are considered to be living in poverty. The median income compares low income families with those in the middle rather than the wealthiest, providing a truer picture of wealth distribution in contemporary society. Income can have a significant impact on health and wellbeing. Having sufficient income for their needs gives individuals more choice about their lifestyle, for instance to eat more healthily and take part in leisure activities.

Additionally, as Figure 1.4 shows, the poorest 10 per cent of society has not seen a rise in income over a ten-year period.

▶ **Figure 1.4** Average changes in household incomes in a ten-year period (from 1998/1999 to 2008/2009)

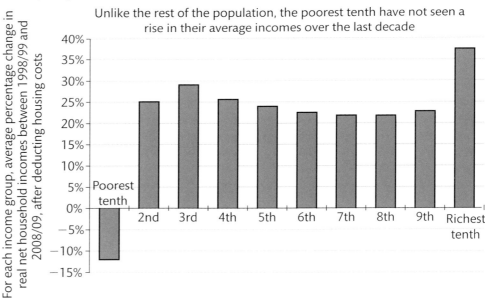

Key groups who are more likely to be on low income include:
▶ lone-parent families
▶ unemployed people
▶ older people
▶ sick people or people with disabilities
▶ families with single earners
▶ unskilled couples (where only one of the couple works, and in unskilled employment).

The impact of low income

Paxton and Dixon (2004) found that children who grew up in poverty in the 1970s underachieved academically at school, were less likely to go to university or college, and one-and-a-half times more likely to go on to be unemployed as those who did not experience poverty as children. They also earned 10 per cent less over their lifetime. Paxton and Dixon point out the following disadvantages of poverty.

▶ Poverty is associated with being a victim of crime.
▶ Poorer communities are more likely to live in polluted areas.
▶ Poorer people have an increased risk of dying young.

Theory into practice

Children living in poverty are almost twice as likely to live in families experiencing fuel poverty. Low income families sometimes have to make the choice between food and heating. Children from low income families often miss out on school trips and holidays and are not able to invite friends home for tea. Produce a fact sheet that provides information on the importance of food banks and fuel poverty. Prepare to share your findings with other learners in your class.

Employment status

Employment status is characterised by whether a person is in work or not, the type of work they do and the type of contract they have.

Being out of work is likely to mean that families live on a low income. According to the Office for National Statistics, 15.9 per cent of households have no adults working. According to Social Trends (2009), this results in 22 per cent of children, about 2.9 million children in England and Wales, living in poverty.

According to the Office for National Statistics, the percentage of households in which no adult has ever worked is 1.5 per cent, and 1.5 million children were living in these households. Of all the regions in the UK, the north east of England has the highest percentage of households where no adult is working (21.2 per cent), with the south east having the lowest (12.3 per cent).

Even when in work, the type of job can affect a person's wellbeing. Work that is low paid, has low status and/or is temporary puts additional stress on individuals which can lead to ill health and possibly depression. Individuals are more likely to have low self-esteem. All types of work can provide social interaction which is important for wellbeing. Work that has status, responsibility and is well paid and secure can boost health and wellbeing and result in high self-esteem. Research has shown that people who are in work are likely to be healthier both mentally and physically.

Research

Working in small groups, research the impact of low income on children and adults. Use the Office for National Statistics, The Joseph Rowntree Foundation and the Child Poverty Action Group websites. Using the statistics you find, produce a chart and short report explaining the extent that poverty rates are improving or worsening. Compare and contrast the different statistics found on the three different websites.

Education

According to the Department for Education, by the age of three, children from poorer families are estimated to be about nine months behind children from wealthier families and, by 14 years old, children from poorer families are nearly a year and a half behind. Children from poorer families do less well in GCSEs, achieving nearly two grades lower in their GCSE results. Generally, children from poor backgrounds fall behind at all stages of their education.

People with few or no qualifications are more likely to be unemployed or employed in low-paid work. This can lead to low self-image. A good education brings wider career and lifestyle choices. In adulthood, individuals are more likely to earn a higher salary and have more job satisfaction. This can lead to positive self-image and high self-esteem. Of course, some 'high-flying' jobs are high pressured which can lead to stress.

Peer groups

As a child becomes more independent, for example after starting nursery school, they begin to learn a lot about social relationships, especially when they start to play with other children. By the time a young person reaches adolescence, peer groups become very important and influential. For example, **attitudes** and beliefs might be copied from other young people, especially if they have similar interests. Peer groups also provide a second source of social learning (**secondary socialisation**) after the family (which provides **primary socialisation**).

Values and attitudes

Beliefs, **values** and attitudes are influenced by how an individual experiences primary and secondary socialisation with family, carers and peer groups. Values and attitudes are also influenced by life experiences (issues like bullying and discrimination) and the culture that an individual is brought up in and the community in which they live. Social networking and access to information found on the internet is becoming increasingly influential, particularly for adolescents. It can have a huge impact on an individual's values, attitudes and life choices and is often blamed for poor choices and unsocial behaviour.

Reflect

What social pressures do people experience to achieve good educational qualifications? Where do these pressures come from? How far have you chosen your own values and attitudes, and how far have you copied them from other people?

Lifestyle

What leisure activities do you engage in? Do you exercise? Are you careful about your diet? How do you dress and present yourself when you are among your friends? These are some of the questions that will explain your **lifestyle**. Your lifestyle represents the way you choose to spend your time and money.

To some extent, your lifestyle is something that you choose. Your choices will be limited by the money that you have and influenced by your culture and the people in your life. People on low incomes have limited choices. Most people develop habits connected to diet, exercise and alcohol use. Many people never actively choose a lifestyle, it happens because of the stress of life events or economic pressure and it can be difficult to change without support.

Nutrition and dietary choices

Some people may choose to eat a diet that includes unhealthy fatty, salty or sugary foods and drink. But others may eat an unhealthy diet because of convenience and cost. Some authors argue that convenience food that has a high fat, salt or sugar content can be cheaper and easier to prepare than healthier alternatives.

A healthy diet has a balance of the carbohydrates, protein, nutrients, fats and fibre that a body needs for health and wellbeing. Deficiencies in diet may affect the health and development of bones, organs and muscles and slow the healing process. Unhealthy diets may also result in obesity that puts increased pressure on the joints and organs and may lead to heart disease and arthritis. Changes in diet can reduce the risk of health conditions such as diabetes in later life.

Exercise

Regular exercise is essential for development. It helps a person to maintain a healthy weight and is important for the skeleton, maintaining mobility and heart function. Regular exercise can also impact on a person's feeling of wellbeing, reducing the likelihood of mental health problems. The Department of Health refers to lack of any exercise as a 'silent killer' as it significantly increases the risk of stroke, heart disease and type 2 diabetes.

Use and misuse of substances

It is accepted that any substance misuse can affect health and may lead to addiction. While substances may cause short-term effects that make people feel good for a while, they will quickly 'come down' from the effects and feel low. There are significant negative effects on the body in both the short and long term.

Drug use

Cannabis is sometimes used for a calming effect but the side effect is that it affects brain function – affecting thinking. It has even been linked with mental health problems, including schizophrenia. If smoked, cannabis can cause respiratory problems or even lung cancer if used with tobacco. Cocaine may give an energy boost but will result in the person feeling unwell and depressed when the effect wears off. Cocaine overstimulates the heart which can lead to a heart attack or even death. Ecstasy and speed can make individuals feel more alert but, in the long term, have detrimental effects. Ecstasy can impact on memory and cause depression, and speed can affect blood pressure and cause heart attacks.

Alcohol

In January 2016, the Department of Health recommended that adults should not consume more than 14 units a week spread over several days – and with some days alcohol free. Social Trends (2009) states that 65 per cent of men and 49 per cent of women reported drinking more than the recommended limits in 2007. Statistics also show that 32 per cent of young men and 24 per cent of young women have a lifestyle that involves heavy drinking. The guidelines from the Department of Health state that no level of alcohol consumption is risk free because research has shown an increased risk to health, particularly in incidences of cancer of the throat, mouth and breasts. Drinking over the recommended limits brings with it a higher risk of heart disease, liver disease and bowel cancer. Binge drinking can result in unintended affects as individuals often behave differently and take more risks. This can result in accidents or unprotected intercourse. Alcohol abuse is a major factor in domestic abuse.

Tobacco

Smoking can have a detrimental effect on health. Smoking can affect all the organs of the body but causes a particular problem for the lungs. It is the cause of most cases of lung cancer. Smoking significantly increases the risk of:

- coronary heart disease
- strokes
- lung disease, including cancer, emphysema and chronic bronchitis.

Smoking can also affect children in the family who inhale nicotine and the unborn baby of a mother who smokes.

PAUSE POINT   Close the book and give four factors that can influence a person's lifestyle.

> **Hint**   Make links from income, employment status and education to lifestyle.

> **Extend**   Identify short- and long-term effects of substance abuse.

B6 Major life events that affect development

As an individual travels through their lifespan, they will experience a number of events that change their life to some degree. Some events are **predictable** and may be chosen or be part of the natural course of life. Other events may be **unpredictable events** that happen when they are least expected. Categorising predictable and unpredictable life events is not straightforward and depends on an individual's circumstances. For some people, issues such as divorce or redundancy may be predictable but others may be shocked to go through a marriage breakdown and divorce or deal with redundancy.

Predictable events

Predicable life events are those events that are expected to happen to an individual at a particular time. Some of these are shown in Table 1.13. For example, starting nursery school may be the first major life event a young child experiences. Many people can recall their first day at nursery school in detail. There will be positive learning experiences for the child as they meet other children and develop social skills and friendships. Experience of nursery school provides opportunities to learn to share toys and take turns in games. Children will develop communication skills as they talk and listen to other children and adults. However, the young child may feel unsupported, stressed and unsafe as their parents or carers are not there. This can lead to becoming withdrawn and isolating themselves from other children. Although predictable life events often involve positive learning, there is also a risk of stress involved.

Key terms

Predictable events – events that are expected to happen at a particular time. While expected they may have a positive or negative effect on a person's health and wellbeing.

Unpredictable events – events that happen unexpectedly and which may have serious physical and psychological effects on the individual. These effects can be positive or negative.

▶ **Table 1.13** Influences of predictable life events on development

Predictable events	Possible influence on development	
	Positive learning	**Risk of stress**
Starting school/nursery	Learning to make new friends and cope with change.	Feeling unsafe – withdrawing from others. Loss of support from parents.
Beginning and changing employment	Choosing a work role and having an income from employment.	Feeling pressured by new demands on time and mental energy. Finding difficulty in adapting. Loss of past lifestyle.
Leaving home/leaving care	Achieving independence – controlling personal environment.	Feeling unable to cope in a new situation. Feeling pressured by all the new tasks. Loss of family/care support.
Leaving prison	Coping with freedom and choice.	Loss of routine, loss of a structured environment, possible lack of support with finding an income and housing. Coping with possible discrimination.
Marriage	Making emotional attachments and experiencing intimacy.	Feeling threatened by intimacy and sharing possessions. Possible loss of independence.
Parenthood	Attachment to infant. Learning parenting skills.	Disruption of previous lifestyle, loss of free time. New demands on time and energy. Feeling tired due to loss of sleep.
Retirement	Controlling own life – disengaging from work.	Loss of previous work roles. Loss of contact with work colleagues. Difficulty establishing a new lifestyle.

Unpredictable events

Unpredictable life events happen unexpectedly and can be a shock. This can impact on an individual's physical and psychological wellbeing. Table 1.14 shows some life events that may be unexpected. When a sudden life event occurs, there is always a risk that an individual will feel out of control, which can cause stress and anxiety. Although people may die at any stage of their lifespan, unexpected death, for example as a result of an accident or unexpected illness, can be a huge shock. The sense of loss and grief can be extremely difficult to deal with. The bereavement period is a time for adjusting to the loss as well as dealing with the emotional upheaval that this entails. Although many older people expect the death of spouses and friends, the death of an adult child can have a devastating effect on their physical and emotional wellbeing. They may find adjustment and adaptation extremely difficult.

▶ **Table 1.14** Influences of some unpredictable life events on development

Unpredictable event	Possible influence on development	
	Positive learning	**Risk of stress**
Birth of a sibling	Learning to make new emotional attachments.	Jealousy and rivalry – emotional tension because role within the family has changed. Older child/children may lose attention from parents.
Redundancy	Learning to adapt to changes in income and lifestyle.	Refusal to accept change. Anger or depression. Failure to cope with loss of income and lifestyle.
Illness and serious injury	Learning to adapt to physical change.	Grief at the loss of good health. Anger or depression and failure to adapt to disability.
Divorce	Learning to cope with a new lifestyle.	Resentment or depression. Grief at the loss of the relationship. Failure to adapt to a new lifestyle. Possible financial hardship.
Bereavement	Learning to cope with loss and a new lifestyle.	Grief at the loss of the relationship. Failure to adapt to an unwanted lifestyle.

The effects of life events on health

Major changes in life may interact with all aspects of growth and development. For example, retirement, redundancy, divorce, bereavement or serious injury might all result in a loss of income or having to live on a low income. Leaving home, marriage or parenthood might all involve changes in your home or in your community and friendship networks. Major life events will change your social, emotional and economic circumstances. Life events may involve feelings of loss and grief and involve lifestyle changes. Being seriously injured or being divorced requires an individual to change and adapt to a new lifestyle, which can have physical, psychological and financial implications. Even predictable and welcome changes can involve learning new things and coping with a range of losses. For example, leaving primary school and starting at secondary school requires adapting to new rules and routines and getting used to a new environment.

 **PAUSE POINT**   Identify five predictable life events and explain their positive and negative effects on health and development.

Hint   These are the events that most people will experience at set points in their life.

Extend   What might help to reduce the negative impact of life events on individuals?

Holmes–Rahe social readjustment rating scale

Psychologists have looked to find ways to rate and measure total stress scores in a way that will help individuals cope with difficult events. Holmes and Rahe (1967) developed a questionnaire called the Social Readjustment Rating Scale (SRRS) (see Figure 1.5), which identified major stressful life events. The SRRS identifies 43 life events each with a different score for a stress level. They asked individuals to score how the events they had experienced affected their stress levels. They discovered that the higher the score and the importance of each event identified, the more likely an individual was to become unwell.

However, each individual is unique and deals with stress factors in different ways. Holmes and Rahe assumed that each stressor would affect people in the same way. Critics of their theory stress that this is not necessarily true, for some people the breakdown of a relationship and getting divorced can be an extremely stressful time, yet, for others, it can almost be a relief, especially if the arrangements for divorce have been amicable. For most people, major life events are not experienced very frequently but they can still experience stresses and strains in daily life, for example losing keys, traffic jams, physical appearance or weight. These are referred to as 'daily hassles'.

Reflect

Think of a life event that you have experienced, for example starting school or breaking up with a friend. Consider how you adapted and describe the feelings that you experienced.

Stress levels

Stress is an automatic response to dealing with challenging situations or life events. When an individual is stressed their body is flooded with hormones that raise heart rate, increase blood pressure, boost energy and prepare them to deal with the problem: this is known as the 'fight or flight' mechanism. If prolonged or out of context, stress responses may interfere with day-to-day life and become a serious psychological and physical problem, making the individual unwell.

It is difficult to define stress. The psychologist Richard Lazarus provided a useful definition, 'stress is experienced when a person perceives that the demands exceed the personal and social resources the individual is able to mobilise.'

The effects of stress and an individual's ability to cope with the demands of stressful events, depend on how threatened and vulnerable they feel rather than on the stressful event itself. There is a focus on stress and stressful events in contemporary society and the word stress is used to describe many situations. Examples range from feeling overloaded with college work, to constant demands via social media to the break up of a relationship or the death of a loved one. Stress can be short term, and may be a positive motivational force, for example waiting to take an exam or performing in a college play. Or it may be longer term, with negative effects on an individual's health, for example someone experiencing chronic health problems, the break up of a long-term relationship or financial difficulties.

Health

Stress can cause an individual to become irritable, fatigued, have headaches, lack motivation and be unable to concentrate. This can lead to over/under eating, smoking or drinking too much alcohol to cope. Chronic stress can lead to anxiety attacks,

Instructions: Mark down the point value of each of these life events that has happened to you during the previous year. Total these associated points.

Life event	Mean value
1. Death of spouse	100
2. Divorce	73
3. Marital separation from mate	65
4. Detention in jail or other institution	63
5. Death of a close family member	63
6. Major personal injury or illness	53
7. Marriage	50
8. Being fired at work	47
9. Marital reconciliation with mate	45
10. Retirement from work	45
11. Major change in health or behaviour of a family member	44
12. Pregnancy	40
13. Sexual difficulties	39
14. Gaining a new family member (ie birth, adoption, older adult moving in etc)	39
15. Major business readjustment	39
16. Major change in financial state (ie a lot better or worse off than usual)	38
17. Death of a close friend	37
18. Changing to a different line of work	36
19. Major change in the number of arguments with spouse (ie either a lot more or a lot less than usual regarding child rearing, personal habits etc)	35
20. Taking on a mortgage (for home, business etc)	31
21. Foreclosure on a mortgage or loan	30
22. Major change in responsibilities at work (ie promotion, demotion etc)	29
23. Son or daughter leaving home (marriage, attending college, joined military)	29
24. In-law troubles	29
25. Oustanding personal achievement	28
26. Spouse beginning or ceasing work outside the home	26
27. Beginning or ceasing formal schooling	26
28. Major change in living condition (new home, remodelling, deterioration of neighborhood or home etc)	25
29. Revision of personal habits (dress, manners, associations, quitting smoking)	24
30. Troubles with the boss	23
31. Major changes in working hours or conditions	20
32. Changes in residence	20
33. Changing to a new school	20
34. Major change in usual type and/or amount of recreation	19
35. Major change in church activity (ie a lot more or less than usual)	19
36. Major change in social activities (clubs, movies, visiting etc)	18
37. Taking on a loan (car, tv, freezer etc)	17
38. Major change in sleeping habits (a lot more or a lot less than usual)	16
39. Major change in number of family get togethers	15
40. Major change in eating habits (a lot more or less food intake, or very different meal hours or surroundings)	15
41. Vacation	13
42. Major holidays	12
43. Minor violations of the law (traffic tickets, disturbing the peace etc)	11

Now, add up all the points you have to find your score.

150pts or less means a relatively low amount of life change and a low susceptibility to stress-induced health breakdown.

150 to 300pts implies about a 50% chance of a major health breakdown in the next 2 years.

300pts or more raises the odds to about 80%, according to the Holmes–Rahe statistical prediction model.

▶ **Figure 1.5** The Holmes–Rahe Life Stress Inventory

depression and cardiovascular problems (caused by high levels of stress hormones). Once an individual is experiencing chronic stress and depression it becomes harder to recover, especially if they have low levels of social support. The individual may be irritable, depressed and apathetic, which may alienate family and friends who could offer support.

High levels of stress hormones over a long period of time can affect many of the body's systems causing a variety of health problems, for example:

- immune system – susceptibility to infections and colds, especially if unhealthy behaviours such as excessive alcohol consumption are used to deal with the stress
- cardiovascular system – high blood pressure, heart attacks, arrhythmias and sudden death
- respiratory system – breathlessness, asthma
- digestive system – loss of appetite, gastric ulcers, duodenal ulcers, irritable bowel syndrome
- musculoskeletal system – tension headaches, taut muscles, muscular twitches
- endocrine system – diabetes, loss of sex drive, absence of menstruation.

People who are stressed can be indecisive, have impaired judgement, muddled thinking and make errors. This can sometimes be through their inability to sleep and feeling fatigued. They may also be more accident prone.

Stress can affect an individual's emotions, especially self-esteem and self-image.

Assessment practice 1.2

B1 B2 B3 B4 B5 B6

Mary was a shy, only child. She enjoyed playing alone and had a small friendship circle. Mary experienced bullying in Year 5 that continued at secondary school which affected her self-image and self-esteem. Mary was very close to her mother and was devastated when she died of breast cancer when Mary was 18.

Mary has been married for 21 years to Bill and they have three children, aged 12, 15 and 18. Bill is a paramedic and works different shifts every week.

Three years ago, Mary had to give up work as a nursing home manager as she needed to be home for the children. Mary was disappointed to leave her job which she loved and which gave her the status needed to boost her self-esteem. Mary missed her colleagues' company. As the children are now older, Mary works part-time as an assistant occupational therapist. She may soon go to university to study for a degree.

Unfortunately, Mary and Bill have begun to experience marital difficulties. They argue a lot about money. Bill has started to spend nights away and has begun divorce proceedings. He wants to sell the house. Mary is distraught, and feels more stressed as their eldest daughter will soon be leaving home to go to university.

Mary has started to drink a little too much alcohol. She is having difficulty sleeping and has put on weight, due to a poor diet and not exercising. Mary's friendship circle has reduced, initially because of her busy lifestyle, but more recently because she is withdrawn and depressed. Mary has stopped taking care of her appearance and her personal hygiene has started to suffer.

1 Identify two predictable and two unpredictable life events that Mary has experienced.

2 Explain, giving two examples of factors that have influenced Mary's development.

3 Discuss Mary's emotional wellbeing in relation to the Holmes–Rahe social adjustment scale.

Plan
- Have I fully understood Mary's situation in the case study?
- What do I know about the Homes-Rahe social adjustment scale?
- How confident do I feel in my own ability to complete this task?

Do
- Am I confident that I know what I am doing and what it is I should be achieving?

Review
- I can explain which elements I found easiest.
- I can explain how I would approach the hard elements differently next time.

C Effects of ageing

C1 The physical changes of ageing

By the time an individual reaches their late sixties, their body functions begin to decline. For example, they may experience hearing loss in higher frequencies. They may become far-sighted and experience impaired night vision. Joints may become stiffer and bones may lose calcium and become brittle bringing an increased risk of fractures. However, each individual is unique and their experience of the ageing process is different. Some people develop serious problems associated with ageing in their fifties, whereas other people have few problems even in their nineties.

> **Research**
>
> Produce a thought shower of as many aspects of physical changes that are due to ageing that you can think of.

These physical changes do not come about just because bodies 'wear out'. If you take regular exercise, you may expect to live longer and stay healthier than people who do not. The physical changes associated with ageing may come about because there is a limit to how many times body cells can repair and renew themselves and because of damage that builds up over a lifetime.

Cardiovascular disease

As an individual ages, they have an increased risk of cardiovascular disease (disease of the heart and blood vessels). The main purpose of the heart is to pump blood around the body. Many older people develop narrowing of the arteries and other blood vessels due to fats such as cholesterol being laid down in the walls of the blood vessels. This process of 'clogging up' is called atherosclerosis. Atherosclerosis can result in higher blood pressure (which puts the person at risk of stroke) and heart attacks. The blood vessels can also start to lose their elasticity causing the heart to work harder, increase in size and raise the blood pressure. Fatty deposits can break away and block the artery. If the coronary artery is partly blocked, it may cause angina, experienced as breathlessness and chest pains. If there is significant blood flow blockage, the person may experience a heart attack.

There were almost 160,000 deaths associated with cardiovascular disease in 2011. Approximately 74,000 of these deaths were caused by coronary heart disease, which is Britain's biggest killer.

Effect of lifestyle choices

There are a number of risk factors associated with cardiovascular disease, including a family history of heart disease, ethnic background, poorly controlled diabetes and a prolonged rise in blood pressure (hypertension). Poor lifestyle choices, such as being overweight/obese, smoking and lack of exercise, increase the risks of cardiovascular disease, and its effects, in older age.

The degeneration of the nervous tissue

An individual's senses depend on the nervous system (nerves, the spinal cord and the brain) which is composed of nervous tissue. Nervous tissue allows an individual to receive stimuli and process information. Some sensory experiences are positive, such as the smell of a cake baking, and some are not. For example, an individual accidentally hitting their thumb with a hammer will experience pain – the sensory impulse travels along nerves to the brain and back and tells the thumb that it hurts.

As the ageing process progresses, brain function begins to decline. However, different aspects of brain function are affected at different rates. For example, short-term memory and the ability to learn new material tend to be affected relatively early. The ability to use words and vocabulary may begin to decline after the age of 70. Cognitive and intellectual ability (the ability to process information) is usually maintained until around the age of 80, if no neurological disorders are present. Reaction time and performance of tasks may become slower as the brain processes nerve impulses more slowly. However, it is important to note that the effect of various conditions that are common in older people, for example strokes, depression, under-active thyroid gland and Alzheimer's disease, can make it difficult to analyse the effects of ageing on brain function. It is worth noting that some areas of the brain may produce new nerve cells and new skills can be learned, for example, after a stroke with the help of occupational therapy.

Blood flow to the brain decreases with the ageing process, especially for people who have some form of cerebrovascular disease, which is more likely in people who have smoked for a long time, have high blood pressure, high cholesterol or diabetes. This may result in the loss of brain cells prematurely, possibly impairing mental function and increasing the risk of dementia, especially if lifestyle changes are not made or medication is not taken.

Having very high blood pressure, diabetes or high cholesterol levels can speed up the age-related decline in brain function. Physical exercise may slow this down.

Nervous tissue degeneration also occurs because, as people age, impulses become slower and age-related changes in function can become more noticeable when the nerves are injured by something, for example diabetes. The self-repairing process in cells occurs more slowly and incompletely making older people more vulnerable to injury and diseases. Decreased sensation, slower reflexes and a tendency to be clumsy can also be a result of the degeneration of nervous tissue within the nervous system. Hence memory, thought and abilities to perform tasks can be affected.

Discussion

A common myth is that all older people become senile and increased confusion may be put down to 'getting old', whereas it might actually be caused by illness. Consider stereotypes of older people. Using the information about degeneration of nervous tissue, discuss to what extent this myth is true or not.

Osteoarthritis

Osteoarthritis is a degenerative disease, a result of wear and tear of the joints and the ageing process. It is one of the commonest types of arthritis in the UK, with over eight million people suffering from the condition. Osteoarthritis causes the joints to become painful and stiff, especially the hips, knee, neck, lower back, hands or feet. The symptoms' severity can vary between individuals. Some experience occasional mild symptoms whereas others experience severe and constant problems, making it difficult to carry out daily activities. Although being overweight and having a family history may add to the chance of developing osteoarthritis, the exact cause is difficult to identify. However, recent research by Coventry University identified multiple injuries in the same joint before an injury has fully healed as a cause.

Women are more likely than men to be affected by osteoarthritis. It can occur at any age, but generally appears between their late forties and 75 years of age.

Physical changes due to osteoarthritis include thinning and roughening of the joint cartilage. **Cartilage** is a protective cushion between the ends of the bones. As the bones start to rub together, moving the joints causes pain and swelling. Eventually, this leads to bony outgrowths, spurs or osteophytes, developing on the ends of the bones, causing damage to the soft tissues around the joints. One of the major impacts is that gradual smooth movements of the affected joint become difficult and this limits movement such as walking, using stairs or lifting heavy objects.

People often confuse osteoporosis and osteoarthritis. Osteoarthritis is a degenerative disease that damages joints at the end of the bones. Osteoporosis is a condition in which the bones become less dense, making them fragile and liable to fracture. Both conditions can cause back pain and height loss, especially in older people.

> **Key term**
>
> **Cartilage** – the soft tissue that protects the surfaces of the bone.

Degeneration of the sense organs

As part of the ageing process, sensory awareness gradually decreases. For example, an individual's sense of balance can become impaired, both hearing and vision may deteriorate, and the ability to taste and smell may diminish. These can all lead to a range of physical problems.

Changes generally begin when people are about 50 years of age. However, they become noticeable when an older person begins to need to turn up the sound on the radio or television, or add more salt and pepper to their food or starts wearing glasses with stronger magnification.

After 45 years of age, the eyes' ability to focus begins to weaken and, for many people, by 65 years old there may be little focusing power left, making small print more difficult to read. Up to half of people over the age of 90 may have serious problems with vision.

Cataracts result from changes in the lens of the eye. As people grow older, the lenses can become hard and cloudy which can result in blurred vision. Cataracts may start forming between the ages of 50 and 60, but often take time to develop and start causing symptoms. The majority of people over 75 years of age have some degree of cataract formation. Diabetes greatly increases the chances of developing cataracts.

Glaucoma is an increase of fluid pressure within the eye. It can affect eyesight in later life with symptoms that can range from hazy or blurry vision or eye pain to sudden loss of vision.

Some older people experience an increase in wax in the outer ear that can block sound transmission to the sensory nerves. Difficulty in hearing high frequency (or high-pitched) sounds also increases with age as the sensitivity of nerve cells in the inner ear decreases. If this is accompanied with a loss of nerve cell function then they may experience partial or complete hearing loss.

For many older people, once they have accepted these ageing processes they will try to make adjustments or adaptations to their environment and use resources to help them perform daily tasks. However, if there is a sudden change in vision, hearing, taste, smell or touch, it is important for older people to seek medical advice.

The reduced absorption of nutrients

Energy requirements may change in older age particularly if physical activity is restricted or reduced. As energy requirements decrease, older people may need more protein-rich foods in their diet, for example eggs, pulses, dairy foods and lean meat.

It is also important that older people's diets include foods containing vitamins and minerals. Minerals such as zinc, calcium, magnesium and sodium are found in dairy products, meat, eggs, fish, bread, cereals, fruit and vegetables. However, absorption of food, including minerals and vitamins, becomes less efficient in older people, meaning that some people can experience malnourishment even though they continue to eat the same diet that was adequate in early adulthood.

Vitamin D is important for good health and essential for absorbing calcium from food. It is largely obtained from sunlight so older people who are housebound, or in residential care, may be at risk of vitamin D deficiency leading to disorders such as osteoporosis and bone fractures. To prevent osteoporosis, some older people are prescribed vitamin D and calcium supplements. Older people may also lack vitamin C, iron and fibre in their diet. Vitamin C is essential for several body functions, including wound healing and forming and maintaining healthy tissues. Many older people do not eat enough fresh fruit and vegetables which provide vitamin C. Some older people find buying fresh fruit and vegetables difficult or expensive, and also have difficulty in preparing and eating them.

Iron absorption may be reduced in older people and, along with a low dietary intake, this can increase the risk of iron deficiency anaemia. Dairy Council research has shown that 30 per cent of older people have an iron intake below the recommended level for the general population. Water helps with digesting food and absorbing nutrients. In older age, people may lose their sense of thirst and, as a result, become dehydrated. This has been highlighted as a particular problem in hospitals where patients do not request drinks.

> **Theory into practice**
>
> Research the food groups essential for maintaining a healthy diet in older age. Make a list of the sources of food containing them and what can happen if older people don't have enough of these food groups in their diet. Produce a leaflet about food groups and the sources of minerals and vitamins that support a balanced diet to offer to older people at your local day care centre.

Dementia

Dementia is more likely to occur in older people. According to the Alzheimer's Society, more than 5 per cent of people over the age of 65 and as many as 20 per cent of people over the age of 80 are affected by dementia. However, the majority of people who live to extreme old age will never develop dementia.

Dementia is a brain disorder that seriously affects a person's ability to carry out daily tasks and activities. A person with dementia is likely to experience problems with understanding what is happening around them, communicating, reasoning, finding their way and remembering recent events. There are different kinds of dementia – two major types are Alzheimer's disease, and **vascular dementia**.

> **Key term**
>
> **Vascular dementia** – symptoms include problems with language, memory and thought processes caused by problems in the blood supply to the brain, for example through stroke.

> **Link**
>
> You looked at the deterioration in intellectual abilities, particularly in relation to dementia, earlier in this unit.

Alzheimer's disease

Alzheimer's disease is the commonest form of dementia. The onset of Alzheimer's disease is usually slow, initially involving parts of the brain controlling thought, memory and language. Individuals with Alzheimer's disease have trouble with short-term memory and recalling the names of people they know. The symptoms gradually worsen. For example, an individual may not recognise family members and may begin to lose the ability to carry out particular tasks, like speaking, reading or writing. As the condition progresses, the ability to carry out simple everyday tasks, like brushing teeth or combing hair may be forgotten. Alzheimer's disease usually begins after the age of 60 and the risk of developing it rises as a person gets older. There is a higher risk of getting Alzheimer's disease if a family member has had the condition. At present, there is no treatment to cure or prevent the disease, but some medications may delay its progress for a limited time.

> **Research**
>
> Research some of the major health problems that you expect older people to have and prepare notes for a class discussion. Historically, many older people have been negatively stereotyped as suffering from disease and dementia. Do you think this is still the case? Provide examples from your research to back up your discussion.

> **Theory into practice**
>
> Working in small groups, research the physical changes associated with ageing. Choose one condition and produce an information leaflet that could be given to care workers about it. Remember to add references to your leaflet.

Effects of illnesses that are common in ageing

Each of the conditions common in ageing brings its own symptoms, but each one can have wider effects on holistic development. Having a chronic condition in addition to the usual physical and psychological changes during the ageing process can worsen stress or depression for many older people (see Table 1.15). Depression affects an individual's mood and can lead to lack of energy, low motivation, interrupted sleep patterns, changes to appetite and headaches. Additionally, physical aches and pains, such as those associated with conditions like arthritis, can worsen.

Social development may be severely affected by chronic conditions. The effects of illness on mobility can restrict a person's social life as they may have difficulty getting out and meeting people. This will reduce their circle of friends causing further emotional stress. The decline of senses or neural capacity can also impact on friendships as they depend upon communicating with others. Individuals may be unable to hear or see sufficiently well to take part in interests and hobbies they used to enjoy, such as reading or going to the cinema. This can reduce motivation and increase isolation.

Illness brings with it a number of physical changes that have been discussed in relation to each of the conditions in section C1: The physical changes of ageing. Many of the conditions will result in losing mobility caused either by neurological problems or because of pain, stiffness of the joints or a reduction in stamina. This can be a vicious circle, as a lack of exercise or even movement can result in the onset or worsening of conditions such as heart disease. A reduction in sensory awareness and neurological illness brings with it an additional problem of dizziness or difficulty in moving that results in an increase in falls in older people, often causing fractures.

A common problem in ageing is incontinence, which is a loss of bladder control. It can happen because of weakness of muscles, enlarged prostate (common in older men) or neurological illness such as Alzheimer's. Whether it is temporary or chronic, it is unpleasant for the individual and can lead to embarrassment and emotional distress.

Many older people experience insomnia or disorders which can disrupt sleep patterns and cause fatigue, stress and anxiety. This can have an adverse effect on their attention span and ability to carry out everyday tasks.

Depression

▶ **Table 1.15** Some of the effects of depression

Physical	Psychological
Difficulty falling or staying asleep, oversleeping, or daytime sleepiness.	Fixation on death, suicidal thoughts or suicide attempts.
Increased use of alcohol or other drugs.	Loss of self-worth, worries about being a burden, feeling of being worthless, self-loathing.
Weight loss or loss of appetite.	Social withdrawal and isolation, not wanting to be with friends, leave the house or take part in activities.
Fatigue.	Sadness.
Giving up or losing interest in hobbies and other pastimes.	

C2 The psychological changes of ageing

The majority of people over state retirement age experience reasonable health, a satisfactory social life and a reasonable standard of living. A minority of older people experience poor health, poverty and isolation. It is important to guard against the stereotype that old age is always a story of decline and isolation.

Old age is like any other life stage, whether or not you lead a happy and fulfilled life depends on a large range of individual issues.

Effects on confidence and self-esteem

Confidence and self-esteem are not fixed and people experience rises and falls in both during their lifespan. An individual's confidence and self-esteem may increase with older age, as they feel that their life is more settled and they may well have achieved many of their life goals. For example, they may have reached a certain level in their job, own their house, and have raised a family – maybe they have grandchildren, and are enjoying a fulfilling retirement. Conversely, older age can mean loss of confidence as the physical effects of ageing make daily tasks difficult or impossible. Older people can feel marginalised by a society that places great emphasis on material possessions and position in life. If an older person had a high status job, they may feel less worthy now they no longer have that function. For some older people, their only income may be their state pension and they may be struggling to cope financially.

Effects of social change

How roles change

The majority of older people enjoy effective social networks with only one person in five experiencing a degree of isolation. For many people retirement provides more opportunity for contact with grandchildren and other relatives. Older people are more likely to vote than any other age group, suggesting involvement in politics and community issues. Conversely, an individual may have viewed themselves as the 'head of the family', the provider and the decision maker, and find it difficult to adjust to their children maturing and taking over many of these functions.

Death of a partner

Loss, grief and bereavement can result in a range of changes, including change of status and result in anxiety and depression. The death of a spouse or partner will bring grief but also a sense of loss which impacts on a person's sense of safety and security. When a partner dies, there is also a loss of intimacy which can cause an additional sense of deep pain and despair. The loss of long-term relationships is particularly difficult as people may have a self-concept as a couple and have lost a sense of who they are as an individual. Being alone will impact negatively on self-image and self-esteem which may result in not wanting to live on alone.

Death of friends

Losing friends is a source of grief and stress and losing social support networks can lead to a sense of isolation and of not being useful. It can also bring a sense of one's own mortality which can lead to depression.

Increase in leisure time

For many people, retirement provides freedom. Retired people may be seen as 'time rich' and free from work stress. But, for some people, retirement may result in losses of income, of purpose, of interest in life and contact with work colleagues. More free time may, however, enable many older people to engage in physical leisure activities such as walking and activity holidays. Gardening is very popular among people aged 50 to 70. Free time may enable many older people to engage in enjoyable social and mental activities such as taking new college courses, maybe through the U3A (University of the Third Age) or Future Learn (free online courses) or they may decide to develop ICT skills. National Statistics Online (2006) reported that 51 per cent of people between 60 and 69 participated in some form of learning.

Financial concerns

Some people over the age of 65 own their own property, have paid their mortgage in full and have sufficient income to live comfortably in their old age. However, there are many who rent, either local authority or privately owned property. For some, paying the rent, including rising rents, or maintaining their own property will cause financial concerns. Some people may have a private pension but others may only have a state pension. Paying household bills, especially with rising costs for heating and other utilities, can be a source of stress for many older people.

Effects of culture, religion and beliefs

Some people can maintain a happy and positive outlook on life despite having serious physical health problems. Other people may appear to be depressed or withdrawn despite being relatively fortunate in terms of physical health. The way in which people react to changes in later life depends on their attitudes and beliefs, which are influenced by social issues such as culture and religion.

▶ Older people, especially those with limited incomes and living alone, may worry about whether they have enough money to pay their household bills

Traditionally, family members have been responsible for caring for older people, providing care within an extended family environment. However, in contemporary society, care of older people is more often provided by the welfare state, or private or voluntary organisations. Sheltered housing facilities enable older people to keep a sense of independence while providing individuals with the care and supervision necessary to stay safe. While care of older people in Britain often focuses on the importance of empowerment and independence, some Asian cultures place greater emphasis on respect and family care for older people. Older people's view of death is also based on the values of their culture. In Britain, it is common to view death as a loss, something to be feared, as opposed to a tranquil and natural transition.

Although the Equality Act 2010 is intended to prevent ageism in society, it is a common form of discrimination in Britain, and negative stereotypes about older people are often portrayed. This type of discrimination can have a negative impact on the care and wellbeing of older people.

Social disengagement theory

Disengagement means to withdraw from involvement. In 1961, psychologists Cumming and Henry proposed that older people naturally withdraw from social involvement as they get older. They concluded that older people have restricted opportunities to interact with others (see Table 1.16). Cumming (1963) further argued that older people experience reduced social contact and become increasingly 'individual' and less concerned with others' expectations. She concluded that it is appropriate and healthy behaviour and that disengagement is a natural part of ageing.

The theory of disengagement was widely accepted in the past. For example, Bromley (1974) argued that 'although some individuals fight the process all the way, disengagement of some sort is bound to come, simply because old people have neither the physical nor the mental resources they had when they were young.'

▸ **Table 1.16** Issues that limit social interaction

Problem	Explanation
Ill health	Poor mobility or problems with hearing or vision may make interaction with other people more difficult.
Geographical mobility	Moving to areas away from friends and relatives in retirement. Family members may move away from older people in order to seek better housing or employment.
Retirement	Retiring from work may mean less contact with people.
Ill health of friends and relatives	Friends or relatives may visit or contact less frequently if they have poor mobility or other disabilities.

However, there is little statistical evidence to support this view. The majority of older people remain socially active and involved with family and friends. Many older people become even more involved with close family as they age. It may be that many older people choose to spend their time with people they feel close to, rather than seeking to make new friends. If people only interact with close friends, does this mean that they are disengaged?

In 1966, Bromley argued that older people needed to disengage but remain 'active' in order to prevent disengagement from going too far. He argued that providing facilities for older people was not enough and that they should be shown how to use them and encouraged not to have negative attitudes or fixed habits. Bromley felt that it was important to remain mentally active, maintain an interest in life and enjoy the company of others.

While many researchers today do not agree with disengagement theory, it is important to remember that when Cumming and Henry first proposed the theory in 1961 there was no internet, no mobile phones or text messaging. Many older people had no access to a car and many would not even have had a phone in their home. Technology helps older people to keep in contact with a wider circle of family and friends.

Activity theory

Activity theory was proposed as an explanation to ageing by Robert Havighurst in the 1960s. His ill health study of older people showed that, rather than an inevitable decline in interest in life and isolation, older people tend to adjust to the ageing process. His theory is based on the assumption that social and psychological needs of older people remain the same.

He recognised that this may involve adjusting to changes in health and/or mobility but theorised that older people's needs can be satisfied by taking on new roles following retirement such as charity work, joining social groups or learning a new skill. Research supports his theory. Many older people look forward to retirement, viewing this part of their lifespan as an opportunity to pursue new hobbies and interests and to meet new friends. When people remain physically and socially active, their overall satisfaction and wellbeing is increased. This is important for reducing the risk of illness and increasing longevity.

One theory is that older people need to engage in telling their life story, reminiscing or reviewing their life to help create self-esteem and confidence. Coleman (1994) argued that some types of reminiscence therapy can be useful for helping individuals cope with the effects of ageing, but that there are wide differences in individual needs.

Close the book and outline reasons why people in older adulthood may be more at risk of falls in their home.

Hint   Consider the conditions that can impact on mobility, the senses and on brain function.

Extend   Explain how injury caused by falls may impact on emotional and social development in older age.

Case study

Retirement

Margery is 65 years of age and about to retire from her job in advertising. She enjoys her job and has many friends at work.

Margery plans to take up painting when she retires. She has already booked herself a painting holiday. She has also been asked by a friend to help out at her local charity shop.

Check your knowledge

1   Justify how Margery's plans when she retires may impact on her health and wellbeing with reference to Activity theory.

C3 The societal effects of an ageing population

Health and social care provision for older people

Older people place more demand on health and social care provision than any other group in society. This increases with age. Often health and social services are required to work closely together to meet the holistic needs of older people. For example, people receiving end of life care may require professionals to work together to monitor and provide medication, psychological support and personal care.

Health care

Health professionals provide a range of different services. These can be thought of as primary or secondary care. The first point of call for older people is usually the primary care services such as their GP surgery, pharmacy or dentist. Those with conditions such as osteoporosis or mental health problems may be referred to specialist secondary health professionals or units to monitor and support their ongoing needs. Acute care is health care that meets immediate needs, such as a broken hip, cancer treatment or specialist health care for chronic conditions. Acute care may be short term for many but, for older people, hospital stays may be extended as they require a longer period for recovery and recuperation.

Social care

Social care services essentially exist to help and support people in need of practical help and/or personal care due to disability or illness. The type of services provided could include having a carer or support worker (**enabler**) to help around the home with practical tasks and personal care. There could also be structural changes to homes which could support an individual to live more independently. Although technically available to everyone, there has to be practical and financial assessment of physical, intellectual, emotional and social needs and abilities to assess how much support can be provided. After completing the assessment, the local authority will decide how much of the care and support services they will provide. Social care

Key term

Enabler – someone who delivers person-centred care in a domiciliary (home) setting, which encourages independence.

services can take different forms, for example help to live at home, day centres, sheltered accommodation, respite care or residential care. Charities and private organisations can also be involved with delivering social care services.

Community equipment

One important aim of health and social care services is to enable people to stay in their own home and keep their independence. Community equipment services, based in each geographical area, do just that by providing support aids for daily living. These may range from large equipment that can be used by family or carers to move people, or walking frames to 'kettle tippers' that take the weight of a kettle to enable a person to make a cup of tea for themselves.

Financial support and entitlements

Many older people will have the advantage of an occupational pension as well as a state pension. Others may have to rely on their state pension only. Older people can claim pension credit to top up their pension to a minimum level and, depending on circumstances, may also claim housing benefit and council tax reduction. For people retiring after 5 April 2016, the minimum pension will increase to meet the minimum level necessary for all pensioners who have made sufficient contributions. Other financial benefits for over 60s include free NHS prescriptions, eye tests and eye care. Concessionary travel fares are available at pensionable age, as well as winter fuel payments, and, for those on low income, cold weather payments. By the age of 75, free television licences and other discounts can make for a comfortable old age, as long as people remain active and lead a healthy lifestyle. Unfortunately, for many older people, retirement years can mean relying on health and social care services for support.

Since the Griffiths report, Community Care, an Agenda for Action, and the introduction of the NHS and Community Care Act in 1990, there has been a move away from institutional care towards independent living. Griffiths was particularly concerned about long-term and continuing care of vulnerable groups within the community, including older people. The report focused on the different types of provision between health and social care services, and the way in which these services could work together in partnership to take responsibility for care in the community.

Social care services can take different forms, for example help to live at home, support for going out in the community, accessing day centres, sheltered accommodation, or even a place in a residential or nursing home. The majority of older people remain in their own home in the community, where they may be supported by friends, family and health and social services.

Some older people choose to move to sheltered housing where they can call for assistance if and when needed. Day Care Centres provide a social setting where people can meet and some NHS providers offer day care to assist with physiotherapy and other health needs. A small proportion of older people choose residential care where 24-hour support is available.

All services for older people aim to provide respect and choice for service users as part of their policy on quality assurance. Many day and residential services provide a range of social and leisure activities for service users. Older people should always have a choice as to how active they wish to be. Quality services will never attempt to force older people to be active and engaged but they will provide opportunities for individuals to maintain the continuity of their lives and remain as active as they wish.

The total population of the UK aged 65 or over has increased from 4.5 million in 1951 to 8.7 million in 2011 and is forecast to increase to 16.6 million in 2051.

Close the book. Note down different types of health and social care services that should be available for older people.

Hint List the main types, eg health service, social care services. Then break them down further, eg home care, residential care.

Extend Explain the importance of professionals working together to meet the needs of individuals with complex needs.

Economic effects of an ageing population

The Office for National Statistics predicts that the population of the UK will rise from 64.6 million in 2014 to 74.3 million by 2039. According to research by The King's Fund, the average life expectancy in 2012 was 79.2 years for men and 83.3 years for women.

Figures from 2012 identified that people over 65 made up 16 per cent of the population. The report also revealed a wide regional variation in the percentage of older people in the population. For example, in Tower Hamlets in the East End of London, people over 65 years of age make up about 6 per cent of the population. This is compared to 25 per cent of the population over the age of 65 living in Dorset, a predominately rural county. Approximately 30 per cent of people aged over 85 will potentially require support from health and social care services. However, meeting increased demand for care services has been made more difficult by government funding to local councils for care being reduced. This could lead to less local authority funding to support older people to live in their own homes resulting in an increase in the number of older people needing residential care.

Reflect

In 2012/2013, 20 per cent of people over 85 years old accessed NHS services compared with just 4 per cent of people under the age of 65. Why do you think this is the case?

Statistics from 2012/2013 identified that people over the age of 85 were more likely to access mental health services. General hospital admissions for people over the age of 85 were more than twice as likely to be emergency admissions (65 per cent), than for people in the 0–64 age group (32 per cent). Home-based services were mostly accessed by older people, who often required adaptations to their homes, for example, installation of stair lifts and wet rooms. These adaptations are very expensive so often the individual may be asked to pay for at least part of the cost. Additional costs may be incurred for other resources and equipment required to ensure that older people can live independently and maintain a good quality of life. Recent research by Age UK identified that, due to an increasing ageing population and government cuts to welfare, there are about two million older people with identified care needs who cannot afford to access social care, health and support.

Reflect

People are living longer and, as the state pension age rises, they may need to work for longer.

What can local and national government do to support people to stay healthy in their later life?

Assessment practice 1.3 | C1 | C2 | C3

Alice is a retired health visitor and was widowed just before she retired. Alice has always had fairly good health but losing her husband and also two of her close friends has affected her deeply.

After retiring, Alice enjoyed theatre trips and holidays with friends, joined a local book group and walked with the local rambling group. She also regularly went to yoga and Pilates sessions. She became involved as a volunteer for an Age UK befriending scheme, visiting vulnerable older people in their homes. Alice's children, Jessica and Matt, visit regularly, although they both live more than 100 miles away.

However, Alice's osteoarthritis gradually prevented her from taking part in the befriending scheme and going out with the rambling group. Recently, she had a bad fall in the shower and broke her hip. Since the fall, Alice has lost confidence and become increasingly housebound and very forgetful. Alice has lost her appetite and is eating just cake and biscuits. Her physical and psychological health have suffered and she will only see her children and a few close friends.

Alice's children have arranged for a care worker to help with her daily living tasks such as personal care and food preparation.

1 Explain, giving two examples, how osteoporosis may have affected Alice's emotional development.

2 Identify two services that could support Alice's health and care needs.

3 Evaluate possible explanations for Alice's development with reference to theories of ageing.

Plan
- How much time do I have to complete this task?
- Do I need clarification of Alice's situation?
- Are there any areas I may struggle with in this task?

Do
- Have I spent time planning out my approach to the task?

Review
- I can identify how this task relates to future experiences, for example in the workplace.
- I realise where I still have knowledge gaps and how to resolve them.

Further reading and resources

Atchley, R.C. (1989) 'A continuity theory of normal aging', *The Gerontologist*, April 29 (2) pp. 183–190

Berryman, J.C., Hargreaves, D., Herbert, M. and Taylor, A. (1991) *Development Psychology and You*, London: Routledge

Boyd, D. and Bee, H. (2015) *Lifespan Development*, 7th edition, Harlow: Pearson Education

Bromley, D.B. (1974) *The Psychology of Human Ageing*, 2nd edition, Harmondsworth: Penguin

Coleman, P. and O'Hanlon, A. (2004) *Ageing and Development (Texts in Developmental Psychology)*, London: Arnold

Haralambos, M. and Holborn, M. (2013) *Sociology Themes and Perspectives*, 8th edition, London: HarperCollins

Havighurst, R.J. (1972) *Developmental Tasks and Education*, 3rd edition, London: Longman

Holmes, T.H. and Rahe, R.H. (1967) 'The Social Readjustment Rating Scale', *Journal of Psychosomatic Research* 11 (2) pp. 213–218

Lazarus, R.S. (1999) *Stress and Emotion*, New York: Springer Publishing Company

Lindon, J. and Brodie, K. (2016) *Understanding Child Development 0–8*, 4th edition, London: Hodder Education

Senior, M. and Viveash, B. (1997) *Health and Illness (Skills-based Sociology)*, London: Palgrave Macmillian

Shaffer, D. R. (2002) *Developmental Psychology Childhood and Adolescence*, 6th edition, Belmont Ca: Wadsworth

Sugarman, L. (2001) *Life-Span Development Frameworks, Accounts and Strategies: Theories, Concepts and Interventions*, 2nd edition, Hove: Psychology Press Ltd.

Websites

www.ageuk.org.uk
Age UK is a charity for older people, providing information, help and support.

www.bhf.org.uk
The British Heart Foundation is a charity providing information about heart disease and research.

www.cpag.org.uk
Child Poverty Action Group is a charity producing research and support for children and families living in poverty.

www.communitycare.co.uk
Specialist website involved in all aspects of social care.

www.dh.gov.uk
Government department responsible for research, develops policies and guidelines to ensure the quality of care of health and social care users.

www.guardian.co.uk/society
Social care reports and research.

www.jrf.org.uk
The Joseph Rowntree Foundation is a charity supporting a wide range of research and development projects in housing, poverty and social care.

www.kingsfund.org.uk
Kings Fund is a health charity that undertakes research for health and social care policies and practices.

www.nhs.uk
Access to NHS services and information on many diseases and conditions.

www.nursingtimes.net
A useful source for NHS and health care news.

www.ons.gov.uk
Produces statistics on a wide range of topics, including health and social care.

THINK ▶▶FUTURE

Lucy Smith, Healthcare assistant

I've been a qualified healthcare assistant for six years. My role is to support other health professionals in the individual care of patients. Much of my work involves helping people with their personal care such as bathing, feeding, toileting and supporting mobility. An important part of my job is to reposition people who are immobile to reduce the risk of bed sores. I also monitor patients' condition when they are admitted and during their hospital stay by taking their respiration, pulse, weight and height.

I recognise how distressing it must be for individuals to suddenly rely on others for their care. I always ensure that patients' dignity and privacy is maintained at all times. In this way, I can help them to maintain their confidence and self-esteem. It is important that I build good relationships with patients, treating each person as an individual. The whole person has to be considered not just their health problem: for instance, culture, religion and values can all impact on an individual's care needs and recovery.

Most people I support are in the later life stage. In this age group, there is a higher risk of conditions that require hospital care such as heart diseases, cancers and osteoarthritis. An increasing number of patients have dementia. I recently attended dementia training so that I can better understand how it might affect them at each stage of the disease and support their needs.

I have to be very well organised and pay attention to detail, especially around making and keeping meticulous records. For example, it is essential that records are kept about patients' food and fluid intake, toileting records and when they have been repositioned to make sure that care plans are followed. I have to make sure that all information is passed to other professionals following correct procedures so that confidentiality is maintained.

Working with other professionals and people using services requires a high level of communication skills. I attend meetings with patients, their families and other professionals such as social workers to discuss patients' needs, progress and develop care plans in preparation for their discharge.

Focusing your skills

Understanding development through all life stages

The knowledge and understanding in this unit will be invaluable to your career in health and social care or further training. To succeed in this unit, you need to understand development through the life stages, the factors that can impact on them and effects of ageing.

Investigating these topics will help you in your examination and your future career. If you can do some voluntary work, you will be able to talk to experienced professionals. While they must observe confidentiality and cannot discuss individual people in their care, they will be able to share their observations of development and how this can be affected, for instance, by life events, chronic illness or ageing.

It could also be helpful to talk to people in your extended family. For example, you could observe any younger relatives at play so that you really get to understand what the milestones mean in practice. You could note down what you see and then research how they are developing. You might speak to a parent, aunt or uncle in middle adulthood and ask what physical changes they have experienced and how it may have affected them. It would be particularly useful to speak to people in later adulthood. You could discuss how they adapted to changes such as retirement, changes in mobility or the onset of disease.

Getting ready for assessment

This section has been written to help you to do your best when you take the assessment test. Read through it carefully and ask your tutor if there is anything you are still not sure about.

About the examination

The examination will last 1 hour and 30 minutes and there are a maximum of 90 marks available. There will be short-answer questions and long-answer questions.

- Short-answer questions are worth 1 to 6 marks.
- Long-answer questions are worth 10 to 12 marks.

Remember, all the questions are compulsory and you should attempt to answer each one.

Preparing for the examination

You should start to plan your revision well in advance.

- Identify the themes and topics in the unit that you feel confident about and those you are less sure about.
- Draw up a timetable for revision of each topic and regularly review your progress.
- Summarise what you have learned on cue cards.
- Recap each topic using your cue cards shortly before the examination.
- Use at least one practice paper so that you are familiar with the layout.

To help plan your revision, it is very useful to know what type of learner you are. Which of the following sounds like it would be most helpful to you?

Type of learner	Visual learner	Auditory learner	Kinaesthetic learner
What it means	Need to see something or picture it, to learn it.	Need to hear something to learn it.	Learn better when physical activity is involved – learn by doing.
How it can help prepare for the test	• Colour code information on your notes. • Make short flash cards (so you can picture the notes). • Use diagrams, mind maps and flowcharts. • Use post-it notes to leave visible reminders for yourself.	• Read information aloud, then repeat it in your own words. • Use word games or mnemonics to help. • Use different ways of saying things – different stresses or voices for different things. • Record short revision notes to listen to on your phone or computer.	• Revise your notes while walking – use different locations for different subjects. • Try and connect actions with particular parts of a sequence you need to learn. • Record your notes and listen to them while doing chores, exercising etc – associate the tasks with the learning.

- **Remember! Take regular breaks** – short bursts of 30–40 minutes are more effective than long hours. Most people's concentration lapses after an hour, so you need breaks.
- **Allow yourself rest** – don't fill all your time with revision. You could schedule one evening off a week.
- **Take care of yourself** – stay healthy, rest and eat properly. This will help you to perform at your best. The less stressed you are, the easier you will find it to learn.

Sitting the examination

All the questions will relate to members of one family. In the first half of the paper, you will be given information about the individuals, such as their age, relationships, lifestyle, their environment, life events and information about their growth and development.

In the second half of the exam paper, you will be given an extended case study relating to one member of the family. This information will contain more detail about the individual so it would be helpful to underline or circle key information that may influence their growth and development.

Short-answer questions will enable you to demonstrate your knowledge and understanding of:

- the key features of human growth and areas of development across the life stages
- factors and life events that may impact on human growth and development
- the effects of ageing.

Short-answer questions are awarded between 1 and 6 marks.

Long-answer questions will require you to analyse, evaluate and make connections between factors, life events, theories and models that help to explain human growth and development. Long-answer questions are awarded 10 or 12 marks.

In both types of question, your answers should demonstrate a thorough knowledge of the topic and relate directly to the stage of development, context or situation described in the case study. Specialist language should be used consistently and fluently. Longer answers must be focused, well structured and have a supported conclusion. Answers should be balanced and show different viewpoints.

Most questions contain **command words**. Understanding what these words mean will help you understand what the question is asking you to do. The following are command words that you may come across in your examination.

Command word	Definition – what it is asking you to do
Describe	Give a full account of all the information, including all the relevant details of any features, of a topic.
Discuss	Write about the topic in detail, taking into account different ideas and opinions and their importance.
Evaluate	Bring all the relevant information you have on a topic together and make a judgement on it (for example on its success or importance, advantages or disadvantages). Your judgement should be clearly supported by the information you have gathered.
Explain	Make an idea, situation or problem clear to your reader, giving reasons to support your opinions.
Identify	State the key fact(s), features or purpose about a topic or subject.
Justify	Give reasons for the point your answer is making, so that your reader can tell what you are thinking. These reasons should clearly support the argument you are making.
Outline	Provide a brief summary or overview of a feature or topic.
To what extent	Assess the evidence and present your argument clearly, coming to a conclusion about the level, importance or extent of something, and exploring factors that may impact on the extent.
Which	Specify which one out of a set of known items.

Remember the number of marks can relate to the number of answers you may be expected to give – if a question asks for two examples, do not only give one! Similarly, do not offer more information than the question needs – giving four examples will not gain you extra marks.

Planning your time is an important part of succeeding on a test. Work out what you need to answer and then organise your time. You should spend more time on long-answer questions. Set yourself a timetable for working through the test and then stick to it – do not spend ages on a short 1–2 mark question and then find you only have a few minutes for a longer 10 to 12 mark question. The space provided on your answer sheet will indicate the length of answer that is expected.

You have 90 minutes and there are 90 marks. This means that you must allow only one minute per mark. For example, for a 6 mark answer, after reading the case study and the question you have less than 6 minutes to write your answer.

If you are writing an answer to a long-answer question, try and plan your answers before you start writing. Check that you have made each of your points and that you have given a valid argument that relates to the information in the case studies or any data provided.

If you finish early, use the time to re-read your answers and make any corrections – this could really help make your answers even better and could make a difference in your final mark.

Hints and tips for tests

- Revise all the key areas likely to be covered – draw up a checklist to make sure you do not forget anything!
- Arrive in good time so you are not in a panic.
- Read each case study and question carefully before you answer it to make sure you understand what you have to do.

- If you are stuck on a question, leave it until later – but remember to go back to it.
- Remember you cannot lose marks for a wrong answer, but you cannot gain any marks for a blank space!

This is an example of a short-answer question

Emily, 42, has two children. Connor aged 13 and Sara aged 8.

Connor has been bullied at school.

Worked examples

Question: Explain one possible effect of bullying on Connor's emotional development and one possible effect on Connor's social development.

(4 marks)

Learner answer:

1. Bullying could make Connor live in fear of what might happen so therefore it may result in him becoming depressed or even suicidal.

2. Bullying may affect Connor's ability to build new friendships because bullying may cause him to become socially isolated.

Questions often state the areas of development that you must explore in your answer. The learner has given one answer relating to emotional and one answer relating to social development. The reasons they give are realistic in Connor's situation. They have shown an understanding of the possible effect of bullying on the individual in the case study.

In **explain** questions, make sure that you have given reasons (explanations) for your answers. Use the words 'because' or 'therefore' to help you make sure you have given reasons.

This is an example of a long-answer question

Emily's brother Frank is 54 years old. Frank worked as a paint sprayer in a car factory for many years but, last year, was made redundant. Frank lives alone now as he divorced at the age of 48. Frank lives in a small flat in the city close to the motorway. Many of Frank's neighbours are now moving out of the area because of increasing vandalism.

Frank has respiratory problems and high cholesterol. He finds difficulty in walking any distance as he soon gets out of breath. After suffering chest pains, Frank visited his GP who diagnosed angina. This concerns Frank as his father had high cholesterol which led to a heart attack and his death at the age of 62.

Emily visits Frank regularly and has tried to encourage him to eat more healthily and to stop smoking. Frank argues that it is not worth cooking for one and relies on ready meals or takeaways. He promises to cut down his smoking but says it is difficult as he has smoked since he was a teenager.

Question: Evaluate possible explanations for Frank's health with reference to the Holmes–Rahe social adjustment rating scale and factors affecting human growth and development. (10 marks)

Learner answer:

Frank's respiratory problems could have been as a result of breathing in fumes when paint spraying at work, exacerbated by smoking. Respiratory problems are linked to the cardiovascular system so this is likely to have led to heart disease. As Frank's father suffered from high blood cholesterol and died from a heart attack, Frank may have a susceptibility to these conditions. Although susceptibility does not make it certain that Frank would suffer high cholesterol and develop heart disease, his smoking over many years and his recent poor diet increases the risk.

Frank's deteriorating health could be explained by the Holmes–Rahe social adjustment rating scale. This scale was based on a study of life events experienced by individuals. Each life event was given a score depending on the level of stress it caused. It was found that those who had a high score were more likely to suffer ill heath. Frank has experienced a number or unpredictable life events, such as his divorce and redundancy, resulting in a level of stress which would have scored highly on the Holmes–Rahe scale. In addition, concerns about his health and living in an unsafe area will have increased his stress level further. Based on this study, Frank would be highly likely to suffer ill health.

Frank's deteriorating health can be explained by influences of nature and nurture. His genetic make-up means that he may have a susceptibility to high cholesterol and heart disease. However, he may not have developed these conditions without the influence of environmental factors, including those that are work and housing related, stress caused by life events and his life style.

You need to have a good grasp of factors, theories and models that may affect human growth and development so that you can make links to the most appropriate ones. This learner has explored a range of factors including environmental, life events, lifestyle and genetic susceptibility to disease.

Learners often show knowledge of theories but fail to make relevant links to the case study. This learner gives an overview of the Holmes–Rahe social adjustment rating scale and then links it directly to Frank's situation. This demonstrates their understanding in context. As the learner explores each factor, they give supported reasons for each point they make with clear links to the details about Frank in the case study.

In the final paragraph, the learner has referred back to the question 'possible explanations for Frank's health'. This has helped them to come to a balanced conclusion as to the likely influence of genetic susceptibility and environmental factors.

Working in Health and Social Care 2

Getting to know your unit

In this unit, you will be introduced to the roles and responsibilities of health and social care practitioners and the organisations they work for. You will see how a wide range of roles, including doctors, nurses, physiotherapists, occupational therapists, social workers, youth workers, care workers and other professionals, work together to ensure that the individual needs of vulnerable people are met.

You will learn how standards in this area are set and monitored and reflect on the role of professionals in this sector in supporting people with health and social care needs.

How you will be assessed

You will be assessed by a paper-based examination, lasting for 1 hour 30 minutes and worth 80 marks. The examination will consist of four sections. There will be short- and long-answer questions. The questions are intended to assess your understanding of how health and care services and health and care practitioners can meet the needs of a range of service users who need professional support. Each section will relate to a different service user group, for example the frail elderly, people with learning disabilities, people with mental health problems or people with long-term illnesses. The questions will make connections between the organisations and professionals that contribute to care and provide opportunities to discuss the challenges associated with providing high-quality health and care provision.

Throughout this unit, you will find assessment practices to help you to prepare for the exam. Completing each of these will give you an insight into the types of questions that may be asked and, importantly, how to answer them.

Unit 2 has four assessment outcomes (AO), which will be included in the external examination. Each assessment outcome also has some 'command words' associated with it – see Table 2.1 for a list of what these command words are asking you to do.

The assessment outcomes for the unit are:

AO1 Demonstrate knowledge of service user needs, roles and responsibilities of workers and working practices within the health and social care sector.

Command words: Identify.

Marks: 2 marks.

AO2 Demonstrate understanding of service user needs, roles and responsibilities of workers and working practices and procedures in the health and social care sector.

Command words: Describe.

Marks: 4 marks.

AO3 Analyse and evaluate information related to the roles and responsibilities of health and social care workers and organisations and how workers and organisations are monitored and regulated.

Command words: Explain.

Marks: 6 marks.

AO4 Make connections between the roles and responsibilities of health and social care workers and organisations, how workers and organisations are monitored and regulated and how multidisciplinary teams work together to meet service user needs.

Command words: Discuss.

Marks: 8 marks

▸ **Table 2.1:** Command words used in this unit

Command word	Definition – what it is asking you to do
Identify	State the key fact(s) about a topic. The word 'outline' is very similar.
Describe	Give a full account of all the information available, including all the relevant details of any features, about a topic.
Explain	Make an idea, situation or problem clear to your reader by describing it in detail, including any relevant data or facts.
Discuss	Write about the topic in detail, taking into account different ideas and opinions.

This table contains the areas of essential content that learners must be familiar with prior to assessment.

Essential content	
A	The roles and responsibilities of people who work in the health and social care sector
B	The roles of organisations in the health and social care sector
C	Working with people with specific needs in the health and social care sector

Getting started

Sheila is nearly 90 and is now quite frail. She lives alone in a ground floor flat and uses a wheelchair indoors. Sheila is on a very low income. Identify and list the health and care services that might be available locally to help her live independently. After completing this unit, see if you can add more services to your list.

A The roles and responsibilities of people who work in the health and social care sector

Roles of people who work in health and social care settings

Doctors

When people are feeling unwell, their first (or primary) point of contact with the medical profession will normally be a **general practitioner (GP)**. GPs provide ongoing care for people in the community. This includes:

▶ caring for people who are unwell, including carrying out simple surgical procedures
▶ providing **preventative care** and health education for service users.

GPs are increasingly based in local health centres, working with other doctors and a range of health and care professionals such as nurses, health visitors and counsellors. GPs may refer people to hospital specialists (consultants) or other care professionals for further assessment and treatment such as X-rays or blood tests, or to social workers for social care support.

The principle responsibilities of doctors in treating illnesses are to:

▶ diagnose an individual's illnesses and ailments
▶ discuss and agree an individual treatment plan
▶ prescribe appropriate medication or treatment
▶ monitor the impact of the agreed treatment.

The preventative care and health education services provided include:

▶ vaccination programmes for people of all ages
▶ health education and advice on issues such as smoking, alcohol consumption and healthy eating.

Research

List the range of preventative care and health education services provided at your GP's surgery. Share this information with the other members of your group. Are there any significant differences in different areas?

Hospital doctors provide specialist medical care. In the UK and the Republic of Ireland, **consultant** is the title of a senior, hospital-based doctor who specialises in a particular field of medicine and manages complex cases. To provide this care, the consultant normally leads a team, or firm, of more junior doctors. This includes newly qualified doctors and more experienced doctors (known as registrars). Consultants are normally known by the name of their specialist field, for example:

▶ cardiologists specialise in treating heart disease
▶ psychiatrists specialise in treating mental health problems
▶ oncologists specialise in treating cancer
▶ paediatricians specialise in treating children
▶ geriatricians specialise in treating older people.

Nurses

Nurses are the largest group of professionals working in the health services. There are many opportunities to specialise and to reach senior levels within the profession, including the role of nurse consultant or **nurse practitioner**.

▶ Adult nurses work with adults of all ages, who may have a wide range of physical health conditions. They may be based in hospitals, clinics or GP practices, or work for specialist organisations such as the armed forces. Many adult nurses work with people in their own homes. Adult nurses will often plan individual care, carry out healthcare procedures and treatments and evaluate their effectiveness. They also work to promote good health by running clinics and health education programmes on topics such as giving up smoking or weight loss.

▶ Mental health nurses are nurses who specialise in mental health work in a range of settings. These may include psychiatric units in hospitals, community healthcare centres, day care settings, residential homes and prisons. Mind, the charity that supports people with mental health problems, estimates that each year one in four people in the UK will experience mental health problems. Remember that most people who experience mental health problems are cared for in the community, not in hospitals.

▶ Children's nurses or paediatric nurses work with children with a very wide range of conditions. A children's nurse works closely with the child's parents or carers. This is to ensure that, as far as possible, the care provided meets their social, cultural and family needs, as well as addressing their health issues. Children's nurses may work in hospitals but also support children at home.

▶ Learning disability nurses work mainly with individuals with learning disabilities living in the community rather than in hospitals. This may include supporting people in schools and workplaces, people living at home with their families and people who live in specialist residential settings. They aim to work with people with learning disabilities and their carers to maintain the person's physical and mental health, provide specialist healthcare and support them to live as fulfilling and independent a life as possible.

▶ District nurses care for people of all ages, supporting them in their own homes or in residential homes. District nurses work closely with family members and other carers. They assess the patient's needs and also the care and support needs of their 'informal' carers. District nurses most commonly care for older people, people with disabilities and people recently discharged from hospital.

▶ Neonatal nurses work with newborn babies, including babies who are born prematurely. They work in specialist hospital settings and in the community. The neonatal nurse works very closely with the baby's parents and actively encourages them to take a practical role in their child's care.

Key term

Consultant – a senior doctor, normally based in a hospital, who provides specialist expert healthcare support in their area of expertise.

Key term

Nurse practitioner – provides expert consultancy service to patients and their carers. They contribute to the management and development of the care provision. They also undertake research and contribute to the education and training of other members of staff.

▶ An adult nurse talking to a patient

▶ Health visitors provide support for families in the early years of their children's life, normally from birth to the age of five. They offer support on health issues and minor illnesses, and advice on feeding and weaning. They carry out routine checks on the child's development and support parents in meeting the developmental needs of their children. Health visitors see the children and their carers in their homes, at clinics, at the GP practice and sometimes at a nursery or in other community settings.

▶ Practice nurses work in GP practices. In small practices there may be only one practice nurse, but increasingly they are part of a larger team of practice nurses. Practice nurses' responsibilities vary according to the GP practice but will normally include taking blood samples, carrying out child immunisation programmes and administering vaccinations for people travelling abroad. Practice nurses often provide **health screening** for men and women, and family planning advice, if they are qualified to do so.

▶ School nurses are usually employed by the NHS but may be employed directly by a school. They provide a variety of services, including developmental checks, administering immunisation programmes and providing health education programmes.

Midwives

Midwives play a central role in supporting women through all stages of pregnancy, providing both **antenatal** and **postnatal** care. This includes helping families prepare for parenthood and delivering babies in the maternity departments of hospitals and in patients' homes.

Midwives may be based in hospital maternity units but an increasing number of midwives work in the community, providing support at local clinics in GP practices, in women's homes and at children's centres.

Healthcare assistants

Healthcare assistants are sometimes known as nursing assistants or auxiliary nurses. They work under the guidance and with the support of qualified healthcare professionals. They may work in GP practices, hospitals, nursing homes and other

---

---

community healthcare settings. Most commonly healthcare assistants work alongside qualified nurses, but they may also work with midwives in maternity services. Duties carried out by healthcare assistants include:

▶ taking and recording a patient's temperature and pulse

▶ weighing patients, and recording the result

▶ taking patients to the toilet

▶ making beds

▶ washing and dressing patients

▶ serving meals and assisting with feeding when necessary.

Social workers

Social workers provide help and support for people of all ages through difficult times in their lives. They aim to ensure that the most vulnerable people are safeguarded from harm and to help people live independent lives. Social workers support children, people with disabilities, people with mental health problems and the frail elderly.

Increasingly, social workers specialise either in providing services for adults or in providing services for children and young people.

▶ Adult services include services for older people, adults with disabilities, people with mental health problems and people who have learning difficulties. They support people living independently and those in residential care. They work very closely with the service users' families and carers.

▶ The children and young people's services provide support for children and their families. They play a key role in ensuring that children are safe and protected from abuse. If children are at risk from harm, social workers take measures to ensure that the children are removed to a safe place. This may, in extreme circumstances, include removing them from their home and family. Social workers also work in residential children's settings and manage fostering and adoption procedures. They provide support for young people leaving care and young people at risk of being in trouble with the law.

Occupational therapists

Occupational therapists work with people of all ages who are having difficulty in carrying out the practical routines of daily life, for example washing and bathing, housework, cooking or getting to the shops. These problems may be the result of a disability, physical or psychological illness, an accident or the frailty of older age. The occupational therapist will agree specific activities with an individual that will help them to overcome their barriers to living an independent life. Occupational therapists may work in people's homes, GP practices, residential and nursing homes, prisons, social services and other council departments and in hospitals.

Youth workers

Youth workers generally work with young people between the ages of 11 and 25. They aim to support young people to reach their full potential and to become responsible members of society. They work in a range of settings, including youth centres, schools and colleges. They may be employed by the local council but youth workers are also employed by a range of religious and other voluntary organisations. Youth workers are not always based in a particular building, especially if they are working with young people on the streets.

Typical youth work activities include:

▶ delivering programmes relating to young people's concerns, such as smoking, drugs, binge drinking, relationships and dealing with violence
▶ organising residential activities and projects
▶ running sports teams
▶ initiating and managing community projects with young people
▶ working with parents to support the healthy development of their children.

▶ Youth work covers a wide range of activities

Care assistants

Care assistants provide practical help and support for people who have difficulties with daily activities. This may include supporting older people and their families, children and young people, people with physical or learning disabilities or people with mental health problems. Care assistants work in a wide range of settings, such as in clients' homes, at day care settings, in residential and nursing homes and in supported or sheltered housing complexes. Their exact duties will vary according to the needs of the clients, but could include:

▶ helping with personal daily care, such as washing, dressing, using the toilet and feeding
▶ general household tasks, including cleaning, doing laundry and shopping
▶ paying bills and writing letters
▶ liaising with other health and care professionals.

Sometimes care assistants will work with only one person, providing intensive support to enable them to manage everyday life.

Care managers

Care managers have a key leadership role within residential care settings. They manage the provision of residential care for:

▶ adults and young adults with learning difficulties
▶ older people in residential care or nursing homes
▶ people in **supported housing**
▶ people receiving hospice care.

> **Key term**
>
> **Supported housing** – shelter, support and care provided for vulnerable people, to help them live as independently as possible in the community.

Care managers are responsible for the routine running of the residential care setting, including appointing suitable staff and managing staff teams, managing the budget and ensuring that the quality of care meets the standards required by the sector. Care managers will manage and supervise the duties of the care assistants working in their setting.

Support workers

The support worker role is closely linked to the healthcare or nursing assistant role discussed earlier. Support workers, however, may work under the supervision of a range of health and care professionals, including physiotherapists, occupational therapists and social workers. Family support workers, for example work with and support social workers. Once the social worker has identified what is needed, the support worker may work closely with the family to help implement the plan. They may provide support with parenting skills, financial management or domestic skills.

Reflect

Consider the range of health and care workers who support people at your work placement. There may be professionals or volunteers who are not included in this unit. The list is not exhaustive! Can you think of other professionals who might promote your clients' or patients' health and wellbeing further?

Keep a list to help you prepare for the exam.

Research

In groups, use the internet and other up-to-date resources to identify the entry qualifications for a health and social care role and the main responsibilities of professionals working in the health and care services. Each group member should research a different job and share their results. You may want to present your work as a chart to help with revision.

Case study

Caring for Imran

Imran has multiple sclerosis. He uses a wheelchair both at home and when he goes out. Imran has a very caring family who are determined that they should look after him at home. He needs help with washing and dressing, he cannot feed himself any longer and he is incontinent.

Check your knowledge

1 Identify the range of care professionals who might support Imran and his family in caring for him at home.

2 Briefly describe the contribution that each of the healthcare professionals you have identified may make to Imran's care and comfort.

3 Discuss your work with other members of your group. Have you missed anything?

4 Present your work in a table.

This will help you prepare for your exam.

⏸ PAUSE POINT   Describe the key roles and responsibilities of a range of health and care practitioners.

Hint   Close the book and list the key health and care practitioners that have been discussed.

Extend   Briefly describe the roles and responsibilities of each practitioner.

Policies – detailed descriptions of the approach, and often the specific procedures that should be followed, in caring for clients.

Procedures – written instructions that outline the expected and required routines that care staff must follow in specific situations, for example reporting accidents or administering medicines, in order to implement agreed policies.

Key term

Safeguarding – policies to ensure that children and vulnerable adults are protected from harm, abuse and neglect and that their health and wellbeing is promoted.

Responsibilities of people who work in health and social care settings

In this section, you will consider the day-to-day responsibilities of people working in health and social care settings. You will examine the strategies that are in place to ensure that the care services promote the health and wellbeing of service users and meet the standards required by the health and care sector.

Following policies and procedures in health and social care settings

Health and social care organisations have guidelines that describe the working procedures that should be followed to ensure that the care provided meets service users' needs. **Policies** and **procedures** aim to ensure that all staff and volunteers work within the law and to the highest professional standards.

The specific policies in place in a care setting will vary according to the client groups served and the particular function of the setting. These policies may include:

▶ health and safety policy
▶ equality and diversity policy
▶ medication policy
▶ **safeguarding** policy
▶ Disclosing and Barring Service (DBS) referral policy
▶ death of a resident procedures
▶ complaints policy.

Research

When you are on work placement, ask your supervisor for a copy of one of their policies. Summarise the policy and explain to the rest of your group how it is used to promote the health and wellbeing of the people you support.

Make notes during other people's presentations in order to gather information about as many policies as possible.

Reflect

Think about the range of policies in place at your work placement setting. Are all staff familiar with them? Are the policies always implemented? What action is taken if staff or volunteers do not follow the official procedures?

Make a note of your answers to help you with your revision.

Healing and supporting recovery for people who are ill

There are clearly many different strategies that may be used to support the recovery of people who are ill. The precise support needed will depend on the service user's condition and also their wider social and personal needs.

The range of treatments and care procedures used in healthcare settings may include:

▶ **Prescribing medication**, this has traditionally been the doctor's role. However, some nurses have undergone additional training and taken on the role of nurse prescriber. Some other healthcare practitioners, such as dentists, chiropodists and physiotherapists, may prescribe some medications in certain circumstances.

Research

Visit the Pharmaceutical Services Negotiating Committee website and research who can prescribe medications and in what circumstances.

▸ **Surgery**, which may play a significant part in supporting an individual's recovery from illness and other physical disorders. For example, cancerous tumours such as breast lumps may be removed by surgery if cancer is diagnosed at an early stage. Older people may require joint replacement surgery, such as hip or knee joints. Health and care workers in the community have an increasingly important role in supporting people recovering from surgery. This may include visits from the district nurse to monitor progress and provide specific treatments, including changing dressings. Physiotherapists and occupational therapists, where necessary, support mobility and promote independence in carrying out daily living activities. Social workers may provide additional emotional support and ensure that the patient is accessing the services available. Home care workers may provide practical help in the home, including preparing meals where this is seen as necessary.
A patient's recovery will continue after discharge from hospital. Community support is particularly necessary as there is a trend to discharge people as soon as possible following surgery.

▸ **Radiotherapy**, is treatment using high-energy radiation. Treatment is planned by skilled radiotherapists working alongside a team that includes radiographers and specially trained nurses. Although radiotherapy is often used to treat cancer, it can be used to treat non-cancerous tumours or other conditions, such as diseases of the thyroid gland and some blood disorders. Patients may need support from their GP on completion of the treatment to ensure full healing. Common side effects of some forms of radiotherapy include itchiness and peeling or blistering of the skin.

▸ **Organ transplant**, involves either moving a body part or organ from one person's body to another's (known as an allograft) or from one part of a person's body to another location in their own body (known as an autograft). The purpose of the transplant is to replace the patient's damaged or absent organ. Organs that can be transplanted include the heart, kidneys, liver, lungs, pancreas and intestines. The most commonly performed transplants are the kidneys followed by the liver and the heart. A living donor can give one kidney, part of their liver and some other tissues, such as bone marrow. However, other transplants come from donors who have recently died, so in the recovery period following surgery the person receiving the transplant may need the support of a counsellor.
Highly skilled surgeons and their teams will carry out the transplant. However, many more care professionals will be involved in preparing the individual physically and mentally for surgery and caring for the person following their transplant. For example, specialist nurses, physiotherapists, occupational therapists, counsellors and social workers may provide post-operative support.

▸ **Support for lifestyle changes**, changing the pattern of daily routines and habits that are damaging to health can be very challenging, but may be very important in improving a person's health. Counselling and the support of **self-help groups** may be crucial in implementing and sustaining lifestyle changes. For example, introducing a more healthy diet, taking more exercise, reducing the amount of alcohol consumed and stopping smoking. Healthcare professionals, such as GPs, practice nurses and district nurses, can assist individuals to set up self-help groups, for example by allowing them to meet in a room in a GP practice.

Key term

Self-help groups – groups formed by people who share a common issue that they wish to address. The members provide advice, support and care for each other. For example, Alcoholics Anonymous is a self-help group for recovering alcoholics.

▶ **Accessing support from specialist agencies**, many specialist agencies support and promote the health and wellbeing of service users, especially those who have specific illnesses or disorders. Healthcare professionals can inform their service users about these agencies, some examples include:

- Age UK – provides services and support to promote the health and wellbeing of older people.
- Mind – provides advice and support for people with mental health problems and campaigns to raise awareness and improve services for people with mental illnesses.
- YoungMind – is committed to improving the mental health of children and young people, through individual support and through campaigning for improved services.
- The Royal National Institute of Blind People (RNIB) – supports people affected by sight loss, both people who are partially-sighted and those who are blind.
- Alzheimer's Society – provides information and support for people living with dementia, their families and their carers. It also funds research and promotes awareness of this condition.

Research

Investigate one specialist organisation or agency that provides specific advice and support for the people cared for at your work placement setting. Write a short report of the aims, objectives and key activities of the organisation. Email this to other members of your group.

 **PAUSE POINT**

Close the book and list the range of policies in place in health and social care settings.

 Hint

Think about the policies in place at your work placement setting.

Extend

Briefly describe the main requirement of one policy at your work placement setting.

Enabling rehabilitation

The purpose of a **rehabilitation** programme is to enable a person to recover from an accident or serious illness and to live, as far as possible, an independent and fulfilling life. These programmes are particularly important after someone has a heart attack or a stroke, or following an accident that has significantly reduced their mobility or their reaction speed. Rehabilitation programmes may also be a central part of treatment for people who have a mental illness. The specific programme will vary according to the person's physical and psychological needs and their home and family circumstances, including the level of support from their family, friends and carers. Rehabilitation may include support from physiotherapists, occupational therapists, counsellors or **psychotherapists**.

Key terms

Rehabilitation – the process of restoring a person to good health following surgery, an accident or other illness, including recovery from addiction.

Psychotherapy – type of therapy used to treat emotional and mental health conditions, usually by talking to a trained therapist one-to-one or in a group.

It may also include using **complementary therapies**. Complementary therapies are not considered **conventional medical treatment**, and so may not be available as part of an individual's NHS care.

Providing equipment and adaptations to support people in being more independent

A vast range of equipment is available to support people to remain independent when carrying out their routine daily activities. There are many reasons for people needing temporary or permanent assistance with mobility or other activities of daily life and their needs are usually assessed by a physiotherapist or occupational therapist. Other healthcare professionals, such as doctors or nurses, may refer a service user to a physiotherapist or occupational therapist for assessment. Care assistants and health care assistants often provide ongoing support in using equipment effectively and adaptions to increase a service user's independence.

Equipment to increase mobility

At the simplest level, mobility appliances allow people to be more physically active and more independent in carrying out daily routines. For example, people with arthritis, people who have broken a limb or are recovering from surgery or a stroke, or who have a progressive disease such as multiple sclerosis, motor neurone disease or muscular dystrophy or are simply ageing and have less strength in their bones and muscles. Mobility aids include:

▶ walking sticks

▶ walking frames, including tripods and tetrapods

▶ wheelchairs, manual or electric

▶ adapted shopping trolleys

▶ stairlifts

▶ adapted cars, or other motorised transport.

Appliances that support daily living activities

Individuals may need a range of other appliances to support daily living activities and to promote their independence. These could include:

▶ special cutlery with thick, light handles that are easy to hold for people with arthritis

▶ feeding cups or angled straws for drinks

▶ egg cups and plates with suctioned bottoms

▶ special gadgets to help people who can only use one hand to take the lids off jars and tins, and others to help with peeling potatoes and buttering bread, kettles on tipping stands and adapted plugs to help with using electrical appliances

▶ special dining chairs and armchairs adapted to meet individual needs

▶ bathing aids such as walk-in baths and showers, bath and shower seats

▶ raised toilet seats for service users who find it difficult to sit down and stand up again

▶ A raised toilet seat is helpful to people who have reduced mobility

> ▶ adapted computer keyboards and, where necessary, screens to support people with a range of physical conditions, including epilepsy, arthritis and visual impairments.

Some people with chronic conditions may need highly sophisticated equipment in their home to manage an independent life. For example, people with chronic bronchitis, emphysema or a coronary heart condition may need oxygen cylinders at home and people with kidney failure may need dialysis equipment.

Technology and other resources that support educational achievement

Assistive technology and a very wide range of other resources are available to support people with disabilities and other illnesses to meet their educational potential. These include:

▶ adapted computers to meet the needs of visually impaired and blind people
▶ availability of signers and other communicators for hearing-impaired and profoundly deaf people
▶ ensuring wheelchair access to all learning spaces
▶ additional time in examinations for learners who are dyslexic
▶ enlarged text for people with poor vision.

> **Key term**
>
> **Assistive technology** – any tool or strategy used to help people with disabilities complete their studies successfully and reach their potential.

> **Research**
>
> Investigate the range of adaptive equipment available to support someone:
> * with arthritis in their hands and fingers
> * who uses a wheelchair
> * who has a degenerative eye condition and is partially sighted.
>
> Which healthcare professionals might be able to help them find the adaptive equipment they need? How might the equipment be paid for? Would they have to buy it themselves?

Providing personal care – including washing, toileting and feeding

Keeping clean, enjoying a meal and using the toilet when needed are tasks and activities that most people are able to take for granted and do for themselves. However, when people become either physically or mentally ill, or they have a disability, these everyday activities become a challenge. There are clearly important reasons, in terms of physical wellbeing, why people should be clean, eat well and be able to use the toilet when necessary. Dealing with these very personal areas of life has an impact on self-esteem and general confidence. It cannot be overemphasised how important it is for health and care workers to approach these intimate areas of a person's daily life with thoughtfulness and sensitivity.

Carers must discuss usual routines and preferences in terms of personal hygiene and diet with clients. For example, when washing the client may prefer a bath to a shower, or a thorough wash to either of these. Most people would prefer to take personal responsibility for these tasks and wash in private. Independence should be encouraged, but where specific help is needed the client's dignity and privacy should be preserved. Toilet and bathroom doors should be closed and shower curtains drawn. You should follow the policies and procedures of your setting to ensure the safety and dignity of your service user while carrying out these intimate tasks.

> **Key term**
>
> **Domiciliary care** – care provided in the service user's own home. This may include district nurses, home care workers and health visitors.

Domiciliary care workers, who provide support for people living in their own homes, will often provide personal care of this type. In a residential home care assistants will provide this support and in hospitals it will be a regular task for health care assistants working on the ward.

A wide range of equipment is available to extend the independence of people in terms of their personal hygiene and to support carers providing personal care. Equipment includes:

▶ walk-in baths
▶ showers suitable for the use of wheelchair users
▶ non-slip bathmats
▶ bath and shower seats
▶ hand rails
▶ bath lifts and hoists
▶ adapted taps
▶ bedpans and commodes
▶ female and male urinals.

▶ An adapted bathroom

Healthcare professionals must also be aware of and respect religious and cultural differences related to personal cleanliness, for example:

▶ Muslims and Hindus normally prefer to wash in running water rather than have a bath
▶ Muslims and Hindus often prefer to use a bidet rather than use paper after using the toilet
▶ Sikhs and Rastafarians do not normally cut their hair
▶ Hindus and Muslims would strongly prefer to be treated and supported by someone of the same sex.

Eating and drinking is vital for life itself, but meal times are also a social activity and ideally an enjoyable occasion. Dining areas should be clean and a pleasing environment. Most people in care settings are able to feed themselves. However there will be clients who experience difficulties because of their physical condition, because they are confused, or because they are emotionally unsettled. They may be depressed or unhappy in the setting and find it difficult to eat.

Some people will be capable of feeding themselves with minimal assistance and often using specially designed eating and drinking equipment, such as those referred to earlier in the unit, will allow them independence.

Many people have specific dietary requirements. This will sometimes be related to religious belief, sometimes to physical disorders and sometimes to personal choice, for example:

▶ vegetarians do not eat fish, meat or meat-based products – this could include jelly

▶ vegans do not eat meat or any animal-related products, including eggs, cheese, cow's or goat's milk

▶ Muslim and Jewish people do not eat pork and they require their meat to be killed and prepared for consumption in a particular way, Muslims eat **halal** products and Jews **kosher** foods

▶ Hindus and Sikhs do not eat beef

▶ people with coeliac disease require a **gluten**-free diet

▶ other people have specific allergic reactions to particular foods – allergic reactions to nuts, strawberries, dairy products and shell fish are particularly common.

Reflect

Use a catalogue or the internet to see the wide range of adaptions and equipment available to support people to wash, use the toilet and eat and enjoy their meals. Think about the people at your placement. Would these adaptions help them?

Make notes so that you can describe key equipment and its purpose. You may need to do this in your final assessment.

Supporting routines of service users in the context of their day-to-day family life, education, employment and leisure activities

Earlier in this unit, the specialist support provided by a wide range of health and care professionals was discussed. Although many health and care staff have expert knowledge and high-level skills in particular areas, they will also try to address the wider personal needs that may emerge while working with their service users. This could include, for example a nurse not just attending to a service user's physical needs but also being aware of their wider social, emotional, spiritual and educational needs. Addressing these may be just as important for a speedy and successful recovery as the medical interventions and physical care that needs to be delivered and monitored.

In attending to the needs of the 'whole' person, health and care professionals will want to support clients in developing and maintaining a fulfilling and satisfying daily life. This will involve being aware of the community in which their client lives, their work, their family circumstances, their general financial position and their interests, hobbies and aspirations. It also includes being aware of the support provided by family, friends and neighbours, who are often referred to as **informal carers**. These wider considerations can be as important to a person's recovery as medicines and other clinical interventions.

Link

You can find out more about caring for the whole person, or holistic care, in the section on Holistic approaches, and also in *Unit 10: Sociological Perspectives*.

Consider how far the care provided at your placement, or at any other care setting with which you are familiar, supports routines that develop good links with families, and promotes opportunities for extending education, employment and leisure activities. Discuss your thoughts, knowledge and experience with other members of your group.

⏸ **PAUSE POINT**   Close the book. List items of adaptive equipment that service users may use to be as independent as possible in daily life.

Hint   Think about the various things people have to do throughout the day, eg get up and dressed, wash, eat, travel etc.

Extend   Explain the impact of using this equipment in promoting health and wellbeing.

Assessment and care and support planning, involving service users and their families

As was discussed earlier in this unit, health and care professionals' skills are wide ranging and cover many specialities. However, despite the differences in skills, experience and specialist knowledge, all health and care professionals are likely to take a similar approach to planning and evaluating care. Often referred to as the care planning cycle (see Figure 2.1), this approach involves:

▸ assessing the individual healthcare needs of their service users

▸ agreeing a care plan that promotes the service user's health and wellbeing

▸ evaluating the effectiveness of the care implemented.

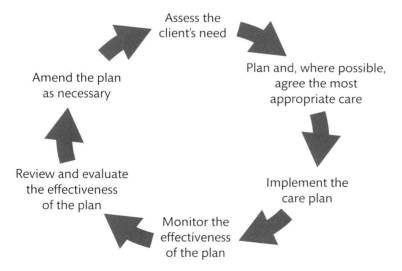

▸ **Figure 2.1** The care planning cycle

The process is cyclical, interventions and changes may be introduced at any point in the process. Adjustments may be necessary, for example in response to changes in the client's health or social circumstances, the resources that are available, the specific expertise of the staff or multi-disciplinary team or changing levels of support from informal carers.

When planning care, professionals will assess needs and agree the appropriate care with the service user and where appropriate with family members and other informal carers. Informal carers often contribute to the reviews and evaluations of care provision and to discussions about alternative strategies.

> **Research**
>
> Read a care plan for a service user at your work placement setting. How closely does the process at your setting match the care planning cycle presented in this unit? Did the planning and review involve informal carers or other members of the service user's family?

Specific responsibilities of people who work in health and social care settings

People working in health and care settings are required to work to high professional standards. They are required to follow agreed policies and procedures and actively promote the health and wellbeing of those in their care. This is underpinned by a value system, which includes commitments to:

▶ promoting anti-discriminatory practice to ensure that care services meet the needs of all people regardless of their religion, culture, ethnic background, disability or other personal differences

▶ empowering individuals, enabling them to take control of their lives and the decisions that relate to their treatment and care

▶ ensuring the safety of staff, and of the people for whom they care

▶ maintaining confidentiality and privacy

▶ promoting good communication between carers, and between carers and their clients.

These principles of good practice are the care value base, established by the Care Sector Consortium in 1992. They are found in the **code of practice** of all health and care professions, for example:

▶ the General Medical Council (GMC) sets and monitors standards of behaviour for doctors

▶ the Nursing & Midwifery Council (NMC) sets and monitors standards of behaviour for nurses and midwives

▶ the recently formed Health and Care Professions Council (HCPC) sets and monitors standards of behaviour for social workers and for a range of other health professions, including physiotherapists, occupational therapists, paramedics and speech therapists.

Promoting anti-discriminatory practice

Implementing codes of practice and policies that identify and challenge discrimination in specific health and social care settings

Anti-discriminatory practice is a core value and principle that guides the work of health and care professionals. It is based on legal requirements as outlined in the Equality Act 2010. It underpins the polices and practices of care settings, and in the codes of practice of all care professionals. Anti-discriminatory practice aims to ensure that the care needs of service users are met regardless of differences in race, ethnicity, age, disability or sexual orientation, and that the **prejudices** of staff or other service users are appropriately challenged.

> **Key terms**
>
> **Code of practice** – standards of behaviour and professional practice required of health and care practitioners, set and monitored by professional bodies such as the GMC, NMC or the HCPC.
>
> **Anti-discriminatory practice** – care practice that ensures that individual and different needs of clients and patients are met regardless of their race, ethnicity, age, disability, sex or sexual orientation, and that prejudices and unfair discrimination are challenged.
>
> **Prejudice** – preconceived opinions or fixed attitudes about a social group that are not based on reason or evidence. Prejudicial attitudes may lead to active discrimination.

Legislation exists (for example, see Figure 2.2) to ensure that vulnerable groups of people are not discriminated against.

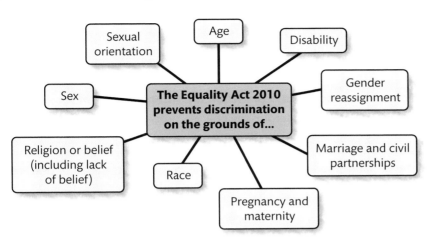

▶ **Figure 2.2** The Equality Act 2010

All citizens in Great Britain (England, Wales and Scotland) have legal protection through the courts. In Northern Ireland, the main legislation protecting workers against discrimination is the Employment Equality (Age) Regulations (NI) 2006 and there is separate legislation for each area of discrimination:

▶ Employment Equality (Age) (Amendment) Regulations (NI) 2006

▶ Employment Equality (Age) (Amendment No.2) Regulations (NI) 2006

▶ Employment Equality (Age) (Amendment) Regulations (NI) 2009

▶ Employment Equality (Age) (Repeal of Retirement Age Provisions) Regulations (NI) 2011.

The Human Rights Act (1998) applies to all parts of the United Kingdom (England, Scotland, Wales and Northern Ireland). The Act guarantees rights to people cared for by 'public authorities' to be treated equally, with fairness, dignity and respect. Public authorities, or organisations, include hospitals, GP practices, social service departments, schools and colleges and many care and nursing homes.

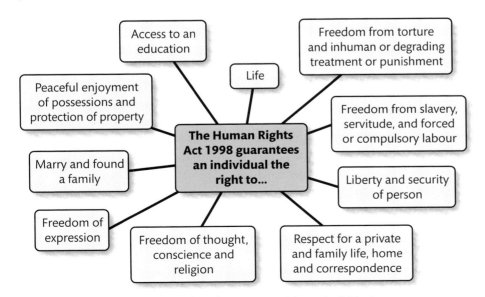

▶ **Figure 2.3** The Human Rights Act (1998) guarantees rights to individuals

Adapting health and social care provision for different types of service users

Despite the legislation that underpins the policies, procedures and codes of practice governing professional practice and the care provided in health and care settings, the world is not free from prejudice and discrimination. Unfair treatment is a daily experience for many people in society. Furthermore, anti-discriminatory practice is more than ensuring that a service user's legal rights are in place. In care settings anti-discriminatory practice involves promoting equal opportunities for all and challenging discrimination at work. This requires health and care workers to:

▶ address their own prejudices and adapt their behaviour to ensure that clients' needs are met, whatever the client's ethnic background, age, disability or sexual orientation

▶ understand and meet the individual needs of all service users, including people from diverse cultures, people belonging to a wide range of religious groups, people who are gay or whose sexuality is unclear, people who have a physical disability, a learning difficulty, a communication problem or people with a mental health problem

▶ celebrate the contribution that a wide and diverse range of people can bring to the setting, and to society

▶ actively challenge both intentional and unintentional discrimination against clients and patients

▶ ensure that the setting is a welcoming and accessible environment for all

▶ compensate for the negative effects of discrimination in society.

In order to ensure that service users' individual needs are met provision has to be adapted according to their needs, for example:

▶ to ensure that people who use wheelchairs have full access to and movement within the setting, ramps may be needed, doors may need to be widened, toilet facilities adapted and kitchens and dining rooms arranged to allow for easy movement

▶ if a service user has a hearing impairment, it may be necessary to use written and visual communication more often than spoken, ensure that a quiet area is available for important conversations and meetings and maybe employ a signer or interpreter to ensure that communication channels are clear

▶ for service users who speak little or no English, information may need to be available in a number of different languages to meet individual needs

▶ in a multi-cultural setting, dietary requirements will need to be met and religious and cultural festivals respected and observed.

Link

Go to *Unit 10: Sociological Perspectives* section C, to find more information about discrimination and the impact of inequalities on health and wellbeing.

Discussion

Identify three ways that provision is adapted at your work placement to meet a service user's needs. Are there other adaptions that should be made to ensure that all needs are met? Discuss your findings and those of other members of your group.

Make notes of the range of adaptions used. Try writing your notes as a table to help with your revision.

Empowering individuals

The importance of fostering and supporting the **empowerment** of service users in health and care settings can often be overlooked. Empowerment means ensuring that service users take a full part in discussions and decisions about their personal care and treatment and that, where possible and appropriate, they are included in discussion of overall policy and provision at the care setting. Empowering service users will help to ensure that meeting individual needs is at the heary of the service provision.

Promoting individualised care

Empowerment enables service users to understand the choices that they can make about their care, to contribute to the decision-making and to take control of their lives. In health and care settings, particularly when service users are feeling unwell or anxious about their future, there can be a tendency to allow the experts to take over and for the service user to just 'do as they are told'. This can lead to service users losing confidence and becoming passive and over-dependent on their care workers.

In most situations, practitioners are required to gain their client's consent before carrying out a care procedure, a treatment or making arrangements for a client's care. If service users are empowered, they will be fully involved in discussion about and planning of their care, and they will fully understand the options open to them. It will ensure **individualised care**, with the service user at the heart of the service.

Promoting and supporting individuals' rights to dignity and independence

Empowering service users means that they are more likely to be treated as individuals. Their needs and preferences will be known and respectfully considered. This provides a context in which their rights to dignity and independence, discussed earlier in this unit, are promoted, which will contribute to boosting their **self-esteem**.

Providing active support consistent with the beliefs, cultures and preferences of service users

Health and care provision in a **multi-cultural society** must address the specific needs of people from diverse backgrounds. The beliefs, languages, traditions, diets and customs of service users will be many and varied. This makes for a stimulating social setting. Diversity can be fun and should be celebrated through sharing festivities and enjoying a wide range of food and music, for example. It can also present challenges for care providers. For example:

▶ if service users speak little or no English, information will need to be presented in a range of languages, translators may be necessary and support may need to be given to access English lessons

▶ there may be a need to provide a wide range of foods for people with different religious requirements, for example Jews and Muslims do not eat pork, Hindus and Sikhs do not eat beef and many Buddhists are vegetarian

▶ religious observances may need to be considered, for example Muslims will need a prayer room and opportunity to pray up to five times a day, Roman Catholics may want to attend Mass on Sundays and other holy days, Jews may want to attend the synagogue on Saturdays.

Key term

Empowerment – supporting people to take control of their lives and futures by taking a full part in discussions and decisions about their care and treatment.

Key terms

Individualised care – care provision tailored to meet the particular and specific needs of each service user.

Self-esteem – a person's sense of self-respect; the confidence a person has in their own worth and value.

Multi-cultural society – a population made up of people from a variety of different ethnic backgrounds and cultural traditions.

A professional carer must be aware of individual differences and ensure, through discussion and planning, that the importance of these needs to the service user are fully respected and are not ignored. If service users are empowered, they will contribute to the planning of their own care and to the policies and procedures at the healthcare setting.

Ⅱ PAUSE POINT　　Can you explain why empowering service users will promote their health and wellbeing?

Hint　　Define the term empowerment.

Extend　　Explain the strategies used at your work placement setting to empower service users. What more could be done?

Supporting individuals who need health and social care services to express their needs and preferences

Of course not all service users will have the confidence or personal skills to participate fully in their care. Some may need specific support to enable them to explain their needs and preferences, or to take part in meetings. This support could be provided by:

▶ translators and interpreters
▶ signers
▶ advocates
▶ family and friends.

Translators and interpreters are concerned with communicating meaning from one language to another. This is obviously essential for many people where English is not their first language, but also includes communication between people using sign language and those using spoken English, for example translating British Sign Language or Makaton to spoken English. Signers play a key role in ensuring that people with hearing impairments can fully participate in meetings and communicate their preferences and care needs.

Sometimes people with communication problems need somebody else to speak for them in meetings, complete forms or write letters for them. For example, the increasing proportion of the population who suffer from dementia, people with a learning difficulty or people who have suffered brain damage following an accident, may not be able to communicate their needs and preferences. In these circumstances, an **advocate** may speak for the client and express their views. In the care sector advocates are often volunteers. They aim to gain the trust of service users who have communication difficulties and find ways of communicating with them to represent their views to the carers. Family and friends can often play a key role in ensuring that the service user's needs are understood and met.

> **Key term**
>
> **Advocate** – a person who speaks for someone else and represents their views and preferences.

Promoting the rights, choices and wellbeing of individuals who use health and care services and balancing their rights with those of other service users and staff

It will not always be straightforward to provide a service user with the care or treatment of their choice, even when their preferences are clear and apparently reasonable.

There may be a conflict between:
▶ the equally valid preferences of one service user and that of another – for example conflicts arising from the choice of music or other leisure-time activities in the sitting room

- the client's right to choice and protecting their personal safety – for example a person suffering from dementia may wish to live independently in their own home but if they are not able to use the cooker and the oven safely, this may pose fire risks and other dangers to themselves and others

- the different rights that service users have – for example the right to confidentiality and the right to protection from harm, if a service user discloses incidents of sexual or physical abuse

- the respect for the cultural or religious values of a service user and promoting their health and wellbeing – for example Jehovah's Witnesses do not believe in blood transfusions, and a blood transfusion may be essential for their own or their children's survival.

Case study

Helping Marjorie

Marjorie is more than eighty years old. She lives in a two-bedroomed terraced house, built just before the First World War. She has always enjoyed good health. In fact she has never been in hospital and rarely visits her GP. She lived for many years with her partner, Jean, who died 10 years ago.

Marjorie has always been very independent and continued to be so after Jean died. Neighbours say she is proud and won't accept help.

However, Marjorie is now very frail and has had a number of falls in the house, and this has made her very anxious about going out. She can't do much in the kitchen and scalded herself recently when making a cup of tea. Marjorie has been reluctant to get help from social services, but has accepted a homecare worker, Mandy, who visits twice a day. Marjorie has cooked meals delivered to ensure she has sufficient nutritious food.

People speak very highly of Mandy, but Marjorie thinks she is unreliable and is convinced she reads her letters and other private correspondence. It seems that before very long Marjorie will need residential care. She has no children and nobody to help her make decisions about her future.

Check your knowledge

1 Identify six hazards for Marjorie in her house when she is at home on her own.

2 Complete a risk assessment for the six hazards and calculate the level of risk.

3 What strategies could be put in place to minimise these risks?

4 If Marjorie is really concerned about Mandy's professional standards, who should Marjorie contact?

5 If Marjorie is to move to long-term residential care, which professional would take a key role in arranging this?

6 What approach should be taken to ensure that when planning this move Marjorie maintains her dignity and right to choice, that she feels empowered, safe and retains her independence?

Write your answers in full. This case study could be very useful in preparation for the final examination.

Discussion

Can you identify situations at your work placement setting where there are conflicts between the valid preferences of one service user and another? How are these conflicts resolved? Discuss your experiences with other members of your group.

Dealing with conflict in health and social care settings

Tension and conflict between service users, and between service users and their carers, is sadly very common. Challenging behaviour could be defined as any behaviour that puts the service user or anybody else in the setting at risk, or significantly affects their quality of life. This may include excessive rudeness, aggression, self-harm or disruptiveness. Professional carers and other staff should be trained to deal with conflict. Conflict may erupt in any care setting, such as in GP practices, hospital wards, residential care homes for the elderly, residential care homes for young adults, residential care homes for people with disabilities or when providing domiciliary care. Conflict may develop between service users and their doctors or nurses, between care workers and their clients, and between the service users themselves or their informal carers. If you are a domiciliary care worker, for example and work alone there should be a **lone workers' policy** in place with specific guidance for dealing with any situation where you feel vulnerable, such as dealing with conflict and aggressive behaviour.

> **Key term**
>
> **Lone workers' policy** – guidance and procedures aimed at ensuring that people working on their own are safe. This is particularly important when providing domiciliary care. Lone workers' policies are in place principally to protect the carer from harm but will also provide additional protection for service users.

When dealing with conflict, a range of skills are needed (see Figure 2.4).

▶ **Figure 2.4** Skills required when dealing with conflict

If it seems that the situation may lead to violence, wherever possible:
- make sure that you know where the doors or other exit points are
- remove anything that could be used as a weapon
- allow the aggressor personal space, do not stand too close to them
- summon help as soon as possible, by using a panic alarm, shouting for help or by phoning the police or security.

> **Research**
>
> Ask your manager or supervisor at your work placement for a copy of the policy that deals with conflict at the setting.
>
> If you have observed incidents of conflict or aggression, describe how closely the procedures were followed. Remember to ensure that confidentiality is respected and all names are changed.

Ⅱ PAUSE POINT Close the book and see whether you can define (i) anti-discriminatory practice and (ii) empowerment.

> Hint   Think about the range of people who might access health and social care.

> Extend   Explain how a health and care provider can promote anti-discriminatory practice and describe its likely impact on service provision.

Ensuring safety in health and social care settings

Risk assessments

It is the responsibility of employers to ensure the health and safety of all who work for their company or organisation. Employers are also responsible for the safety of volunteers, learners on work placement and all visitors, including those visitors providing technical or professional services, for example plumbers, electricians and visiting care professionals. The Health and Safety at Work Act (1974) governs the requirements of employers and employees to ensure that they maintain a safe working environment for all.

Employers must:

▶ ensure that the organisation has a robust health and safety policy and that there is someone with official responsibility for health and safety at the setting

▶ undertake a **risk assessment** to identify the **risks** and **hazards** at the workplace, and take action to reduce the likeliness of harm or injury

▶ provide up-to-date information on health and safety issues

▶ provide health and safety equipment to carry out all procedures and treatments

▶ provide health and safety training

▶ keep a record of all accidents and incidents.

> **Key terms**
>
> **Risk assessment** – identifying and evaluating the possible consequences of hazards and the level of risk that the hazard will cause harm.
>
> **Risk** – the likelihood, high or low, that a person will be harmed by a hazard.
>
> **Hazards** – anything that could potentially cause harm, such as climbing stairs, wet floor surfaces, trailing electricity cables, the disposal of waste or bathing a service user.

Employees must:

▶ take reasonable care of their own safety and that of others in the workplace, including service users, colleagues and visitors

▶ cooperate with their employer to carry out the agreed and required health and safety procedures of the workplace

▶ not intentionally damage health and safety equipment at the setting, for example hoists and lifts.

When employers carry out risk assessments, they examine all the procedures and activities that take place in their organisation and assess the level of risk involved. In a care home, for example this will range from risks associated with routine care procedures to organising social events and taking service users on outings. The responsibility for carrying out the risk assessment will often be delegated to a senior member of staff or a supervisor, for example a senior care assistant in a residential home may have responsibility for assessing the risks associated with the bathing of a new resident. It is the responsibility of the care home manager to ensure that the senior care assistant has had the training to carry out this task.

▶ Even seemingly harmless household items can be hazardous for frail elderly people

Step by step: Carrying out a risk assessment

5 Steps

1 Identify the hazards at the setting, or in carrying out an activity.

▼

2 Identify those at risk, including service users, staff, volunteers and other visitors.

▼

3 Evaluate the level of risk – usually rated on a scale of 1 to 4, with 1 being the lowest level of risk.

4 Identify ways to limit the risk – this will include specific actions to minimise risk.

▼

5 Review measures taken to minimise the risk.

When assessing the level of risk that may arise from a particular hazard, a guide similar to Table 2.2 could be helpful.

▶ **Table 2.2** Assessing the level of risk

Score	Likelihood of risk	Score	Severity of the injury
1	Most unlikely to happen	1	If it did happen the harm would be negligible and could be dealt with by an untrained person, eg applying a plaster.
2	Unlikely to happen	2	Slight injuries, eg catching a cold or the need for a few stitches.
3	Likely to happen	3	Serious injuries, they may be physical or psychological and may take months or years to heal.
4	Very likely to happen	4	Could be permanent disability or even death.

The risk rating for a particular activity or procedure can be helpfully expressed numerically by multiplying the rating for the likelihood of the risk happening by the severity of the likely injury that could arise.

Risk rating = likelihood of risk × severity of the injury

Rating 1 or 2 = a minimal risk rating – the existing practice would be seen as adequate.

Rating 3 or 4 = a low risk rating – the existing practice should be reviewed to lower the level of risk.

Rating 6 or 8 = a medium risk rating – this should lead to specific action to improve safety.

Rating of 9, 12 or 16 = a high rating – this must lead to immediate action to improve safety and the activity should be stopped until proper measures are in place to reduce the risks identified.

Taking service users with a mild learning difficulty on a bus, for example, would normally be considered low risk because the likelihood of harm is low. It is rare for such service users to come to harm on public transport. Of course in the unlikely event of an accident, the harm could be serious. However, if the same group were going swimming, the risk may be higher and the potential harm could lead to death.

Research

Ask to see a risk assessment that has been used at your work placement for taking service users on an outing. Do you think it identifies the key hazards? Do you agree with the level of risk identified? Would the measures taken lessen the risk of harm?

Summarise the key points of the risk assessment using a grid similar to Figure 2.5.

As a group, complete a risk assessment form for the risk of frail elderly service users falling on stairs (you could use a form similar to that shown in Figure 2.5). Are you able to agree on the level of risk and the measures that should be taken?

Keep copies of your risk assessments to help you with your revision.

Potential hazard	Who is at risk	Existing measures to minimise risk	Risk rating	Preventative measures	Responsibilities (identify the job role)

▶ **Figure 2.5** Example of a form that could be used to carry out a risk assessment

Safeguarding and protecting individuals from abuse

If a child or vulnerable adult shares information that raises concerns about their personal safety, or they disclose that they are being abused, you should follow the setting's safeguarding policies. As an employee or volunteer, you should listen carefully and avoid asking questions. Let the service user tell their story in their own way and in their own words. In this instance, you will have to explain to the service user that the information must be shared with somebody more senior. All care settings will have a designated safeguarding officer who will take over responsibility for investigating the claim or accusation. The safeguarding officer will ask you to provide a written record of what you have been told.

Reflect

Read the safeguarding policy at your work placement setting. If some areas are unclear or you are confused, ask your supervisor or manager to explain the procedures for you. Write down in your own words what you are required to do if a service user discloses abuse.

Protecting service users, staff and volunteers from infection

Working in a care environment requires all staff and volunteers to ensure that they maintain a clean and hygienic working environment and minimise the likelihood of passing on infection. In order to keep yourself and service users safe from infection, you must ensure that you are familiar with the policies and procedures in place at your setting to minimise the spread of infection. Procedures are likely to include the following requirements.

▶ Washing your hands before you start work and before you leave work, before eating, after using the toilet and after coughing or sneezing and before and after you carry out any personal care, particularly if this involves contact with body fluids, **clinical waste** or dirty linen. Alcohol hand rubs are a further effective and swift procedure to ensure that hands are clean and provide further protection from contamination.

▶ Safe handling and disposal of sharp articles such as needles and syringes to avoid needle-stick injuries and to ensure that infection is not passed on through viruses carried in the blood or bacteria.

Key term

Clinical waste – waste contaminated by blood, urine, saliva or other body fluids, which could be infectious.

- Keeping all soiled linen in the designated laundry bags, or bin, and not leaving it on the floor. Soiled linen should always be washed in a designated laundry room. When handling soiled laundry a protective apron and gloves should be worn. Hands must be thoroughly washed after handling soiled linen. Separate trolleys should be used for soiled and clean laundry to avoid cross-contamination and the spread of disease.
- Wearing protective disposable gloves and aprons when you have contact with body fluids, or when you are caring for someone with open wounds, rashes or pressure ulcers, for example.
- Cleaning all equipment according to the agreed procedures of your setting.
- Wearing protective clothing for any activities that involve close personal care or contact with body fluids.

Control and disposal of substances harmful to health

To protect all service users, staff and visitors from harm and infection, you must ensure that **hazardous waste** is disposed of properly. This includes disposing of protective clothing, syringes, soiled dressings, nappies, incontinence pads and bodily fluids.

There are different disposal requirements for different types of substances and equipment. This includes cleaning fluids, harmful vapour and fumes. The Control of Substances Hazardous to Health (COSHH) Regulations (2002) provide guidance approved by the Health and Safety Executive for the safe disposal of hazardous waste. The policies and procedures used in your care setting will be based on this guidance.

In care settings, different coloured bags are often used to ensure the safe and efficient disposal of hazardous waste. Table 2.3 shows examples of waste disposal that are widely used.

> **Key term**
>
> **Hazardous waste** – waste containing substances that can cause serious harm to people or equipment, including soiled dressings and items contaminated with bodily fluids, explosives, flammable materials and substances that poison or destroy human tissue.

Table 2.3 Examples of types of waste and appropriate methods of disposal

Type of waste	Method of disposal
Clinical waste, eg used bandages, plasters or other dressings	Yellow bag: waste is burned in controlled settings
Needles and syringes	Yellow 'sharps' box which is sealed: waste is burned in controlled settings
Body fluids, eg urine, vomit or blood	Flushed down a sluice drain: area must then be cleaned and disinfected
Soiled linen	Red laundry bag: laundered at the appropriate temperature
Recyclable equipment and instruments	Blue bag: returned to the Central Sterilisation Services (CSSD) for sterilising and reuse

Source: adapted from Nolan, Y (1998) *Care NVQ Level 2*, p.78.

> **Safety tip**
>
> Check the approved procedures for disposing of substances harmful to health at your work placement setting.

Reporting and recording accidents and incidents

There are particular illnesses, diseases and serious accidents that health and care providers must officially report. These are called 'notifiable deaths, injuries or diseases' and are covered by the Reporting of Injuries, Diseases and Dangerous Occurrences Regulations (RIDDOR) (2013). Notifiable illnesses include diphtheria, food poisoning, rubella (German measles), tuberculosis (TB) and notifiable incidents occurring at work include broken bones, serious burns and death.

However, less serious accidents and incidents must also be recorded. If somebody slips on a wet floor or trips over the trailing straps of a shoulder bag a record must be made, regardless of whether or not there is an injury. Providers of health and care services use an accident form to report the details of all accidents and incidents, which are then recorded in an accident book. These reports are required by law and are checked when care settings are inspected.

EXEMPLAR ACCIDENT FORM

About the person completing the form:

Full name: _____

Job title: _____

Signature _____

About any witnesses:

Full name: _____

Job title/Status _____

Signature _____

About the injured person:

Name: _____

Home address: _____

_____

_____

Post code: _____

Home tel no: _____

Date of birth: _____ **Age:** _____

Gender: _____

About the accident:

Date of accident: _____ / _____ / _____

Time of accident: _____ : _____ **hrs**

Location of accident: _____

_____

Injury (e.g. fracture) _____

Part of the body injured: _____

About the type of accident:

What happened? (tick if applies)

☐ Equipment failure

☐ Slip on wet surface

☐ Tripped over object

☐ Injured while moving something

☐ Fell

☐ Trapped by something collapsing

☐ Inhaled gas/fumes

☐ Electric shock

☐ Asphyxiation

☐ Assault

☐ Exposure to fire

☐ Struck by moving object

☐ Other

Describe the accident using factual information:

About prevention of a recurrence:

Can you identify any way the accident could have been prevented?

Date form completed: _____ **Review date:** _____

▶ **Figure 2.6** A sample accident form

Provision of first-aid facilities

The provision of first aid in health and care settings is governed by the Health and Safety (First-Aid) Regulations (1981). Provision for first aid should be 'adequate and appropriate'. What is deemed as adequate and appropriate will vary from setting to setting. It is proposed that from September 2016 all newly qualified early-years practitioners will be required to complete paediatric first-aid training.

All first-aid incidents occurring in care settings must be recorded, either in the accident book or by completing the setting's accident form. The report should include:

▶ the name of the casualty

▶ the nature of the incident/injury

▶ the date, time and location of the incident

▶ a record of the treatment given.

These records must be truthful and accurate. They may be used in courts of law, particularly if the casualty is claiming compensation for injury, or if there is an accusation of criminal negligence.

Complaints procedures

All care organisations must have complaints procedures and these are also checked when the setting is inspected. Complaints should not be regarded as a purely negative activity but rather as a source of information that will help improve the service. Complaints procedures vary in different organisations but will follow a very similar format. If a service user, a member of staff or a volunteer complains, they have a right to:

▶ have their complaint dealt with swiftly and efficiently

▶ have a proper and careful investigation of their concerns

▶ know the outcomes of those investigations

▶ have a judicial review of the facts, if they think the action or the decision is unlawful

▶ receive compensation if they have been harmed either physically or psychologically as a result of the situation about which they are complaining.

ⅠⅠ PAUSE POINT	Identify the responsibilities that care providers have to ensure the safety of service users, staff and visitors at their settings.
Hint	Think about all the potential hazards in your care setting. How likely is an accident and what could be the consequences?
Extend	Complete a risk assessment for organising a simple birthday party for a service user at your setting.

Information management and communication

Health and social care organisations hold a wide range of diverse information about service users. This ranges from mundane concerns about preferred TV programmes or planned holiday arrangements to very personal and sensitive information, including addresses, telephone numbers, family details, information about criminal convictions and health issues. It is important that service users are able to trust that their personal information is treated as confidential, and only shared with people who have a legitimate reason to know about their circumstances and preferences.

The Data Protection Act 1998

The Data Protection Act (1998), which came into force in March 2000, sets out the rules governing the processing and use of personal information in health and social care settings and in many other organisations, including credit agencies, clubs and many other organisations that hold information about their members. The act covers information stored electronically on computers, mobile phones and on social media sites. It also covers most paper-based personal information. It is against the law to have photographs of service users without their permission.

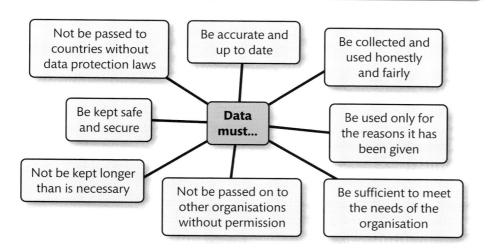

Not be passed to countries without data protection laws

Be accurate and up to date

Be collected and used honestly and fairly

Be kept safe and secure

Data must...

Be used only for the reasons it has been given

Not be kept longer than is necessary

Not be passed on to other organisations without permission

Be sufficient to meet the needs of the organisation

▶ **Figure 2.7** The Data Protection Act (1998) has eight key principles

Recording and storage of data

The Act covers the policies, procedures and systems for:

▶ Storing information – confidential information should be stored in locked filing cabinets, in a locked room. Information held electronically should be protected by a secure password.

▶ Accessing information – members of staff in the organisation who are allowed access to this information should be clearly identified. Staff should never have access to personal information that they do not need to know. Where information is stored electronically, only the relevant staff should have personal access passwords.

▶ Sharing information – information should only be shared with other professionals who have a need and a right to know it.

Legal and workplace requirements

▶ The principles and requirements of the Data Protection Act (1998) and the requirement for confidentiality are within the policies and procedures of all health and social care settings. They are also embedded in the codes of practice of the professional bodies that regulate health and care staff, discussed earlier in this unit, such as the General Medical Council, Nursing & Midwifery Council and the Health and Care Professions Council.

▶ All employees and volunteers in organisations have a responsibility to ensure that the confidentiality of service users' information is protected. They also have a duty to actively promote respect for confidentiality throughout the setting. If they spot weaknesses in the procedures, for example the location of offices where personal care is discussed, they should feel confident to suggest improvements in the systems and arrangements. This is necessary to ensure the safety and security of service users and to respect their right to the confidentiality of personal information.

Confidentiality, safeguarding and legal disclosure

All personal records must be kept safely and securely and used only for the purpose that they are intended for. They must not be available to people who do not have a valid professional need to know the details. If a child or vulnerable adult discloses to any member of staff or volunteer that they are at personal risk or that they are the subject of abuse, the setting's safeguarding policies should be followed. In this situation, you will have to explain to the service user that their disclosure will be shared with a senior member of staff who will then support them. The safeguarding officer at the setting will then take over responsibility for dealing with the concerns.

Accountability to professional organisations

As you have seen, the standards of professional practice expected of professionals working in health and care settings are regulated and monitored by a range of professional bodies, including the General Medical Council (GMC), Nursing and Midwifery Council (NMC) and the Health and Care Professionals Council (HCPC).

The specific regulations vary according to profession. However, each professional organisation monitors the:

▶ level and content of the initial education and training of members of their profession
▶ ongoing professional development and the requirement to keep up to date, and to complete further training – often called continuing professional development (CPD)
▶ standards of professional practice in their everyday work
▶ standards of personal conduct, both at work and in leisure time.

Codes of professional conduct

Professional organisations publish codes of practice for members which must be followed. If a member is accused of failing to meet the standards set, this will be investigated and, in extreme circumstances, the member can be removed from the professional register and barred from professional practice.

The professional organisation's regulations outline the formal procedures that will be used following a complaint or concern about the qualifications or professional practice of its members. This will include specific procedures to investigate unprofessional practice reported by professionals about their colleagues, known as **whistleblowing**.

Revalidation procedures

Each of the professional bodies requires its members to complete regular CPD in order to remain on the register. This may include, for example:

▶ training on the use of new procedures or new treatments
▶ training on the use of new equipment
▶ providing evidence that a registered person reviews and learns from their own practice.

CPD requirements will always include evidence that members have current and up-to-date understanding of safeguarding regulations.

Safeguarding regulations, raising concerns and whistleblowing

In April 2015, a Care Certificate was introduced for newly appointed health and social care workers who are not members of the regulated professional bodies that were discussed earlier, that is the GMC, the NMC and the HCSC.

> **Key term**
>
> **Whistleblowing** – a situation in which an employee reports poor or dangerous practice at their workplace to the press or to another organisation outside of their work setting, for example the GMC, NMC or HCPC, in order to bring about change for the better.

Employees who would normally complete this new programme include health or social care assistants, support workers and homecare workers.

The Care Certificate is not a statutory requirement, it is voluntary, and would normally be used alongside the specific induction programme for a work setting. It does, however, provide an identified set of standards that health and social care workers should follow in their daily working life. Employers are expected to implement the care certificate for all new starters from April 2015. They will be required to meet its standards before they can work with patients. It replaces the Common Induction Standards (CIS) and the National Minimum Training Standards (NMTS).

The code of conduct incorporated into the new certificate requires that healthcare support workers and adult social care workers in England:

- are accountable, by making sure they can answer for their actions or omissions
- promote and uphold the privacy, dignity, rights, health and wellbeing of people who use health and care services, and that of their carers, at all times
- work in collaboration with colleagues to ensure they deliver high-quality, safe and compassionate healthcare, care and support
- communicate in an open and effective way to promote the health, safety and wellbeing of people who use health and care services, and of their carers
- respect a person's right to confidentiality
- strive to improve the quality of healthcare, care and support through CPD
- uphold and promote equality, diversity and inclusion.

Multi-disciplinary working in the health and social care sector

Different care professionals often work together as a team to promote the health and wellbeing of their service users. For example, the care manager of a residential home may work with GPs, district nurses and physiotherapists to meet the needs of their residents. Social workers with responsibility for children may work with the health visitor, the school nurse, school teachers and the educational psychologist to meet the children's needs. These teams may include not only the health and care workers discussed earlier in the unit but also representatives from voluntary organisations. The emergency services, including the police and the education services, may also be represented. When professionals co-operate in this way by working together as a team, it is called a **multi-disciplinary team**.

> **Key term**
>
> **Multi-disciplinary team** – a team in which health and care workers from different professional backgrounds and with different work roles, plan, implement and monitor an individual's care.

The need for joined-up working with other service providers

If a service user is known to and supported by a number of different agencies or professionals, it is essential that those carers work as a team. There have been a number of high-profile cases of child abuse, for example the abuse and tragic death in February 2000 of Victoria Climbié while in the care of her aunt, and the death of Baby P (Peter Connelly) in 2007 following months of abuse. Part of the reason for the death of these children was identified as a lack of 'joined-up working'. Both children lived in the London Borough of Haringey. The professionals and the agencies working there did not pass on crucial information.

Involving service users, carers and advocates in the multi-disciplinary team

At formal team meetings it will be expected that, where possible, the service user will be present, their advocate, translator and/or interpreter will be there, informal carers will be invited along with all other professional staff who contribute to the support, planning and evaluation of the care provided. The service user's presence and/or their representatives is crucial to ensure the empowerment of the client or patient. It is the key opportunity for the service user to express their views and preferences and to contribute to the planning and delivery of their support.

Holistic approaches

The work of a multi-disciplinary team ensures that a **holistic approach** is taken to planning and implementing a care programme. It means health and care professionals must not only provide their specialist support but also see this in the context of the wider needs of the service user. At a care planning meeting the physical, social, emotional, spiritual and intellectual needs of the service user will be considered. The care plan must meet the needs of the 'whole person'.

> **Key term**
>
> **Holistic approach** – an approach to care that addresses the individual's physical, social, emotional and spiritual health, so addressing the needs of the whole person.

PAUSE POINT

Can you list and describe the impact of using specialist equipment to promote health and wellbeing?

Hint List all the different health and care practitioners who provide support at your work placement setting.

Extend How do they ensure that there is good communication between them in planning and delivering care?

Monitoring the work of people in health and care settings

Line management

In addition to working in interdisciplinary teams as discussed in the previous section, people who work in health and care settings normally also work in hierarchical organisations and their work is monitored by senior members of staff. For example, in a care home, the care assistants will be managed by the care manager who will allocate tasks and set the routines and standards for the setting. The care manager will expect employees to follow these routines and meet the standards set. In a larger setting, there will often be senior care workers who manage a team of care assistants on behalf of the manager. In an early-years setting, for example, the nursery manager will manage the early-years' practitioners at the setting and in a reception class the nursery teacher will manage the early-years educator. If staff performance falls short of the practice expected, it will be the **line manager's** responsibility to address the issues with the staff concerned and take the appropriate action. In the first instance this may be an informal

> **Key term**
>
> **Line manager** – person responsible for managing the work of an individual or of a team in an organisation, usually the position they hold will be at least one level above the person/people they manage.

conversation or warning. If the concerns are serious or there is no improvement in performance more formal action may be taken which could finally lead to suspension or dismissal.

▶ A range of adults work with young children

External inspection by relevant agencies

All health, care and early-years settings in the United Kingdom are regularly inspected by independent, government-financed agencies. For example in:

▶ England, health and care provision is inspected by the Care Quality Commission (CQC)

▶ Northern Ireland, health and care provision is inspected by the Regulation and Quality and Improvement Authority (RQIA)

▶ Wales, care provision is inspected by the Care and Social Service Inspectorate Wales (CSSIW) and health by Healthcare Inspectorate Wales (HCIW)

▶ Scotland, on 1st April 2011 the work of the Care Commisioner passed to a new body, the Care Inspectorate; regulation of independent healthcare has passed to Healthcare Improvement Scotland.

Early years and education services are inspected by:

▶ Ofsted, in England

▶ the Education and Training Inspectorate (ETI), in Northern Ireland

▶ Her Majesty's Inspectorate for Education and Training in Wales

▶ Education Scotland, in Scotland.

Whistleblowing

Whistleblowing is when a member of staff is aware that the quality of care at their workplace is dangerously poor and reports this to bring about change. They may inform the press or another, usually powerful, organisation outside the setting in which they work such as the police or a professional body. Whistleblowers may be employees at any level and working in any part of the organisation as a care worker, an administrator or a manager.

Service user feedback

Settings will have a range of different systems for ensuring that service users and their families, friends or other informal carers can formally comment on the strengths and weaknesses of the service that they receive. This may include:

▶ regular meetings for service users to report concerns and to share ideas for the improvement of provision

▶ at a large setting, there may be a committee that represents all service users, for example a parents and carers association at a pre-school setting

▶ a suggestions box

▶ service users may request a private meeting with a manager or governor of a setting

▶ service users reporting good practice or areas of concern to the external agencies – for example Ofsted, CQC or CSSIW. If organisations responsible for inspecting settings receive complaints this may lead to a prompt and often unannounced inspection of the care setting.

Criminal investigations

In extreme circumstances, such as cases of sexual, physical, financial or emotional abuse, or in other circumstances in which it is suspected that criminal law has been broken, the police may investigate. There have been high-profile cases where care staff have been found guilty and imprisoned following criminal investigations, for example following a Serious Case Review of the Winterbourne View residential home. This may also lead to health and care workers being removed from their professional register and being barred from professional practice.

Assessment practice 2.1

Aziz was born in Pakistan, and came to England in the 1960s. He is a devout Muslim and has a large, caring family. However, he now needs some additional help. He has chronic bronchitis, he doesn't have a very good appetite and he is beginning to lose his balance when walking into town.

1 Identify two health professionals who might be involved in Aziz's care.

2 Describe the role of the two professionals in delivering healthcare.

3 Explain how the care provision may need to be adapted to meet Aziz's cultural needs.

4 Discuss how Aziz may be supported in planning for his future.

B The roles of organisations in the health and social care sector

Roles of organisations in providing health and social care services

Health and social care services are provided and managed by a wide range of organisations. Some services are directly funded and delivered by government or public sector organisations, such as the National Health Service and local authority social work support. Many other services are provided by independent charitable organisations, such as Shelter, Barnardo's and the Samaritans. Services are also provided by a growing number of private companies, such as Bupa or Priory Group Hospitals. These are profit-making businesses that deliver health and care services.

The public sector

The public sector organisations that provide health and social care services are financed and directly managed by the government. For example, the National Health Service is a public sector service. It is primarily funded by taxation and a smaller proportion of funds come from National Insurance contributions. The majority of the services available are free to service users when they need them, but they do pay for them through their regular tax and National Insurance contributions. The public sector health services and systems of organisation in the four countries that make up the United Kingdom generally work independently of each other, but there is no discrimination when individuals/service users move from one part of the UK to another. The four organisations are:

▶ National Health Service England (NHS England)

▶ Health and Social Care in Northern Ireland

▶ NHS Scotland

▶ NHS Wales.

The range of services that the National Health Services in the four countries provide includes:

▶ **Primary health care** is provided by GPs, dentists, opticians and pharmacists. Primary health care services are normally accessed directly by the service user when needed.

▶ **Secondary health care** includes most hospital services, mental health services and many of the community health services. These are normally accessed via the GP, who makes an appropriate referral to a consultant or other healthcare specialist, such as a hospital physiotherapist, a psychologist or community nurse, and requests an appointment for further examination or specialist treatment. Members of the public and the emergency services have direct access to the accident and emergency services of hospitals.

▶ **Tertiary health care** provides specialist, and normally complex, services. For example specialist spinal injury units or hospice support. Referral to these services is by health professionals who have identified the need.

NHS Foundation Trusts

In England, hospitals are managed by hospital trusts, most of which are now **NHS Foundation Trusts**. Foundation trusts were established in 2004. Although their services are largely financed by government, they are independent organisations. NHS Foundation Trusts are managed by a board of governors, which may include patients, staff, members of the public and members of partner organisations. The aim of the NHS Foundation Trust is to move decision-making from a centralised NHS to local communities, in order to respond to local needs and wishes. Trusts that have not achieved foundation status are still managed centrally.

Mental health services may be provided through your GP, or support may be needed from more specialist service providers, for example counsellors, psychologists or psychiatrists. More specialist support is normally provided by Mental Health Foundation Trusts. Mental Health Foundation Trusts are managed by the community, including people who use the mental health services. Patients, their families

Key terms

Primary health care – care provided by doctors, dentists and opticians, for example.

Secondary health care – care which includes most hospital services, normally accessed via the GP or other professional.

Tertiary health care – specialist and often complex care provided in highly specialised units and hospitals, for example spinal injury units.

NHS Foundation Trusts – health services, largely financed by government that manage the delivery of hospital services, many mental health services and community health services in England.

and friends, local organisations and local residents can become members of the foundation. The members elect governors who have responsibility for the quality and range of care provided.

The services provided by a Mental Health Foundation Trust include provision of psychological therapies, the support of psychiatric nurses and very specialist support for people with severe mental health problems.

Community Health Foundation Trusts work with GPs and local authority social services departments to provide health and care support. The services provided by the trust may include:

▶ adult and community nursing services

▶ health visiting and school nursing

▶ physiotherapy and occupational therapy and speech therapy services

▶ **palliative**/end of life care

▶ walk in/urgent care centres

▶ specialist services, such as managing diabetes, sexual health or contraceptive services.

> **Key term**
>
> **Palliative care** – specialist care for people with serious illnesses, which aims to provide relief from symptoms and to reduce stress for patients and their families.

The aim of the Community Health Foundation Trust is to provide care for service users that will enable them to live as independently as possible in the community, rather than in settings such as hospitals or residential care.

Adult social care

Adult social care provision is for people over 18 years of age who have disabilities, mental health problems or who are otherwise frail, due to age or other circumstances and who are unable to support themselves without specific and planned assistance.

Adult social care services are the responsibility of local authority social service departments. The support provided can take many forms, including:

▶ care in the service user's own home – such as help with cooking, cleaning, shopping and a wide range of other personal daily needs

▶ day centres to provide care, stimulation and company

▶ sheltered housing schemes

▶ residential care for older people, people with disabilities and people suffering from mental illness

▶ respite care or short-term residential care provided principally to give families caring at home a rest and a break from their responsibilities

▶ training centres for adults with learning difficulties.

In some parts of the country, care trusts have been established that are responsible both for the NHS mental health services and the local authority provision for people with mental illnesses. Primary Care Trusts (PCTs) were launched in April 2000 and fully established across the country in April 2002, to provide better continuity of care between the NHS provision and the social care support necessary for people with mental health problems.

▶ Adults receive support in a range of settings

Children's services

Children's services are the responsibility of local authorities. Their aim is to support and protect vulnerable children and young people, their families and also young carers. The local council's children's departments are required to work in close collaboration with other care providers, and crucially with the NHS and the education services.

Support for children and their families can include:
▶ services to safeguard children who are at risk from abuse or significant harm, including sexual, physical, emotional harm or neglect
▶ day care for children under 5 years old, and after-school support for older children
▶ help for parents and carers with 'parenting skills'
▶ practical help in the home
▶ support of a children's centre
▶ arrangements for fostering and adoption.

GP practices

General practitioner (GP) practices are often the first point of access to health and care provision. GPs have an extensive knowledge of medical conditions, including a wide range of physical disorders, and they also offer preventative healthcare. GPs work in local communities. Their role is to make initial diagnoses and to refer individuals, if necessary, to a specialist for further investigation and treatment. However, GPs increasingly work as members of multi-disciplinary teams, which may include nurses, health visitors and healthcare assistants. They also work closely with other agencies, including the education services, local authority social services and also the police. The GP and their team aim to use a holistic approach to care.

GP practices are funded from central government as part of the National Health Service. They are funded according to their assessed workload from their patients. This takes into account:
▶ the age of their patients
▶ their gender
▶ levels of **morbidity** and **mortality** in the area

Key terms

Morbidity – the levels of ill-health in a particular area, in this case the GP practice area.

Mortality – the death rate in a particular area.

- the number of people who live in residential or nursing homes – this generates a higher workload
- patient turnover – newer patients generate more work than established patients.

In addition, GP practices receive further payments from the NHS for the following:
- if they are deemed to give a high quality service
- for certain additional services they may provide, such as flu immunisations
- for seniority, based on a GP's length of service
- to support the cost of suitable premises and other necessary equipment, such as computers
- to cover additional costs if the GP practice also dispenses medicines.

Research

Find out whether your GP practice is a dispensing service. Do they dispense medicines to their patients?

Discussion

In groups, discuss reasons why people who live in residential and nursing homes, and new patients should generate higher levels of work in a GP practice than people living in their own homes or more established patients.

Voluntary sector

Voluntary sector organisations are often known as charities. Voluntary organisations vary enormously in their size, history and the services they provide. They include some well-known groups, such as Shelter, the NSPCC and the Samaritans, and some very small organisations that are run solely by volunteers for specific needs or for a particular local community. Voluntary groups often rely heavily on charitable donations for their survival but may also receive support from central or local government.

The social services provided by the voluntary sector (sometimes known as 'third sector' services) are managed independently from government, but government departments may sometimes pay charities to provide services on their behalf. Charities often provide services for the NHS, adult social services and children's services. For example, MENCAP provides residential care, day care and educational services for people with learning difficulties, and service users can use their personal funding to access these services. Nacro (the National Association for the Care and Resettlement of Offenders) receives government funding for their work with offenders.

The key features of a voluntary organisation are that they:
- are not run for personal profit, any surplus income is used to develop their services
- usually use volunteers for at least some of their services
- are managed independently of central government or local authorities.

NCVO (the National Council for Voluntary Organisations) is the body that supports and promotes the work of the voluntary sector. They have over 12,000 members that range from the smallest community group to the largest of the very well-known charities.

Private sector

Private sector health and care provision is managed by commercial companies. These are organisations that need to make a profit in order to stay in business. Private care providers work in all sectors, including the provision of:
- private schools
- nursery and pre-school services
- hospitals
- domiciliary day care services
- residential and nursing homes for older people
- mental health services.

Private sector companies often provide services for central government and local authorities, including services for the NHS, adult social care and children's services.

Private sector companies are funded by:
▶ fees paid directly by service users
▶ payments from health insurance companies, such as Bupa, Saga or AXA – many people who choose private healthcare will subscribe to a health insurance scheme
▶ grants and other payments from central and local government for services provided on their behalf.

⏸ PAUSE POINT   Close the book and briefly describe the role of the public, private and voluntary sectors in providing health and care services.

> Hint   Think about who they care for, their funding and the services they provide. Could these services be provided by the NHS?

> Extend   Why is it important that these agencies work closely together?

The range of settings that provide health and care services

The settings in which health and care services are provided vary enormously. Settings range from domiciliary care services provided in the service user's own home to day care centres, residential care homes to hospital departments providing highly technical and sophisticated specialist treatments.

Hospitals

Hospitals provide both inpatient and outpatient services. Outpatient services include regular clinics, day surgery and other specialist daytime care. Inpatient services include treatment for individuals whose condition requires 24-hour specialist support. If you need to visit a hospital for specialist care, you will normally be referred by your GP. When a service user is referred to a hospital for specialist care, they have the right to choose which hospital they wish to attend as well as the consultant they would like to see. In hospitals, clinical departments are organised according to medical speciality. Some hospitals have accident and emergency services, which individuals can access directly for emergency treatment.

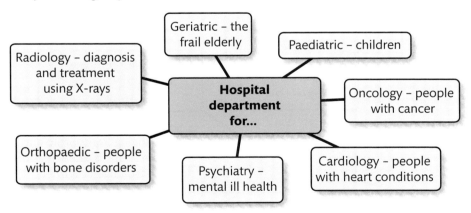

▶ **Figure 2.8** Examples of specialist hospital departments

Day care centres/units

Day care centres, or day care units, are normally provided for specific client groups. In most places there will be day centres for older people, for people with disabilities, people with learning difficulties, people with mental health problems and for people with specific conditions such as dementia or visual impairment. The day service provision is designed to provide a friendly, stimulating and supportive environment for people who otherwise would be socially isolated. Day centres normally offer educational facilities and support, where appropriate, to help people progress into employment. Day care services may be provided by statutory, voluntary or private providers.

Hospice care

Hospice care aims to improve the quality of life for people who have an incurable illness. Care may be available from when the diagnosis of a terminal illness is made until the end of the individual's life. Hospice care is holistic, providing for the physical, social, emotional, spiritual and practical needs of the individual, their family and their carers. Care may extend to support during the bereavement period.

Residential care

Residential care refers to the long-term care of adults and children needing 24-hour care, which cannot be provided adequately or appropriately in their own home. Residential care units are usually specialist units providing care for specific client groups, such as people with mental health problems, people with learning difficulties or older people unable to look after their daily needs. There are two types of care home:
- a residential care home, which provides help with personal care such as washing, dressing and taking medication
- a nursing home, which provides personal care but also provides 24-hour nursing care by a qualified nurse, who may also contribute to the planning, supervising and monitoring of healthcare tasks.

Domiciliary care

Domiciliary care, sometimes called home care, is care provided in a client's home, rather than in a specialist care setting. The care may be short-term, for example providing support following discharge from hospital or for a family with a new baby, or may be needed as a long-term solution for a service user with a disability or for a frail older person. The support can vary from one visit a day to 24-hour care, providing both support with domestic tasks and intimate personal care.

Appropriate domiciliary care being provided can ensure that service users are able to live as independently as possible in their own home.

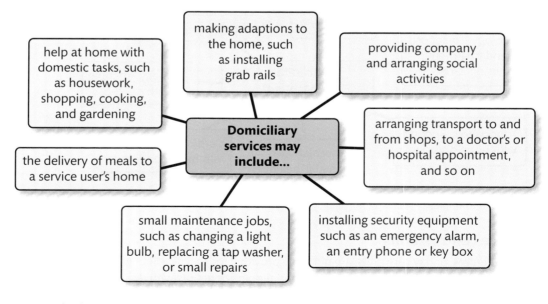

▶ **Figure 2.9** Examples of domiciliary services

The workplace

Occupational health services aim to keep a workforce fit and healthy so that they are able to carry out the duties for which they are employed, or to assist employees to regain fitness following an injury or illness. These services are normally provided by an employer to support the people that they employ. This can include access to nurses based in the workplace or referral to a doctor or other health professionals. Referrals may be to a counsellor, if the employee is thought to be suffering from work-related stress, or to a physiotherapist if there is a problem with the employee's posture or a repetitive strain injury. Advice, information and treatment will vary according to the individual employee's needs.

⏸ **PAUSE POINT**   Close the book. List and describe as many different health and social care settings with which you are familiar as you can.

> Hint > Think about the times that you, or someone you know, needed care. Where did you/ they receive that care?

> Extend > Briefly describe the main purpose of four different care settings and the range of needs that they aim to meet.

Issues that affect access to services

Referral

Health and care organisations are accessed by those in need through referral systems. These are normally classified in three ways.

▶ **Self-referral** is when a person contacts a care provider personally, by letter, email, phone call, making an appointment or attending a care setting or surgery and requesting help. Access to the primary healthcare services, such as doctors, dentists and opticians, is normally through self-referral. Many social care services for children and adults are accessed by self-referral.

▶ **Third-party referral** is when a friend, neighbour or relative contacts a health or care service on another person's behalf. For example, a neighbour may ring the social services department on behalf of a frail elderly person to request care support, or a relative concerned about the general health of a person with Down's syndrome may contact the GP. These referrals are usually to services that are accessible through self-referral.

▶ **Professional referral** is when a health or care professional contacts another service provider to request support for a service user. For example, a GP referring a service user to a hospital consultant, or a head teacher referring a child with learning difficulties to an educational psychologist, or a social worker contacting the domiciliary care services for a client with disabilities.

Assessment

Local authorities have a duty to carry out a **community care assessment** for anyone who appears to be finding it difficult to look after themselves without additional help. The adult social services department is usually responsible for this, and it would normally be a social worker who completes such an assessment. It may be that the service user needs:

▶ reassurance and information about local or national organisations that could help

▶ simple devices that can help the client to live independently, such as aids to open tins or jars, or equipment to help them use their bath

▶ a higher level of care, such as domiciliary care, or they may need residential care.

> **Key term**
>
> **Community care assessment** – professional assessment of care needs provided by a local authority adult social services department, which also provides help and advice in accessing services to best meet the service user's need.

Key term

Carer's assessment – assessment of the needs of informal carers providing support for a vulnerable person, such as a person with a physical disability, a person with a mental health need or a frail older person.

If a client is supported in their home by family, friends or neighbours, these carers also have a right to a **carer's assessment** to see whether they need support to carry out their caring activities. These unpaid carers are often called informal carers to distinguish them from professional care staff, or representatives of charitable groups. The Care Act (2014) sets out carers' legal rights for assessment and support.

When the assessment for a service user or their carer is complete the service users must be provided with a written copy of the report outlining the needs identified and the action agreed.

Eligibility criteria

In order to decide whether a person is entitled to care and support from the local authority, a social services department assessor, usually a social worker, has to consider whether these needs arise from:

1 a physical and/or mental impairment or illness, plus
2 an inability to achieve at least two of the following daily activities (called outcomes):
   - prepare and eat food
   - wash themselves or their clothes
   - manage their toilet needs
   - dress appropriately, especially in cold weather
   - move around their home easily
   - keep their house safe and clean
   - maintain family or other close relationships, in order to avoid social isolation
   - access work, training, education or volunteering
   - use local facilities, including shops, recreational facilities and other services
   - carry out caring responsibilities, including caring for their children
   - meet the outcomes likely to affect their health and wellbeing.

An adult is eligible for support only if they meet both criteria. If a person meets these criteria for support, called **national eligibility criteria**, the local authority has a duty to make sure the identified needs are met.

Key terms

National eligibility criteria – criteria applied to decide whether a service user is entitled to support from the local authority social services department.

Personal budget/direct payment – a cash payment made directly to the service user so that they may pay for identified and necessary care services to be provided.

However, social care is not usually free of charge and people may have to contribute to the cost of their care. The local authority carries out a financial assessment which will take into account the service user's regular income and their savings. The financial assessment will decide whether the service user must contribute to the cost of care and if so how much they will contribute. Service users, if they are eligible, will normally receive a **personal budget**, sometimes called a **direct payment**, which are cash payments. These payments are available to all client groups across the UK, including older people, people with physical and learning disabilities and carers. People with disabilities normally receive a personal budget to allow them to purchase care services from people or companies of their own choice. The local authority, however, still has a duty to ensure that service users' care needs are met.

Discussion

Discuss the advantages and disadvantages of providing service users with personal budgets rather than the local authority directly providing the care services for people who are eligible.

Barriers to accessing health and care services

As you have seen, the health and care services available in the UK are many and various and accessing these services can be very confusing for service users, particularly when people are unwell or have complex personal difficulties. These difficulties may lead to service users and their families not receiving the care they need and have a right to.

Some of the barriers to accessing services may be:

▶ language, for example if English is not a service user's first language and there is no interpreter available, or the service user is hearing-impaired and there is no signer available to support communication

▶ inconvenient location of the service, particularly if the service user has to rely on public transport, additionally, the cost of travelling may be a barrier as financial help for travel is not always available

▶ financial, such as the cost and difficulty in providing care for children or other dependants while a service user attends a care setting, or the potential loss of wages

▶ scarce resources, for example long waiting times for hospital appointments or treatment, lack of beds available in hospitals or appropriate residential care settings, restricted opening times or specialist resources not easily available

▶ communication, such as service users feeling unable to communicate easily with care providers and other service users, because they feel discriminated against or that there is prejudice against them, or that there are negative stereotypes associated with their community. For example, some groups in society, such as travellers, may not feel comfortable at care settings where they may feel that they are discriminated against.

> **Link**
>
> Go to *Unit 10: Sociological Perspectives*, section C, Inequalities within society, to find more information about prejudice, stereotyping and labelling, and its impact on health and wellbeing.

Additionally, barriers to accessing care are made worse if an individual is poor or on a low income.

Ways organisations represent the interests of service users

Charities and patient groups

Many voluntary organisations or charities represent their service users when they need to contact and liaise with other official agencies. For example, MENCAP will represent their service users and support them if they are liaising with other organisations such as their local council housing department, social services or other health and care professionals. Shelter provides advice, guidance and support for people with housing problems and will represent them when they liaise with council officials, are applying for housing benefit or negotiating with landlords. These organisations also provide support if service users need to make a complaint. Patient groups in hospitals represent the needs of patients and also support individuals making complaints.

Many charitable groups act as **pressure groups** and campaign on behalf of the individual members that they represent. For example, they may write to the papers, use social media, organise demonstrations and contact Members of Parliament or local councils to raise awareness of their service users' needs and to request improvements to the services offered. For example, the NSPCC campaigns to encourage the government to introduce policies and laws that support the protection of children.

> **Key term**
>
> **Pressure groups** – people who come together to campaign to improve the services offered to their members. They aim to influence public opinion and government decisions.

Advocacy

If a client has a serious communication problem, an advocate may speak on their behalf. For example, clients may have a learning difficulty, a speech impediment, poor literary skills, a limited grasp of English or lack confidence when talking with professional health and care workers.

In health and care settings, advocates are usually volunteers. They work with individual service users, getting to know them well and building a trusting relationship so that they can accurately represent the needs, wishes and preferences of their client to the professional workers and to official organisations when needed. This may be through attending care meetings with the service user or completing forms, writing letters or emails on the client's behalf.

Complaints policies

All care settings must have formal complaints procedures. The settings have a responsibility to ensure that their service users and, where appropriate, their families and other informal carers, understand how to access and use complaints procedures if they are unhappy with the quality of care provided. The procedures and the outcome of any complaints will be checked whenever the setting is inspected.

If a service user complains, they have a right to:

▶ have their complaint dealt with efficiently and in a timely way

▶ have their complaint formally investigated

▶ be told the outcome of their complaint.

Research

Investigate the complaints procedure at your work placement setting or at your school or college, and make brief notes to summarise it.

Keep your notes in the correct section of your file to help you with your revision.

Whistleblowing policies

Care organisations are required to have whistleblowing policies, as discussed earlier in this chapter. Whistleblowing policies provide protection for staff who tell the press or another organisation outside the setting in which they work that the quality of care at their workplace is dangerously poor. For example, if they report the situation to the media, the police or to a professional body in order to heighten awareness of the problem and to bring about change.

Link

See section A, Accountability to professional organisations, for the earlier discussion on whistleblowing.

 **PAUSE POINT**
Close this book and briefly describe the different methods of referral to health and care services.

 Hint
There are three main types of referral, can you remember what they are?

Extend
Explain the barriers that service users may have to accessing services.

Roles of organisations that regulate and inspect health and social care services

There are independent organisations with responsibility for the inspection and regulation of health and care services in England, Wales and Northern Ireland. This section will deal with each country in turn, but you should concentrate on the country in which you live or in which you expect to work.

England

The Care Quality Commission (CQC)

The CQC is responsible for monitoring and inspecting health services and adult social care services in England. Its aims to ensure that health and social care services are of a high quality and that they are delivered safely, effectively and compassionately.

The CQC monitors and inspects:

▶ NHS Trust hospitals and independent hospitals

▶ GP provision, including GP practices, walk-in services and out-of-hours provision

▶ clinics, including family planning clinics, slimming clinics and clinics run by GPs and hospitals

▶ dentists

▶ residential care homes and nursing homes

▶ domiciliary or home care services

▶ community care provision, including day centres and other community support for people with physical, social or mental health problems, or people who have a learning disability

▶ mental health provision, including provision for people who are detained, for people whose rights are restricted under the Mental Health Act (2007) and for those who voluntarily receive care, either in hospital or in the community

▶ accommodation for people requiring treatment for substance misuse.

All providers of these services must register with the CQC. A service provider can be an individual, a partnership or an organisation – for example a company, a charity, an NHS Trust, or a local authority.

Reflect

If your work placement setting is a registered care provider, identify **three** ways in which they meet the standards of the CQC.

Make notes and add any relevant information that other members of your group collect. These notes will be useful in preparing for the final assessment.

The National Institute for Health and Care Excellence (NICE)

Following the Health and Social Care Act (2012) the National Institute for Health and Clinical Excellence (NICE), was renamed as the National Institute for Health and Care Excellence (which is still abbreviated to NICE). This name change reflects its new responsibilities for social care. NICE is responsible for providing guidance on current best practice in health and social care. It publishes guidance and advice that aims to control and improve health and social care provision. For example, NICE provides:

▶ guidance on the most appropriate treatments for people with specific conditions and diseases, such as cancer or diabetes

- evaluation of whether procedures are sufficiently safe and effective to be used within the health and care services
  - guidance about the use of specific health technologies and procedures, including the use of new and existing medicines, treatments and procedures
  - assessment of the cost and the effectiveness of treatments
  - recommendations about best practice, based on the most recent research
  - support for health promotion campaigns and healthy living advice.

NICE recommendations are for the use of NHS practitioners, local authorities, charities and any organisations financed by the government who provide health and social care services.

As part of NICE's new responsibilities for social care it aims to provide a smoother transition for service users moving from health services to social care services, and from children's services to adult social services. NICE has jurisdiction in England and Wales and its recommendations are national, providing consistent approaches for service users wherever they live.

Public Health England (PHE)

PHE is an executive agency sponsored by the Department of Health that was set up on 1 April 2013, following the implementation of the Health and Social Care Act (2012). It aims to protect and improve the **public health** and wellbeing of people in England, and to reduce health inequalities. The focus of all public health organisations is on the protection and improvement of the health of a community or population, in contrast to the individual support of a service user discussed earlier.

> **Key term**
>
> **Public health** – organised strategies to prevent disease, promote health and prolong life in a population.

Some measures that PHE uses to carry out its responsibilities are through:
- setting up health promotion programmes to improve the nation's health, for example PHE ran a high-profile campaign 'Be Clear on Cancer', with a particular focus on the prevention of lung, bowel, kidney and liver cancer
- research projects to improve our knowledge of public health issues and generate strategies to address problems, for example in 2015 PHE published a report on the prevalence of breastfeeding at 6–8 weeks after birth
- taking measures to protect the nation's health when there is a public health concern, such as when an epidemic is threatened or a new virus is circulating.

Examples of campaigns supported by PHE include, in 2013, helpful advice for people who may be affected by flooding, and in the autumn of 2015 PHE launched their largest flu vaccination programme, 'Stay well this winter'.

> **Research**
>
> Write brief notes about **one** public health campaign, including the:
> 1 aims and objectives
> 2 activities or strategies
> 3 outcomes.
>
> Share your information with other members of your group. Always keep clear notes as this will make revision much easier.

Ofsted

The Office for Standards in Education, Children's Services and Skills (Ofsted) regulates and inspects services that educate children, young people and adults or care for children through the inspection of:

▶ state funded schools and colleges, and some independent providers

▶ adult education providers

▶ initial teacher education

▶ many private agencies who provide training in the workplace, particularly those that educate and train apprentices

▶ education provision in prisons and the armed forces.

Ofsted also regulates and inspects care provision for children and young people, for example by inspecting:

▶ nurseries, pre-schools and child minders

▶ fostering and adoption agencies

▶ settings providing residential care for children.

Inspectors make a judgement about the overall effectiveness of the provider based on their judgements relating to the:

▶ effectiveness of leadership and management

▶ quality of teaching, learning and assessment

▶ personal development, behaviour and welfare

▶ outcomes for children and learners.

Following inspection, Ofsted publishes a report and the provision is graded: Grade 1 – Outstanding, Grade 2 – Good, Grade 3 – Requires Improvement or Grade 4 – Inadequate.

(Source: adapted from Ofsted: Common inspection framework: education, skills and early years from September 2015)

▶ Ofsted inspects schools on a regular basis

Wales

In Wales, health services and social care services are inspected separately. The Care and Social Services Inspectorate Wales (CSSIW) is responsible for monitoring the quality of care and social service provision and the Healthcare Inspectorate Wales (HIW) is responsible for monitoring the quality of provision of healthcare services.

The Care and Social Services Inspectorate Wales (CSSIW)

The CSSIW is responsible for the regulation and inspection of care provision, which includes:

▸ residential care homes and nursing homes for adults
▸ domiciliary or home care provision
▸ nurses' agencies
▸ children's homes
▸ child minders and day care services for children under the age of eight
▸ fostering and adoption agencies
▸ boarding schools, including residential schools for children with specific needs
▸ further education colleges that accommodate learners under 18.

CSSIW publishes reports on the outcomes of each of its inspections.

The CSSIW aims to:

▸ provide independent assurance about the quality and availability of social care
▸ safeguard adults and children, making sure that their rights are protected
▸ improve care, by encouraging and promoting improvements in the safety, quality and availability of social care services
▸ provide independent professional advice to those who plan health and care provision in Wales.

(Source: www.cssiw.org.uk)

Healthcare Inspectorate Wales (HIW)

The HIW inspects all healthcare provision provided by the NHS and by other independent organisations, including private or charitable organisations. Its responsibilities are wide ranging, and include:

▸ hospitals and clinics
▸ mental health and substance misuse services
▸ nursing agencies and midwifery provision
▸ Youth Offending teams
▸ deaths in prisons, and homicide investigations.

HIW aims to:

▸ contribute to improving the safety and quality of healthcare services in Wales
▸ improve citizens' experience of healthcare in Wales, whether as a patient, service user, carer, relative or employee
▸ strengthen the voice of patients and the public in the way health services are reviewed
▸ ensure that timely, useful, accessible and relevant information about the safety and quality of healthcare in Wales is made available to all.

(Source: www.hiw.org.uk/about-us)

The National Institute for Health and Care Excellence (NICE)

NICE was discussed in relation to its responsibilities in England. However, it has jurisdiction in both England and Wales and its areas of responsibility, and the recommendations it makes, apply in both countries.

Her Majesty's Inspector of Education and Training in Wales (Estyn)

Estyn is the organisation responsible for the inspection of education and training in Wales. Unlike Ofsted, their work is specifically linked to education and training. The inspection of children's social services is largely the responsibility of CSSIW.

Estyn's responsibilities include the inspection of:

▶ schools
▶ further education colleges
▶ work-based learning providers, eg apprenticeship programmes
▶ adult and community learning provision
▶ initial teacher education and training
▶ education in the justice sector, including prisons and young offenders' institutions.

Estyn makes judgements about the quality of provision by addressing three questions.

1 How good are outcomes? (This includes exam results and other evidence of achievement.)
2 How good is provision? (This is concerned with the quality of learning and teaching.)
3 How good is leadership and management? (This is concerned with the management and governance of the setting.)

A four-point scale is used to describe the quality of provision as judged by the inspectors: Grade 1 – Excellent, Grade 2 – Good, Grade 3 – Average, Grade 4 – Unsatisfactory.

Northern Ireland

The Regulation and Quality Improvement Authority (RQIA)

In Northern Ireland, the RQIA has similar responsibilities to the Care Quality Commission in England. That is, it is responsible for the regulation of both care and health services. It inspects services provided by both statutory and independent organisations, including:

▶ children's homes
▶ day care settings for older people, people with disabilities, people who have learning difficulties and people with mental health problems
▶ boarding schools
▶ domiciliary care services
▶ residential family centres
▶ nursing agencies.

Public Health Agency for Northern Ireland (PHA Northern Ireland)

The PHA Northern Ireland was established in 2009 and brought together a number of different public health organisations. Its overall responsibility is to improve the health and social wellbeing of all people living in Northern Ireland. The PHA manages this by:

▶ developing effective health protection strategies, such as an immunisation programme
▶ developing policy to improve the health and wellbeing of the population
▶ conducting research and development activities to identify the causes of poor health
▶ recommending strategies to improve the health of the nation.

In 2015, PHA Northern Ireland ran a campaign to urge people to take steps to reduce their likelihood of having a stroke, as part of World Stroke Day in October, and another related to Global Handwashing Day.

The National Institute for Health and Care Excellence (NICE)

NICE does not have direct responsibility for the control and improvement of health and social care services in Northern Ireland, as it does in England and Wales. However, NICE has a direct link with the Northern Ireland Department of Health, Social Services and Public Safety (DHSSPSNI). This department regularly and systematically reviews NICE recommendations and applies them in Northern Ireland where it is thought appropriate.

Education and Training Inspectorate (ETI)

The ETI are responsible for the inspection and improvement of educational services in Northern Ireland, which includes educational services provided in:

▶ early years, largely pre-school education

▶ primary and secondary schools

▶ further education colleges

▶ youth work

▶ initial teacher education

▶ prisons and young offenders' institutions in Northern Ireland, and other areas of the criminal justice system.

When reporting on the quality of provision in schools and colleges, the ETI uses the following descriptors to report on the quality of provision:

▶ achievements and standards

▶ provision for learning

▶ leadership and management.

Following inspection, a grade is awarded for the overall performance of the provider, based on the judgement of these three areas. A six-point scale is used to describe the quality of provision, as judged by the inspectors: 1 is outstanding, 2 is very good, 3 is good, 4 is satisfactory, 5 is inadequate, 6 is unsatisfactory.

The roles of the organisations which regulate or inspect health and care services

How regulations and inspections are carried out

The CQC in England, the CSSIW and the HIW and the RQIA in Northern Ireland all require service providers to register with them before offering care services. When a service provider applies for registration, there are checks to ensure that it meets the necessary standards of safety, and has the resources to ensure high standards of care (including an appropriate number of sufficiently experienced and qualified staff). Once registered, the services are continually monitored. This includes regular inspection.

Inspectors are drawn from a range of backgrounds, including experienced health and care professionals, members of other related professions and also care users and their informal carers. The inspection teams make judgements supported by robust evidence, on the quality of provision, such as whether the care provision is safe, caring, effective in carrying out its services, well-managed and well led.

Each of the national regulators publishes National Minimum Standards (NMS) of provision in these areas for the types of settings that they inspect. The main sources of evidence used to support their judgements are:

▶ feedback from service users, their families and friends, and from staff at the setting

▶ written reports of care practice and procedures

▶ information from other linked local organisations

▶ records of complaints

▶ on-site inspection of practical care provision.

How organisations and individuals respond to regulation and inspection

Inspection can be a stressful experience. Weaknesses in provision may be identified that managers were unaware of being areas of concern. Managers and staff may feel vulnerable and, on occasion, angry. They may feel that they cannot make the improvements needed. To support care providers, the regulators publish clear guidance that outlines what they expect to see. Following an inspection, the regulator publishes a report. The CQC publishes the outcomes of each inspection and the health and care provision is graded according to the quality of care provided. In Northern Ireland, the RQIA assesses whether the National Minimum Standards are fully met, partially met, or not met.

Changes in working practice required by inspection

Following an inspection where the practice does not meet the required standards, the regulator can enforce change, which may include:

▶ requiring or recommending improvements to the provider's policy and practice in specific respects, for example to share good practice in the provision of care

▶ issuing a requirement notice or warning notice, to set out what improvements the care provider must make, and by when

▶ making changes to a care provider's registration to limit the range of care that they are able to provide

▶ pursuing a criminal prosecution in extreme cases, such as when there is inadequate safeguarding of service users from abuse and improper treatment.

 **PAUSE POINT**   Can you explain why inspection of health and care provision is important?

     Do you remember earlier discussions about health and safety, safeguarding and confidentiality?

     Find an online inspection report and summarise strengths and areas for improvement identified. Compare with a report for a different type of provision.

Organisations that regulate professions in the health and social care services

Here are organisations that regulate professions in the health and social care services.

England, Wales and Northern Ireland

The Nursing and Midwifery Council (NMC)

The NMC is a statutory authority set up by parliament in 2002. It is responsible for regulating the standard of professional practice of all nurses and midwives in the United Kingdom (England, Scotland, Wales and Northern Ireland) wherever they are working. This applies whether they are in paid employment or working as a volunteer.

The NMC exists to protect the public and it sets high standards for:

- initial education and training of nurses and midwives
- continuing professional development
- standards of professional practice
- standards of personal conduct, both at work and in leisure time.

The NMC sets the standards and formal code of practice required of all nurses and midwives. Nurses and midwives have to provide evidence of continuing learning and training in order to remain on the register. All practising nurses and midwives are required to register with the NMC, who investigate any allegations that their members are not meeting the standards set. The NMC has the power to restrict a nurse's practice, for example to require that they work under supervision, take specific training or are restricted to working in a limited number of areas, or to remove them from the register. If a nurse or midwife is removed from the register they are no longer permitted to practice.

The Royal College of Nursing (RCN)

The RCN, although not an inspectorate or regulator of nursing practice, is the world's largest union and professional body representing the nursing profession. It represents nurses in the public, private and voluntary sectors. The RCN aims to maintain high standards in nursing practice through their education and research activities.

The Health and Care Professions Council (HCPC)

The HCPC (formerly the Health Professions Council) was set up in 2012 under the Health and Social Care Act (2012). The HCPC promotes good practice and also exists to protect the public, throughout the United Kingdom, from poor standards of care. The HCPC regulates a wide range of health and care related professionals, sixteen different professions in all, including physiotherapists, occupational therapists, speech therapists, social workers and paramedics. Members of these professions must register with the HCPC. To register as an HCPC approved practitioner, individuals must:

- have achieved the relevant qualifications
- meet the standards of professional practice and personal behaviour required by the council.

If a member of the public feels that a professional registered with the HCPC is not meeting the standards set, they have a right to complain. The HCPC will investigate complaints and take the appropriate action. In cases of serious misconduct, this can include suspension or permanent removal from the register.

The General Medical Council (GMC)

The GMC is an independent organisation for the registration and regulation of doctors. The GMC:

- oversees UK medical education and training
- decides which doctors are qualified to work in this country
- sets the standards that doctors must meet in their professional practice
- takes action to address shortfalls in the standards of treatment that may put patients' safety at risk, or brings the medical professions into disrepute.

When a serious concern is raised about a doctor's behaviour or professional practice, the GMC investigates. If the concern is upheld, the GMC may restrict the doctor's right to practice. The doctor may be required to work under supervision or to undertake further training or in extreme circumstances they may be removed temporarily or permanently from the register.

▶ Andrea Spyropoulos, RCN President

Wales

All the organisations that operate In England also operate in Wales.

Care Council for Wales (CCW)

The CCW was set up under the Care Standards Act (2000) with the aim of registering and regulating the social care workforce in Wales. The CCW confirms and registers staff working in children's or adult social care and early years in Wales. This includes social workers, social care workers, pre-school staff, nursery staff and play workers. The CCW checks that practitioners:

▸ have the necessary qualifications

▸ are physically and mentally fit to practice and work in this area

▸ are of good character, which will involve a Disclosure Barring Service check

▸ comply with the CCW Code of Practice for Social Care Workers.

As with the other regulatory bodies, the CCW investigates complaints and takes appropriate action to protect the public if their members are not reaching the professional standards required of them.

Northern Ireland

All the organisations that operate In England also operate in Northern Ireland.

The Northern Ireland Social Care Council (NISCC)

The Northern Ireland Social Care Council was set up under the Health and Personal Social Services Act (Northern Ireland) (2001). This was during the time that the CCW in Wales and the General Social Care Council in England (the organisation that preceded the HCSC) were established. The overall aim of the NISCC is to protect the public and all service users by regulating the registration and practice of social work and the social care workforce.

The NISCC has responsibility for:

▸ monitoring and regulating the social care workforce in Northern Ireland, which includes social workers, social care workers and social care managers, and probation officers – these professionals work in a wide range of settings, including residential and day care, other community settings and in service users' own homes

▸ setting standards for the training and professional practice of members of the care workforce

▸ promoting the professional development of the workforce.

How services are improved by regulation

The overall purpose of regulation is to protect the public by setting standards of education, training, professional conduct and professional practice, to ensure high standards are maintained throughout a health and care professional's career. Health and care work is a fast changing area, with constant new developments that require new approaches to work. This can be stressful for care workers and requires significant continuing professional development.

If an allegation is made that a practitioner is not meeting the standards of education, skill or professional conduct expected, their regulator will investigate that complaint. The regulators have the power to suspend their members, require them to take additional training, restrict the types of work that they can do or, in extreme circumstances, remove them from the professional register.

Respecting preferences

Paul is a paediatric nurse and has worked on children's wards in general hospitals for more than ten years. He enjoys his work and has always been regarded as an excellent professional nurse. Ali is a Muslim woman. She has requested that Paul does not care for her daughter, Shameena. Ali would like a female nurse to provide Shameena's care.

Furthermore, Ali has accused Paul of unprofessional conduct. She claims that Paul provided intimate personal care for her daughter without drawing the curtains, and that he has helped other children with bathing without closing the bathroom doors. Ali has informed Paul's line manager.

Check your knowledge

1. Do you think that Ali should be able to request nursing care from a woman for her daughter? Please give reasons for your answers.

2. If the accusation of providing intimate care without a concern for privacy is found to be true, will Paul have contravened the Nursing and Midwifery Council's Code of practice?

3. Paul is a member of the Royal College of Nursing (RCN). How might the RCN support Paul?

4. If the allegations are found to be true, what is the likely outcome for Paul?

5. How do you think codes of practice can lead to improvement in healthcare?

Responsibilities of organisations towards people who work in health and social care settings

Organisations providing health and social care services are required to ensure that all employees understand how to meet national standards in their professional practice.

Implementing the organisation's code of practice

The Health and Social Care Act (2008), and the linked regulations of 2014, require that registered providers of care services must ensure that they have sufficient numbers of appropriately qualified staff to meet the needs of their service users at all times. They must also provide or support training and professional development to ensure that their staff can carry out their caring role.

In social care settings, new staff are required to complete an induction programme and to meet the requirements of the Common Induction Standards (2010) within 12 weeks of commencing their new job. This requires the manager to ensure that all new employees understand how to implement the codes of practice in their workplace and how to meet the current National Occupational Standards (NOS) for their role.

Meeting National Occupational Standards

National Occupational Standards (NOS) describe best practice. They are the standards of professional practice that should be met in the workplace. The NOS for people working in the health and social care sector are applicable throughout the UK and were updated in 2012. The NOS underpin the codes of practice in care settings and the curriculum for the training of practitioners and cover the standards that are also included in the codes of practice for professional bodies, for example the Nursing & Midwifery Council (NMC).

Undertaking continuing professional development

In order for health and care practitioners to maintain the high standards required in the sector, they need to continually update their skills. This will ensure that they are following the best practice and most up-to-date procedures, based on recent research. As discussed earlier in this unit all members of the GMC, the NMC and the HCPC are required to complete regular professional training to remain on their registers. It is the responsibility of care managers to ensure that support staff who are not members of professional organisations also regularly update and extend their skills.

Supporting and safeguarding employees in health and social care

Internal and external complaints

All care organisations are required by their regulators, which include the professional organisations and the inspection agencies, to have formal procedures to address complaints. Where allegations of poor practice are made against staff, this will normally initially be addressed through the organisation's internal disciplinary systems. However, in more serious instances the regulatory body, for example the GMC, the NMC or the HCPC may be involved. In extreme circumstances, for example in cases of assault or death thought to be caused by negligence or active abuse, the police may also deal with the complaints.

Membership of trade unions/professional associations

Many practitioners will be members of trade unions or professional associations, which support them if they are accused of professional misconduct or are in conflict in other ways with their employer. For example, many doctors belong to the British Medical Association (BMA), nurses may belong to the Royal College of Nursing (RCN), midwives to the Royal College of Midwives (RCM) and social workers are often member of the trade union UNISON.

Following protocols of regulatory bodies

Protocols are accepted codes of practice and behaviour required of professionals by their regulatory bodies. The regulatory bodies, such as the GMC, the NMC and the HCPC, also provide protection for employees by ensuring that the standards expected of them are clear and transparent. As part of their induction and ongoing training, health and care practitioners must fully understand their professional responsibilities and the protocols by which they must practice.

Whistleblowing

Whistleblowing procedures can be a form of protection for all staff. If the quality of care in an organisation is poor and this is going unchecked, whistleblowing will protect not only the service user but also other members of staff and sometimes the provision itself. Poor practice damages the reputation of the sector. It may lead to investigations by professional organisations, the inspectorate and, in extreme cases, by the police. Poor practice is a matter for the organisation to check and remedy.

 **PAUSE POINT**   Explain how care organisations ensure that health and care workers are protected and supported in their jobs.

Hint   Check that you understand the importance of codes of practice, NOS, CPD and safeguarding policies and practice.

Extend   Which of these areas do you think are important for you to know about at your work placement setting?

Assessment practice 2.2

Muriel is 40 years old and visually impaired. Her sight is deteriorating, and her doctors have predicted that she will be totally blind within two years. Muriel lives alone and feels lonely.

Muriel had an emergency admission to hospital to have her appendix removed but will soon be going home.

1 Identify one voluntary organisation and one statutory service that could support Muriel in maintaining an independent life at home.

2 Describe two barriers that Muriel, and other people who are visually-impaired, might face when going into hospital.

3 Explain which care provision may be most helpful in supporting Muriel to remain independent.

4 Discuss how the nurses who provided care during Muriel's stay in hospital are monitored to ensure they provide professional services.

C Working with people with specific needs in the health and social care sector

People with specific needs

Physical and mental ill health

When supporting people with physical and mental illnesses, a multi-disciplinary approach is usual and normally essential. When people are supported by health and care professionals, it is not at all unusual that the service user has a range of concerns in addition to the one first presented. As discussed earlier in this unit, care professionals, whatever their speciality, aim to take a holistic approach to meet the needs of the whole person. People with mental health problems often have associated physical ill health. Poor physical health can lead to serious anxiety and depression. It is the care professional's role to judge when it is necessary to work professionally with other specialists to ensure that the service user's needs are fully met.

Mental illness is difficult to define and, therefore, difficult to monitor. What is regarded as normal and acceptable behaviour varies from one society to another, and at different times in history. In addition, the evidence available is derived largely from medical statistics, recording the number of people who present themselves for treatment. Mind, the charity that works with and supports people with mental health problems, estimates that one in four people experience a mental health problem each year.

Table 2.4 identifies a wide range of symptoms that are linked with stress and mental ill health. However, people experiencing these symptoms may not necessarily regard themselves as ill and therefore may not seek professional help.

▶ **Table 2.4** Some common signs of stress

Physical	Psychological	Behavioural
tiredness	anxiety	increased smoking or drinking
a feeling of tightness in the chest	tearfulness	withdrawal or aggression
indigestion	feeling low	lateness
headaches	mood changes	recklessness
appetite and weight changes	indecision	difficulty concentrating
joint and back pain	loss of motivation	
	increased sensitivity	
	low self-esteem	

There may be many reasons why people with mental health problems do not seek professional help, for example:

▶ they may not regard themselves as mentally ill, perhaps they think they are just having a hard time at the moment

▶ they might not want to admit that they have a mental health problem, some people feel that there is a particular stigma linked to mental illness that is not associated with physical illness

▶ they may be frightened to seek medical help, worried that being diagnosed as depressed or phobic would affect their employment prospects. There is some basis for this concern as people with mental health problems have the highest rate of unemployment among people with disabilities.

It is the health and care practitioner's role to be aware of changes in both a service user's mental and physical wellbeing.

Learning disability

MENCAP, the organisation that supports people with learning disabilities, defines a learning disability as 'a reduced intellectual ability and difficulty with everyday activities... which affects someone for their whole life'. This may include difficulties with regular household tasks, shopping, using public transport or managing their money. Many people with learning difficulties also have other health needs, for example people with Down's syndrome, a common condition that leads to learning difficulties, often have heart problems and sight and hearing impairments.

Research by The Foundation for People with Learning Difficulties has found that between 25 per cent and 40 per cent of people with learning difficulties also suffer from mental health problems. The prevalence of dementia is much higher amongst older adults with learning difficulties compared to the general population.

Until relatively recently, many people with learning disabilities were cared for in large institutions or hospitals and were almost invisible to the rest of society. However, the Community Care Act (1990) increased the number of people with learning disabilities who were cared for and supported in the community rather than in large institutions. Importantly, the Disability Discrimination Act (1995) provided legal protection from discrimination in employment, access to public buildings and in renting of accommodation. However, MENCAP (2015) reports that despite recent progress, just 7% of adults with a learning disability are in paid employment, yet 65% want to work and, more importantly, have the capability to work. (This compares with one in two people with a physical disability being in work.) Of those people with a learning disability that do work, most only work part-time and are in low paid employment. Additionally, only a third of people with a learning disability take part in some form of education or training.

(Source: MENCAP 2015)

Key terms

Impairment – physical or mental loss of function, whether permanent or temporary, that restricts an individual's ability to perform daily activities independently.

Disabling environment – a social context in which adaptions and other necessary facilities are not in place to ensure that people with impairments can take a full part in social life.

Braille – system of writing and printing for blind or visually impaired people in which raised dots are used to represent the letters of the alphabet, numbers and punctuation marks.

Link

See *Unit 10: Sociological Perspectives*, section B for a fuller discussion of the difference between disability and impairment.

Physical and sensory disabilities

Prior to the Community Care Act (1990), many people with physical and sensory disabilities and **impairments** also lived in hospitals and other large institutions in which the focus was predominantly concerned with their physical care. There was less awareness of the need for a holistic approach. People with disabilities tended to be segregated from the community rather than included in the wider life of our society.

A sensory impairment refers to a condition where a person's sensory organs, for example their eyesight or hearing, function abnormally poorly, which limits their ability to perform day-to-day activities. However, a person with an impairment may only be disabled if adaptions and services are not in place to ensure they are able to perform their daily routines and other activities of daily life independently. A **disabling environment** describes a situation where appropriate adaptions and services are not in place to support people with impairments. For example, a person with a hearing impairment is only disabled if they do not have access to a hearing aid. Or a person with a visual impairment does not have access to information in **Braille,** if this is the system of communication they prefer.

Poverty and disabilities

The poverty rate for adults with disabilities is twice that for adults without a disability. The main reason for this, despite the Disability Discrimination Act (1995), is the high rate of unemployment among people with disabilities. According to the Poverty Site (a website containing statistics on poverty and social exclusion), approximately one in five adults with any type of disability who wants to work is unable to find employment. This compares with one in 15 adults without a disability. Furthermore, people with disabilities face extra costs related to managing their impairment, such as the extra expense of paying for to their homes, social care support and other mobility and communication aids.

Specific age groups

Early years

Human growth and development is usually described in terms of life stages, which begin with conception and range through infancy, childhood and adolescence to the final stages of adult life. The development of infants and young children can be regarded as a journey, influenced both by their physiological changes and social environment. The care and education services supporting children in early childhood are required to follow a curriculum, the Early Years Foundation Stage (EYFS) curriculum. The EYFS, which was updated in 2014, sets standards and measures progress from birth to 5 years of age. All schools and Ofsted-registered early-years providers must follow the EYFS. This includes childminders, pre-schools, nurseries and school reception classes. The EYFS covers seven key areas of learning and development, which together form a holistic model that addresses the development of the 'whole child'.

The EYFS areas of learning and development are:
1 communication and language
2 physical development
3 personal, social and emotional development
4 literacy
5 mathematics
6 understanding the world
7 expressive arts and design.

Link

See *Unit 1: Human Lifespan Development* for further discussion of human growth and development.

Later adulthood

Adulthood is the stage in human development associated with reaching physical and emotional maturity. Early adulthood, the period between the age of 18 and about 40 years of age, is associated with the cessation of physical maturation and is when the ageing process gradually begins. In the middle adult period, approximately between the ages of 40 and 65 years, people begin to notice a decline in their physical stamina. People begin to move and run more slowly than in previous years and their eyesight often deteriorates. There is a loss of skin elasticity, with an increase in wrinkles. Women will also experience the onset of the **menopause**.

However, the effects of the ageing process for most people are most acute in later adulthood. At this stage, there are changes in the brain structure that result in noticeably slower intellectual and physical reactions, poorer memory and less effective problem-solving skills. Physical changes include poorer hearing and eyesight, a loss of muscle tissue leading to less strength and generally less stamina. Older people often experience changes in sleep patterns and their immune system is less efficient, making them prone to infections that take longer to clear.

Many older people, however, live active and busy lives. They may contribute to community activities, extend their education, online or through attending courses, for example, and provide essential family support for their children and grandchildren.

Key term

Menopause – stage in life, usually between the ages of 45 and 55, when a woman's menstrual cycle gradually stops and she is no longer able to become pregnant naturally.

▶ Many people stay active in retirement

⏸ PAUSE POINT Can you explain how provision of services will need to vary according to individual need?

    Hint Briefly describe the range of people with specific needs that may need health and care support.

    Extend In more detail, describe the range of provision for one type of service user. Compare your notes with other group members.

Working practices

Relevant skills to work in these areas

As we have discussed throughout this unit, the specific knowledge and skills required for working in the health and care sector varies according to the wide range of specialist job roles within this sector. Health and care is a rapidly changing sector in which changes in the size and structure of the population present new challenges, legal requirements change and new treatments and procedures are introduced at a fast pace.

Link

Go to section A to remind yourself of the range of roles, responsibilities and skills required of people working in the health and care sector.

In December 2012, the Chief Nursing Officer for England launched a three-year strategy for all nurses and midwives entitled 'Compassion in Practice'. Central to her campaign was the focus on six key values, which came to be known as the Chief Nursing Officer's 6Cs (see Figure 2.10).

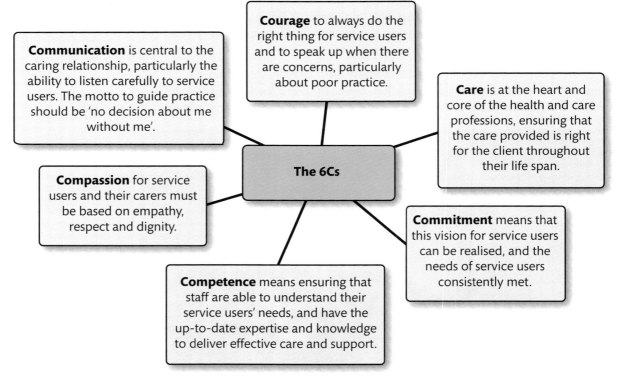

▶ **Figure 2.10** The Chief Nursing Officer's 6Cs

The 6Cs are now incorporated into the introductory Care Certificate for healthcare support workers and adult social care workers that was introduced in April 2015.

Research

Using the internet, investigate the requirements of the Care Certificate for healthcare support workers and adult social care workers, introduced following the Cavendish Report in April 2015.

How policies and procedures affect people in these areas

The policies, procedures, codes of practice and codes of conduct for the caring professions have become more specific in recent years. They are presented so that professionals, service users and their carers can understand them clearly, and they are more rigorously enforced. The inspection agencies have a specific responsibility to monitor standards of provision, and to require immediate action where significant failings are identified. Since the publication of Robert Francis's report in 2013 into the failings of the Mid Staffordshire NHS Trust, issues of patient safety and the quality of care have been even more in the public eye.

> **Research**
>
> Using the internet, investigate the failings at the Mid Staffordshire NHS Trust reported in 2013.

How regulation affects people working in these areas

As has been discussed, all staff working in care settings are affected by regulation and inspection, both of their provision and their professional practice.

Where provision is failing to meet the standards required, immediate action can be required and its implementation carefully monitored. Where care professionals fail to meet the standards set by their regulators, they can be disciplined and in the most serious cases removed from their professional register. This means they can no longer practice either voluntarily or in paid employment.

> **Link**
>
> Go to section B to see the codes of practice members of the health and care professions must abide by, such as that of the GMC, NMC and HCPC, and the Code of Conduct required of healthcare support workers and adult social care workers in England.

How working practices affect people who use services in these areas

Of course, the overall aim of all health and care provision is to meet the individual needs of service users. The policies, procedures, legislative requirements and regulation of health and care providers is in place to ensure that standards are high, and also to ensure that service users can take action where there are failings in provision.

Recent examples of how poor working practices have been identified and addressed

Changes in policy and the regulation of care services have often been introduced following the investigations of failings in the health and care settings. The following are examples of where this has been the case.

Victoria Climbié

Victoria Climbié was abused, and finally died, while living with her guardians in the Borough of Haringey, London, in February 2000. Victoria was born in the Ivory Coast, West Africa, and came to live in London with her great aunt and her great aunt's boyfriend. They claimed to be able to offer her a better life. In January 2001, the great aunt and her boyfriend were convicted of Victoria's murder. While Victoria was living in London, and during the period she suffered horrific abuse, several organisations had contact with the 'family' and had noted signs of abuse. These included the police, social workers from four different local authorities, two housing authorities, the National Health Service, the National Society for the Prevention of Cruelty to Children (NSPCC) and local churches.

Following Victoria's death, an enquiry was set up under the direction of Lord Laming to investigate how and why, despite being known to the authorities, this tragedy was allowed to happen. Lord Laming identified countless examples of poor practice **within** these services and organisations; and very poor levels of communication **between** them. The report by Lord Laming led to the government taking the following steps.

▸ Every Child Matters (ECM), this initiative was launched in 2003. ECM was to ensure that all children, regardless of their background, should have the chance to reach their full potential by reducing levels of ill health, eradicating abuse and neglect and improving educational success for all children. The five outcomes to achieve for all children are for them to:
  • stay safe
  • be healthy
  • enjoy and achieve
  • make a positive contribution
  • achieve economic wellbeing.
▸ The Children Act (2004), which led to the:
  • appointment of a Director of Children's Services in every local authority, who has responsibility for the care and education of children in their area
  • 'duty to cooperate' for all services concerned with the care and safeguarding of children
  • setting up of local Safeguarding Boards, which are responsible for monitoring the professional practice of agencies in the safeguarding of children in their area
  • creation of a Children's Commissioner, with responsibility for representing and promoting the interests of children and young people, particularly the disadvantaged and children whose voices are rarely heard.

Jessica Chapman and Holly Wells

In August 2002 two primary school children, Jessica Chapman and Holly Wells, were reported missing from their home. Less than two weeks later, their bodies were found. The girls had been sexually abused and murdered by their school caretaker. It emerged during the investigations that the caretaker had been investigated in the past for sexual offences and burglary, but he had still been appointed to work in a school. An enquiry, led by Sir Michael Bichard, was set up to investigate this tragedy. One of the key recommendations of the Bichard Report was that there should be a statutory agency with responsibility for vetting all individuals wanting to work with children or vulnerable adults, whether as a paid member of staff or as a volunteer. This was initially the responsibility of the Criminal Records Bureau (CRB) set up in 2002. In 2012, the responsibility for vetting staff and volunteers was given to the newly created Disclosure and Barring Service (DBS).

Peter Connelly (Baby P)

In 2008, seventeen-month old Peter Connelly, still often referred to as Baby P, died after suffering serious physical and psychological abuse over a nine-month period. Just as in the case of Victoria Climbié, he had been seen by numerous health and care professionals during this period, but they failed to intervene and avert the tragedy. Further, just like Victoria Climbié, Baby P was also living in the Borough of Haringey. Lord Laming conducted a review to establish why, despite the changes in legislation, the tragedy had occurred. He found that yet again communication had been poor, practice unprofessional and the standards of care inadequate. As part of his review, Lord Laming recommended that there should be:

▶ a review of the recruitment, training and supervision of social workers to ensure that they received better child protection training

▶ improved safeguarding training for staff with a responsibility for the care of children.

The Mid Staffordshire NHS Trust

In 2013, the Francis Inquiry reported on the failings in the standard of care at the Mid Staffordshire NHS Trust. Concerns were raised in 2007 by the then Healthcare Commission about the apparently high death rate at the Mid Staffordshire Hospital Trust. Its final report did not conclude that the higher number of deaths was caused by inadequate provision, but serious failings were identified in the quality of care provided. As a result of these concerns, a number of investigations, including the influential Francis Inquiry, led to reports of widespread failures in the quality of care within the Trust. These included:

▶ chronic staff shortages

▶ patients having inadequate access to food and water

▶ patients left in soiled bedding

▶ a culture where raising concerns about the quality of care was discouraged

▶ a failure in the management and leadership of the trust.

As a result of the Francis Inquiry, a further report by Camilla Cavendish was set up to investigate the quality of recruitment, training and support for non-registered staff in hospitals and other care settings. This included all staff who were not professionally trained doctors, nurses or other regulated and professionally trained health and care staff; that is, most care assistants and healthcare assistants. The Cavendish Review recommended that improved induction training should be in place for all healthcare assistants and support workers, and this was introduced in March 2015. Employers are required to ensure that all newly appointed support staff complete the Care Certificate, which covers fifteen units of study, including:

▶ understanding the role as a support worker

▶ a carer's duty of care

▶ equality and diversity

▶ communication

▶ privacy and dignity

▶ safeguarding

▶ health and safety

▶ infection prevention and control.

(Source: adapted from: http://www.nhsemployers.org/your-workforce/plan/
education-and-training/care-certificate)

The Care Quality Commission (CQC) are responsible for ensuring that the Care Certificate is effectively delivered. Their guidance is that it should be completed within 12 weeks of a new entrant beginning their job.

 **PAUSE POINT**   Can you identify and describe how good health and care practice is promoted, and the quality of provision monitored?

        Hint   You should refer to the impact of policies and procedures, and of inspection.

        Extend   How have investigations into failures in provision led to improved policies and practice?

Assessment practice 2.3

Peter is nineteen. He has a range of health and care needs. He is grossly overweight, has high blood pressure and suffers from bronchitis. He was bullied at school and left with few qualifications. He has never worked. His self-esteem is low and he has recently been diagnosed with clinical depression.

1 Identify two of the health and care professional who may be involved in Peter's care.

2 Describe the key skills that the two professionals need to effectively support him in living an independent life.

3 Explain why a multi-disciplinary team is likely to be involved in Peter's care.

4 Discuss the importance of good communication between members of a multi-disciplinary team and the possible consequences of poor communication between professionals.

Plan
- First collect all your notes and handouts that relate to these questions.
- Divide them into sections according to the theme of the question.

Do
- Highlight the key points for quick reference.
- Make separate notes that directly answer the questions set. Extending bullet points may help.
- Learn your work. Write your answers without looking at your notes.
- Remember that for the final question you need to discuss different aspects of Peter's care and how they are linked together. Also to take into account different ideas and opinions.

Review
- Try to identify the strengths and weaknesses in your answers.
- Fill in any gaps that you identify.
- If you have time re-do the 'test' without looking at any of your notes.

Further reading and resources

Ayling, P. et al. (2012), *Preparing to Work in Adult Social Care Level 3*, Cheltenham: Nelson Thornes.

Maclean, S. (2013), *Level 3 Diploma in Health and Social Care*, London: City and Guilds.

Marshall, T. (2012), *Learning Disabilities Care: A Care Worker Handbook*, London: Hodder Education.

Morris, C. (2012) and Collier C., *End of Life Care: A Care Worker Handbook*, London: Hodder Education.

Nolan, Y. (2009), *Illustrated Dictionary in Health and Social Care*, Oxford: Heinemann.

Nolan, Y. (2011), *Level 3 Health and Social Care, Adults, 3rd edition*, Oxford: Heinemann.

Nolan, Y. (2012), *Health and Social Care: Dementia Level 3 Candidate Handbook (QCF) (Level 3 Work Based Learning Health and Social Care)*, Harlow: Pearson Education

Pilgrim, D. (2014), *Key Concepts in Mental Health, 3rd edition*, London: Sage Publications.

Rowe, J. and Collins, A. (2013), *Key Concepts in Health and Social Care*, London: Collins

Websites

www.gmc-uk.org
The General Medical Council regulates doctors in the UK.

www.nmc.org.uk
The Nursing and Midwifery Council regulates nurses and midwives in the UK.

www.hcpc-uk.co.uk
The Health and Care Professions Council regulates health care workers.

www.nice.org.uk
National Institute for Health and Care Excellence (NICE) provides guidance and advice to improve health and social care.

https://www.cqc.org.uk/
The Care Quality Commission regulates health and social care in England.

www.ccwales.org.uk
The Care Council for Wales regulates social care in Wales.

www.niscc.info
The Northern Ireland Social Care Council (NISCC) registers social care workers in Northern Ireland.

cssiw.org.uk
Care and Social Services Inspectorate Wales (CSSIW) inspects social care and social services in Wales.

www.estyn.gov.wales
Estyn (The education Inspectorate Wales) inspects education and training standards in Wales.

www.hiw.org.uk
The Healthcare Inspectorate Wales inspects healthcare organisations in Wales.

www.gov.uk/government/organisations/ofsted
Ofsted regulates and inspects services for children and those providing education and training.

www.gov.uk/government/organisations/public-health-england
Public Health England works to protect and improve the health and wellbeing of the national population.

www.publichealth.hscni.net
The Public Health Agency for Northern Ireland works to protect and improve the health and wellbeing of the population in Northern Ireland.

www.etini.gov.uk
The Education and Training Inspectorate (Northern Ireland) inspects educational standards in Northern Ireland.

www.rqia.org.uk
The Regulation and Quality Improvement Authority regulates health and social care in Northern Ireland.

www.mind.org.uk
Mind is a charity that supports people suffering from mental health problems.

www.mencap.org.uk
MENCAP is a charity that supports people with learning disabilities.

www.nspcc.org.uk
The National Society for the Prevention of Cruelty to Children (NSPCC) is a charity that helps children who are at risk of abuse and neglect.

www.ageuk.org.uk
Age UK is a charity that helps and supports older people.

THINK ▶️FUTURE

Leo Watkins

Domiciliary Care Worker

I've been working as a domiciliary care worker for over two years. Most of my service users are older people, including Alf, whose wife has just died. I also support Mohammed, who has mild learning difficulties, and Julia, a single parent who has three children under the age of four and needs practical care support. So many of my friends are surprised that I do this work and even more surprised that I don't just do the cleaning. They don't realise the level of responsibility, particularly as I'm normally working on my own in the client's home.

I have to check that my service users are safe, that they are eating properly, that they are keeping well, both physically and emotionally, and that they are managing to carry out the normal routines of their daily life. My aim, and the aim of our service, is that they should be able to live independently in their own home for as long as possible.

Of course, our service users are individuals with their own needs, preferences and choices. Some are able to live more independently than others. We aim to work with the individual service user to ensure that they are safe and that their rights, including the right to choice, dignity and independence, are respected.

Focusing your skills

Respecting the rights of service users

It is important to ensure that the rights of service users are respected. Here are some tips to help you do this.

- It is essential that you know that your service users are safe. Consider the hazards and risks that Alf, Mohammed and Julia may encounter.
- How might you expect the specific care needs of Alf, Mohammed and Julia to differ?
- How can you be sure that you provide care consistent with your service users' culture, beliefs and preferences? What particular religious needs may Mohammed have?
- It is important that service users are empowered, that they take a full part in the discussions about their care. How can you be sure that your service users exercise their right to choice and their independence is promoted?

Your safety and protection as a domiciliary care worker

- How can you be sure that you are safe as a lone worker in other people's homes?
- What is a code of practice? How will this help to ensure that you are safe?
- Are there professional organisations or trade unions that would protect your rights if necessary?
- If you are concerned about your safety at work, or travelling to work, what should you do?

Getting ready for assessment

This section has been written to help you to do your best when you take the assessment test. Read through it carefully and ask your tutor if there is anything that you are still not sure about.

About the test

The assessment test will last 1 hour and 30 minutes and there are a maximum of 80 marks available. The test is in four sections. Each section will be based on a different short scenario briefly explaining the situation of a person with health and social care needs. Each scenario is relevant to a different service user group.

Each section of the paper will be structured with questions awarding 2, 4, 6 or 8 marks. These will require:

- short answers, worth either 2 or 4 marks, responding to the command words identify and describe respectively
- longer answers, worth 6 or 8 marks, responding to the command words explain and discuss.

Remember that all the questions are compulsory and you should attempt to answer each one.

Sitting the test

Listen to, and read carefully, any instructions you are given. Lots of marks can be lost through not reading questions properly and misunderstanding what the question is asking.

The questions will contain command words. Understanding what these words mean will help you to understand what the question is asking you to do.

Arrive in good time so you are not in a panic.

Command word	Definition – what it is asking you to do
Analyse	Identify several relevant facts of a topic, demonstrate how they are linked and then explain the importance of each, often in relation to the other facts.
Assess	Evaluate or estimate the nature, ability, or quality of something.
Consider	Think carefully about (something). The question will often require you to make a decision on the issue as part of your answer.
Define	State the meaning of something, using clear and relevant facts.
Describe	Give a full account of all the information, including all the relevant details of any features, of a topic.
Discuss	Write about the topic in detail, taking into account different ideas and opinions and how they relate to each other. You will examine how the opinions are similar or contrast with each other.
Evaluate	Bring all the relevant information you have on a topic together and make a judgement on it (for example on its success or importance). Your judgement should be clearly supported by the information you have gathered.
Explain	Write about the origins and functions or objectives of the subject, with examples and reasons to support an opinion, view or argument, where possible.
Identify	Name and briefly give the main features of something and its qualities.
Justify	Give reasons for the point your answer is making, so that your reader can tell what you are thinking. These reasons should clearly support the argument you are making.

Work out what question you need to answer and then organise your time, based on the marks available for each question. Set yourself a timetable for working through the test and then stick to it – don't spend ages on a short 1–2 mark question and then find you only have a few minutes for a longer 7–8 mark question.

If you are writing a longer answer, try and plan before you start writing. Have a clear idea of the point your answer is making, and make sure this comes across in everything you write, so it is all focused on answering the question.

Remember you can't lose marks for a wrong answer, but you can't gain any marks for a blank space!

Try answering all the simpler questions first then come back to the harder questions. This should give you more time for the harder questions.

Sample answers

For some of the questions, you will be given some background information on which the questions are based. Look at the sample questions that follow, and our tips on how to answer these well.

Answering short-answer questions

☐ Read the question carefully.

☐ Highlight or underline key words.

☐ Note the number of marks available.

Make sure you make the same number of statements as there are marks available. For example, a two-mark question needs two statements.

> **Scenario:** Peter is 70 years of age. He has mild learning disabilities and now has mobility problems. He is using a wheelchair most of the time. It is thought that he needs twenty-four-hour care. Three weeks ago he moved into a residential care home for older people.

Worked example

Question: Identify **one** social care practitioner and **one** healthcare practitioner who may support Peter with his mobility problems. He is using a wheelchair. [2]

Look carefully at how the question is set out to see how many points need to be included in your answer.

Answer: The healthcare practitioners could include (any one of) nurses, doctors, healthcare assistants, physiotherapists and occupational therapists.

The social care practitioners could include (any one of) social workers, care assistants in the residential home, social work assistants or support workers.

This answer names the occupational roles of a range of health and care practitioners and that is what you are asked for. You do not need to explain how they would contribute to care for this 2-mark question.

Worked example

Question: Describe **two** responsibilities of care assistants who work in residential homes for older people. [4]

Answer: The responsibilities could include any of the activities that are part of the care assistant's routine duties, for example:

- Helping residents to eat and drink – care assistants provide support at all meal times and when residents are having a snack or a cup of tea to ensure that residents can enjoy a nutritious diet and the social aspect of meal times. Most residents will be able to feed themselves but others will need some help. The care assistant may suggest special cutlery or adapted plates and cups to support the resident's independence.

- Helping residents to maintain and improve their mobility – care assistants encourage and support residents in taking exercise to keep supple and to maintain mobility. They may suggest mobility equipment, walking sticks or walking frames to support mobility and independence.

- Enabling residents to maintain their personal hygiene – care assistants support residents with washing, showering, bathing, hair washing, shaving and general personal cleanliness and hygiene. Most residents will be able to do some of these tasks. The care assistant provides support, as necessary, but always tries to maintain the resident's independence. They may suggest specially designed clothes, dresses without buttons or zips, for example.

- Enabling residents to use the toilet facilities – care assistants monitor the continence of residents and provide support when people are not able to use toilet facilities in the way they used to. Care assistants should provide support and minimise the resident's embarrassment. For example, they may suggest the use of continence pads.

- Promoting communication with residents and supporting their communication with each other – care assistants support clients in maintaining their social skills, which includes good communication. They may arrange social activities for the residents, support them in making meal times a social occasion, and encourage them to communicate with visitors.

> These answers are by way of illustration. You should be able to suggest other responsibilities of care assistants in residential settings. They give brief descriptions of the responsibilities of care assistants. You do not need to give any more detail for a 4-mark question of this sort. There will be 2 marks for each of the responsibilities that you describe.

Worked example

Answering extended-answer questions

Question: Explain how the physiotherapists who support Peter are monitored by the Health and Care Professions Council (HCPC) to ensure that they maintain high professional standards in their care practice. (6)

Answer:

The Heath and Care Professions Council (HCPC) was set up in 2003, with the aim of promoting high standards of practice in a range of health and care professions throughout the United Kingdom. It monitors practice for some 16 professions including physiotherapists, social workers, speech therapists and occupational therapists. The HCPC also exists to protect the public, throughout

> For a question using the word 'explain', you must do more than just describe. You must show that you understand the functions and purposes of the organisation. You must show that you understand the origins of the subject or organisation and why it is important. You need to show that you understand its suitability for purpose and give reasons to support your opinion, view or argument.

the United Kingdom, from poor standards of care. Members of these professions must register with the HCPC. They cannot practice in the UK unless they are members of the HCPC.

In order to register with the HCPC, all physiotherapists must have achieved the approved qualifications, must complete ongoing training after they have qualified, and they must meet the standards of professional practice required by the HCPC. If Peter or any member of the public feels that a professional physiotherapist is not meeting the standards set, they have a right to complain. The council will investigate and take the appropriate action. In cases of serious misconduct, this can include suspension or permanent removal from the register. The HCPC is not very well-known by the public and a service user with learning disabilities, like Peter, may find it very difficult to make a formal complaint. Peter would need support if he really was going to follow the complaints procedure.

This answer describes the origins of the HCPC and its main purpose. It describes why the HCPC is important and its role in maintaining high standards within physiotherapy. Some of the ways of maintaining these standards are shown. Reasons why it may be difficult for members of the public to lodge complaints is considered. The answer clearly explains how the HCPC can be important in protecting service users such as Peter. You may write more than one paragraph.

Worked example

Question: Discuss the effectiveness of using an advocate to ensure that Peter has the care he needs from the care practitioners who support him. (8)

Answer:

An advocate is a person who represents a service user and speaks for them. They will try to ensure that the professionals and other people who support Peter understand his wishes and his needs. People with learning disabilities often have difficulties in communicating with officials, writing letters and filling in forms. The best and most effective advocates will get to know their client very well and build a trusting relationship with their client so that they can accurately convey their needs, wishes and preferences to the professional workers, and to official organisations. If this works well, it is an excellent provision and ensures that, despite his mild learning difficulty, Peter's needs and wishes can be clearly explained. However, most advocates are volunteers and not everyone who needs advocacy can get that support. It just depends on the number of volunteers. Advocates do not need to have formal qualifications. The training of advocates varies and so the quality of the support is not very reliable. There is no professional organisation to monitor the quality of their work.

The advocate, therefore, is a very important and helpful service. However, advocates are not usually paid and so it is difficult to ensure that there are enough advocates and that the quality of service is consistent.

For a question using the word 'discuss', you must do more than just explain. You might need to talk about the issues or the advantages and disadvantages of an approach, and take in different opinions.

This answer explains what an advocate is and describes their role in representing the wishes and needs of service users.

The learner discusses both the value of good advocacy in helping people communicate effectively with professionals and formal organisations and also explores the limitation, such as the scarcity of provision that may leave some service users vulnerable. For a higher mark, the learner could explain how important this can be in empowering service users.

The learner will usually write a longer section here, perhaps even multiple paragraphs. However, the important thing is that they look at different aspects of the topic, take in different opinions and look at the advantages and disadvantages.

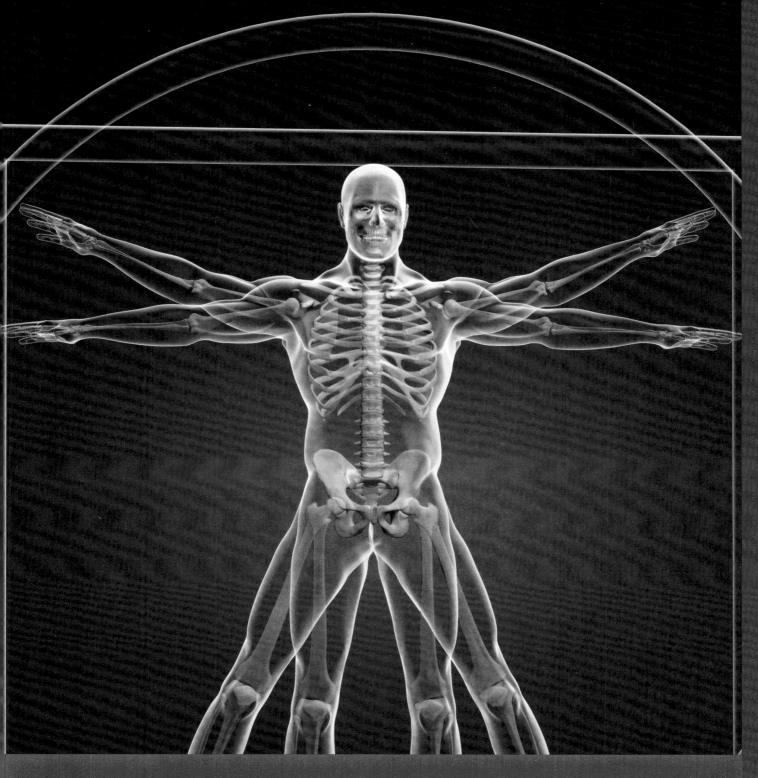

Anatomy and Physiology for Health and Social Care

3

Getting to know your unit

Assessment

You will be assessed using a paper-based examination worth 90 marks

Understanding basic human anatomy and physiology is essential to understanding how the body works. You should know how the body functions normally to appreciate what happens when something goes wrong and also how solutions, in the form of treatments, may work. This unit provides basic anatomy and physiology at detailed cellular level, both in body organs and of the major body systems. You will explore how certain body systems work together to create functional units to maintain the limits essential to life of elements such as temperature, water content and energy supply. This is known as homeostasis. The key features of some common disorders will be studied, together with an introduction to epidemiology and clinical drug research.

How you will be assessed

You will be assessed by a paper-based examination, lasting for 1 hour 30 minutes, worth 90 marks and consisting of short- and long-answer questions. The questions will assess your understanding of cells and tissues, human anatomy and physiology of major body systems, homeostatic mechanisms and fundamentals of medical research. The questions will make connections between structures and functions, and provide opportunities to analyse and evaluate information associated with life processes.

Throughout this unit you will find assessment practices that will help you prepare for the exam. Completing each of these will give you an insight into the types of questions that could be asked and, importantly, how to answer them.

Unit 3 has four assessment outcomes (AO), which will be included in the external examination. Each assessment outcome also has some 'command words' associated with it.

The assessment outcomes for this unit are:

AO1 Demonstrate knowledge of the structure, organisation and function of the human body.

AO2 Demonstrate understanding of the structure, organisation and function of the human body and relevant medical research.

AO3 Analyse and evaluate information related to anatomical and physiological systems and medical research related to disorders affecting these systems.

AO4 Make connections between common disorders and how they affect human anatomical and physiological systems.

This table contains the areas of essential content that learners must be familiar with prior to assessment.

Essential content	
A	The structure and orginisation of the human body
B	The structure, function and disorders of body systems
C	Medical research

Getting started

Work in small groups of between four and six people. On four large pieces of paper write 'cells', 'tissues', 'organs' and 'body systems'. On four smaller slips of paper, each group member should write the name of a type of cell, a type of tissue, an organ and a body system. Mix up the slips of paper and give four slips to each person. Each group member should place their slips under the correct label on the larger sheet of paper. Discuss the reasons for everyone's choices and the accuracy of their decisions.

If working on your own, you can sort the following examples into cells, tissues, organs and body systems: heart, bone, blood, skeleton, red blood cell (or erythrocyte), cartilage, nervous system, kidney, brain, digestive system, skin, stomach, muscle cell.

A The structure and organisation of the human body

This learning aim explains the basic anatomy and physiology of the human body before moving on to look at selected body systems.

How cells work

Every individual is composed of billions of microscopic units called **cells**. Cells carry out vast numbers of chemical reactions and processes that make up the essence of life itself. After looking at the structure and functioning of cells you will discover how cells work together, managing the energy you use.

Cells rarely exist in isolation. They are usually grouped together with other similar cells, which carry out particular tasks. Groups of cells are known as **tissues**.

Different types of tissues are commonly grouped together to form an **organ**, which carries out a particular function.

Groups of organs responsible for major tasks or functions in the body are called organ systems, or body systems.

The largest cell in the human body is the female ovum, which can just be seen with the naked eye. Most cells are much smaller than this and microscopes are needed to view them. Ordinary light microscopes, such as those found in school or college laboratories, are quite good for viewing tissues and organs but not very useful for looking inside individual human cells.

Electron microscopes are necessary to see the detail of cell contents. These are highly expensive instruments requiring trained operators to prepare and interpret the specimens. It is possible to take photographsof objects magnified using a microscope (**photomicrographs**) so that other people can use them, and also diagrams made from them, instead.

Function and structure of cells

Details of the interior of a cell are often referred to as the ultrastructure of the cell ('ultra' means 'beyond what is considered normal'). This is because they can only be seen with immense magnification. Before the electron microscope was developed,

> ### Key terms
>
> **Cell** – the basic unit of living material.
>
> **Tissues** – groups of cells joined together to carry out a particular task.
>
> **Organ** – a collection of tissues joined together to carry out a specific function.
>
> **Electron microscope** – a very powerful type of microscope, needed to see inside cells.
>
> **Photomicrograph** – a photograph taken of an object magnified using a microscope.

the inside of a cell was considered to be a granular sort of 'soup', but it is now known that the ultrastructure is highly organised and composed of many different bodies that carry out their own functions.

Do you remember the definition of an organ? The very tiny bodies inside a cell are known as **organelles** because they have different physical (and chemical) compositions and carry out their own functions.

Although you will learn about a typical human cell, there are actually lots of different types of cells each with their own characteristics. The 'typical cell' exists only for study purposes and has no specialisation. When studying actual cells in the body, you must adapt your knowledge to the specific type of cell being considered. For example, a mature red blood cell does not have a nucleus, so any description of the ultrastructure of a red blood cell would not include the nucleus.

The living material that makes up whole cells is called **protoplasm**, and is subdivided into the **cytoplasm** and the **nucleus**.

Under a light microscope cytoplasm appears granular with no distinct features. The cytoplasm is the site where most complex chemical reactions occur, mainly directed by the nucleus. The nucleus, which is also responsible for inherited characteristics can be seen as a dark body, usually centrally placed. Both the whole cell and the nucleus are surrounded by a membrane, which appears as a single line (see Figure 3.1).

Key terms

Organelle – a tiny body inside a cell, which carries out its own functions.

Protoplasm – means 'first material', refers to anything inside the cell boundary.

Cytoplasm – 'cell material', refers to anything inside the cell boundary and outside the nucleus.

Nucleus – the central part of the cell, which is enclosed in a membrane and is usually darker than the rest of the cell because it contains genetic material.

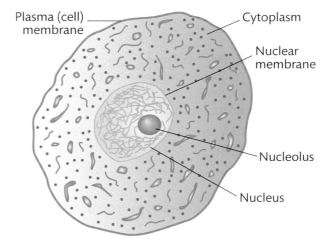

Plasma (cell) membrane
Cytoplasm
Nuclear membrane
Nucleolus
Nucleus

▶ **Figure 3.1** Diagram of a cell viewed with a light microscope

Cell ultrastructure is so complex and highly organised that it has its own branch of science – cytology, the study of cells. In this unit you will learn about the structure and functions of the cell membrane, the organelles in the cytoplasm and the nucleus.

Cell membrane

The electron microscope shows the cell membrane to be a phospho-lipid-protein bilayer. The lipids are small, fatty molecules in two layers (bilayer), with larger protein molecules inserted at intervals partly or completely through the bilayer. The lipid molecules are phospholipids. The phosphate head is water soluble and the two lipid chains are insoluble in water. This is why the two layers align themselves, with the lipid chains facing one another. The fluid surrounding cells (called tissue fluid) and the cytoplasm are both watery environments next to the phosphate heads (see Figure 3.2).

Protein molecules often form channels through the membrane for substances to pass to and from the cell. The protein molecules also act as identity markers or reception sites for other molecules such as hormones, which are important to those cells. This structure is often termed the 'fluid mosaic model' of the cell membrane.

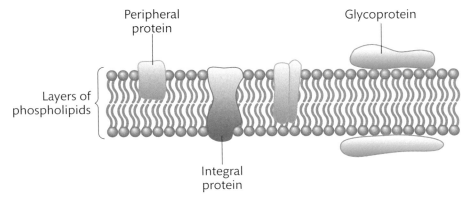

Peripheral protein

Glycoprotein

Layers of phospholipids

Integral protein

▶ **Figure 3.2** Model showing the structure of a cell membrane

Cytoplasm

Cytoplasm is a semi-fluid material, likened to a gel, capable of flowing slowly. Many chemical reactions are carried out here. The collective term for these reactions is **metabolism** and you will find that this term is frequently used in physiological and biological texts. Complex storage sugars, such as glycogen and melanin (the dark pigment responsible for skin and hair colour), are found in cytoplasm.

Nucleus

This is usually the largest structure inside the cell and, when viewed under a microscope, it stands out as a dark shape as it takes up dyes or stains very easily. Most cells have a single, central, spherical nucleus but there are many variations. Some muscle cells have many nuclei and are, therefore, called 'multinucleate'. Red blood cells and platelets do not have a nucleus and are said to be 'anucleate'. Some white blood cells have distinct, lobed nuclei. Apart from red blood cells and platelets (which cannot reproduce and have a limited lifespan), most cells separated from their nuclei will die.

The nuclear membrane has a structure similar to that of the cell membrane, but with gaps or pores, through which proteins and nucleic acids pass.

The cell is said to go through cycles of division (mitosis), replication (synthesis) and resting (interphase). When a cell is not dividing it is said to be 'resting' or interphase and the nuclear material appears like a thick, tangled mass and is called the **chromatin network**. A smaller, darker sphere is often visible, the nucleolus. This is a source of **ribonucleic acid (RNA)**, one of the nucleic acids. There may be more than one nucleolus present in some cells. When a cell is in the process of dividing (mitosis), the chromatin network separates into distinct black threads known as **chromosomes**.

There are 23 pairs of chromosomes in a human cell, containing specific sequences of **deoxyribonucleic acid (DNA)**, another nucleic acid. DNA is responsible for all our inherited characteristics, such as hair and eye colour. The sequences of DNA are our genes.

The nucleus controls nearly all the activities of the cell and has been likened to the architectural drawing or blueprint from which the cell operates.

Key terms

Metabolism – the sum of all the chemical reactions occurring in human physiology that involves using or releasing energy from chemical substances.

Chromatin network – the dark tangled mass seen in the nucleus of a resting cell.

Ribonucleic acid (RNA) – nucleic acid found in both the cell and the nucleus, responsible for the manufacture of cell proteins such as pigments, enzymes and hormones.

Chromosomes – long threads of DNA and protein seen in a dividing cell, which contain the genetic material, or genes, responsible for transmitting inherited characteristics.

Deoxyribonucleic acid (DNA) – nucleic acid found only in the chromatin network and chromosomes of the nucleus, which is responsible for the control of the cell, and passing on of inherited characteristics.

PAUSE POINT Which nucleic acids are found in cells?

Hint There are two different nucleic acids.

Extend Why are nucleic acids important in cells?

Cell organelles

Organelles are various components of a cell with a distinct structure and their own functions and can be likened to miniature organs (hence the term 'organelles').

Organelles include:

▸ centrioles

▸ mitochondria

▸ the endoplasmic reticulum

▸ ribosomes

▸ the Golgi apparatus

▸ lysosomes.

Before looking at the organelles in detail, you will see in Figure 3.3 a diagram of a typical cell as it might be seen under the electron microscope. Refer to the diagram as you learn about the organelles. Note that the magnification is still not sufficient to make out the full structure of the cell and nuclear membranes.

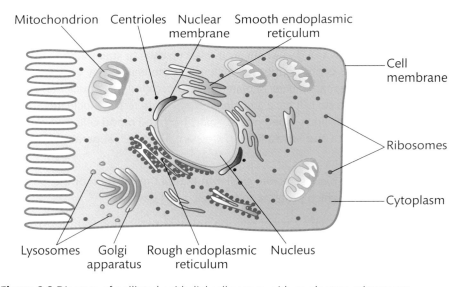

▸ **Figure 3.3** Diagram of a ciliated epithelial cell as seen with an electron microscope

<table>
<tr><td>

Key term

Centrioles – organelles that play an important part in spindle formation during cell division.

</td></tr>
</table>

Centrioles

Every cell in the body has two small organelles called **centrioles**. Centrioles play a part in cell division and are usually found near the cell nucleus lying at right angles to each other. However, they cannot be seen unless the cell is dividing when they may be seen through the microscope as one or two black dots. They are made of protein strands called microtubules (see Figure 3.4), which move to opposite ends of the cell at the start of cell division, where they make even more microtubules, which are known as the mitotic spindle. These threads connect to chromosomes to give the new cells formed the correct amount of DNA.

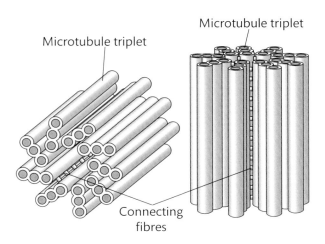

▶ **Figure 3.4** Structure of a centriole

Mitochondria

Every cell in the body has at least 1000 rod-shaped or spherical bodies, known as **mitochondria**, which are concerned with energy release. Very energy-active cells (like muscle and liver cells) will have many more. Each mitochondrion (singular) has a double-layered membrane, like the cell membrane but the inner layer is folded at intervals, producing a series of 'shelves' or ridges known as **cristae**. The enzymes responsible for the end stages of glucose oxidation (or cell respiration) are located on the cristae. The energy released from glucose is trapped and stored until required by a 'chemical battery' called **adenosine triphosphate (ATP)**. When energy is required for building complex molecules, or for doing work such as contracting muscles, the ATP breaks down to **adenosine diphosphate (ADP)**, releasing energy. The ADP is then recycled, to be built up once more into ATP, using the energy released from glucose.

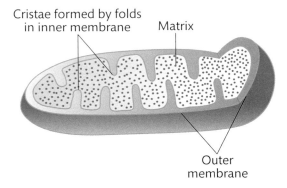

▶ **Figure 3.5** Structure of a mitochondrion

Endoplasmic reticulum (ER)

There are two variations, called rough and smooth ER. 'Endo-' means 'within' and 'reticulum' is a technical term for 'a network'. ER is a branching network that fills the cell interior. The membrane of the channels is similar in structure to the cell membrane and continuous with the nuclear membrane. The channels form passageways for transporting materials to and from different parts of the cell.

▶ Rough ER is studded with tiny black bodies, known as ribosomes, and has the function of making cell proteins and acting as a temporary storage area. Sometimes sugars are added to the cell proteins to make glycoproteins, in secretions such as mucus.

▶ Smooth ER has no attached ribosomes and is involved in the metabolism of lipids or fats.

Key terms

Mitochondria – spherical or rod-shaped bodies scattered in the cytoplasm, concerned with energy release.

Cristae – folds of the inner layer of mitochondrial membrane on which the enzymes responsible for the oxidation of glucose are situated.

Adenosine triphosphate (ATP) – a chemical in mitochondria capable of trapping and storing energy, to supply to the cell when needed.

Adenosine diphosphate (ADP) – a chemical left after ATP has released its stored energy to do work.

Ribosomes

There are thousands of ribosomes in a cell. They are only visible with an electron microscope and appear as black bodies located on the rough ER, or lying free in the cytoplasm. They contain different forms of RNA and their role is to manufacture proteins, as instructed by the DNA in the nucleus. Proteins are part of the cell structure – they are important for growth and repair of cells. Enzymes and peptide hormones are proteins that are important in physiological processes such as digestion.

Golgi apparatus

Like the ER, the Golgi apparatus is responsible for packaging proteins for delivery to other organelles. It appears as a series of flattened, fluid-filled sacs stacked like pancakes. Many tiny fluid-filled globules or bags lie close to the main stack and these are often known as vesicles. The Golgi apparatus is also responsible for producing lysosomes.

Lysosomes

Lysosomes can be found in all parts of the cell cytoplasm and are also small vesicles produced by part of the Golgi apparatus. Because they contain powerful enzymes capable of digesting all major chemical components of living cells, they are sometimes called 'suicide bags'. Lysosomes can travel freely throughout the cell and, by releasing their contents they can destroy old or damaged organelles and even entire cells. Another of their functions is to destroy bacteria and other foreign materials, such as carbon particles, that enter the cell. They do this by taking the foreign matter into their vesicles. After destroying the foreign matter with their enzymes, the lysosomes release the digested or broken-down material.

Some types of white blood cells – phagocytes (literally 'eating cells') and monocytes – and tissue cells known as macrophages (meaning 'large eaters') are loaded with lysosomes because their function is to destroy bacteria, viruses and foreign material entering the body cells and tissues.

Many disease-causing agents are thought to be capable of damaging lysosome membranes, bringing about internal cell destruction.

> **Reflect**
>
> The electron microscope enables you to see extremely small objects to identify their structure but it does not tell you what the structures do. Researchers with a range of expertise (such as chemists, physicists and biochemists) have to separate out the different structures and carry out many tests to identify the functions of the tiny objects they observe.

❚❚ PAUSE POINT   Identify the organelles in a cell that will remove old worn-out parts of cells and foreign materials.

   There are many of these organelles scattered throughout the cytoplasm. They are linked to the Golgi apparatus.

Extend   Can you think of some types of cells or organs where these might exist in larger numbers?

Characteristics of tissues

Tissues are groups of similar cells carrying out specific functions. In this unit, you will learn about the following tissues:

- epithelial
- muscle
- connective
- nervous.

Epithelial tissues

Epithelia are the linings of internal and external surfaces and body cavities, including ducts (tubes or channels) carrying secretions from glands. They may be composed of several layers of cells, called compound epithelia, or just a single layer known as simple epithelia. The lowest or bottom layer of cells is attached to a basement membrane for support and connection. Part of the basement membrane is secreted by the epithelial cells. There are nerve supplies to epithelia but they are supplied with oxygen and nutrients from deeper tissues by **diffusion**. As they are surface tissues and exposed to friction, their capacity for growth and repair is greater than other tissues and usually occurs during sleep.

Simple epithelia

Simple epithelial cells may be squamous, cuboidal, columnar or ciliated. Squamous epithelial cells are very flat, with each nucleus forming a lump in the centre (see Figure 3.6). (Squamous means scaly and refers to the flatness of the cells, which fit together closely rather like crazy paving.) Clearly, such delicate thin cells cannot offer much protection and their chief function is to allow materials to pass through via diffusion and **osmosis**. Simple squamous epithelium is found in the walls of:

▶ lung alveoli

▶ blood capillaries

▶ Bowman's capsules of nephrons.

As their name suggests, cuboidal epithelial cells are cube-shaped, with spherical nuclei. They often line ducts and tubes and can allow materials to pass through in a similar way to squamous epithelia. They often occur in glandular tissues making secretions. For example, they can be found in:

▶ kidney tubules

▶ sweat ducts

▶ the thyroid gland and breast tissue.

> **Key term**
>
> **Diffusion** – the passage of molecules from a high concentration to a low concentration.

> **Key term**
>
> **Osmosis** – the passage of water molecules from a region of high concentration (of water molecules) to one of low concentration through a partially permeable membrane, such as the cell membrane of simple epithelial cells.

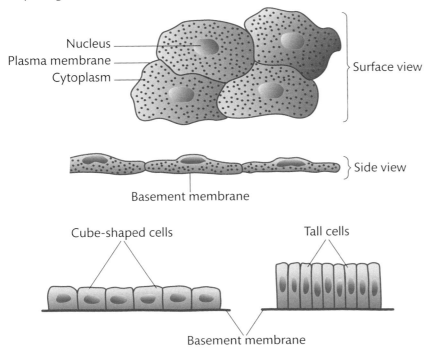

▶ **Figure 3.6** Simple squamous, cuboidal and columnar epithelia

Columnar epithelial cells are much taller, with slightly oval nuclei. They can often be associated with microscopic filaments known as cilia and are then called ciliated epithelia. Cilia move in wave-like motions, beating towards the orifices. They are commonly found associated with goblet cells, which secrete mucus in the respiratory and alimentary tracts. The mucus traps unwanted particles like carbon, and the cilia transport the flow of 'dirty' mucus towards the exterior.

Columnar cells are found lining:
▶ the trachea and bronchi
▶ villi in the small intestine.

Compound epithelia

The principal function of compound epithelia is to protect deeper structures and multiple layers of cells, and to hamper the passage of materials. The vagina, mouth, tongue and oesophagus are lined by stratified epithelia consisting of layers of squamous, cuboidal or columnar cells, which gradually become flattened by pressure from below as they reach the surface. The lowest layer of cells on the basement membrane actively divides and the older cells are pushed upwards. This type of epithelium is usually a pink colour and is often termed mucous membrane.

The skin has an outer layer of epithelium similar in structure to the stratified epithelium but with the important addition of a layer of flattened dead cells on the outside. This is known as the epidermis. As the cells advance from the basement membrane, they gradually become filled with a protein called keratin and are said to be keratinised, or cornified. This layer is vital to prevent micro organisms invading deeper structures, and it has a waterproofing effect on the skin. The skin can be variously coloured, with pigment produced by pigment cells in the lowest layer. For example, the pigment melanin darkens under the influence of the sun. The numbers of pigment cells in the skin is genetically inherited, although they can divide and increase during exposure to sunshine.

Link

You can learn more about the structure and function of skin in section B, Body control.

Connective tissues

These tissues are the most widely distributed in the body and lie beneath the epithelial tissues, connecting different parts of the internal structure.

Various types of cells lie in a background material known as a matrix. The matrix may be liquid as in blood, jelly-like as in areolar tissue, firm as in cartilage or hard as in bone. The matrix of a tissue is usually secreted by the connective tissue cells.

The functions of these tissues are to transport materials (as in blood), give support (as in areolar tissue and cartilage), and strengthen and protect (as in bone). Many tissues contain different fibres secreted by the cells to provide special characteristics.

In this unit, you will learn about the connective tissues of:
▶ blood
▶ cartilage
▶ bone
▶ areolar tissue
▶ adipose tissue (fatty tissue).

Blood

Blood consists of straw-coloured plasma (the matrix), in which several types of blood cells are carried. Plasma is mainly water in which various substances are carried, such as dissolved gases like oxygen and carbon dioxide, nutrients like glucose and amino acids, salts, enzymes and hormones. There is also a combination of important proteins, collectively known as the plasma proteins, which have roles in blood clotting, transport, defence against invading organisms (part of the immune system) and osmotic regulation.

The most numerous cells by far in the plasma are red blood cells, also known as erythrocytes. These are very small cells with an elastic membrane, which is important because the membrane often has to distort to travel through the smallest capillaries. Erythrocytes have no nucleus in their mature state. The loss of a nucleus produces a depression in the top and bottom of the cell, making them biconcave, which provides a larger surface area to be exposed to oxygen. They are packed with haemoglobin, which gives them a red colour. (This is why blood is red.) In oxygenated blood (**arterial blood**), the oxygen and haemoglobin form the compound oxyhaemoglobin, which is bright red. In deoxygenated blood (**venous blood**), after the dissolved oxygen is delivered to body cells, the reduced haemoglobin is dark red in colour.

Due to the absence of nuclei, erythrocytes cannot divide and have a limited lifespan of around 120 days.

White blood cells (or leucocytes) are larger, nucleated and less numerous. There are several types but the most numerous are the granulocytes (also known as polymorphs, neutrophils and phagocytes). They are called granulocytes because they contain granules in their cytoplasm, as well as lobed nuclei. They are capable of changing their shape and engulfing foreign material, such as bacteria and carbon particles. This process is known as phagocytosis. A granulocyte acts rather like an amoeba and is sometimes said to be amoeboid. Granulocytes, because of their ability to engulf microbes and foreign material, are very important in defending the body against infection. The number of granulocytes increases significantly during infections and a blood count may be valuable in diagnosis.

Lymphocytes are smaller white blood cells with round nuclei and clear cytoplasm – they assist in the production of antibodies. Antigens are found on the surface coats of disease-causing microbes or pathogens and act as identity markers for different types of pathogens (rather like name tags on a school uniform). Antibodies neutralise antigens and prevent the microbes from multiplying. They can then be phagocytosed by granulocytes and monocytes. Antibodies are chemically globulins (types of protein carried in the plasma).

In a completely different way from granulocytes, lymphocytes also contribute to the defence of the body because of their role in the production of antibodies. They form an important part of the immune system.

Monocytes are another type of white blood cell, larger than lymphocytes. They also have large, round nuclei and clear cytoplasm. They are very efficient at phagocytosis of foreign material and, like granulocytes, can leave the circulatory blood vessels to travel to the site of an infection and begin phagocytosing pathogens very rapidly.

Thrombocytes are not true cells but are usually classed with the white blood cells. They are more commonly called platelets. They are products of much larger cells that have broken up and they have an important role in blood clotting.

Granulocytes, monocytes and red blood cells are all made in the bone marrow. Lymphocytes are produced by the lymphoid tissue, for example in the spleen.

Key terms
Arterial blood – flows from the heart and is usually bright red oxygenated blood.
Venous blood – flows towards the heart and is usually dark red deoxygenated blood.

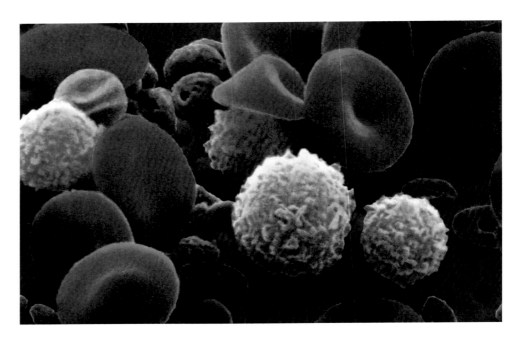

▶ **Figure 3.7** Blood cells

Reflect

Doctors often take samples of blood if they suspect a service user has an infection. What changes in blood counts would you expect to see if the service user has an infection such as pneumonia?

Cartilage

This is the smooth, translucent, firm substance that protects bone ends from friction during movement, and forms the major part of the nose and the external ear flaps, called pinnae. The matrix is secreted by cartilage cells called chondrocytes and is a firm but flexible glass-like material of chondrin (a protein). ('Chondro-' is a prefix associated with cartilage.) The cells become trapped in the matrix and sometimes divide into two or four cells, giving a very characteristic appearance. It does not contain blood vessels and is nourished by diffusion from underlying bone.

Bone

Bone is a much harder substance than cartilage but it can be worn away by friction. The rigid matrix has two major components:

▶ calcium salts, which form around collagen fibres and give bone its hardness

▶ collagen fibres, which offer some ability to bend under strain and prevent bone from being too brittle and, therefore, likely to fracture.

Osteocytes (or bone cells) are trapped in the hard matrix on concentric rings called lamellae. A system of these rings is known as a Haversian system or osteone. (Osteo- is a prefix associated with bone.) Blood vessels and nerves pass through the hollow centre of each osteone.

Bone is designed to bear weight and the limb bones are hollow like girders (the strongest mechanical structures). Bone is also used to protect vital weaker tissues such as the brain, lungs and heart. Bones contain marrow in their central hollow. In some bones, the marrow makes vital blood cells.

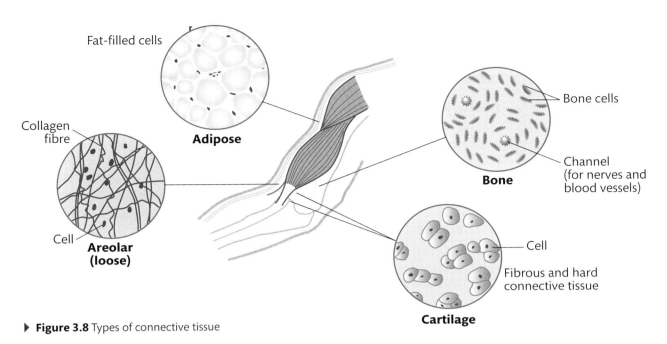

▶ **Figure 3.8** Types of connective tissue

Areolar tissue

This is the most common tissue in the body and you have probably never heard of it before! If you eat meat, you will have seen it many times. It is the sticky, white material that binds muscle groups, blood vessels and nerves together. The matrix is semi-fluid and it contains **collagen** fibres and elastic fibres secreted by the cells found in this loose connective tissue. Elastic fibres give flexibility to the tissue, which is located around more mobile structures. The deeper skin layer known as the dermis is a denser type of areolar tissue, with extra fibres and cells. Areolar tissue offers a degree of support to the tissues it surrounds.

> **Key term**
>
> **Collagen** – structural protein in the form of fibres for extra strength.

Adipose tissue

Adipose is a technical term for fatty tissue and it is a variation of areolar tissue, in which the adipose (or fat) cells have multiplied to obscure other cells and fibres. When mature, an adipose cell becomes so loaded with fat that the nucleus is pushed to one side and, as fat is translucent, the cell takes on a distinctive 'signet ring' appearance. Adipose tissue is common under the skin and around organs such as the heart, kidneys and parts of the digestive tract. It helps to insulate the body against changes of external temperature, acts as a 'hydraulic shock absorber' to protect against injury, and is also a 'high-energy storage depot'.

⏸ PAUSE POINT   Compare and contrast two connective tissues – blood and cartilage.

> **Hint**   Consider the types of matrix, the types of cells and main functions.
>
> **Extend**   Cartilage does not contain blood vessels. How does cartilage receive the nutrients it requires?

Muscle tissue

Muscle is an excitable tissue because it is capable of responding to stimuli. There are three different types of muscle in the human body:

▶ striated

▶ non-striated

▶ cardiac.

Each is composed of muscle fibres that are capable of shortening (or contracting) and returning to their original state (known as relaxation). Contraction causes movement of the skeleton, soft tissue, blood or specific material such as urine, food and faeces. Muscle has both blood and nerve supplies.

Striated muscle

Most striated muscle (also called voluntary, skeletal or striped muscle) is attached to the bones of the skeleton, although some facial muscles are attached to skin. Striated muscle makes up the familiar animal meat seen in the butcher's shop. This type of muscle will contract when it receives nerve impulses controlled by conscious thought from the **central nervous system** – hence its alternative name of voluntary muscle. The name striated means 'striped'. Each individual fibre shows alternate dark and light banding from the muscle protein filaments from which it is made.

Each fibre is cylindrical and multinucleate, lying parallel to its neighbours. There may be hundreds or thousands of fibres in a muscle, depending on its size. Some fibres are 30 centimetres long and one-hundredth of a millimetre wide. Muscle fibres contain many thousands of mitochondria to supply ATP for the energy used in muscular contraction.

Key term

Central nervous system – the brain and spinal cord.

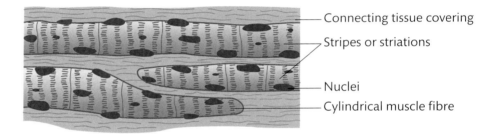

Connecting tissue covering
Stripes or striations
Nuclei
Cylindrical muscle fibre

▶ **Figure 3.9** Striated muscle tissue

Non-striated muscle

Although this type of muscle tissue (also called involuntary, smooth or plain muscle) still contains protein filaments, they do not lie in an ordered pattern and, therefore, do not produce the banding that is characteristic of striated muscle. The muscle fibres are spindle or cigar shaped, with single central nuclei, and dovetail with each other. This type of muscle tends to form sheets. Although still requiring nervous stimulation to effect contraction, it is not under conscious thought, but supplied by the **autonomic nervous system** (which is why it is called involuntary muscle). This type of muscle is found around hollow internal organs such as the stomach, intestines, iris of the eye, bladder and uterus. It is not attached to bones.

Key term

Autonomic nervous system – part of the nervous system responsible for controlling the internal organs.

Nucleus

Connecting tissue

Smooth muscle cells

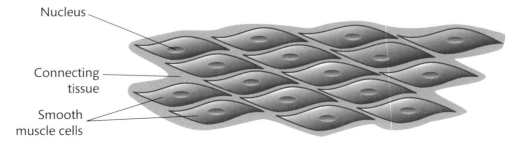

▶ **Figure 3.10** Non-striated muscle tissue

Non-striated muscle frequently occurs in two sheets running in different directions, known as **antagonistic muscles**. In the digestive tract, one sheet runs in a circular fashion around the intestines, while another outer sheet runs down the length. The two sheets are said to work antagonistically (against each other) to propel the food contents down the tract. This type of movement is known as peristalsis.

In the iris of the eye, one set of muscle runs radially outwards from the centre like the spokes of a wheel, while the other set runs in a circular fashion around the central pupil. This arrangement allows for the control of light entering the eye, causing the pupil to dilate (open) and allow in more light, or to constrict (narrow) allowing less light.

Cardiac muscle

This type of muscle, also called myocardial muscle, is found only in the four chambers (atria and ventricles) of the heart. It is said to be myogenic because it can rhythmically contract without receiving any nervous stimuli, and in this it differs from other muscle. The muscle cells branch repeatedly to form a network through which contraction spreads rapidly. Each cell has a central nucleus and is both horizontally and vertically striped. The divisions between cells are known as intercalated discs and are specially adapted for transmission of impulses.

Under normal healthy circumstances, cardiac muscle is not allowed to contract myogenically because the atrial or upper chamber muscle has a different contraction rate to that of the lower ventricular muscle and this would lead to inefficient and uncoordinated heart action. The autonomic nervous system controls the rate of contraction via the nerves in order to adapt the flow of blood to specific circumstances such as rest and exercise.

> **Key term**
>
> **Antagonistic muscles** – one muscle, or a sheet of muscles, contracts while the opposing muscle or sheet relaxes. For example, when the biceps contract the triceps relax.

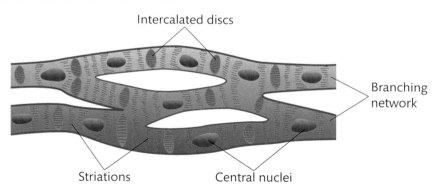

Intercalated discs

Branching network

Striations   Central nuclei

▶ **Figure 3.11** Cardiac muscle

🔘 **PAUSE POINT**   Explain the special features of cardiac muscle that allow the whole of the heart to contract very rapidly.

Hint   Compare the structure of cardiac muscle with other types of muscle.

Extend   Research the conduction system through the heart, key terms: sinoatrial node, atrioventricular node and the bundle of His.

> **Reflect**
>
> When muscles contract regularly such as during exercise, they produce heat, which contributes to maintaining body temperature. Glucose can be stored in muscles as a more complex molecule called glycogen.

Nervous tissue

Nervous tissue is only found in the nervous system, which consists of the brain, spinal cord and nerves. Receiving stimuli from both external and internal sources, it serves to create consistency (particularly regarding **homeostasis**), co-ordination, and communication between different parts of the body. The nervous system interprets stimuli from the sense organs so that vision, hearing, smell and the other senses become apparent.

Nervous tissue is composed of:

▶ neuron(s) – highly specialised nerve cells that transmit nervous impulses. They are present only in the brain and spinal cord, but their long processes (nerve fibres) form the nerves

▶ neuroglia – also known as glia or glial cells, connective tissue cells, intermingled with neurons in the brain and spinal cord, that offer support and protection, form **myelin** and assist in homeostasis.

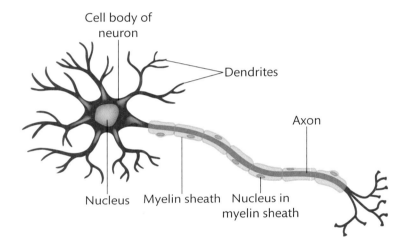

▶ **Figure 3.12** General structure of a neuron

The structure and function of body organs

You will need to know the location, structure and function of major organs. The details of the organs will primarily be found in the sections on body systems but Table 3.1 provides a summary of this information.

▶ **Table 3.1** The location, structure and function of the major body organs

Name of organ	Location of organ	Structure of organ	Main functions
Heart	Between the lungs in the chest, with apex to the left.	Cardiac muscle and epithelial linings.	Pumps blood to the lungs and round the body.
Lungs	One on either side of the heart, filling the chest cavity.	Simple epithelia and elastic fibres allowing expansion and contraction.	Inhalation and exhalation of gases linked to respiration.
Brain	Inside the skull, in the head.	Nervous tissue consisting of neurons and neuroglia.	Receives and sends nervous impulses as a means of communication.
Stomach	In abdomen, on left side beneath the diaphragm.	Non-striated muscle in three layers, epithelium, gastric glands.	Churns and mixes food into a paste (chyme), begins digestion.
Liver	In the abdomen, on right side beneath the diaphragm.	Cuboid epithelial cells in lobules.	Large number of functions such as secretes bile and salts, stores glycogen etc.

▶ **Table 3.1** – *continued*

Pancreas	Lies between the stomach and duodenum on left side of abdomen.	Glandular epithelium.	Secretes digestive juice down ducts to small intestine, also secretes insulin and glucagon.
Duodenum	C-shaped part of the small intestine lying beyond the stomach.	Two coats of non-striated muscle, lined by columnar epithelium.	Passes chyme to ileum and secretes major digestive secretions.
Ileum	Long coiled part of the small intestine joined to duodenum.	Two coats of non-striated muscle, and villi lined by columnar epithelium.	Passes undigested chyme to colon. Absorbs nutrients into bloodstream.
Colon	Joins to ileum in right-hand side of the abdomen, runs up to the liver in front of the stomach and down the left side to join with the rectum.	Two coats of non-striated muscle, but outercoat not complete.	Absorbs water, producing semi-solid faeces.
Kidneys	One on each side of the back wall of the abdomen below diaphragm. Left kidney is higher than the right, due to position of the liver.	Composed of nephrons.	Eliminate waste products and water, maintaining homeostasis.
Bladder	Lies centrally at front of lower pelvis.	Non-striated muscle lined by epithelium.	Collects and stores urine until appropriate time for release.
Ovaries	One on each side of the pelvis below the kidneys.	Connective tissues and blood vessels, epithelial cells that form follicles.	Produce ova or eggs, secrete hormones.
Testes	One on either side of penis, in skin sac called the scrotum. Lie outside the body cavity.	Connective tissues and blood vessels, epithelial cell forming convoluted seminiferous tubules.	Produce spermatozoa, secrete hormones.
Uterus	Centrally in the pelvis connected on each side to ovaries by oviducts (Fallopian tubes).	Non-striated muscle lined by special epithelium.	Produces new epithelium monthly, supports and protects foetus until birth, contracts powerfully to expel foetus and placenta during birth.
Skin	Covers whole body.	Keratinised, compound epithelium above dermis of areolar tissue.	Water – and bacteria-proof covering, assists body temperature regulation and homeostasis.

Energy in the body

Energy can exist in several forms and chemical energy is the most common. This energy is in the chemical bond that unites atoms or molecules with each other. When a new bond is made between two atoms, energy is required to form it. This is usually in the form of heat, although light and electrical energy can be used. When a bond is broken and atoms are released, the energy in the bond is released as well. Forms of energy include heat, light, sound, electrical and nuclear energy.

Transformation of energy

Energy can neither be created nor destroyed – it merely changes its form. This is known as the law of conservation of energy. Think about placing a lump of wood or coal on a fire, as the wood burns it gives out heat and light and makes a crackling sound. The chemical energy trapped within the wood has been released by burning to give heat, light and sound. The chemical energy of the wood was formed using the sun's rays in the process of photosynthesis and stored as glucose.

Discussion

Discuss the transformation of energy from the sun to handclapping at a concert.

Energy metabolism

The role of energy in the body

At this stage, you may be wondering why there is so much emphasis on energy and be thinking that it is only concerned with muscular activity and movement. However, energy is also needed to circulate blood, lymph and tissue fluid throughout the body, it is necessary for breathing and taking in oxygen, it is necessary for making new cells for carrying out growth and repair, it is used to transmit nerve impulses so that you can respond to changes in the environment and it is needed to build different complex molecules, such as enzymes and hormones, from the simple molecules produced after the digestion of food.

Anabolism and catabolism

You have already learned about metabolism and how some chemical reactions involve breaking down molecules and releasing energy – these are **catabolic** reactions. The oxidation of glucose inside cells is a catabolic reaction and there are many more. The opposite process is building complex molecules from simple substances and using energy – these are **anabolic** reactions.

Key terms

Catabolism – the breaking down of molecules into smaller units, releasing energy.

Anabolism – the building up of complex molecules using the energy released in catabolism.

Case study

An illustration of energy forms

Ian slid down a climbing rope in the gym wearing only a vest and shorts. A little while later, he noticed that the skin on his hands and inner legs was red, swollen and painful. Ian had friction burns from the slide. The kinetic (motion) energy had been partly converted into heat energy, which had caused the burn. Friction is the resistance to motion when two bodies are in contact.

Check your knowledge

1 Which two items were in contact to cause the friction burn?

2 Name the two forms of energy in the slide and the relationship between them.

3 What is the name given to the law associated with this example?

4 What type of energy had Ian used to climb the rope?

Aerobic and anaerobic respiration

Aerobic respiration uses oxygen to release energy from glucose but this can only take place inside cells as many cellular enzymes are required. The energy is used to do the work of the cells, tissues, organs and organ systems. All cells respire aerobically producing water, carbon dioxide and energy as products. However, there are some cells that, when they are very active, use up energy faster than the body can take in oxygen by breathing. These are striated muscle cells and this happens during vigorous exercise such as a 100 m sprint. For a short time these muscle cells can respire anaerobically, that is, without oxygen. Once again, many cellular enzymes are needed but the products formed are energy and lactic acid. The body and blood can only tolerate certain levels of acidity for the enzymes to work efficiently, so this is the reason why anaerobic respiration can only occur for short periods of time. Anaerobic respiration is less efficient than aerobic and produces less energy.

> **Reflect**
>
> Observe video footage of short-distance sprinters. The fastest sprinters do not take a breath until the race is over – they are running anaerobically. Why is this not possible for an 800 m race?

> **Research**
>
> Find out what happens to the lactic acid produced after an athlete like Usain Bolt has run a 100 m race anaerobically.

Basal metabolic rate

Cells require energy for living processes. Even when the body appears to be totally inactive, energy is being used to pump blood round the body, breathe, digest food, produce urine etc. This amount of energy is known as basal metabolism and it varies with age, size and gender. When asleep for approximately eight hours, the average energy consumption is 2400 kJ, which would equate to 2400 x 3 for a 24-hour day, making 7200 kJ when there has been no physical activity. Energy is usually measured in kilojoules (kJ), which replaced calories.

However, on a normal day there are eight hours of being physically inactive such as watching TV, texting or reading – using 3000 kJ, and a further active eight-hour period using 6600 kJ. This means a total energy consumption of 12 000 kJ per day. Men require more kJ than women as they are physically bigger and have a greater surface area for losing heat. Very active occupations such as labouring or blacksmithing will need more energy, as will playing sports.

Human genetics

Genetics is the name given to the biological study of heredity, including attempting to predict the characteristics of offspring from mating. In the mid-19th century Gregor Mendel, an Austrian monk, studied how the characteristics of pea plants were passed on in each generation of plant. Mendel is considered to be the founding father of genetics. (Remember that the structure of DNA was only discovered in 1953.)

Principles of Mendelian inheritance

In each sperm and ovum there is a single set of chromosomes (haploid state) and when fertilisation occurs the resulting zygote will have two sets (the diploid state) – one from the mother and one from the father. A specific place on each chromosome represents a characteristic, such as handedness (which hand will be dominant) and this location, known as a **gene**, must have two parts or halves called **alleles**.

The two alleles might have the same characteristic, when they are known as **homozygous**, or have two different characteristics, called **heterozygous**. Some characteristics show in the offspring while others do not. Those that show, such as right-handedness, are said to be **dominant** alleles and those that only show when

> **Key terms**
>
> **Gene** – unit of heredity on a pair of chromosomes.
>
> **Allele** – half a gene, or the location of a characteristic on one chromosome.
>
> **Homozygous** – having two dominant or recessive alleles.
>
> **Heterozygous** – having one dominant and one recessive allele.
>
> **Dominant** – the allele that, when present, displays in the individual.

Recessive – an allele that does not show when a dominant allele is present.

Punnett square – a diagram, named after the British geneticist Reginald C. Punnett, used to determine the probability of an offspring having a particular genotype.

dominant alleles are absent, such as left-handedness, are known as **recessive** alleles. When representing alleles, it is common to use an upper case initial letter for a dominant allele and a lower case for the recessive allele.

Using R to represent right-handedness alleles, and r for left-handedness alleles, we find that:

▶ right-handedness could be RR (homozygous dominant) or Rr (heterozygous)
▶ left-handedness could be rr (homozygous recessive).

Any sperm can fertilise any ovum so all combinations must be considered. A **Punnett square** is a visual representation of the potential combinations.

▶ Punnet square **A**

Sperm and ovum	R	r
R	RR	Rr
R	RR	Rr

▶ Punnet square **B**

Sperm and ovum	r	r
R	Rr	Rr
R	Rr	Rr

Square **A** represents the potential offspring of two right-handed people. Where one person is homozygous dominant and the other is heterozygous all the offspring will be right-handed, although half are heterozygous and half homozygous.

Square **B** represents two different homozygous parents. They will have all right-handed heterozygous children despite one parent being left-handed rr. However, if one of these children mated with another heterozygous right-hander, 25 per cent of their offspring could be left-handed. It is usually the case that transmission of recessive alleles misses a generation.

Remember when looking at the predictions of offspring and inherited characteristics, any sperm (carrying an allele) can fertilise any ovum (also carrying an allele) and the statistics are only valid for very large numbers of people.

Reflect

Can you construct a Punnett square for predicting the offspring of two heterozygous parents?

Externally, nobody can tell the difference between Rr and RR, both appear right-handed and this is said to be the **phenotype**. However, genetically there is a difference, and RR and Rr are said to be the **genotypes** for handedness.

Genetic variation

A spontaneous or unplanned change in a gene or a chromosome is known as a mutation and usually has a harmful effect in humans. There are 23 pairs of chromosomes in human cells and most mutations occur during cell division when the copying of DNA in chromosomes and genes goes wrong. If the mutation happens in a body cell the effect will be minimal, and only cause harmful effects in the new cells resulting from the divisions of that cell. However, if the mutation occurs during the formation of sperm or ova (known as **gametes**) and that gamete becomes a **zygote** that divides multiple times to form a new human being then every cell in that

Key terms

Phenotype – the outward display of a characteristic that is observable.

Genotype – an individual's genes, which are not outwardly observable, or the identification of alleles an individual inherits for a gene.

Gamete – reproductive or sex cells, each cell is haploid and carries only one copy of each chromosome.

Zygote – cell produced when a sperm fertilises an ovum, it contains all the genetic material for a new individual – half from the sperm and half from the ovum.

individual will carry the mutation. When the mutation affects a gene this is a genetic or gene mutation. Sometimes a mutation happens in a chromosome and this has serious effects. A piece of chromosome breaks off or joins with another during cell division. The number of chromosomes is vital to the species and incorrect numbers are often devastating to normal anatomy and physiology.

Genetic and chromosome disorders

Down's syndrome

Down's syndrome is caused by a chromosome mutation resulting from an extra chromosome at the 21st pair, instead of 46 chromosomes in total there are 47. A syndrome is a group of characteristics and in this instance short height, flattened nose and high cheek bones together with wide hands and folds of skin around the upper eyelids give rise to a characteristic look. Individuals with Down's syndrome have learning disabilities and often heart defects. Pregnant women who are older have a greater risk of having babies with Down's syndrome, possibly because their ova are quite old. A baby girl is born with her quota of immature ova, she does not make any more as she ages.

> **Research**
>
> Older mothers-to-be are offered tests for genetic disorders such as Down's syndrome. What are these tests? What might be the disadvantages of having the test?

Phenylketonuria (PKU)

Phenylketonuria is a genetic disorder caused by a recessive allele that makes an affected individual unable to process an amino acid called phenylalanine. Consequently, infants who are affected develop a high level of phenylalanine in their blood, causing damage to the brain and severe mental disabilities. By providing a diet without phenylalanine this can be avoided, so all newborn babies are tested for the condition at birth, using the blood from a small heel prick.

> **Research**
>
> Find out which foods a child with PKU must avoid eating.

Sickle cell disease

Sickle cell anaemia is caused by a defective allele that interferes with the normal production of red blood cells, which carry oxygen in the blood. The abnormal haemoglobin is contained inside crescent-shaped red blood cells that are short-lived and not replaced as quickly. The abnormal cells are unable to bend and flex like normal red blood cells and get stuck in the smaller blood vessels such as the capillaries and arterioles, causing damage to body cells and intense pain (a sickle cell crisis). It is most common in African, Caribbean and Mediterranean populations. The sickle cell allele is a recessive allele. To inherit full sickle cell anaemia an individual must inherit both alleles from both parents. However, inheriting one allele gives what is known as the sickle cell trait in which the individual will produce some sickled cells but which contain normal haemoglobin. This individual may pass the allele on to their children and, if they have offspring with another individual with the sickle cell trait, then a child could have sickle cell anaemia. The effects of sickle cell anaemia are breathlessness, lack of energy and tiredness – all worse after exertion. Individuals have an increased risk of stroke and infections. Pregnant women are offered screening tests for this disorder.

Cystic fibrosis

Cystic fibrosis is a genetic disorder that mainly affects white people in Northern Europe. It is a serious condition caused by a recessive allele so both parents must possess this faulty allele. Individuals with one faulty allele may not know that they have it and are unaffected by it. They are often called 'carriers'. Various glands are affected by this fault, chiefly the glands lining the bronchi, which produce very thick mucus (phlegm) that is difficult to cough up. Therefore, respiratory infections are common. The pancreas is also affected and the pancreatic enzymes are inadequate for digestion. The main treatments are physiotherapy to aid in mucus removal and pancreatic medication. In severe cases, a lung transplant may be needed. Generally life expectancy is shorter than average.

Huntington's chorea now known as Huntington's disease

This is a rare genetic disorder with a delayed onset that is caused by a faulty dominant allele. Individuals are usually in their 40s before the signs and symptoms are apparent. This means it is likely that they may already have children. The incidence of offspring developing the disease is 50 per cent. The faulty allele causes brain damage resulting in personality changes, irritability, mood swings, dementia and fidgety or jerky movements (chorea).

PAUSE POINT   Explain the difference between an individual's phenotype and genotype.

> **Hint**   You could use a simple example such as having brown eyes which is dominant and blue eyes which is recessive.
>
> **Extend**   Some genetic disorders are carried on the so-called sex chromosomes X and Y. Find out some sex-linked disorders.

Diagnostic testing for genetic and chromosome disorders

There are many ways that diagnosis can be achieved for genetic and chromosome disorders including blood tests, considering signs and symptoms and using scans. PKU can be diagnosed shortly after birth using a heel prick blood test to look for high levels of phenylalanine. Sickle cell anaemia can be diagnosed by a blood test that identifies red blood cells that show sickling. A sweat test is used to diagnose cystic fibrosis looking to see if the individual's sweat is abnormally salty. There are specific external features that may provide a diagnosis for Down's syndrome. Huntington's disease can now be confirmed by chorionic villus sampling. This technique, and amniocentesis, provide information about several genetic and chromosome disorders. Genetic counselling will ensure that prospective parents are fully informed about their options.

Chorionic villus sampling (CVS)

This prenatal test involves taking a small sample of cells from the placenta after the tenth week of pregnancy. The chorion and amnion are two membranes surrounding a developing foetus. The chorion has tiny protuberances known as villi that form part of the placenta. The placenta is located by ultrasound or endoscopy and a small sample of villi are removed, either via the abdominal wall or through the cervix. The cells of the villi have the same genetic makeup as the foetus. Once the sample has been prepared in the laboratory, the chromosomes can be extracted and paired up to form a karyotype or chromosomal picture. Correct genetic counselling can be given and the parents can be offered a termination to avoid disorders. There are some risks involved in CVS, such as miscarriage and infection, which must be explained before the test is carried out. However, the technique can be carried out sooner in the pregnancy than amniocentesis.

Amniocentesis

In this technique, a hollow needle is used to take samples of amniotic fluid through the abdominal and uterine wall. The amniotic fluid surrounds the foetus and contains flaked-off skin cells from the foetus that can be grown in a laboratory and then examined after processing. The amniotic fluid may also be analysed by biochemical tests, such as for bilirubin and alpha-fetoprotein to exclude other congenital disorders. Women should be informed that the additional risk of miscarriage following CVS may be slightly higher than that of amniocentesis carried out after 15 weeks gestation. However, as the test can only be carried out between the 15th and 20th week of pregnancy if it is positive for a disorder and termination of the pregnancy is chosen, then it will be at a much later stage of pregnancy and is likely to be more distressing.

Assessment practice 3.1

1 Explain the main function of striated muscle.

2 Which types of connective tissue occur in the skeleton?

3 Identify the cells present in brain tissue.

4 Compare the processes of osmosis and diffusion.

5 Identify the type of organelle inside a cell that is responsible for releasing energy.

6 Explain the importance of mucus in the body.

7 Describe a tissue associated with the flow of mucus.

8 In which genetic disorder is the composition of mucus a problem?

9 Outline the key features of the genetic disorder identified in question 8.

The structure, function and disorders of body systems

You will learn about ten body systems and how the internal composition of the body, often called the internal environment, is kept within a narrow range of limits. These limits are essentially to make sure that enzymes controlling metabolism are working to the best of their ability. People tend to think of enzymes in terms of digesting food, which they do, however, cellular enzymes control all the chemical reactions taking place in the body and there are at least a thousand in each cell.

Homeostatic mechanisms

Definition of homeostasis

Homeostasis is the technical term for the process of maintaining a constant internal environment despite external changes.

Internal environment

The 'internal environment' comprises blood, tissue fluid, body cell contents and all the metabolic processes taking place.

It is important to realise that the use of the term 'constant' in this context is not absolute and fixed. It is more flexible and dynamic and refers to the physical and chemical composition of the body being kept within a limited range of variables for maximum efficiency and well-being of the whole body and, indeed, maintaining life itself. This limited range of variables is regulated by homeostasis.

The concept of negative feedback as regulatory mechanism

Negative feedback occurs when an important variable, sometimes known as a key variable, such as the pH of blood and tissue fluid, deviates from the accepted range or limits, and triggers responses that return the variable to within the normal range. In other words, deviation produces a negative response to counteract or nullify the deviation. It is a 'feeding back' of the disturbance to the status quo. When you study the liver, as part of the digestive system, you will learn that when blood glucose levels fall, the liver glycogen is converted into glucose, in order to top up crucial energy levels in cells. This is an example of a negative feedback system and you will study this further in due course.

The brain and nervous system play a vital role in controlling homeostatic mechanisms and they also help you to anticipate when key variables might rise or fall beyond the accepted range. For example, if it is several hours since your last meal and you are beginning to feel tired and cold, you will try to eat a warm, energy-giving meal to counteract these feelings. This can be termed 'feedforward' (rather than feedback), as you are taking steps to avoid a low energy state before it has happened.

Negative feedback systems require:

▶ receptors to detect change
▶ a control centre to receive the information and process the response
▶ effectors to reverse the change and re-establish the original state.

Most control centres are located in the brain.

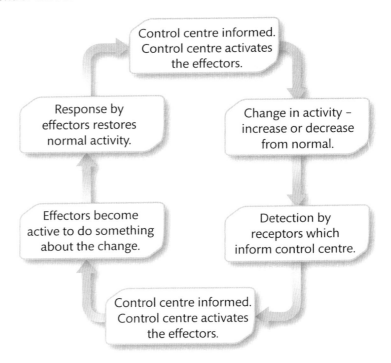

▶ **Figure 3.13** Feedback control systems

Body temperature

Human beings are the only animals that can survive in both tropical and polar regions of the earth. This is largely due to efficient thermoregulatory homeostatic processes and the use of intelligence (for shelter, sources of warmth and clothing), which mean that body temperature varies only minimally.

The fundamental principle is to keep the inner core of the body (containing the vital organs) at normal temperatures while allowing the periphery (skin, limbs and so on) to adapt to changes in external temperature.

At very low temperatures, such as –30°C, the water component of the body would freeze and at high temperatures, such as +50°C, enzymes and body proteins would be permanently altered or **denatured**. Life would not be possible under these conditions so homeostatic regulation of body temperature or thermo-regulation is vital. The skin plays an important role in this, so learning will start with an explanation of its structure and functions.

The role of skin in maintaining body temperature

The skin covers the outer surface of the body and is the largest body organ. New cells are continually forming to replace those shed from the surface layers. The skin is a significant part of our in-built, or innate, immunity and forms not only a waterproof layer but also a microbe-proof covering. It plays an important part in the homeostatic regulation of body temperature and is considered to be part of our nervous system because of its sensitivity.

The skin varies in thickness throughout the body, being thinnest over the eyelids and lips and thickest on the soles of the feet. For study purposes, it is divided into an outer thinner layer, the epidermis, and a deeper layer called the dermis. The dermis is connective tissue, mainly areolar, in which blood vessels, nerves, sweat glands, elastic and collagen fibres intermingle. Nerve endings in the dermis form specialised receptors for temperature changes, pain, touch and pressure.

> **Key term**
>
> **Denature** – permanent change to the active site (where molecules bind and reaction occurs) of an enzyme. Enzyme functioning is affected by pH and temperature.

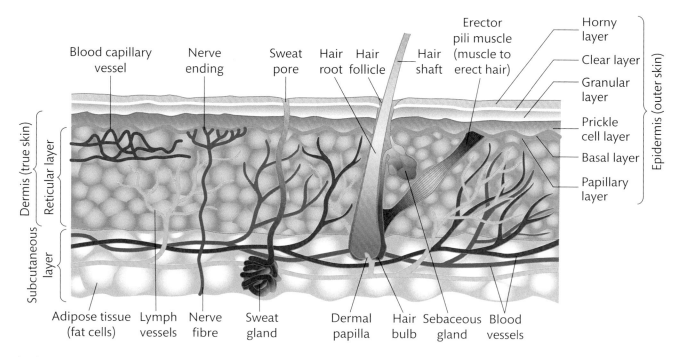

▶ **Figure 3.14** Structure of skin

You have already learned about the structure of the epidermis as a tissue and the keratinisation of its cells. Hair follicles are also extensions of the epidermis, they run down into the dermis and produce hairs made of keratin. Attached to these are the sebaceous (or oil) glands that coat the surface in hairy parts, assisting the waterproofing. Sweat ducts penetrate the epidermis as they emerge from the actual sweat gland in the dermis. In the basal layer, there are collections of pigment cells known as melanocytes that produce skin colour. The pigment melanin protects against damage to deeper structures from ultra-violet light radiation.

Hair erector muscles have their origins low down on the hair follicles, and their attachments to the basal layer of the epidermis. When hair erector muscles contract (usually from fear or the sensation of coldness) the hair becomes more erect, making the skin surface lumpy (known as goosebumps).

The major functions of skin are:

▶ to protect the underlying tissues against friction damage
▶ to waterproof the body
▶ to protect deeper structures from invasion by microorganisms
▶ to protect against ultra-violet radiation
▶ for thermoregulation (control of body temperature)
▶ to relay nerve impulses generated from the specialised skin sensory receptors for heat, cold, touch, pain and pressure, thus informing the brain of changes in the environment
▶ to synthesise vitamin D from sunlight acting on the adipose layers.

Production of heat by the body

Heat is generated by the metabolic processes taking place in the body. Although energy released during chemical reactions is used to drive processes, such as muscle contraction (heart pump, breathing, movement, nerve impulses and so on), some of the energy is always released as heat. For example, hundreds of chemical reactions take place in the liver every day and the liver is a massive generator of body heat. The blood distributes this heat around the body, particularly to the extremities. Some heat is also gained from hot food and drinks and, under some circumstances, from the sun's rays.

Loss of heat from the body

Skin capillaries form networks just below the outer layer or epidermis. When you are hot, you need to lose heat from the skin surface to cool yourself down. There are four ways of losing heat from the skin.

1 **Conduction** – warming up anything that you are in contact with (like clothes and seats), even a pen becomes warm from your hand when you are writing!

2 **Convection** – this is when you warm up the layer of air next to your skin and it moves upwards (because hot air is less dense and rises), to be replaced by colder air from the ground.

3 **Radiation** – you can think of this as being rather like diffusion but of heat temperature. In other words, heat will pass from your skin to warm up any colder objects around you and, conversely, you will warm up by radiation from any object hotter than yourself, like a fire or the sun.

4 **Evaporation of sweat** – when liquid water is converted into water vapour (the technical term is evaporation), it requires heat energy to do so. When you are hot, sweating will only cool the skin if it can take heat energy from the skin surface to convert to water vapour and evaporate.

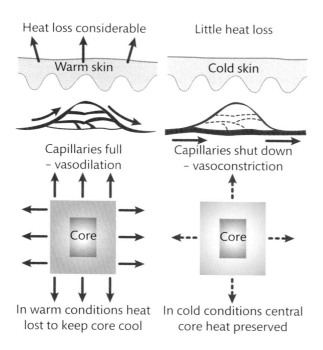

▶ **Figure 3.15** Changes in skin radiation

Although conduction and convection take place, they cannot be changed significantly to alter body temperature. The main methods of regulating temperature are by changing radiation and sweat evaporation processes.

Body temperature varies according to the location of the measurement, for example mouth, axilla (armpit), ear canal and rectum. The latter is only used when the other sites are unavailable and in patients who are unconscious and/or very seriously ill, as the procedure causes raised anxiety and stress levels. Rectal temperatures are nearer to actual body core temperatures but are slower to change. Mouth or oral temperatures are about 0.5°C higher than axillary temperatures.

Normal body temperatures range from 36.5 to 37.2°C. Most people will quote 37°C as normal body temperature but, given the range of influencing factors, this is rather too precise.

Role of the hypothalamus and the autonomic nervous system

The receptors for temperature, both heat and cold, are located in the peripheral skin and around the internal organs. These are specially adapted cells with nerve fibres that run up the spinal cord to the temperature control centre in the **hypothalamus** of the brain. The hypothalamus sends nerve impulses to muscles, sweat glands and skin arterioles (small blood vessels) via the autonomic nerves to cause changes that counteract the external changes. You can see the precise effects of a rising and falling external temperature in the flow charts in Figures 3.16 and 3.17. When there is conflict between information from skin receptors and those around internal organs, the hypothalamus will always respond to the central receptors.

Key term

Hypothalamus – an important part of the brain lying in the centre of the base of the brain just above the pituitary gland. It controls heart rate, body temperature and breathing rate by the autonomic nerves.

 **PAUSE POINT**   Ahmed felt hot so he ate an ice-cream but did not feel cooler. Explain why he would have felt cooler drinking a warm coffee.

Hint   Eating a large mass of cold food will affect the central thermoreceptors.

Extend   Try to explain why we feel cold if we stay in wet swimwear, even on a hot day.

Effects of shivering

Rhythmic involuntary contractions of the skeletal muscles are known as shivering. Muscular activity generates heat so in a cold environment as well as the involuntary act of shivering, people may stamp their feet, swing their arms, rub their faces, hands and feet. These are very effective ways to generate heat, and readily available to warm up the body.

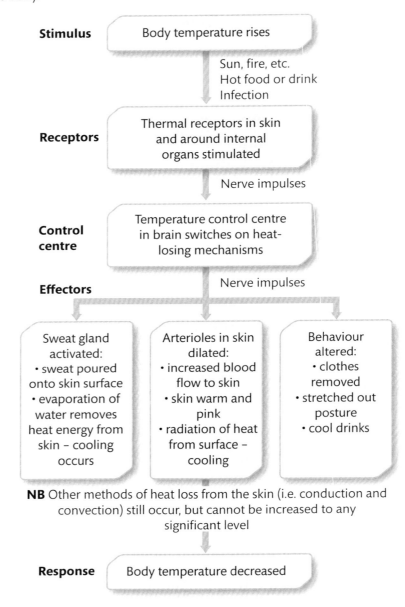

NB Other methods of heat loss from the skin (i.e. conduction and convection) still occur, but cannot be increased to any significant level

▶ **Figure 3.16** Homeostatic control of an increasing body temperature

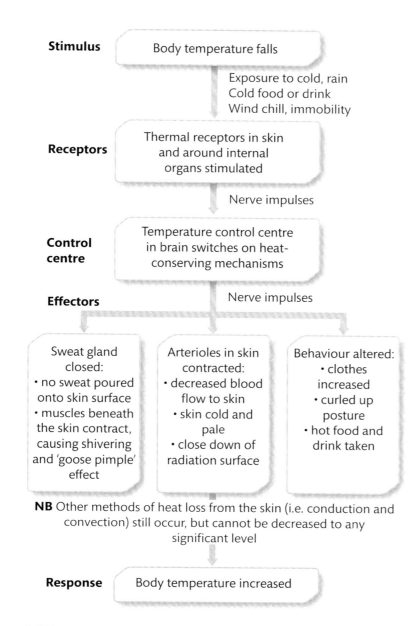

Stimulus — Body temperature falls

Exposure to cold, rain
Cold food or drink
Wind chill, immobility

Receptors — Thermal receptors in skin and around internal organs stimulated

Nerve impulses

Control centre — Temperature control centre in brain switches on heat-conserving mechanisms

Nerve impulses

Effectors

Sweat gland closed:
• no sweat poured onto skin surface
• muscles beneath the skin contract, causing shivering and 'goose pimple' effect

Arterioles in skin contracted:
• decreased blood flow to skin
• skin cold and pale
• close down of radiation surface

Behaviour altered:
• clothes increased
• curled up posture
• hot food and drink taken

NB Other methods of heat loss from the skin (i.e. conduction and convection) still occur, but cannot be decreased to any significant level

Response — Body temperature increased

▶ **Figure 3.17** Homeostatic control of a falling body temperature

Implications of surface area to volume ratios

Small bodies have a large surface area compared to their volume. They lose heat to their surroundings very quickly. Larger bodies, by contrast, have a small surface area compared to their volume and may experience difficulties with overheating.

As babies have a larger surface area to volume ratio than adults and cannot effect changes to gain or lose heat for themselves, they are more at risk of developing **hyperthermia** or **hypothermia**. Babies do not sweat much and newborn babies do not shiver. Therefore, it is important to wrap babies warmly in cold weather, including the extremities and the head, and to guard against overheating in hot weather.

Fever

A high body temperature is often associated with confusion or delirium, and with fits in babies as they are less able to control their own body temperature. Fever tends to occur as a result of infection. This is because bacteria and viruses release toxins and the body's reaction is to raise the temperature to try to neutralise the microbe invaders.

Key terms

Hyperthermia – a body temperature above the normal range, similar to fever. The heat-losing processes are unable to work properly.

Hypothermia – a body temperature lower than the normal range when heat-conserving processes are unable to cope. Tends to occur in older people and infants as their nervous systems are weak.

Blood glucose levels

Role of the pancreas, liver, insulin and glucagon

You will learn how carbohydrates are broken down by digestive enzymes to produce simple soluble sugars, mainly glucose. After a meal rich in carbohydrates (such as rice, bread, pasta and certain vegetables), blood glucose will start to rise. This increased level of glucose stimulates the production of the hormone insulin from the beta cells in the **islets of Langerhans** in the **pancreas**. Insulin has two main functions:

▶ to regulate the concentration of glucose in the blood

▶ to increase the passage of glucose into actively respiring body cells by active absorption.

In the absence of insulin, very little glucose is able to pass through cell membranes (with the exception of liver cells) and so the plasma level of glucose rises. Individuals with untreated diabetes mellitus (caused by a lack of insulin secretion) have high plasma glucose levels, which leads to other biochemical disturbances. In healthy people, the plasma glucose hardly varies at all because liver cells, under the control of insulin, convert glucose into liver **glycogen** for storage (glycogen is also stored in muscle tissue). When blood glucose starts to fall as a result of fasting or being used up by respiring cells, another hormone, glucagon, from the alpha cells in the islets of Langerhans, is secreted and this converts liver glycogen back into glucose for release into the bloodstream. These two hormones regulate the amount of glucose in the blood plasma by negative feedback mechanisms. Both have receptors attached to their islet cells to identify rising and falling plasma glucose levels.

Insulin also promotes the conversion of glucose into fat (once again removing surplus glucose from the circulation) and delays the conversion of amino acids into energy.

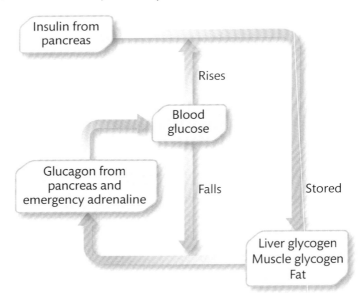

▶ **Figure 3.18** Negative feedback mechanism to maintain blood glucose levels

Fluid balance

Water intake, output and loss

To maintain a balance of water in the body the fluid intake must roughly equal the fluid output; most substances (even respiratory gases) and chemical reactions are dissolved in water so it is crucial to body systems. Fluid intake is through liquids drunk and food eaten whereas fluid lost is from urine, faeces, sweating, expired air which is saturated with water and occasionally tears and vomiting.

Role of the kidneys and renal system

The renal system is responsible for maintaining the composition and volume of body fluids. This is carried out by the action of the kidneys, which also filter out many waste products such as breakdown products of proteins (urea) enzymes, hormones and drugs from the blood.

Failure of homeostatic mechanisms

The processes for maintaining physical and chemical regulation can sometimes fail and, for reasons referred to earlier, this can be life-threatening.

Hypothermia

Hypothermia is recognised as body temperature lower than 35°C. It can occur at any age if someone is exposed to cold and damp for a long time. However, mostly it happens to older people living in poorly heated houses, who may or may not also have a physical or mental disorder. For example, having hypothyroidism (due to lowered metabolism), dementia (as a result of poor cognitive function) and arthritis (due to immobility) can influence the onset of hypothermia. The signs and symptoms of hypothermia are drowsiness, low pulse and breathing rates and confusion, which will eventually lead to coma and death if untreated. Brain function declines during the onset of hypothermia meaning that people do not even feel cold and, therefore, do not take appropriate action. People with this condition must be warmed up slowly.

> **Safety tip**
>
> If you suspect an older service user has developed hypothermia, **never** give them hot water bottles, hot baths or sit them in front of a fire. These methods warm up the skin, increasing blood flow to the skin and taking more heat from the inner core, which may hasten death. Send for the emergency services and, in the meantime, wrap the person in warm blankets and keep them in a warm room to slowly warm up their body.

Dehydration

Dehydration is when the water content of the body is too low. Symptoms include feeling thirsty, dry lips and mouth and producing only small volumes of dark urine. If dehydration is due to a lack of water in a very hot climate, there is likely to be a salt shortage as well through excessive sweating. Water loss can arise through environmental conditions, fever and excessive vomiting and urine production, such as in severe food poisoning and diabetes insipidus. Severe dehydration is life-threatening, with drowsiness and coma preceding death. Dehydration is treated by supplying fluid, either by mouth or intravenously. In hot climates salt may also need to be added.

The structures, function and main disorders of the cardiovascular system

The heart is a muscular pump that forces blood around the body through a system of blood vessels – namely arteries, veins and capillaries. Together this is known as the cardiovascular system. Blood carries dissolved oxygen to the body cells and at the same time removes the waste products of respiration (carbon dioxide and water). However, blood is also important in distributing heat around the body, along with hormones, nutrients, salts, enzymes and urea.

The structure of the heart

The adult heart is the size of a closed fist, located in the thoracic cavity between the lungs and protected by the rib cage. It is surrounded by a tough membrane, the pericardium, which contains a thin film of fluid to prevent friction.

The heart is a double pump. Each side consists of a muscular upper chamber (the atrium) and a lower chamber (the ventricle). The right side of the heart pumps deoxygenated blood from the veins to the lungs for oxygenation. The left side pumps oxygenated blood from the lungs to the body, and the two sides are completely separated by a septum. The blood passes twice through the heart in any one cycle and this is often termed a 'double circulation' (Figure 3.19 shows a schematic diagram of this).

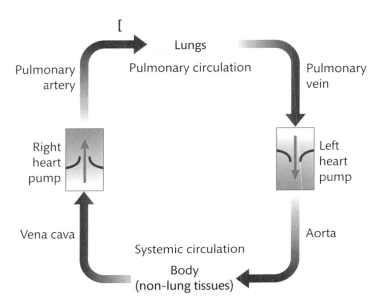

▶ **Figure 3.19** Schematic diagram of the double circulation of blood

Each of the four heart chambers has a major blood vessel entering or leaving it. Veins enter the atria, and arteries leave the ventricles. To help you remember the structure, atria (A) have veins (V) entering (AV) and ventricles (V) have arteries (A) leaving (VA). So, never two As or two Vs together.

The circulation to and from the lungs is known as **pulmonary circulation** and that around the body is **systemic circulation**. Arteries are blood vessels that leave the heart, while veins take blood towards the heart.

In pulmonary circulation, the pulmonary artery carrying deoxygenated blood leaves the right ventricle to go to the lungs. You will realise that it must divide fairly soon after leaving the heart because there are two lungs to be supplied – hence the right and left pulmonary arteries. The pulmonary veins (there are four of them), now carrying oxygenated blood from the lungs, must enter the left atrium.

The main artery to the body leaving the left ventricle is the aorta, and the main vein bringing blood back to the heart from the body enters the right atrium and is the vena cava. The vena cava has two branches – the superior vena cava returning blood from the head and neck, and the inferior vena cava returning blood from the rest of the body. In many diagrams of the heart, these are treated as one vessel.

Key terms

Pulmonary circulation – blood circulation to and from the lungs.

Systemic circulation – blood circulation around the body.

It is important that the blood flows in only one direction through the heart, so there are special valves to ensure that this happens. There are two sets of valves between the atria and the ventricles, one on each side. Sometimes these are called the right and left atrioventricular valves but their older names are also still used – the bicuspid, or mitral (left side), and tricuspid (right side) valves. These names refer to the number of 'flaps', known as cusps that make up the valve. The bicuspid has two cusps and the tricuspid has three cusps. Each cusp is fairly thin so, to prevent them turning inside out with the force of the blood flowing by, they have **tendinous cords** attached to their free ends and these are tethered to the papillary muscles of the ventricles. The papillary muscles tense just before the full force of the muscle in the ventricles contracts, so the tendinous cords act like guy ropes holding the valves in place.

Key term

Tendinous cords – fibrous cords that attach the papillary muscle to the atrioventricular valves, preventing backflow of blood during the cardiac cycle.

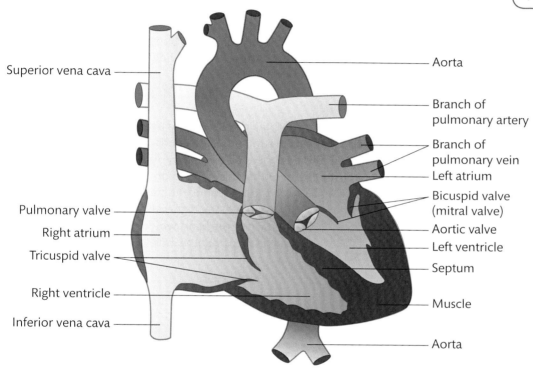

▶ **Figure 3.20** Section through the heart

The two large arteries, the pulmonary artery and the aorta, also have exits guarded by valves called semilunar valves (so-called because the three cusps forming each valve are half-moon shaped). These valves are needed to prevent blood forced into the arteries by ventricular muscle contractions from flowing back into the ventricles when they relax. These valves are also called the pulmonary and aortic valves.

Labelling the heart chambers correctly can be confusing. When you look at an image in front of you, it is like a mirror image, so the left side of the image is opposite your right hand and vice versa. To help you visualise this, you could place a paper-based image on the front of your chest facing outwards, making the sides of the diagram the same as your left and right hand. A heartbeat makes a 'lubb-dup' sound, with a very short interval between each beat, which can be heard using a stethoscope, or by putting your ear against someone's chest. Valves, like hands clapping, make sounds when closing not opening. 'Lubb' represents the atrioventricular valves closing while 'dup' is the sound made by the semi-lunar valves closing. In some people, swishing sounds can be heard between heart sounds and these are called heart murmurs. All murmurs should be investigated but most are not related to disease. Murmurs are the result of disturbed blood flow.

Heart muscle is cardiac (myocardial) muscle, composed of partially striped interlocking, branched cells. It is myogenic, which means that it is capable of rhythmic contractions without a nerve supply. However, the atrial muscle beats at a different pace from the ventricular muscle, so the contractions are organised and co-ordinated by a nerve supply to ensure that the heart is an efficient pump. The heart muscle also has its own blood supply, provided by the coronary arteries and veins.

The muscular walls of the atria are much thinner than the ventricular walls, as the flow of blood is aided by gravity and the distance travelled is merely from the atria to the ventricles. The ventricles are much thicker than the atria but they also differ from each other. The right ventricle is about one-third the thickness of the left ventricle, which has to drive oxygenated blood around the whole of the body, including against the force of gravity to the head and neck. The right ventricle only has to deliver blood a short distance – to the lungs on either side of the heart.

The cardiac cycle

The cardiac cycle comprises the events taking place in the heart during one heartbeat. Taking the average number of beats in a minute (60 seconds) at rest to be 70, then the time for one beat or one cardiac cycle is 60 divided by 70 seconds, which works out at 0.8 seconds. You must remember that this is based on an average resting heart rate. When the heart rate rises to say 120 beats during moderate activity, the cardiac cycle will reduce to 0.5 seconds. As you can see, the higher the heart rate, the shorter the cardiac cycle, until a limit is reached when the heart would not have time to fill between successive cycles and there is a risk that the individual may experience cardiac arrest.

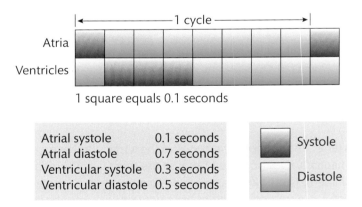

1 square equals 0.1 seconds

Atrial systole	0.1 seconds
Atrial diastole	0.7 seconds
Ventricular systole	0.3 seconds
Ventricular diastole	0.5 seconds

Systole

Diastole

▶ **Figure 3.21** Timing of events in the cardiac cycle

The cardiac cycle is shown in Figure 3.21 as a series of boxes, each one representing 0.1 seconds, to show the events occurring in the heart. Red boxes signify when contraction is occurring and green boxes signify relaxation time. The technical term for contraction is **systole** and the term for relaxation is **diastole**. The activity of the atria is shown on the top line and the ventricles at the bottom.

Key terms

Systole – time in heartbeat when cardiac muscle contracts.

Diastole – time in heartbeat when the cardiac muscle relaxes.

Step by step: The events in the cardiac cycle **6 Steps**

1 Both atria contract, forcing blood under pressure into the ventricles.

▼

2 Ventricles are bulging with blood and the increased pressure forces the atrioventricular valves shut (giving rise to the first heart sound – lubb).

▼

3 Muscle in the ventricular walls begins to contract, pressure on blood inside rises and forces open the semilunar valves in the aorta and pulmonary artery.

▼

4 Ventricular systole forces blood into the aorta (left side) and pulmonary artery (right side). These arteries have elastic walls and begin to expand.

▼

5 As the blood leaves the ventricles, the muscle starts to relax. For a fraction of a second, blood falls backwards, catching the pockets of the semilunar valves and making them close (the second heart sound – dup).

▼

6 With the ventricles in diastole, the atrioventricular valves are pushed open with the blood that has been filling the atria. When the ventricles are about 70 per cent full, the atria contract to push in the remaining blood rapidly, and the next cycle has begun.

You can see that when the chambers are in diastole and relaxed, they are still filling. The heart is never empty of blood. The cycle is continuous. With a high heart rate, it is the filling time that has shortened.

Theory into practice

Listen to your heartbeat with a stethoscope, or count your pulse three times and find your average resting heart rate.

Run on the spot for a few steps and then listen to your heartbeat again. What do you notice? Count your heart rate again in one minute.

Copy two sets of boxes like those in Figure 3.21 and discover how much time the atria and ventricles have to fill when the heart rate is at the new level. Work out the new value for the length of the cardiac cycle and shade in the boxes for atrial and ventricular systole. On your chart, mark the places where the heart sounds will be heard.

Heart rate and stroke volume

The **cardiac output** is the quantity of blood expelled from the heart in one minute. To calculate this, you need to know the quantity of blood expelled from the left ventricle in one beat (known as the **stroke volume**) and the number of heartbeats in one minute (or the **heart rate**). The average individual has a stroke volume of 70 ml and a heart rate between 60 and 80 beats per minute. An individual who trains regularly might have a lower heart rate but a higher stroke volume. To calculate cardiac output, you need to multiply the heart rate by the stroke volume. For example, for an adult with a heart rate of 70 beats per minute and a stroke volume of 70 ml, their cardiac output will be 4900 ml/min.

> **Key terms**
>
> **Cardiac output** – the quantity of blood expelled from the heart in one minute, usually expressed in millilitres (ml) per minute.
>
> **Stroke volume** – the quantity of blood expelled from the left ventricle in one minute, usually expressed in millilitres (ml).
>
> **Heart rate** – the number of heartbeats in one minute.

> **Case study**
>
> ## Fit and fast or is it slower?
>
>
>
> Cheryl trains every day by doing cross-country running, while Louis enjoys playing computer games.
>
> | Heart features | Cheryl | Louis |
> | --- | --- | --- |
> | Stroke volume (cm³) | 95 | 72 |
> | Resting heart rate (beats/minute) | 62 | 72 |
>
> **Check your knowledge**
>
> 1 Calculate the cardiac output of both adults in ml/min.
>
> 2 Explain the figures in the table in the light of their different lifestyles.
>
> 3 Explain how exercise benefits the cardiovascular system.

Research

Sometimes an individual's heart is not pumping blood onwards adequately, a condition called heart failure. This causes fluid to collect in the tissues making feet and legs swell – this is called oedema. The fluid collects in the lowest position so an individual sitting in bed will have fluid collecting in the lower back rather than the lower limbs. Find out how to test for oedema.

The regulation of the heart rate

The heart is controlled by the autonomic nervous system, which has two branches – the **sympathetic nervous system** and the **parasympathetic nervous system**. These two systems act rather like an accelerator and a brake on the heart. The sympathetic nervous system is active during muscular work, fear and stress, causing each heartbeat to be stronger and the heart rate to be increased. It is boosted by the secretion of the hormone adrenaline during periods of fright, flight and fight. The parasympathetic nervous system calms the heart output and is active during peace and contentment.

Blood pressure

The force blood exerts on the walls of the blood vessels it is passing through is known as the blood pressure (BP). It can be measured using a special piece of equipment called a sphygmomanometer, often abbreviated to 'sphyg' (pronounced *sfig*).

Systolic blood pressure corresponds to the pressure of the blood when the ventricles are contracting. Diastolic BP represents blood pressure when the ventricles are relaxed and filling. BP is usually written as systolic/diastolic (for example, 120/80) and the units are still millimetres of mercury (mm Hg). The SI (International System of Units) units are kiloPascals (kPa) but few establishments have converted.

The standard BP for a young healthy adult is regarded to be 120/80 mm Hg (or 15.79/10.53 kPa).

BP is highest in blood vessels nearer the heart, like the aorta and the large arteries. BP drops rapidly as blood is forced through the medium-sized arteries and the arterioles, as these muscular vessels present considerable resistance. BP in the capillaries is very low and blood in the veins has to be assisted back to the heart by a so-called 'muscle pump'. Veins in the limbs are located between muscle groups and, as they have thinner walls than arteries and possess valves at intervals, muscle action 'squeezes' the blood upwards in columns, and the valves prevent backflow. The slightly negative pressure in the chest during breathing also tends to 'suck' blood back towards the heart.

Key terms

Sympathetic nervous system – part of the autonomic nervous system that acts in opposition to the parasympathetic nervous system, by speeding up the heart rate and causing blood vessels to contract, particularly in times of stress (fight or flight mechanism). It also regulates sweat glands.

Parasympathetic nervous system – the most active part of the autonomic nervous system, which conserves energy by slowing the heart rate, increasing intestinal and gland activity, relaxing sphincter muscles in the gastrointestinal tract.

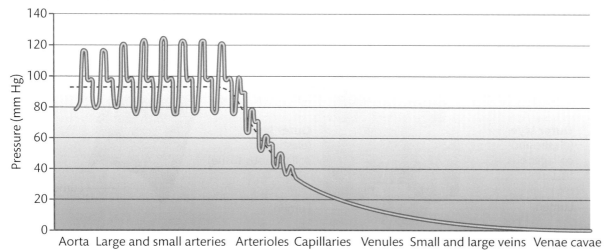

◀ **Figure 3.22** Graph to show the effect on blood vessels of blood pressure

Blood vessels

Arteries and arterioles

Arteries leave the heart and supply smaller blood vessels (known as arterioles), which in turn supply the smallest blood vessels, the capillaries. Arteries usually carry oxygenated blood. The exceptions are the pulmonary arteries which carry deoxygenated blood to the lungs for oxygenation, and the umbilical arteries, which carry deoxygenated blood from the foetus to the placenta in pregnancy. The arterioles provide an extensive network to supply the capillaries and, in overcoming the resistance of these muscular vessels, BP drops significantly at this stage. Arteries and arterioles are lined by endothelium and have a thick muscular coat. Their lumen (or central hole) is round.

Capillaries

These single-cell-walled vessels are supplied with blood by the arterioles. Body cells are never very far from capillaries, on which they rely for nutrients and oxygen. A protein-free plasma filtrate is driven out of the arterial ends of capillaries to supply the cells with oxygen and nutrients. This is called tissue (or interstitial) fluid. Tissue fluid re-enters the venous ends of the capillaries, bringing the waste products of the metabolic activities of the body cells (such as dissolved carbon dioxide and water).

> **Link**
>
> See more information in the section on Lymph.

Venules and veins

Venules are small veins, which are supplied by capillaries and feed into veins. The largest vein is the vena cava, which enters the right atrium of the heart. Limb veins contain valves to assist the flow of blood back to the heart because of the low BP in the veins. Veins have a much thinner muscular coat than arteries, more fibrous tissue and an oval lumen. BP is low in veins and venules. Generally, veins carry deoxygenated blood, with the exceptions of the pulmonary veins which bring oxygenated blood back from the lungs, and the umbilical vein which carries oxygenated blood from the placenta to the foetus.

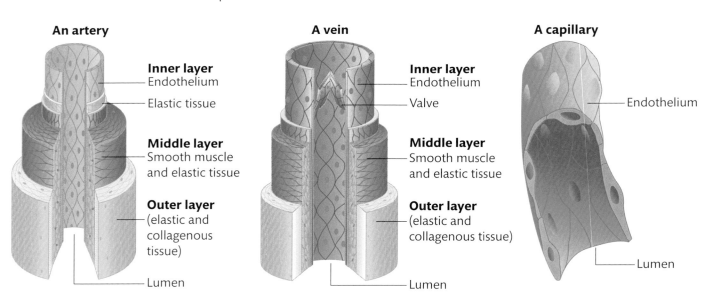

▶ **Figure 3.23** Arteries, veins and capillaries

▶ **Table 3.2:** The roles of different blood vessels

Arteries	Veins	Capillaries
Carry blood away from heart to organs.	Carry blood to heart from the organs.	Connect arteries to veins.
Carry blood under high pressure.	Carry blood under low pressure.	Arterioles and capillaries cause the greatest drop in pressure due to overcoming the friction of blood passing through small vessels.
Have thick, muscular walls and a round lumen.	Have thin, muscular walls and an oval lumen.	Have single-cell walls.
Usually contain blood with a high oxygen content, and low carbon dioxide and water content.	Usually contain blood with a low oxygen content, and high carbon dioxide and water content.	Deliver protein-free plasma filtrate with a high oxygen content to cells, and collect respiratory waste products (carbon dioxide and water).
Large elastic arteries close to the heart help the intermittent flow from the ventricles become a continuous flow through the circulation.	Veins in limbs contain valves at regular intervals and are sandwiched between muscle groups to help blood travel against gravity.	Walls are formed from a single layer of epithelium cells.

⏸ **PAUSE POINT**   Jasmine (who has 8 children) has varicose veins in her calves. Her legs feel heavy and her ankles swell if she stands for a long time. Explain why damaged vein valves would give Jasmine these signs and symptoms.

Hint   The blood in Jasmine's legs is unable to travel back to the heart efficiently.

Extend   What might be the relationship between varicose veins and having a large family?

Pulmonary and systemic circulation

The pulmonary circulation consists of the blood vessels going to and returning from the lungs. The pulmonary arteries carry deoxygenated blood and the pulmonary veins transport oxygenated blood. This is opposite to blood vessels in the systemic circulation because the lungs are the organs that oxygenate the blood.

The systemic circulation delivers and returns blood to and from all organs and body systems, except for the lungs. Arteries run from the heart and transport blood with a high oxygen content and low carbon dioxide content, whereas veins carry blood with a high carbon dioxide content and low oxygen content back to the heart.

The structure and function of the blood

You have already learned about blood in the section on tissues. You might like to read this section again before reading about haemoglobin.

Erythrocytes (red blood cells) contain haemoglobin, an important respiratory pigment that is essential for human life.

Haemoglobin is a very special iron-containing protein because:

▶ in an environment containing a high concentration of oxygen, such as in the blood of the lung capillaries, the haem part of the molecule forms a strong chemical bond with oxygen, becoming oxyhaemoglobin (a bright red pigment), which carries oxygen to tissue cells

▶ in an environment containing a low concentration of oxygen, the oxygen is released to pass down a concentration gradient to body cells. Haemoglobin is now said to be reduced haemoglobin (a dark red pigment).

Hint

Think about colour and pressure differences between arteries and veins.

Extend

As well as calling for help and applying pressure, first-aid advice includes raising the affected limb. Why does this help?

Disorders of the cardiovascular system

Disorders arising in this system are from the heart, blood vessels or the blood.

Coronary heart disease (CHD)

The heart muscle, like all other organs, must have its own supply of nutrients and oxygen to function. The left and right coronary arteries leave the aorta first and this supply has both the highest oxygen content and the greatest blood pressure, they then run over and into the cardiac muscle. When one or both of these arteries become narrowed, it causes angina (a severe pain in the chest) usually on exertion. The blockage is due to fatty plaques sticking to the artery walls (**atheroma**) on which clotting (**thrombosis**) can take place. If the artery becomes blocked, the segment of muscle it supplies starts to die, this is a heart attack (myocardial infarction) or coronary thrombosis.

Key terms

Atheroma – weakening of the blood vessel by the deposits of fatty plaques, usually leading to thrombosis.

Thrombosis – clotting in part of the circulatory system, such as in the coronary arteries: coronary thrombosis.

Link

Go to *Unit 14: Physiological Disorders and their Care, section B* to find more information about coronary heart disease.

Stroke (cerebrovascular accident (CVA))

Blood flow to the brain is disturbed or prevented due to atheroma, a leaking vessel wall or a portion of a clot broken off from elsewhere such as the legs (deep vein thrombosis). Signs and symptoms depend on the area of the brain supplied by the artery and partial paralysis is common.

Anaemia

There are several different types of anaemia but the most common is iron-deficiency anaemia, which occurs when iron, an essential component of haemoglobin, is lacking in the diet or not fully absorbed from the digestive tract. The main signs and symptoms are tiredness, breathlessness and pallor. This type of anaemia is easily treated with iron supplements.

Hypertension

This is a raised BP (more than 140/90 mm Hg) over a long period of time, which can increase the risk of an individual developing angina, a heart attack or a stroke. The heart has to push against the increased pressure so it works harder and needs more oxygen. When blood vessels are narrowed by atheroma or become hardened, called **sclerosis**, disorders such as coronary thrombosis and stroke are more likely to occur.

Key term

Sclerosis – hardening of tissue.

The structure, function and main disorders of the respiratory system

Respiration can be artificially subdivided into four sections to facilitate study, three of which are grouped under 'external respiration', which comprises: breathing, gaseous exchange and blood transport. The fourth is internal or tissue respiration, carried out inside the body cells.

Role of the air passages in the nose and the ciliated epithelial cells

The nose contains fine bones on its side walls (the turbinates), which are curled like scrolls and covered with moist ciliated mucous membrane, rich in blood capillaries. This arrangement produces a large surface area over which incoming air flows. During the passage through the nose, the air is warmed and moistened by the close contact with the mucous membrane and filtered by the ciliated epithelial cells. By the time the air reaches the throat, it is warmed to almost body temperature, moistened to almost saturation point and most foreign materials (such as dust, carbon particles and many pathogens) have been filtered out.

The structure and function of the trachea, bronchi and bronchial tree

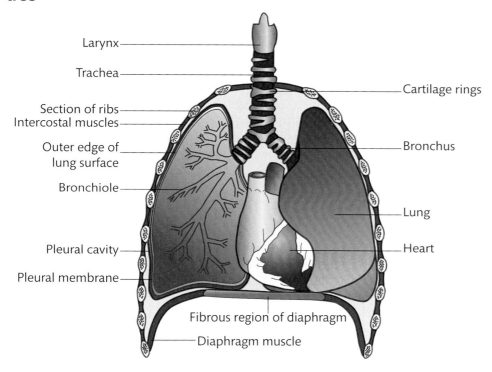

▶ **Figure 3.24** Section through the thorax to show respiratory organs

The trachea starts at the back of the throat, or pharynx, and divides into two main bronchi, each serving one lung on either side of the heart. The first part of the trachea is specially adapted to produce sound and is called the larynx, or voice box. It is protected by a moveable cartilage flap, the epiglottis, which prevents food entering during swallowing. When any material, such as a crumb, manages to pass the epiglottis it provokes an intense bout of coughing by reflex action, to expel the foreign body.

The trachea (or windpipe) and the bronchi have rings of cartilage to prevent them collapsing. Those in the trachea are C-shaped, with the gap at the back against the main food tube, the oesophagus. This is because, when food is chewed in the mouth, it is made into a ball shape (called a bolus) before swallowing. The bolus stretches the oesophagus as it passes down to the stomach, and whole rings of cartilage in the trachea would hamper its progress. The gap is filled with soft muscle that stretches easily, allowing the bolus to pass down the oesophagus. The bronchial tree is the pattern formed by the branching bronchi and their smaller branches, the bronchioles (see Figure 3.24).

The structure and function of the lungs and the alveoli

Each lung is a pale pink, smooth structure that closely mimics the interior of half the chest in shape. Each is divided into lobes (the right lung has three lobes, and the left has two) and has a hilum, or root, that marks the entry of the bronchus, blood vessels and nerves on the inner side.

The lungs themselves have a spongy feel to them, and are lined on the outside by a thin, moist membrane known as the pleura. The pleura continue around the inner thoracic cavity so that the two pleural layers slide over one another with ease and without friction. The **surface tension** of the thin film of moisture does not allow the two layers to pull apart but does allow them to slide. This means that when the chest wall moves when breathing, the lungs can move with it.

Each bronchus, after repeatedly dividing, ends in a group of single-layered globe-shaped structures called alveoli, which look rather like a bunch of grapes on a stem. The walls of the alveoli consist of very thin, flat, simple squamous epithelium, and each alveolus is surrounded by the smallest blood vessels known as capillaries. The walls of the capillaries are also composed of simple squamous epithelium, in a single layer. This means that the air entering the alveoli during breathing is separated from the blood by only two single-layered, very thin walls. There are elastic fibres round the alveoli, enabling them to expand and recoil with inspiration and expiration respectively. A film of moisture lines the inside of each alveolus to enable the air gases to pass into solution. As the two layers of epithelium are very thin and semipermeable, the dissolved gases can easily and rapidly pass through, in a process called gaseous exchange (see Figure 3.25).

Respiratory muscles

Diaphragm

The diaphragm separates the chest (or thorax) from the abdomen. It is dome-shaped with fleshy muscle fibres attached to the ribs and a tendinous part in the centre. When the muscular part contracts, the tendinous section is flattened and pulled down, increasing the space inside the chest thus drawing air in from outside – the process of inspiration. When the muscle relaxes, the reverse happens and the tendinous part rises to decrease the chest space forcing air out – the process of expiration.

Intercostal muscles

There are two sets of intercostal muscles running between the ribs and diagonally attached to them: the outer (or external) and the inner (or internal) intercostal muscles. Usually the recoil of the lungs and chest wall are enough to drive air out of the chest during expiration, but when more air needs to be exchanged, such as when running, forced breathing involves the intercostal muscles. The internal muscles pull the ribcage downwards increasing expiration and the external muscles pull the rib cage upwards, increasing internal chest space. The action of the internal and external intercostal muscles is antagonistic. Note that during exercise, the abdominal muscles also contract to help push the diaphragm upwards.

Ventilation, or breathing, and the respiratory muscles

Ventilation is the movement of air in and out of the thorax to replenish the oxygen supply and remove surplus waste products (carbon dioxide and water). Ventilation has two phases, namely inspiration (or inhalation) and expiration (or exhalation). The movements in these phases are effected by respiratory muscles attached to the skeleton. Two sets of intercostal muscles run obliquely at right angles to each other between the ribs, and the diaphragm is a dome-shaped muscle attached to the lower ribs and separating the thorax from the abdomen.

Discussion

Using your knowledge, discuss why there is a limit to the length of a snorkel for swimming underwater. Find out the meaning of 'dead space air' to help you.

Key term

Surface tension – a thin elastic skin of a liquid that allows it to resist an external force, for example it is what causes some objects to float and why some insects can walk on water. Surface tension is caused when similar molecules stick together.

Inspiration

When the intercostal muscles contract, the ribs move upwards and outwards and at the same time the contraction of the diaphragm causes it to flatten. All these movements increase the volume of the thorax and the lungs and thus reduce the pressure inside the lungs, causing air to rush in from the environment. This is known as inspired, or inhaled, air.

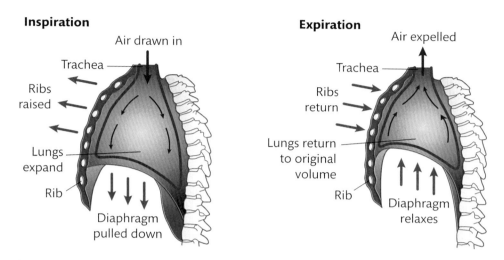

▶ **Figure 3.25** Changes in the thorax during inspiration and expiration

Expiration

The main force in expiration during quiet breathing is the elastic recoil of the fibres around the alveoli, and the relaxation of the diaphragm. However, during exertion, more forcible expiration can occur with the assistance of the other set of intercostal muscles contracting to move the ribs downwards and inwards. The volume of the thorax decreases, the pressure increases above that of the environmental air, and air rushes out.

Normal ventialation rate is 16 to 20 breaths per minute but this rises significantly during exertion.

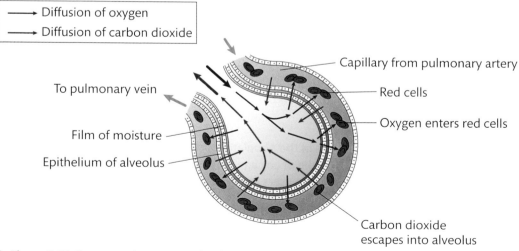

▶ **Figure 3.26** Gaseous exchange in an alveolus

Gaseous exchange

The composition of inspired air, breathed in from the environment around us, and expired air, as breathed out, is shown in Table 3.3.

Component	Inspired air	Expired air
Oxygen	20%	16%
Nitrogen	80%	80%
Carbon dioxide	Virtually 0 (0.04%)	4%
Water vapour	Depends on climate	Saturated

Although the largest component of air is nitrogen and this too passes into solution, it takes no part in the process of respiration. Breathing in fresh air replenishes the high concentration of dissolved oxygen molecules in the lung alveoli, and the removal of diffused oxygen by the bloodstream maintains the low concentration. With carbon dioxide, the situation is reversed – the high concentration is in the blood and the low concentration is in the refreshed air, so diffusion (see below) moves dissolved carbon dioxide from the blood into the expired air from the lungs. Carbon dioxide and water are waste products from internal respiration in cells.

Diffusion

Diffusion occurs in liquids or gases because the molecules are in constant random motion, and diffusion is an overall 'equalling up' of a situation where you have a lot of molecules meeting a few molecules. Diffusion will stop in time, as the numbers of molecules become more evenly distributed. This is said to be equilibrium. (Note that this does not mean the molecules stop moving, only that there are now equal numbers of molecules passing in all directions.)

In the human body, where diffusion is a common method of transport, the state of equilibrium is not desirable as it means overall transport ceases. To prevent equilibrium being attained the high concentration must be continually be kept high, and the low concentration must also be maintained.

Diffusion can only occur where there is no barrier at all to the molecules or where the barrier (in gaseous exchange, this is cell membranes) is thin. The rate of diffusion is enhanced by having an increased surface area (usually created by folds or similar structures to alveoli) and a raised temperature, since warmth increases the random motion of molecules.

Disorders of the respiratory system

Smoking-related diseases

The diseases of the respiratory system considered to be smoking-related are asthma, bronchitis and emphysema, chronic obstructive pulmonary disease (COPD) and lung cancer although many other disorders of the body are also affected by smoking cigarettes.

Asthma

Asthma affects large numbers of the population and, although associated mainly with children and adolescents, people of any age can have it. The chest becomes tight and wheezing can be heard as service users try to expel air from their chests. The muscle bands of the trachea and bronchial tree contract and narrow the air outlet. This is often caused by an allergen such as traffic fumes, dust, cigarette smoke, pollen, animal fur and colds. The mucus inside the respiratory tract becomes thick and the linings of the airways swell making it difficult to breathe.

Chronic obstructive pulmonary disease (COPD)

Smoking irritates and inflames the lungs, which results in scarring. This may lead to repeated attacks of chronic bronchitis and emphysema, and to COPD. A service user

Research

Use the NHS choices or ash (Action on Smoking and Health) website to research bronchitis, emphysema and lung cancer.

with COPD will have difficulty breathing and often have bluish lips, fingers and toes due to poor oxygenation, or if not they have a higher than normal breathing rate as they compensate to overcome narrowed airways. Coughing and breathlessness are features of COPD, which is serious and irreversible.

The longer you smoke, and the more cigarettes you smoke, the more likely you are to develop COPD.

Pneumonia

Inflammation of the lungs is called pneumonia and this is often found in service users who are frail and ill. It is caused by infection by bacteria, fungi or viruses, causing fever and coughing up of infected mucus (phlegm). Pneumonia is often accompanied by infection of the pleural membranes covering the lungs, so breathing becomes painful. Fluid can often be seen building up in the lungs and pleural cavity on an X-ray.

> **Discussion**
>
> Smoking damages the action of cilia. Discuss how this relates to the fact that smokers have more chest infections than non-smokers.

The structure, function and main disorders of the skeletal system

The structure of the skeletal system

The bony skeleton that forms the framework of the body is divided into the axial skeleton, in the midline of the body, consisting of the skull and vertebral column (spine) and the appendicular skeleton, the limb bones and the girdle muscles that attach them to the vertebral column and the ribs.

Types of bone

▸ **Long bones** – such as those of the limbs. The humerus, radius and ulna in the arm, and the femur, tibia and fibula in the leg. They support the weight of the body and provide attachments for powerful muscles that enable movement.

▸ **Short bones** – the phalanges of the hands and feet, the clavicle (collar bone) and the ribs. These bones provide stability and some movement.

▸ **Flat bones** – the sternum and bones forming the cranium, which holds the brain. They provide protection.

▸ **Irregular bones** – such as the scapula or shoulder blade, the vertebrae and the bones making up the pelvis. Their shape helps to protect internal organs.

▸ **Sesamoid bones** – develop in tendons to protect the parts they lie over and the tendon itself. The largest is the patella (kneecap). Other smaller sesamoid bones can be found in the hands and feet.

The function of the skeletal system

▸ **Support** – keeps the body upright even in movement and supports soft tissues such as skin.

▸ **Protection** – forms a hard case over vital organs like the brain and spinal cord, heart, lungs, liver and reproductive organs.

▸ **Attachment for skeletal muscles** – to produce movement muscles must be attached at both ends and lie over a joint. The fibrous ending of a muscle is the tendon and this merges strongly with the outer surface of a bone.

▸ **Source of blood cell production** – the red marrow found in the shafts of the ribs, sternum, vertebrae and the heads of long bones produces all the blood cells with the exception of lymphocytes.

▸ **Store of minerals** – bone is a store of both calcium and phosphate and interchange occurs when needed between bone and blood levels.

Structure and function of cartilage and ligaments

The structure of **cartilage** has been described earlier in the unit. It is the forerunner of bone in the foetus and as bone tissue increases in infancy, childhood and adolescence it does so from a plate of cartilage just below the head of each bone. This is called the epiphysis or epiphyseal cartilage. Parts of the ears, nose, ribs and pelvis remain cartilaginous enabling a degree of flexibility. For example, the cartilage in the pelvis forms a cartilaginous joint (the pubic symphysis) between the two pubic bones, which is important during childbirth. Cartilage also provides a smooth, glassy surface around the ends of bones to protect and reduce friction at a joint.

Ligaments are strap-like bands that run from bone to bone across a joint. They are made of yellow, elastic fibres of protein and have a limited degree of stretch. Their function is partly to hold the joint together but also to prevent overstretching at the joint.

The location of major bones

You will need to know the location of the bones featured in the diagram below.

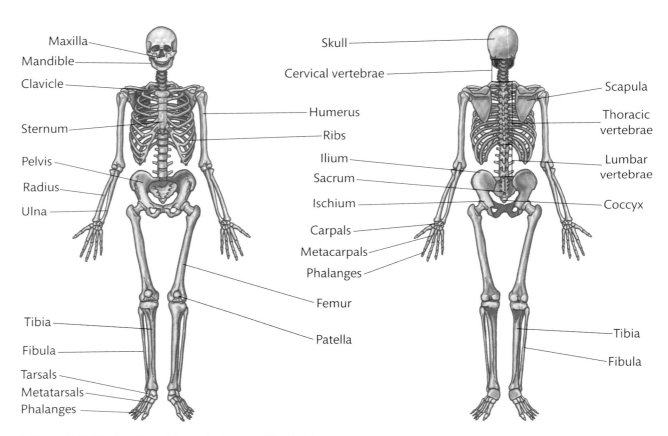

▶ **Figure 3.27** The location of the major bones of the skeleton

The classification of joints

Joints are where bones meet and move against one another. Joints fall into three groups:

▶ fibrous joints which are fixed, meaning that they allow no movement, for example between the bones of the skull

▶ cartilaginous joints, which allow little movement, for example the pubic symphysis

▶ freely moveable synovial joints, which are the commonest type of joint.

Synovial joint structure

Where two or more bones meet and move against each other, their ends are covered by a thin layer of smooth cartilage which prevents friction. There is a fibrous joint capsule enclosing the joint and this is lined by a delicate synovial membrane, which secretes a small volume of synovial fluid that fills the capsule and also prevents friction. The joint capsule is reinforced at interval by ligaments, to prevent overstretching.

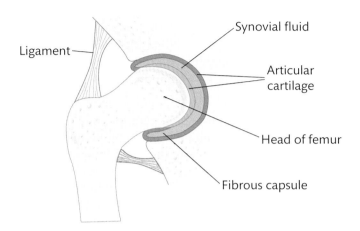

▶ **Figure 3.28** Section through a synovial joint

Movement at joints

It is important to be aware of the range of movements allowed by different types of joint to avoid injuring yourself, people working with you and service users. The key joint actions that you should know are:

- ▶ **flexion** – where the angle between two bones decreases, as in touching the shoulder with same arm
- ▶ **extension** – where the angle between two bones increases, such as straightening the arm after flexion
- ▶ **circumduction** – turning a limb in 360°, for example 'windmilling' the arm in a circle
- ▶ **abduction** – moving the arm or leg away from the central trunk
- ▶ **adduction** – the opposite of abduction, returning the limb towards the central trunk
- ▶ **gliding** – sliding one bone against another, for example the interverterbral joints and the small bones of the ankle and wrist.

Disorders of the skeletal system

Fractures

A fracture is the medical term for a crack or break in a bone. This is usually caused by an accident or fall. Healthy children and adults are at low risk of breaking bones but as people age, their bones become more brittle and even a minor trip or fall may lead to a broken bone. Additionally, some physical disorders such as osteoporosis (see below) cause bones to be thinner and more susceptible to breaking.

Minor breaks and cracks in healthy bones should heal quite quickly. However, when a large bone, for example one of the leg or arm bones, is broken then the limb may need to be immobilised and rested. When the bone is broken and sticks through the skin, known as an open fracture, the person is likely to need surgery to stabilise the bone and close the open wound as bone tissue is very susceptible to infection.

Osteoarthritis

Excessive wear of joints will cause the cartilage on the ends of bones to break up causing friction on movement. This is known as osteoarthritis and it usually causes a lot of pain, restricting the person's mobility. Although it is a disorder associated with older people, younger people may get osteoarthritis as a result of their occupation or lifestyle, for example some ballet dancers, weightlifters, body builders and athletes.

Osteoporosis

In osteoporosis, bones lose density and have less material in them. They become brittle and fragile and are more likely to fracture. Osteoporosis in women is often associated with a decrease in oestrogen secretion in the years following the menopause. It can also be caused by deficiency of calcium or of vitamin D.

Increase in people with rickets

Rickets affects children (in adults it is called osteomalacia) and is due to vitamin D deficiency, which causes the bones to become softer and weaker as vitamin D aids the absorption of calcium. Since the beginning of the 20th century, rickets has been rare. However, the number of cases is now increasing due to various reasons. For example, children not playing outdoors as much as they used to, and the number of people who for religious reasons are heavily covered by clothing and so not exposed to much sunlight – a good source of vitamin D. Also, people are eating less fatty food and drinking less milk (fats and dairy produce are also good sources of vitamin D).

Case study

Ivan's legs

Ivan was a ballet dancer until he was 37 years old. He gave up when the pain in his knee joints became too much to bear, even with strong painkillers. He had his left knee joint replaced and is shortly due to have his right knee joint replaced. His hip joints grate when he walks a lot, but otherwise he is in good health.

Check your knowledge

1 What condition do you think Ivan has developed?

2 How could this be linked to his former occupation?

3 Name the bones that form his knee joint.

4 Describe how his joints have been affected.

The structure, function and main disorders of the muscular system

This section deals with striated, skeletal or voluntary muscle attached to the skeleton.

The structure of striated muscle

You have already learned about striated muscle.

How muscles are attached to the body

Generally muscles are attached to bone by **tendons** at either end of the muscle, or by fascia in some parts of the body where the bones do not move, such as in the skull.

Tendons

Tendons are inelastic soft tissues made of strong collagen fibres that merge into the bone coverings. Tendons and muscles work together to move bones.

Reflect

It is important that the tendon is inelastic otherwise movement would be hindered.

A muscle straddles a joint to cause bones to move when it contracts. What would happen if the tendon stretched?

Anatomy and Physiology for Health and Social Care

Fascia

In some parts of the body, such as the skull, the bones do not move but facial movements are necessary. In this case, muscles are attached to fascia. Earlier in this unit you learned about areolar tissue. Fascia is a strong, often thick sheet of areolar tissue to which smaller muscles can be attached, such as the many muscles in the face responsible for facial expressions.

Link

You can learn more about fibrous joints in Section B, and about areolar tissues in section A.

Types of contraction

Different types of contraction are involved with various forms of movement. For example:

▶ **isometric contraction**, when muscles contract but there is no movement, such as in a tug-of-war when neither team is winning
▶ **concentric contraction**, when muscles contract and increase tension and shorten, as in a bicep curl or climbing stairs
▶ **eccentric contraction**, when the muscle contracts it lengthens often carrying a load, such as in a tricep curl – it is the opposite of concentric contraction. Muscle damage, especially during exercise, is more likely to occur in eccentric contraction.

Function of the muscular system

Movement – antagonist pairs (agonist/antagonist), synergist and fixator

The function of the muscular system is to enable parts of or the whole body to move. Muscles only pull bones into a new position, they never push. Striated muscles work in pairs, the main 'puller' is known as the **agonist** (or **prime mover**) and its opposite muscle is the **antagonist**. However, most movements require several muscles. For example, the muscle carrying out the main movement in flexing the forearm is the agonist known as the biceps brachii. The opposite muscle, the antagonist, is the triceps brachii, which returns the limb to its former position – extension. As one muscle contracts to move the bone, the other must relax and lengthen to allow the movement. Other muscles nearby also have roles in movement such as **fixators**, which steady nearby bones so that there is a firm support for the agonist. A **synergist** helps the movement by reducing movement that is not part of the action being carried out. Muscles can change roles depending on the particular movement being carried out.

Key terms

Agonist/prime mover – the main contracting muscle in a movement.

Antagonist – the muscle opposite to the agonist, it relaxes to allow the agonist to move the bone.

Fixator – a muscle that holds surrounding bones and joints steady to form a stable base for the movement.

Synergist – a muscle that cooperates in a movement but is not the agonist, it also stabilises the movement. Synergist comes from synergy, 'working together'.

The location and main actions of the major muscles

Table 3.4 and Figure 3.29 show the location of the major muscles and the table also explains their actions.

▶ **Table 3.4** The location and main actions of the major muscles

Name of muscle	Location in body	Action
Erector spinae	Alongside back of vertebral column	Extends and strengthens spine
Rectus abdominis	Front of abdomen – 'abs' or ' six-pack'	Flexes trunk forwards
Internal/external obliques	Side and front of abdomen	Sideways movement of trunk
Biceps brachii	Front of forearm	Flexes forearm and turns it upwards (supinates)
Triceps brachii	Back of forearm	Extends the forearm and helps adductors
Deltoids	Top of shoulder and shoulder joint	Raises arm from side – abducts
Pectoralis major	Front of chest and armpit –'pecs'	Adducts arm and lowers it
Trapezius	Upper back and neck from spine	Raises shoulder and retracts scapula
Latissimus dorsi	Lower back from spine	Adducts and inwardly rotates arm
Gluteus maximus	Rounded prominence of lower back – 'the bottom' or 'buttocks'	Extends the femur and helps maintain erect posture
Semimembranosus	Back and inner part of thigh	Rotates leg inwards
Semitendinosus	Back and inner part of thigh	Rotates leg inwards
Biceps femoris	Back of thigh	Rotates leg outwards
Adductors (3 muscles)	From pubic bone to femur	Adduct leg and carry across to other side
*Rectus femoris	Middle of front of thigh	Extends leg
*Vastus lateralis	Outer side of upper leg	Extends leg on thigh
*Vastus medialis	Inner side of upper leg	Extends leg on thigh
*Vastus intermedius	Centre of upper leg	Extends leg on thigh
Tibialis anterior	Outer side of lower leg	Flexes foot at ankle joint
Gastrocnemius	Major part of calf at back of lower leg	Extends foot at ankle
Soleus	Below gastrocnemius, in lower leg	Extends and steadies foot at ankle joint.

*Note: You may be familiar with a muscle called the quadriceps, this is the four muscles comprising the rectus femoris and the three vastus muscles.

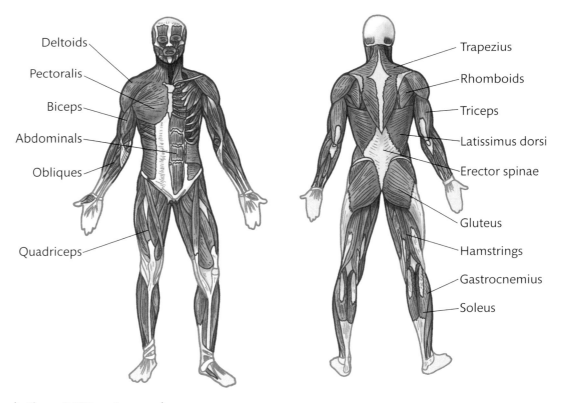

▶ **Figure 3.29** Locating muscles

Disorders of the muscular system

Muscular dystrophy

A group of genetic muscle disorders that affects muscle action, causing increasing disability. Muscles gradually become weaker and may cease to function. Some types of muscular dystrophy are life-threatening as they affect the cardiac and intercostal muscles, whereas other types are less severe.

The structure, function and main disorders of the digestive system

Alimentary canal

The alimentary canal is a tube that extends from the mouth to the anus. It is dilated, folded and puckered in various places along its length. You will need to know the names of the various regions, their main purpose and the outcomes of their activities. Many glands are associated with the alimentary canal, and they have important roles to play in digestion.

When food is taken into the mouth it is mixed with saliva, chewed (or masticated) by the action of the tongue and teeth, rolled into a small ball known as a bolus, and swallowed. This process is called mechanical digestion and it is an important part of physically breaking the food down at an early stage.

The salivary glands

There are three pairs of salivary glands that pour their secretions, known as saliva, into the mouth. Saliva, a digestive juice, contains an **enzyme** known as salivary amylase, which begins the digestion of carbohydrates, as well as lubricating the mouth and helping bolus formation.

The oesophagus

The oesophagus (or gullet) transports the food bolus from the back of the mouth (the pharynx) to the stomach in the abdomen. The swallowed bolus is in the oesophagus for a few seconds only and no enzymes are secreted here, although salivary amylase will continue to act during this brief journey. The oesophagus is mainly a transit for food boluses, which it moves by muscular contractions known as **peristalsis**. A moveable flap called the epiglottis covers the opening of the trachea during swallowing to prevent food entering the respiratory system.

Key terms

Enzyme – biological catalyst that alters the rates of a chemical reaction (usually speeding them up) but which is itself unchanged at the end of the reaction.

Peristalsis – muscular contractions of the circular and longitudinal muscle in the gut wall which pushes food along the alimentary canal.

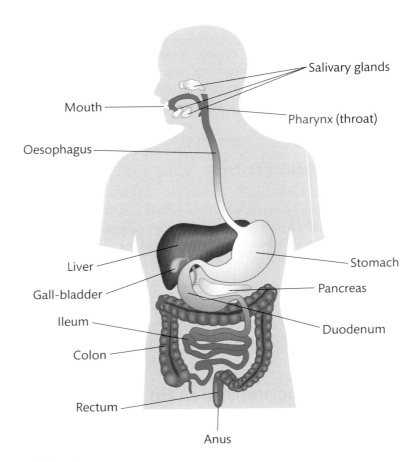

Mouth

Salivary glands

Pharynx (throat)

Oesophagus

Liver

Gall-bladder

Ileum

Colon

Rectum

Anus

Stomach

Pancreas

Duodenum

▶ **Figure 3.30** The digestive system

Reflect

You cannot eat and breathe at the same time so if you are assisting a service user with eating you must allow a little time between mouthfuls for breathing.

What happens if a crumb enters the trachea? Why is this dangerous?

The stomach

The stomach is the widest part of the alimentary canal, tucked mainly behind the rib cage under the diaphragm on the left side and receives food from the mouth by way of the oesophagus. Food can stay in the stomach for up to three hours, with a protein meal remaining the longest and food not containing protein passing through relatively quickly. During this time, the strong stomach walls roll and churn the food around and pour on secretions from the gastric glands. The resulting paste-like material is called chyme.

Gastric glands produce gastric juice that contains the enzyme gastric protease and hydrochloric acid. The gastric juice works on proteins. In babies, another enzyme, rennin, solidifies and digests milk protein. The pH of the stomach is 1–2 which is strongly acidic. The epithelial lining of the stomach contains goblet cells which produce thick mucus to protect the stomach lining from acid erosion.

The stomach empties the chyme in spurts into the duodenum through the pyloric sphincter, a thick ring of muscle that alternately contracts and relaxes.

The duodenum

The next part of the alimentary canal is the small intestine, so-called because of its small diameter – certainly not its length, for it is around 6 metres long! The first C-shaped part, and the shortest, is called the duodenum. It is mainly concerned with digestion and is helped by two large glands, the liver and the pancreas, that pour their secretions or juices into this area. The duodenal wall also contains glands which secrete enzyme-rich juices that continue the digestive process on proteins, carbohydrates and lipids (or fats).

The ileum

The remainder of the small intestine, known as the ileum, is mainly concerned with the absorption of the now fully digested food. It is specially adapted for this by its:

▶ long length

▶ folded interior

▶ lining covered in many thousands of tiny projections called villi

▶ epithelial cell lining being covered in microvilli, projections so small that they can only be detected using an electron microscope.

These adaptations enormously increase the surface area for absorption of nutrients from digested food.

Small intestine showing the internal folds and the villi   **A villus and its blood supply**

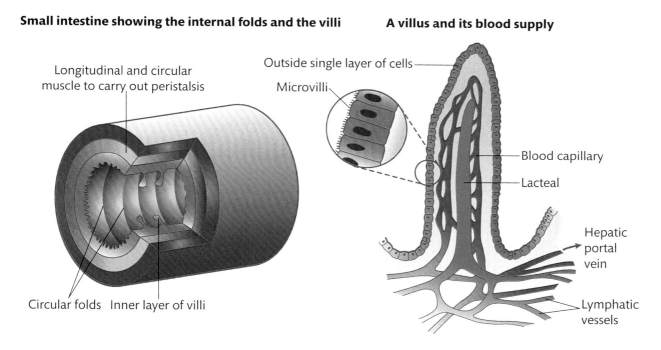

▶ **Figure 3.31** Section through the small intestine and a villus

Each villus is lined by columnar cells and goblet cells only one-cell thick, with an extensive internal capillary network and a blind-ended branch of the lymphatic system called a lacteal.

The chief products of protein and carbohydrate digestion pass into the capillary network, which drains to the liver via the hepatic portal vein. Products of fat digestion pass into the lacteal and eventually they pass, via the lymphatic system, into the general circulation.

The colon

In the right-hand lower corner of the abdomen, the small intestine meets the large intestine. There are two biological remnants at this point, the caecum and the appendix. In grass-eating animals the caecum is a large structure with the worm-like appendix at the end. They are known as biological or evolutionary remnants because, in the human species, neither the caecum nor the appendix has any function. The appendix can become inflamed or pustulous and threaten life – a condition known as appendicitis. As well as the caecum and appendix, the large intestine consists of the colon and rectum, which ends in a sphincter, the anus, for controlling the elimination of faeces.

The colon runs up the right side of the abdomen and turns to travel across to the left side before ending at the anus. There are no enzymatic juices in the large intestine.

The colon has a puckered appearance because the outer longitudinal muscle coat splits into three bands and the circular muscle bulges out between the bands. During the journey down the alimentary canal, many glands have poured watery juices onto the chyme. The body cannot afford to lose so much water and the purpose of the large intestine is to slow down the passage of food waste. (Food waste is all that is left at this stage because all the absorption of nutrients occurred in the small intestine.) This means that water can be reabsorbed and the motion, or faeces, becomes semi-solid. It can then be eliminated by muscular action of the rectum, and relaxation of the anus at a convenient time.

Faeces contain:

▶ cellulose (fibre or roughage) from plant cell walls left after digesting fruit and vegetables

▶ dead bacteria, including the usually harmless bacteria living in the large intestine that have died a natural death, and other bacteria, which are often killed by the hydrochloric acid in the stomach

▶ cells scraped off from the gut lining.

Mucus, secreted by enormous numbers of goblet cells in the gut lining, reduces friction as chyme and waste are moved along by peristalsis.

The liver and pancreas

The liver

The liver is a large, dark-red organ occupying the top right half of the abdomen and partly overlapping the stomach. It has many vital functions in the body, one of which is to produce bile. Bile flows down the bile duct into the duodenum, after temporary storage in the gall bladder on the under surface of the liver. Bile contains no enzymes at all, but it provides important bile salts that cause the **emulsification** of fats (lipids) in the duodenum. You will recall that protein and carbohydrate have already experienced enzymatic action. Lipids, like all fats, do not readily mix with water, so the enzymes have only a small water/lipid surface on which to work.

Emulsification results in the fats forming millions of tiny globules, each with a water/lipid surface so that enzymes can work efficiently over a massively enlarged surface area. Bile also contains bile pigments – bilirubin and biliverdin. These are the waste products of degraded haemoglobin from the breakdown of old red blood cells, which gives the brown colour to faeces. Bile is secreted continuously by the liver and temporarily stored in a sac called the gall bladder. When a lipid-rich meal arrives, the gall bladder releases bile into the small intestine.

The liver also removes glucose and other sugars from the blood coming from the small intestine and converts them into glycogen for storage. Surplus amino acids that

> **Key term**
>
> **Emulsification** – occurs when an emulsifier causes oil or lipids to be suspended as a large number of tiny globules in water.

are not required for manufacturing cell proteins are broken down in the liver to form glycogen and urea – a nitrogenous waste product transported by the bloodstream to the kidneys for elimination in urine.

Reflect

The liver carries out hundreds of chemical reactions and produces much heat. The blood distributes this heat around the body to maintain body temperature.

Although this heat is used in the body it can only be regulated through homeostasis rather than by the liver as chemical reactions are always taking place in this organ.

The pancreas

The pancreas is a slim, leaf-shaped gland located between the intestines and the stomach, close to the duodenum. It secretes enzyme-rich pancreatic juice as well as alkaline salts needed to neutralise the acidic secretions from the stomach. Pancreatic enzymes go to work on all three macronutrients (protein, fat and carbohydrate) and are important agents for the complete breakdown of complex food molecules into amino acids, glucose and similar simple sugars, fatty acids and glycerol.

The pancreas also makes the hormones insulin, required to metabolise glucose, and glucagon, required to release stored glucose, in the islets of Langerhans.

Breakdown and absorption of food materials

Ingestion, digestion, absorption, egestion

It is vital to understand that without the organs and glands of the digestive system, you would be unable to use the substances collectively called food by means of **digestion**. Taking food in through the mouth (what is called 'eating') is known technically as **ingestion**. Food is generally composed of large complex molecules of protein, carbohydrate and lipids (or fats) that would be unable to pass through the lining of the alimentary canal. Converting these complex molecules into simple soluble molecules enables their **absorption** into the bloodstream and onward transit for metabolic processes. Waste material that has not absorbed is passed out through the anus periodically. The technical term for this is **egestion**.

Key terms

Digestion – conversion of food into simple, soluble chemicals capable of being absorbed through the intestinal lining into the blood to be used by body cells.

Ingestion – taking in food, drink and drugs by the mouth.

Absorption – taking up of substances to be used by the body cells and tissues.

Egestion – process involved in eliminating waste material from the body as faeces.

Peristalsis

Food and chyme move down the alimentary canal by a process known as peristalsis. Note that in Figure 3.32 there are two sheets of muscle surrounding the tube – one sheet runs in a circular fashion around the tube while the other runs down the tube. Behind the bolus or chyme, the inner circular muscle contracts (and the longitudinal muscle relaxes), pushing material in front of it. This is rather like your fingers pushing toothpaste up the tube. In front of the material, the circular muscle relaxes and the longitudinal muscle contracts, to hold the tube open to receive the food. Two sets of muscles acting in this way are said to be antagonistic.

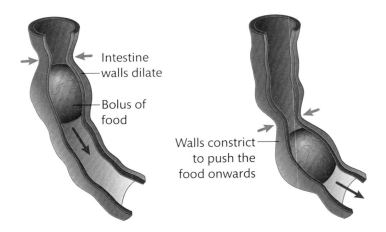

Intestine walls dilate

Bolus of food

Walls constrict to push the food onwards

▶ **Figure 3.32** Peristalsis

The role of enzymes in digestion

To break down large complex molecules in the laboratory you would use heat (as in cooking) or add chemicals such as acids or alkalis.

Body cells are able to produce substances called enzymes that can alter the rate of chemical reactions to build up or break down other molecules, without using heat or harmful chemicals.

Enzymes are biological catalysts. This means that they are substances that can act within living organisms to enable the breakdown or building-up of other chemicals, but they remain unchanged themselves at the end of the reactions or tasks.

Enzymes are specific to the material on which they act (called a substrate). For example, a protease only acts on protein and a lipase only acts on lipids or fats. You may have noted that adding '–ase' at the end of the substrate name signifies that it is an enzyme. Not all enzymes are named in this way, but most are.

The main bulk of the human diet consists of protein, fat and carbohydrate so these are called macronutrients. They provide calories or joules of heat energy. Vitamins and mineral salts are only required in tiny amounts and are called micronutrients. They do not provide energy but are often important in energy release processes, oxygen carriage, metabolic rate, red blood cell formation and so on.

Enzyme reactions have some special features.

▶ Enzymes are sensitive to temperature. At low temperatures they work very slowly, or stop working. At high temperatures, they become distorted (denatured) and permanently stop working. Enzymes work best, or optimally, at body temperature.

▶ Enzymes are sensitive to the acidity or alkalinity of their surroundings, known as pH. Some digestive enzymes, such as pepsin (also known as gastric protease), work best in an acidic environment. The stomach lining secretes gastric protease and hydrochloric acid for maximum efficiency in breaking down proteins. Lipase prefers alkaline conditions and the pancreas secretes alkaline salts, such as sodium hydrogen carbonate, to provide optimal conditions. Salivary amylase prefers neutral or pH7 conditions. (Amylum is the Latin name for starch, so amylase works on starch.)

▸ Relatively few molecules of enzymes are required to break down lots of large food molecules because they are catalysts.

▸ Amylases work on cooked starch substrates (bread, rice, potatoes and so on), converting the molecules to simple sugars like glucose.

▸ Proteases act on proteins, breaking them down into amino acids and peptides (two amino acids joined together chemically). Proteases in the stomach and pancreas are secreted as inactive precursors (something that comes before) and are activated once they enter the cavities of the stomach and duodenum and mix with chyme.

▸ Lipases convert lipids to fatty acids and glycerol.

▸ **Table 3.5:** summary of the sites of enzyme secretion and their role in digestion.

Location	Gland and juice secreted	Contents	Substrate	End product	Special comment
Mouth	Salivary glands, saliva	Salivary amylase	Carbohydrate starch	Disaccharides or double sugar molecules	Mixed during chewing, needs neutral pH 7
Oesophagus	None	None	None	None	Salivary amylase still active
Stomach	Gastric glands, gastric juice	Protease Hydrochloric acid Rennin, in babies	Protein	Amino acids and peptides	Contents must be acidic, pH1–2, churned into paste called chyme kills bacteria in raw food
Duodenum	Intestinal glands, intestinal juice (succus entericus)	Peptidases Carbohydrases	Peptides Disaccharides	Amino acids Glucose	Needs to be alkaline, pH 8
Ileum	None	None	None	None	Main area for absorption
Colon	None	None	None	None	Reabsorbs water
Rectum	None	None	None	None	Stores faeces until evacuation (egestion)
Associated glands					
Liver	Bile	Bile salts Bile pigments No enzymes	None	None	Bile salts emulsify fats
Pancreas	Pancreatic juice	Lipase Amylase Protease Salts	Fats Carbohydrates Proteins	Fatty acids and glycerol Glucose Amino acids	Turns acid contents of stomach alkaline

The role of microorganisms in the gut

Microorganisms flourish in the large intestine. There are estimated to be 100 trillion bacteria doing a variety of tasks. The bacteria release locked-in nutrients through fermentation, and manufacture vitamins such as biotin and vitamin K (needed for blood clotting). It is thought that microorganisms play a role in immunity and research is actively trying to unravel the process, and also that of using hormones for fat storage. The bacteria live in harmony within us, with both the bacteria and us benefitting – this is known as symbiosis. By having a healthy population of bacteria, pathogens (disease-causing micro organisms) are 'crowded out' and disease is prevented. Oral antibiotics may destroy 'good' bacteria and so should be taken only when really necessary.

Major products of digestion

Roles in the body, storage and deamination

▸ **Peptides and amino acids** are nitrogenous compounds. They travel via the bloodstream to areas of need in body cells. They are important in making enzymes, some hormones, plasma proteins, new cells (growth) and in repair processes. Surplus amino acids are broken down in the liver as they cannot be stored. Some parts of the molecules are used for energy but the nitrogen-containing part is converted into urea in the liver by a process called deamination, and excreted by the kidneys in urine.

▸ **Sugars**, chiefly glucose, are transported to cells to be broken down in internal respiration to release energy. Excess carbohydrate is stored in liver and muscles as glycogen or converted into fat to be stored around organs or under the skin. Glycogen is converted back to glucose when energy is required to top up the blood glucose supply to cells, or for muscle contraction. The end products of internal respiration, carbon dioxide and water, are removed by the respiratory and renal systems.

▸ **Glycerol** is used for energy, or reconverting fatty acids into a form of fat that can be stored.

▸ **Fatty acids** travel from the lacteals through the lymphatic system into the main veins of the neck. This circuitous route enables smaller quantities of potentially harmful lipids to enter the circulation gradually. Fatty acids are used in internal respiration to release energy to drive metabolic processes. The end products of internal respiration, carbon dioxide and water, are removed by the respiratory and renal systems.

▸ **Fat** is stored under the skin and around organs, where it forms a long-term energy store to be used after glycogen stores are depleted.

The absorption of food

The ileum is mainly concerned with the absorption of the now fully digested food. It is specially adapted for this.

Disorders of the digestive system

There are many disorders that can affect the digestive system, ranging from mouth ulcers to various types of cancer. Minor disorders can lead to uncomfortable symptoms such as dyspepsia or indigestion. However, more serious disorders will affect an individual's appetite, may prevent efficient or sufficient absorption of nutrients and may cause severe pain.

Ulcers

Ulcers can occur singly or in groups and occur mainly in the mouth, stomach and duodenum. An ulcer is a localised inflammation that has destroyed a small area of skin or mucous membrane, producing an open sore. The ulcer can be painful and the symptoms affected by eating. Ulcers in the stomach and duodenum are known by the general term peptic ulcer. They may be caused by bacterial action and can be treated with antibiotics. If peptic ulcers are left untreated, they may bleed, usually requiring immediate surgical repair.

Hepatitis

This is inflammation of the liver and can be caused by viruses or chemical substances, including alcohol. The symptoms of hepatitis may include nausea, vomiting, lack of appetite and jaundice – a yellowing of the skin and white of the eyes, and passing of dark-brown urine. The condition can be acute or chronic (long-term). Treatment is usually rest, good nourishment and avoiding alcohol. In severe cases, the individual may have liver failure and require a liver transplant.

Coeliac disease

Coeliac disease is an autoimmune disease that runs in families and so is thought to have a genetic base. An intolerance of gluten, a protein found in wheat and other cereals, triggers an immune response that can lead to loss of weight, some vitamin deficiencies and often diarrhoea.

Research

You can find out more about coeliac disease by visiting the Coeliac UK website: www.coeliacuk.org.

The structure, function and main disorders of the nervous system

The central nervous system, the brain and spinal cord

The central nervous system (CNS) consists of the brain and spinal cord and together they control and coordinate both the voluntary and involuntary actions of the body. Voluntary actions are those under the will, such as walking or reaching for a drink, whereas the involuntary actions of the body are those that are not under conscious control, such as the heart beating and peristalsis pushing food along the alimentary canal.

The peripheral nervous system

The peripheral nervous system consists of the nerves of the body which connect to the CNS. **Nerves** are the long processes of the neurons (nerve cells), gathered together in bundles and wrapped in connective tissue sheaths, rather like the wires in a cable. Nerves carry **nerve impulses** away from and towards the CNS. Individual neuron processes are often referred to as nerve fibres, which carry impulses concerned either with voluntary or involuntary activities.

Motor nerves carry impulses from the CNS to muscles or glands from **motor neurons**. The muscles and glands are known as effectors because they effect actions, such as contracting muscle or causing glands to secrete. Sensory nerves carry impulses towards the CNS, they transfer information to the CNS from body parts via receptors in the **sensory neurons**.

Key terms

Nerve – bundles of nerve fibres travelling together and wrapped in connective tissue.

Nerve impulse – wave of electrical discharge passing along a nerve fibre.

Motor neuron – nerve cell carrying information from the CNS, associated with muscles or glands known as effectors.

Sensory neuron – nerve cell associated with specialist receptors carrying information into the CNS.

Motor neurons have cell bodies lying in the spinal cord, and long processes called axons that are the motor nerve fibres; the processes within the spinal cord are very short and called dendrons. Sensory neurons, however, have long dendrons coming from receptors via nerves to the CNS, and short axons as their cell bodies lie in a chain of ganglia close to the spinal cord. Figure 3.33 will help you to understand.

Dendrons and axons are likely to be myelinated – surrounded by a fatty sheath of myelin. The myelin is formed inside **Schwann cells** that are wrapped spirally around the nerve fibres. The point between two Schwann cells is the **node of Ranvier**, this enables nerve impulses (which are electrical phenomena) to leap from one node to the next and not have to travel down the whole nerve fibre. There is a small gap between the end of one neuron and the next, known as a **synapse**. Impulses can only cross a synapse if an appropriate **neurotransmitter** is secreted into the synaptic space. The impulse can only travel in one direction as the neurotransmitter is only secreted at one ending.

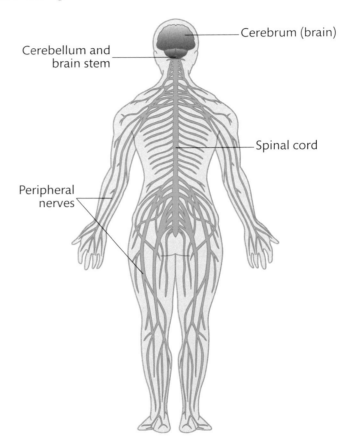

Cerebellum and brain stem

Cerebrum (brain)

Spinal cord

Peripheral nerves

▶ **Figure 3.33** The nervous system

The parasympathetic and sympathetic nervous systems

Conduction of nerve impulses to and from the CNS

Together these form the autonomic nervous system, which you have learned about in homeostatic regulation. As stated earlier, the nerves of these systems generally run with other nerve fibres in bundles, although there are a few nerves that are completely autonomic (involuntary or unconscious). The actions of the parasympathetic and sympathetic nerves are often opposite to one another. The sympathetic system has a branch supplying the adrenal medulla and is enhanced by the secretions, such as adrenaline, from this gland. The sympathetic system is associated with the 'fright, flight or fight' response to emergency situations, whereas the parasympathetic system is linked to peace and contentment. For example, the sympathetic system speeds up both the heart and breathing rates, while the parasympathetic system slows them down – rather like an accelerator and a brake on a vehicle. Both systems communicate with the CNS via nerve impulses to and from the brain.

Disorders of the nervous system

Parkinson's disease

Dopamine is an important chemical substance for healthy brain function and it is released by the endings of neurons in a synapse. In Parkinson's disease the level of dopamine falls due to damaged nerve cells deep in the brain and this affects muscular movements. Service users with this condition experience tremors, stiff muscles and they can only move slowly. It takes many years to develop fully.

Dementia

Nowadays people are living longer due to better living conditions and better medicine. More people are developing dementia as the chances of developing dementia increase with age. Most service users with dementia are over 65 years old. There are several types of dementia but the most well-known are Alzheimer's disease, vascular dementia and dementia with Lewy bodies (DLB), which has some features of Parkinson's disease as well as dementia. Some dementias arise following a head injury, due to poor blood supply to the brain.

Dementia causes a decline in brain function leading to memory loss, a reduction in the understanding and speed of thought, such as not being able to find the right words and a lack of feeling for other people. An individual's sleep patterns are often disturbed and they may begin to wander at night.

> **Research**
>
> There is still much to learn about dementia. Visit www.alzheimers.org.uk and www.dementiauk.org for further information.

Multiple sclerosis (MS)

The majority of nerve fibres are covered with a fatty sheath of myelin, which serves to speed up the passage of nerve impulses along the fibres. In MS, a disease that is both progressive and disabling, this myelin sheath breaks up in patchy areas. The symptoms depend on the area of brain, spinal cord and nerves affected but range from a tingling sensation to complete paralysis. MS is thought to be an autoimmune disease.

The structure, function and main disorders of the endocrine system

The endocrine system is a collection of ductless glands that secrete hormones directly into the bloodstream. Figure 3.34 shows the location of the endocrine glands, which are always close to blood vessels. Like the nervous system, the endocrine system communicates and coordinates internal body organ functions but depends on the circulation to affect destination organs, often called the target organ, and so its actions are slower.

The hypothalamus

You have learned about the role of hypothalamus in homeostasis, particularly in the control of water and body temperature, but it also has a role in the endocrine system. The pituitary gland used to be called the master gland but is actually controlled by the hypothalamus. This part of the brain is about the size of a cherry and secretes substances known as releasing factors, which can stimulate other endocrine glands to secrete hormones and inhibit the secretion of others. The hypothalamus also plays a role in daily bodily rhythms, including sleep control.

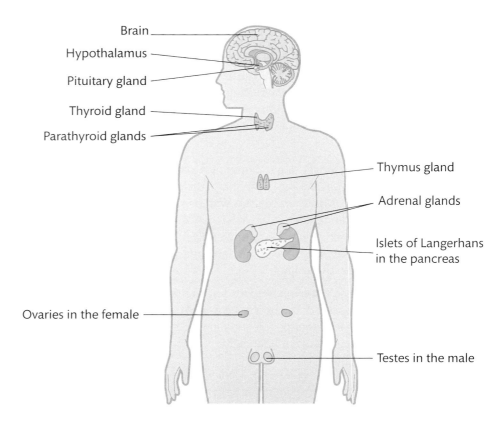

▶ **Figure 3.34** Structure of the endocrine system

The pituitary gland

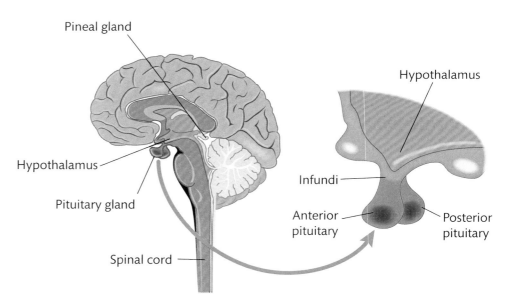

▶ **Figure 3.35** The hypothalamus and pituitary gland

The pituitary gland is connected by a stalk to the hypothalamus and lies directly beneath it in a small bony depression at the base of the brain. It has three parts and secretes several hormones. The anterior pituitary secretes six important hormones:

- **growth hormone**, which controls the growth of bone, muscle and soft tissue
- **adrenocorticotrophic hormone (ACTH)** or corticotropin, which stimulates the release of cortisol from the adrenal cortex
- **follicle stimulating hormone (FSH)** or follitropin, which stimulates the release of ova or sperm from the sex organs
- **luteinising hormone (LH)** or lutropin, which causes ovulation and the formation of the corpus luteum in the ovary, which secretes progesterone, and secretion of testosterone from the testes in the male
- **thyroid stimulating hormone** or thyrotropin, which stimulates the thyroid gland to produce thyroxine
- **prolactin**, which stimulates production of breast milk after childbirth.

The intermediate lobe of the pituitary gland secretes:

- **melanocyte stimulating hormone (MSH)**, which controls darkening of the skin.

The posterior pituitary secretes two hormones:

- **antidiuretic hormone (ADH)** also known as vasopressin, which causes water reabsorption in the renal tubules (osmoregulation)
- **oxytocin**, which causes contractions of the uterine muscle during childbirth.

The thyroid gland

The thyroid is an H-shaped gland that straddles the trachea in the neck. Embedded within it are several patches (usually four) of a different structure – the parathyroid glands, which secrete parathyrin to regulate blood and tissue calcium levels. Thyroxine is the main product of the thyroid gland, which affects many body systems and has roles in controlling growth, development and metabolic rate.

The manufacture of thyroxine is dependent on iodine from the diet. In geographical areas where the soil is iodine-poor, individuals may get a neck swelling, known as a goitre. This is due to a failure of the negative feedback system causing continued stimulation of the thyroid gland by the hypothalamus and pituitary gland. This condition is usually easily treated by giving the individual daily doses of thyroxine. However, it is also a preventable disease and iodine may be added as a dietary supplement to ordinary table salt.

The pancreas

See page 203.

The adrenal glands

The adrenal glands are two triangular glands that sit one on top of each kidney. Each gland consists of a central medulla surrounded by a cortex, both the medulla and cortex secrete different hormones.

- The adrenal cortex produces aldosterone, which causes sodium and water to be reabsorbed from the kidneys consequently increasing blood volume and, therefore, blood pressure. Aldosterone also plays a role in maintaining the blood chemicals. Cortisol and the sex hormones, androgens and oestrogen, are also produced by the adrenal cortex. Androgen hormones are converted elsewhere in the body to female hormones (oestrogens) and male hormones (androgens). However, these steroid hormones are produced in much larger amounts by the ovaries (oestrogen) in women and testes (androgens) in men.
- The adrenal medulla secretes noradrenaline, which promotes vasioconstriction and adrenaline, which boosts the action of the sympathetic nervous system in both strength of response and the length of the action. It is also responsible for the 'fight, fright or flight' response.

The ovaries

Responding to follicle-stimulating hormone (FSH) from the pituitary gland, some ova start to grow (but only one fully matures as a rule). As growth of follicle cells surrounding the ovum increases, the cells secrete oestrogen, which causes secondary sexual characteristics to appear and thickens the lining of the uterus. After ovulation, the follicle forms the corpus luteum, which secretes progesterone that makes the thickened uterine lining glandular and ready for the fertilised ovum or zygote to become embedded.

The testes

Follicle stimulation hormone (FSH) from the pituitary gland causes the testes to produce androgens, causing the seminiferous tubules to produce sperm and the supporting cells to secrete testosterone, which is responsible for secondary sexual features, such as facial and body hair growth and, therefore, 'maleness'.

Disorders of the endocrine system

Diabetes mellitus

Diabetes mellitus is a serious disorder due to an absence of insulin, or to a resistance to insulin. Insulin helps glucose to enter body cells so that the process of internal respiration can take place to release energy. Being overweight means an individual has more body cells and so an increased demand for insulin. Additionally, older insulin-producing cells cannot deliver the extra needed. In younger diabetics, a viral infection may have destroyed the cells producing insulin. There are two types of diabetes mellitus. Type 1, in which little or no insulin is produced and type 2, in which there is insufficient insulin produced for the body's needs.

Treatment for type 1 diabetes is by insulin injection, type 2 diabetes can usually be treated by diet and taking tablets that stimulate insulin production.

Case study

Sally is slightly overweight but quite active for 72 years of age. She enjoys gardening and a bit of walking. She had a letter from the GP asking her to go for a fasting blood glucose test. Sally was told to not eat or drink anything except water for 14 hours overnight before going to the health centre for her blood test.

When the results of the blood glucose test came back, Sally's result was on the upper limit of the normal range. Sally's GP informed her that she would have the same test every year from now on.

Check your knowledge

1   Explain why it is important to fast for several hours before having a blood glucose test.

2   Explain why Sally is now more at risk of diabetes mellitus.

3   What else could the GP have advised Sally to do to help prevent this condition developing?

4   Identify why it is important to diagnose this condition.

Discussion

In small groups, discuss the value of 'MOT'-type tests for older people, which use both financial and staffing resources of local healthcare centres and the NHS. Make lists of the type of tests that could make up the health 'MOT' and debate this with other groups.

Diabetes insipidus

Diabetes means 'a running through' and refers to the large volume of urine produced due to a lack of antidiuretic hormone, which controls the reabsorption of water from the renal tubules. Diabetes insipidus is a rare disease. Because it causes an excess of urination, an individual with diabetes insipidus feels very thirsty and so drinks large volumes of water. If they do not drink a lot of water, they quickly become dehydrated.

Hypothyroidism

Hypothyroidism is a reduction of production of the hormone thyroxine, which governs growth. In children a lack of thyroxine causes delayed growth, and results in mental disability and slow metabolism (a condition that used to be known as cretinism). In adults, the slow metabolism leads to a slow heart and breathing rate, slow digestion and constipation and slow mental processes, such as in the ability to add up purchases. An individual with hypothyroidism may look bloated, due to increased weight and constipation and always feels cold, due to a slower heart rate and poor circulation. Treatment is usually with daily replacement by taking thyroxine tablets.

⏸ PAUSE POINT To what extent do you think the hypothalamus, rather than the pituitary, is the 'master gland'?

 **Hint** How is the pituitary gland controlled?

Extend Compare the ability of the nervous system with that of the endocrine system to communicate with other parts of the body.

The structure, functions and disorders of the lymphatic and immune systems

The lymphatic system is important in the transport of some fats and in maintaining your body's fluid balance. It is also part of the body's immune system, an important defence against infections. The lymphatic system (see Figure 3.36) is made up of lymphatic capillaries, lymphatic vessels and lymph nodes, which collect and transport lymph.

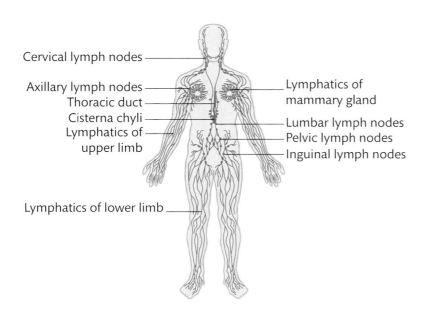

Cervical lymph nodes

Axillary lymph nodes
Thoracic duct
Cisterna chyli
Lymphatics of upper limb

Lymphatics of mammary gland

Lumbar lymph nodes
Pelvic lymph nodes
Inguinal lymph nodes

Lymphatics of lower limb

▸ **Fig 3.36** Structure of the lymphatic system

Lymph

Lymph is a clear fluid that circulates in the lymphatic system. Lymph is formed when body cells secrete a protein-free plasma filtrate (carrying dissolved oxygen, glucose, enzymes, hormones and nutrients) that bathes cells, known as tissue fluid, and passes into the venous end of the lymphatic capillaries. The lymph is carried to the lymph vessels and lymph nodes, and eventually passes into the subclavian vein and back into the blood.

Lymph also contains white blood cells, which are part of the body's defence system.

Lymphatic vessels

The lymphatic vessels have thin walls and valves. They push lymph from the lymph capillaries towards the heart and into the thoracic duct, which empties into the main blood circulation via the subclavian vein.

Lymphatic organs

The lymphatic organs include the lymph nodes and also include the thymus, spleen, tonsils and appendix.

At certain places in the body, such as the groin, axillae and neck, there are swellings through which the lymph must pass. These are lymph nodes, and they act as filters for microorganisms, mainly bacteria and other cells, such as cancer cells. They also add their manufactured lymphocytes to the flowing lymph.

The thymus, spleen, tonsils, appendix and other special lymphatic tissue found in the gut, have specialised functions. For example, the thymus is involved in the maturation of lymphocytes and the spleen filters blood, removing old or damaged red cells, and releasing lymphocytes in response to infection.

Reflect

Have you ever visited your GP or dentist because you are in pain from an infection? They have probably felt the sides of your neck for lumps. These are swollen lymph nodes, which some people call swollen 'glands'.

Why can these nodes be felt when you have an infection when normally they cannot be felt?

Lymphocytes

Lymphocytes are present in circulating blood and play a role in defending the body against invading microorganisms, and abnormal cells such as cancer cells. There are two major types, called T and B lymphocytes, of which T lymphocytes are the most numerous. The T lymphocytes are programmed in the thymus gland in the neck. This gland is large in babies and children but, although still present, it shrinks in adulthood. T lymphocytes recognise abnormal cells and destroy them with special chemicals. B lymphocytes are also programmed to recognise specific proteins, called **antigens**. Antigens are on the surface coatings of microorganisms and stimulate the B lymphocytes to produce specific **antibodies** against the antigens causing then to stick together until the **macrophages** in the blood destroy them by phagocytosis. The spleen also produces lymphocytes. Every time the same invading microorganism attacks, the lymphocytes produce thousands of antibodies to destroy them, this is called **immunity**.

The spleen

The spleen is a reddish-purple organ lying in the upper abdomen behind the stomach. It is a spongy organ that makes lymphocytes, passing them into the circulation. It also

Key terms

Antigen – protein found on the surface of micro-organisms, specific to that organism.

Antibody – large protein that recognises antigens and helps remove them. Different antibodies recognise specific antigens.

Macrophage – large white blood cell that engulfs and destroys invading micro-organisms, such as bacteria in the process of phagocytosis.

Immunity – having adequate body defences to fight infection and disease.

filters out abnormal and worn-out red blood cells, breaking them down and recycling the pigments. The spleen also acts as a reservoir of blood but is not necessary for life.

Disorders of the lymphatic and immune systems

Hodgkin's disease

Hodgkin's disease is also called Hodgkin's lymphoma and is an uncommon cancer. In this condition, the B lymphocytes multiply abnormally, causing lymph nodes to swell and lose their ability to fight infection. This type of lymphoma is most often found in young adults and people over the age of 70. The cause is unknown but it is usually associated with people who are immunosuppressed, probably through taking immunosuppressant medication, for example after having a transplant, people who have weak immune systems through other illnesses, or people who have had glandular fever in the past.

Leukaemia

Leukaemia is cancer of the white blood cells. It is classified as acute or chronic, and according to the different type of cell involved, the main types are lymphocytic and myeloid. Acute means that the disease progresses rapidly whereas chronic means that the progress is much slower. The symptoms may include pale skin, tiredness, breathlessness, having repeated infections over a short space of time and unusual and frequent bleeding, such as nosebleeds.

Due to the immense number of abnormal cells being produced there is a reduction of red blood cells, causing anaemia.

Structure, function and disorders of the renal system

The renal system consists of two kidneys with emerging tubes (called the ureters) running down the posterior abdominal wall to a single pelvic collecting organ, the bladder. The passage from the bladder to the exterior is via the urethra, and the flow of urine is controlled by a **sphincter muscle** located just below the bladder. The kidneys are supplied by short renal arteries coming off the main artery of the body, the aorta. Renal veins take the blood from the kidneys straight into the vena cava, the main vein of the body.

> **Key term**
>
> **Sphincter muscle** – circular muscle controlling an aperture (opening). When the muscle contracts the aperture closes and when it relaxes the aperture reopens.

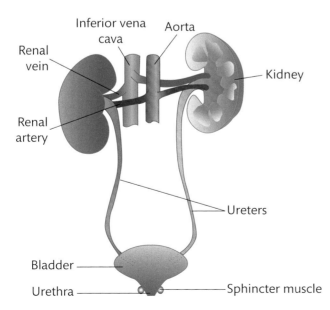

Inferior vena cava
Aorta
Renal vein
Kidney
Renal artery
Ureters
Bladder
Urethra
Sphincter muscle

▶ **Figure 3.37** The renal system

The kidneys

Each kidney holds about a million units called nephrons, which are responsible for filtering blood to produce urine. Each tubule has a knot of capillaries (the glomerulus) in a cup-shaped Bowman's capsule leading to a long coiled and bent tubule.

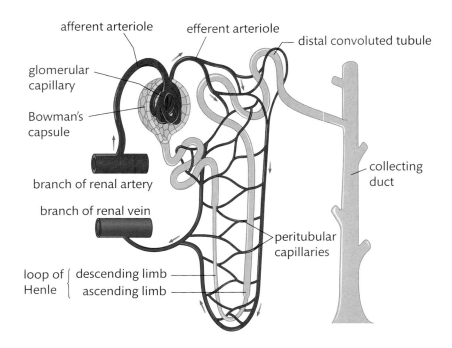

▶ **Figure 3.38** Structure of a nephron

High pressure develops in the glomerulus due to a narrowing of the capillaries forcing fluid and dissolved substances through the two layers of epithelia (one from the capillary and one from the Bowman's capsule).

Protein-free plasma filtrate leaks from the glomerulus into the cup and as the filtrate passes down the tubule useful substances such as glucose, amino acids and some water are reabsorbed back into a network of capillaries around the tubules. Protein molecules and blood cells are too large to pass into the Bowman's capsule unless the nephron has been damaged.

Antidiuretic hormone (ADH) from the pituitary gland controls fluid balance, known as osmoregulation. If a lot of water has been drunk and absorbed into the blood, volume increases and ADH production is reduced so that less surplus water is reabsorbed and more goes into urine until the balance is restored. On the other hand, if body water is lacking water, more ADH is secreted and more water is reabsorbed to regain balance. Fluid balance is maintained in this way by excreting either dilute or more concentrated urine.

The kidneys also remove toxins and drugs, which are broken down in the liver and their products eliminated by the kidneys in urine. The pH (a measure of acidity and alkalinity) of blood must be kept just on the alkaline side of neutral (pH 7.4). The kidneys have a role in maintaining pH as they can manipulate the pH of urine to get rid of extra acids or alkalis, as necessary.

The amount of salts (electrolytes) in the blood is regulated through a special process in the bends of the tubules, and the action of the hormone aldosterone.

Ureters

Ureters are the slim tubes that leave the kidneys and pass down to the bladder in the pelvis. No further modifications take place in the ureters. Urine passes mainly by gravity but the muscular walls of the tube can also carry out peristalsis.

Bladder

The bladder is a hollow organ with muscular walls, capable of great expansion. Its function is to store urine until a convenient time for expulsion from the body. A healthy bladder can hold about 300–400 ml in the day and up to 800 ml during sleep.

Urethra

The urethra is the tube that carries urine from the bladder to the exterior. In females it is quite short but in males it runs through the penis and so is longer. The urethra in males also carries semen during sexual intercourse or excitement.

Disorders of the renal system

Urinary tract infections (UTIs)

UTIs are more common in females due to the short urethra and the proximity of the anus and vagina. Cystitis is inflammation of the bladder that causes a burning pain on urination, with a sense of urgency and the frequent need to urinate, although the volume may be smaller. Urinary infection can arise from sexual intercourse and sexually transmitted infections. There is always the danger that, if left untreated, the infection will pass up to the kidneys via the ureters.

In men, an enlarged prostate which may cause an inability to pass urine could lead to urinary tract infections.

Renal failure

The kidneys may lose function due to damaged renal tubules, for example as a result of infection, hypertension or drug use. This is known as renal failure. The symptoms include decreased urine output, fluid retention (causing swelling in the legs, ankles or feet) drowsiness, shortness of breath, fatigue and in later stages there may be confusion, nausea, seizures or, in severe cases, coma.

Treatment usually includes a special diet limiting protein, salt and fluid. Eventually kidney function will need to be replaced either by dialysis (haemodialysis) or by a kidney transplant.

Haemodialysis means the service user will spend an average of four hours for three days a week connected to a haemodialysis machine. Alternatively, dialysis fluid can be run into the abdominal cavity where exchange of materials occurs. The dialysed fluid is removed from the abdomen and replaced with fresh dialysis fluid. This may be done two or three times each day, but the service user can remain mobile in between treatments. A kidney transplant is cheaper, but the kidney will not last for ever, and the service user has to take immunosuppressive drugs for the remainder of their life.

 **PAUSE POINT**   Can you explain what the kidneys do? Explain why urine containing protein is 'abnormal'?

   Hint   List the functions of the kidneys and describe the way blood is filtered from the glomerulus.

   Extend   Research 'podocytes' to see how the inner layer of the Bowman's capsule helps prevent large molecules and blood cells passing through.

The structure, function and disorders of the reproductive system

Female

Figure 3.39 shows the female reproductive system, which consists of the ovaries, Fallopian tubes (oviducts), uterus, cervix and vagina.

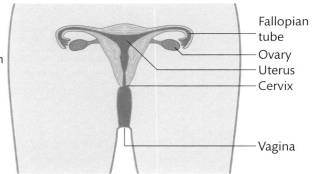

▶ **Figure 3.39** Diagram showing the female reproductive system

Fallopian tube
Ovary
Uterus
Cervix
Vagina

The ovaries

Ovaries are almond-shaped organs lying one on each side of the pelvis close to the oviducts. The main functions of the ovaries are to produce monthly ova and to secrete the two hormones, oestrogen and progesterone.

A female infant is born with ovaries containing immature ova and she does not make any more in her lifetime. Each ovum is surrounded by a single layer of follicle cells. When adolescence begins, one ovum grows a little and the follicle cells produce the hormone oestrogen, which causes the uterine lining to thicken. After about 14 days, the follicle is mature and releases the unfertilised ovum, a process called ovulation. The remainder of the follicle is converted into a corpus luteum or 'yellow body', which secretes progesterone and oestrogen. After another 14 days, if the ovum remains unfertilised, the corpus luteum degenerates, the lining of the uterus is shed (menstruation) and the cycle starts again.

The fallopian tubes

The Fallopian tubes, or oviducts, lie in close proximity to the ovaries and are attached to the uterus. The ends of the oviduct nearest the ovaries are funnel-shaped and fringed. The unfertilised ovum enters the oviduct after ovulation and passes down by the action of cilia in the epithelial lining. If sexual intercourse has taken place recently, the ovum will meet the sperm and be fertilised at the junction of the middle and outer parts of the oviduct. Whether fertilised or not, the ovum proceeds down the tube to the uterus.

The uterus

The uterus, or womb, is shaped like an inverted pear and lies centrally in the pelvis. It has thick muscular walls (myometrium) and a special lining, the endometrium, which undergoes cyclic changes in thickness. In a non-pregnant female, the lining breaks down and is expelled with a variable volume of blood during menstruation. The corpus luteum hormones thicken the endometrium in preparation for a fertilised ovum. When the ovum remains unfertilised, this lining is shed. A fertilised ovum or zygote, however, will embed into the thickened endometrium and develop into an embryo, and then a foetus. The muscular myometrium will expel the foetus in childbirth, approximately 40 weeks after fertilisation.

The cervix

The cervix is a ring of muscle at the narrow end of the uterus that projects into the vagina. It is normally closed by a thick plug of mucus. However, around the time of ovulation the plug softens and, following sexual intercourse, allows sperm through to travel into the uterus and Fallopian tubes to fertilise the ovum.

The vagina

The vagina is a muscular tube, well lubricated with glands and capable of stretching during sexual intercourse. When the erect penis is inserted into the vagina, rhythmic movements cause sperm to be deposited just below the cervix. During childbirth the cervix is thinned and the uterus and vagina become the birth canal through which the foetus/baby is born.

The vulva

The vulva is the area hidden by fleshy lips of the external genitals, called labia, which conceal the external opening of the vagina.

Disorders of the female reproductive system

Endometriosis

Endometriosis is patches of endometrial cells that are found elsewhere in the body, but which are under the same hormonal influences, so they go through the same cyclical changes of building up, breaking down and bleeding. However, the blood and debris from the patches has no outlet. Some of the symptoms include pain, especially in the pelvis and lower back, bladder and bowel problems, painful sexual intercourse and sometimes infertility.

Polycystic ovary syndrome

A cyst is a fluid-filled sac and in this condition the ovaries contain many cysts. Ovulation is irregular and, therefore, menstruation is either irregular or absent altogether. Women with this syndrome find it difficult to become pregnant and may also have problems with their weight and insulin control. The condition tends to run in families.

Male

The testes

The primary sex organs in males are the testes, which lie outside the body cavity. Each testis is composed of a mass of tubules, known as seminiferous tubules. Sperm are produced in the seminiferous tubules, triggered by hormones from the pituitary gland and testosterone. Sperm production begins at puberty.

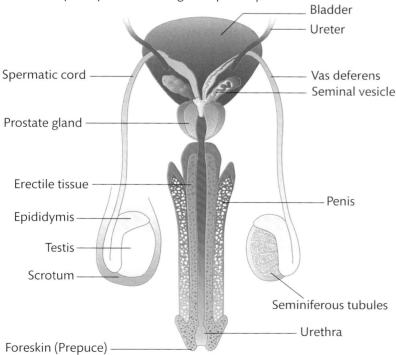

◀ **Figure 3.40** Diagram of the male reproductive system

Scrotum or scrotal sac

The scrotum is a skin bag holding the testes outside the abdomen, just behind the penis. Sperm need a cooler temperature than body temperature for normal development. This location is generally 1–2°C cooler.

Vas deferens, seminal vesicles and prostate gland

The vas deferens is a tube connecting the testis to the urethra. It stores and passes sperm towards the exterior.

The seminal vesicles are small ducted glands that join the vas deferens above the bladder and the prostate gland encircles the base of the bladder. These glands pour secretions into the vas deferens to make the sperm mobile and give them nourishment. The sperm and secretions are called semen.

The prostate is a small gland that lies at the base of the bladder and the penis, in front of the rectum and encircling the urethra. It also secretes fluid that nourishes and protects sperm. During ejaculation, the prostate squeezes this fluid into the urethra.

Urethra

The urethra runs from the bladder through the prostate to the penis. Urine is expelled through the urethra, and during sexual intercourse semen is expelled.

Penis

The penis is normally limp and soft but when a male is sexually aroused two columns of spongy tissue on either side of the urethra become engorged with blood, causing the penis to become stiff and erect. In this state it is capable of being inserted into the female vagina to deposit semen.

Disorders of the male reproductive system

Hydrocele

A hydrocele is a soft painless swelling in the scrotum due to fluid accumulation. It can be caused by infection or injury or have no obvious cause. The fluid can be removed easily through a hollow needle.

Prostate cancer and benign prostatic hypertrophy (BPH)

As males age, the prostate gland enlarges and becomes 'woody', squeezing the bladder outlet so it becomes narrower. This may cause some urine to remain in the bladder, which is likely to become infected. This condition is called benign (not cancerous) prostatic hypertrophy (overgrowth or increase in cell size).

Prostate cancer produces the same symptoms as BPH. A rectal examination may reveal the difference. The shape of the prostate gland can be felt through the wall of the rectum and a cancerous enlargement is usually felt as lumpy and irregular. If cancer is suspected, a blood test and biopsy will confirm the diagnosis.

The way in which natural conception occurs and patterns of prenatal growth

The production of gametes and meiosis

Body cells all contain 23 pairs of chromosomes, 46 chromosomes in total – this is the species number called **diploid** and serious errors occur if any variation arises. New human beings are formed when one sperm fertilises one ovum, and the nuclei fuse to form a zygote. If each ovum or a sperm (known as gametes) had 46 chromosomes, this would double up at fertilisation. It follows, therefore, that in the production of gametes there must be a halving of the chromosomes, and this is the **haploid** number.

> **Key terms**
>
> **Diploid** – cell that has paired chromosomes, one from each parent.
>
> **Haploid** – cell with half the usual number of chromosomes, such as a sperm or an ovum.

Medical research

How data are collected and used

Clinical trials

Medical research is a continuous process. However, it is not something that only scientists working in laboratories all over the world do. Many doctors, nurses and people working in professions allied to medicine (such as pharmacologists, occupational therapists and physiotherapists) may also be taking part in research projects with the aim of benefitting their service users.

People working with service users will observe, record and evaluate diagnosis, treatment and support and contribute to research by answering questions such as:

▶ Would it be better if we did 'x' rather than 'y'?

▶ Should we use 'x' drug rather than 'y' drug?

▶ Would doing it 'x' way save time and enable us, for example to see six more service users in each clinic?

Ordinary everyday working dialogue is important and can prompt a programme of official research somewhere in a health and social care workplace environment, known as a clinical trial.

Clinical trials might look at standardised treatments or at new treatments to see which has greater benefits for service users, or whether there is any difference between them at all. Research might be carried out into how services are organised or provided and whether these services can be improved or delivered more cheaply without losing quality.

Double blind trials

A double blind, or randomised clinical controlled trial (RCCT), is where volunteers are randomly assigned to one of at least two groups. There are several ways of doing this, such as each individual is given a number and a computer generates two lists of random numbers. One group is given one treatment, say, drug 'X' and the other drug 'Y'. The individual conducting the trial does not know which group has been given which drug, and neither do the group members – hence the name double blind. This information is held by a third party and is not revealed until the study has ended.

In a double blind trial, one group receives specific treatment but the other group may get different treatment, no treatment or a dummy drug (**placebo**). At the end of the trial, or sometimes after a specified period, the results are compared. This type of clinical trial can be conducted at the same time as, or at different times from, similar trials in different global locations, or with service users from different ethnic groups or environments. However, it is important in experimental work to attempt to keep everything the same except for one thing, known as the **variable**, and to be able to repeat the trial and get the same results. This can be problematic as human beings are unique.

Placebo trial

Earlier it was stated that a chemically inactive dummy drug, or placebo, could be used in clinical trials. A placebo has the same appearance and method of treatment as drugs used in the trial. Using a placebo avoids the problem of people taking part in the trial cheating and eliminates psychological bias. Additionally, in a double blind trial, even the doctors and nurses will not know whether a trial subject is taking the real drug or a placebo.

> **Key terms**
>
> **Placebo** – chemically inactive substance used in a clinical trial that resembles, and is taken in the same way as, an active drug but has no effect in the body.
>
> **Variable** – something that changes or is not consistent. In a clinical trial this will include factors such as age, sex and ethnicity.

Epidemiological studies

Epidemiology looks for patterns of disease or illness in groups of people to try to identify or promote further knowledge about causative factors relative to a specific disease. Information can be gathered about the effects of diet, race, culture, employment, age, gender, occupation and specific local environmental conditions, which can be correlated with the incidence, distribution, time and place of the disease under investigation. However, strong links do not necessarily indicate a cause, rather it is an indication that further research is needed. Sometimes a study may compare a group of service users with a disease to one without that condition over a period of time to see what happens.

Mortality and morbidity statistics

Mortality statistics

Mortality is the death rate in a population. Every death, along with the cause of death, must be reported to the authorities and registered within a specified time. These data are a vital tool in the study of disease.

The number of deaths each year per 1000 of the population is the mortality or death rate, which is often standardised by age and/or gender. The Office for National Statistics collects the data and keeps records, which it publishes annually.

Infant mortality rates refer to the number of infant deaths in the first four weeks after birth divided by the number of live births in the same year multiplied by 1000.

Morbidity rates

There are two ways of looking at morbidity rates. The first looks at the prevalence of the specific disease – the number of service users suffering from the disease at any one time. The media often use prevalence statistics when reporting about an infectious disease, such as when telling readers how many people had 'flu in February 2012 compared with, say, February 2015.

The other way of expressing morbidity is to provide the incidence, which is the number of service users diagnosed with 'flu in a given period – usually a year.

Data analysis skills to evaluate the efficacy of medical procedures and effects of lifestyle choices

Most researchers use technology to great advantage when analysing data. Therefore the ability and skill to use information technology correctly is crucial, particularly when considering ways to present information in a clear and concise way. However, before deciding how to display results, the researcher must be clear about the precise nature of the subject and able to narrow the variables to as few as possible. Many young researchers for examination work or coursework decide to use questionnaires without giving due consideration to their goals. It takes skill to produce questionnaires that provide the desired results or alternatively conducting observations or interviews.

Examine a professional newsletter or magazine for ways in which they display statistical evidence, for example as a pie charts or histograms. Make a list of the different ways that these publications use graphical images. Did you find the images, charts and graphs easy to interpret? Was this quicker than reading the relevant text?

❚❚ PAUSE POINT   Explain the meaning of 'clinical trial'.

> **Hint**   You should consider the plan, method, collection of results and interpretation and analysis of the data collected.

> **Extend**   Why might pregnant women be excluded from standard clinical drug trials?

Assessment practice 3.3

Using the internet to research answers to these questions.

1   Research the mortality statistics for prostate cancer for the most recent year and ten years before this.

2   Compare and contrast the statistics for the two years.

3   Explain how these differences can arise.

Further reading and resources

Waugh, A. and Grant, A. (2010) *Ross and Wilson Anatomy and Physiology in Health and Illness*, Oxford: Elsevier Health Sciences.

Bassett, S. (2011) *Cliffs Notes Anatomy and Physiology Quick Review*, New Jersey: Wiley Publishing Ltd.

Patton, K. (2015) *Anatomy and Physiology*, 9th edition, Elsevier Health Sciences.

Peate, I. and Nair, M. (2015) *Anatomy and Physiology for Nurses at a Glance*, Oxford: John Wiley & Sons.

Toole, G. and Toole, S. (2015) *AQA Biology* (2nd ed.), Oxford: Oxford University Press.

Baggaley, A (ed), (2001) *An Illustrated Guide To Every Part Of The Human Body and How it Works*, London: DK publishing.

Boyle, M. and Senior, K. (2008) Collins *Advanced Science – Biology*, 3rd edition, Glasgow: Collins Educational.

Bradfield, P. (2010) *Edexcel International GCSE Human Biology*, Harlow: Pearson Education.

BMA A–Z Family Health Encyclopaedia (2004), London: DK Publishing.

Lowrie, P. et al. (2008) *OCR AS and A2 Human Biology*, Harlow: Pearson Education.

THINK ▶FUTURE

Liam Doyle
Assistant physiotherapist

I've worked at a Football League club with the senior physiotherapist for two years now and hope to become a senior physiotherapist with a Premier League club in about ten years' time. My job involves working mainly with very fit young men, although we're starting a women's team next season, and of course we have an academy of young men aged 16+ who are hoping to become first-rate footballers. I have to be capable of diagnosing a problem quickly and giving treatment promptly and just about daily. We aim to get the individual back to almost full fitness very rapidly as footballers are paid well and need to be available for both training and match days. You'd be surprised at the degree of psychological support we also provide, as well as treating bruises, fractures and injuries to tendons, ligaments and cartilages. All footballers go through periods when they make more errors than they should, can't score goals or are sitting on the bench for weeks and they easily become depressed. So, although our job is mainly treating physical injuries, we all have to assist the coaches and try to lift spirits. I need to know the musculoskeletal system very well but also when to call on the club doctors to diagnose or treat other abnormalities. It's a great job and I love it.

Focusing your skills

As an assistant to the senior physiotherapist, I have to be able to work within the coaching team but be prepared to make some decisions on my own. I agree most treatments and techniques with the team but then carry them out personally. This is a role where knowledge, skills and understanding are vital to be successful.

I require an extensive knowledge of anatomy and physiology but particularly of the musculoskeletal system, the cardiovascular and respiratory systems. I need the skills for managing various treatments from simple massage techniques to using specialist equipment such as infra-red light rays as well as complying with health and safety issues.

At the unit I need to show commitment and a positive approach every day and use psychological techniques to encourage the individuals needing treatment to exercise diligently and maintain a positive self-concept. I need to keep up to date with the latest pain-relieving medication and techniques that are permitted by the rules of the governing body so research skills are used regularly. Every day can be a different challenge such as individuals presenting with colds, digestive upsets, bruising, sprains, strains and fractures but I love the variety.

Getting ready for assessment

About the test

The assessment test will last 1 hours and 30 minutes and there are a maximum of 90 marks available. The test is in two sections. Section A is a series of short answer questions, some of which are multiple-choice questions. Section B includes a longer question worth up to 12 marks. There are three types of question in the test:

- multiple-choice questions
- short answer questions, worth 1–2 marks
- a longer answer question, worth up to 12 marks.

Remember all the questions are compulsory and you should attempt to answer each one.

Sitting the test

Listen to and read carefully, any instructions you are given. Marks may be lost through not reading questions properly and from misunderstanding what the question is asking. Use your common sense and remember you have your own body with you, which is useful for some questions, particularly those on the musculoskeletal systems.

Most questions contain command words. Understanding what these words mean will help you understand what the question is asking you to do.

Arrive in good time so you are not in a panic. Make sure you have writing materials.

Command word	Definition – what it is asking you to do
Analyse	Identify several relevant facts of a topic, demonstrate how they are linked and then explain the importance of each, often in relation to the other facts.
Assess	Evaluate or estimate the nature, ability, or quality of something.
By how many	Calculate an item in relation to another.
Compare and contrast	Identify the main factors relating to two or more items/situations or aspects of a subject that is extended to explain the similarities, differences, advantages and disadvantages.
Complete	Learners provide all items. For example, 'Complete the diagram…'.
Consider	Think carefully about (something). The question will often require you to make a decision on the issue as part of your answer.
Deduce	Reach a conclusion about something by reasoning.
Define	State the meaning of something, using clear and relevant facts.
Describe	Give a full account of all the information, including all the relevant details of any features, of a topic.
Discuss	Write about the topic in detail, taking into account different ideas and opinions.
Evaluate	Bring all the relevant information you have on a topic together and make a judgment on it (for example on its success or importance). Your judgment should be clearly supported by the information you have gathered.
Explain	Show understanding of the origins, functions and objectives of a subject and its suitability for purpose. Give reasons to support an opinion, view or argument, with clear details.
Identify	State the key fact(s) about a topic of subject. The word 'Outline' is very similar.
In which	Learners specify a particular item. For example, 'In which trimester is the woman likely to…'.
Justify	Give reasons for the point your answer is making, so that your reader can tell what you are thinking. These reasons should clearly support the argument you are making.
Outline	Provide a summary or overview or a brief description of something.
Provide a key	Learners correspond an item to another. For example, 'Provide a key for Graph…
State	Express facts about something definitely or clearly
To what extent	Show clear details and give reasons and/or evidence to support an opinion, view or argument. It could show how conclusions are drawn (arrived at).
What	Specify one or more items from a definite set.
Which	Specify one or more items from a definite set.

- Allocate a few minutes to work out which questions you need to answer and then organise your time, based on the marks available for each question. Set yourself a timetable for working through the test and then stick to it – don't spend ages on a short 1–2 mark question and then find you only have a few minutes left for a longer 7–8 mark question.

- If you are writing a longer answer, try and make a plan before you start writing. Have a clear idea of the point your answer is making, and make sure this comes across in everything you write, so it is all focused on answering the question.

Remember you can't lose marks for a wrong answer, but you can't gain any marks for a blank space! So make an attempt at all questions.

Try answering all the simpler questions first and then come back to the harder questions. This should give you more time for the harder questions. There is no need to repeat the question in your answer.

Sample answers

For some of the questions you will be given some background information on which the questions are based. Look at the sample questions that follow and our tips on how to answer them well.

Answering multiple-choice questions

You need to be careful when choosing answers. Some may look sensible, but aren't suitable for the CONTEXT of the question. Always read the question carefully and choose the MOST APPROPRIATE answer.

Worked example

Examples:
Which statement accurately reflects the main action of insulin?   [1 mark]

A   to control the rate of metabolism

B   to stimulate ovulation

C   to raise the level of glucose (sugar) in the blood

D   to lower the level of glucose (sugar) in the blood

Read the question very carefully. Sometimes more than one answer is required.

Answer -------------D------------------------

Answering short answer questions

☐ Read the question carefully.

☐ Highlight or underline key words.

☐ Note the number of marks available.

Make sure you make the same number of statements as there are marks available. For example, a 2-mark question needs two statements.

Worked example

Give one difference between a tendon and a ligament. [2]

Look carefully at how the question is set out to see how many points need to be included in your answer.

Answer: A tendon joins a muscle to a bone whereas a ligament runs from bone to bone.

This answer gives a clear difference by using the word 'whereas'. You need to be sure that you have provided a difference. In this example, the difference is one of location, but you could have used their function – for example, a tendon causes a bone to move when the muscle contracts whereas a ligament strengthens a joint. Asking for differences is a common question in anatomy and physiology and will usually be allocated one mark for each correct 'half' of the answer.

Answering extended answer questions

Example 1:

Outline the path of a red blood cell from the renal vein to the renal artery, include the location of the site of oxygen uptake by the red blood cell and its delivery of oxygen to body cells. (8)

To answer this question you need to know the pattern of the circulatory system including the route through the heart and basic information on the respiratory system.

Answer:

An excellent answer will know that the renal vein containing deoxygenated blood will empty into the main vein going back to the heart called the vena cava. The vena cava enters the right atrium and the blood passes into the right ventricle to be forced out during a heart contraction into the pulmonary artery to the lungs. Here the red blood cell will pick up dissolved oxygen and return to the left atrium of the heart via the pulmonary veins. Blood passes from the atrium into the left ventricle and during contraction it is forced out into the aorta and then the renal artery where it will deliver oxygen to the renal tissues.

A weak answer will refer simply to the heart and the lungs and may use incorrect names of some blood vessels. The uptake and delivery of oxygen will be vague.

Example 2:

Explain how the volume of water in the human body is kept within a narrow range. (10)

To answer this question you will need to know the homeostatic control of fluid (water) involving the nervous system, the renal system and the endocrine system.

Answer:

An excellent answer will look at both increased blood volume through say drinking and absorbing fluid disturbing the osmoregulation and the hormonal process by which the excess fluid is passed out in urine. When excess water is lost from the body by say sweating in a hot climate then more water is reabsorbed by the kidneys through ADH secretion and urine is concentrated.

A weak answer might look at only one side, perhaps the excess being removed by the kidneys in urine. They may know the name of the hormone but not the role of the hypothalamus and pituitary gland or where ADH acts in the kidneys.

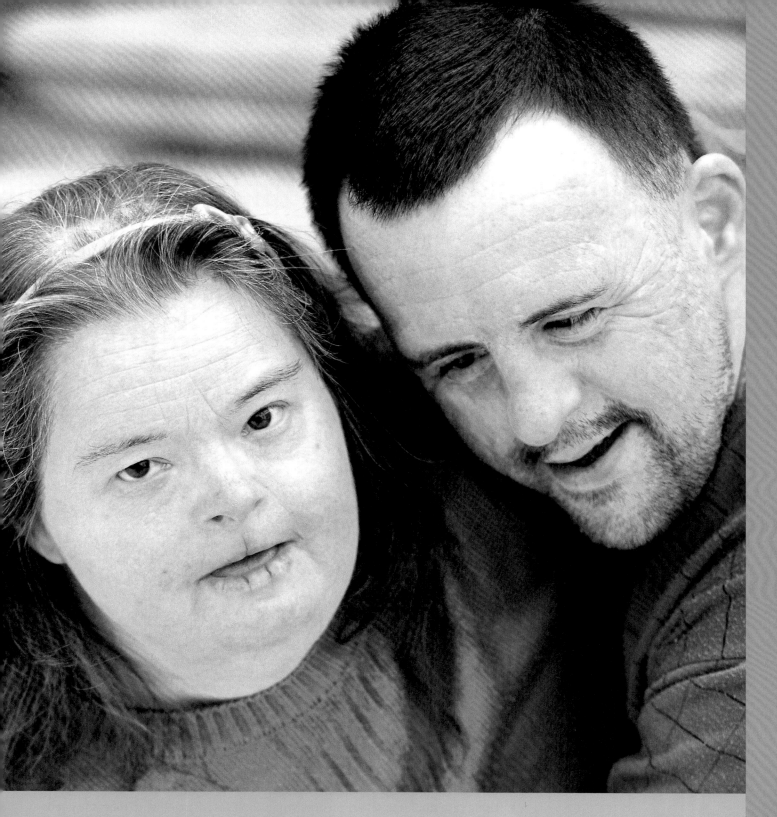

Meeting Individual Care and Support Needs 5

Getting to know your unit

To be able to provide the care and support that meets the needs of an individual in a health and social care environment, it is important that you understand the principles and practicalities that are the foundation of all the care disciplines. This unit introduces you to the values and skills that you will need for a career in social care or health care. Ethical issues will arise and challenges will need to be overcome when personalising care. You will reflect on the different methods used by professionals working together in a multi-agency team to provide a package of care and support that meets individual needs.

How you will be assessed

This unit will be assessed internally by a series of tasks set by your tutor. Throughout this unit, you will find assessment practices that will help you prepare for your final assessment. Although these activities do not contribute towards your final grade, it is important to complete them because they provide you with an opportunity to practise or they suggest useful research to undertake, both of which will be good preparation for your final assessment.

You should check that you have met all the Pass grade criteria as you work your way through the assignment. If you fail to meet one of the Pass grade criteria, you will be unable to gain a Merit or Distinction even if the rest of your work reaches the required standard. To pass you need to be able to explain and describe the information asked for in your assignment. To gain a Merit or Distinction, you need to make sure that you present the information in the style that is required by the relevant assessment criteria shown in the table below. For example, to gain a Merit you need to be able to successfully analyse and assess and, to gain a Distinction, you need to be able to use the higher-order skills of evaluating and justifying.

The final assessment set by your tutor will consist of a number of tasks designed to meet the criteria in the assessment criteria table. This is likely to consist of a written or oral activity such as:

▶ analysing and evaluating situations in case studies to reflect on the promotion of equality and diversity, and the values and skills needed to care and support others
▶ writing a report on how an ethical approach to providing support benefits service users
▶ preparing a presentation on the communication techniques used when providing care for service users with different needs
▶ using case studies to reflect on how professionals work together to meet the needs of individuals.

Assessment criteria

This table shows you what you must do in order to achieve a **Pass, Merit** or **Distinction** grade, and where you can find activities to help you.

Pass	**Merit**	**Distinction**

Learning aim **A** Examine principles, values and skills which underpin meeting the care and support needs of individuals.

Pass	**Merit**	**Distinction**
A.P1 Explain the importance of promoting equality and diversity for individuals with different needs. Assessment practice 5.1	**A.M1** Analyse the impact of preventing discrimination for individuals with different needs. Assessment practice 5.1	**A.D1** Evaluate the success of promoting anti-discriminatory practice for specific individuals with different needs. Assessment practice 5.1
A.P2 Explain the skills and personal attributes necessary for professionals who care for individuals with different needs. Assessment practice 5.1	**A.M2** Assess different methods professionals might use when building relationships and establishing trust with individuals with needs. Assessment practice 5.1	

Learning aim **B** Examine the ethical issues involved when providing care and support to meet individual needs.

Pass	**Merit**	**Distinction**
B.P3 Explain how to incorporate ethical principles into the provision of support for individuals with different needs. Assessment practice 5.2	**B.M3** Analyse how an ethical approach to providing support would benefit specific individuals with different needs. Assessment practice 5.2	**BC.D2** Justify the strategies and techniques used to overcome ethical issues and challenges experienced by individuals with different needs when planning and providing care. Assessment practices 5.2 and 5.3

Learning aim **C** Investigate the principles behind enabling individuals with care and support needs to overcome challenges.

Pass	**Merit**	**Distinction**
C.P4 Explain the strategies and communication techniques used with individuals, different needs to overcome different challenges. Assessment practice 5.3	**C.M4** Assess the strategies and communication techniques used to overcome different challenges faced by individuals with different care and support needs. Assessment practice 5.3	
C.P5 Explain the benefits of promoting personalisation when overcoming challenges faced by individuals with different needs. Assessment practice 5.3		

Learning aim **D** Investigate the roles of professionals and how they work together to provide the care and support necessary to meet individual needs.

Pass	**Merit**	**Distinction**
D.P6 Explain why meeting the needs of the individuals requires the involvement of different agencies. Assessment practice 5.4	**D.M5** Assess the benefits of multi-disciplinary and multi-agency working for specific individuals with care and support needs. Assessment practice 5.4	**D.D3** Justify how organisations and professionals work together to meet individual needs while managing information and maintaining confidentiality. Assessment practice 5.4
D.P7 Explain the roles and responsibilities of different members of the multi-disciplinary team in meeting the needs of specific individuals. Assessment practice 5.4	**D.M6** Analyse the impact of legislation and codes of practice relating to information management on multi-disciplinary working. Assessment practice 5.4	**D.D4** Evaluate how multi-agency and multi-disciplinary working can meet the care and support needs of specific individuals. Assessment practice 5.4
D.P8 Explain the arrangements for managing information between professionals. Assessment practice 5.4		

Getting started

Think about an occasion when you've been asked by a friend to do something, that you believe to be wrong. Did you do it so that you didn't upset your friend? Did you say 'no' and explain why? Write down what makes you feel that something is right or wrong. Imagine that this happened if you were working in a health or social care environment. How might this affect how you respond to service users and providers?

 # A Examine principles, values and skills which underpin meeting the care and support needs of individuals

Promoting equality, diversity and preventing discrimination

Definition of equality, diversity and discrimination

Equality

Equality in the health and social care sector means everyone having equal access to the services they need, that is, receiving a service of equal quality that meets their personal needs, no matter where they live or how they live their lives. This is not the same as everyone receiving the same service. For example, everyone has the right to register with a doctor but a seriously or chronically ill person will need more of the doctor's time. Treating people as individuals by taking into account their different **beliefs** and abilities is crucial when caring for others, and service providers should acknowledge an individual's personal beliefs, even if they do not share them. If a person's religious beliefs mean they can only eat certain foods or have to pray at a certain time, they would feel unvalued if a hospital did not accommodate these beliefs, and it might slow down their recovery.

> **Reflect**
>
> In a group of three or four, discuss your differences and similarities. Think about your appearance, how you each live your life, your preferences in music, clothes and so on, and your dislikes. Reflect on how many differences you find.

Link

Principles, values, skills and qualities underpin work in all health and social care disciplines. Links can be found between this unit and almost every other unit in this qualification. Look out for them.

Diversity

Diversity means a variety or range of differences. To value diversity is to respect and value the **cultures** and beliefs of other people. If you are unwilling to do this, and so dismiss or ignore the cultures and beliefs of others, you will be unable to learn about them or from them. You will be unable to understand them or meet their needs if you are caring for them. Similarly, you must respect and value differences such as age, gender and disability. It is a legal requirement for health and social care organisations to respect and value all individuals, irrespective of their religious or cultural beliefs, attitudes or other differences.

Britain is a **multicultural** society and this has an impact on health and social care delivery. Not only do health and social care professionals come from a diverse range of backgrounds, but so do the people receiving health and social care services. Living and working in a culturally and socially diverse society can provide access to a wide range of skills and expertise from different traditions and cultures. For those working in health and social care, this can create exciting opportunities such as new forms of treatment, different ways to deliver social care and, most importantly, learning opportunities for professional practitioners. A good service provider will be open to other people's life experiences and differences, will value their diversity and form good relationships with their colleagues and the people who use the services. A team of service providers who have different interests and skills is more likely to be able to handle a range of tasks when helping an individual, and the team will enjoy working together.

Discrimination

Discrimination is when someone has a **prejudice** against a person or a group of people. This might be for reasons such as age, gender, race, ethnicity, social class, religious beliefs, secular beliefs, family structure, sexuality, ability, health, disability, address (where they live), dress or appearance. They might then discriminate against that person or group and treat them differently.

There are four types of discrimination.

▸ **Unfair discrimination** is when a person is treated unfairly compared with someone else. For example, when someone is not considered for a job because they are older than another candidate, despite having the same qualifications and experience.
▸ **Direct discrimination** is when someone is rude, hostile or offensive to someone because they see them as being different. For example, when someone who is overweight is called names. This form of discrimination is easy to prove because it is heard or witnessed by other people.
▸ **Indirect discrimination** is harder to prove. For example, a manager may appear to be supportive and friendly towards a member of staff, but may show disrespect for their ideas by dismissing them in a jokey way.
▸ **Positive discrimination** is when a decision is made in a person's favour because there is something different about them. For example, when an advertising agency seeks to hire a person who has red hair and fair skin because they are to play the part of the sister of someone who has these characteristics; or when a service has few people from an ethnic minority at a certain level, so they appoint someone from that ethnic minority.

Importance of preventing discrimination

It is crucial to prevent discrimination, so that everyone receives a service of equal quality, which meets their personal needs. Some of the possible effects of discriminatory practice are shown in Figure 5.1.

> **Link**
>
> Learning aim A in *Unit 6: Work Experience in Health and Social Care* also looks at diversity and equality.

> **Key terms**
>
> **Beliefs** – strongly held opinions stored in the subconscious mind.
>
> **Diversity** – a variety or range of things.
>
> **Culture** – the beliefs, language, styles of dress, ways of cooking, religion, ways of behaving, etc. shared by a particular group of people.
>
> **Multicultural** – many cultures or ethnic groups living in one area.
>
> **Discrimination** – treating a person or group of people differently from others.
>
> **Prejudice** – an unreasonable feeling against a person or group of people.

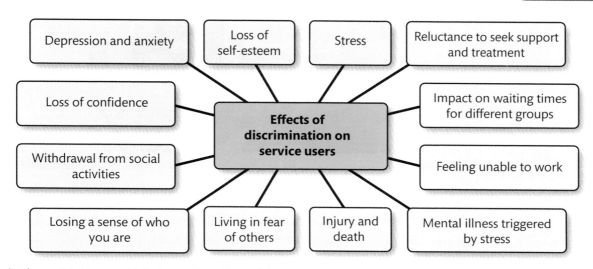

▸ **Figure 5.1:** Can you think of any other effects of discrimination on service users or service providers?

In some cases, this can lead to malpractice and abuse, putting individuals at risk of significant harm. Care workers need to understand the importance of avoiding discriminatory language and behaviour in order to employ anti-discriminatory practices in their own work. Don't forget that discrimination, whether from other service providers or from service users, affects service providers too.

Initiatives aimed at preventing discrimination in care

There are many ways in which care services can be adapted to meet individuals' specific needs and prevent discrimination.

▶ **Access:** the environment can be adapted, for example by having wide corridors, ramps, disabled toilets, lifts, wide automatically opening doors, counters and signs at wheelchair level, no obstacles or clutter, hearing loops.

▶ **Diet:** there is choice for those with medical conditions, religious requirements or cultural preferences.

▶ **Support:** appropriate resources and information are provided in a wide range of formats and languages to reflect local cultures, with advocates, translators, interpreters and carers available to help.

▶ **The use of advocacy services:** someone, referred to as an advocate, can speak on behalf of someone else (who maybe can't speak for themself due to illness, disability or lack of confidence).

Discussion

In groups, consider this statement from The Children's Society's website: 'Many children who are looked after in care or who are in the child protection system are not consulted about matters affecting their lives. Choices are made for them, often without their consent.'

What sort of choices and decisions do you think are being referred to? How do you think having choices made for them will make the children feel? How do you think advocacy services will help?

▶ Can you think of any health care situations where advocacy services could help older adults?

 **PAUSE POINT** Can you explain what has been covered in the learning aim so far? What elements did you find easiest?

> **Hint** Close your book and write down what is meant by the words equality, diversity and discrimination.

> **Extend** Why is it important to prevent discrimination? Give at least five reasons.

Skills and personal attributes required for developing relationships with individuals

In order to care for and meet the needs of others, you need to develop relationships with them, and to do that you need certain **skills** and **personal attributes**. A skill is an ability to undertake a task, such as being able to communicate or give an injection correctly. Personal attributes are qualities you have that make you the person you are. These are based on your values: the things you believe to be important in life, such as being kind and treating others with respect. The way professionals work in each health and social sector is underpinned by a set of basic values that influence working practices and enable relationships to be developed between service providers and users. One example is the 6Cs.

The 6Cs

Compassion in Practice is the national strategy for nurses, midwives and care staff. It was launched in December 2012, following nationwide concern about the standard of nursing care after the failings at the Mid Staffordshire Hospital and Winterbourne View, a hospital for people with learning disabilities and autism. A key part of this strategy is a programme of work based on the 6Cs: six values or behaviours felt to be essential to providing quality care. The 6Cs (see Table 5.1) have rapidly been adopted by many organisations across the whole spectrum of health and social care.

> **Key terms**
>
> **Skill** – the ability to do something well or to be expert in something.
>
> **Personal attributes** – the qualities or characteristics that make an individual who they are: ie their personality.

▶ **Table 5.1:** The 6Cs

Value	Definition
Care	Looking after and providing for the needs of a person.
Compassion	The awareness of the needs of others and the desire to help them.
Competence	The ability to understand a person's needs, combined with the expertise and knowledge to deliver effective care to meet those needs.
Communication	The exchange of information between two or more people that helps to provide care and support.
Courage	The personal strength and vision to do the right thing for the people being cared for.
Commitment	The determination to improve care and meet the needs of people.

> **Research**
>
> Research the charity Compassion in Action. Look at the ways in which it and different health and social care organisations are implementing holistic approaches similar to the 6Cs. Produce a slideshow presentation that would be suitable for explaining to patients in a health centre what the Compassion in Action strategy is, and how it could help them.

> **Discussion**
>
> Research the review of the failings at the Mid Staffordshire Hospital and Winterbourne View Hospital. In small groups, discuss and compare what you have found out.
>
> How do you think the use of the Compassion in Action approach to the 6Cs would help to prevent such situations happening again?

People skills

People skills are the skills that help us to get on with other people, and so develop relationships with them. Some of these skills are:

- **empathy** – the ability to share and understand the emotions of others, such as sadness, anxiety or happiness
- **patience** – the capacity to accept or tolerate problems without becoming annoyed or anxious
- **engendering trust** – the ability to get people to trust you
- **flexibility** – being able to fit in with others and change your own plans if necessary
- **a sense of humour** – being able to see the funny side of situations
- **negotiating** – the process by which two parties with different interests or perspectives attempt to reach agreement, for example a doctor and a patient
- **honesty** – being truthful and sincere
- **problem solving** – the ability to ask the right questions and find an answer to a problem.

Case study

Different perspectives

Toni, a 45-year-old woman with chest pain, is brought to the Accident and Emergency Department (A&E) in the middle of the night. The junior doctor tells her that she has had a minor heart attack and needs a surgical procedure on her heart to make sure that this doesn't happen again. However, the pain has receded and Toni feels much better. She is worried and agitated because her husband, who is severely disabled, is home alone and she is his only carer. She says she'd rather come back the next day. The junior doctor is near the end of a double shift, is very tired and, although he clearly tells Toni the risks, he is rather abrupt and aloof with her and doesn't ask her why she wants to go home, before he is called

away to another emergency. Toni discharges herself, but is brought back in an ambulance a few hours later in cardiac arrest, which leads to more serious damage to her heart.

Check your knowledge

1 Which of the people skills did the doctor use in dealing with Toni? How do you know this from the case study?

2 Which people skills could the doctor have used better? Explain your answer.

Communication skills

Good communication skills are vital for people working in health and social care as they help them to:

- develop positive relationships with people using services and their families and friends, so that they can understand and meet their needs
- develop positive relationships with work colleagues and other professionals
- share information with people using the services, by providing and receiving information
- report on the work they do with people.

Link

Refer to learning aim C of this unit and learning aim A of *Unit 6: Work Experience in Health and Social Care* for more information about communication skills and techniques.

Active listening and responding

Listening to people involves more than just hearing what they say. To listen well, you need to be able to hear the words being spoken, think about what they mean and then think what to say in reply. You can also show that you are listening and what you think about what is being said through your body language, facial expressions and eye contact.

By yawning, looking at your notes or watch, or looking around when someone is speaking, you will give the impression that you are bored by what is being said. This is not only very rude but can also cause the person distress and negatively affect their self-esteem.

The process of active listening and responding involves:

▶ allowing the person who is talking time to explain

▶ not interrupting

▶ giving encouragement by smiling, nodding and making encouraging remarks such as 'Really?' and 'Oh yes.'

▶ asking question for **clarification**, such as 'Can you explain that again please?'

▶ showing empathy by making comments such as 'That must be so difficult for you.'

▶ looking interested by maintaining eye contact and not looking at anything else

▶ not being distracted by anything else – switch off your mobile

▶ summarising to check that you have understood what has been said. For example, 'So what you mean is ...'

> **Key term**
>
> **Clarification** – making something clear and understandable.

▶ How can you tell that the service providers in this picture are interested and listening carefully to each other?

Tone of voice

It is not just what you say but also the way in which you say it that is important. If you talk to someone in a loud voice with a fixed tone, the person will think that you are either angry with them or treating them as though they are less intelligent than you. It is important to speak calmly and quietly, with a varying tone, so that the other person will think you are being friendly and kind, and are interested in what they are saying. If the person has difficulty hearing, you might speak more loudly, but still calmly and with a varying tone.

Use of appropriate language

You probably wouldn't like it if your tutor started to use slang and text language in an attempt to appear cool while they were teaching you. You would feel embarrassed for the tutor. It is important to adjust your language to match the situation you are in and the person you are talking to. People usually do this without even realising it, unconsciously changing their dialect or accent depending on who they are speaking to. For example, when they are speaking to a friend on the phone they will be less formal than if they are ringing up the optician for an appointment.

> **Reflect**
>
> Work with a partner and decide who will be the speaker and who will be the listener. The speaker should tell the listener about a recent visit to a health care service, such as the dentist or doctor. They should talk for three minutes. The person listening must listen carefully and they are not allowed to take any notes or to interrupt. The listener has to repeat what they have heard. The listener must then reflect on how well they feel they have listened. The speaker will then feed back whether they agree or not, and say why. The speaker then reflects on whether they spoke clearly and used appropriate language so that the listener could understand what was being said. Swap and repeat the activity, this time taking the other role. Do you think that you could have been a better listener and/or speaker?

Observation skills

Observing changes in an individual's condition

A carer has to be constantly alert to changes in patients' conditions, and the implications of this in terms of care. For example, if a person lapses from being asleep to being unconscious, they will need immediate medical help. If you do not have good observation skills, you may not notice that a person's condition has changed. There are two types of observations: ones that are measurable, such as volume of blood in the urine, pulse rate, blood pressure and temperature, and ones that you can see, such as whether the patient is pale or flushed, alert or sleepy, sad or happy, or eating properly. Both of these types of observation are important when maintaining a watch on a patient's overall condition.

Monitoring children's development

Another area where good observation skills are essential is in child development work. It is important to watch a child carefully and take note of all aspects of their development, including their physical condition, non-verbal communication, behaviour, relationship to others and how they play, so that problems can be identified quickly and addressed before they get worse.

Other observations

Good observation skills also help a service provider to note signs of abuse or negligence and identify any areas of care that could be improved. For example, the manager of a care home noticing that a service user is unclean and bruised, and investigating in order to remedy the situation.

Dealing with difficult situations

Having a range of skills and personal attributes that allow you to develop relationships with individuals means that, as a service provider, you will find it easier to deal with difficult situations.

Case study

Breaking bad news

Aurel is a patient of Dr Kumah's, and has a good relationship with him. Aurel is 62 years old and has been having difficulty passing water for the last few months. He is worried that he has something wrong so, although he is embarrassed, he goes to see the doctor. He has blood tests and, when the results come back, the doctor explains that one of the things in his blood showed higher levels than usual. He tells Aurel that this may mean that there is something wrong and he'd like Aurel to see a specialist.

Dr Kumah refers Aurel to a consultant in the urology department at the local hospital. In a ten-minute appointment, Aurel is told in a very forthright manner that he has prostate cancer. He is upset but does not let it show in front of the consultant. The consultant tells Aurel to go to his own doctor to have his Prostate Specific Antigen (PSA) levels monitored. This is to watch for any signs of the cancer spreading to other parts of his body. Aurel has only heard the words 'cancer' and 'spreading'. Because he is upset, and thinks that he is not going to receive any treatment, he is convinced he is not going to survive.

Aurel goes back to his doctor and is tearful and resentful. Dr Kumah spends a long time with him,

explaining that many men with prostate cancer do not die of it because it is one of the most easily controlled cancers. Dr Kumah goes over the treatment with Aurel, explaining how often he has to come for a blood test and to have his condition monitored. He even teases Aurel about it not stopping him going to watch his favourite football team. Aurel feels much better and by the time he leaves he is feeling more optimistic about the future.

Check your knowledge

1 How did having a good relationship with Dr Kumah help Aurel when he first became aware that he had a problem?

2 How do you think Aurel felt when he was told by the consultant that he had prostate cancer? Why do you think he felt like this?

3 What, if anything, could the consultant have done differently? Was it his fault that Aurel was upset?

4 How did having a good relationship with Dr Kumah help Aurel to come to terms with his condition?

5 What did Dr Kumah do that helped? What skills and personal attributes did Dr Kumah use to deal with a difficult situation?

❚❚ PAUSE POINT   Can you explain what this section of the learning aim was about? What elements did you find hardest?

> Hint   Close your book and draw out a concept map about skills and personal attributes.

> Extend   Why are good observation skills so important in health and social care?

Empathy and establishing trust with individuals

Empathy is the ability to understand another person's condition from their point of view, by placing yourself 'in their shoes' and imagining what they are feeling or thinking. You need to have an overview of the different methods of establishing positive relationships using an empathetic approach with individuals in your care.

Attachment and emotional resilience theory

John Bowlby (1907–1990) first proposed the theory (theory of attachment) that highlights the importance of a child having a significant adult (a person who is important to the child) with whom to form a close bond. This is usually the mother but it can be any other adult, such as the father, a grandparent or a main carer. Bowlby

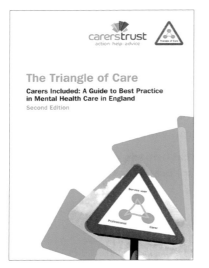

▶ The Triangle of Care. Do you know anyone who is a carer struggling to get information and support because they are not the actual service user? https://professionals.carers.org

said that children who are not able to bond in this way do not develop as successfully as infants that they may and who can have difficulties forming relationships with others later in life. The bonding process comes about through touch, eye contact and making contact through sounds. Children who have had support and a safe, secure and stable upbringing will form a secure **attachment** with their carer and are most likely to be **resilient** as they grow and develop. This means that they will be able to deal better with disappointments and overcome problems. They will trust others and expect people to be good to them, and so will want to spend time with others and develop relationships with them. They will feel and act confidently, secure in the knowledge that their needs are being met, that they are loved and that they can depend on their carer for emotional and practical support when they need it. This will enable them to become increasingly **autonomous** as they will have the confidence to make decisions independently.

The triangle of care

The 'triangle of care' is used in mental health care and is a three-way partnership between the service user, the service provider and the carer, with each being able to contribute their views and influence care and treatment decisions. It was launched in July 2010, after a number of years of research into the information and support that mental health carers need from service providers. This approach leads to the best possible care by promoting safety, supporting recovery and sustaining wellbeing. It acknowledges the essential role that a carer plays every day with the service user: for example, in looking after a person with dementia.

Carers are often the only constant in the service user's mental health care journey. They are there on both good and bad days, and they understand the service user's needs and condition really well. This makes the carer a key partner in the service user's care. Carers wish to be trusted, involved and thought of as part of the care team as they are delivering routine, daily care. This will only happen if the service provider and the carer are willing to engage with each other and share information. It is the responsibility of the service provider to actively encourage this partnership. This not only helps the service provider and the service user, but also improves the wellbeing of the carer, as they feel valued and included.

Reflect

Think about the words empathy and sympathy. What do you think is the difference in meaning between these two words? Would you rather someone had sympathy for, or empathy with, you? Why?

Empathy theories

Empathy theory attempts to offer a psychological explanation of empathy as being not only a person's capacity to share emotions with others, but also their ability to engage emotively with the world around them and with the intentions underlying art, music and literature. A few empathy theories are mentioned very briefly below.

Johannes Volkelt

Johannes Volkelt (1848–1930) was a German **philosopher**. He said that you could only really appreciate an object, such as a work of art or piece of music, if your personal identity and the object become one, so you not only see an object or hear music but also feel it with your body.

Robert Vischer

Robert Vischer (1847–1933) was also a German philosopher. He invented the term *Einfühlung*, which was later translated in English as empathy. He said this word referred to when you imagine yourself as being one with a piece of art or literature and feel the emotions that the artist tried to reproduce, so **imbuing** the piece with relevant emotions.

Max Scheler

Another German philosopher, Max Scheler (1874–1928) said that we should look at objects differently, so we didn't just give the facts about an object, such as it being big and a particular colour, but also give our opinion of it, such as it being beautiful, ugly, bland or majestic.

Martin Hoffman

Martin Hoffman is a contemporary American **psychologist**. His work is based on social and emotional development, especially empathy, and its bearing on how we develop morally. Our moral development includes our principles, how we behave and our sense of right and wrong.

> **Key terms**
>
> **Philosopher** – someone who studies or writes about the meaning of life.
>
> **Imbuing** – filling up with, or becoming soaked in, an emotion.
>
> **Psychologist** – someone who studies people; how they think, how they act, react and interact.

Assessment practice 5.1   A.P1   A.P2   A.M1   A.M2   A.D1

Dooriya is from the traveller community. Her three-year-old daughter, Rosie, is ill and she takes her to see the local GP, accompanied by several members of their extended family. The GP allows only Dooriya and Rosie into her room. However, after speaking to Dooriya, she learns that within the traveller community, family members expect to be included in discussions about health. She arranges for the extended family to wait outside while she examines Rosie and then invites them to come in.

Task 1

Write a thank you letter to the GP from Dooriya which:

- explains how she felt at different points in the appointment

- gives her opinion of how the GP has conducted herself today, and the skills and personal attributes she demonstrated.

Task 2

Create a presentation that the GP will deliver to the practice staff which:

- analyses how the service could further promote anti-discriminatory practice in the future

- assesses and evaluates different ways that the service staff could build relationships and establish trust across different groups.

Plan

- Have I read the task carefully? What exactly am I being asked to do?
- Is there anything I am unclear about? Is there anything I need to speak to my tutor about so I do not struggle to complete this task successfully?

Do

- Could I start by writing an outline plan that sets out what I need to include in each paragraph of the letter, and check this against the task?
- Have I covered all of the assessment criteria in my letter?

Review

- Which bits of this task did I find challenging? Why do I think this is?
- Would I approach a task of this nature differently next time? If so, why and how?

B Examine the ethical issues involved when providing care and support to meet individual needs

Ethical issues and approaches

Ethical working includes respecting the basic values and principles that underpin practice, but ethics also involves facing **moral** questions such as whether to prolong life against the wishes of a terminally ill patient.

Discussion

Discuss the following issues in small groups and try to come to an overall decision before sharing this with the rest of the class.

- There should be women-only carriages on trains to stop men harassing them, especially late at night.
- The death penalty should be brought back for murderers.
- The UK should have tougher rules on immigration to stop so many immigrants entering the country.

Once all groups have shared their views, reflect on your own about how the discussion went. Was there much difference of opinion within your group and between the groups? Did you find it hard to accept the views of others when they differed from your own? Were you able to justify your own opinions to others? Were you able to change the opinions of others?

Ethical theories

For centuries, philosophers have come up with theoretical ways of telling right from wrong and for giving guidelines about how to live and act ethically. When you are faced with a difficult situation in life, you can use ethical theories to guide your decisions. Each theory emphasises different points, in order for you to reach an ethically correct decision. You will have your own individual choice of theory based on your life experience. Some of the key theories are described briefly here.

Consequentialism

Early writers on consequentialism were Jeremy Bentham (1748–1832) and one of his students, John Stuart Mill (1806–1873). A modern writer on consequentialism is Peter Singer (born 1946). This theory says that the correct moral response is related to the outcome, or consequences, of the act, not its intentions or motives. If you were making a decision about a person's health or social care using this theory, you would look at the likely results of your decision for that person's wellbeing and the wellbeing of others. For example, a critically-ill child needs a very expensive surgical treatment and has low survival expectancy. Should the NHS do the operation or should the money be allocated to carry out hundreds of tonsillectomy operations? What are the consequences of spending the money either way? Which is the most important?

Deontology

Writers on deontology include Immanuel Kant (1724–1804) and W.D. Ross (1877–1971). Deontology theory says that you should stick to your obligations and duties to a person or society when making a decision because this is ethically correct. It focuses on your intentions rather than the outcomes of your actions. This means, for example, that rules about who receives what treatment are applied universally and consistently.

All patients are owed the duty of care and the duty of not being harmed. This theory does not take various factors into account, such as a lack of resources making it impossible to give everyone the same care everywhere.

Principlism

Writers on principlism include Tom L. Beauchamp and James F. Childress. This approach uses the following four key ethical practices.

▶ **Autonomy**: respecting the decision-making capabilities of autonomous people by enabling them to make independent, reasoned and informed choices about their own care.

▶ **Beneficence**: balancing benefits of treatment against the risks and costs, so acting in a way that benefits the patient and promotes the wellbeing of others. For example, using the cancer drug trastuzumab (Herceptin®) costs £22,000 to treat one person for one year (correct in August 2015). Would this money be better spent on saving many people who suffer a heart attack each year?

▶ **Non-maleficence**: doing no harm, so avoiding causing harm. For example, by making sure that any side effects of a treatment do not outweigh the benefits of that treatment.

▶ **Justice**: being morally right and fair, distributing a fair share of benefits, doing what the law says and looking at the rights of the people involved.

The aim of principlism is to bring together the best elements of the various other ethical theories that match with most social, individual or religious belief systems.

Virtue ethics

This theory, which has its roots in the work of Plato and Aristotle, focuses on the moral character, or virtues, of the individuals. If using this theory as a health or social care professional, you would make decisions based on your morals and what you feel is the right way to behave towards patients and colleagues. For example, you might take time to explain treatment options to a patient and find out what they want to happen.

Theory into practice

Jenna is 23 years old. She has a baby who is 6 months old and a partner, and they have just moved into their first flat together. She smokes 40 cigarettes a day to cope with the cravings she now has because, when she was 16, she became addicted to drugs. She has been clean for two years now.

David is 60 years old and has always made healthy lifestyle choices, so he is fit and active. He lives with his wife in a cottage in the countryside and has four grown-up children who are all married, or with a long-term partner, and have their own homes.

Both Jenna and David have a life-threatening illness and need very expensive treatment to save their lives. There is only enough money in the budget to give one of these two patients the treatment. Who should it be? Apply each of the ethical theories to the situation. Explain your thinking using each theory. Then identify the decision that you personally think is the most ethical.

Hint

Read them all again. If there are any you still don't understand, ask your tutor to explain them to you again.

Extend

What is the difference between consequentialism and deontology?

Managing conflicts

It is important that you know how to handle conflict if you work in the health and social care sector because, as a group, health and social care professionals probably face more conflict and greater complexity than any other profession. Conflict happens with service users, carers and/or families for reasons such as disagreement over care decisions, concern about the quality or cost of care, or the behaviour of staff. People may be more critical or overwrought and their emotions may be less controlled than usual because they feel ill or are concerned about a friend or family member. Conflict can also occur between colleagues, maybe over decisions made based on different ethical theories.

▶ **Table 5.2:** NHS checklist for running a meeting to manage conflict

Do	Don't
Make sure that the issues are fully outlined.	Conduct your conversation in a public place.
Acknowledge emotions and different styles.	Leave the discussion open – instead create an action plan.
Have a comfortable environment for any meetings.	Finish people's sentences for them.
Set a time frame for the discussion.	Use jargon.
Establish good rapport.	Constantly interrupt.
Use names and, if appropriate, titles, throughout.	Do something else whilst trying to listen.
Work to cool down the debate in a hot conflict.	Distort the truth.
Convince parties in a cool conflict that something can be done.	Use inappropriate humour.

Conflicts of interest

Key term

Conflict of interest – a situation where the concerns or aims of two or more different parties are incompatible.

When working with groups of vulnerable people in health and social care settings, there are times when care workers are faced with a **conflict of interest** for which they will need to find an ethical solution. Often, ethical dilemmas will not have a 'correct' answer and the solution will depend on a number of considerations.

Nevertheless, the care worker is faced with a dilemma and is expected to make a decision. Before making a decision, the care worker must consider the following questions.

▶ What are the risks to the individual and any other people?

▶ What are the professional and legal responsibilities?

▶ What are the policies of the organisation?

▶ Have I got all the facts of the case?

Examples of potential dilemmas include:

▸ being asked to prescribe the contraceptive pill to a girl under the age of 16 without parental consent

▸ having to involve social services when parents have drug addictions

▸ having to decide on the allocation of scarce resources

▸ deciding whether to pass information on to other agencies.

One of the most controversial dilemmas involves the treatment of terminally ill patients, who are very close to death and may be in a great deal of pain. In such cases, a doctor may not wish to prolong the situation and may, therefore, withhold treatment; this is known as an act of omission.

> **Discussion**
>
> Aman is a 23-year-old man who has been rushed into A&E in an ambulance. He is unconscious, seriously ill and urgently needs intensive care support. The intensive care unit (ICU) is full with some patients who are critically ill and others who have improved slightly and are in a stable condition. Evidence shows that moving a patient out of ICU too soon can increase their chances of complications. There is an intensive care bed available in another hospital 50 miles away, but Aman may not survive the journey. The consultant has to decide what to do.
>
> In a group, discuss the situation and decide what the consultant should do.

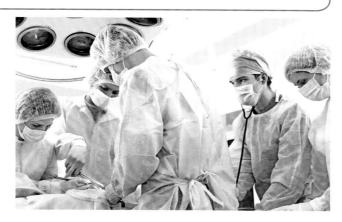

▸ Does the hospital have a moral responsibility to provide intensive care even if a person's chance of survival is small and it involves potential risk to other patients?

Balancing services and resources

There has been a lot of discussion about the way in which health and social care services should be provided, especially when there is limited funding and almost unlimited demand. The funding pressures will continue to rise due to issues such as an ageing population, rising expectations and innovative but very expensive medical technologies. Practical decisions on how resources should be allocated are often difficult to make. Should children and young people get priority, as they have their whole lives ahead of them? Or should consideration be given to the ageing population, as they have paid their national insurance contributions and taxes for longer? Should the focus be on people living in poverty or people who have disabilities? These sorts of situations require ethical decisions to be made by groups of people such as hospital boards. For example, any decisions on health care research are made by research ethics committees that review research proposals using policies which lay down the principles, requirements and standards they are expected to adhere to.

Minimising risk when promoting individual choice

When working with vulnerable people receiving social care services, there can quite often be a conflict of interest between the individual and the organisation.

> **Reflect**
>
> In small groups, discuss the various questions asked and points made in this section. Then reflect on your own thoughts and reach your own conclusions. If you had to make such decisions would you be able to make strong enough arguments to support your decision?

For example, an older person who uses a wheelchair and is living in a residential care home might be a smoker who is unable to give up their habit; yet the legal requirements and policies and procedures of the organisation state that the environment does not permit smoking. Should the older person have to go outside the building or should the care home manger provide a space for the person to smoke inside? What about the rights of those who are caring for that person not to be exposed to smoke in the workplace when they go into that space inside? A possible solution is to have a covered veranda-type smoking shelter, open at the sides, that is not near the front door, so that other residents, carers and visitors are not exposed to the smoke, but which the person can access via a wheelchair-friendly path, wearing a call button round their neck in case they need urgent assistance. An alternative solution is to help the older person to give up smoking by providing the resources necessary.

For people with learning disabilities, the conflict of interest could be related to whether they live on their own or not. It has to be decided whether the benefits of the person having their own independence are worth any possible risk to that person or to others. In situations like these, policies and procedures have to be followed closely and a risk assessment could be undertaken to assess the level of potential harm to the individual concerned and to other people. It is important that the individual is able to express what they would like; vulnerable people can be more involved in decisions about their lives when supported by an independent advocate.

Sharing information and managing confidentiality

Workers in health and social care have a duty of confidentiality that protects the rights of individuals. This means keeping information private by not sharing information about individuals without their knowledge and agreement, even with the service user's friends, family or other individuals. Health and social care workers should never:

▶ discuss one individual with another

▶ discuss matters relating to service users outside the care setting, or in a public place where they might be overheard

▶ share written information without permission

▶ leave any form of records insecurely stored

▶ leave records that are in use unattended, where they may be read by unauthorised people.

Maintaining confidentiality also safeguards service users. If, for example, a member of staff puts a photo on social media of people living in a shelter for victims of domestic abuse to escape their abusive partners, then this could lead to abusive partners discovering their whereabouts.

However, there are occasions when confidential information has to be shared. For example, if an individual is at risk of being harmed or of harming another person. All health and social care settings have procedures in place that must be followed with regard to the breeching of confidentiality.

Link

For more information about confidentiality turn to learning aim D of this unit, and learning aim A of *Unit 6: Work Experience in Health and Social Care.*

Reflect

There is a clear difference between breeching confidentiality by sharing information with a care setting manager and telling a friend. Do you know the difference? Have you ever told someone a secret told to you by someone else and caused a problem by doing so? Has anyone shared your secrets with someone else? If so how did it make you feel?

Managing confidentiality

Fred is 91 years old and has lived on his own for many years, since his wife Sheila died. His niece, Elizabeth, is his next of kin and regularly visits to help him when he needs it. One day, shortly after moving into a care home, he is taken into hospital as a non-emergency with pain in his back. Elizabeth is on holiday. She rings the hospital several days running to try to find out what is wrong with Fred and what his treatment is. However, Elizabeth is repeatedly told that they are not allowed to give out information over the telephone unless she goes into the hospital and sets up a password on the system. She is unable to do this as she is many miles away.

After three days, one nurse, who is more understanding than the others she has spoken to, sets up a password for Elizabeth over the telephone, so that she is then able to get the information she requires. After six days, Fred is sent back to the care home and the day after, on returning from her holiday, Elizabeth goes straight to the care home to see him. She is met by the manager of the home who is very relieved to see Elizabeth. The hospital has sent Fred home with a back brace but no information about how to put it on, how long for or what it is for. The care home manager has rung the hospital but, although the home cares for him on a day-to-day basis, the hospital has refused to give any information because the manager is not a family member. Elizabeth is able to provide this information and Fred can then wear his back brace.

Check your knowledge

1 How do you think the hospital's reluctance to release information made Elizabeth feel while Fred was in hospital?

2 How do you think the hospital could have dealt with this situation better?

3 What effect has the hospital's refusal to share information with the care home manager had on:
   a Fred
   b the care home manager and other care home staff looking after Fred?

4 Think back to learning aim A. How would a triangle of care approach have helped:
   a Elizabeth as his closest family member, who looks after him as best she can despite living an hour's drive away
   b the care home staff, as the people who provide his day-to-day care?

PAUSE POINT Can you explain the ethical issues and approaches described in this section? What elements did you find easiest?

Hint Close your book and draw a mind map of what you know about managing conflict.

Extend Why should all information about a service user be password protected? What could happen if someone gained access to a person's records and found that they were currently in a care home for respite care, or in hospital having an operation?

Legislation and guidance on conflicts of interest, balancing resources and minimising risk

There are organisations, legislation and guidance that influence or advise on ethical issues within the health and social care sector. These play a vital role in solving conflicts of interest, balancing resources and minimising risk to service users, their carers and/or families and service providers.

Organisations

Within the UK, there are a number of organisations – publicly and privately funded – that are involved in health and social care provision. Table 5.3 looks at some of them.

Name	About the organisation
National Health Service (NHS)	• Launched in 1948 from the ideal that good health care should be available for all, regardless of wealth • Provides a wide range of health services, the vast majority of which are free at the point of delivery for people legally resident in the UK • Made up of four, mainly independent, publically funded health care systems: NHS (England), Health and Social Care in Northern Ireland, NHS Wales and NHS Scotland • All services are often referred to as the NHS, although only the English NHS is officially called the National Health Service
Department of Health (DH)	• A ministerial department of the government • Helps people to live better for longer • Leads, shapes and funds health and care in England by creating national policies and legislation
National Institute for Health and Care Excellence (NICE)	• Set up in 1999 to help prevent ill health and promote healthier lifestyles • Provides national guidance and advice to improve health and social care, officially only in England, but does provide certain NICE products and services to Wales, Scotland and Northern Ireland • Accountable to its sponsor department, the DH, but operates independently from the government • Role is to improve outcomes for people using the NHS and other public health and social care services
Health and Safety Executive (HSE)	• Set up as the national independent watchdog for work-related health, safety and illness • Executive public body, sponsored by the Department for Work and Pensions • Acts in the public interest to reduce work-related death and serious injury across the UK's workplaces • Shapes and reviews policies, reviews regulations, produces research and statistics and enforces the law

> **Research**
>
> Research the organisations listed in Table 5.3 that you know least about. Prepare a presentation, in whatever form you want, to show a range of ways in which the chosen organisation benefits the service user.

> **Key terms**
>
> **Statutory** – required by law and governed by legislation.
>
> **Legal guidance** – policies or procedures that support the implementation and practice of laws or regulations.

Legislation

An Act of Parliament creates a new law or changes an existing law. Legislation refers to those laws that parliament makes. These laws reflect the **statutory** rights of organisations, groups and individuals; some examples are given in Table 5.4. In a health and social care setting, you need to understand the importance of adhering to **legal guidance**, as this protects against poor practice. Legislation also ensures that everyone is clear about their rights and responsibilities within the care environment.

▶ **Table 5.4:** Some of the legislation affecting health and social care in the UK

Legislation	Brief summary
Human Rights Act 1998	• Means that public organisations including the government, police, hospitals and local councils must treat everyone equally, with fairness, dignity and respect • Gives everyone the right to defend their rights in the UK courts • Sets out fundamental rights and freedoms that individuals in the UK have access to: for example, the right to life, liberty, security and a fair trial, freedom of thought and expression, and protection from discrimination
Mental Capacity Act 2005	• Designed to protect and empower people aged 16 and over who may lack the mental capacity to make their own decisions about their care and treatment • States that individuals must be given the help they need to make a decision themselves • States that treatment and care should be the least restrictive of their basic rights and freedoms possible, while providing the required care and treatment

▶ **Table 5.4:** – *continued*

National Health Service Act 2006 Section 140	• Act brought in to promote an improved health service with regard to physical and mental health and the prevention, diagnosis and treatment of illness • Section 140 is about primary care trusts giving financial assistance to people to do preparatory work for pilot schemes providing local pharmaceutical services without involving a primary care trust. This could lead, for example, to setting up pharmacies in supermarkets.
Mental Health Act 2007	• Changes the definition of mental disorder • Makes it no longer possible for patients to be compulsorily detained, unless appropriate treatment and all other information is available to that patient • Broadens the role of practitioners • Gives relatives and civil partners more rights • Provides more help, such as age-appropriate services, independent mental health advocacy, quicker tribunals, more safeguards around electro-convulsive therapy (ECT), and supervised community treatment
Equality Act 2010	• Protects people from discrimination in the workplace and in wider society • Ensures consistency in making workplaces a fair environment for both employees and employers • Replaces previous legislation (eg Sex Discrimination Act 1975, Race Relations Act 1976, Disability Discrimination Act 1995) with a single Act, making the law easier to understand • Sets out the ways in which it is unlawful to treat someone
Care Act 2014	• Replaces numerous previous laws to provide a coherent approach to adult social care in England • Aims to give clearer, fairer care and support for the physical, mental and emotional wellbeing of both the person needing care and their carer • Aims to speed up the provision of care and support where needed • Gives people control of their care

Case study

Bournewood Hospital

This is a true story. In 1994, HL, a 49-year-old man with autism, left Bournewood Hospital, where he had lived for 32 years, and moved in with carers. People with autism have problems with social interaction and communication, and have restrictive and repetitive patterns of thought, and so they become upset when set routines are disrupted. HL couldn't talk and needed help with basic tasks, such as washing and getting dressed, but he grew in confidence and made significant progress.

In 1997, on his set weekly trip to a day centre, a new driver took him on a different route, which caused HL to become agitated. He was taken back to Bournewood Hospital, without his consent or the knowledge of his carers and, because he couldn't speak, he was unable to object. He was kept there for three months. During this time, his carers were not allowed to see him and, when he was finally allowed to return to them, they found him to be half-starved, with blackened toenails

and scabs on his face. They took the case to the High Court, then the House of Lords and, finally, to the European Court of Civil Rights, who, in 2004, found that HL had been deprived of his liberty and hadn't been allowed his right to have the lawfulness of his detention reviewed by a court. This case led to the introduction of the new Deprivation of Liberty Safeguards in 2009, and is also reflected in the Mental Capacity Act 2005 as amendments to the Mental Health Act of 1983.

Check your knowledge

1 Why do you think HL became agitated when the new driver took him on a different route?

2 Which parts of the Mental Health Act 2007, listed in Table 5.4, do you think came about as a result of the Bournewood Case?

3 Do some research into the details of this case. Write an article for a magazine that covers the facts and ethics of this case, including how other Acts now help protect people like HL.

Guidance

Some of the key pieces of guidance that help health and social care services tackle issues such as conflicts of interest, balancing resources and minimising risk are described in this section.

The DH Decision Support Tool

If it is considered that if an individual needs extra support from a healthcare setting, such as an older person who is no longer able to live in their own home, the first step will be an assessment by a professional using a screening tool called the NHS Continuing Healthcare Checklist. If the results suggest that the individual is **eligible** for NHS continuing healthcare, a full up-to-date assessment of their needs will be arranged using a tool called the Decision Support Tool. Multi-disciplinary teams set out the individual's needs in relation to twelve care domains, and then make a recommendation as to whether the person is entitled to NHS continuing health care.

Five Step Framework

This approach is a model that can be used to help with making an ethical decision or to support improvement projects, from the initial idea through to completion. It can be applied to all walks of life and is used extensively by health and social care services. A step-by-step approach can be used to make an ethical decision, as shown below.

Step by step: Using a Five Step Framework to make an ethical decision   `5 Steps`

1. Recognise the decision or issue; identify the need to make a decision.
- Are you being asked to do something that may be wrong or illegal?
- Are you aware of others involved who are behaving unethically or illegally?
- Are you unsure about the ethical course of action to take?

2. Think before you act; make a prediction about which decision is most likely to give a good outcome.
- Summarise the issue so that it is clear to you, and explain why it is bothering you.
- Consider the various options and consequences.
- Consider who may be affected and consult others for their views.

3. Decide on a course of action; identify your feelings.
- Identify your responsibility in this process.
- Review all the relevant information.
- Assess any risks and how they can be reduced.
- Decide on the best course of action.

4. Test your decision; can you live with your decision?
- Review it against ethics and values.
- Consult polices, laws and professional standards.
- Consult others about your plan of action.

5. Proceed and evaluate; can you explain your reasoning clearly and engage with others in a discussion about the morals of your decision?
- Communicate the decision and reasoning to all involved, so that the action taken becomes the norm.
- Celebrate achievement by sharing successful outcomes with other stakeholders.
- Record and reflect on anything you have learned and any principles decided.

Ⅱ PAUSE POINT Try using the Five Step Framework to make a decision about whether to do something your friends want you to do but your parents would prefer you not to do.

> **Hint** Check that you understand the command words used in the Five Step Framework to make an ethical decision.

> **Extend** Try to use the Five Step approach to plan and complete a task that you have been given for homework.

NICE and NHS guidance on care pathways and care plans

The steps taken to care for and treat a service user are called care pathways; care plans are drawn up for the service user based on the care pathway. These pathways are designed to implement national standards of care, such as those produced by NICE and the NHS. The pathways are developed by multi-disciplinary teams to reflect local services and staffing arrangements. They identify who carries out key parts of the care or treatment and where care or treatment should be delivered. The pathways usually include decision support systems to help make ethical decisions about appropriate care in specific circumstances, and to help reduce unnecessary variations in treatment and outcomes between service users. One example is the controversial *Liverpool Care Pathway*, withdrawn in 2015, which aimed to improve end-of-life care, making the final hours of life as pain free and dignified as possible. Details of a wide range of NICE and NHS guidance can be found on their websites.

Managing Conflicts of Interest: Guidance for Clinical Commissioning Group (2013) (NHS)

Clinical Commissioning Groups (CCGs) manage conflicts of interest as part of their routine activities. This guidance was put in place to help CCGs manage this efficiently, to avoid the risk of loss of confidence in their decisions and the risk of undermining the integrity of clinicians. The National Health Service Act 2006, later amended by the Health and Social Care Act 2012, sets out clear guidance for CCGs to make arrangements for managing conflicts of interest. This means that they can demonstrate that they are acting fairly and transparently, and in the best interest of their patients and local populations.

HSE guidance on risk assessments

The Health and Safety Executive (HSE) provides guidance to businesses about carrying out risk assessments in order to:

▸ control risks in the workplace
▸ keep everyone working in the business (employers and employees) as safe as possible
▸ ensure that businesses do not break health and safety laws.

How guidance may be counterbalanced by other factors

There are other factors that need to be taken into account when using any of this guidance, including religion, personal choice and government policies. For example, if a piece of guidance leads a person down a care pathway which suggests the use of certain drugs for a particular condition, but something along that path is against their particular religious beliefs, adjustments have to be made to allow for this. For example, an alternative to porcine-based drugs should be found for those who are of Jewish or Muslim faith as they are forbidden to eat pork. Similarly, alternatives to bovine-based drugs or cattle-derived cartilage transplants are needed for those of the Hindu faith and also for some vegans and vegetarians.

> **Key term**
>
> **Clinical Commissioning Groups (CCGs)** – groups of general practices (in England) working together to ensure best delivery of local health services: for example, buying health and care services such as hospital care.

Assessment practice 5.2

Jamie has Down's syndrome. He lived at home with his family until the age of 21. Recently Jamie moved into a residential home for younger adults with moderate learning difficulties so that he can make the first steps towards living independently without his parents. The home has 15 single bedrooms, and a number of communal areas. Jamie will receive independent living training while he lives there.

He quickly settles in and becomes very friendly with Susan, who is 23 and has learning difficulties. They spend more and more time together and one day one of the carers walks into Jamie's room and finds Jamie and Susan kissing. The carer reports the incident to her manager, Dawn, who decides that Jamie and Susan are not to be left alone together in future. Jamie and Susan are very upset by this and do not understand what they have done wrong. The decision is not discussed with them and they feel confused, hurt and betrayed.

Task

Imagine you are the area manager for the chain of care homes of which this one is a part. Write a report (no longer than two pages of A4 paper) that can be used across the whole chain, which:

- explains the ethical dilemma that managers and carers face in such a situation
- suggests and analyses an ethical solution to this problem, with guidance for future similar situations, and that allows residents such as Jamie and Susan their independence and enables them to have a safe relationship
- evaluates whether the home is promoting anti-discriminatory practice and justifies the strategies used to overcome the ethical issue arising from Jamie and Susan's relationship.

Plan

- How should I set about starting this task?
- What do I need to understand in order to complete this task successfully?

Do

- I can use the Five Step Framework to help me decide what I think is the right course of action to solve this dilemma.
- I will draw up a rough draft, so I know what to include in each part of my report.

Review

- I can justify what I have suggested if my tutor disagrees with me.
- I know how I would tackle this task better.

C Investigate the principles behind enabling individuals with care and support needs to overcome challenges

Enabling individuals to overcome challenges

Different types of challenges

Individuals with care and support needs face different types of challenges. The following are examples based on older people, but other groups will also face many of these challenges.

▸ **Awareness and knowledge**: an older person may not be aware of the funding help available if they need to move into a care home, and so may be worried about how they can afford this type of care. Similarly, if service providers are not aware of the latest guidance or do not consistently refer to it, they will not change their way of working, so those they care for will not benefit from the guidance.

▸ **Practical challenges**: an older person may find it increasingly difficult to cook meals or wash themselves as they become less mobile. A service provider may find it cannot offer the best care possible because it does not have the resources to do so.

▶ **Skills challenges**: an older person who can no longer get out of the house may want to find out what help is available but doesn't have the ICT equipment or skills to find the relevant phone numbers or to research online. Likewise, service providers may need time to learn and practice new ICT skills.

▶ **Acceptance and belief challenges:** an older person who has lost most of their mobility may find it hard to accept that they can no longer manage on their own, and may feel that they have lost their independence. An older person with certain beliefs may find the challenge of the approach of the end of life easier to deal with due to their religious beliefs. Similarly, a service provider's response to new guidance is affected by whether they think the change is right, or whether they believe they are capable of adapting to it.

▶ **Motivational challenges**: an older person who is morbidly obese may find it very hard to find the motivation to start what they see as the very long task of trying to lose weight. Similarly, a service provider may lack the drive to improve, wanting to stick to the 'old way' of doing things, so that change for the better doesn't happen.

▶ **Communication challenges**: an older person may start to lose their sight or hearing, or become very hesitant in their speech and find it increasingly hard to communicate with others. A person who provides a service may also have communication difficulties, either because they have a disability or develop a problem.

Case study

Children's Centre Advisory Boards

Children's centres were set up as part of the Sure Start programme to improve the outcomes for young children and their families, with a particular focus on the most disadvantaged families. In some local authority areas, children's centres are **governed** by an **advisory board**. These can have up to about 20 people on them and are made up of people such as children's centre managers, primary school head teachers, health professionals, and representatives from the local authority and various other organisations offering services for children and families. There are also two representatives of governors from local primary schools.

There are meant to be at least two parent representatives on the board but some struggle to find anyone willing to join them. One particular board meets between 4 and 6 pm four times a year. The meeting is mainly taken up by each organisation delivering a report on their own areas of expertise, including details such as how far they have come towards meeting their targets for the year and what difficulties they are facing. The reports are full of **acronyms** and **abbreviations**.

Check your knowledge

1 What are the challenges facing children's centre boards in terms of recruiting parents to attend?

2 What will happen if these challenges are not overcome?

3 Suggest ways in which these challenges could be overcome.

Key terms

Children's centre – a place providing services for young children and their families.

Govern – exercise a controlling influence.

Advisory Board – a group of people who meet and give advice.

Acronym – a word made from using the initial letters of other words or phrases, such as AIDS (acquired immunodeficiency syndrome) or FAST (face, arms, speech, time)

Abbreviation – a shortened form of a word or phrase, such as Mon for Monday.

Methods of identifying challenges

There are various methods for identifying challenges, such as the following.

▶ **Observation**. One of the most important skills you will learn if you become a care worker is observation. This skill will help you identify problems quickly, so they can be addressed before they get any worse. Observing and identifying patterns of behaviour, and any changes, may point to a developing problem that needs attention: for example, a change in the way a person walks, signs of abuse or negligence, or noticing any areas of care that could be improved, such as hand washing.

▶ **Focus groups**. A focus group is a small group of, typically, around eight people. They are invited to discuss a particular issue, such as introducing new early intervention services, in a session run by a facilitator and, maybe, an assistant. The group shares ideas and explores issues rather than reaching decisions. The information gathered is used to clarify situations and identify challenges. Health and social care services can then provide the services needed to meet these challenges.

▶ Have you taken part in discussions in a group of this size? Did you manage to speak up and contribute?

▶ **Talking to individuals informally**. Chatting casually to individuals, using plain language instead of jargon or technical words, can help to identify any challenges that an individual is facing without them feeling that they are being questioned or watched. This could be used to gather opinions on a new procedure being introduced at a dental surgery or on a hospital ward.

▶ **Using questionnaires**. Questionnaires are sets of questions used to collect people's opinions on certain topics, to get a snapshot of the views of a large number of people. They could be used, for example, when a primary care trust is looking for feedback from a group of practice-based GPs within their area. A well-designed questionnaire is useful because it can collect a lot of information from a large group of people much more quickly than other methods. Questionnaires are also relatively inexpensive to administer. However, they do not allow for follow-up questions and the response rate may be poor.

Strategies used to overcome challenges

Educational information materials

Educational information materials can take a range of forms, such as leaflets, posters, games, slide presentations, wall displays, CD-ROMs, DVDs, flyers, web-based materials and newspaper or magazine adverts or articles, TV and radio coverage. These materials inform people about current thinking on how to live healthily and also give advice on how to overcome challenges, such as giving up smoking, or how to apply for funding. They help raise awareness and knowledge, and can provide information for people who have communication difficulties, as they are presented in so many different forms, including Braille. Such materials also alert service providers to changes in practice and provide a resource that they can continually refer to.

Reflect

Think about health promotion materials that you have seen. How could they be changed to make you pick them up, read them, and act on them?

Training courses

Courses are available to help people with care and support needs to overcome challenges. For example, if you are a carer for a family member who has an illness or disability, you can go on a course to learn how to help them move around so that you don't hurt them or yourself. If a person has had a stroke and has been left with a disability, they can access training to learn how to overcome the problems associated with their disability: for example, how to do routine tasks with reduced use of part of their body. Organisations such as local councils and hospitals run these courses, and there are also courses available online, covering a wide range of challenges. Training courses are also used to educate service providers about the latest developments in their area of care.

Opinion leaders

An opinion leader is a well-known individual or organisation that has the ability to influence public opinion. An opinion leader can be anyone who has an active voice in a community, who speaks out and is often asked for advice. In health and social care, this tends to be people who are chief executives of bodies such as the NHS, Skills in Care or Care England, but, equally, it could be a local GP. They could be asked to use their influence to discuss, for example, how to cope with the challenge of caring for the ageing population as the demand for services rises but the resources shrink as funding is cut. They can use their influence to motivate health and social care service providers to achieve the best possible care for service users.

Discussion

In a small group, discuss people who live or work in your community and decide between you who you consider to be a local opinion leader. Write down their name and why you have picked them. Be prepared to share your choice with the rest of your class.

Clinical audits

A clinical audit is a systematic review of care based on standards of best practice and explicit criteria. Based on the results, changes are then implemented, wherever necessary. For example, a clinical audit of the level of care that GPs provide individually for continuing care for a certain long-term condition may show that patients have been on the same medication for a number of years, and highlight the fact that new drugs have been developed that might be of more help to those patients. Such audits highlight challenges for both service users and providers.

Computer-aided advice systems

These are online decision support systems that supply service providers with specific information when they need it, such as to pharmacists and doctors when they are prescribing medication. These systems provide prompts designed to reflect best practice and remind service providers to take or avoid a certain action. They are effective in the delivery of preventative services.

Patient-mediated strategies

Patient-mediated strategies provide information via mass-media campaigns to service users and the wider public about the latest evidence-based practice. Evidence shows that this enables service users to be more able to influence decisions made during a consultation about their own care, and more accepting of any changes because they are already well informed about them. These strategies also educate and motivate service providers about changes in practice.

Ⅱ PAUSE POINT Can you identify the different types of challenge faced by individuals with care and support needs, and the methods for identifying them?

Hint Write out the types of challenge in alphabetical order. Then devise a way to remember them.

Extend Draw a concept map that shows the different strategies used to overcome challenges.

Policy frameworks

A policy framework is a structure used to organise sets of principles and long-term goals into a logically documented set of rules, providing guidance and an overall direction for planning and development. Many policy frameworks are used in the health and social care sector to reduce inequality of care and improve integration of services. Some include ways in which to assess needs, and some include ways in which to decide whether a service user is eligible for help with their needs.

NHS Patient Experience Framework

This framework sets out a working definition of a positive patient experience, built around the eight elements of the definition of good patient care. It uses these elements as a framework for measurement and improvement of the patient experience. 'When using this framework, the NHS is required, under the Equality Act 2010, to take account of its Public Sector Equality Duty, including eliminating discrimination, harassment and victimisation, promoting equality and fostering good relations between people.' (DH)

▶ **Table 5.5:** The NHS Patient Experience Framework (2011)

	Elements critical to the patients' experience of NHS Services
1	Respect for patient-centred values, preferences and expressed needs, including: cultural issues; the dignity, privacy and independence of patients and service users; an awareness of quality-of-life issues; and shared decision making.
2	Coordination and integration of care across the health and social care system.
3	Information, communication, and education on clinical status, progress, prognosis and processes of care, in order to facilitate autonomy, self-care and health promotion.
4	Physical comfort, including pain management, help with activities of daily living and the provision of clean and comfortable surroundings.
5	Emotional support and alleviation of fear and anxiety about such issues as clinical status, prognosis and the impact of illness on patients, their families and their finances.
6	Welcoming the involvement of family and friends, on whom patients and service users rely, in decision-making, and demonstrating awareness and accommodation of their needs as care givers.
7	Transition and continuity regarding information that will help patients care for themselves away from a clinical setting; and co-ordination, planning, support and empowerment to ease transitions.
8	Access to care, giving attention, for example, to time spent waiting for admission or time between admission and placement in an in-patient setting, as well as waiting time for an appointment or visit in the out-patient, primary care or social care setting.

Health Action Plans

Health Actions Plans are plans that set out the NHS's commitment to patients and how services will improve. These plans aim to minimise challenge by looking at future pressures on the health service and planning ahead. These pressures are:

▶ an ageing society

▶ a rise in long-term conditions, such as dementia, and those due to unhealthy lifestyle choices

▶ increasing expectations of the health service by the general public and service users.

These pressures have to be dealt with at the same time as considering:

▶ the increased costs of providing care

▶ the limited productivity gains, which means that there is not much improvement in services after a lot of time and money have been spent

▶ **constrained** public resources.

There are plans in place for tackling issues such as obesity, late HIV diagnosis and many other areas of health. Individuals may have their own health action plan to minimise the risks from their own challenges, such as lack of exercise, giving up smoking or coping with mental health issues.

Research

Research some of the areas of health for which Health Action Plans have been created in the last ten years. Draw a table on a single sheet of A4 paper to summarise the key points of each, such as its topic, the year it was created, its aim and other points that you think are important.

Adult Social Care Outcomes Framework

Launched in 2011, the framework measures performance against the aim of ensuring that the most vulnerable people in our society receive high-quality care, regardless of where they live. The framework covers four areas:

▶ **enhancing** quality of life for people with care and support needs

▶ delaying and reducing the need for care and support

▶ ensuring that people have a positive experience of care and support

▶ safeguarding adults whose circumstances make them vulnerable, and protecting them from avoidable harm.

The framework also provides yearly results about how each local authority performs against the framework, which allows people to see how well their own local authority is performing and how it compares with other local authorities.

Common Assessment Framework (CAF)

If a service provider, such as a teacher, has any concerns about a child, they complete a CAF pre-assessment checklist.

Key terms

Constrained – restricted, limited or forced to follow a particular course of action.

Enhance – to improve.

Worked Example: Complete the pre-assessment checklist for Carly, who lives with her father as her mother has died, referred by her teacher to the Special Educational Needs Coordinator (SENCO).

Step 1: Complete identifying details (name, date of birth, contact name and telephone number, address)

Carly, age 8

Step 2: Does the unborn baby, child or young person appear to be healthy?

No. Carly is looking thinner and paler. She is also tired all the time and increasingly scruffy

Step 3: Does the child appear to be safe from harm?

Yes

Step 4: Does the child appear to be learning and developing?

No, Carly has started to miss days from school every couple of weeks and is quiet and withdrawn when she does attend

Step 5: Does the child appear to be having a positive impact on the others?

No, she is falling out with her friends more often or being left out because she has been missing from school. She is becoming isolated.

Step 6: Does the child appear to be free from the negative impact of poverty?

Not sure. Her weight loss suggests she may be undernourished and her scruffiness may suggest there is less money for uniform.

Step 7: If you answered no to any of the previous questions, what additional services are needed for the unborn baby, infant, child or young person or their parent(s), carer(s) or families?

I feel that Carly is not having all her needs met at the moment. I would like someone to have a chat with Carly's father to look at every aspect of her care to try to identify why Carly has changed in recent months.

Step 8: Can you provide the additional services needed?

No

Step 9: If you answered 'No' or 'not sure' to any of the previous questions, or it is not clear what support is needed, would an assessment under the Common Assessment Framework help?

Yes

Step 10: If you answered 'yes' to the previous question, who will do this assessment?

Another practitioner

Step 11: Sign and date the form

If the pre-assessment checklist suggests there is a need, the service provider will use a CAF to assess the child's needs. This is a simple, early intervention process for gathering and recording information in a standard format, on a CAF form, identifying the needs of the child at an early stage and how those needs can be met. The framework is common to all children's services and all local authority areas in the UK; it plays a central role in delivering integrated services focused on the needs of children and young people. A CAF aims to provide early intervention, to improve communication and joint working between all service providers and also to help stop children and their families having to repeat their details to each separate service or agency. It is voluntary, so the child or young person and their parent or carer has to give their permission at the start of the process and then again for the information to be stored and shared with other service providers.

The CAF is for children and young people who have additional needs in one or more of the three areas shown on the sides of the triangle in Figure 5.2.

Safety tip

All service providers using CAF must have an enhanced **DBS check**.

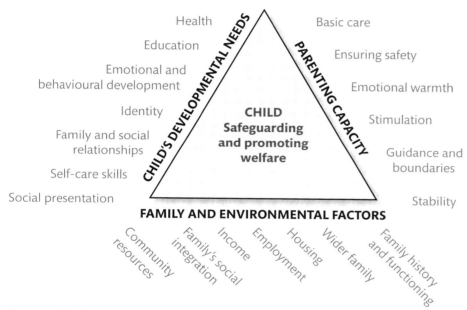

▶ **Figure 5.2:** Make sure you know what all these different terms mean

Key term

DBS check – Disclosure and Barring Service check, carried out on anyone working with or adopting children and anyone working in other areas such as health care, to make sure the individual does not have a criminal record.

Completion of a CAF does not always ensure that the child or young person will have access to all the services they need locally, as the local area will prioritise the services it provides based on local need.

Reflect

Have you ever been in hospital or visited someone in hospital and noticed how every member of staff checks their name and date of birth? Why do you think they do this? Would you feel less irritated by repeating the same information if you knew the reasons why? How does a CAF stop a service user having to keep repeating their story?

Impact of not enabling individuals to overcome challenges

It is difficult to ensure that all service providers know about the latest guidance in their particular field of care, what needs to change as a result of it and be motivated or accepting enough to make changes. Sometimes there are several sets of guidance coming from different bodies, which can make it hard to get service providers and users to engage with the guidance. If service providers don't make the changes, then service users aren't able to make the changes necessary to improve their health and wellbeing. A challenge, such as the ageing population not being effectively tackled, could become a crisis in the future. The NHS could reach breaking point because it has reached its capacity, and environments such as care homes may have to turn people away. Services and outcomes for service users won't improve, and early identification and intervention won't happen, which leads to a greater need for specialist services.

❚❚ PAUSE POINT

Do you know the policy frameworks available to minimise challenges?

Hint

Close your book and draw a table with two columns. Write the names of the four frameworks in the first column and what they are for in the second column.

Extend

Why are these frameworks so important to minimising challenges? What do they all have in common that makes them so useful?

Promoting personalisation

Personalisation

Personalisation is the term used for ensuring that every person receiving care and support is able to set their own personal goals, and have choice and control over the shape of their care and support. Service users can be given control over the services they receive by being allowed to control how some of the budget for their support is spent. They can decide the service they want, the provider they wish to purchase it from and how they want it delivered. For example, older people in need of care and support can claim Attendance Allowance. This is a weekly amount that they can choose how to spend. For example, they could put this towards the cost of paying for **supported living services** in their own home, ranging from 15-minute visits to 24-hour assistance, or it could be used to pay towards living in residential care, either in a care home or in sheltered housing. Similarly, a parent may decide to spend their childcare vouchers on a childminder or on a nursery place for their child.

If an adult of any age has care and support needs (such as those shown in Figure 5.3), the local authority will start by carrying out a care and support needs assessment to decide whether the person's needs meet the **national eligibility criteria**: that is whether their needs:

▶ arise from, or are related to, a physical or mental impairment or illness

▶ make them unable to achieve two or more specified outcomes

▶ mean that there is likely to be a significant impact on their wellbeing if these two or more outcomes are not met.

If the person does not meet the national eligibility criteria, the local authority will give the person information about other services and ways in which they can find funding. If, however, their needs do meet the national eligibility criteria, the local authority will have to meet these needs. The local authority starts by drawing up a care and support plan, and discussing with the person how they wish to live their life. This may be in their own home or in residential care. The local authority will look at preventative services, such as aids to make it possible for the person to stay in their own home, and/or information about other support available, such as help in the home or care in a care home. The person will be involved throughout the whole process, if necessary with the help of a family member or advocate. If the local authority is paying for the person's care it is allowed to choose what it feels is the most cost-effective method.

Key terms

Supported living services – services that can help a person live in their own home on a long-term basis.

National eligibility criteria – a minimum threshold of needs for adult care and support.

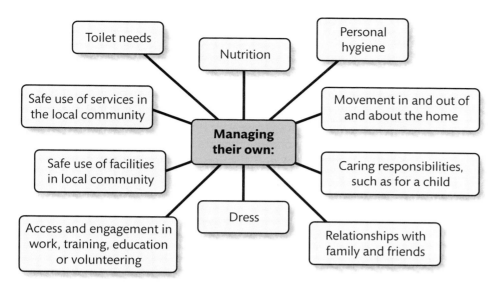

▶ **Figure 5.3:** Specified outcomes for assessment for eligibility threshold

However, if the person is **self-funding** their care, then they can make the choice. From April 2020, there will be a cap on the costs of meeting eligible care needs (not including normal daily living costs and residential care), above which the local authority will take over payment.

Methods of recognising preferences

Plans

There are several methods available to help a service user recognise their preferences for how their care and support needs will be met. These include various types of plan, all of which are written documents drawn up as an agreement between a person and their care and support professional, describing, in an accessible way, the services and support being provided. However, as every plan is developed for the individual concerned, they are not standardised.

Key term

Self-funding – a person paying all the costs of their care and support services.

▶ **Table 5.6:** Three types of plan

Type of plan	What does it plan?	Who do they help?
Care	The care services and support to be provided.	Individuals needing extra help with daily living.
Learning	A programme of learning that takes into consideration the person's strengths and weaknesses.	Individuals with learning difficulties.
Behavioural	How a person's behaviour may be changed.	Individuals with conditions such as autism.

Specialist support from health and social care professionals

The local authority adult social services department will carry out a care and support needs assessment. This is usually done in a person's own home. However, it may be carried out in a hospital if, for example, an older person has had a fall or illness and the hospital staff and family do not think the person will be well enough, or safe, to be discharged to their own home to look after themselves. This will always involve the adult concerned, unless they are too unwell or have severe learning difficulties. Once the assessment has been carried out, other health and social care professionals will be involved, depending on the needs identified.

The importance of promoting choice and control and the financial impact of this on care

A basic aim of all service providers is to promote a way of life for service users that allows them to enjoy, as far as possible, their rights as individuals. One of the most important rights we have is to be independent, to make our own decisions and our own choices, and to feel in control of our own lives. How would you feel if you were never allowed to choose which clothes to wear, or how to style your hair? Often, a carer will select clothes to be worn because they are easy to put on, or easy to wash when food is spilled down them. However, the person being cared for might prefer a different outfit because it suits them better and makes them feel better about themselves. Having choice and control helps people maintain their independence and positive self-esteem.

By providing personalised care, people are helped to live with **long-term conditions**, such as arthritis, asthma or depression. The emphasis has moved to being proactive, that is, acting before the condition worsens, and allowing people choice and control, rather than services reacting when something goes wrong. By acting early and by making it possible for people to live in their own homes, supported by family and friends, limited health care resources can be used more appropriately, which should lead to reduced use of urgent and emergency care.

The aim is to find cost-effective solutions to managing long-term conditions in the community so as to reduce the cost of funding this care. Promoting choice and control should reduce the cost of this area of care provision.

⏸ **PAUSE POINT**   Do you feel that you understand personalisation?

> **Hint**   Close your book and try to draw a spidergram to summarise everything you have learned about personalisation.

> **Extend**   How might personalisation of care help the economy of the UK in the long term?

Communication techniques

Good communication skills are vital for people working in health and social care as they help them to:

▸ develop positive relationships with services users and their families and friends, in order to understand and meet their needs

▸ develop positive relationships with work colleagues and other professionals

▸ share information and feelings with people using the services, by providing and receiving information

▸ report on the work they do with people.

Communication between service users and providers is almost always **interpersonal**. However, service providers may never actually meet, and so communication may be by telephone, text or email.

> **Key term**
>
> **Interpersonal** – between people present in the same place, face-to-face.

> **Reflect**
>
> Write down all the different ways you communicated with somebody yesterday. Reflect on how effective your communication was. Did other people always seem to be listening to, and understanding you? Did you listen to, and understand, all the various forms of communication that came your way?

Different approaches for effective communication

Health and social care providers use a range of techniques to communicate with, and gather information about, service users. Some of the psychological approaches are summarised in Table 5.7. A service provider, such as a therapist, has to ask themselves questions such as whether a particular approach fits the problem, whether they have the right skills to use a certain approach, etc. before deciding which approach to use. The strengths and weaknesses of each approach need to be considered as well as the impact it will have on the service user.

▸ **Table 5.7:** Psychological approaches to effective communication

The approach	Strengths	Weaknesses
Humanist Person-centred	• Non-intrusive, meet as equals • Unconditional, depends on basic trust in the service user • Uses a positive manner, thoughts and actions, empathy, shows respect • Gives person choices and believes they can change their lives • Positive approach • Used in lots of situations	• Ignores behaviour • Short term • Relies on good communication skills • Uses complicated terms • Hard to be non-judgemental

The approach	Strengths	Weaknesses
Behavioural Looks only at observed behaviour	• Objective, so people can agree about what is happening • Easy to understand • An approach that comes naturally • Doesn't rely on communication skills, so works with all ages and abilities, eg a baby imitating adults to acquire language skills	• Doesn't look at what's going on inside someone's head, so limited • Deals with symptoms not causes, so can be short term • Can only be used to change behaviour
Cognitive Structured approach of understanding and changing behaviour	• Easy to understand, logical and makes sense to service users • Takes notice of what service users think and feel • No interpretation or hidden meaning	• Relies on good communication skills, need to express thoughts and to understand what service providers want the individual to do • Rational approach, so not suitable for those who don't have a rational mind • Only one problem worked on at a time
Psychoanalytical Interprets what the person says and does	• Effective • Gives service users insight into why they think or feel as they do, so gets deeper into problems • Can change many parts of lives, not just behaviour • Can be used for a wide range of problems	• Very complicated to use • Needs specialist training • Based on service providers' analysis • Lengthy
Social Studies individuals in a social context	• Uses real-life situations when studying behaviour • Uses the results from experiments, such as the BBC prison study, to explain and offer solutions to an individual's problems • Helps understanding of social behaviour in general	• Presence of observer may have a negative effect on participants • Findings are generalised • Members of the group being studied may not be representative of population as a whole, ie they may be more motivated

---

Theory into practice

Work with a partner on one of the theories listed in Table 5.7. Your tutor will tell you which one to look at.

- Research to find more details about your theory, so you understand it better.
- Think of one example of a situation in a health and social care setting where a professional could use the theory to work with a service user.

Write a clear, easy-to-read guide for workers in that setting to explain how to use the theory in a session with a service user. You should give details explaining why it is the best approach to use.

Types of communication

Verbal

Verbal communication uses words to present ideas, thoughts and feelings. Good verbal communication is the ability both to explain and present your ideas clearly through the spoken word, and to listen carefully to other people. This involves using a variety of approaches and styles appropriate to the audience or person you are addressing.

Discussion

In pairs, discuss a TV soap opera or drama that you both watch. Choose two characters and a recent storyline. How did the storyline convey the feelings and moods of the characters? List as many ways as you can remember, and discuss how well the soap did this.

Body language

Body language is very important. It often gives service providers a better idea of how someone is feeling than what the service user says. It is also important, as a carer, that you understand what messages your own body is giving to the person you are trying to help. Body language includes the following.

▸ **Posture**: the way you sit or stand can send messages. Even the way you move can give out messages. For example, shaking your head while someone else is talking might indicate that you disagree with them, or waving your arms around might mean you are excited. Sitting facing the person you are talking to, with your arms unfolded and a smile on your face shows a positive and warm response.

▸ **Facial expression**: the human face is very expressive. It is able to express countless emotions without any words being used. The facial expressions for happiness, sadness, anger, surprise, fear and disgust are the same across cultures. It is important to match your facial expressions to the conversation: for example, not smiling when someone is talking about something sad.

▸ **Eye contact**: most people find that what they see affects them most so eye contact is especially important. You can often tell what someone is feeling by their eyes. Our eyes become wider when we have positive feelings, for example, when we are excited or happy, attracted to, or interested in someone. Eye contact is also important in keeping a conversation going and for judging the other person's response.

▸ **Appropriate use of touch**: touching another person can send messages, for example care and affection or power and control. It is important to think about the setting you are in and what you are trying to convey before touching a person in a health and social care environment.

▸ **Gestures**: there are certain common signs or gestures that most people automatically recognise, but it is important to understand cultural norms so that you do not unintentionally cause offence. For example, in Western cultures, thumbs-up can mean that all is well and is perfectly acceptable whereas in the Middle East, it is not only unacceptable but also one of the biggest insults possible. It also causes offence in countries such as Greece and Russia.

▸ **Non-threatening body language**: it is important not to give out negative messages through your body language. Turning away slightly with your arms folded portrays negative feelings of boredom, coldness and lack of interest. Getting too close to someone, and so invading their personal space, can cause discomfort, intimidation or distress.

▸ **Personal space**: getting too close to, or too far away from, someone can create unease. The size of a person's personal space depends on cultural norms. For example, Americans tend to require more personal space than many other cultures. Also, getting too close to someone with a mental illness can be very distressing for them. If a person backs away a little when you are speaking to them, don't try to close the gap as this will make them feel uncomfortable. How close you can move into a person's personal space depends very much on individual preference and context.

▸ Can you tell the emotions of these two people by looking at their facial expressions?

To tell or not to tell

Charles is 70 years old and lives on his own since his wife died last year. About 6 months ago he had a heart attack, from which he has made a good recovery. However, the doctors have told his daughter, Laura, that he is to take regular exercise, watch his diet and have as little stress as possible. Laura (aged 40) and his granddaughter Chloe (aged 6) try to visit him every week and he very much looks forward to their visits. Laura's husband, Alex, occasionally joins them.

Chloe and Laura are walking home from school one day when a cyclist mounts the pavement and knocks Chloe down. She bangs her head on the pavement and is taken to hospital, where she has to stay due to her injuries. Laura and her husband decide not to tell Charles about the accident as they don't want to cause him any stress. Alex and Laura visit Charles. They tell him that Chloe is absent as she is at a sleepover and then carry on a different conversation to distract him. Charles feels uneasy but doesn't know why. Laura and Alex make cups of tea and change the subject whenever they think Charles is going to mention Chloe, and make an excuse to leave earlier than normal.

Check your knowledge

1 How will Laura and Alex be feeling?
2 What signals is Charles likely to pick up from Laura and Alex?
3 In a group of three, role play Laura and Alex's visit to Charles.
4 What could have been the better course of action to take, rather than leaving Charles feeling uneasy and worried?
5 Role play an alternative way of handling the situation.

Written

Written communication is central to keeping records and writing reports when anyone is providing a service in a health and social care environment. Different types of communication need different styles of writing and different ways of presenting information, but all require **literacy skills**. Meaning has to be clear and writing needs to be well structured and legible, with grammar, spelling and punctuation used correctly. A more formal style of writing and language are needed when recording information about a patient.

Formal

Formal communication tends to start with a greeting such as 'Good afternoon. How are you feeling today?' It can be used to show respect for others. Formal conversation is often used when a professional person, such as a health or social care worker, speaks to a service user. It is clear, correct and avoids misunderstanding.

Informal

Informal communication is more likely to start with 'Hi, how are you?' and allows for more variety, according to the area someone lives in. Informal communication is warm and friendly. People usually communicate more informally with friends, including those they work closely with on a day-to-day basis.

PAUSE POINT   Can you remember what you have been taught so far about communication techniques?

Hint   With a partner, take it in turns saying something new that you have learned about communication techniques.

Extend   How is communication important in the health and social care sector?

Alternative communications

It is sometimes necessary to find an alternative form of communication to meet people's differing needs, such as when someone has visual or hearing impairment or learning difficulties.

Makaton

Makaton is a method of communication that uses signs and symbols. Unlike British Sign Language, it uses speech as well as actions and symbols. Makaton uses picture cards, and ties facial expressions to a word to make the word more easily recognised by those with learning difficulties.

British Sign Language (BSL)

BSL is a language in its own right. It was first recognised in the UK in 2003. BSL uses visual signs instead of sounds. These are made up of the shapes, positions and movements of the hands, arms or body and facial expressions. Sign language is commonly used by communities that include the families and friends of deaf people, as well as by those who are deaf or hard of hearing.

Braille

The Braille system is a method widely used by blind people to read and write. It was devised in 1821 by Louis Braille, a Frenchman. Braille is a system of raised marks that can be felt with the fingers. Each Braille character is made up of six dot positions, arranged in a rectangle. A dot may be raised in any of the six positions to form sixty-four possible combinations and these raised dots are read by touch.

▶ Have you ever tried to read Braille? It's harder than it looks.

Communication boards

Pictures can be used to communicate with people who have no ability to speak or use a language: for example, many people with autism use picture cards as they tend to learn visually and communicate with images and pictures. Communication boards are also used with people who have suffered a stroke or other brain injury. They are a universal means of communication, understandable by people of all ages and abilities.

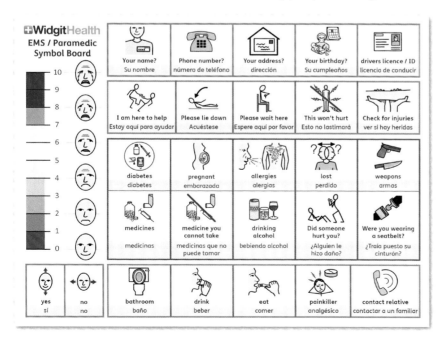

▶ Can you see how you could use this board to communicate your needs to a family member if you couldn't speak?

Symbol systems

Every day, we see and immediately understand symbols such as traffic signs or no smoking signs. Makaton and communication boards are examples of systems that use symbols. Symbol systems are used with children and adults who are either not able to use speech effectively or cannot use speech at all. These systems enable them to share information with others and to receive messages back, by pointing to the symbol that conveys what they want to communicate. Some symbols are pictures or photos and others may be tactile – actual objects or parts of objects to touch. Symbols can be arranged in order, for example in a series of trays or compartments called a calendar box, to let the person know what will be happening on a particular day. These systems are often designed for a particular person, to meet their specific needs as well as possible.

Commercial symbol systems are also available. For example, Bliss symbols, sometimes written Blissymbols or Blissymbolics, are used to provide people with severe speech disabilities with a written language that is based on concepts rather than words. Blissymbolics was originally developed by Charles Bliss, as a universal written language in which people speaking any language could learn and communicate.

Case study

A smile is worth a thousand words

Harry is 15 years old and has Rett syndrome. This is a rare **genetic condition** affecting the development of the brain. It causes severe physical and mental disabilities in early childhood. Harry developed normally at first; however, Rett syndrome was diagnosed when he was three after he lost the ability to walk or even crawl, and was still showing no signs of talking.

His parents loved him very much but struggled to cope with meeting his increasing needs as he was unable to communicate effectively with them. At the age of 12, he moved into a local residential school for children with severe special needs, where he could be given the expert help he needed. His parents were able to visit him every day. Harry has always responded well to any form of music and, in music therapy, he was taught to hit a drum if he liked a piece of music. Once Harry got the hang of hitting the drum, he was given a tambourine to hit whenever he wanted more of anything, such as a particular food or activity. The school staff and his parents are now rewarded with a huge smile every time he uses his tambourine to ask for, and receive, more.

Check your knowledge

1 How do you think Harry's parents managed to communicate with him at home before he moved to the residential school?

2 How do you think this limited communication might have affected family life?

3 How has music therapy helped Harry to communicate?

> **Key term**
>
> **Genetic condition** – a condition present at birth, passed on by a defective gene or abnormal chromosome.

Theories of communication

Charles Berner

In 1965, Charles Berner developed the idea of looking at communication as a cycle in twelve parts.

Step by Step: Communication cycle

`12 Steps`

1. **You choose:** to communicate (independently).

2. **They choose**: to communicate (independently).

3. **Be specific**: you find a specific idea to communicate.

4. **Put it out**: present the idea in such a way that the other person can understand it.

5. **Take it in**: the other person receives the idea as presented.

6. **Directed connection:** the other person is connected with you.

7. **Do the work:** the other person interprets what the words mean.

8. **Acknowledge sender:** the other person decides to acknowledge the idea they have just received back to you.

9. **Put out acknowledgment:** the other person sends a body-language signal or uses some other process to let you know that he or she understood what was said.

10. **Take in acknowledgment:** you receive the acknowledgment from the other person.

11. **Acknowledgment is valid:** you are reacting appropriately to the message sent.

12. **New reality:** you have a reality shift due to the completion of a communication cycle.

Michael Argyle

Michael Argyle (1925–2002), a social psychologist, specialised in the study of interpersonal behaviour, social skills and body language, or non-verbal communication. In the 1960s, he found that non-verbal signals can be more important than verbal communication in conveying people's attitudes. His research showed that, when you talk to a stranger, your gaze tends to be averted but, with a close friend, you make direct eye contact more often. Argyle said that feelings of friendship and a positive attitude can be encouraged simply by looking at people in the right way. He also said that it was important not to let verbal and non-verbal signals conflict. For example, if you speak sternly to a child with a smile on your face this will undermine the main point of the communication, namely, to tell them off, because they will remember the smile more than the words.

In 1972, he built on Berner's work by developing the simpler communication cycle (shown in Figure 5.4) that we refer to today. He said that interpersonal communication was a skill that could be developed, and involved building an understanding of listening, observing and reflecting on what another person is trying to communicate.

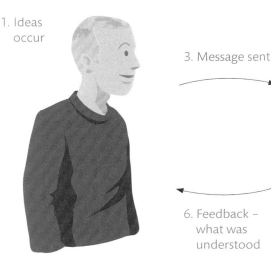

1. Ideas occur

2. Message coded

3. Message sent

4. Message perceived

5. Message decoded

6. Feedback – what was understood

Reflect

Work in a group of four. Two of the group should sit opposite each other and talk about an agreed topic, such as what they did last weekend. The other two observe and see if they can spot the six different stages of the communication cycle. Repeat this with two different people talking to each other, but, this time, one has to keep interrupting the other. What happens to the communication? Is it as effective? Which part of the cycle is missed out when this happens?

Reflect on your own communication with a parent or carer. Do you always allow the communication cycle to work effectively? If not, how can you improve this in future?

▶ **Figure 5.4:** The communication cycle happens very quickly and subconsciously. Do you know that we think three times faster than we speak?

Bruce Tuckman

In a formal group brought together for a specific purpose, such as a committee or working party, communication is regulated as it is led and controlled by a chairperson. Bruce Tuckman (born 1938) carried out research on how groups develop and operate. In 1965, he suggested that, when groups work together, they go through a series of stages as they become more effective at communicating as a group.

Step by step: Stages to achieve effective communication between members of a group

`5 Steps`

1 Forming
- A group of strangers come together; there is high dependence on the group leader.
- They talk about themselves and share information.

▼

2 Storming
- The members of the group starts to fall out with each other as they compete for position, so there are tensions within the group.
- There is disagreement about how the group acts.

▼

3 Norming
- Things calm down in the group.
- The group comes to an agreement on **group values,** either consciously or unconsciously.

▼

4 Performing
- The group is sorted, with any disagreements resolved positively.
- The group works effectively and members look after each other.

▼

5 Adjourning (added around 1977)
- The group breaks up when the task is completed successfully.
- All feel good about achievements, but there is some sadness about loss of the group.

New technologies and communication techniques

Technology is developing rapidly and there are now many electronic aids to help communication. The following are some examples of these developments.

▶ **Voice activated software** can turn the spoken voice into movement and the written word, such as instructing the user's wheelchair to move.

▶ **Voice output communication aids (VOCA)** can turn small movements into written word and then into speech, such as that used by the scientist Professor Stephen Hawking. These devices are now being used more widely: for example, NHS Wales announced plans, in 2015, to provide electronic devices such as VOCA and Augmentative and Alternative Communication (AAC) devices.

▶ **Mobile phones and minicoms** can be used to send text messages and emails. Those who are hearing impaired can feel a vibration when a message arrives.

▶ **Hearing aids** are devices with small microphones that pick up and increase the volume of sound. They are battery operated, very small and light and many are hardly noticeable as they are tucked behind the ear. However, in a noisy environment, hearing aids will amplify background noise which may cause problems for the user.

▶ **Text relay service** is operated by the charity Action on Hearing Loss. This service makes it possible for a person who can't speak and/or hear to text their message to an operator, who then reads it to a hearing person. The operator types the reply so that the original sender can read it.

▶ **A loop system** is cable that surrounds a given area, such as a lecture theatre. The cable amplifies sound from various sources, such as a music system or from a speaker wearing a microphone. This loop produces sound that can be heard by a person wearing hearing aids set to a special setting.

▶ **Braille software** is used by those who are visually impaired. It creates Braille that is printed out using a special printer. The software comes in a wide range of packages, including those that create mathematical, musical and text Braille, and those that translate different languages.

▶ **Speech recognition software** can be used by the visually impaired, or those with dyslexia, to generate messages without using a computer keyboard.

> **Key term**
>
> **Group values** – a common system of beliefs and values shared by all members of a group.

Assessment practice 5.3

`C.P4` `C.P5` `C.M4` `BC.D2`

Imagine you are the owner of a newly opened residential care home for older people who need extra help and support. Some of the new residents have conditions such as dementia. The home has 33 rooms and your prospective new residents range in age from 72 to 101.

Task

Prepare a presentation to deliver at an open day for the older people planning to move in and for their families.

In your presentation, you should explain and assess the strategies and communication techniques that you and your staff plan to use with individuals with different needs, to overcome different challenges.

You should explain the personalised care that you will be delivering and what its benefits are. You should also justify the strategies and techniques that you will use to overcome any ethical issues and challenges that may arise.

Plan
- What am I being asked to do?
- Do I need clarification about anything?
- What strategies will I use to tackle this task?

Do
- I can evaluate whether my planning strategies are working.
- I can set myself small milestones and evaluate my progress and success each time I reach one.

Review
- I can explain which elements I found the hardest.
- I can explain how I would approach the hard elements differently next time.

D Investigate the roles of professionals and how they work together to provide the care and support necessary to meet individual needs

How agencies work together to meet individual care and support needs

Research shows that, in areas of high unemployment, where there are issues with housing and a lack of public transport, people struggle to be healthy. Historically, one of the major problems with health and social care has been the lack of co-ordination between services. A family living in an impoverished area of the UK could be dealing with tens of different agencies at a time, repeating their stories each time to a different agency. They may find that they are dealing with the same agencies a year later, still repeating their stories. They may have services forced on them, rather than agencies working with them to meet their needs, with little or no progress towards better health or wellbeing. In recent years, there has been a drive to integrate services, to make the system more efficient and cost effective. You can see, in Figure 5.5, all the different organisations that may be involved in providing care.

Role of organisations responsible for commissioning healthcare services

There are a number of key organisations responsible for the **commissioning** of healthcare services. These are explained in Table 5.8.

▶ **Table 5.8:** Organisations responsible for commissioning healthcare services

Organisation name	Formation (when and why)	Roles	Members
Clinical Commissioning Groups (CCGs) in England	• Formed in April 2013 by NHS England • To take on greater delegated commissioning responsibilities for GP services • To give patients, communities and clinicians more scope in deciding how local services are developed and more influence over the wider NHS budget	• Assess the health needs of the area • Commission most of the hospital and community NHS services in their local area, including most planned hospital care, **rehabilitative care**, urgent and emergency care (including out-of-hours), most community health services, mental health services and learning disability services • Overseen by NHS England	GP practices Other health professionals, such as practice nurses
Local Health Boards in Wales	• Formed in October 2009 • Consists of seven Health Boards working alongside three NHS Trusts • To redesign the delivery of the NHS in Wales, to improve health outcomes and deliver care effectively with its partners	• Plan, source and deliver primary care, hospital and community health services, and provide information in their local area • Provide more care close to people's homes • Strong emphasis on public health and long-term planning	Representatives at executive level: GPs and other health professionals, such as nurses, dentists, pharmacists and **optometrists**; people from areas such as public relations and finance
Health and Social Care Board in Northern Ireland	• Formed in April 2009 • Consists of five Local Commissioning Groups and five Health and Social Care Trusts (covering the same local areas) • To reform and modernise the management of health and social care services • To integrate provision of services in an efficient, effective and economic manner	• Effective commissioning of health and social care services, resource management, performance management and service improvement	Representatives at executive level of various health and social care services; also people from areas such as public relations and finance

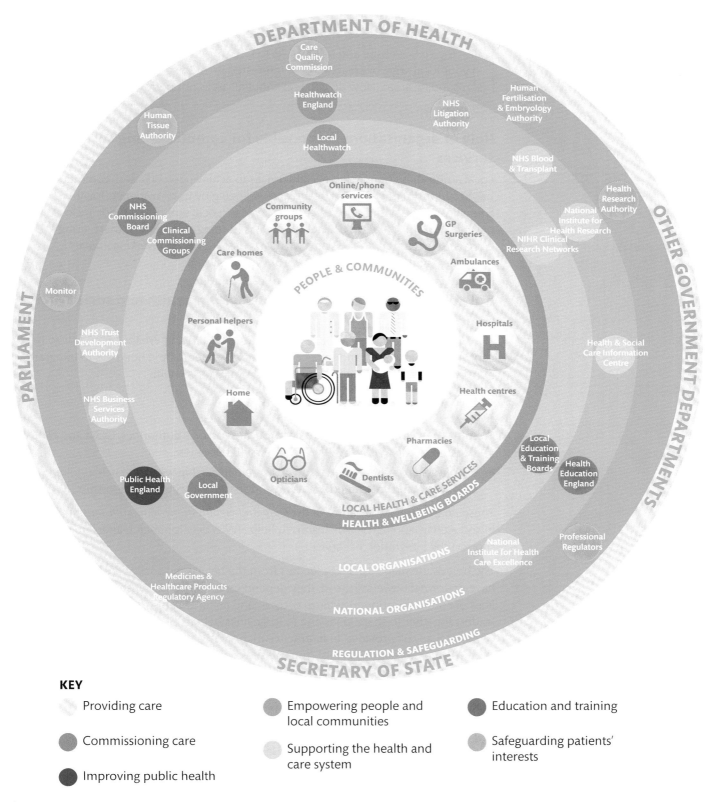

KEY

Providing care

Commissioning care

Improving public health

Empowering people and local communities

Supporting the health and care system

Education and training

Safeguarding patients' interests

▸ **Figure 5.5:** This diagram was produced by the Department of Health to show how health and social care would look in England from 2013. Can you spot all the different organisations involved?

Role of organisations responsible for commissioning social care services

Local authorities commission social services to achieve personalised, community-based support that promotes health and wellbeing by using evidence, local knowledge, skills and resources as best they can. Local authorities work in close partnership with other organisations, such as housing and NHS partners, using guidance such as the *Adult Social Care Outcomes Framework*, *Making it Real* statements and the *Public Health Outcomes Framework*.

Role of bodies responsible for integrating health and social care

Health and Wellbeing Boards (HWB)

The Health and Social Care Act 2012 introduced Health and Wellbeing Boards to be a forum for local health and social care leaders. The aim of the boards is to integrate public services for health and social care. They are tasked with:

▶ assessing the needs of their local population

▶ reducing inequalities in provision

▶ setting out strategies and shared approaches for local authorities, CCGs and NHS England to use to improve their commission decisions

▶ encouraging greater integration and more partnership working, such as joint commissioning, integrated provision and shared budgets and leadership.

These boards are at the centre of the *Care and Health Improvement Programme*, introduced in April 2015, which aims to help HWBs develop their leadership and better support the integration of services.

The boards are made up of key leaders from the health and social care system. HWBs have no formal powers; instead, they depend on building relationships and strong lines of communication to achieve success, and are invaluable in getting all key local leaders together to share ideas and to forge links between local services. The website www.local.gov.uk provides an interactive map for health and wellbeing priorities (you will need to search for this). You can select an area of England and a theme, such as alcohol and drug abuse, to find a summary of local priorities and links to various reports and examples of good practice in the area. This allows sharing of information and practice.

Role of assessment and eligibility frameworks

In learning aim C, you learned what policy frameworks are. Frameworks that include ways in which to assess needs, and eligibility to have those needs met, are also called assessment and eligibility frameworks. These frameworks are key to integrating health and social care. Their use should lead to:

▶ reduced inequalities in service provision

▶ greater clarity, transparency and consistency

▶ greater emphasis on the individual person rather than the services

▶ better integration of services

▶ reduced repetition of a person's story

▶ greater focus on prevention, by earlier consideration of people's care and support needs.

 **PAUSE POINT**   The roles of the *Common Assessment Framework* (CAF), the *National Eligibility Criteria* (Care Act 2014) and the *National Framework for NHS Continuing Healthcare* were covered in learning aim C. The role of the Department of Health was covered in learning aim B. Draw a mind map to summarise the roles.

Extend   How do you think such frameworks contribute towards the way in which agencies work together to meet individual care and support needs?

The Education, Health and Care Plan (EHC)

An EHC plan is for children and young people aged up to 25 who need more support than is available through special educational needs (SEN) support. An EHC plan can be requested by a parent, someone from the child's school, a doctor, a health visitor or a nursery worker. If it is thought that a child needs an EHC plan, the local authority carries out an assessment.

> **Theory into practice**
>
> Research to find out what SEN support for a child of school age includes, how your local authority assesses a child for an EHC plan, and what legally must be included as a minimum in any EHC plan. Draw up an EHC plan for a child aged 5 with hearing difficulties.

Roles and responsibilities of key professionals on multi-disciplinary teams

Multi-disciplinary teams, members and formation

A multi-disciplinary team is made up of professionals from the same service who have different roles. These professionals work together to support an individual or a family facing complex situations. Effective multi-disciplinary working means that the individual gets a better service and better outcomes from the service provider. This is possible because the team takes a holistic approach to providing care, looking at all the person's needs and how they can be met. Multi-disciplinary working also helps avoid duplication of roles and responsibilities. The team must work together to be aware of conflicts that may arise between professionals, or between the service provider and user, to make sure the service user's wishes are acknowledged. You need to know the specific roles and responsibilities of a variety of health and social care professionals within a multi-disciplinary team which relate to meeting an individual's health and social care needs.

Healthcare professionals

Multi-disciplinary teams are formed based on the individual's specific needs. For example, for someone diagnosed with cancer, the team might be made up of an oncologist, a radiologist, a haematologist, a dietician, a clinical nurse specialist and other specialist nurses. Each team member has a different role and responsibilities (see Table 5.9).

▶ **Table 5.9:** An example of a multi-disciplinary team of health care professionals

Professional	Role	Responsibilities
GP	• First point of contact with NHS • Assess problem, make a diagnosis and decide on appropriate course of action, treatment or referral to another service, such as a hospital consultant • Provide a complete spectrum of care within the community	• Maintain the health of patients through preventative care and health promotion • Ease difficulties of individuals with **chronic conditions** • Help patients access specialist secondary care services when needed
Nurse	• Provide hands-on care to patients • Provide emotional support to patients and their families	• Help patients, eg by administering medicines, monitoring conditions, maintaining records, providing health promotion and other information, communicating with doctors
Paediatrician	• Manage medical conditions affecting babies, children and young people • Provide health maintenance for healthy children • Provide medical care for child who is acutely or chronically ill	• Reduce infant and child mortality • Control infectious disease • Foster healthy lifestyles • Ease difficulties of children and young people with chronic conditions
Clinical psychologist	• Reduce psychological distress • Enhance and promote psychological wellbeing	• Use psychological methods and research to make positive changes to their clients' lives • Offer treatment for a variety of different mental or physical health problems

Key term

Chronic condition – a long-term or recurrent condition, such as arthritis, asthma or diabetes.

Reflect

Think about times you have needed a doctor. Have you ever needed any of the other health professionals mentioned above? How did they work together? Do you think they could have worked together better? Can you think of other health care professionals who might be involved in a team to help a child who has had a serious accident and faces a long stay in hospital.

Research

Draw up a table similar to Table 5.9 for *each* of the following:

- social care professionals, to include at least social worker, occupational therapist
- education professionals, to include at least SENCO (Special Educational Needs Coordinator), educational psychologist
- allied health professionals, to include at least a speech and language therapist.

Think of a situation for the social care team, such as an adult who has had a stroke, where a person may need the support of the multi-disciplinary team you have just drawn up, and write a case study to illustrate how the team would help that person. Be prepared to share your case studies with others in your class.

▶ A Macmillan nurse. You can read her story, and that of others on the Macmillan website

Voluntary sector workers

A multi-disciplinary team of voluntary sector workers may include:

▶ **Macmillan nurses**: Macmillan nurses are funded by the charity Macmillan Cancer Support. They are specialist nurses who provide guidance and support to individuals with cancer, and to their families.

▶ **Family support worker**: a family support worker's job is to provide emotional and practical help and advice to families with short- or long-term difficulties, such as drug or alcohol addiction, marital or financial difficulties, disability, problems accessing services due to a language barrier or having a parent in hospital or prison.

The family support worker helps the family to deal with the situation, maybe by teaching them new skills or encouraging them to seek help from various other health and social care professionals. A family may be referred to a family support worker by a social worker.

Case study

Maria's story

When Maria was 27 years old she was involved in a serious road traffic accident, and has to use a wheelchair. She is now 33 years old and stays at home to look after her 5-year-old son and 3-month-old daughter. Her husband Sven, works on a production line in a local factory and has just been diagnosed with bowel cancer. He needs radiotherapy and chemotherapy. Sven has been told that he may need

an operation later on and regular tests to make sure the cancer has not spread to other parts of his body.

Check your knowledge

1 How do you think Maria will be feeling?

2 What practical problems will the family now face?

3 How could a multi-disciplinary team of voluntary sector workers help them?

How multi-agency and multi-disciplinary teams work together to provide coordinated support

A multi-agency team is made up of professionals from different health and social care services (see Figure 5.6). For example, a local authority social services department may work with a mental health organisation such as Mind (a mental health charity) to help a service user with mental health problems live in the community.

The benefit of working in partnership is that all the professionals are working together, communicating and planning as a team, so support is coordinated. Professionals can use their skills more effectively by concentrating on meeting just some of an individual's needs, rather than all of them, and focus on what they do best. There will also, hopefully, be no gaps in care and, because the care is planned and resources are not wasted, costs are reduced. However, some difficulties may also arise, such as professional animosity between agencies, poor communication, manipulation by service users, logistical problems, limited budgets and breakdown in services. It is important to have a strong leader of the team to minimise these difficulties.

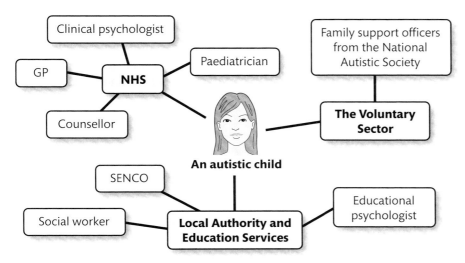

▶ **Figure 5.6:** What do you know about autism?

Use Figure 5.6 and carry out some research into autism, to draw a table, similar to Table 5.9, which shows all the different agencies working to help young people, and their roles and responsibilities towards the child.

Draw your own mind map to create a multi-disciplinary and multi-agency team to help a young mother who has tried to abandon her 6-week-old baby girl. She is struggling to breast feed the baby and feels no attachment to her. Her partner thinks she is suffering from postnatal depression.

PAUSE POINT

Can you explain what this section on roles and responsibilities of key professionals on multi-disciplinary teams was about? What elements did you find easiest?

Hint | Close your book and write out an example of a multi-disciplinary team and an example of a multi-agency team.?

Extend | What sort of multi-disciplinary team might include a charity such as Blood Bikes?

Maintaining confidentiality

Definition of confidentiality

You were reminded, in learning aim B, that confidentiality means keeping information private, and not sharing information about individuals without their knowledge and agreement, even with a service user's friends, family or other individuals. Confidentiality refers to all information relating to those using health and social care services, as well as the records associated with them, no matter what format those records are in.

Working practices to maintain confidentiality

Confidentiality is one of the most important values when caring for others. By breaking confidentiality you can destroy the trust and relationship between you and the person you are caring for, as this may cause that person embarrassment, loss of dignity or harm. Safety might be put at risk if sensitive information is disclosed to those who should not have access to it. For example, if an abused child has been removed from their family and adopted by a family living in a different part of the country, for the child's safety, it may be important that their whereabouts are not disclosed.

Keeping yourself informed of the relevant laws

The law and the underpinning values of care practice demand that all health and social care professionals maintain people's confidentiality at all times. The law sets out duties, which combine the decisions made by the courts, known as the common law of confidentiality, and legislation such as the Data Protection Act 1998 and the Human Rights Act 1998. The Data Protection Act aims to protect the right of the individual to privacy with respect to the processing of personal data. The Human Rights Act reflects this when it says that everyone has a right to respect for private and family life.

It is, therefore, very important that as a health or social care service provider you keep yourself informed of, and up to date with, the relevant laws. Every organisation or workplace in the health and social care sector must have a confidentiality policy, as well as procedures in place that must be followed with regard to breaching of confidentiality. *A guide to confidentiality in health and social care* (2013) gives clear user-friendly guidance for processing confidential information about an individual's care. It states that service providers should not hide behind the Data Protection Act to avoid taking decisions that benefit the service user. For example, if they do not share that an older person is struggling with their own care, that person may struggle for longer as they may not know how to get the extra help they need.

Keeping information locked away or password protected

It is very important that information stored on paper should be kept locked away when not in use. Decisions have to be made about paper records such as where they should be stored, how to keep them safe, who can have access to them, how long they should be kept, what information should be stored and how often it needs to be reviewed and updated.

Although most health and social care settings still use paper records, many records are now stored electronically. Some form of electronic patient record (EPR) system is in place in most GP practices and hospitals, and is used to record information about a patient's medical history, diagnosis and treatment. As people can now make appointments and order prescriptions via their computer, smart phone or other devices, it is necessary to have secure passwords and networks to avoid unauthorised people accessing an individual's personal information. When using EPRs, decisions have to be made about who has access to passwords and who will train staff, given the confidential nature of the records. When working in health and social care, it is very important that you do not store or transmit data and photographs of service users using your insecure smart phone, or share information about service users on social networking sites.

▶ What happens when the system fails? Who will carry out the repairs and will they see any of the information?

Sharing information only with people who are entitled to have access to the information

The need to respect a service user's wishes in relation to how their information is used has to be weighed against the duty of staff to share information to ensure safe and effective care for that service user. Times when confidentiality needs to be broken include:

▶ if an individual is at risk of being harmed or killed
▶ if an individual is at risk of causing harm or death to others
▶ if an individual is about to break, or has already broken, the law.

Information should only be shared with people who are entitled to it, for example other people in a multi-disciplinary team, service users and their carers or families, depending on the situation.

Being professional about how information is shared

If information is to be shared, it is important that this is done professionally. You should first ask the individual concerned for their agreement to pass it on, even if it is something like an address. It is also vital that the information is accurate; there have been cases where a patient has had the wrong organ removed in an operating theatre. Information should never be passed on in an offensive way, or anywhere where it can be overheard.

Codes of practice for care workers establishing the importance of confidentiality

Concern about confidentiality led to the *Caldicott Report*, published in April 2013. It set out seven principles (known as the Caldicott principles). These principles are the following.

▸ Justify the purpose(s): every proposed use or transfer of personally identifiable information within or from an organisation should be scrutinised to make sure it is necessary.

▸ Don't use personally identifiable information unless it is absolutely necessary: only use personally identifiable information if there is no alternative.

▸ Use the minimum that is required: if it is essential to use personally identifiable information, then only the item required should be disclosed. For example, the whole of a person's medical details should not be sent if only one small part is needed.

▸ Access to personally identifiable information should be on a strict need-to-know basis: only those people who need access to the information should be allowed that access.

▶ Everyone with access to personally identifiable information must understand their responsibilities: anyone, both clinical and non-clinical staff, handling the information should understand the need to respect the service user's confidentiality.

▶ Understand and comply with the law: every use of personally identifiable information must be lawful, and not go against the principles of, for example, the Data Protection Act 1998. There should be someone in every organisation who is responsible for making sure that the organisation complies with the law.

▶ The duty to share information can be as important as the duty to protect service user confidentiality: health and social care professionals should have the confidence to share information in the best interests of service users, within the framework set out by these principles. They should be supported by the policies of their employers, regulators and professional bodies.

The Caldicott principles were drawn up to guide decisions about the storage and disclosure of confidential information. A new code of practice, based on this report, was published as a working document in December 2014 by the Health and Social Care Information Centre (HSCIC). The HSCIC is committed to building on this code and to updating it regularly.

Relevant aspects of legislation

The Data Protection Act 1998 and the Human Rights Act 1998, have been mentioned earlier. Another important piece of legislation about confidentiality is the Health and Social Care Act 2012. The HSCIC was given statutory responsibility under this Act to produce a Code of Practice for processing confidential information, based on the Caldicott principles, and the five confidentiality rules they came up with. In September 2013, the HSCIC published a document called *A guide to confidentiality in health and social care*. The confidentiality rules are the following.

1 Confidential information about service users or patients should be treated confidentially and respectfully.

2 Members of a care team should share confidential information when it is needed for the safe and effective care of an individual.

3 Information that is shared for the benefit of the community should be **anonymised**.

4 An individual's right to object to the sharing of confidential information about them should be respected.

5 Organisations should put policies, procedures and systems in place to ensure that the confidentiality rules are followed.

The Act states that all health and social care bodies in England must have regard to this code, as must any person other than a public body who provides health services, or adult social care, in England.

The role of the Health and Social Care Information Centre (HSCIC)

The UK government website states that the HSCIC is 'the national provider of information, data and IT systems for **commissioners**, **analysts** and **clinicians** in health and social care.' Sponsored by the Department of Health, the HSCIC was set up in April 2013, and has powers to provide advice and guidance 'on any matter relating to the collection, analysis, publication or other dissemination of information'. Health and social care service providers must have regard to any guidance that the HSCIC produces.

Research

Produce a two-page summary of the *Code of Practice on Confidential Information* published in 2014.

Key terms

Anonymised – made so that an individual cannot be identified.

Commissioner – someone who contracts a service provider to provide a service.

Analyst – someone who studies data to learn something from it, such as a trend or pattern.

Clinician – a health care practitioner who has direct contact with service users.

PAUSE POINT Can you remember the working practices required to maintain confidentiality?

Hint
Close your book and imagine that you are working in a nursery. Think about all the ways you might try to keep information confidential. List them.

Extend
How do codes of practice written by bodies such as the HSCIC protect both service users and service providers when dealing with issues of confidentiality?

Managing information

Working practices for managing information

All organisations must have policies and codes of practice for managing information. These policies and codes will include the following procedures.

Identifying why information is needed

Most organisations will need information to formally identify a service user. This is to avoid mistakes, such as the wrong treatment being given or information sent to the wrong address, resulting in delays or the wrong person seeing confidential information. Service providers will also need information about an individual in order to identify, provide and monitor care and support. Records should be legible, factual, **unambiguous**, dated, consistent and accurate. Service users have the right to see their own records.

Identifying what information is needed

A key principle in identifying what information is needed is that a service user's records are made by the service provider to support that person's care. This information will include the service user's name, address, date of birth and maybe a photo. In certain cases, additional data may also be required: for example, a hospital number and NHS number, medical history and medical details, such as images (X-rays, scans).

Searching for the information

When asking for personal information, a service provider should inform the service user that the information will be recorded and that it may be shared, in order to provide appropriate care. In some instances, a service user's personal information may be used to support other work, such as research. The information required should be gained directly from the service user unless they are unable to provide it. For example, an infant or child, an unconsciousness person, or a person with a physical or mental condition that makes them unable to communicate is unlikely to be able to provide the information. In these cases, a family member or other advocate may be asked, usually in the presence of the service user. The service user should also be told where they can find more information to help them understand what is happening to them, such as websites and information leaflets. If a service provider needs information from another provider, such as a doctor, permission should be obtained from the service user to release those records.

Using information ethically and legally

Service users trust service providers to gather sensitive information relating to their health and other matters, so it is legally and ethically essential that the information is kept confidentially. Information should not be used or disclosed in a way that can identify the person without their consent. The extent to which information needs to be shared to meet a service user's needs should also be disclosed to the service user. If the service user decides that they are not happy for their information to be disclosed, for example, to other health professionals involved in providing their care, it should be made clear that this might mean that it will not be possible to offer certain treatment options.

Key term

Unambiguous – clear, no chance of being misunderstood.

However, confidential information can be very useful and provide benefits for society, for example, through medical research. Although using this information does not affect the care of the service user, they should be asked for their consent to share the information, which will usually be in an anonymised form.

The NHS confidentiality model is shown in Figure 5.7. It outlines how patients are to be provided with a confidential service.

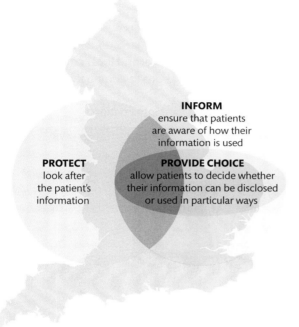

INFORM
ensure that patients
are aware of how their
information is used

PROTECT
look after
the patient's
information

PROVIDE CHOICE
allow patients to decide whether
their information can be disclosed
or used in particular ways

▸ **Figure 5.7:** This diagram is taken from Confidentiality: NHS Code of Practice. Can you see how this would work in other health and social care settings by changing the word patient to service user?

The importance of sharing information

It is important that relevant information is shared with colleagues and other health and social care providers to make sure that a person gets the care and support they need. For example, if a GP decides that a service user has a problem that needs more specialised care, the GP will need to share information with a hospital consultant. It is also important to share as much information as possible with the service user and their family. This ensures that everyone is informed and reassured that the best possible care is being given, and helps them to prepare for what happens next. However, there should always be **protocols** in place that set out the principles and procedures for sharing confidential information. If someone telephones or appears in person asking for information about a service user, the service provider must check that the person asking is who they say they are, and that they have the right to access the information.

Key term

Protocols – procedures following specific guidelines.

Impact of new technologies on managing information

The impacts of advances in technology, such as electronic patient records (EPRs), are:

▸ improved and faster communication
▸ increasing quantities of data available
▸ more detailed information.

However, care must be taken to make the means of transferring information, such as emails, faxes and surface mail, as secure as possible.

The HSCIC's vision is that, by 2020, there will be full service user access to national and local data, for the user to view and manage their own records, communicate with care providers and increasingly manage their own health, care and wellbeing. Service providers will also have access to the information and support systems they need to deliver safe and effective care. The HSCIC has set out a strategy with five objectives towards achieving this vision.

1 Ensure that every citizen's data is protected.
2 Establish shared architecture and standards so that everyone benefits.
3 Implement services that meet national and local needs.
4 Support health and care organisations in getting the best from technology, data and information.
5 Make better use of health and care information.

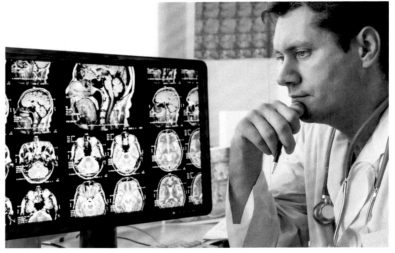

▸ Information about a service user is not made up of only words and numbers. What other forms of information can you think of?

Research

Read the HSCIC document *Information and technology for better care*. Produce a summary that explains clearly and concisely what each of the HSCIC objectives above is actually promising.

Ⅱ PAUSE POINT Do you remember the working practices for managing information?

> Hint Think about a time when you have been in a health or social care setting as a service user. What information were you asked for and why was it needed? How was it collected?

> Extend In what ways has new technology both helped and hindered the safe management of information?

Bodies that control the management of information

The National Adult Social Care Intelligence Service (NASCIS)

The NASCIS has been developed by the HSCIC to provide a single national online resource of relevant, useful and up-to-date information for social care services across England. It is made up of a collection of tools and resources designed to meet the needs of, for example, those who plan services, manage services, carry out research and write policies. One such tool is an analytical processor, which allows easy access to a wide range of health and social care data against which a service provider can compare their performance.

Legislation and codes of practice that relate to the storage and sharing of information in health and social care

There are many examples of legislation and codes of practice relating to the storage and sharing of information, such as the *Confidentiality: NHS Code of Practice*, mentioned in Figure 5.7. Some of the most important are explained in Table 5.10.

▶ **Table 5.10:** Legislation and codes of practice that relate to the storage and sharing of information in health and social care

Act or code of practice	Notes
Data Protection Act 1998	• The main piece of legislation that governs the protection of personal data in the UK • Controls how your personal information is used by everyone responsible for using data, by providing rules called data protection principles • Provides legal protection for more **sensitive personal data** • Gives you the right to access to your own personal data • Enables health and social care providers to share information with other professionals directly involved in providing clinical care, for example transferring case notes when you change GP
The Freedom of Information Act 2000	• Provides public access to information held by public authorities in England, Wales and Northern Ireland, and UK-wide public authorities based in Scotland • Does not give access to your own personal data • Makes public authorities **accountable** for their actions. Allows public debate to be better informed and, therefore, more productive
Mental Health Act 2007	• Allows people in England and Wales to be admitted to hospital, detained and treated against their consent, for their own health and safety and for that of others, so allows the storing and sharing of their personal information without their consent
Mental Capacity Act 2005	• Requires professionals to consider a person's mental capacity to consent to share information • Outlines correct procedures for making decisions in the best interest of a person who lacks the mental capacity to consent
Care Quality Commission (CQC) codes of practice	• CQC is an independent body that speaks up for the rights of people who use care services, their families and carers, and checks that services stick to the Health and Social Care Act 2008 • One example is the 2010 code of practice for health and adult social services in England, which: • sets out the practices to be followed in obtaining, handling, using and disclosing confidential personal information • is based on a set of nine principles • includes a necessity test to decide whether it is necessary to obtain, use or disclose personal information
The Health and Care Professions Council (HCPC) codes of practice	• HCPC is a regulator set up to protect the public, by keeping a register of health and social care professionals who meet HCPC standards for training, professional skills, behaviour and health • Confidentiality – guidance for **registrants** 2008, slightly amended in 2012, sets out the standards of conduct, performance and ethics expected from the professionals it regulates, including management of information

> **Key terms**
>
> **Sensitive personal data** – information about a person's physical or mental health.
>
> **Accountable** – has to justify actions.
>
> **Registrants** – a person who is registered.

Case study

A canine partner

Edi is a 49-year-old woman. Edi suffered a brain injury at the age of 20 that left her unable to function without daily help. She spent almost 30 years relying on others for help, until someone told her about Canine Partners. This charity trains dogs to assist with practical tasks, enabling people with a disability to regain independence. Canine Partners have recently provided Edi with a dog called Molly. Molly helps with a range of tasks, from helping Edi to dress and retrieving the remote control to loading the washing machine. Trainers from Canine Partners are visiting frequently to start with, to help Edi and Molly get into a routine.

Check your knowledge

1 What sort of information will the charity have about Edi?

2 What are some of the things that could happen to Edi if the information got into the wrong hands?

3 Research the Data Protection Act 1998. How does this Act protect Edi?

▶ Do you know of other ways in which animals are being used in health and social care to meet the needs of service users?

Research

Pick one of the acts mentioned in Table 5.10. Research what the act says about storing and sharing information. Then imagine that you are working at a residential centre for young offenders. What might be the consequences for the young offenders, the centre and for you if you did not store and share the information lawfully? Produce a colourful poster that could be displayed in such a centre to remind staff about what they need to do to stay within the law when they store and share information.

> **Reflect**
>
> Search online for the 2010 code of practice and see what it says about keeping personal information safe. Then find the CQC easy-access document *Our rules for keeping private information safe*. Did you get the same messages from each? Why do you think the code of practice is produced in two different forms?
>
> Now try to write your own version for the HCPC's code of practice *Confidentiality – guidance for registrants*. How successful have you been in completing this task?

Assessment practice 5.4

D.P6 | D.P7 | D.P8 | D.M5 | D.M6 | D.D3 | D.D4

A serious spinal injury, after a fall from her horse at the age of 17, meant that Josie had to lie flat on her back in hospital for months. She was eventually able to return home, but faced using a wheelchair for the rest of her life.

Tasks

1 Draw up two lists of the professionals and agencies from which Josie will need help:
  * from the moment she arrives at the hospital after her accident until her discharge home
  * for her continuing care on leaving the hospital.

2 Write a report to:
  * explain each of their roles and responsibilities
  * explain why she needs so many service providers to be involved in her care
  * assess, justify and evaluate how these professionals, all working together, can meet her specific needs
  * analyse the arrangements for managing information between the professionals that will reflect the law and current codes of practice.

Remember to try to use all the correct terms, such as multi-disciplinary and multi-agency.

Plan
  * Exactly what do I need to include in my report?
  * What are the success criteria for this task?

Do
  * Have I spent some time planning my approach to the task?
  * I understand what to reflect on and what action to take.

Review
  * I can explain what the task is.
  * I can draw links between this task and prior learning.

Further reading and resources

DK Publishing – *First Aid Manual 10th edition* (Dorling Kindersley, 2014)

Parker L – *The Early Years Health and Safety Handbook 2nd edition* (Routledge, 2011)

Websites

https://professionals.carers.org
The *Carers Trust Professionals* website describes the Triangle of Care for mental health.

www.cyf.govt.nz
The *Child, Youth and Family (New Zealand)* website has information about attachment and resilience.

http://www.compassioninaction.info
Compassion in Action is a charity which helps meet the needs of people in crisis.

www.hscic.gov.uk
The *Health and Social Care Information Centre* provides a guide to confidentiality in health and social care, codes of practice on confidential information and the Caldicott principles.

www.local.gov.uk
The *Local Government Association* has links to Health and Wellbeing Boards.

www.nhs-chaplaincy-spiritualcare.org.uk
The *NHS chaplaincy* service provides information about meeting NHS standards of quality and professionalism and questions of policy and practice relating to the Church's ministry in health care.

www.england.nhs.uk
The *NHS England* website has useful information about the 6Cs, health action plans, personalised care and support, multi-disciplinary and multi-agency working. It also gives guidance for CCGs: for example, *Managing Conflicts of Interest: statutory guidance for CCGs.*

www.scottishhealthcouncil.org
The *Scottish Health Council* was established to listen to the views of users, including through the use of focus groups and to promote public involvement.

www.gov.uk
The *UK government* website contains much information, including the *Adult Social Care Outcomes Framework.*

THINK ▶FUTURE

Laura Hope

Nursing home manager

I've worked with older people for more than 20 years. People are surprised that I still have day-to-day contact with the residents now I'm a manager, but, if an older person needs help, there is no way I wouldn't give it. The residents are usually very grateful for the help, but sometimes they can be bad tempered. I don't mind that because I know it's just frustration as they feel they have increasingly less control over their lives and don't like having to depend on others so much. In a nursing home, the residents are even more dependent on our help than in a care home, as they are all here due to having at least one medical condition they need help with, as well as with day-to-day living. It's good to talk to the residents so that I can hear their preferences regarding their own care, whether that's to do with the food, the type of chair they have in their own room or the time they go to bed.

As well as working with the residents, I have to do a whole range of tasks to manage the home. One of these is to write policies and guidelines so that all the staff are informed and know the correct procedures to follow, from administering medicines to keeping records, to addressing the residents respectfully. I also have to make arrangements for various health professionals to visit each resident and make sure that each person receives the care and support they need.

Focusing your skills

Communicating with a person with impaired hearing

It is important to be able to communicate with those who have some form of disability. Here are some tips to help if you think that someone is losing their hearing.

- Do they think the TV is too quiet and keep turning it up? Do they say you are mumbling? If so, they need to have a hearing check with an audiologist.
- In the meantime, always attract their attention before you start to speak. Rephrase things if they don't understand you, as some words are easier to hear than others.
- Use natural hand gestures, but don't over-exaggerate or cover your mouth when speaking to them.
- Finally, be patient! They will feel frustrated and will be grateful that you are willing to work out how to help them.

Observing a person who is unwell

If someone who can't speak is in your care, how will you know if they are unwell?

- Look out for any changes in a person's condition. Try to do this in a room where there is good light.
- Has their colour changed? Is their skin paler, darker, yellow or bluish? Are their lips or insides of their eyelids pale? Do they have a rash?
- Are their lips or fingernails going blue? Is the white part of their eyes normal, red or yellow? Have their pupils become larger (dilated) or smaller (constricted)?
- Are they sweating? Is their breathing faster, more shallow or laboured?

Getting ready for assessment

Ryan is working towards a BTEC National in Health and Social Care. He was given an assignment for learning aim B with the following title: 'Is it right that that some of the UK's biggest charities put pressure on vulnerable people to give money?' The task was to write an article about this issue for *Yours*, a magazine aimed at people in later middle age and older people. The article had to:

▶ include information on the ethics of managing the conflict of interest between the charities needing to raise money and vulnerable people feeling they are being hounded to donate money

▶ discuss how adults can cope with these demands, and how charities could change their approach but still raise the money they need to help others.

Ryan shares his experience below.

How I got started

First I read the assessment criteria for learning aim B, so I knew what I was trying to achieve. While doing this, I made a note of the command words from the criteria. Then I did some research online to see if something had happened recently to make the way in which charities ask for money an issue in the media, before reading all the ethical theories in my textbook several times until I felt I understood them. I was undecided as to what I thought about this issue so I draw a concept map, which included everything I knew and felt about this topic.

I decided to divide the facts for the article into four sections, the first about why and how the charities work to raise money, the second on how this affects people, the third about how charities could change their ways and the fourth about how others could deal with this problem. I intended to finish the article with a few sentences giving my conclusions on the matter.

I arranged to visit a local charity's office to speak to a volunteer about how they tackle asking for donations. They gave me permission to use what they had said in my assignment.

How I brought it all together

I decided to use a variety of fonts and colours to make the work look appealing. To start the article, I wrote a short introduction to the article explaining the dilemma. For each of the four sections I:

▶ wrote a case study based on real-life stories I'd read when researching the problem

▶ included photos to make the article more eye catching and to show different aspects of this situation.

I used comments I'd noted down during my visit to the local charity to help explain the charity's point of view. Finally, I wrote a short summary as a conclusion to the article.

What I learned from the experience

I wish I'd made more notes during my visit to the charity as I didn't have as much information as I would have liked, and forgot some of the points they made. Next time, I'll write a list of questions to ask before my visit. I also wish I'd thought to visit my local newspaper office to talk to them about how they structure articles like these. Another idea, which came to me too late, was to have a proper discussion about the issue with a group of friends or family members to gather more opinions. I felt very undecided as to how the situation should change, seeing both that charities are competing for much-needed funds but also that some people are feeling pressurised into giving money they can't afford to a number of charities.

Think about it

▶ Have you written a plan with timings so that you can complete your assignment by the agreed submission date?

▶ Have you read your course notes on learning aim B, and read the relevant section of the textbook so you are clear on the general subject of ethical issues and approaches?

▶ Is your information written in your own words, and referenced clearly where you have used quotations or information from a book, journal or website?

Principles of Safe Practice in Health and Social Care

7

Getting to know your unit

This unit has been designed to guide you through the principles of safe practice in health and social care, and to support your learning about the wider concepts of working in the caring professions. Safe working practices are vital for protecting you and your service users from harm, and for promoting their safety and wellbeing. You need to have an understanding of the policies and procedures that protect individuals from harm, the rights and responsibilities of care workers and the importance of recognising and reporting poor practice. Service users are likely to be vulnerable and you will need to know how to respond to situations and emergencies in a professional manner.

How you will be assessed

This unit will be assessed by a series of internally assessed tasks set by your tutor. Throughout this unit, you will discover assessment practices to help you work towards your assessment. Completing these practices will not mean that you have achieved a particular grade, but that you will have carried out useful research or preparation for your assessment tasks.

In order to achieve a Pass in your assignments, it is important that you meet all of the Pass grading criteria. You can check on this as you work your way through your assignment.

If you are hoping to achieve a Merit or Distinction, you should also ensure that you present the information in your assignment in the style that is required by the relevant assessment criterion. For example, Merit criteria require you to assess and analyse, and Distinction criteria require you to evaluate and justify.

The assessment set by your tutor will consist of a number of tasks designed to meet the criteria in the Assessment criteria table. This is likely to consist of a written assignment but may also include activities such as:

▶ creating a report identifying types of abuse and neglect and the procedure for documenting and reporting safeguarding concerns

▶ analysing and reflecting on case studies of accidents and/or incidents in health and social care settings

▶ creating a file of policies, practices and protocols for promoting safe practice in health and social care settings.

Assessment criteria

This table shows what you must do in order to achieve a **Pass**, **Merit** or **Distinction** grade, and where you can find activities to help you.

Pass	**Merit**	**Distinction**

Learning aim Examine how a duty of care contributes to safe practice in health and social care settings

Pass	**Merit**	**Distinction**
A.P1 Explain the implications of a duty of care in a selected health or social care setting. Assessment practice 7.1	**A.M1** Assess the importance of balancing individual rights with a duty of care in a selected health or social care setting. Assessment practice 7.1	**A.D1** Evaluate the significance of a duty of care and complaints procedures in promoting safe practice in a selected health or social care setting. Assessment practice 7.2
A.P2 Discuss ways in which complaints and appeals procedures address failure in a duty of care in a selected health or social care setting. Assessment practice 7.1		

Learning aim Understand how to recognise and respond to concerns about abuse and neglect in health and social care settings

Pass	**Merit**	**Distinction**
B.P3 Describe the types and signs of abuse and neglect that may be experienced by different individuals. Assessment practice 7.2	**B.M2** Assess the importance of recognising and responding to evidence or concerns about different types of abuse and neglect in health and social care. Assessment practice 7.2	**B.D2** Justify procedures for responding to concerns about abuse and neglect in the selected health or social care setting. Assessment practice 7.2
B.P4 Explain the factors that may contribute to and reduce the likelihood of abuse and neglect for service users in health and social care. Assessment practice 7.2		
B.P5 Explain how to respond to concerns about abuse and neglect in the selected health or social care setting. Assessment practice 7.2		

Learning aim Investigate the influence of health and safety legislation and policies in health and social care settings

Pass	**Merit**	**Distinction**
C.P6 Compare the influence of different health and safety laws or policies on health and social care practice in a selected setting. Assessment practice 7.3	**C.M3** Analyse how health and safety legislation or policies influence safe practice in a selected health or social care setting. Assessment practice 7.3	**CD.D3** Justify the effectiveness of health and safety legislation, policies and procedures in maintaining health and safety in a selected health or social care setting. Assessment practice 7.3

Learning aim Explore procedures and responsibilities to maintain health and safety and respond to accidents and emergencies in health and social care settings

Pass	**Merit**	**Distinction**
D.P7 Explain how different procedures maintain health and safety in a selected health or social care setting. Assessment practice 7.4	**D.M4** Analyse how individual responsibilities and health, safety and emergency procedures contribute to safe practice in a selected health or social care setting. Assessment practice 7.4	**CD.D4** Evaluate the importance of safe practice principles in maintaining and promoting the health, safety and welfare of service users in a selected health or social care setting. Assessment practice 7.4
D.P8 Explain the health and safety responsibilities of employers, employees and others in a selected health or social care setting. Assessment practice 7.4		

Getting started

Working in health and social care means that you must consider the public's confidence in your ability to safeguard the welfare and best interests of service users. A duty of care is a responsibility to behave in a way that promotes welfare and does not cause harm and applies to all health and social care workers. You will owe a duty of care to many people including service users, colleagues (both voluntary and paid staff), your employer, yourself, visitors, family and friends of service users and also the 'public interest' – this means anyone likely to observe or be affected by your actions.

Examine how a duty of care contributes to safe practice in health and social care settings

Safe practice in health and social care involves employers and care workers understanding their rights and responsibilities, performing duties competently and minimising risks. In *Unit 2: Working in Health and Social Care*, you looked at what it is like to work in a health and social care setting. In this unit, you will be examining the principles of duty of care and safe practice.

Duty of care

Legal obligation to protect wellbeing and prevent harm

Duty of care is defined simply as a **legal obligation** to always act in the best interests of the service user and any others that may be affected by your actions. You should not act, or fail to act, in a way that results in harm. You should know your limits and act within your competence level.

Part of your code of professional conduct is to set relationship boundaries. It is important to understand that a professional relationship has boundaries. It is very different to your relationships with family and friends. 'Professional detachment' means that you can provide care objectively and without becoming emotionally involved.

Safety tip

You should not take on tasks that you do not think you can perform safely.

Upholding the rights and promoting the interests of individuals experiencing abuse or neglect

In the workplace, you may find that service users trust you and you have to act as an advocate for a vulnerable service user, to ensure that they are treated fairly and with dignity. All service users have rights. However, they may not feel able to ask for what they need because they are scared or physically intimidated by another service user, a member of their own family, a friend or even a member of staff.

All service users are individuals with unique needs and abilities. Some service users may lack the capacity to protect their rights because they do not have the mental capacity to understand the implications of their circumstances or the consequences of their actions.

> **Safety tip**
>
> Never promise to keep a secret for a service user as this may put you and the service user at risk of harm. Always tell the service user that you will **not** keep a secret and make sure that you follow the disclosure policy of the organisation you are working for.

You should always consider how disrespectful remarks or actions may impact on the service user's self-esteem. You must work on the principle that the service user is telling the truth – it is not your job to judge them or tell them that they are wrong.

Protecting health, safety and wellbeing

In the workplace, you are in a position of trust in relation to all service users. It is important to understand that a service user may be vulnerable and you have to take responsibility for the unequal distribution of power, so that the service user is not exploited, intimidated or unjustly treated.

When you are working with service users, you should be able to explain to your managers how your actions were safe, fair, considered, and proportionate or warranted.

You have a duty as an employee to take care of yourself. You must also consider the impact of your actions or failings on others, and take care of them as well.

Ensuring safe practice

Whatever care setting you work in, including in a service user's home, you must ensure that you follow and put into practice the safe workplace policies set by your employing organisation. This is for the benefit of your employing organisation, the service user, yourself and anyone else in your working environment. Not observing safe practices may lead to accidents that can be painful and sometimes cause irreversible damage. In the worst scenario, accidents can be fatal. As well as causing injuries to people, accidents have to be investigated and may be costly both in terms of damaged health and confidence, and in loss of time and money.

All work environments present hazards but this can be particularly true of the service user's home where there may be additional problems such as large pieces of furniture or thick carpets. Both of these will create problems when using equipment such as a hoist. It is important that you consider additional environmental obstacles before you start a task with a service user. You must plan tasks carefully in order to minimise risks and the floor should be as clear as possible.

> **Safety tip**
>
> Remember that the floor should be as clear as possible. Pets, such as cats and dogs, can prove to be hazards. Pets should be moved to a different room before you perform any task involving large equipment, such as hoists or wheelchairs, or if your service user needs assistance to walk.

▶ Make sure that you explain to your service user why you need to remove their pet from the room before starting a procedure where their pet may present a hazard.

The Care Quality Commission (CQC) requires that health and safety training should be part of your induction to the care workplace. Training is an important part of safe and effective working practice and you should ensure that you attend your training sessions to learn about this important aspect of your working life. After training, you should have a working knowledge of the fundamental health and safety procedures for your workplace, in order to practice and promote safe working procedures. You should adopt and promote a culture of safe practice and set and maintain high standards of care for yourself and others.

Part of your personal professional development should include reflective practice. In health and safety terms, this should include questions such as: 'Did I use the correct health and safety procedures in my work?' and 'If not, how could I improve safety in the care setting next time?' Share your skills and understanding, and also be open to other people's experience. Care is a team effort and you need to be part of the open analytical reflection of the practices of your workplace. It is also important to use **constructive criticism** to improve your professional practice.

Code of conduct

A code of conduct is a framework to work to. It tells you how to behave when interacting with others, maintain and improve the quality of your service, be effective in what you do, stay safe and promote the safety of others. The code of conduct sets the standards for your profession. It gives people an idea of what to expect and an indication of how to tell when things do not meet these standards, or when things can be improved.

 **PAUSE POINT**

Why can a 'code of conduct' improve the care experience for both service users and staff?

Hint — Think about the importance of people's expectations of a service.

Extend — How might the way in which a healthcare professional dresses make an impression on the wider public?

Balancing individual rights with risks

We live in a complex, multicultural society in which needs, rights and associate risks may be interpreted very differently. We do not live in isolation, so one person's choices usually have an effect on other individuals, whether positively or negatively. Healthcare professionals may have power over those in their care that service users find difficult to challenge. Many service users fear losing their independence, which can cause conflict with healthcare professionals and friends and family, who may feel that the service user will not be able to cope with independent living. Additionally, service users have the right to accept or reject any course of treatment or care that is offered to them.

Research

Using the internet, research Ashya King. His parents took him abroad for brain tumour treatment as they did not agree with the treatment offered in the UK. Discuss the following questions. Do you feel that Ashya's parents had the right to remove Ashya? What risks were they taking on Ashya's behalf?

Before examining duty of care and the policies and procedures involved, it may be helpful for you to think about the service user as an individual. Service users have the right to make informed choices even if those choices may involve a small amount of risk.

> **Safety tip**
>
> Different care settings have different policies and procedures, depending on the needs of the service users. Always familiarise yourself with the policies and procedures of the organisation that you are working for **before** you start to deliver care.

Acting in a person's best interests

When working in care, you may be concerned about the choices that some service users are making. You may think that the choices that you would make in a particular situation would be better. You may think that you are acting in a person's best interests by preventing them from doing something. You can only do this if you have their consent unless you have evidence that the person lacks the capacity to make that particular decision at the time it needs to be made.

Case study

Jimmy's choices

Anil works for an agency that provides care for people in their own homes. He cares for Jimmy, an elderly man with chronic lung disease and limited mobility. Anil has to get his shopping for him and help Jimmy

with his personal care needs. Jimmy has started getting breathless and sometimes needs oxygen in addition to his medication.

He likes to smoke and is strong willed and assertive.

Jimmy has run out of cigarettes and asks Anil to go to the shop and pick up three packs of twenty cigarettes. Anil reluctantly goes to the shop. He thinks that what he is doing is wrong. Anil knows that he has a duty of care to Jimmy. When he gets back, Jimmy's sister is at the house and is cross with Jimmy for smoking. She threatens to report Anil for encouraging him.

Check your knowledge

1 What do you need to consider when acting in someone's best interests?

2 How do you ensure that someone is making an 'informed choice'?

3 What should you do if you have concerns about a service user's behaviour?

4 How should Anil protect himself from complaints by Jimmy or his family in this situation?

PAUSE POINT   Can you give examples of when and where you may try to act in someone's best interests?

> Hint   Think about health care, social care and home care settings.
>
> Extend   What might happen if someone tried to make decisions for the service user without their consent?

Complaints procedures

Complaints policies and procedures

Most of the time in care settings, things do not go wrong. However, if they do, people have the right to complain.

The CQC has the power to respond to complaints about the quality of service that you, or the organisation that you work for, may have delivered. This is shown in Table 7.1.

▶ **Table 7.1** CQC complaints procedure

Organisation/service complaint is about	How to complain	If you are not satisfied with the response
NHS hospital, GP, dentist or other NHS service.	Complain to the organisation that commissions (pays for and arranges) the service. For example, in England this is NHS England.	• You can find information about the Health Service Ombudsman at www.ombudsman.org.uk.
Private health care that you have paid for yourself.	Complain to the organisation directly. For larger organisations you will need to contact their head office.	• You can contact the Association of Independent Healthcare Organisations (AIHO).
Care home, nursing home, home-care agency or other social care service.	Contact the service directly to make your complaint. This gives them the chance to try to put things right for you.	• You can complain to your local council, if they paid for the care. You can find contact details for your local council by visiting www.gov.uk. • You can also contact the Local Government Ombudsman at www.lgo.org.uk.
The use of the Mental Health Act (2007), whether the person is detained in hospital or on a community treatment order.	Contact the CQC.	• Service users detained under the Mental Health Act (2007) are entitled by law to have access to an Independent Mental Health Advocate (IMHA). IMHAs are trained in the Mental Health Act and can advise you about your health or social care service rights. For more information about IMHAs, visit www.scie.org.uk.
Social services decisions.	The local authority.	You can find out the contact details for your local authority at www.gov.uk.
The NHS.	Contact the Parliamentary and Health Service Ombudsman (PHSO).	

The reasons why complaints are made

There are many reasons why people may complain about the care that they or their relatives or friends receive.

▸ Service users not having their needs met. This can happen in both health and social care settings and may result in harm being done to the service user. Remember, not all harm is physical; some service users may be emotionally harmed by poor quality care.

▸ Care worker's behaviour or attitude. Care workers may be abrupt, disrespectful or careless. Some care workers find it hard to maintain a level of professionalism in their work and may speak to the service users in the same casual or off-hand way that they would speak to their friends.

▸ Discrimination. People may be discriminated against for any perceived difference, such as gender, race, disability or sexuality. Discrimination and being treated less favourably can sometimes be passed off as a joke or the person discriminated against is considered to be 'over-sensitive' by the people perpetrating it.

▸ The cost of care. Care can be very expensive and in a free-market, costs can vary a lot. Some service users may feel like they are not being given value for their money.

▸ Abuse or neglect. Everyone has the right to expect a high standard of care, but some care workers cannot or will not provide high levels of service. The consequences of abuse or neglect are serious, and can be fatal.

Discussion

Why is it important for people to complain if they are not satisfied with the levels of care that they receive?

Case study

Sara needs help

Sara is 53 and has early onset dementia. Her family live nearby and visit her daily but they cannot be there all of the time. To begin with, Sara just needed help with daily tasks such as shopping, cooking, cleaning and maintaining a safe environment. However, recently Sara has started to need more help with personal care. Sara's new home help is always in a hurry. She rushes Sara, leaving her confused and anxious.

Last week Sara's daughter came round to visit and was surprised to see bruises on Sara's upper arms. She asked the carer how she got them and the carer said that Sara had banged into the door frame as she was passing through the doorway.

This week Sara had bruises on her wrists. When Sara's daughter asked Sara what had happened she said that the carer was rough with her and was always trying to make her rush and, if she was not quick enough, then the carer would shout at her.

There was no documentation about the bruising on either occasion. The carer had left herself open to criticism or even prosecution by not keeping appropriate documentation. The carer had failed in her duty of care to Sara by not keeping her safe. She had also failed to observe her code of professional conduct because she gave poor quality care and had lost the trust of her service user. The carer's manager had also failed in their duty of care by not providing enough time for the carer to discharge her duties.

Check your knowledge

1 What do you do if you have concerns about the quality of care that an individual is receiving?

2 What do you need to consider before making a complaint?

3 What changes are required in Sara's care provision to ensure that it is satisfactory?

PAUSE POINT   Some people do not complain even if they are not receiving the care that they need. Suggest reasons why this happens.

Hint   Think about the patient's capacity, their isolation or their vulnerability.

Extend   How could you support someone who feels that they ought to make a complaint?

Investigating complaints

NHS organisations must make arrangements for dealing with complaints in accordance with The Local Authority Social Services and NHS Complaints (England) Regulations 2009. According to these regulations, a complaint should be made within 12 months of the cause of the complaint, unless there are **extenuating circumstances**.

Under these regulations, the complaint must be investigated in a timely fashion and the complainant kept informed of the progress of the investigation. The regulations state:

▶ complaints should be investigated by someone of appropriate standing who is not involved in the cause of the complaint – the complainant must have confidence that the investigation is going to be thorough and impartial

▶ people making a complaint should be told which organisation will be investigating their complaint

▶ complaints should be investigated properly – the investigation should be thorough and documented

▶ complaints should be taken seriously and complainants treated with courtesy and respect

▶ the complainant should give permission for disclosure of the circumstances, or their personal information relating to the complaint, and who can be informed of the events leading to the complaint

▶ everyone needs to have confidence in the process – the investigation should be proportional to the complaint made and it is important to remember that investigations can be stressful for staff

▶ the person who complains should be told the outcome of the investigation into their complaint

▶ action must be taken, where necessary, to safeguard the welfare of future service users – it is not enough to deal with problems on an issue-by-issue basis, especially if the problem is within the care delivery system.

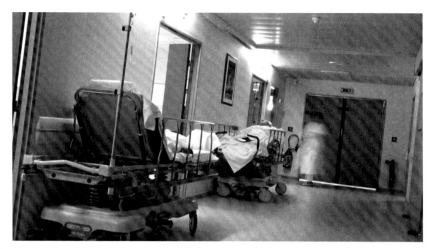

▶ Why might a person left on a trolley in a hospital corridor complain?

Complaints can be made orally (face-to-face or by telephone), in writing or electronically (by email or via an organisation's website). If they are made orally, then a written transcript must be produced. The Citizens Advice Bureau website provides some useful help about making a complaint.

Step by step: Making a complaint   `4 Steps`

Joyce is 83 and she was found wandering in the street in her nightclothes in the middle of the day. She was confused and disorientated. She was taken to hospital but had to wait on a trolley in the accident and emergency department for six hours following her initial assessment. This was because there were no inpatient beds free and she could not be admitted until one became available the next day.

Joyce's daughter, Ailish, decided to complain and was informed of the complaints procedure. Ailish used the following complaint procedure.

1 Ailish wrote a letter of complaint to the hospital.

2 The complaint was acknowledged within three days. The hospital discussed with Ailish how her complaint would be managed, and how long this would take.

3 The complaint was investigated. Ailish was informed of the outcome, and the proposed actions to minimise the risk of this happening again. The outcome of the inquiry stated that the incident occurred as a result of the 'winter-bed crisis' and that the hospital could not be held liable for extraordinary levels of demand. No action would be taken over the fact that Joyce did not have a psychiatric assessment.

▼

4 Ailish was not satisfied with this outcome and appealed to the Parliamentary and Health Service Ombudsman.

Responding to complaints with respect and treating them seriously

There are some key things that those investigating a complaint must do. The person making the complaint may not know their rights so it is important that you, as a health worker, are fully informed and able to support them.

If you are not sure yourself, do not just guess or dismiss the request for help and support. Refer the complainant to someone who can help them, such as a senior carer or a manager.

A person dealing with a complaint about the care a service user has received, about health care or social care, must treat the complainant with dignity and respect, and treat the complaint seriously.

> **Research**
>
> Visit the CQC website (**www.cqc.org.uk**) and find out the advice they offer to service providers who are responding to complaints.

Using complaints to improve the quality of service provision

Complaints can highlight areas of care that can be improved on. As a care worker, it is important that you can see the positive effects of the complaints procedure. Service users are entitled to high-quality care and, where opportunity for improvements has been identified, it is important that those improvements are made. There may be simple steps that can be taken to improve care, or there may need to be a major overhaul of the practice employed by the institution that you work for. Whatever the outcome of an investigation, it is important that you adopt the new procedures identified and follow any new policies.

Ⅱ PAUSE POINT Can you give examples of complaints that people make about health or social care provision?

Hint Think about the things that can go wrong and the potential outcome for the health or welfare of the service user.

Extend What happens if recommendations for improvements are not communicated to staff, are ignored or not followed properly?

Legal proceedings and clinical negligence

Most service users receive excellent care. However, when care falls below standard it can become negligent or even dangerous enough to cause harm to the service user. When this happens, the service user or their advocate may decide that the problem is serious enough to be considered a criminal act. Everyone within society is entitled to the protection of the law and access to justice including both the service user and the care worker.

The Care Act 2014 replaces 'No Secrets' guidance (Department of Health, 2000) and makes safeguarding adults a statutory duty. Practitioners and managers who suspect that an adult service user has been the victim of criminal behaviour, or is at risk of becoming a victim, must inform the police immediately. For example, conduct that amounts to neglect and abuse, such as physical assault or theft from a patient, can be a specific criminal offence (eg under the Theft Act (1968)).

For example, if a patient dies as a result of abuse or deliberate neglect by a care worker, legal proceedings can result in a charge of manslaughter.

Legal proceedings are taken against healthcare practitioners who have caused harm to a service user, whereas a clinical negligence action is about claiming compensation. In these cases, the court cannot:
▶ discipline the healthcare professional (disciplinary procedures are performed by employers)
▶ force a healthcare worker or an organisation to change the way it works, or how it delivers a service
▶ make a healthcare worker apologise to the person making the claim.

Some causes for a claim of clinical negligence may be:

▶ a late diagnosis, or a misdiagnosis

▶ an error made during surgery by a healthcare professional

▶ a medication error, for example the wrong medication was given or an incorrect dosage

▶ informed consent not being given by the service user before treatment (the service user must understand what they are consenting (saying yes) to)

▶ the service user not understanding the risks involved in a particular treatment.

An individual injured as a result of negligent medical treatment may be able to take legal action for compensation. A service user's next of kin can also take legal action on their behalf, for example if the service user lacks the mental capacity to take the action or if the service user has died. If you have concerns about your service user's welfare, you must ensure that you share them with your line manager in accordance with the policies and procedures of your organisation. If your service user is unlikely to remember the details of an incident, or even that they have made a complaint, this should also be recorded.

Case study

Baby P

Peter Connelly, known as Baby P, died in 2007 in Haringey, London, aged 17 months. At autopsy, he was found to have swallowed one of his teeth after being punched in the face, he had a broken back, broken ribs and mutilated finger tips. His mother's boyfriend was found guilty of causing his death. The family were known to social services and had made numerous visits to healthcare professionals, where injuries and incidents of suspected abuse were noticed.

Peter's death led to a Serious Case Review as failings had been identified in the practice of the social workers, their managers and the medical professionals directly involved in Baby P's care.

Check your knowledge

1 How did the healthcare professionals involved in this case fail in their duty of care to Peter Connelly?

2 Why is it important to ask specific and directed questions of the carers and relatives of service users with regard to their care, if the service user cannot speak for themselves?

3 What should you do if relatives refuse to answer your questions or become hostile?

4 Why is it important to follow up the actions on concerns that you have reported?

5 What should you do if you feel that the parents or carers of your service user are trying to prevent you from doing your job competently or efficiently?

Safety tip

Accurate record keeping is essential in all care settings. This is especially the case once a complaint has been made. If legal proceedings are started, an absence of time/dated documentation may weaken a case and make the defendant vulnerable.

Discussion

Why is it important for the law to be used to investigate acts of deliberate neglect or abuse?

A care worker works in a home for people with learning difficulties. One day, she is with a colleague when a service user mentions that they are in love with someone and would like a relationship with them.

Her colleague says that this is impossible for someone like 'them'. The service user starts to cry.

- Produce a short report on the duty of care with regard to maintaining dignity, why this would be important to the service user and a step-by-step guide to reporting breaches of a duty of care.
- Discuss how complaints and appeals procedures address a failure in duty of care.
- Evaluate the importance of the duty of care and complaints procedures in promoting safe practice.

Explain the importance of advocating for vulnerable individuals in health and social care settings, and assess the importance of balancing individual rights with duty of care.

Plan
- What am I being asked to do?
- How confident am I with this task? Are there areas where I might have problems?
- Am I confident that I know what the operative verbs mean? Do I understand the difference between 'explain' and 'evaluate'?

Do
- I know what I am doing and what I want to achieve.
- I can check my work to see where I have made mistakes and make changes to correct them.

Review
- I can explain what the task was and how I approached it.
- I know what I would do differently next time, and how I would approach the parts that I found difficult this time.

B | Understand how to recognise and respond to concerns about abuse and neglect in health and social care settings

Key terms

Abuse – an action deliberately intended to cause harm or distress.

Civil rights – the right to political and social freedom, and equality.

Legal rights – the rules set by a legal system about what a person is entitled to, such as the protection of property or person.

Human rights – the principles of human behaviour expected of everyone regardless of nationality, place of residence, sex, national or ethnic origin, colour or religion.

Abuse is mistreatment of a service user by one or more people which violates the service user's **civil**, **legal** or **human rights**. Abuse can take many forms and the impact on the service user, their family and the wider community can be devastating.

Recognising the signs and symptoms of abuse or neglect and acting appropriately is the responsibility of all care workers. You need to know what you are looking for and how to act if you find it. You must report your concerns to your manager. Never be tempted to 'take matters into your own hands' or act outside the policies and procedures that govern your profession.

You should not let emotions about the situation cloud your judgement. Your role is to support the service user and to remain professional. In order to support your service users properly when working in care, you will need to be resilient and set aside your own thoughts and feelings about a particular situation.

Be aware that sometimes you may see incidents of abuse or neglect that will distress you. Always ensure that you also get the support that you need to deal with the feelings or emotions that you may experience. Individuals have civil rights, legal rights and human rights. It is important that you are aware of the difference between these terms, but that all of these rights are applied equally.

Types and signs of abuse and neglect

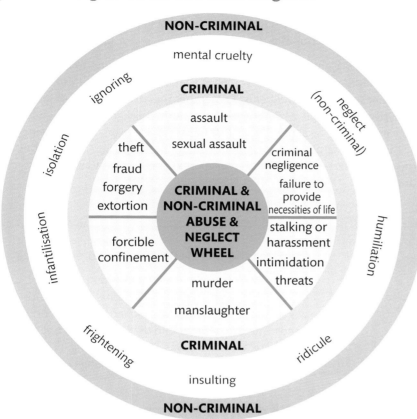

▶ **Figure 7.1** There are many different forms of abuse and neglect, the effects of which can be long-term and devastating

Types of abuse and neglect

Neglect and acts of omission

Neglect can occur when a service user's needs are simply not met. Failing to leave a drink within reach of a service user is neglect, *deliberately* leaving a drink out of reach is abuse.

Neglect can take many forms. It may be physical, for example poor cleanliness. This may be self-neglect, where an individual simply stops taking care of their personal hygiene or nutritional needs. The neglect may be visible, where you can see that their clothes are not laundered, that personal hygiene has not been observed or that the person may be inadequately dressed for the season. You may notice, for example that they are wearing a thin summer jacket in the middle of winter.

However, there may be no physical signs of neglect. Instead, neglect may show as a range of behaviours that cause concern. For example, the service user may be left alone in a darkened room with no means of contacting anyone for help.

Neglect is also the failure to protect a vulnerable individual from emotional harm. For example, it is neglect if you allow a service user to be shouted at by another service user or a relative when you know this causes them distress.

An **act of omission** may occur when a health or social care professional fails to meet the required standards of their professional code of conduct. It can relate to failing to observe a service user's preferences or failing to maintain their dignity. It may include

> **Key term**
>
> **Neglect** – failure to provide proper care.

> **Key term**
>
> **Act of omission** – failing to provide something which is needed, such as medication or respect.

things that are not done for the service user, for example because of a conflict with the carer's preferences. An example of this may be that the service user has a strong faith but the carer does not take them to their place of worship, meaning that the service user's spiritual needs are not met.

Service users have a right to expect to be treated with dignity and to have their privacy protected. As a care worker, you have a vital role to play in this aspect of the service user's emotional wellbeing. Remember that people are all different and the value systems of people of different ages, cultures, backgrounds or genders will not necessarily be the same. Things that upset service users, such as being called by the wrong name, may not bother you but the key thing to remember in person-centred care is that it is the service user's preferences that are most important.

Case study

Mrs Richardson

Mrs Richardson is 78 and becoming increasingly frail. She lives with her daughter in a two bedroom flat on the tenth floor of a tower block. As her daughter does not work and Mrs Richardson's friends have moved away or died, they have very few visitors. Usually, they stay together and keep each other company.

Mrs Richardson likes getting dressed up, even if she is not going anywhere.

When her daughter went into hospital, a homecare worker was sent to help Mrs Richardson with her basic needs. The care worker said that, as she was not going anywhere, then there was no point 'getting all dolled up' and that all that was needed was a change of nightdress so that she would feel fresher.

Check your knowledge

6   Why has the care worker been neglectful? Why should Mrs Richardson complain?

7   What support will Mrs Richardson need to make a complaint?

8   Why is it important to maintain a service user's dignity and respect their choices?

9   What do you need to consider when delivering personal care?

Physical abuse

Physical abuse includes many aggressive acts such as hitting, punching, pushing or burning. Using medication in a way that it is not prescribed in order to subdue the service user is also abuse. Physical abuse also includes force feeding, slapping or breaking bones by inappropriate movement, for example causing a fracture by forcing a service user's arm into a sleeve awkwardly.

You may see other carers pinching or poking or slapping a patient and saying things like, 'It's only a joke' or 'We're playing, it's fine'. Nothing is fine if it causes harm or distress to a service user who may not feel empowered to complain. You have a responsibility (duty of care) to report your concerns so that they are properly investigated.

Always read a service user's care plan before you start caring for them, so that you can confidently and professionally manage any atypical behaviour, such as a service user displaying aggression. Inappropriate reaction to this type of behaviour could leave you vulnerable to accusations of abuse.

Ⅱ PAUSE POINT   Why should you take another care worker with you to perform a personal care task if a service user is unpredictable?

  Hint   Think about the risk of physical harm to yourself and the service user if they become aggressive.

  Extend   What may happen to you if a service user in your care is found to have unaccounted-for bruising?

Psychological abuse

Psychological abuse is caused by someone behaving in such a way as to cause a **psychological trauma**. As a carer, you may notice a change in your service user. For example, they may become very anxious, or depressed, they may be self-harming or deliberately placing themselves in high-risk situations such as running into busy traffic, as an expression of their emotional pain, or they may develop anorexia.

An individual may be subjected to psychological abuse for a long time. Although it can be just as devastating as physical abuse, without any obvious physical signs it may not be noticed for a longer period of time.

Psychological abuse is the act of inflicting emotional abuse, verbal abuse or humiliation. It includes name calling and undermining someone's confidence.

Emotional abuse may include:

▶ threatening to withdraw affection if the person does not behave in a certain way or perform a particular action

▶ acting in an inconsistent way, sometimes being affectionate and sometimes not, in order to manipulate someone and leave them unsure of how to behave to get the affection back

▶ threat of punishment

▶ saying hurtful things in order to exercise control by reducing a person's self-confidence or sense of self-worth.

Verbal abuse may include:

▶ deliberately using language that a service user will find disrespectful

▶ shouting or threatening a service user

▶ criticising a service user in a way that makes them feel insecure, unsafe or lowers their self-esteem – this may be done over a long period of time and gradually reduce the service user's sense of self-worth.

Humiliation may include:

▶ belittling a service user in the presence of family, friends, other care givers or even strangers

▶ deliberately undermining a service user

▶ deliberately embarrassing a service user by disclosing private information.

> **Key term**
>
> **Psychological trauma** – a feeling of helplessness and vulnerability following very stressful events.

> **Reflect**
>
> Psychological abuse of elderly people may be unnoticed for a long time as they may be more isolated. Elder abuse can include emotional abuse, verbal abuse, humiliation, or threats of punishment.
>
> Find out the steps that you can take if you think that an elderly person is being abused. You can access 'Report abuse of an older person' at **www.gov.uk.**

Sexual abuse

Sexual abuse is forcing a person to take part in sexual behaviour for which they have no desire. It does not have to include touching genitalia (private parts), it can also include non-touching activities. Sexual abuse involving touching may include genitals, penetration of the mouth, vagina or anus, or forcing another to touch genitals against their will. Examples of non-touching sexual abuse include forcing a person to watch pornography, photographing them in sexual poses, forcing them to watch or listen to sexual acts or exposing genitalia to a person when they do not want to see them.

Sexual harassment may be passed off as a joke by the perpetrator but may rapidly escalate into behaviour that is not only unprofessional but can also lead to emotional harm.

Care workers often have to deliver personal care when the service user is naked. Do not forget that having no clothes on often makes people feel very vulnerable and they may display a range of reactions to this feeling.

Service users may try to abuse carers by using lewd or suggestive language or by inappropriate touching. It is important that you maintain your professionalism, remind the service user of what is and is not appropriate behaviour and report such incidents to your line manager.

You will need to use **empathy** to help you to understand why people are reacting in a certain way to their own personal care needs, how you can make them feel more secure and what you need to do to in order to support them in their care needs so that they do not get upset and potentially make accusations against you for sexual abuse.

You must be aware of your behaviour at all times. You should not do or say things which may be misinterpreted. It is not acceptable for care workers to joke about or direct a sexual remark at a service user or at another member of staff in the presence of a service user.

You must report any such activity to your manager in order for the matter to be dealt with. In severe cases, sexual harassment can lead to prosecution under the Equality Act (2010) as it is a form of discrimination.

Sexual activity where the individual cannot give consent

You need to be aware of the signs of sexual activity without consent for service users with complex needs as they may be unaware themselves that abuse has occurred. A service user cannot consent to sexual activity if they are unconscious or they lack the capacity to give informed consent.

Case study

Changing relationships

Beryl developed Alzheimer's disease when she was 74. She had been married for 50 years by then and she and her husband Bert had always been so happy. As her health deteriorated, Bert found it increasingly hard to cope. Eventually, after two years, and very reluctantly, he asked that she should be moved to a nursing home. Bert visited every day and took Beryl out for lunch every Sunday. Bert still lived in the home that they had shared all their married life.

Beryl deteriorated to the point where she did not recognise Bert or anyone else. She was incontinent, could not feed herself and required all her care needs to be met by the carers.

Bert's feelings for Beryl had not changed and he had spoken before about them having a full sexual relationship, even after Beryl's diagnosis and up until she moved to the care home. He had also spoken about how he missed that intimacy. One Sunday, Bert brought Beryl back and mentioned to staff that there had been sexual intimacy that afternoon between himself and Beryl because he just loved her so much and missed that side of the relationship.

Check your knowledge

1 Why is what happened to Beryl abuse if she is still married to Bert?

2 Why might Bert think that he has not done anything wrong by having sexual intercourse with Beryl?

3 Why is it important that all incidents of concern are investigated by the appropriate professionals?

4 What does your manager need to consider before referring the matter to the police?

Financial abuse

Financial abuse is a type of theft. It is another name for stealing money or valuables from a service user or of **defrauding** them of their money or property. Often the people who defraud vulnerable service users of their property or inheritance are considered 'friends' by the service user. They can be very close to or get very close to the service user, they may have **power of attorney** or they may simply steal a service user's bank details or property. You may notice that small objects of high value, such as jewellery, are missing. Remember to be tactful if you ask questions about where things have gone as there may be a very simple explanation. If there is a cause for concern, then you must report this to your manager.

Financial abuse is a crime and should always be investigated. However, some service users are reluctant to press charges when they are being financially abused by a relative and/or their primary carer.

It is often a very difficult issue to address because the service user may assume that they have made a mistake or they may be perceived as an unreliable witness because of their vulnerability/frailty.

As a care worker, you should try to ensure that vulnerable people do not fall victim to scams and 'Get rich quick' schemes and that someone is not trying to defraud them of their property or inheritance. Many elderly or vulnerable people are victims of cybercrime or literature received through the post asking for upfront payments, for example to retrieve a jackpot prize, or requesting bank details. You should alert your service users to the dangers of these scams. As a care worker, you are also vulnerable to accusations of financial abuse. If a service user asks you to take money out of their purse or wallet to 'Buy yourself something nice for being so kind', always refuse politely. Remember that you are just doing your job. If they forget that they told you to take the money, or they later deny it, you would have no defence.

Abuse by discrimination

It is important, as a care worker, that you are aware of the different types of discrimination and can recognise them when you see them.

People can be discriminated against on many different grounds, including:

▸ age
▸ sex/gender
▸ race
▸ culture
▸ religion
▸ ability
▸ sexual orientation.

Key terms

Defraud – to trick or deceive someone into giving you money.

Power of attorney – the legal authority granted to an individual to make decisions on behalf of someone else.

Sometimes it is hard to know whether someone is being discriminated against, so ask yourself some simple questions such as: Can everybody who wants to take part in this event participate (whatever it is – a meal, sport or a fun activity)? If not, why not? Has it been organised or arranged so that a particular section of society cannot participate? Has that group been offered an alternative of equal value or importance to them?

The Equality Act (2010), which replaced the Disability Discrimination Act (1995), enshrines the principle of inclusivity.

Research

The Equality Act (2010) identifies nine protected characteristics. What are these characteristics? Why do you think they were chosen?

Ⅱ PAUSE POINT Why should you reflect on your own practices and evaluate your handling of situations involving vulnerable service users?

Hint Think about the principle of minimising risk for yourself and the service user.

Extend How can self-evaluation of professional practice improve your performance in the workplace?

Domestic abuse

Domestic abuse can be defined as an incident, or number of incidents, where a person is subjected to behaviours that control, scare, threaten or try to persuade them to do something against their will. There is a government definition for domestic abuse. This definition includes the following ideas about what domestic abuse is. It occurs between people who are over 16 and are, or have been, intimate or are, or have been, a family. It can also occur between people who simply live at the same address. Domestic abuse may take the form of physical, sexual, financial or emotional abuse.

Controlling and **coercive behaviours** are now recognised as abusive within domestic relationships. For example, in a relationship where someone tries to dominate another person by only allowing them to go to certain places or to see certain people. They may also try to manipulate the other person by threatening violence. For example, a service user may feel coerced into handing over money because they are threatened with violence although they have never actually been hit.

You will need to be aware, as a care worker, that some service users may feel too intimidated or **disempowered** to seek help. There are some practical steps that you can take:

▶ do not be critical, the service user needs to be supported not judged

▶ report your concerns to your line manager

▶ make sure your concerns are recorded and sign the documentation appropriate to your workplace

▶ never promise the service user that you will keep it a secret.

Key terms

Controlling behaviour – domination and manipulation of one individual by another.

Coercive behaviour – manipulation of one person by another, usually through threats.

Disempower – make a person or a group less confident or less likely to succeed.

Discussion

Some people do not think that they are being abused when the evidence suggests that they are. What should you do if the service user does not want your support?

Signs of abuse and neglect

Signs of neglect and acts of omission

As a care worker, you are in a good position to note changes in a service user's physical appearance.

There are many key physical indicators of neglect or acts of omission, such as:

▶ unkempt appearance
▶ unexplained weight loss
▶ ulcers, especially to the legs
▶ pressure ulcers (also called bed sores).

It is important to report your concerns to your line manager so that they can be properly investigated.

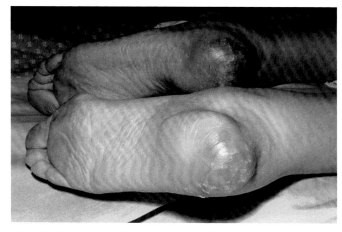

▶ A pressure ulcer (bed sore) can take a long time to heal and may become infected

Signs of physical abuse

You may think that you have identified signs of physical neglect such as bruises, but are concerned that there may be an innocent explanation and that you are making a fuss. Elderly people tend to bruise very easily. Poor manual handling techniques are a form of neglect. If you see 'finger mark bruises' or marks to parts of the body that are not usually touched when supporting a service user in their daily living activities, for example on the face, neck or feet, then this could be a sign of abuse. You should document any bruises that you notice and report this to your manager immediately.

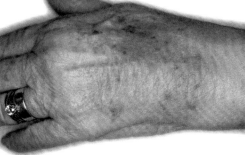

▶ Elderly people tend to bruise very easily

> **Discussion**
>
> Other signs of physical abuse or neglect may include burn marks, malnutrition or broken bones. Is it acceptable to believe the service user's explanation of an injury to their body?

Signs of psychological abuse

Psychological abuse can change a service user's behaviour in a way that you might notice. For example, they may become anxious or withdrawn, perhaps they are chatty and then stop abruptly in the presence of their abuser, or they may cry a lot. There is not necessarily one definitive sign that will show you that your service user is being abused, you are looking for a **change in behaviour** – particularly an unexplained change. It can be difficult to see and some service users will try really hard to cover up what is happening to them.

Pedro's mother

Yolanda is 67. In less than two months she has changed from being outgoing and confident to being withdrawn and suspicious. She has always had a strained relationship with her son, Pedro. Recently, following his divorce, Pedro has moved in with Yolanda.

Pedro is always very brusque with the carers and appears to be hostile towards them. Whenever Amina, the practice nurse, comes to dress Yolanda's leg ulcers and Pedro is there, Amina notices the cowering looks that Yolanda gives him. Yolanda is afraid to speak, is fidgety and far too keen to please her son. When her son is not in the room, Yolanda just looks very sad and frail. Pedro's mother is a changed woman.

Check your knowledge

1   What do you think has caused the change in Yolanda?

2   What should Amina do?

3   How can the practice nurse support Yolanda?

4   What should happen if Yolanda refuses help?

5   Who could Amina report her concerns to if she fears that Yolanda is in danger?

6   What could happen if Amina does not report her concerns?

Signs of sexual abuse

As a carer, you must be aware of the signs of sexual abuse such as bruising or bleeding around the anal or genital areas, or the symptoms of sexually transmitted infections or pregnancy. If you observe any of these signs or symptoms, you must report them to your line manager. Preserve any evidence, such as blood- or semen-stained underwear. Remember to be compassionate and respect the dignity of your service user.

 **PAUSE POINT**

Why must you act quickly and professionally, following your workplace policies and procedures when you suspect abuse?

 Hint

Think about the possibility of any legal proceedings that may follow.

Extend

How can identifying incidents of abuse affect the emotional welfare of the care giver?

Signs of financial abuse

Financial abuse can be perpetrated by anyone that the service user trusts with their financial information. Vulnerable adults are statistically more likely to be subject to financial abuse than other members of society. They are often targeted by people who want to take advantage of their intellectual or emotional vulnerability. The individual targeted is then manipulated into thinking that they are not being exploited.

As a carer, you may see that valuable items are missing from the service user's home or that the service user is short of money. Even a small loss can have a big impact on the service user's welfare. They may be left unable to pay for the services that they need or unable to pay their rent or household bills. The service user may also suffer the range of emotions usually associated with being the victim of a robbery.

Signs of discriminatory practice

Discrimination is treating someone less favourably because of a perceived difference. It can lead others to behave in a similarly discriminatory manner leaving the subject of this kind of abuse feeling targeted, helpless or vulnerable. Anyone can be the object of discrimination. It may take the form of sexual harassment, bullying or racism and lead to the person discriminated against being subjected to:

▶ denial of choice about their care, or even what care is offered to them

▶ denial of privacy and dignity, and maybe of personal belongings

▶ punishments, such as being denied food and drink

▶ refusal of access to services, denial of disabled access or even being excluded from care settings inappropriately.

Being discriminated against can lead to a spectrum of feelings ranging from anger and frustration to being withdrawn, anxious or having low self-esteem. You need to advocate for your service users who are subjected to discriminatory practices.

Reflect

Think about your reaction the last time that you thought that you were treated unfairly. Could something have been done so that you did not think that you had been treated less favourably than someone else? How will this make you treat others in the future?

Factors that could contribute to an individual being vulnerable to abuse or neglect

Vulnerable groups

Service users may be vulnerable for a number of reasons outside of their control. Anyone reliant on assistance from others in order to perform the activities of daily life is vulnerable to abuse and neglect. Everyone has different physical, intellectual, emotional and social (PIES) needs. People with similar needs may be classed as groups within society and a person may be part of different groups at different times in their lives. A person may be considered vulnerable by reason of any of their PIES needs.

Discussion

Why is it important to be aware of the reasons for a person's vulnerability when trying to minimise the risk of abuse or neglect?

Physical vulnerability

There are many reasons that your service user could be physically vulnerable and these may contribute greatly to the risk of abuse or neglect. A service user may have a **chronic medical condition** such as arthritis or they may have a physical disability such as quadriplegia. As people age, their physical frailty increases and their strength may diminish. This can make them more vulnerable to physical abuse and more susceptible to neglect. Younger people may also be vulnerable to physical abuse as they are often smaller (shorter and less heavy) than their abuser.

Key term

Chronic medical condition – a persistent or long-lasting disorder, such as osteoarthritis.

Discussion

Suggest reasons why people with physical disabilities, chronic medical conditions or sensory impairments such as blindness, may be more at risk of abuse or neglect.

Cognitive impairment

Cognitive impairment can have a large range of causes. A person with cognitive impairment may have difficulty protecting themselves from abuse, exploitation or neglect.

Causes of cognitive impairment can include head injury or being born with learning disabilities. The extent of the cognitive impairment will have an impact on how likely the service user is to be able to protect themselves from abuse or neglect. Each service user is an individual and their circumstances are unique. When you are working in care it is important to assess each situation separately and not to make assumptions based on an individual's diagnosis.

Emotional vulnerability

Emotional vulnerability can impair an individual's judgement. A person with depression, anxiety or phobias may react differently to the dangers around them or may not even perceive a danger at all. They may be more vulnerable to persuasion or coercion. You need to be alert to the signs or symptoms of abuse or neglect as individuals may be unwilling or unable to complain about what is happening to them.

Social vulnerability

Social vulnerability can happen for many reasons. Elderly people may outlive their friends and relatives and lose confidence in making new friends. They may fear going out or have problems accessing support that may be available. People can be lonely for all sorts of reasons. New mothers who are coping with a baby may feel socially isolated and vulnerable, as may children in care who are moved from one home to another. Social vulnerability may also affect those who cannot afford to engage in social activities. A sense of belonging is an emotional need that you as a care worker may have to foster or support in your service users.

> **Key term**
>
> **Cognitive impairment** – condition, ranging from mild to more severe, in which an individual has trouble remembering, concentrating and learning, or in making decisions.

> **Key terms**
>
> **Emotional vulnerability** – a feeling of nervousness and uneasiness that may be caused by an individual thinking that they are in some way inferior to or not as worthy as other people.
>
> **Social vulnerability** – the lack of ability to deal with adverse events in life.

> **Research**
>
> Research social activities aimed at elderly people in your local area. What problems could elderly people encounter in trying to participate in these groups or events?

Case study

Rakesh's lonely day

Rakesh is 36. He has Down's syndrome and he used to live with his mother. When his mother became too frail to look after him he moved in with his brother, Karan, who lives eight miles away. Rakesh can use the bus to go and see his mum but Karan is afraid that Rakesh will get lost and has asked him not to go on his own. Karan and his wife both work full time and Rakesh is often alone. Rakesh is well fed and his clothes are clean. Rakesh's old friends miss him but as Karan does not want him to go out on his own, Rakesh has told them that he has new friends where he now lives so that they do not need to worry about him. Rakesh has not joined any groups. He does not go out and feels very lonely and isolated.

Sabrina, Rakesh's social worker, wants to help Rakesh to meet new people.

Check your knowledge

1   Is Rakesh neglected?
2   What could Sabrina do to improve the quality of Rakesh's life?
3   How can Sabrina support the rest of the family?
4   What should Sabrina do if Rakesh refuses help?
5   What could happen to Rakesh if his social needs are not met?
6   Why is it important for Sabrina to document all of her interventions and keep a check on Rakesh's progress?

 **PAUSE POINT**   Why is it important for a care giver to consider all of an individual's PIES needs when trying to prevent abuse or neglect?

> **Hint**   Think about the quality of life of the individual that you are supporting.
>
> **Extend**   What are the potential long- and short-term consequences of abuse or neglect?

Staffing issues that may lead to institutional abuse and neglect

Sometimes health and social care systems let service users down. To deliver an acceptable level of care, correct numbers of staff must be employed, trained and on duty. Staff disputes, low morale and sickness can impact on a care team's performance.

Healthcare and social care workers should be treated fairly, their views should be heard and they should feel part of a team. If you have concerns about staffing levels or other issues that may affect your ability to deliver an acceptable level of care, it is vital that you report these concerns.

If you notice that staffing levels are consistently low and the institution refuses to act, you may take your concerns to the CQC. This may also be your course of action if you are concerned about the quality of leadership in the institution you work for and/or feel that they may be creating a culture of poor care.

For other shortcomings, such as lack of training for new or established staff, you should first take your concerns to your manager.

> **Discussion**
>
> Why is it important to raise your concerns with the appropriate authorities if you are concerned that an institution is failing in its duty of care to either the service users or its own staff?

Responding to concerns of suspected abuse or neglect

Following safeguarding policies and procedures

Policies and procedures can vary depending on the type of institution but all are covered by the Care Act (2014). This act sets out a clear framework for how local authorities and service providers should protect adults from the risk of abuse or neglect.

Local authorities have new safeguarding duties. These include:

▶ establishing multi-agency Safeguarding Adults Boards, made up of health professionals, the local authority and the police, to share information and help plan and formulate safeguarding strategies to identify where abuse may occur, to prevent it or to intervene quickly

▶ carrying out a Safeguarding Adults Review when someone dies as a result of abuse or neglect, or if there is concern that the local authority or the other members of the board could have done more to protect the vulnerable person

▶ providing an independent advocate to support the service user and to explain the Safeguarding Adults Review process to them.

The different agencies involved

Many agencies work together to ensure that the most vulnerable in society are protected from potential abuse. Table 7.2 shows the different agencies involved.

Organisation	Checks and balances	Potential action
Social services	Social services are regulated by the Care Quality Commission to ensure that complaints of poor quality service are investigated.	• This may include leading a multi-agency local adult safeguarding system in an enquiry. • Should be represented on Safeguarding Adults Boards, and carry out safeguarding adults reviews, where necessary. • Advocates may also be provided by social services.
Health services	The ambulance service has developed a system for recognising 'cluster calls' from people at risk of abuse or neglect.	• Staff in all front-line health and social care services should be trained in the identification of indicators of abuse.
Police	Neighbourhood Harm Register to raise an alert when there are repeat calls from individuals at risk of exploitation, neglect or abuse.	• Data is shared with the appropriate agencies so they can work together to provide a joint response.
Voluntary organisations	Disclosure and Barring Service (DBS).	• It is an offence for those convicted of particular crimes to work with vulnerable people, and it is an offence for voluntary organisations to knowingly employ them, even in voluntary situations. • The voluntary organisation must report barred applicants who are trying to gain access to vulnerable individuals.
Care Quality Commission (CQC)	Fundamental Standards.	• A specific regulation on safeguarding people from abuse and improper treatment, which providers have to guarantee. • CQC inspections to ensure the regulation is complied with.

Reflect

Why is it so important to have a coordinated multi-agency approach to safeguarding vulnerable groups within society?

Professional roles and legal responsibilities

Adult protection coordinator

The role of the Adult Protection Coordinator varies from region to region, but essentially it involves implementing a safeguarding policy, and coordinating the flow of information between the different agencies involved in protecting vulnerable service users.

Research

Research the role of the Adult Safeguarding Boards. What are the six safeguarding principles and how do you think that these will help improve the service provided for vulnerable people?

Child safeguarding boards

The local Safeguarding Children Boards are made up of key contributors, such as the police, the NHS, local authority, youth offending teams and voluntary and community services. These boards provide advice and training for those working directly with children, young people and their families. Workers are trained in safeguarding procedures and in identifying the signs and symptoms of abuse or neglect, as well as in promoting children's welfare. People who work with children need to know how to be proactive as well as reactive. It is always preferable to intervene before harm is caused to a child, but staff must be trained to do this in a way that does not cause unnecessary suffering or distress to the child.

Responding to disclosure

When responding to an adult at risk who is making a disclosure, you should follow the guidelines in the disclosure policy of the establishment you work for. If your service user begins to disclose an allegation, it is important that you consider the following points.

▸ Assure the person that you are taking them seriously.

▸ Stay calm and do not jump to conclusions.

▸ Do not ask too many questions. The service user will have to repeat the information to those investigating the allegations and it can be distressing to go over information repeatedly.

▸ Do not promise to keep it a secret or agree to complete confidentiality.

▸ Report your concerns to your manager.

Reporting and recording procedures

Information about adult safeguarding issues is considered to be sensitive and personal. The use of this type of information is governed by the common law duty of confidentiality.

It is never acceptable to disclose information to individuals not directly involved in the care of a service user. As a care worker, you will have access to information that your friends and family who do not work in care will not have. You may all know these people or you may have friends in common.

The Data Protection Act (1998) states that 'personal data' and 'sensitive personal data' must be managed in accordance with the law. The Human Rights Act (1998) gives individuals the right to respect for private and family life, home and correspondence.

All information must be stored safely and all staff must be trained in how to share the information for safeguarding purposes appropriately.

Case study

Everybody knows Dave

Dave is popular in the town where he lives. He is 43 and lives with his mother. Dave was born with cerebral palsy, which caused cognitive impairment. He does not work but is often seen around the town with his bags of shopping and small dog. Dave always has a smile and a wave for everyone. Dave has told his care worker, Carla, that his uncle keeps touching him 'down there' and he does not like it. Carla knew she had to report it. So she followed the procedures of her organisation, reported the disclosure to her manager and filled out, signed and dated the documentation.

When she got home, Carla's mum asked her if anything exciting had happened. Carla's mum does not work with Carla but she likes to gossip and knows lots of people in the local area, including Dave.

Check your knowledge

1 Why should Carla respect the confidentiality policy of the organisation that she works for?

2 Why might Carla be tempted to tell her mother about Dave?

3 What sensitive data does Carla have?

4 What are the potential consequences for Dave and Carla if Carla breaches confidentiality?

5 What is the potential emotional impact on Dave of a breach of confidentiality?

6 What other agencies could become involved in Dave's situation?

PAUSE POINT   Why do care workers sometimes choose to ignore disclosures or incidents of abuse or neglect that they have witnessed?

Hint   Think about the potential reliability of some service users as witnesses.

Extend   What may happen to the care worker and the service user if evidence or concerns are ignored?

Whistleblowing

Key term

Whistleblowing – the mechanism by which staff can voice their concerns about the conduct of other members of staff without fear of repercussion.

You should be aware of the actions of other staff and be familiar with the policy for reporting incidents or the action of others that you consider unlawful or immoral. This is commonly called '**whistleblowing**'. People are often afraid of whistleblowing because they may be intimidated by the person that they are reporting, worry that the managers may not deal with the situation effectively or even feel that they simply like the person that they are reporting and do not want to get them into trouble. Bad practice continues when people do not report their concerns. When you are working in care, it is important to remember your duty of care to the service user and to advocate for them effectively. Although the whistleblower should be protected by law, this is not always the case. Indeed, it can sometimes be impossible for the whistleblower to continue working in the organisation that they have exposed.

Case study

Whistleblowing

Winterbourne View was a residential unit designed for people with a range of learning disabilities. It was owned by a company called Castlebeck. In 2011, the BBC *Panorama* programme sent an undercover reporter to investigate the quality of care there following reports that patients were being systematically abused and neglected by the staff.

The CQC relies on service users, staff and managers to inform them when care is not delivered to the required standards. The CQC had received various warnings that things at Winterbourne View were not right, but no action had been taken. A senior nurse at Winterbourne View reported his concerns to the CQC, but these were not followed up. So, eventually, the senior nurse alerted the BBC who sent their undercover reporter to investigate.

Check your knowledge

1. Why would the CQC be unlikely to hear about problems at Winterbourne View from the service users?

2. What issues could the CQC face if they are dealing with a 'culture of abuse and neglect'?

3. How important is the documentation when pursuing a criminal investigation in a case of this kind, even if the records kept did not reflect what was going on?

4. Why is it important to be a whistleblower, even if it means that you risk losing your job?

PAUSE POINT   Can you give examples of behaviour that may require 'whistleblowing'?

Hint   Not all poor quality care is abuse, some is neglect.

Extend   How should an employer respond, both to the whistleblower and to the allegation?

If you are concerned about safeguarding issues in your workplace, you should tell your employer first so that they have the opportunity to make a thorough investigation.

There may be more people involved in the abuse or neglect than you are aware of. In order for abuse or neglect to stop, everyone involved must be dealt with according to the policies and procedures of your workplace.

If you do not want to tell your employer, you can get legal advice or tell a prescribed person or body. For example, in the case of a care home this would be the CQC.

Reducing the likelihood of abuse and neglect

When working in care, you may find that there are opportunities for you to have a direct role in reducing a service user's risk of abuse or neglect. Everybody is responsible for identifying how and why an individual may be vulnerable.

Sometimes a person's vulnerability is obvious. They may be very young or they may be very old and frail and it is easy to see why they may fall victim to the abusive behaviour of someone who could dominate or control them. Other vulnerable individuals are more difficult to identify and you need to use a range of skills to do so.

Identifying people at risk and the importance of observation

Some abusers are aware of the care worker's role in reporting concerns and will not abuse or neglect a service user in front of others. You need to be aware of changes in patterns of behaviour. You must familiarise yourself with your service user's personality and habits so that you can spot any changes. Also, be aware of any changes in how the service user interacts with others as this may indicate that something is wrong. They may change how they react to someone who is abusing them. You should also look out for any physical signs of abuse or neglect.

If you identify behaviour changes, report them quickly and appropriately. Document your concerns in the service user's files.

> **Safety tip**
>
> If you think someone may be at risk but you are not sure, tell your line manager anyway. Once concerns have been raised about a vulnerable adult who may be at risk, it is easier for all care workers in contact with the service user to be more vigilant.

Awareness raising, providing information, advice and advocacy

It is not uncommon for vulnerable people to be unaware of their risk of being abused or neglected. Sometimes their vulnerability, disability or social exclusion can make them a target for abusers. The vulnerable person may engage with their abuser, or try to maintain a friendship or relationship with them, because they fear being lonely. Vulnerable people, such as those with learning difficulties, may be unaware of the risks posed by certain individuals, or certain circumstances. They may, for example, be more likely to comply with an abuser's instruction to steal from a shop or to drink alcohol excessively.

> **Research**
>
> Research the 'No Secrets' policy. How can this policy help to protect vulnerable individuals in the community?

Would the 'No Secrets' policy have protected Mo Ncube?

Mo was 41 when he died. He had learning disabilities. Before he died he was tortured and eventually murdered by people who targeted him because of his learning disabilities.

Mo thought that Paul aged 29, Ben aged 19 and Marie aged 17 were his friends. Mo wanted to 'belong' and they told him that he was in their 'gang'.

Mo let Paul, Ben, Marie and their other friends into his home many times in the months before his death. Paul, Ben and Marie even moved in for a time. Paul was well known to the police and social services for his violent and unpredictable behaviour. Paul liked to dominate people who were younger or more vulnerable.

Mo was often made to crawl around his flat on all fours and had to call the 'gang' members 'sir' or 'madam'. They took control of his money and ensured that he broke off contact with social services.

On the night of his death, Mo was told to steal some sweets from a shop. He was clumsy and likely to be caught and the others thought that would be funny. When Mo was not caught, they injected him with heroin and pushed him off a nearby bridge. Mo fell 20 metres to his death.

Check your knowledge

1 Why did the members of the 'gang' force Mo to break off contact with social services?

2 Why would it be important to communicate with Mo in a way that he could understand?

3 Before his death, Mo had made numerous calls to a number of agencies, including the police, health and social care services, so they should have been aware that he was in danger. Why is it important to follow up on calls for help?

Inter-agency collaboration and multi-agency working

When working with vulnerable people who are at risk of abuse, neglect or exploitation, different agencies in health care must work as a team, and follow the appropriate disclosure policies.

As a care worker, you should remember that service users should be able to expect a certain level of confidentiality. If you are disclosing information, always ensure that you are the person that should be disclosing it and that the person to whom you are disclosing it has a right to that information.

If you are unsure whether you should be disclosing a particular piece of information then you should ask your line manager. Do not disclose confidential information over the phone without your line manager's permission.

Knowledge and understanding of legislation, regulation, policies and procedures

Legislation can be defined as the process of making or applying laws or Acts of Parliament, such as the Mental Health Act (2007). Regulations are the rules or directives of the organisation that you work for – for example staff not wearing nail varnish when at work.

You will need to know and understand the legislation that helps you to perform your job safely and effectively. In the workplace (if you are performing duties in the service user's home, this is your workplace), your activities are governed by the Health and Safety at Work etc Act (1974). Both you and your employer have responsibilities under the legislation that covers the caring professions.

All care settings are subject to different sections of different acts. The legislation for your workplace informs you about what is and is not legal practice, and regulations inform you about what is and is not permissible practice. You will also to have knowledge and understanding of policies and procedures that are in place at your place of work.

Research

Research the Care Act (2014), which replaced the 'No Secrets' legislation, for the rules on safeguarding vulnerable adults in the UK. How can this framework help care workers and employers use policies and procedures to protect vulnerable people in their care?

Link

This unit links to *Unit 2: Working in Health and Social Care*, which covers the roles and responsibilities of people working in health and social care.

Staff training and continuing professional development

When you start a job as a care worker, there should be an induction process that will include an introduction to your employer's policies and procedures regarding safeguarding. If this does not happen, then the employer is failing in their duty of care to you as an employee.

However, basic training will not provide you with everything that you will ever need to know about working in health and social care. For example, legislation changes over time and the policies and regulations relevant to your work will change when the legislation changes. To deliver safe, appropriate and effective care, it is important that you keep up to date with current policies and practices.

Continuing professional development is the way that professional practitioners maintain and update the knowledge and skills related to their professional lives. During your employment, your employer may offer you training courses related to specific issues. However, it is also your responsibility to keep your knowledge and skills up to date.

Legislation is there to protect both the service user and the care worker. If you fail to take advantage of appropriate training and something goes wrong, not knowing the law will not protect you from prosecution.

Discussion

What are the benefits, to the service user and the staff, of the care worker actively participating in continuing professional development?

 **PAUSE POINT**   What are the benefits to the service user of having a well-trained and dedicated team of carers who can advocate for them?

Hint   Think about the range of ways in which service users may be vulnerable.

Extend   What might happen to the service user if the policies and procedures are not applied consistently?

Promoting empowerment and choice for service users

Service users should be encouraged to make informed choices, even if those choices contain a small amount of risk. The risk should be proportional to the service user's ability to cope with the consequences. Empowering people means allowing them to recognise their action, possibly stop them and avoid harm. They should be encouraged to balance risks with quality of life decisions.

Service users should feel confident in their ability to make their views and choices known. You should listen to them and work with them to help them achieve the outcomes that they want, where possible. If a service user is not in a position to make decisions about their care because they lack the mental capacity, then someone else has to make decisions for them. The service user is entitled to an advocate to speak on their behalf in order to protect their rights. The decisions made must be in the best interests of the service user.

Case study

Terry's options

Terry is 91 and was in the Army for most of his working life. After retirement, he remained active and often volunteered to drive the mini bus at a local centre for elderly people. Terry still insists on driving when there are outings. However, his mobility has become steadily worse as he has aged and his eyesight has also deteriorated significantly. Tariq works at the centre and is concerned that Terry may be endangering the other service users by refusing to let anyone else drive the bus.

Check your knowledge

1 Why might it be important to Terry that he is the one to drive the bus?

2 How might Terry's insistence on driving the bus impact on the other service users?

3 How could Tariq approach this issue with Terry, while still promoting choice, empowerment and dignity for Terry?

4 What are Terry's rights and responsibilities?

5 What are the potential consequences of Tariq doing nothing?

Assessment practice 7.2

B.P3 B.P4 B.P5 B.M2 B.D2

Orchid View home opened in November 2009 for residents with dementia and closed in October 2011. Several safeguarding alerts were triggered and investigated by the CQC in that time.

Although there was insufficient evidence to pursue criminal convictions, the senior coroner found that five residents 'died from natural causes contributed to by neglect' and that several other people 'died as a result of natural causes' but that there was insufficient evidence 'to show that this suboptimal care was directly causative'. The Serious Case Review found that residents were subjected to physical and financial abuse in the understaffed care home and that record keeping was inadequate.

- Write a short report outlining signs or symptoms of abuse that the investigators may have discovered.
- Explain why the abuse may have occurred and how it could have been prevented.
- Justify methods for investigating claims of abuse in situations like this.

Explain how to respond to claims of abuse or neglect and assess the importance of responding to those claims.

Plan
- What am I being asked to do?
- How confident am I with this task? Are there areas where I might have problems?

Do
- I know what I am doing and what I want to achieve.
- I can check my work to see where I have gone off topic and make changes to put this right.

Review
- I can explain what the task was and how I approached it.
- I know what I would do differently next time and the approach I would take with the parts that I found difficult this time.

C

Investigate the influence of health and safety legislation and policies in health and social care settings

Health and safety legislation and policies in health and social care

It is important that you follow the current legislation for the country that you live in. You will find an outline of some of the major legislation and regulations that you will come across in your work below.

Health and Safety at Work etc Act (1974)

The Health and Safety at Work etc Act (1974) or HASAWA is legislation aimed at reducing risk to employees, volunteers and visitors to a workplace. It applies to all workplaces and the policies can vary in response to the needs of the organisation. For example, a residential home for individuals with unpredictable, challenging or aggressive behaviour may have a restraint policy, whereas a nursery probably would not.

HASAWA is the legislation on which most of the health and safety policies you will follow in the workplace are based.

Complaints are investigated by the Health and Safety Executive (HSE), who can impose unlimited fines and pursue prison sentences for individuals or companies that breach these regulations.

Data Protection Act (1998)

Confidentiality is key when working in health and social care and is the basis of the professional relationship that you form with a service user. Maintaining confidentiality helps you to preserve the service user's dignity. You must comply with the principles of the Data Protection Act (1998) that information must be:

▸ held only with consent of the service user

▸ held securely

▸ shared only on a 'need to know' basis

▸ accessible to the service user.

However, there are some limits on confidentiality which apply when there is a risk of harm to other people.

Care Act (2014)

Data sharing is covered by the Care Act (2014). Data sharing enhances the quality of care for the service user and the health and safety of the care worker, whether this is in **statutory care**, voluntary care or private care provision. Data sharing should:

▸ enable inter-agency communication and support decision making

▸ clarify the channels of communication and procedures for sharing information

▸ be inclusive of all **safeguarding partners**.

Key terms

Statutory care – care provided as a legal requirement by the NHS, social care services, education and early years services.

Safeguarding partners – members of the safeguarding boards such as representatives from the police, the NHS, the local council, appropriate charities and the probation service. The CQC or similar organisations may also be represented.

Jeanie uses the drag lift

Jeanie is very proud of the fact that she has worked in care for 30 years. She likes her job as a healthcare assistant in a care home and is keen to work with the new recruits. Jeanie's employer offers Jeanie manual handling training which she has regularly attended. However, Jeanie likes to use the drag lift.

When using the drag lift, the carers stand either side of the bed, parallel to the service user's shoulder and look in the direction of the head of the bed. The carers each hook an arm under the armpit of the service user, who is then dragged back up the bed towards their pillows.

This manoeuvre can shear the skin off the sacrum and should never be used.

Jeanie feels that it was the most effective lift and she does not see why she cannot use it when working with service users.

Jamilia is a new recruit and has been trained in manual handling. She knows that this technique should not be used.

When Jeanie and Jamilia are repositioning Mary in her bed, Jeanie suggests the drag lift. Jamilia does not feel confident to refuse. As they drag Mary back up the bed, the friction shears the skin off Mary's sacrum. Mary is left in pain, with a high risk of infection in the open wound.

Check your knowledge

1 Why should this incident be reported to the care home manager?

2 What should Jamilia have done when Jeanie suggested the lift?

3 What rights does Mary have with reference to the quality of care she received?

4 Which pieces of legislation have been breached?

5 What action should be taken against Mary's carers?

6 What liability does the employer have for ensuring the safety of the staff and the service users?

Care Standards Act (2000)

This act established a National Care Standards Commission to provide for the registration and regulation of children's homes, independent hospitals, independent clinics, care homes, residential family centres, independent medical agencies, domiciliary care agencies, fostering agencies, nurses agencies and voluntary adoption agencies. The act sets minimum standards of care and requires that these institutions are inspected and regulated.

In 2000, the Care Standards Act (2000) set up the Commission for Social Care Inspection which established a new system of national minimum standards for all residential and nursing homes, and domiciliary services. Its primary function is to promote improvements in social care.

According to the Alzheimer's Society, in 2015 there will be 850,000 people in the UK with dementia. One third of these people live in residential care and many may be suffering from depression.

Care standards have a role in ensuring that care homes promote, recognise and support mental health within the care establishment. The standards require care homes to access primary and secondary care and health services for their residents regularly so that the service users' mental health is cared for and treated appropriately.

Equality Act (2010)

The Equality Act (2010) replaces previous anti-discrimination legislation, such as the Disability Discrimination Act (1995), the Race Relations Act (1976) and the Sex Discrimination Act (1975). This act protects people from being discriminated against because of their disabilities or because of their caring responsibilities.

> **Research**
>
> Research the impact of the Equality Act (2010) on reported incidents of discrimination by comparing the statistical data available for the number of reports before the act came into force with the data available for after the act came into force.

Care Act (2014)

The Care Act (2014) replaces a number of existing acts. The purpose of the act is to implement a system of support, putting the service user at the centre of care while integrating the needs of carers so that support is in place before the service user's situation is in crisis. Recognising the needs of the carer for training and support is essential to promoting the health and safety of the service user.

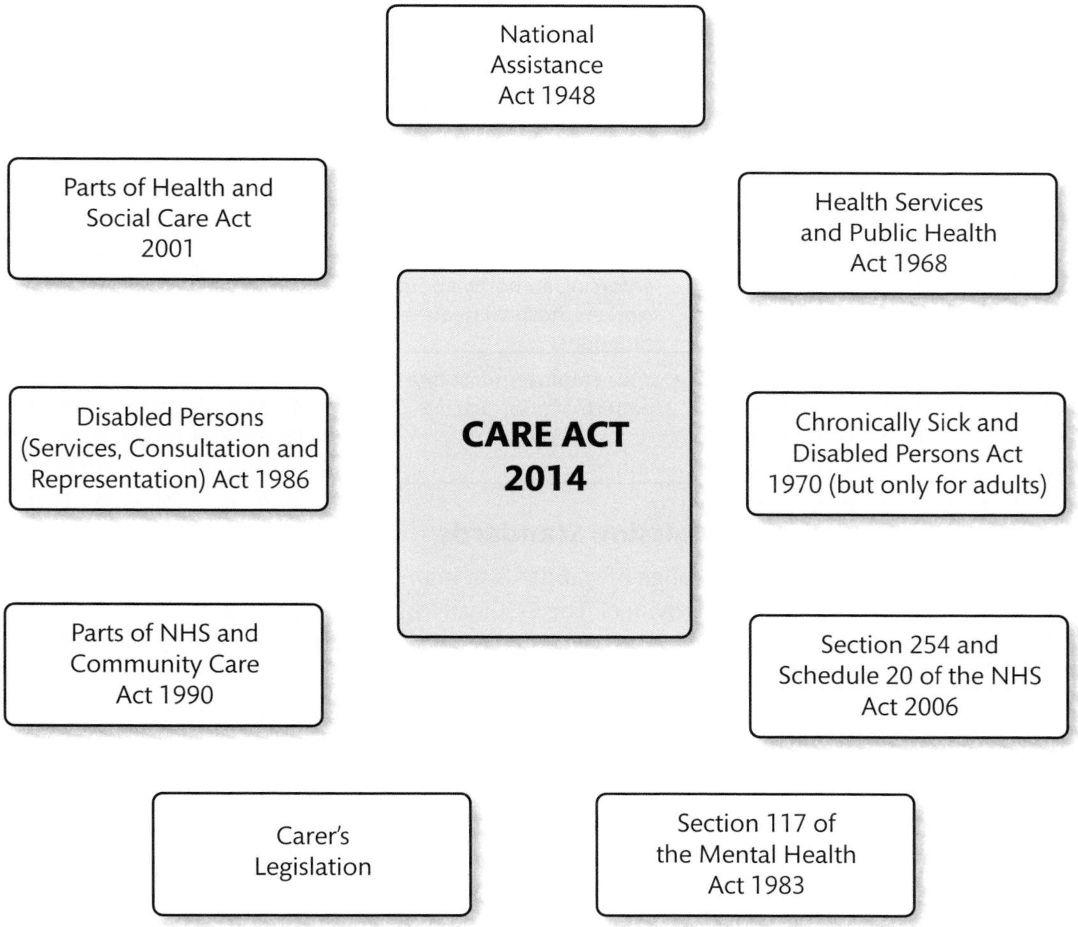

National Assistance Act 1948

Parts of Health and Social Care Act 2001

Health Services and Public Health Act 1968

Disabled Persons (Services, Consultation and Representation) Act 1986

CARE ACT 2014

Chronically Sick and Disabled Persons Act 1970 (but only for adults)

Parts of NHS and Community Care Act 1990

Section 254 and Schedule 20 of the NHS Act 2006

Carer's Legislation

Section 117 of the Mental Health Act 1983

▶ **Figure 7.2** The Care Act (2014) replaces previous legislation, consolidating it into one act

Name and date of legislation	Application in relation to care	Your role in the workplace
The Manual Handling Operations Regulations (1992) Amended (2002)	• There are no 'blanket bans' in relation to manual handling if it leads to a service user being denied care. • Solutions must be found for manual handling issues that maintain dignity as much as possible and use appropriate equipment where necessary.	• You must know your limits and not attempt to exceed them, being forced to do so by an employer increases risk. • If risks cannot be eliminated you should try to minimise them. • You should monitor and review your practices regularly for potential improvements. • You should receive manual handling training.
The Food Hygiene Regulations (2006) Amended (2013)	• These regulations apply if you are preparing food for a service user. • If the service user is preparing food for their own consumption, this is considered a 'domestic arrangement'.	• You must ensure that your hands and clothing are clean and your hair is tied back or in a net before preparing food. • You must make sure that the area that you are working in is clean. • You must check that the food you are preparing is fit for purpose. • You must prepare the food according to directions and to the correct temperature. (Many foods are dangerous if not prepared correctly; some may be lethal.)
Control of Substances Hazardous to Health (COSHH) 2002	Legislation that requires employers to control substances that may be harmful to health, for example: • products containing chemicals such as cleaning products • gases and fumes • medication.	• You must follow the instructions on the label of the product that you are using. • You must store products safely, in accordance with the workplace policy, eg controlled drugs must be in a locked cabinet that is fixed to the wall. • You must not assume that you know the contents of unmarked containers. If it is not labelled then it must not be used. • You should not decant substances from their original container to a container that was designed for a different purpose, eg putting bleach in a lemonade bottle.
Reporting of Injuries, Diseases and Dangerous Occurrences Regulations (RIDDOR) 2013	• Requires employers and designated people in an establishment to report death or serious workplace accidents, occupational diseases and specified dangerous occurrences to the HSE.	• You must report accidents, illnesses and near misses to your employer, either directly or through the responsible person. • The responsible person in your organisation must inform the enforcing authority about accidents resulting in: death, injuries to workers, hospital treatment and other dangerous occurrences or situations. • Your employer must take improvement actions if there is a pattern of poor practice.

Care Quality Commission Standards

The CQC introduced a range of standards to improve the service levels offered by health and social care providers. The CQC can inspect your workplace, look at what you do and how you do it, and ask you about your training and competence. The CQC publishes its findings as a rating so that people can choose the highest quality of care. The CQC is independent of care providers but works with them and with the public to improve the quality of care provided. The CQC can issue warning notices with deadlines for improvement. It can impose 'special measures' to improve the quality of care provided. A hospital, for example, could be put in special measures for having unusually high mortality (death) rates.

There are 13 fundamental standards in the CQC framework. They follow the Francis Report (2013) into the care delivered in hospitals in the Mid Staffordshire NHS Foundation Trust.

❚❚ PAUSE POINT   Why is it important to legislate on the quality of care that service users should receive?

Hint   Think about the range of service providers and the types of service that they provide.

Extend   What might happen to the service user if each institution is allowed to define its own standards?

Disclosure and Barring Service checks

Care work is exempt from the Rehabilitation of Offenders Act (1974). This means that if an individual commits certain offences they can never work in care. In order to find out if an individual has committed an offence that they have not disclosed, an employer may request a Disclosure Barring Service (DBS) check on a job applicant.

There are three levels of DBS checks in England and Wales. The rules are slightly different for Scotland and Northern Ireland.

▸ Standard – checks for spent and unspent convictions, cautions, reprimands and final warnings.

▸ Enhanced – includes the same as the standard check plus any additional information held by local police that is considered reasonably relevant to the role being applied for.

▸ Enhanced with list checks – like the enhanced check but includes a check of the DBS barred lists. If an individual is named on the barred lists they cannot work with children or vulnerable adults.

Influence of legislation and policies on health and social care practice

Safeguarding vulnerable adults, children and young people

The service user's welfare is the most important aspect of care. Your service user has a right to feel safe and secure in your care. However, an important and often overlooked role of safeguarding legislation is to protect you, the care giver, from allegations of improper or unprofessional behaviour. You are responsible for your own behaviour and should avoid putting yourself in situations that would lead any reasonable person to question your motives.

It is vital that you act in such a way that your professionalism is not questioned. If you think that a service user is likely to misread a situation, ask for a chaperone and make your manager aware of your concerns. You may be doing all you can to meet the needs of the service user and you may be professional and polite, but the service user may see your care on a different emotional level. They may read their own meanings into your actions and think that you feel the same about them as they do about you.

You need to communicate clearly and unambiguously so that your service user does not have the opportunity to misread a situation. When communicating with service users, you need to check that the message you think you have given is the same as what the receiver understands it to mean.

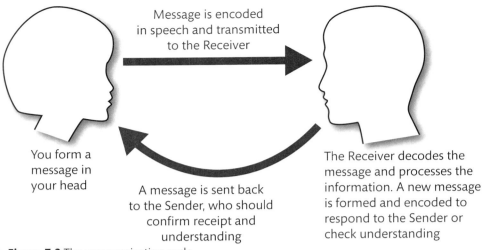

Message is encoded in speech and transmitted to the Receiver

You form a message in your head

A message is sent back to the Sender, who should confirm receipt and understanding

The Receiver decodes the message and processes the information. A new message is formed and encoded to respond to the Sender or check understanding

▶ **Figure 7.3** The communication cycle

Protection from accidents, injuries and illness, including infection control, food preparation, hazardous substances

The Health and Safety at Work etc Act (1974) requires employers to ensure the health and safety of all employees and anyone else affected by the work of the organisation, as far as is reasonably possible. Employees have a duty not to put themselves or others in danger. Employees are required to use any safety equipment provided and must be trained to do so.

As a carer, you must use the equipment provided in a correct manner whether it is a hoist, an antibacterial hand gel or a temperature probe for ensuring that food is heated to the correct temperature. Once you are trained, you are responsible for your actions.

You should follow the instructions on any pieces of equipment that you use. For example, you should not fill a sharps bins beyond the line indicated, as trying to force extra sharps in may lead to a needle-stick injury.

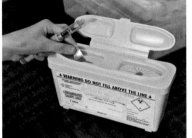

▶ Filling a sharps bin beyond the line indicated could lead to a needle-stick injury from the sharps already in the bin

Managing risk assessments and maintaining a safe working environment, including safe moving and handling

Before starting any task you need to ask yourself: is the task really necessary? Are you equal to the task and could the task be made simpler and safer?

Remember ELITE:

▶ E – environment, is the environment dark, cluttered with trip hazards or is the floor surface uneven?

▶ L – load, is the load stable, slippery or awkward? How can you stabilise the load?

▶ I – individual capability, are you equal to the task? Has your individual capability changed for any reason, for example because you have a sprained wrist or are pregnant?

▶ T – task, is it possible to break down one large task into a couple of smaller ones? For example, could you make two trips with half a bale of sheets rather than one trip with a large bale?

▶ E – equipment, is it designed for the task you want to use it for? Has it been safety checked?

Case study

Harley could do with more guidance

Harley has just started working as a home carer. During his induction, he was shown how to use a care plan and how to record the duties that he performs. He was then shown how to wash, dress and feed a typical service user. He was also told what to wear. When Harley makes his first service user visit, he finds that the other carer has not turned up. Harley knows that the service user is a man who needs two people to help him to stand, wash and dress.

Harley decides to try to meet the service user's needs on his own as he has another call to make shortly after. As he is helping the service user to stand up, the service user falls and bruises his leg badly.

Check your knowledge

1 What has Harley done wrong?

2 How would understanding the risk assessment process have helped Harley and his service user?

3 Why is it important to follow the manual handling policy for your workplace?

4 What steps should Harley have taken before beginning the task?

5 What are the potential consequences of Harley's actions for Harley, and for his line manager?

6 Why is it is only possible to minimise risk not eliminate it?

Promoting health and wellbeing, including handling medication

You should encourage your service users to make informed choices about their health and wellbeing. For example, eating a nutritious diet or taking regular exercise. There are also many lifestyle changes that people can make to help prevent ill health such as stopping smoking and reducing alcohol consumption. You can help your service users to spot the early signs of disease as many diseases, such as bowel cancer, are more successfully treated if diagnosed early.

Handling medication safely is important when working in health and social care settings. You must never handle medication until you are trained to do so. There are many rules governing the safe handling of medication and errors could cause various complications, including death.

Before administering medication to a service user, you need to know:

▶ whether it is a repeat prescription, a new prescription or an over-the-counter drug

▶ how the drug is to be administered – for example orally (by mouth), by injection, through a drip (intravenously), by suppository (into the rectum or vagina)

▶ how to store the medicine safely – should it be refrigerated or kept somewhere dry

▶ how to complete records of the administration of medicines so that the service user is not given two doses by mistake.

Research

Research the principles of handling medication safely. How do these promote health and wellbeing?

Providing confidence and reassurance for families and other carers

Service users and their families will have expectations about your conduct and performance as a carer. They will often need reassurance. While you can tell them that they are 'in the best place' and that everyone is 'doing all they can', you should never promise them that 'everything is going to be alright'.

It is always important to act professionally when providing care. Do not lose your temper with service users and remember to be polite and considerate to their relatives and friends. It is important that service users have confidence in your competence and understanding of the principles of care-giving. In stressful situations you must remain calm and keep your own emotions under control. Wherever possible, try to gather as much information as you can before deciding on the best course of action. Do not jump to conclusions or assume that you always know what is best for a service user before you have properly assessed the situation. You should always strive to maintain your professionalism so that your colleagues can also have confidence in your competence.

PAUSE POINT

Can you think of examples of situations where people might want you to promise them that everything will work out?

Hint   Think about people in danger or despair.

Extend   What harm could you do by promising a service user something you cannot deliver?

Discussion

When you are working in health and social care, dealing with the families of service users will often be a large part of your workload. Why can it sometimes be difficult to find a balance between keeping the service user's family happy while promoting the rights and wellbeing of your service user?

Meeting legal and regulatory requirements, including record keeping

In health and social care work, accurate record keeping is vital for effective continuity of care. If a service user requires the input of a number of carers or services, it is important that each service knows what the other has done. Your employer will have regulations covering clear and accurate record keeping and it is important that you follow these procedures. Remember the care setting is your workplace and you have to abide by the Health and Safety at Work etc Act (1974). You have a duty to maintain a safe environment and report incidents and accidents that could endanger others and to see that this information is recorded. There are many other pieces of legislation that could have an impact on the way that you do your job, for example the Mental Health Act (2007). It is important that you follow your workplace policies and procedures which have been written in accordance with this legislation.

Link

For more information on legislation, see the section Health and safety legislation and policies in health and social care, earlier in this unit.

As a carer, you may be required to follow a care plan (see Table 7.4) and to sign a log of the tasks you have performed. You are accountable for the care you give and should be able to show a record of the care you delivered and when, should the CQC inspect the establishment where you work.

▶ **Table 7.4** A simple care plan

	Morning	**Lunch**	**Evening**
Mon	8 am carer assists up, wash, dress	Meals on wheels	9:30 pm carer assists ready for bed
Tues	8 am carer assists up, wash, dress	District nurse	9:30 pm carer assists ready for bed
Wed	8 am carer assists up, wash, dress	Meals on wheels	9:30 pm carer assists ready for bed
Thu	8 am carer assists up, wash, dress	District nurse	9:30 pm carer assists ready for bed
Fri	8 am carer assists up, wash, dress	Meals on wheels	9:30 pm carer assists ready for bed
Sat	8 am carer assists up, wash, dress	Son visits	10:00 pm carer assists ready for bed
Sun	8 am carer assists up, wash, dress	Daughter visits	10:00 pm carer assists ready for bed

Recruitment of staff in health and social care

In order to be an effective care practitioner you need to think about how the 6 'C's apply to you. The 'C's stand for: care, commitment, communication, courage, competence and compassion. Employers will be looking for staff who have an understanding of the job role and a range of coping strategies for the pressures faced by people working in health and social care. They are looking for people of good character, with integrity and a real desire to support service users. It is also important to be able to meet the care needs of people that you do not like, people who may have done bad/criminal things, or who are difficult and unyielding. When you work in care, you are providing a service for the service user based on the service user's needs, not on how much you like them.

Disclosure Barring Service checks

The murders of Holly Wells and Jessica Chapman, in 2002, by a caretaker at their school, led to the establishment of the CRB (Criminal Records Bureau) system in England and Wales and the Disclosure Scotland and Access Northern Ireland systems for checking applicants for posts involving children or vulnerable adults.

By March 2012, figures from CRB revealed that 130,000 unsuitable people including paedophiles and rapists had been prevented from working with children. DBS replaced CRB in December 2012 in order to simplify the system for employers.

It is important to remain vigilant, though, as DBS will only show up offenders that have come to the attention of the authorities. It will not reveal offenders that have not yet been reported to the police.

It is an employer's duty to report employees they dismiss for abuse or neglect or who they were going to sack but the employee left before they could do so. If these individuals are not identified, then they could go on to work somewhere else.

PAUSE POINT How influential has health and safety law been on providing safe practice in health and social care?

Hint   Think about the broad range of services available and the need for some service users to have a multi-agency approach.

Extend   In what ways could the law be strengthened to meet the demands of a consumer-led service?

The Francis Report into the treatment of patients in hospitals in the Mid Staffordshire NHS Trust revealed very poor quality care.

The first inquiry heard from service users and their families about the appalling care they received, including cases where:

- service users were left for lengthy periods in bedclothes soiled with excrement
- assistance was not provided with feeding for service users unable to eat without help
- water was left out of the service users' reach
- service users were not assisted in their toileting – despite persistent requests for help
- wards and toilet facilities were in a filthy condition
- privacy and dignity, even in death, were denied
- triage in the accident and emergency department was undertaken by untrained staff
- staff treated service users, and those close to them, with what appeared to be callous indifference.
- Produce a short report identifying which health and safety policies could have prevented patients suffering.
- Analyse how applying these policies could improve service user's care.
- Justify the assertion that correctly applying health and safety policies can maintain a safe environment for staff and service users.

Plan
- What am I being asked to do?
- How confident am I with this task? Are there areas where I might have problems?

Do
- I know what I am doing and what I want to achieve.
- I can check my work to see where I have made mistakes and put them right.

Review
- I can explain what the task was and how I approached it.
- I know what I would do differently next time and the approach I would take with the parts that I found difficult this time.

D   Explore procedures and responsibilities to maintain health and safety and respond to accidents and emergencies in health and social care settings

Procedures to maintain health and safety

Infection control and prevention

Infections are caused by pathogens, which are microbes that infect your body. A contagious disease is one that is transmitted by physical contact with someone who has that disease. An infectious disease can be transmitted by air, water or a vector such as a mosquito.

As a carer, you should make sure that your vaccinations are up to date.

> **Research**
>
> Use the internet to research the list of vaccinations recommended for care workers. In what ways are care workers particularly vulnerable to exposure to disease?

If you know that you have an infection such as a cold, you could expose your service user, who may be a sick, frail or vulnerable individual, to your disease.

If you are not meticulous with your hygiene when you are working with service users who are ill, for example hand washing and using protective clothing, you could pass their diseases to someone else without necessarily catching them yourself.

The easiest way to prevent spread of disease is to wash and dry your hands thoroughly (see the step-by-step guide) at appropriate times. You must take responsibility for deciding when it is appropriate to wash your hands. To judge when the time is right, you should think about how your actions will affect your service user. Would you want a carer to touch you without washing their hands if they have just met the personal care needs of someone else? Would you like them to serve your food if they have just been to the toilet and not washed their hands?

Step by step: Guide to handwashing

1. Lather hands with soap

2. Rub both palms together

3. Rub each finger and between fingers

4. Rub palms with finger nails

5. Rub back of hand with finger nails

6. Wash thoroughly and towel dry

Safe moving and handling of equipment and individuals

You should be trained in moving and handling people and loads before you attempt a moving and handling task in the workplace.

There are some basic checks (see step-by-step guidance on lifting heavy objects safely) that you can perform to reduce the risk of harm either to yourself or a service user.

▶ Avoid. Is the task really necessary? Is there another way of reaching the same outcome without putting yourself or others at risk? For example, can an elderly person get themselves out of the chair if you just give them a little more time?

▶ Assess. Do you know exactly what the task involves? For example, what are the loads involved? Have you done a risk assessment of the task?

▶ Reduce. Have you reduced the risks as much as you can?

▶ Review. Reflect on your practice. Is there a better way of performing the task that would reduce the risks still further next time? If you are using equipment, is it fit for purpose? For example, a hoist should be serviced regularly. Is the environment that you are working in clear of obstacles? Do you need to move anything, such as a bedside table, before you start?

▶ Correct procedures should be used for picking objects up, and also for putting them down

Research

Use the internet to research manual handling and how it applies to people working in care (either informally or professionally). The NHS provides excellent information for informal carers. Search their website (**www.nhs.uk**) for 'Moving and handling the person you care for'. You should also check the official guidance from the HSE (**www.hse.gov.uk/**) about manual handling.

Food preparation and storage

It is vital that food is stored and prepared correctly and safely.

Food preparation

You must keep cooking surfaces clean and wash your hands before preparing food. If you handle raw meat when preparing food for your service users then you must ensure that you clean down surfaces that the meat may have touched and wash your hands before you handle food that does not need to be cooked.

Raw meat can contain a range of bacteria that can cause serious illnesses. If your service user is already frail or has existing health conditions, then contracting food poisoning can have very serious implications. You must check the use-by dates on the food that you serve to your service users if you are caring for them in their own homes. You should also make sure that you are scrupulous in your personal hygiene when handling food. Tie back long hair and keep nails short. Any cuts on your hands should be properly covered.

You must ensure that you heat food to the correct temperature. The only way to ensure that food is heated thoroughly is to use a temperature probe. When reheating meals in a microwave, follow the manufacturer's instructions about cooking times. If the service user's food is regularly prepared by relatives and does not have instructions about heating times, you should use a food thermometer to check that the food is thoroughly reheated. As a care worker, you may feel pressured by time, or by the service user, to rush the food preparation process and to serve food before it is ready. You must not take this risk. Explain to the service user the importance of thorough reheating and try to organise your time so that you can perform all of your duties competently and efficiently.

Food must be covered until it is ready to be served and eaten, to minimise the risk of airborne pathogens landing on it. Houseflies are a particular risk for transmitting germs such as *E. coli*, which can cause serious health problems.

▶ Overfilling dustbins creates a breeding ground for flies, which may then get into kitchens and serving areas and settle on food

Food storage

Fridges must be set at the correct temperature, between 3°C and 5°C, in order for the food to be safe but for nutrients not to be lost. (Freezers should operate at around minus 18°C or below although there are no defined regulations for freezer temperature.)

Reheated food cannot be refrozen and must be thrown away. Try to get to know your service user's dietary requirements so that you can avoid excessive wastage. If their food is prepared by friends or relatives, you should work on the principle that it has already been frozen, so leftover food should be discarded unless you are specifically told that it is fresh. Check that the freezer is properly maintained as a build-up of ice can mean that the door does not shut properly and the food in the freezer will defrost. If you find that this is the case and the food has thawed, you should not refreeze the food.

When an ice box in a fridge overfills with ice, it tends to force open the ice box, and also prevents the fridge door from closing. This will mean that the fridge is not operating at the correct temperature and the food stored in it could be spoiled. If this happens, you should report the situation to your manager. The service user and their relatives will also need to be told so that the situation is dealt with.

It is important that you store food in the correct packaging and that food taken out of its original packaging is labelled and dated.

Sansome's curry

Sansome is hungry and cannot wait to try the new recipe for chicken curry that his sister has found on the internet. Sansome has learning difficulties and lives in a supported living complex. He has his own kitchen and is very proud of how clean he keeps it. His carer Jane comes in to help him cook.

Jane is late and Sansome is hungry. He is a big man and shouts a lot if he does not get his own way. He always feels sorry afterwards as he does not mean to scare people but he cannot control his temper.

He shouts at Jane when she arrives and says he wants his food straight away. Jane starts to cook the chicken curry. Sansome is impatient to eat it and does not know about the dangers of undercooked chicken. He demands to be allowed to eat it before Jane thinks that it has been on for long enough to have cooked through properly. Jane lets Sansome have his curry.

Check your knowledge

1 What risks is Jane taking with Sansome's health?

2 Why is it vital to follow the food safety guidelines when working with service users?

3 Would a child be as much at risk as Sansome or more at risk?

4 What safety precautions should Jane take when handling food?

5 What is the best way to check that food is thoroughly cooked?

PAUSE POINT Why is it important to wash your hands thoroughly after catching your sneezes in a tissue and putting the tissue in the bin?

Hint Think about the number of surfaces, objects and even people you need to touch when performing a caring role.

Extend How else could you minimise the risk of transmitting infection?

Storage and administration of medication

Legislation covering the receipt, storage and administration of medicines includes:

▸ Care Standards Act (2000)
▸ Health and Social Care Act (2008)
▸ Health Act (2006)
▸ Medicines Act (1968)
▸ Misuse of Drugs Act (1971)
▸ Misuse of Drugs (Safe Custody) Regulations (1973, amended 2007)
▸ Misuse of Drugs Regulations (2001)
▸ Misuse of Drugs (Safe Custody) (Amendment) Regulations (2000, amended 2007).

Individuals should be encouraged to self-medicate where possible. In care settings and in situations where individuals cannot manage self-medication, medication should be stored centrally in hygienic and secure conditions. The keys to the medicine storage facilities should not be part of a master key system. Medication should be administered only by individuals who are trained and qualified to do so.

The facility should be large enough to contain the maximum number of medicines expected to be used. Badly organised or overcrowded cupboards may lead to errors.

All medications should be stored in the correct conditions. Sunlight, temperature and humidity can have adverse effects on medications.

All medicine containers should be labelled with the following information:

▶ service user's name
▶ name of the medicine
▶ the dosage amounts and frequency
▶ route for administration
▶ whether it needs to be taken with food
▶ expiry date
▶ dispensing pharmacist's name
▶ warnings about specific side-effects, eg may cause drowsiness.

A record must be kept of any medication administered to reduce the risk of overdose.

You should talk to your line manager if you are unsure about whether you should be administering medicine to your service user, the appropriateness of the medications or any adverse effects on your service user.

Why do you think that it is important not to take medication prescribed for someone else, even if you have the same symptoms?

Storage and disposal of hazardous substances

COSHH applies to virtually all substances considered hazardous to health. However, there are certain exclusions, including:

▶ lead
▶ asbestos, covered by The Control of Asbestos Regulations (2012)
▶ radioactive materials
▶ substances considered hazardous to health but administered by a qualified medical practitioner, such as a doctor or dentist, covered by the Medicines Act (1968).

You must follow the policies and procedures for the environment that you are working in. Medication should be stored according to the policies and procedures of your workplace, and cleaning materials must be kept in their original packaging in a secure and appropriate place.

If cleaning materials need to be diluted before use, you must follow the instructions on the packaging. You should also remember that industrial products are often bought in bulk and the solutions may be stronger than the products you use at home.

In the workplace, there will be different disposal techniques and containers for different products. Dressings, for example are clinical waste and should be disposed of in the appropriate bag or container.

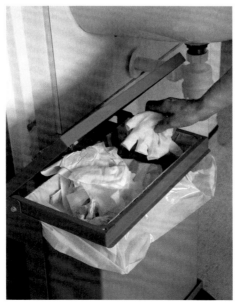

▶ You must dispose of waste appropriately, both for your own safety and also as part of the duty of care that you have for others

> **Research**
>
> Research the role of the COSHH Risk Assessor. How can they promote safe practice in the workplace?

Procedures for responding to accidents and emergencies

Responding to accidents and illness, including basic first aid

There are many reasons why people become ill at work. Find out who the first aider is in your workplace and where the first-aid kit is kept. Unless you are a first aider you should not treat minor accidents and injuries. First-aid training is part of the continuing professional development offered by most employers. You may feel more confident if you are properly trained and it will give relatives and colleagues more confidence in you. However, if someone needs help, you should assist them to get it and keep them safe until help arrives.

In the case of a major incident such as a heart attack, you must dial 999 and follow the specific instructions given by the operator to help stabilise the situation. You must listen carefully to the instructions and, if you are unsure, ask the operator for clarification. If you are in an isolated situation such as caring for service users in their own homes, basic first-aid training should be provided for you. It is important that you keep your training up to date as the advice given about dealing with some situations may change periodically. In the case of a service user whose heart has stopped, the advice will be different for babies than adults. This is also the case with choking.

You should notify your employer if you are allergic to any substance that you are likely to encounter in your workplace or if you have been prescribed medication that is likely to affect your concentration or cause drowsiness.

There are a number of common reasons why healthcare workers have to take time off work – back pain and stress are the biggest causes of sickness absence. The majority of back injuries are caused by poor posture when performing tasks, misuse of equipment and the frequent repetition of tasks. To avoid accidents and injuries you must attend your manual handling training sessions and apply the skills that you learn. You should always use equipment appropriately and not take unnecessary risks.

Health care is a demanding vocation, both physically and emotionally and you cannot be a useful member of the team if you do not take good care of yourself. If you feel stressed or overwhelmed by your work, seek help before the situation becomes a crisis. Early intervention is important to maintaining your mental health. You must be aware of your own limitations and intervene early if you feel that your health is at risk. If your health status changes, you must adapt accordingly. This may mean that you are unable to do as much as you could before. Broken limbs, pregnancy and depression are all examples of changes to a person's state of health.

There are other causes of illness in the workplace such as burns, fainting, bleeding, choking, fractures, poisoning, shock, stroke or heart attack. These examples could apply to the service users you support, to yourself or to your colleagues. If your service user, a visitor or one of your colleagues becomes ill or has a serious accident, you should follow the policy of your workplace and, if necessary, report the events to the person responsible under RIDDOR regulations.

Slips and trips also account for a number of sickness absences in health and social care. Floors are often made hazardous by fluid spillages (such as blood, urine, food or drink). If you are providing care in a service user's own home, trip hazards may include wires trailing across floors, rugs (especially if they are frayed or the edges are curling) and pets or small pieces of furniture. Your line of vision may be obscured by trying to manoeuvre large equipment in a confined space so you will need to be aware of the risks of bumping into objects and harming yourself or your service user.

You should take responsibility for your own welfare and the welfare of others by minimising the risk of accidents. You should:

▶ wear suitable clothing

▶ be aware of your environment – look where you are going

▶ keep the environment where you are working tidy – do not drop things on the floor and then leave them there

▶ clean up spillages, if appropriate, or report them so that the right person can do so.

Fire safety, evacuation and security procedures

In England and Wales, The Regulatory Reform (Fire Safety) Order 2005 requires a managed risk approach to fire safety. This means that the management of premises providing care must take reasonable steps to reduce the risk from fire and, if there is a fire, to make sure that people can escape safely. A responsible person should draw up the fire policy which should include how to minimise fire risks, provide and maintain fire-fighting equipment such as extinguishers, plan escape routes and ensure that training is provided.

In the event of a fire, most of your service users will require some degree of help to evacuate a building safely. Therefore it is an essential part of your orientation to the workplace, during your induction, for you to familiarise yourself with the evacuation procedure in the event of fire, including your duties and your responsibilities.

As an employee, you are required to follow the fire policy so that you do not increase the risk of causing a fire. You should report any concerns you have about the workplace environment that may increase the chances of a fire occurring. You should be aware of the colour coding for the different contents of fire extinguishers and in what circumstances they should be used.

Research

Research the colour coding system for the contents of fire extinguishers. Why is it important to use the correct extinguisher?

Safety tip

Never prop fire doors open just because you need to open them frequently or want some fresh air. In the event of a fire, fire doors will slow the progress of the fire and give valuable extra time for evacuation procedures.

 **PAUSE POINT**   Why is it important for you to check the dates when the policies for your workplace were written?

      Hint   Think about how the needs of the service users may change over time.

      Extend   What are the potential implications for an existing policy if the law or the regulations change?

Reporting and record keeping

Accurate record keeping is fundamental to safe practice in the caring professions. Accurate information (data) means that the service user receives the care they need and that you are delivering this care in a safe and appropriate manner. The data held within the service user's records must refer to the service user and/or their condition. You must never falsify information in order to hide errors or omissions.

The appropriate handling of data is covered by regulation 20 of the Health and Social Care Act 2008 (Regulated Activities) Regulations 2010. These regulations require that there is a registered person responsible for ensuring that records are kept accurately to avoid the risk of unsafe treatment or even the wrong treatment being administered. At your workplace, there should be a person with responsibility for ensuring that data is stored safely and securely. This person will also take responsibility for records relating to you and the performance of your work duties as well as any documents detailing how these duties are to be performed.

Health and safety responsibilities

Responsibilities of employers

Employers have a key role to play in reducing the risks to the health and safety of their employees. They are uniquely placed to identify needs and **hazards**, instigate protocols and policies and monitor and regulate by implementing the measures necessary to promote safe practice.

The employer has a range of responsibilities for reducing the risks to their employees, including:

▸ following the recommendations of the risk assessment and implementing the health and safety measures identified as necessary

- ensuring that a competent person has responsibility for implementing the health and safety recommendations
- ensuring that procedures such as a fire evacuation policy are established
- making sure that employees understand the health and safety responsibilities of their job role
- providing training opportunities and information to keep their employees safe
- providing and maintaining the equipment that helps employees to do their jobs.

Responsibilities of employees

When you are working for an employer, you have a duty to take reasonable care of yourself. You must remember the guidance from your health and safety training, consult your line manager if you are unsure of what to do in a particular circumstance, document any incidents or near misses and get into the habit of looking for risks in order to minimise the hazards for yourself and others.

You will also often be responsible for the personal safety of your service user. For example, a service user may not process information effectively and, therefore, make poor judgements about personal safety. People in pain may lack concentration and act irrationally or the service user may experience mental health issues that make them unable to make informed choices. For whatever reason, the service user may be susceptible to hazards.

Responsibilities of others in the setting

Health and safety legislation extends to anyone in the workplace including visitors. You should ensure that visitors to a workplace such as a nursing home, are aware of relevant health and safety guidance and emergency procedures. For example, visitors should sign in so that they can be accounted for in the event of a fire.

Visitors to hospital settings should be informed of where they can and cannot go on a ward or department. For example, store rooms, the sluice, dressings rooms, areas where medications are stored and operating theatres are places where visitors are not allowed – either for their own protection or for the protection of staff and service users.

Discussion

What potential risks does a visitor pose to a service user in their own home? (Think back to all the sections that you have covered in this unit.)

Assessment practice 7.4

D.P7   D.P8   D.M4   CD.D4

Fire evacuation drills should be run regularly in your workplace so that staff and service users have a chance to practice the procedure.

Everyone should know what their role is in the event of a fire and who they need to assist, and how, during an evacuation. They must be capable of carrying out that role. If the health status of a member of the team changes and this stops them performing their role (eg pregnancy) then a substitute member of staff should be found for that role.

- Write a short report explaining how different policies and procedures can maintain health and safety in the care setting.
- Explain the importance of staff meeting the obligations of their job role.
- Analyse how different policies and procedures and individual responsibility contribute to safe practice.
- Evaluate the importance of safe practice principles in maintaining and promoting the health, safety and welfare of service users.

Plan
- What am I being asked to do?
- How confident am I with this task? Are there areas where I might have problems?

Do
- I know what I am doing and what I want to achieve.
- I can check my work to see where I have made mistakes and can make changes to put them right.

Review
- I can explain what the task was and how I approached it.
- I know what I would do differently next time and the approach I would take with the parts that I found difficult this time.

Further reading and resources

Mantell, A. and Scragg, T. (2011) *Safeguarding Adults in Social Work* (Transforming Social Work Practice Series) Exeter: Learning Matters

Stewart, A. (2011) *Supporting Vulnerable Adults: Citizenship, Capacity, Choice (Policy and Practice in Social Care, no. 13)* Edinburgh: Dunedin Academic Press

Shaffer, D. R. (2002) *Developmental Psychology: Childhood and Adolescence*, 6th edition, Belmont Ca: Wadsworth

Sugarman, L. (2001) *Life-Span Development: Frameworks, Accounts and Strategies, Theories, Concepts and Interventions*, 2nd edition, Hove: Psychology Press Ltd.

Websites

www.direct.gov.uk

DirectGov has information about health and safety legislation.

www.cqc.org.uk

The *Care Quality Commission* website has information about making complaints.

THINK ▶▶FUTURE

Hardeep Bansal

Learning Disabilities Nurse

I became a Learning Disabilities Nurse after volunteering at a sports facility for young people with learning difficulties when a friend asked me to help out. His brother went there and it was really helping with his balance and coordination as well as his social skills. During the first session I went to, I realised that young people with learning difficulties can be very isolated as their needs are all so very different. I started thinking of ways of tailoring games so that they were more inclusive and everyone could take part. I wanted the young people to feel that there was a purpose to what they were doing and it wasn't just 'somewhere to go and hang out'.

As I took on more responsibility, I realised just how much training in health and safety, child protection and safeguarding that I needed. I began to realise the level of responsibility that came with trying to meet the physical, social, emotional and intellectual needs of these young people. After I completed my nursing degree, I started to work in a respite care unit. Every day is different and every achievement that each young person makes is very, very special.

Focusing your skills

Safe handling of medication

It is important that medication is stored and handled safely. Here are some tips to help you.

- Medication should be administered by designated and appropriately trained staff.
- All individuals taking medication should be monitored to make sure they are not having a reaction. Any reactions should be reported to a doctor.
- All medicine should be stored safely and in the correct conditions – for example, some medications must be kept in a fridge.
- If you are administering a medication, you must ensure that the full dose is taken as prescribed and that courses of medication are completed.

To lift or not to lift

Moving and handling questions.

If a young service user has fallen on the floor, should you pick them up or assume that they must have fallen and may need first aid?

- If you are not sure why they are on the floor, you should assume that they have fallen and address the situation as a first-aid incident.
- Check the safety of the environment.
- Call for assistance from another care giver. You should not try to deal with a potential fall on your own. Even if the service user is not hurt and only needs assistance to get back up again, it is safer with two carers present.
- Check for injuries.

After you have dealt with the situation, remember to document your actions.

Getting ready for assessment

Dominic is working towards a BTEC Extended National Diploma in Health and Social Care. He was given an assignment to write a report entitled 'Evaluate the importance of safeguarding and duty of care procedures in promoting safe practice in a care setting', for learning aim A. The submission had to:

▶ include an overview of the principles of duty of care and safeguarding

▶ evaluate the factors that have an impact on safe practice in health and social care settings

▶ evaluate the importance of the complaints and appeals procedures and duty of care in promoting safe practice.

How I got started

First, I looked at the notes that I had made on discussions on promoting safe practice in care settings. Different people place a different emphasis on what is needed most to promote safe practice. It was informative to consider their opinions. I also needed to look at my notes for information on safeguarding and duty of care to ensure that I fully understood the concepts and could put them in the context of a specific care situation. I separated out safeguarding, safe practice and duty of care into separate headings. I needed to make sure I included enough information to achieve all the criteria.

I divided my notes into two sections on how first safeguarding and then duty of care could have both a positive and a negative impact on promoting safe practice. I arranged to visit a nursing home to shadow and interview one qualified member of staff and one healthcare assistant on their experience of safeguarding policy, how often there were incidents and whether the management were effective in meeting their duty of care.

How I brought it all together

I decided to write in the first person past tense in order to make the piece seem more of a narrative. After that I:

▶ created a spidergram of safeguarding and another for duty of care and their applications in care

▶ wrote up my observations and interviews from the shadowing exercise in the form of a personal account

▶ researched statistical data on the impact of safeguarding incidents and the management of incidents in relation to duty of care and compared it with the anecdotal evidence gathered from the interviews.

I anonymised the anecdotes from the nursing home and referenced my research using the Harvard system. Finally, I wrote a short summary as a conclusion to the report.

What I learned from the experience

I got some useful insights from the nursing home, but I was unfamiliar with the environment and was occasionally distracted by events going on and, therefore, I was not always focused on what they were saying. I felt embarrassed at asking staff to repeat themselves and this meant that I didn't get as much out of the experience as I could have. Next time, I would ask to do a short orientation visit in order to feel more at ease and more focused on the person that I was interviewing.

I hadn't considered how the duty of care that staff had for themselves and their peers might impact on my report. I focused my research heavily on the employer's responsibility and the report turned out to be more descriptive than evaluative. I should have concentrated more on the operative verbs and checked that I was staying on task rather than concentrating heavily on an area that interested me more. I struggled to write the conclusion to pull the whole thing together. Next time, I must be more disciplined in my approach to following my plan for the assignment as I felt that my plan was better than the finished article.

Think about it

Have you written a plan with timings so that you can complete your assignment by the agreed submission date?

▶ Do you have notes on the skills, qualities and attributes that employers in the care field are looking for in their staff?

▶ Is your information written in your own words and referenced clearly to show where you have used quotations or information from a book, journal or website?

Getting to know your unit

In this unit, you will study the different approaches that sociologists have used to explain health and social care issues. You will consider different definitions of health and illness, and examine the impact that family, occupation, social class and other aspects of our environment and culture have on our health and wellbeing. Why are birth rates falling in European countries? Why are we living longer? Why, despite the equal pay acts, are women still paid less than men? These are the kinds of questions that concern sociologists.

How you will be assessed

This unit will be assessed internally by a series of tasks, which will be set and marked by your tutor. Throughout this unit, you will find assessment practices that will help you prepare for your final graded assignment. Completing these activities will not mean that you have achieved a particular grade for this unit, but they will provide useful opportunities for research and other preparation for your final graded assignment.

In order to achieve a Pass in your final assignment, it is important to check that you have met all of the Pass grading criteria. You can do this as you work your way through the assignment. To gain a Merit or Distinction, you will need to present the information in your assignment in the style that is required by the relevant assessment criteria. For example, Merit criteria require you to analyse and discuss sociological issues as they relate to health and social care, and Distinction criteria require you to evaluate their importance and impact.

The final assignment will consist of a number of tasks designed to meet the criteria in the table below. It is likely to include a written assignment, but may also include activities such as the following:

▶ a presentation describing and discussing how social inequalities arising from poverty, disability or ethnic origin, affect health and wellbeing
▶ the preparation of a booklet describing how social differences may affect health and wellbeing
▶ analysing case studies drawn from work experience, using the sociological concepts and approaches introduced in this unit.

Guidance is included, throughout this unit, to help you prepare and present your work.

Assessment criteria

This table shows what you must do in order to achieve a **Pass**, **Merit** or **Distinction** grade, and where you can find activities to help you.

Pass	**Merit**	**Distinction**

Learning aim Understand how sociological concepts and perspectives are applied to the study of health and social care

A.P1

Explain how sociological perspectives are applied to the understanding of health and social care.

Assessment practice 10.1

A.M1

Analyse the contribution of sociological perspectives to the understanding of health and social care and society.

Assessment practice 10.1

AB.D1

Evaluate the role of sociological perspectives in the understanding of society and models and concepts of health in relation to service provision in a local health and social care setting.

Assessment practices 10.1 and 10.2

A.P2

Explain how sociological perspectives contribute to the understanding of society.

Assessment practice 10.1

Learning aim Examine how sociological approaches support understanding of models and concepts of health

B.P3

Compare the biomedical model of health with an alternative model of health.

Assessment practice 10.2

B.M2

Analyse how the biomedical and an alternative model of health, and concepts of health, ill health and disability affect service provision in a local health and social care setting.

Assessment practice 10.2

B.P4

Explain the contribution of concepts of health, ill health and disability to service provision in a local health and social care setting.

Assessment practice 10.2

Learning aim Examine how social inequalities, demographic change, and patterns and trends affect health and social care delivery

C.P5

Explain how social inequality affects different groups in society.

Assessment practice 10.3

C.M3

Analyse the impact of social inequality on different groups in society.

Assessment practice 10.3

C.D2

Evaluate sociological explanations for patterns and trends of health and ill health in different social groups, and how demographic data is used in service provision in a local health and social care setting to reduce social inequality affecting those groups.

Assessment practice 10.3

C.P6

Explain how demographic data is used in service provision in a local health and social care setting.

Assessment practice 10.3

C.M4

Analyse the impact of the use of demographic data in a local health and social care setting in enabling the enhancement of service provision for different social groups.

Assessment practice 10.3

C.P7

Explain patterns and trends in health and ill health within different social groups.

Assessment practice 10.3

C.D3

Evaluate the importance of the sociological perspectives used in a health and social care setting in relation to understanding society, reducing social inequality and improving service provision for different social groups.

Assessment practice 10.3

Getting started

Sociologists claim that the groups we belong to (for example, our family and friends) influence how we behave. Create a spidergram to show all the social groups you belong to. Select two groups and identify how each has influenced your behaviour. In what ways have they had a positive or negative effect on your development?

 Understand how sociological concepts and perspectives are applied to the study of health and social care

Sociology is the scientific study of human behaviour. Sociologists are concerned with the study of human societies, and, most specifically, the different groups within these societies. They study how these groups relate to each other and influence individual behaviour. Throughout this unit, you will explore how these groups affect people's health and wellbeing.

Concepts and terminology used within sociology

Diversity of culture and identity

Societies can be viewed as the sum of their **social institutions** (their major building blocks). As Figure 10.1 shows, these may include the family, the education system, the economic system, the political system, religious organisations and health and social care services. Sociologists look at the way these institutions are structured, how they relate to each other and how they influence individual behaviour.

Sociologists describe, for example, the different forms of the family in our society, the changes that are taking place within the family, how our family influences our behaviour, and how the family relates to other social institutions. They examine how our family background may influence our **values**, attitudes, religious beliefs, educational achievements, employment prospects and our health and wellbeing.

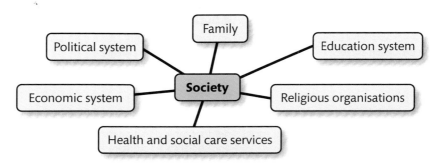

▶ **Figure 10.1:** Many institutions make up a society

Research

Write a brief description of a family structure that is different from your own. Use the internet, sociology textbooks, TV programmes or films to support your work. In small groups, discuss your findings and identify how each family structure could support healthy development.

Socialisation

The study of sociology is based on the idea that most of our behaviour is learned through the process of **socialisation** (and very little of our behaviour is instinctive). Socialisation is the process by which individuals learn the **culture** of their society – that is, the language, values and beliefs, customs and ways of behaving that are seen as usual and acceptable. It may be argued that the most critical period of socialisation occurs in the early years of life.

▶ Why do sociologists think that what happens in our early years is so important for our later development?

For most people, this period of **primary socialisation** takes place within a family. This could be the birth family, a family of adoption or a foster family. **Secondary socialisation** is the process that continues as our social life develops and extends, through playgroups, nursery, school, friendship or peer groups, religious groups, access to the mass media and employment.

Discussion

Consider the values, beliefs, attitudes and ways of behaving that you learned during your primary socialisation. How were these reinforced or challenged later in life during your secondary socialisation? Discuss your thoughts in small groups.

Socialisation affects people's attitudes towards the care and support of vulnerable people, children and older people. For example, whether we care for the very old at home, as part of the family, or use the range of residential and day services to support their care. In Islamic and Hindu cultures, care would normally be provided at home by grown-up children and grandchildren, whereas, in British families, residential care and other support services are more commonly used. Sociologists would argue that this is largely because of a difference in the values, beliefs and expectations learned during primary and secondary socialisation.

It is argued that the **norms**, or expected behaviour of the society or group to which we belong, are learned by absorbing and copying the behaviour of others in our social group. We normally adopt the main values and beliefs of the society to which we belong. Those who do not conform to expectations, that is, those who disregard the norms of the society or group, are said to be **deviant**.

Key terms

Socialisation – the process of learning the usual ways of behaving in society.

Culture – values, beliefs, language, rituals, customs and rules associated with a particular society or social group, and seen as normal.

Primary socialisation – early socialisation that normally takes place within the family.

Secondary socialisation – socialisation that takes place in social settings beyond the family, such as in nursery, in friendship groups or in a wide range of other institutions.

Norms – rules or guidelines that govern how we behave in society or in groups within society.

Deviant – an individual who does not conform to the norms of a society or social group.

Reflect

Think of a group of people who are regarded as deviant in our society. How are they represented by the media? How is this group treated by the wider society? Do you think their social experience as an 'outsider group' would affect their health and wellbeing?

Key term

Social role – expectations about the way an individual acts and behaves that are linked to their position in society, for example being a child, a parent, a lawyer, a nurse or a politician.

Social roles and expectations

Membership of a group brings a range of expectations and obligations. In sociology, these expectations are called **social roles**. For example, there are expectations linked with the social position of being a parent, a son or daughter, or a student. The generally accepted social role (or social expectation) of parents in our society is that they will protect their children, ensure that they are kept safe and warm, provide a home, teach them acceptable ways of behaving, and ensure that they attend school ready to learn.

PAUSE POINT   Can you explain what socialisation is about?

> **Hint**   Close your book and list the main social institutions in society.
>
> **Extend**   Explain how these institutions may influence people's behaviour.

Case study

Growing up in a traveller community

Rosie is seven years old and is a member of a travelling community. She lives with her mum and dad, both sets of grandparents and members of her extended family (aunts, uncles and cousins). Rosie has never attended a playgroup or nursery. Her parents did not see the need as there were always plenty of children to play with in her community.

Rosie has already been to four schools but her attendance was poor. Her parents have very poor literacy skills and they don't see any value or benefit in Rosie getting an academic education. Rosie has no friends outside her travelling 'family'. She is not registered with a doctor and has never seen a health visitor. Her mother never liked going to the baby clinic and they missed many appointments. Rosie's dad earns an adequate living in a number of ways. He works at fairgrounds during the summer and sells Christmas trees in the winter. He tidies gardens and can turn his hand to a very wide range of housing repairs. Rosie often goes with him to work.

Check your knowledge

1 How was the culture of Rosie's community and her socialisation similar and different to yours as you were growing up?

2 Identify and discuss three aspects of Rosie's family and community life that may contribute positively to her health and wellbeing.

3 Identify and discuss three aspects of Rosie's family and community life that may impact negatively on her health and wellbeing.

4 Suggest reasons why Rosie didn't go to pre-school, is not registered with a doctor, was rarely taken to baby clinics, and why her parents rarely visited school. What impact might this have had on her health and wellbeing?

Sociologists study the different social groupings in society and how membership of different groups influences our values, attitudes and ways of life. For example, they study the impact of differences in social class on our life style, and on our health and well being. They study the impacts of racial, ethnic and religious groupings, and of gender and sexual orientation.

Social class

Social stratification is a term used by sociologists that is borrowed from geology. In geology, 'strata' refer to different layers of rock laid on top of each other. In sociology, the term is used to describe hierarchies in society, highlighting the fact that some groups of people are seen as having higher status than other groups. People identified as being of higher status are often wealthier and have easier access to the possessions and way of life most valued in that society. Almost all societies have some form of stratification.

Social class is the form of stratification that describes the social hierarchies in most modern industrialised societies. Social class is largely based on economic factors (such as occupation, income, property ownership and other forms of wealth). Sociologists are particularly interested in the link between our social class position and other aspects of our lives such as educational achievement, lifestyle choices and our health and wellbeing.

The official classification of social class used by British governments to measure and analyse changes in the population began in 1851, when broad classification of occupations into social 'grades' (later called social classes) was used for the analysis of death rates.

The five social classes identified by the Registrar General in 1913, based largely on perceived occupational skill, remained in place until 1990, when they were renamed as *Social Class based on Occupation*. Government statisticians and others used these categories to analyse population trends until very recently. The Registrar General's Scale of Social Class included:

▶ I: Professional occupations

▶ II: Managerial and technical occupations

▶ IIIN: Skilled non-manual occupations

▶ IIIM: Skilled manual occupations

▶ IV: Semi-skilled occupations

▶ V: Unskilled occupations.

Since 2001, the National Statistics Socio-economic Classification (NS-SEC) has been used for official government statistics and surveys. It is still based on occupation but has been altered in line with employment changes and has categories that include the vast majority of the adult population.

▶ **Table 10.1:** NS-SEC analytic classes

Class 1	Higher managerial, administrative and professional occupations in large organisations
Class 2	Lower managerial, administrative and professional occupations
Class 3	Intermediate occupations
Class 4	Small employers and own-account workers
Class 5	Lower supervisory and technical occupations
Class 6	Semi-routine occupations
Class 7	Routine occupations
Class 8	Never worked and long-term unemployed

Race and ethnic or national origin

In African countries following colonisation, and in America before the Civil War (1861–1865), groupings were based on race. Black communities had far less social status than white communities. Some people would argue that, despite changes in legislation, such hierarchies and inequalities still exist.

> **Key terms**
>
> **Social stratification** – a term (borrowed from geology) describing hierarchies in society, where some groups have more status and prestige than other groups.
>
> **Social class** – describes a person's social and economic standing in society.

> **Discussion**
>
> Some people think that class differences in our society have disappeared. In groups, try to agree two arguments in favour of and two against the view that social class is no longer significant in modern Britain.

In India, the Hindu caste system has four clearly defined social levels, into which people are born:

1 Brahmins – the highest caste, priests
2 Kshatriyas – the military, rulers and administrators
3 Vaisyas – the merchants and farmers
4 Shudras – the manual workers.

In addition, there are people excluded from society altogether, regarded as having no caste at all. They are sometimes referred to as the 'untouchables', the Chandalas, or by their Hindi name, the Dalits.

There is rarely intermarriage and very little social contact between the castes. There is very little **social mobility** (meaning that there is very little opportunity to improve or change your position in society). It is a closed system of social stratification. Indian governments have passed laws attempting to remove the inequalities of the caste system but with limited success.

In feudal England, the different social strata were called 'estates' and were based on ownership of land. The monarchy and the knights, barons and earls formed the highest estate, the church and clergy were in the second estate and the merchants, peasants and serfs were in the lowest estate.

Key term

Social mobility – the process of moving from one social stratum (level) to another. Social mobility can be upward or downward.

Social class differs from the more closed caste and feudal systems, or those based on race or gender, in that:

▸ the class differences are more difficult to define
▸ social class differences are not backed by law or regulation
▸ social class barriers are far less rigid
▸ there is the possibility of social mobility – people can rise, or indeed fall, in the class system.

Ⅱ PAUSE POINT Can you explain what is meant by the term social stratification?

Hint Close the book and briefly describe two different forms of social stratification.

Extend How do you think a person's social position or status in a social hierarchy may affect their health and wellbeing?

Gender

Gender is a term used by sociologists to describe the different and often distinct social roles of men and women in society: that is, the social expectations and patterns of behaviour that are linked with being a man or a woman; this varies from society to society and at different times in history. Gender is contrasted with differences that are defined biologically by our sex. The sexual differences are defined by physical differences such as internal or external genitalia, the ability to bear and suckle children and the pitch of the adult voice.

Key term

Gender – refers to the social or cultural expectations of men and women in society as contrasted with the biological, sexual or physical differences between men and women.

Probably, the most significant change in gender roles since the Second World War has been the changing role of women, both within the family and in the wider society. There have been significant moves towards increasing social and economic opportunities for women. For example, more women continue in full-time employment after marriage and after the birth of their children. Additionally, there are increasing numbers of women in professional occupations, such as medicine, architecture and the legal profession, and women are taking a more significant role in public life and within the community. However, despite these changes, there is considerable evidence that inequalities between men and women still exist. Women's hourly rates of pay, despite equality legislation, stubbornly remain lower than men's.

Reflect

Despite the Equal Pay Act 1970, the average hourly rate of pay for men has been persistently higher than the for women in full-time employment. Using the internet and other suitable sources:

1   compare the current average earnings of men and women
2   suggest reasons why, despite legislation, differences remain.

Despite changes in attitudes, and significant evidence that men take a fuller part in childcare and housework than in the past, there is evidence to suggest that women are still seen as having the main responsibility for the home and family. Jenny van Hooff ((2013) *Modern Couples?: Continuity and Change in Heterosexual Relationships*, Routledge) studied dual earning couples. In all but one instance, women were doing most of the housework.

Theory into practice

Think about a family (either your own or another that you know well) that is headed by a man and a woman who are both in full-time employment. Identify who normally takes responsibility for the following domestic tasks:

*   making evening meals
*   cooking
*   ironing
*   small repairs around the house
*   gardening
*   household shopping
*   taking time off work to look after members of the family who are sick.

1   Collate the information gathered by each member of your class and present it as a bar chart.
2   Do the results confirm or disprove the view that women take a larger responsibility than men for household tasks?

Age

In many societies, social status increases with age. Older people, or elders, have a high status and an important role in the family and wider community. In China, in many parts of Africa and on the Indian subcontinent, older people are treated with great respect. In the contemporary UK, however, older people have a less clear position in society. They may feel they have less of a stake in society or, if they are not working, that they are less important. They may be unclear as to what their new role should be.

Link

There are references throughout this chapter to the use of statistics to understand society. You may often find it helpful to present statistics as a table or as a graph.

Reflect

Respecting your elders

1   Why do you think that older people in our society may not feel that they are respected in the way that elders are revered in many developing nations?
2   How may this affect their health and wellbeing?

There is widespread evidence that older people are the subject of discrimination. In 2006, the Age Discrimination Act was passed in response to the extent of discrimination against older people, particularly in employment. The Equality Act 2010, and subsequent changes in 2011, made it illegal to require a person to retire because of their age unless the employer could provide a clear and objective reason why they should.

There have also been a number of studies pointing to the higher incidence of poverty among older people, compared to the population as a whole. Recent research supported by Age UK confirmed that 1 in 6 pensioners, that is 1.8 million or approximately 16 per cent of pensioners, in the UK live in poverty. Further, that poverty is not evenly spread across the older people in our society and that low income in retirement is often linked to:

▶ low pay during working life

▶ time out of paid employment, often due to caring responsibilities – both for children and adults needing care

▶ disability

▶ periods of unemployment, for example following redundancy where people are without work but seeking employment

▶ no occupational pension.

▶ What are the positive and negative impacts on older people of working beyond age 65?

Key term

Morbidity rates – rates of illness or disease in a particular population.

Research

Using the internet, find the region of the UK with the highest and lowest levels of diagnosed lung cancer. Make sure that you record the source of your data.

Suggest reasons why the rate of lung cancer is so different in these two parts of the country.

Studies, for example, Joseph Rowntree Trust (2002) *Work History and Income in Later Life*, have found that people who have worked continuously in professional and managerial jobs are far less likely to face a poor retirement than people who have worked in manual or unskilled occupations. In 2006, Age UK published *Older People, Decent Homes and Fuel Poverty*. In 2010, The Centre for Social Justice published *The Forgotten Age: Understanding Poverty and Social Exclusion in Later Life*. Manual workers will typically have earned lower wages, enjoyed less secure employment and are less likely to have an occupational pension.

Region

There are regional variations in the level of poverty in the UK, and regional differences in patterns of health and illness. Mortality and **morbidity rates** vary in different parts of the country and also within towns and cities. It should come as no surprise that the poorer regions and the poorer parts of cities have higher recorded levels of illness.

For example, research published by Cancer Research UK in 2015, *Lung Cancer Incidence Statistics*, confirmed that there are clear regional trends in the incidence of lung cancer across the UK. Rates for lung cancer are highest in Scotland and are higher in the north than the more affluent south of England. The differences reflect regional variations in the prevalence of smoking.

Religion or belief systems

Earlier in this unit, you looked at how societies can be defined by their culture, that is, the values, beliefs, language, rituals and rules that members see as usual and acceptable. Sociologists see religious beliefs as examples of belief systems that influence and potentially control behaviour. They are not concerned about whether the beliefs are valid or not, but they are concerned with how these beliefs affect our behaviour. For example, Jehovah's Witnesses do not allow their members to have blood transfusions, which can lead them to refusing life-saving treatments. This becomes a particularly complex, distressing and, in fact, a legal issue when parents refuse blood transfusions for their critically ill children.

Britain is a country of many faiths. The traditional practice of the Christian faith through church attendance and regular prayer is in decline. People from other faiths, such as Muslims, Jews or Buddhists, are often more devout. As care workers within a diverse multicultural society made up of people from many nations and many different ethnic and religious groups, it is essential that we understand the religious customs of our patients and clients, respect them and celebrate the variety that they bring. **Multiculturalism** promotes the view that people from all ethnic and cultural groups should be able to practise their faith and enjoy the associated customs, celebrations and feasts. Furthermore, there should be an atmosphere of interest and tolerance. People should learn about each other's culture with respect and understanding.

Key term

Multiculturalism – acceptance and celebration of the different cultural and religious practices in our society.

Research

Using the internet, textbooks and other sources, find out about the celebrations of various religions and cultures: for example, the Chinese New Year, the Christian festival of Easter, the Muslim celebration of Eid, the Jewish festival of Passover, or Diwali, the Hindu Festival of Lights. How could you arrange to celebrate these festivals in a care setting?

Sexual orientation

Homosexual men and women have a long history of oppression and discrimination against them, both in this country and abroad. There have been recent changes in the law, including the introduction of civil partnerships in 2004 under the Civil Partnerships Act, the Marriage (Same Sex Couples) Act 2013, and the protection provided by the Equality Act 2010. However, many people who do not regard themselves as heterosexual still feel unable to reveal their sexual orientation. As a result, the true number of people who are lesbian, gay, bisexual, transgender or intersex (LGBTI) is not known.

Attitudes to sexuality can have a major impact on health. For example, the Trevor Project website states that lesbian, gay and bisexual young people are four times more likely to attempt suicide than their heterosexual peers. It is reasonable to explain this, in part, as a result of the prejudice and discrimination that lesbian, gay and bisexual people experience and their fear of 'coming out'.

Disability

It is helpful, at this stage, to introduce the distinction between the related ideas of **disability** and **impairment.** Like many of the other sociological terms introduced in this unit, the words 'disability' and 'impairment' can be used in different ways, and the term 'disability' is not easy to define. It is important that you are absolutely clear about how you are using these terms when discussing the strategies to promote the health and wellbeing of service users.

Tom Shakespeare (1998) formalised a helpful distinction between impairment and disability. He defined impairment as focusing on the individual, and referring to the day-to-day restrictions that may arise because of a long-term physical or mental condition, such as the loss of a limb, loss of sight or depression. People with impairments often receive the support of a range of health and social care professionals to limit the restrictions caused by the impairment. These professionals may include doctors, nurses, occupational therapists, physiotherapists, social workers and other care staff.

Disability, in contrast, is seen by Tom Shakespeare as a problem that arises when the wider society does not take into account the needs of people with impairments. For example, there may be no ramps into buildings, and doorways may be too narrow for people who use wheelchairs. A person with a hearing impairment may only be disabled if they do not have access to a hearing aid, or they have not been taught to lip-read. Disability, from this point of view, is seen as a restriction on the opportunity to take part in the normal life of the community because of physical, social or attitudinal barriers. In this context, writers will sometimes refer to the **disabling environment**: an environment where facilities are not in place to ensure that people with impairments can take full part in a social life. This is a **social model of disability**.

> ### Key terms
>
> **Impairment** – restrictions on day-to-day activity caused by a physical or mental dysfunction or abnormality, such as the loss of a limb, loss of hearing or a learning difficulty, such as Down's syndrome.
>
> **Disability** – restrictions that arise for a person with an impairment because of attitudes and lack of appropriate services and facilities to meet their needs.
>
> **Disabling environment** – a social context where adaptions and other necessary facilities are not in place to ensure that people with impairments can take a full part in social life.
>
> **Social model of disability** – focuses on the environmental factors that impact on the health and wellbeing of people with physical or mental impairment. For example, the impact of poverty, of poor or unadapted housing and social isolation.

 **PAUSE POINT**
Describe the main social groupings in our society and how their health needs may vary.

 Hint

List the main social groupings that are part of our very diverse society.

Extend

Suggest, for each social group, two ways in which their health and care needs may vary.

The main social institutions

Family networks

The family, for the majority of people, is the place of earliest socialisation – primary socialisation. Although the form and structure of families and households varies considerably and the roles and relationships within families are diverse, the rearing and protection of the young and the mutual support of other members are probably the key functions of the family in modern Britain.

The popular image of the small family group consisting of a married couple and their children, known as the **nuclear family**, cannot be regarded as the 'typical' family in contemporary Britain. Small families of this sort may, for example, be headed by same sex couples. Their children may be born of surrogate mothers or produced by new technologies involving sperm donation. Some stable nuclear families consist of unmarried couples and their children. Lone parent families may be the result of divorce, separation or widowhood. Equally, it may be the choice of an adult to have children without having a long-term partner.

Larger family groups are known as **extended families** and these can take many forms. An extended family may include members of three or even four generations of a family and also include aunts, uncles and cousins. They may be step families, or reconstituted families in which one or both partners have children from a previous relationship. This can include same sex couples where children are the result of previous heterosexual relationships. In the African and Asian subcontinents, the extended family is the typical family form. The wider kinship group is expected to provide support and care for its members, old and young. In modern Britain, however, health and social care services take a greater responsibility for the care and support of children and other dependent members of society.

> **Key terms**
>
> **Nuclear family** – normally two generations, consisting of adult carers (who may be the birth parents) and their children.
>
> **Extended family** – normally at least three generations who form a close-knit kinship group, and provide support and care for their members.

> **Discussion**
>
> In groups, draw on your own experiences to discuss the advantages and the disadvantages of living as a nuclear or extended family in the UK today.

Education

For many people, the education system continues the socialisation process that has begun within the family, providing a formal environment for learning and training for work. In less developed, non-literate societies, education is provided informally by the family and the community. Children acquire knowledge and develop skills by following the example of their elders. In more complex, industrialised societies, formal educational systems have developed.

The UK education system, consisting of pre-schools and nurseries, schools, colleges and universities, provides a formal curriculum to guide learning, but it is also the context in which we meet and work with a much wider range of people. This will include our peers and friends, nursery nurses, teachers and other adults who are not members of our family. For most people, this is where secondary socialisation begins.

It is well documented that educational success in our society is also linked with higher paid work, good health and a longer life. There are a number of explanations for this. For example, educational success is linked with higher earnings, which allows for a healthier lifestyle through a better diet, better housing and the possibility of regular holidays.

Statistics, gathered by the Office for National Statistics, relating to wages and income over a lifetime show that the higher the qualifications people have achieved, the higher their earnings will be (see Figure 10.2). Although graduates may start work on a relatively low annual income, their pay increases at a fast pace, levelling at about 38 years of age to £35,000 per year, on average. The salary of people educated to A Level, or equivalent, reaches approximately £22,000 per year, while those whose highest level of achievement is GCSE A*– C average £19,000 in their early 30s.

The lower a young adult's qualifications, the more likely they are to be low paid. Half of all employees aged 25 to 29 with low or no qualifications are low paid.

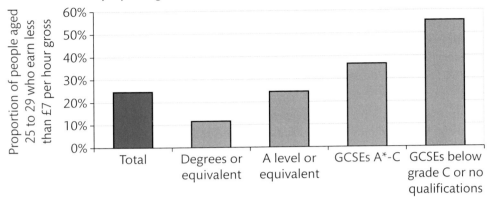

▶ **Figure 10.2:** Over half of all young employees with low or no qualifications are low paid

Health and social care services

In all societies there are people who are vulnerable and need specific support to ensure good health and wellbeing. These may include the very young, frail elderly people, people who have disabilities and are unable to work and those with mental health problems. The strategies to support groups such as these, however, vary from society to society, and at different times in history. In some societies, the care of the vulnerable is seen as the responsibility of the family and the immediate community; in other societies, such as in the UK, formal, professional health and care services play a far bigger role.

In addition to support from family and friends, health and care services in the UK are provided by a very wide range of organisations, which are financed in different ways.
▶ The **statutory sector**, organisations funded and directly controlled by the government.
▶ The **private sector** organisations, such as private hospitals and many care homes for older people and people with disabilities, which are run as commercial, profit-making businesses.
▶ The **not-for-profit sector** is made up of non-profit making organisations. All their income, whether from fees, donations or government grants, is used to finance the services they offer. This sector includes many charities, such as the National Society for the Prevention of Cruelty to Children (NSPCC), Mind, YoungMinds and many housing associations.

Many private and not-for-profit providers are contracted by the statutory sector to provide care services on their behalf. The non-statutory sectors are often referred to as the **independent sector**, as they are managed independently of both central and local government.

The specific arrangements for the delivery of health and care vary over time, and in different localities. On occasion, there is rapid change. The strategies for delivery and the specific forms of care will be influenced by the dominant attitudes of the society, government policy, the wealth of the nation and how that wealth is distributed.

Key terms

Statutory sector – organisations funded and controlled by the government.

Private sector – organisations run as commercial, profit-making businesses.

Not-for-profit sector – organisations, such as charities, that are non-profit making care providers; any surplus income is used to improve their provision, eg NSPCC.

Independent sector – private sector and not-for-profit organisations together are often referred to as the independent sector because they are not directly managed by the government.

Research

Identify health and care services in your area for *one* client group (eg older people, children under five, or people with a sensory impairment) that are provided by:
• statutory providers
• the private sector and
• the not-for-profit sector.

The key sociological perspectives

The main sociological perspectives

You will find the key terms and vocabulary introduced earlier helpful as you consider the key sociological perspectives, or approaches, that have been used to describe and understand societies and the behaviour of individuals within societies. You will also explore how these approaches (shown in Figure 10.3) can help explain the way that society affects people's health and wellbeing.

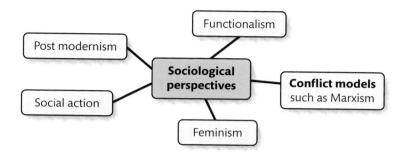

▶ **Figure 10.3:** Key sociological perspectives

The first two perspectives to consider, functionalism and conflict theory, are **structuralist** approaches. Structuralists are interested in describing and understanding the main institutions of societies, how these institutions relate to each other and how they influence and mould individual behaviour. In industrialised societies, these institutions include the family, the education system, the health services, the economy, the political institutions, religious groups and the media. The two structuralist approaches you will look at are known as **functionalism** (or the consensus model) and the conflict model developed by Karl Marx. Feminism will be considered separately, as an example of a conflict model that focuses on the continuing oppression of women in our society.

Functionalism

The functionalist approach to sociology can be best understood by likening society to the human body. Just as the body functions through the efficient interrelationship of major organs (such as the lungs, heart, liver and kidneys) and has mechanisms to deal with disease, so the different institutions in society each have particular contributions to make. They work together, and use methods of social control to deal with deviant members or groups, to ensure that society functions smoothly.

Talcott Parsons (1902–1979) played a vital role in the development of functionalism as a sociological approach. He saw society as a system made up of interrelated institutions, which contribute to its smooth running and continuity. He thought that the main role of an institution was to socialise individuals and ensure that they understood the underlying values of their society and behaved in acceptable ways. From a functionalist point of view, it is **value consensus** that ensures order in society.

As an example, the family can be seen as a key institution that contributes to the order and stability of society, or the social system (a term that functionalists often use). George Peter Murdock (1897–1985), in his classic 1949 study of the family, examined over 250 societies, ranging from small hunter–gatherer communities to large industrialised societies, and found some form of the family in all of them.

Key term

Conflict model – a sociological approach, first associated with Karl Marx, which sees the institutions of society as being organised to meet the interests of the ruling classes.

Key term

Structuralism – describing and understanding the main institutions of society, how they influence each other and how they mould individual behaviour.

Key terms

Functionalism – sees the institutions in a society as working in harmony with each other, making specific and clear contributions to the smooth running of that society.

Value consensus – general or common agreement about the values and beliefs of a society.

Talcott Parsons (1951), writing about American society, argued that the family had two 'basic and irreducible functions':

▶ the primary socialisation of children

▶ the stabilisation of adult personalities – in a complex, stressful and demanding world the family provides warmth and emotional security, especially, as Parsons saw it, for the male breadwinner.

Limitations of functionalism include the following.

▶ Probably the most fundamental criticism of the functionalist approach is that it does not address areas of conflict, which certainly characterise modern societies and, in principle, could be found in all societies. Functionalists emphasise consensus and agreement, and paint a rather rosy picture of institutions having clear, positive functions and cooperating effectively for the good of all. However, this does not seem to reflect many people's experience of the contemporary world, where there are often clear winners and losers and many non-conformists.

▶ Functionalism is based on the idea that, in all societies, members share some basic values and beliefs – and that this value consensus underpins the socialisation process and the working of the main institutions. Researchers have not been able to find that common values are clearly shared in contemporary societies.

▶ Functionalists are also very clear that the way we behave is a direct result of the socialisation process and that very little of our behaviour is the result of our personal choice. They believe that we are largely 'programmed' to behave in particular ways. The social action or interactionist model, considered later, provides an alternative to this view.

▶ Finally, functionalists tend to present a picture of a socialisation process that never fails. They give no clear explanation of deviant behaviour, especially the extreme forms of deviance found in crime, delinquency and abuse, which are destabilising for society as a whole.

Discussion

In small groups, consider the social functions of the following institutions:

- the family
- school or college
- health and social services.

1 Compare and discuss the range of answers produced by your groups.

2 Are you able to agree on the principal functions of these institutions?

Conflict perspectives

Conflict theorists focus on social differences rather than on consensus and harmony. They have identified, particularly, the inequalities between the wealthy and powerful groups in society and the relatively powerless. They have discussed the conflicts and tensions between the rich and the poor, men and women, people from different ethnic groups and employers and employees. Conflict theorists do not think that there is value consensus but groups of people with very different values and concerns from each other.

Marxism

Marxism is a conflict model and also a structuralist model. This approach was first developed by Karl Marx (1818–1883). He also thought that individual behaviour was shaped by society, but he believed that the economic system defined society and people's place within it. Marx held the view that, in the industrial society of his time, there were two social classes:

▸ the **bourgeoisie**, or **capitalists** – the small powerful group who owned the factories and other places of employment

▸ the **proletariat** – a much larger, poorer group of 'workers' (the people, or 'hands', that the bourgeoisie employed).

His view was that these two social class groups would always be in conflict: the owners of the factories, land and offices would want high profits; and the employees would want higher wages, which would eat into the profits. This is why Marxism is often called a conflict model. He thought that this conflict would lead to revolution. There was an unequal relationship between the bourgeoisie and the proletariat and conflict was inherent in the economic system.

Marxists argue that members of the bourgeoisie (the ruling class) also hold power in other social institutions and shape society because they control the mass media and the legal system, and it is their ideas that influence the curriculum in schools. Through the socialisation process, it is the values and attitudes of the ruling class that are passed on, rather than the common value system of the functionalists. This is so successfully achieved that the majority of the proletariat do not realise that they are being exploited or that they are serving the interests of the bourgeoisie rather than of their own class. This lack of awareness by the proletariat is called **false consciousness** – and it is used to explain why the conflicting interests seldom erupt into actual conflict or revolution.

Like functionalists, Marxists have a structuralist perspective. They see the family as contributing to a stable social system but regard the family as the servant of the capitalist system. They believe that it provides the context for the socialisation of children, preparing them for the disciplines and routines of work. Children have limited power in the family. They are required to be obedient at school in preparation for adult life, when they are required to be obedient to their bosses at work. In addition, Marxists see the family as providing a secure emotional base, a home, from which people will return to work rested and refreshed, ready to make larger profits for their employer. As a servant of the capitalists, the ordered family is necessary for passing on inheritance. Children born within the nuclear family are the rightful inheritors of the family's wealth.

Limitations of Marxism

Like functionalists, Marxists believe that individual behaviour is the direct result of the socialisation process, with very little individual choice. In the case of Marxist theorists, however, they see socialisation as meeting the values and interests of only the ruling classes.

Closely linked with this point is the view that Marxists put too much emphasis on different class interests and potential conflicts of interest. Although clear inequalities exist, the standard of living in industrialised societies has improved immensely over the last 100 years and, arguably, employers and employees share some common interests. All will potentially benefit from a successful company.

Some writers believe that the Marxist model, which sees the economy as the institution that drives all others, does not give sufficient emphasis to the power of other institutions – religion, race and family life – in moulding our behaviour.

Key terms

Bourgeoisie – the powerful social class who own the factories, land and other capital and are able to organise the economy and other important social institutions to their own advantage.

Capitalist – another word for a member of the bourgeoisie.

Proletariat – the 'working class'; they have only their labour to sell. They work for, and are exploited by, the bourgeoisie.

False consciousness – lack of awareness by the proletariat that they are supporting the views and beliefs of their class enemy, the bourgeoisie. For example, by working hard, they are serving the interests of the capitalist class much more than their own.

Reflect

Can you identify ideas or systems in our society that serve the interests of the powerful but are supported by most people, whether it benefits them or not?

Feminism

Feminism is normally seen as an example of a conflict model. There are three main types of feminist approach:

▶ Marxist feminism
▶ radical feminism
▶ liberal feminism.

Feminists have argued that sociology, as an academic discipline, was developed and dominated by men. Hence the term **malestream sociology** was introduced. Pamela Abbott, Claire Wallace, and Melissa Tyler (1997) clearly summarised feminist concerns and criticisms of mainstream (or malestream) sociology. They argued that this male dominance has produced biased descriptions and analyses and that not enough attention has been paid to the issues of women and their unequal place in society.

▶ Has women's changing status made a difference to their social standing and relative power in society?

Key terms

Feminism – the belief that women should have the same rights and opportunities in society as men.

Malestream sociology – the view that, because sociology has largely been written by men, and from their point of view, there has been insufficient attention paid to the position of women in society.

Patriarchal society – led and dominated by men.

Marxist feminism

Marxist feminists see women, especially working-class women, as oppressed both by capitalism and by men, or the **patriarchal society**. Women produce the next generation of workers. They meet the physical, social and emotional needs of their children, so that they are ready to work in the offices and factories of the future. They support their husbands and partners, cook meals, care for their children and clean their houses – for no pay! Thus, women are dominated by their husbands and they are also subsidising industry. The family would not be ready for work if somebody did not take responsibility for domestic life and this, it is argued, remains the primary responsibility of women.

Radical feminism

For radical feminists, it is not capitalism that dominates women, but men. The family is seen as a patriarchal institution. They see the socialisation of women as housewives and mothers as a form of oppression and this oppression as a characteristic of the nuclear family.

Liberal feminism

Liberal feminists would argue that changes have taken place. They believe that, through changing attitudes and legislation, such as the Equal Pay Act 1970, the Sex Discrimination Act 1975 and the Equality Act 2010, there is more equality. Liberal feminists believe that improvements will continue by means of legislation and policy changes.

Limitations of feminism

Feminism is probably the sociological approach that has generated the most discussion in the academic literature and in the popular press. Criticisms include the following.

▶ Feminists have tended to assume that all women share the same experiences of oppression; they ignore the many differences that arise from income, social class, employment opportunities, religion and ethnicity.

▶ Feminists tend to understate the many legal and social changes that have taken place in our society that have improved the position of women, eg in education, employment and most aspects of our social and political life.

▶ The female role is defined, particularly in the advanced stages of pregnancy, childbirth and early infancy, when women are likely to be more reliant on men. Some modern feminists would argue that women should celebrate this role within an equal and respectful relationship. They fear that the feminists of the 20th century undermined the value of child rearing.

Reflect

Are there equal opportunities for all? Do some groups have advantages over others?

If there are inequalities in society, what could be done to reduce them?.

Social action theory

Interactionism, or the social action approach, contrasts with the structuralist perspectives in that the focus is not on how the large institutions function and link with each other. Instead, the focus is on the interaction in small groups and how this influences individual behaviour and shapes society. **Interactionists** may study groups as diverse as teenage gangs, staff, patients and visitors on hospital wards, or social interaction in school classrooms. They will study the dynamics within these groups. For example, they may ask these questions.

▶ How do different members of the group see themselves?

▶ Do some have more power than others?

▶ Who are the formal leaders?

▶ Are there some informal leaders who actually have power in the group?

Social action or interactionist theorists do not believe that we are 'programmed' by the socialisation process. They see individuals as being influenced by the socialisation process but still having the power to choose how they will actually behave and to create their own roles. These theorists have very little interest in social structure as a whole. They see our behaviour as driven by the way we interpret situations, how we see ourselves and other people, and how they see us.

In the family, a mother may understand what is expected of a 'good' mother but social action theorists think that social roles are not clearly defined. They believe that the mother will interpret what that means for her in the context of her family, her relationship with her children and her links with the wider society. There is no blueprint. For the social action theorist, the main aim is to understand how people interpret situations and behave in small-group face-to-face situations.

Key terms

Interactionism – a sociological approach that focuses on the influence of small groups on our behaviour rather than the impact of large institutions.

Interactionists – believe that our behaviour is driven by the way we interpret relationships in smaller groups and settings, such as a hospital ward. They suggest that our behaviour is influenced by how we see ourselves in relation to other people in a group, and how they see us.

Limitations of interactionism

Social action theorists, although emphasising individual choice, accept that social roles exist – even if they are not clearly defined. They are criticised for paying insufficient attention to issues of power in society. Although they would say that social roles are only defined in broad outline, they do not explain how these roles develop, and they do not explain why, on the whole, people behave in very predictable ways.

In addition, social action theorists are sometimes criticised for describing social behaviour 'in a vacuum' as they tend to focus on the interactions within the group, rather than on wider issues. For example, they describe behaviour in delinquent gangs, or the relationship between staff and patients in a hospital ward, but do not describe the wider social factors that have influenced this, or the historical factors that might have defined or caused the situation.

Key terms

Social dynamics – the study of relationships within a group and how they influence our behaviour.

Post modernism – a view that society is characterised by rapid change, that there is no longer value consensus and that there is fragmentation into many different groups, interests and lifestyles.

Post modernism

Post modernism emerged in the 1980s. It is an approach to sociology, or understanding of society, that focuses on the rapid change and uncertainty (some would even say chaos) in our society. Post modernists would suggest that we can no longer talk about established institutions like the family, religion or the economy because nothing stays the same. Domestic arrangements are so varied these days that it is no longer possible to talk about the 'typical' family. Post modernists hold the view that, because of the constant change, structuralist perspectives, such as functionalism and Marxism, no longer help us to understand society. The social institutions have become fragmented. Individuals and groups of people now make their own lifestyle decisions, choosing from the many leisure activities and consumer goods that are available, and these commodities have become more important than human relationships.

Criticism of post modernism

Post modernists reject the grand theories of the structuralists. Although they criticise the power of the media, big business, consumerism and the world of advertising, they do not concern themselves with how our behaviour is still influenced and shaped by the many groups and institutions we belong to. They do not discuss the extent to which choices are limited by the growing inequalities in wealth and income in our society. Some people have a far greater choice than others when selecting from the increasing range of goods and services, including the range of health and care services available.

PAUSE POINT Can you explain what the key sociological perspectives are?

Hint What are the main sociological perspectives used to describe and analyse society?

Extend Which perspective do you find most helpful when considering health and social care issues?

Assessment practice 10.1

1 You are working for an organisation that provides day care support for people with learning disabilities. You have been asked to work in a team that will open a day centre for your service users. It will be located in a multicultural area of a large city. It is an area of high unemployment and wages are low. Many people live in cold, damp houses. Most people seem to spend their leisure time watching television. Their educational opportunities have been few.

Produce a brief report which explains the sociological factors that should be taken into account when setting up the day centre.

You will need to use the terminology introduced in this unit (eg socialisation, social class, race and ethnicity, disability and sexuality) and explain how the main social institutions may have affected the service users' development.

2 Write an essay (approximately 1,000 words) that explains, analyses, and evaluates how the sociological perspectives you have studied can be applied to the understanding of society, and to this day care setting.

Plan

- I will collect together my notes relating to:
  - the main social institutions that influence development and behaviour
  - the diversity in society
  - the sociological perspectives studied.

Do

- I will identify the areas I am most confident about and those which I might struggle with.
- I will use my notes and textbooks to check areas of concern. I can discuss these areas with my tutor and others in my group before I start writing.

Review

- I can explain what the task was and how I approached the task.
- I can explain how I would approach the difficult elements differently next time, ie what I would do differently.

B Examine how sociological approaches support understanding of models and concepts of health

The biomedical model of health and alternatives

The biomedical model

Origins and influence

The model of health that has dominated Western industrialised societies, certainly since the industrial revolution of the mid-19th century, has been the **biomedical model**. This view of health underpins the policies and practice of the National Health Service (NHS). According to this model, health is largely regarded as being the absence of disease, and the intervention of health professionals is necessary in times of illness. The main purpose of the health services is to cure disease, and health professionals will use scientifically tested methods to address diagnosed illnesses.

The biomedical model fits well with the functionalist perspective introduced and developed by Talcott Parsons, in which illness is regarded as, in itself, dysfunctional for society. If people are ill, they cannot make their normal contribution to the smooth running of society. For the functionalist, if people are ill, or adopt the **sick role** (a term introduced by Talcott Parsons), and are exempt from their usual social responsibilities, they also have a responsibility to cooperate with health professionals and take all reasonable steps to get better.

Criticisms

Sociologists believe that the focus of the biomedical approach to health and illness pays insufficient regard to the environmental and social factors that may have led to ill health. The causes of illness may be many and varied, but the biomedical approach

> **Key terms**
>
> **Biomedical model of health** – the identification of health as the 'absence of disease', with a focus on diagnosing and curing individuals with specific illnesses and other medical conditions.
>
> **Sick role** – the view that illness is a social role and considers the sick, where possible, to have a social duty to resume their active place in society as soon as they are able.

tends to focus on the individual, while largely ignoring the environmental factors that might cause disease.

Further, by focusing on the diagnosis and treatment of specific conditions, the overall health and wellbeing of the patient may be ignored or seen as unimportant.

Implications for professionals and service users

Health and care workers using a biomedical approach, often referred to as a negative model of health, adopt a view that a person can, or even should be, regarded as healthy if they do not have the symptoms of an illness or disease. This diagnosis of the biomedical professional is likely to be accepted by the patient. By focusing only on the symptoms of illness, it ignores the importance of feeling fit, energised, happy and optimistic as an aspect of good health.

The alternatives

Social model of health and illness

The **social model** of health, often referred to as a positive model of health, focuses on the social factors that contribute to health and wellbeing in our society. Research indicates that **life expectancy** rose, and death rates, especially infant mortality rates, began to fall during the late 19th and early 20th centuries. This coincided with improvements in sanitation, the provision of clean water, the building of new council houses and generally improved standards of living. This was long before 1948 and the introduction of the NHS, with universal personal health care. This sort of evidence supports the view that environmental and social conditions are a significant source of disease, and the causes of ill health are not solely located in the individual.

The social model fits more easily with the beliefs of the conflict theorists, such as Karl Marx, than the functionalists. Conflict theorists would explain the current shorter life expectancy and relatively higher rates of ill health among lower-income groups as being consequences of the inequalities in society and the life circumstances of the disadvantaged. They would suggest that the poor are more likely to have an inadequate diet and live in damp houses, often in inner-city areas where unemployment and environmental pollution tend to have the greatest impact. They would also say that the ruling groups in society (the politicians and the owners of industries) are not willing to make the changes needed to protect the poor from ill health and disease.

The biomedical model of health has a clear focus on individual diagnosed illness, and the social model is concerned with the environmental causes of illness. They can, though, be seen as two complementary approaches to the study of health and illness.

Complementary medicine

Complementary approaches and complementary therapies (**complementary medicine**) include a diverse range of health-focused practices and treatments, such as aromatherapy, reflexology and acupuncture. Most of these are not currently part of conventional or **orthodox medical practice**.

Aromatherapists use special oils, impregnated with plant extracts, for external massage. Reflexology uses massage in the belief that there are reflex points on the feet, hands and head that are reflected or linked to other parts of the body. Many reflexologists will use herb-impregnated oils as they work. Acupuncture is a form of ancient Chinese medicine in which needles are inserted through the skin at specific points, or energy lines, in the body to treat disorders.

Despite scepticism by some health professionals, complementary or alternative therapies are being used alongside conventional medicine in some health and care settings.

Key terms

Social model – an approach that focuses on the social and environmental factors that influence our health and wellbeing, including the impact of poverty, poor housing, diet and pollution.

Life expectancy – a statistical measure of how long a person is expected to live.

Orthodox medical practice – a scientific approach to the diagnosis, treatment and prevention of illnesses and disease as practised by the medical profession and other healthcare professionals.

Complementary medicine – an approach to improving health and wellbeing (eg aromatherapy or acupuncture) not usually prescribed by the medical profession. Complementary medicine is sometimes used as an alternative to, and sometimes alongside, standard treatments as prescribed by the medical profession.

Research

Use the internet, or other available resources, to investigate different forms of complementary therapies.

Are complementary therapies used at your placement or by your service users? Do they seem to be effective?

⏸ PAUSE POINT

Can you describe the models of health that you have studied so far?

Hint   Close your book and briefly describe the biomedical, the social and the complementary models of health.

Extend   How will the response of health and care professionals vary according to the model they use?

The concepts of health, ill health and disability

Defining health is not easy and there is certainly no clear agreement on definition among scholars. In fact, most sociological research concerned with studying and comparing levels of health within and between societies actually focuses on issues of ill health. For example, sociologists use a great deal of information about death rates, visits to GPs' surgeries, incidence of serious diseases, admissions to mental-health units and suicide statistics. This data is often analysed by social class, occupation, ethnicity, gender, age and geographical location.

Physical and mental ill health and disability as social biological constructs

Physical and mental ill health can be regarded and treated as an individual concern, requiring diagnosis and treatment and the expertise of the medical professions to ensure recovery. Alternatively, the symptoms of physical and mental ill health may best be addressed by considering environmental factors that are leading to distress and increased infirmity. Ill health may be a result of poor housing and a poor diet, and mental illness the result of abuse or loneliness.

It could be argued that,in order to address the needs of the patient or service user, both approaches often need to be used. The expertise and resources of the medical professions are used to address ill health and the expertise of social care staff is needed to identify and address the underlying social causes that may have led to ill health.

Definitions of health

As we have seen health can be defined in negative terms, as 'the absence of disease'. This is contrasted with a positive definition, such as that provided by the World Health Organization (WHO) in 1948, which described health as 'not merely an absence of disease, but a state of complete physical, mental, spiritual and social wellbeing'. A negative concept of health (as the absence of disease), therefore, contrasts with the positive concept of health that is concerned with people's physical, intellectual, social and emotional wellbeing.

In the health and social care sectors, care professionals usually adopt a **holistic approach** to care and support. They see their role as addressing the needs of the 'whole' person, rather than single issues or identified problems.

Key term

Holistic approach – addresses the patient's or client's physical, emotional, social and spiritual health, attempting to meet the needs of the 'whole' person.

Medicalisation

With the rapid development of scientific knowledge and skill in the early 19th century, the biomedical or negative model became the prevailing model of health in the growing industrial societies. This gave doctors significant status and power over their patients. It is argued that this led to increasing areas of life falling under the remit of doctors that would more properly be considered as social issues, such as gambling, alcoholism, drug use, some forms of crime and aspects of pregnancy, childbirth, death and dying. This extension of the remit of doctors and their staff is known as **medicalisation**, a concept famously developed by Ivan Illich in *Limits to Medicine* (1976). Illich explored the view that activities and conditions that may previously have been seen as social problems, or a normal part of life, came to be seen as medical problems despite, he claimed, the strong evidence that medicine had very little success in treating some of these conditions or life events.

Case study

Helping Alf

Alf is 50 years old and a laboratory technician. He lives alone in a large rambling house that he says he can't afford to keep warm. He is lonely and depressed. He has never enjoyed cooking and normally eats ready-made or takeaway meals. His house is unclean, untidy and fast deteriorating. He smokes heavily and takes very little exercise. Every winter, he suffers from bronchitis and has recently been diagnosed as having lung cancer. Alf is not poor, but he has no interest in looking after himself.

Check your knowledge

1 Briefly describe the approach that a practitioner using the biomedical model of health would use when caring for Alf.

2 Briefly describe the approach that a practitioner using the social model of health would use when caring for Alf.

3 Using the internet, explore complementary therapies that might help Alf give up smoking.

4 What do you think would be the most appropriate model of health to apply when considering Alf's care?

5 Explain why you have chosen this approach.

The sick role

The functionalist approach to considering health and illness derives from the work of Talcott Parsons. Using the traditional functionalist approach, Parsons described how, for society to function efficiently, its members need to be healthy. He described illness as a form of deviance and members who are ill as performing a social role – the sick role. This became a very powerful concept in the sociology of illness. In his view, if people declared themselves ill, specific rights and responsibilities came with their new role.

The rights associated with the sick role were:

▶ to be exempt from normal social obligations, for example, going to school, college or work, and from meeting normal family obligations

▶ to be cared for.

Parsons would see it as one of the key functions of the family to care for the sick and other dependent members of the family group.

The responsibilities associated with the sick role included the individual:

▶ taking all reasonable steps to get better and seeking to resume their normal place in society as soon as possible

▶ cooperating with medical professionals, particularly doctors and their staff.

The functionalist view (and the view of most governments) is that illness has social consequences. The sick are not normally at work and they may need to be cared for, and this must, whenever possible, be swiftly dealt with, in order for society to run smoothly.

Clinical iceberg

The term clinical iceberg is used to describe the large amount of illness that is not reported; this is illustrated in Figure 10.4. Government statistics on the levels of ill health and disability are based on information provided by doctors and other health and care services. This data will certainly be unreliable and will underestimate levels of illness and stress because, for a very wide range of social, personal and economic reasons, people will not always seek professional help when they feel unwell.

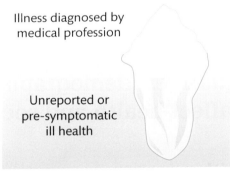

Illness diagnosed by medical profession

Unreported or pre-symptomatic ill health

▶ **Figure 10.4:** Can you think of reasons why an individual may not seek professional help when they are physically or mentally unwell? (Source: ONS)

⏸ **PAUSE POINT**   Can you explain what learning aim B was about? Which element did you find easiest?

> **Hint**   Close your book and briefly describe the models of health, ill health and disability that have been introduced.

> **Extend**   Discuss how these models and concepts will influence health and social care provision that may be provided.

Reflect

Consider the reasons why people who feel ill may not access medical help. Can you think of friends or family members who are reluctant to visit a doctor? Why do you think this is the case?

Winston and Christiana were born in Jamaica. They have lived in England for more than 40 years and are now in their sixties. They are both in very poor health. They live in a large three-bedroomed house. Their children have left home and rarely visit.

Winston has a serious heart condition and is unable to climb the stairs at home or walk to the shops. He has few friends and is becoming very depressed. Christiana is diabetic and overweight. She finds running the home too much and does not know how to cheer Winston up.

Write an essay (approximately 1,000 words) to:

- Compare the biomedical model of health with one other model you have studied and explain how these models affect the approach to meeting Winston and Christiana's needs.
- Explain how the concepts of health, ill health and disability may contribute to the planning of service provision for people such as Winston and Christiana. You should refer to the definitions of health, the concept of the sick role and the clinical iceberg.
- Analyse how these models and concepts may affect the provision of health and care services.
- Evaluate the contribution that the

a sociological perspectives you have studied make to the understanding of Winston and Christiana's position

b different concepts of health will make to the services they receive.

Plan
- I will collect together my notes on:
  - different models of health
  - concepts of health and ill health and disability.
- I will identify areas I am confident in and those I find more difficult.

Do
- I know what it is I am doing and what I want to achieve.
- I must make sure that I:
  - **analyse** how the models and concepts may affect the type of provision
  - **evaluate** the contribution of these concepts in understanding society and planning provision.

Review
- I can explain what the task was and how I approached the task
- I can explain how I would approach the difficult elements differently next time, ie what I would do differently.

C Examine how social inequalities, demographic change and patterns and trends affect health and social care delivery

Inequalities within society

How people experience inequality

Inequality has many faces. Health and care workers need to understand the inequalities that affect the health and wellbeing of their service users. By knowing which groups of service users are most vulnerable to poor health and social disadvantage, and the reasons why this is the case, health and care professionals can use their resources in the best way to meet all service users' needs.

There is evidence that patterns of health and illness vary with:
- social class
- race and ethnic or national origin
- age
- gender
- sex
- disability
- sexual orientation
- geographical region.

Social class

As you saw earlier in the unit, different sociologists define the term 'social class' in slightly different ways. Despite the difficulties of definition, and different views on the continuing importance of class in our society, there is overwhelming evidence that there is variation in health and wellbeing by social group, and, especially, by social class, in:

▶ the incidence of ill health or morbidity

▶ life expectancy.

Although statistics must be treated with caution, there is evidence that members of the higher social classes are living longer and enjoying better health than members of the lower social groups and, if people from any of these groups are also poor, the differences are even greater.

The most influential studies that consider the reasons for this difference are the *Black Report* (1980) and the *Acheson Report* (1998). These reports provide detailed and comprehensive explanations of the relationships between social and environmental factors and health, illness and life expectancy.

In fact, the findings of the *Black Report* exposed such vast differences in the levels of health and illness between different social classes that the government of the time suppressed its publication. A small number of duplicated copies were circulated and made available just before an August bank-holiday weekend, when they would expect to get very little press coverage. Nevertheless, this study has been extremely influential and the explanations offered in it are still used by sociologists today when examining and considering these issues.

The *Black Report* considered four types of explanation (see Table 10.2) that might account for the differences in the levels of illness and life expectancy experienced by different social classes. The researchers were persuaded that the differences in health and wellbeing were an effect of the level of people's income, the quality of their housing and the environment in which they lived and worked.

▶ **Table 10.2:** Sociological explanations that might account for differences in levels of illness and life expectancy

Explanation	Comment
The statistical artefact explanation	Researchers working on the *Black Report* suggested that the differences could be explained by the fact that the statistics themselves produced a biased picture. They argued that the lowest social classes had a higher proportion of older people and people working in traditional and more dangerous industries. So, it would be expected that they would have higher levels of illness than more prosperous, younger people working in offices, call centres and other service industries.
	This explanation suggests that it is not really social class, but the age structure and patterns of employment of people in the lowest social classes that explain the differences. However, more recent studies have shown that, even when the researchers account for this bias in employment and age, they still find a link between low social class, high levels of illness and lower life expectancy.
Natural or social selection	This explanation suggests that it is not low social class and the associated low wages, poverty and poorer housing that cause illness, higher infant mortality rates and lower life expectancy for adults; instead, it is, in fact, the other way round. People are in the lower classes because of their poor health, absenteeism and lack of energy needed for success and promotion. This explanation has been rejected by sociologists because there is evidence to show that ill health is caused by deprived circumstances rather than causing them.
Cultural or behavioural explanations	This explanation focuses on the behaviour and lifestyle choices of people in the lower social classes. There was evidence that people in the lower social classes smoked more, drank more heavily, were more likely to eat junk food and take insufficient exercise. Their poor lifestyle choices were linked to a range of chronic illnesses including heart disease, some forms of cancer, bronchitis and diabetes. However, the fact is that many people in economically deprived circumstances use smoking and alcohol to help them cope with their difficult circumstances. It is their difficult circumstances that lead to their lifestyle choices, not the other way round.

Explanation	Comment
Material or structural explanations	Material explanations claim that those social groups for whom life expectancy is shorter, and for whom infant mortality rates are higher, suffer poorer health than other groups because of inequalities in wealth and income. Poverty and persistently low incomes are associated with poorer diets, poor housing in poor environments and more dangerous and insecure employment. It is these inequalities and the associated deprivation that lead to the differences in health and wellbeing. This is an explanation that can be traced back to the work of Marx and Engels in the 19th century. The writers of the *Black Report* presented very persuasive evidence to support the materialist explanation. Shaw *et al* (1999) completed a major review of all the research in this area and concluded that the major factors contributing to these differences in health and illness were social factors. Put simply, poor health and lower life expectancy is a consequence of poverty in a community.

Race and ethnic or national origin

Evidence for a link between race (or ethnicity) and illness is difficult to study systematically because there are difficulties in defining a person's racial type, particularly in the context of the increasing numbers of people who are of mixed race. In addition, a high proportion of people from minority ethnic groups live in areas of deprivation: in inner-city areas with associated poor housing, pollution and relatively high unemployment. It is, therefore, difficult to know whether their poorer health is due to poverty or to ethnicity. Nevertheless, compared to the white majority ethnic group, there is evidence that:

▶ there is a higher incidence of rickets in children from the Asian subcontinent because of a deficiency of vitamin D, although, according to *The Lancet* in February 2014, hospitalisation rates for rickets in England are now the highest in five decades
▶ most minority ethnic groups have a shorter life expectancy
▶ most minority ethnic groups have higher infant mortality rates.

In addition to the health implications of higher levels of poverty, there are issues of access to the health services. Language problems and other cultural barriers may limit full use of the health services. Asian women are often reluctant to see a male doctor, many of them speak little English and, despite improvements, translators are in short supply and much important information is not translated into minority languages. In addition, racism, or the fear of racism, is stressful. Unless health and social care workers understand the religious and cultural beliefs and practices of minority ethnic groups, their care needs are unlikely to be fully met, leaving those groups vulnerable to higher levels of ill health.

Research

Use the internet to research the specific health risks for members of minority ethnic groups living in the UK.

Age

Many people over retirement age are fit, healthy and making valuable contributions to our society through paid work, voluntary activities, and caring for their families. In fact, the Office for National Statistics (*Labour Market Statistics*, December 2013) reported that, in 2013, the employment rate for people over the age of 65 was 10 per cent, the highest since comparable records began in 1992 and an increase of 0.8 per cent over the previous year. The 2011 census revealed that almost 1.3 million people over the age of 65 had a caring responsibility. This is a 35 per cent increase on the proportion reported in 2001. The number of carers over the age of 65 is growing faster than for any other age cohort in the population, with 342,032 people aged 65 and over providing 50 hours or more unpaid care each week. However, it is also true that there are higher levels of illness among the older population, particularly among those people over the age of 75. During a three-month period in 2003, 24 per cent of people over the age of 75 had attended the casualty or out-patient department of a hospital, compared with 14 per cent of people of all ages (*General Household Survey*, 2003). In 2007, research published by the Alzheimer's Society found that one in 79 people in the UK population suffer from dementia. For people over the age of 65, the figure rises to one in 14, and to one in six for people over the age of 80.

Sex

Although women's life expectancy is higher than that of men (with women in our society typically living five years longer than men, and with the infant mortality rates for boys being persistently higher than those for girls), studies consistently report higher levels of illness for women than for men. The social factors that contribute to these differences (as shown in Table 10.3) can be identified as differences in lifestyle, economic inequalities and the perceived role of women in society. However, it may also be the case that women have a higher rate of diagnosed stress-related illness due to their willingness to discuss mental health issues with their doctor, rather than actually having a higher rate of stress-related illnesses.

▶ **Table 10.3:** The social factors that can have an impact on women's health

Risk factors	Impact of the key risk factors
Lifestyle factors	The higher death rate for men can be linked with higher levels of cigarette smoking and drinking by men, and their participation in more risky and dangerous sports and other activities. The relatively high death rate of young men between 17 and 24 is specifically linked with this risk-taking behaviour and the associated deaths from road accidents.
Economic inequalities	As discussed earlier in this unit, there are clear and direct links between poverty and poor health. Despite changes in the law, women still earn less than men. For example, a recent survey by the Higher Education Statistics Agency showed that women who have degrees are paid, on average, less than men. Men earn £1000 more than their female classmates within three years of leaving university. They are much more likely to go straight into highly paid jobs, with 40 per cent of men earning over £25,000 a year three years after graduating, compared with only 26 per cent of women earning this three years after graduating. A higher proportion of women than men are in low-paid part-time work. They are also far more likely to be the main carer in a lone-parent family, and are more likely to be on means-tested state benefits. In older age, they are more likely to be in poverty because they are less likely to receive an occupational pension and may not, because of family responsibilities, have a full state pension either.
Impact of the female role	Women still take responsibility for housework in most homes, and the higher incidence of depression in women may be linked with the dull repetitive nature of this work. Popay and Bartley (1989), studying the hours spent on domestic labour in 1700 households in London, found that women spent more time doing housework than their male partners even if they had a full-time job. Often, women will be managing on a limited budget, working long hours and will have little time to themselves.

Research

Use the internet to find out whether women in the family still perform more household tasks than their male partners.

Disability

Disability arises when society does not address the specific needs of people with impairments. Anti-discriminatory legislation, particularly the Disability Discrimination Act 1995 and the more recent Equality Act 2010, has attempted to ensure that people with impairments will be able to participate fully in society. Evidence suggests, however, that the aims and objectives of the legislation are yet to be realised. Sociological research has consistently found a high correlation between disability and poverty.

According to the Office for National Statistics:

▶ in 2012, 46.3 per cent of working age people with a disability were in paid employment, compared with 76.4 per cent of the rest of the population of working age (Labour Force Survey, Quarter 2, 2012)

▶ the number of people with disabilities, over the age of 19, who have no formal academic or vocational qualifications is three times higher than for people with no disability (Labour Force Survey, Quarter 2, 2012)

▶ approximately a third of people with disabilities experience difficulties in accessing shops, leisure activities, offices and other businesses due to their impairment (Opinions Survey, 2010)

▶ a significantly higher proportion of people living in households where a person has a disability live in poverty, compared with people living in households where no one has an identified disability (Family Resources Survey, 2011 to 2012).

You may find it helpful to revisit the passage on disability and impairment earlier in this unit. You will notice that government statisticians use the term disability where health and social care practitioners might normally use impairment. These terms are sometimes used differently by different writers.

Reflect

How easy is it for someone using a wheelchair to access the shops and other facilities in your local high street or shopping centre?

Sexual orientation

There is significant evidence, as discussed earlier in this unit, to show that people who are lesbian, gay, bisexual, transgendered, intersex or who are uncertain of their sexual orientation, have higher levels of mental illness than heterosexual adults.

YoungMinds, the mental health charity that specifically supports young people with mental health problems, reports that:

▶ more than half (55 per cent) of lesbian, gay and bisexual school pupils have experienced direct bullying on account of their sexual orientation; those who are bullied are at a higher risk of suicide, self-harm and depression

▶ two in five (41 per cent) have attempted, or thought of attempting, suicide because of bullying, and the same number say that they self-harm because of bullying (Stonewall School Report, 2012).

Region

As discussed earlier in the unit, the patterns of health and illness vary in different regions of the UK and in different parts of the same town or city. Levels of ill health and reported disability are lower in more affluent areas than in the poorer areas. As well as this, life expectancy and **healthy life expectancy** is higher in richer areas than poorer ones.

Between 2012 and 2014, statistics (reported in the ONS Statistical Bulletin, November 2015) showed that the life expectancy for boys born in England and Wales was highest, at 83.3 years, in the west London borough of Kensington and Chelsea, whereas, in Blackpool, it was just 74.7 years

For girls, the life expectancy for those born in this period was highest (86.7 years) in the Chiltern areas and lowest in Middlesbrough (79.8 years).

For both boys and girls, the highest life expectancy is in areas of greater affluence and the lowest in areas of high unemployment and low wages. The areas with the lowest life expectancy across England and Wales were in the relatively poor areas of the North East, the North West and Wales.

Key term

Healthy life expectancy – a statistical measure of the average number of years a person can expect to live in 'full health', unhindered by disease or injury.

Ⅱ PAUSE POINT Can you explain how social differences can influence health and wellbeing?

> **Hint** Close your book and list the social differences that can influence our health and wellbeing.

> **Extend** Explain how four of these social differences may influence health and wellbeing.

How different social groups experience inequalities

Prejudice

Disadvantaged groups in society often become the subject of **prejudice**. Prejudice is a term that is not easy to define. It refers to a set of fixed **attitudes** or beliefs about particular social or ethnic groups. People are normally unwilling, unable or uninterested in changing these attitudes. An example of a prejudiced view would be that people of working age who receive state benefits are lazy; they do not want to work: if they did, they would find a job because there are plenty advertised. A person with this prejudice would not easily change their minds about this, even if you presented clear examples of unemployed people who had applied unsuccessfully for many jobs. Prejudicial attitudes are very often negative and based on oversimplified views of a social group.

Stereotyping

Stereotyping is a term closely linked to the concept of prejudice. Stereotyping defines a group, such as immigrants or older people, as if they all share the same characteristics and ignores their individual differences. It is very important that health and social care professionals confront any issues of stereotyping and always meet the individual needs of their service users, whatever their personal or cultural backgrounds.

▶ Are stereotypes in the media of teenagers largely positive or negative? Why do you think this may be?

Labelling

When a stereotype is widely held, it is sometimes said that the group is the subject of **labelling**. This means that the stereotypical qualities and characteristics are applied to them, their individual differences are ignored and they are treated accordingly. For example, ex-prisoners may be labelled as anti-social and never to be trusted, which may lead to discrimination and exclusion from many social activities.

Discrimination and attitudes

Prejudicial attitudes, which in themselves are a state of mind, can easily lead to **discrimination**. This means treating a person differently (usually, less favourably) because of their particular personal characteristics such as their age, race, colour or gender. Men may be discriminated against when applying for work with young children because this has traditionally been seen as work better suited to women.

Marginalisation

Groups who are discriminated against can quickly feel **marginalised** by society in general or by the groups to which they belong. They feel 'out on the edge' and excluded from the life and status enjoyed by the rest of the group or society. For example, immigrants can often feel marginalised by the community in which they now live.

Key terms

Prejudice – preconceived opinions or fixed attitudes about a social group that are not based on reason or evidence.

Attitudes – fixed beliefs or ways of looking at issues.

Stereotype – a fixed image or view of a social group that ignores individual differences, for example, all unemployed people are lazy and do not want to work.

Labelling – applying the stereotypical view of a particular group and ignoring individual differences.

Discrimination – treating individuals or a social group in a different way to other individuals or groups, eg treating members of a particular racial group less favourably than other people.

Marginalisation – when a group of people are discriminated against and prevented from enjoying equal rights or accessing services in society.

A matter of class?

Nikola is 18 years of age. She is Polish and has been living in England for six months, but her spoken English is still very poor. Nikola lives with her brother in a large four-bedroom house, with ten other single adults from Poland. The house is damp and overcrowded. Most of the residents smoke. All the residents are in paid work, but it is mainly low-paid and insecure employment. Nikola has just discovered that she is pregnant and does not want any further contact with the father of her child.

Felicity and Charles are married and live in Kensington. Charles is a senior civil servant. They have two children, Hilary and Edmund, who both attend fee-paying schools. Both children play the piano and are excellent tennis players. Edmund plays rugby for his school.

Check your knowledge

1 Which social classes do you think that Nikola and Felicity would be assigned to using the National Statistics Socio-economic Classification described in Table 10.1, earlier in this unit?

2 Briefly describe how the health and wellbeing of people in the higher social classes differs from that of people in the lower groups.

3 Identify two pieces of research that discusses these differences.

4 How might Nikola's circumstances provide a serious challenge to the health and wellbeing of her new baby?

5 With the support of the health and care services, how might Nikola try to minimise the inequalities in opportunity for her new child compared to Felicity's children?

⏸ PAUSE POINT Can you explain how the attitudes and prejudices of a society could influence health and well being?

Hint Close your book and define the following terms: prejudice, discrimination, labelling and marginalisation.

Extend Explain how the inequalities that arise from these attitudes and behaviours may influence our health and wellbeing.

Demographic change and data

Demographic change

Key terms

Demography – term used to describe the study of changes in the size and structure of the population.

Policymaker – someone who makes the plans carried out by a government or a business.

Demography is the technical term used to describe the study of changes in the size and structure of the population. Social scientists, commercial institutions, governments and other **policymakers** all study changes in the size and make-up of the population. At first, governments were concerned with measuring:

▶ natural changes in the population – changes in the birth rates and death rates

▶ changes in migration (emigration and immigration).

Now demographers examine wider changes in the population, such as changes in educational achievements, employment, spending patterns and the use of leisure time.

It is important, when planning health and social care provision, to know, for example:

▶ the overall size of the population

▶ the age structure of the population, including how many people over retirement age and how many school children there are to support

▶ the numbers of people with disabilities and with mental health problems

▶ any regional or geographical differences in levels of health and ill health.

Birth rates

Natural changes in the population include changes in the **birth rates** and **death rates**. The birth rate, measured as a proportion of live births per thousand of the population, fell during the 20th century from an average of six children per family in 1870 to 1.7 children in 2007.

It is not possible to explain the fall in the birth rate with full certainty, but it is reasonable to account for it by considering changing social circumstances, such as:

▶ the availability of reliable contraception for women from the late 1960s

▶ women pursuing their own careers and choosing to have smaller families

▶ the wish to have smaller families in order to enjoy a higher standard of living

▶ the development of the welfare state, which meant that it was not necessary to have a large family to ensure that parents were cared for in their old age.

The 2001 UK **census** showed that, for the first time, there were fewer children under the age of 16 than people over the age of 65. Birth rates subsequently rose between 2001 and 2012 by 23 per cent bu,t if present trends continue, it is expected that, by 2044, only 17 per cent of the UK population will be under the age of 16 and 25 per cent of the population will be over the age of 65 (as shown in Table 10.4).

> **Key terms**
>
> **Birth rate** – the number of live births per thousand of the population over a given period, normally a year.
>
> **Death rate** – the number of deaths per thousand of the population over a given period, normally a year.
>
> **Census** – a compulsory, official and detailed count of the population in the UK, held every ten years. It includes demographic information about households.

▶ **Table 10.4:** Age distribution of the UK population (* = predicted)

Year	Age 0–15 (%)	Age 16–64 (%)	Age 65 and over (%)
1984	21	64	15
1994	21	63	16
2004	20	65	16
2014	19	64	18
*2024	19	61	20
*2034	18	58	24
*2044	17	58	25

Death rates

Death rates, or mortality rates, are the statistical measure of the number of deaths in a population and they are normally expressed in terms of the number of deaths per thousand of the population. Throughout most of the 19th and 20th centuries, the mortality rates in the UK were falling, or, to see this from another point of view, the life expectancy in the UK was increasing (see Figure 10.5). A number of explanations may be given for this including:

▶ improved living standards – more people were living in smaller, warmer houses

▶ improved diets

▶ introduction of immunisation programmes: in the 1920s, vaccinations were widely available for diphtheria, tetanus, whooping cough and tuberculosis and, in 1955, for polio

▶ the National Health Service, which was established in 1948

▶ improved medical knowledge

▶ improved social care for vulnerable people, including the frail and elderly, people with disabilities and people with mental health problems

▶ improved health education programmes.

▶ **Figure 10.5:** Life expectancy at birth in the UK, according to mortality rates experienced in given years (Source: ONS)

Key terms

Infant mortality rate (IMR)
– the number of deaths of babies under the age of one year per thousand live births over a given period, normally a year.

Perinatal mortality rate
– the number of deaths of babies during the first week of life per thousand live births over a given period, normally a year.

The **infant mortality rate (IMR)** is defined as the number of deaths of babies under the age of one year per thousand live births over a given period, normally a year. The **perinatal mortality rate** refers to babies who die during the first week of life. The number of babies who died in infancy declined in the UK during the 20th century, and it remains very low (see Figure 10.6). Immunisation programmes, improved maternity care and the general resources of the NHS are significant contributors to this change.

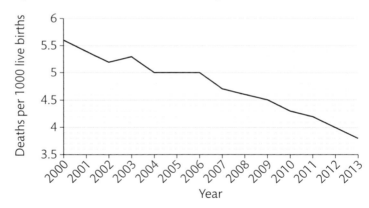

▶ **Figure 10.6:** Infant mortality rate in the UK (deaths per 1,000 live births), 2000 to 2013 (Source: ONS)

A high infant mortality rate will often point to inadequacies in a range of social and economic services and to high levels of poverty and economic hardship. Much of the decrease in overall death rates can be attributed to this fall in the infant and child mortality rate.

Family and household size

When the UK government collects statistics about family and household size, a family is defined as a household consisting of:

▶ a married couple, with or without children, or

▶ a civil partnership or cohabiting couple, with or without children, or

▶ a lone parent with at least one child.

A household also includes the family types listed above and: one person (single), two or more unrelated people living together, multiple families.

▸ Household size (as summarised in Figure 10.7) has remained relatively static during the first years of the 21st century. However, in the period between 1971 and 2011, the average household size fell. In 1971, the average household size was 2.91 people and in 2011 the average was 2.35 people. This is accounted for by the increase in the number of people living alone. In 1971, the proportion of people living on their own (one-person or single households) was just 17 per cent; this had risen to 29 per cent in 2014.

Migration

Emigration is the movement of people from their home country to make a permanent residence in another, for example when people from the UK move to Australia or the USA to settle and work there, and make a new life. **Immigration** is the arrival of people from one country to make a permanent home in another country. For example, in recent years many people from Eastern Europe have come to the UK hoping for work opportunities. **Net migration** refers to the difference between the number of immigrants and the number of emigrants over a given period.

For many years, the UK has been a multicultural country, with many races from a variety of backgrounds. Immigration often occurred because people were escaping religious or political persecution. For example, in the 17th century, French Huguenot protestants came to Britain to escape religious persecution, and Jewish people sought refuge in Britain at the time of the Second World War. During the same conflict, men and women from Commonwealth countries (particularly India, Pakistan and the Caribbean) and from Eastern Europe, (especially Poland and the former Czechoslovakia) served in the British armed forces. In the mid-20th century, people from Commonwealth nations were offered inducements to emigrate to the UK to help solve labour shortages in:

▸ the health services
▸ textile industries
▸ public transport.

In recent years, statistics show that net migration to the UK has increased. This is partly the result of movement of people from within the European Union (EU). Since its formation, there have been few restrictions on migration between the EU member countries. There are currently 28 member states.

In 2004, seven countries from Eastern Europe joined the union, and, in 2007, Romania and Bulgaria also became members. 53,000 Romanian and Bulgarian people moved to the UK between March 2014 and March 2015; this was almost double the number (28,000) for the previous 12 months. In March 2015, net migration to the UK was 330,000, an increase of 94,000 on the previous twelve months.

In the late 19th century, and until the 1930s, emigration was more common than immigration. There were more emigrants from the UK starting new lives in other countries than immigrants making new homes in the UK. However, in most years since the early 1930s, the reverse has been the case. There have been more people entering the country than leaving. Health and social care settings can play a key role in promoting multiculturalism and celebrating the diversity and variety of cultures within our society.

Life expectancy

Since the mid-19th century, there has been a steady fall in the death rate or, to look at it another way, an increase in life expectancy.

The fall in the death rate in the mid-19th century was certainly linked to the public health measures of the time, including improved sanitation and cleaner water (in place from the

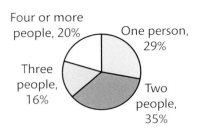

Four or more people, 20%
One person, 29%
Three people, 16%
Two people, 35%

▸ **Figure 10.7:** Percentage of UK households by household size in 2014 (Source: ONS)

Key terms

Emigration – movement of people from their home country to make a permanent home in a different country.

Immigration – arrival in a country of people from their home country who wish to make the new country their permanent home.

Net migration – the difference between the number of immigrants and the number of emigrants in a country over a given period, normally a year.

1840s onwards). In the 20th century, further public health measures included the increase in immunisation programmes and the introduction of NHS care, free at the point of need. Public health measures continue to improve the health and wellbeing of the nation.

In 2014–15, Public Health England, in collaboration with the NHS, developed health education programmes to reduce the number of premature deaths by reducing the levels of:

▶ obesity
▶ alcohol consumption
▶ tobacco smoking
▶ diabetes
▶ tuberculosis.

Public Health England aims to improve the nation's health and to reduce inequalities in health and life expectancy. Their health programmes and the linked campaigns are informed by the most recent and respected research.

Uses of demographic data

Assessing the potential needs of the population

Governments need to measure and monitor changes in the size and structure of the population in order to plan provision and anticipate changes in social need. For example:

▶ an increase in car ownership has implications for transport policies
▶ an increase in life expectancy has implications for care provision for older people
▶ a fall in the birth rate has implications for child-care provision.

Statistical data that explain levels of health and illness are generated from three main sources (see Table 10.5). Throughout this book, you will find references to evidence drawn from all these sources.

▶ **Table 10.5:** Some sources of statistical data

Source	Data
Government statistics, the census	• The Office of National Statistics (ONS) provides current data on a wide range of health and care issues. Publications include *Social Trends* and *Population Trends*. • ONS publications provide a wide range of statistics on birth rates, death rates, infant mortality rates and suicide rates, as well as data for appointments at GPs' surgeries and hospital admissions, often analysed by social class, gender, geographical location and age. • Data from the UK Census is collected every 10 years, with the most recent in March 2011. The Census gathers data about population and other statistics needed to plan and allocate resources.
Charitable organisations and pressure groups	• Many charitable groups and special interest groups also collect and publish statistical data and other information that informs discussion on issues of health and illness. • For example, Mind and Young Minds are charities that support adults and young people with mental health needs, and Youreable is a website run by the Disability Living Foundation that provides a disability-related news service on the internet. • All provide ongoing and up-to-date information relating to their areas of concern.
Academic researchers and other authors	• Largely based in universities, researchers and authors also contribute to the evidence and debate on a wide range of health and social care issues.

Planning and targeting services

Demographic information of this type will be used to set specific targets for planners, for example:

▶ the number of child-care places needed in nurseries and schools over the next decade
▶ the range and size of provision for older people
▶ the size of the building programme needed to meet these demands
▶ the training needed to support the plans.

PAUSE POINT Can you explain how demographic information may be used to plan health and social care provision?

> Hint Close your book and list the range of demographic information that is available to health and social care practitioners.

> Extend How might this information be used to plan provision?

Patterns and trends in health and ill health within social groups

Difficulties in measuring health

As you saw earlier, defining what is meant by health and wellbeing is not easy and there is no clear agreement on it among scholars. In fact, most sociological research concerned with studying and comparing levels of health within and between different social groups focuses on issues of ill health. For example, sociologists use a great deal of information about death rates, visits to GPs' surgeries, incidence of serious diseases, admissions to mental health units and suicide statistics. This data is often analysed by social class, occupation, ethnicity, gender, age and geographical location.

This type of information can be measured statistically and is, generally, clearly defined. It is much more difficult to measure the positive indicators of health (people's physical, intellectual, social and emotional wellbeing), as defined by the WHO (World Health Organization).

Mortality rates

People in our society are living longer and well beyond the usual retirement age, leading busy and active lives. Many remain in paid employment and contribute to a wide range of voluntary and community activities. Many retired people give practical support to their children and grandchildren and often say that they don't know how they found the time to work!

Growing older is a natural process and, while it may lead to slower reactions, poorer eyesight, loss of hearing and restricted mobility, it need not of itself be an issue or a problem. However, it does become a problem if there is insufficient support and if routine activities become too big a challenge. The fall in the death rate and the fact that people are living longer, presents new and pressing issues for health and care workers.

In 1901, life expectancy in the UK for men was 45 years and for women 49 years. By 2012, this had increased to 79.2 years for men and 83.3 years for women. However, people on low incomes and living in areas of deprivation have shorter lives than the more affluent. The gap between the life expectancy of the poor and the rich remains, and evidence shows the gap is increasing (ONS *Statistical Bulletin*, 2011). In 2008–2010, the life expectancy of those living in areas with the highest levels of deprivation in England and Wales was 76.5 years for men and 80.9 years for women. Of children born in England and Wales between 2007 and 2011, boys born to families from the highest social class could expect to live until they were 82.5 years and the lowest class 79.1 years. For girls, the expectation of life ranged from 85.2 years to 82.4 years for these social groups.

The causes of death also vary by social class. The incidence of lung cancer, respiratory diseases, coronary heart diseases and strokes are lowest in the higher social classes. The incidence of these as causes of death increases with social disadvantage.

As discussed earlier in this unit, infant mortality rates have declined. However, Figure 10.8 shows that infant deaths are still far more common in babies born to parents working in manual, low income occupations than they are in babies whose parents are in non-manual occupations.

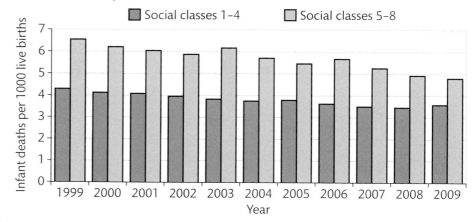

▶ **Figure 10.8:** Infant deaths are more common in babies born to parents in manual occupations

Suicide rates

In 2013, there were 6,708 suicides in the UK and the Republic of Ireland, of which 6,233 suicides were registered in the UK. This was a 4 per cent increase from 2012. As with many of the other data you have looked at, there are considerable variations in the suicide rates among different groups in the population. For example, in the UK:

▶ the overall suicide rate was 11.9 per 100,000, but the rate for men was more than three times higher (19.0 per 100,000 in the population) than for women (5.1 per 100,000)

▶ male suicide rates in Wales (26.1 per 100,000 of the population) are at their highest since 1981

▶ for both men and women, the age group with the highest suicide rate is 45–59 years

▶ the north east of England has the highest rates, at 13.8 deaths per 100,000 of the population; London has the lowest rate of 7.9 per 100,0000.

There are difficulties, however, in relying on suicide rates as a fully accurate record of the number of suicides in a region. For example, it is not always easy to be sure of the true cause of death. Also, in the UK, suicide rates do not include children under 15 years of age. It is widely accepted that the suicide rates are probably higher than those registered and used in the official statistics.

Incidence and prevalence of disease and illness

The **incidence** of a disease or illness refers to the number of new cases of a specified illness or disease occurring in a specific population over a given time. The **prevalence** of a disease or illness is the total number of cases of the illness in a population at a given time. The population would normally refer to a geographical region but could refer to an ethnic group or to a population of health and care workers.

Local and national patterns and trends of care for different groups of people in society

The underlying principle of the National Health Service was that health care should be equally available to all, and free at the point of use, regardless of income, age, gender, social class, geographical region, or any other differences between groups of people. However, research has indicated that access to health care provision is lower in areas of highest need. In an article for *The Lancet*, J. Tudor Hart (1971) introduced the concept of the **inverse care law**. This describes situations where access to health and care services is lowest for the people who most need them. This particularly includes people living in poverty (which is closely linked with chronic health conditions), who are least likely to receive care.

The marketisation of health and social care

Since the National Health Service (NHS) and Community Care Act 1990, an increasing proportion of health and care services, financed by government or local authorities, have been provided by private companies or other independent organisations rather than the NHS or the local council. The Health and Social Care Act 2012 created a more competitive market, whereby it was established that, although the government would still *finance* health care provision, it no longer had the responsibility for *providing* comprehensive health care. This could be done by a range of private or not-for-profit organisations. For example, most residential care homes and nursing homes, most day nurseries and pre-schools are owned and run by private companies. Politicians, governments and sociologists supporting this way of organising services hold the view that competition between the different companies or service providers will improve standards. They suggest that the private companies will deliver high quality services in order to get the business and be contracted by the NHS or the local council, who will only contract the best providers. However, other politicians and sociologists are concerned that the private providers will have different values to the NHS and local authorities, and be more concerned with making a profit than caring for service users.

> **Key terms**
>
> **Incidence** – the number of new cases, for example of an illness or disability, in a particular population over a given period of time.
>
> **Prevalence** – the total number of cases, for example of an illness or disability, in a particular population over a given period of time.
>
> **Inverse care law** – a situation in which those most in need of health care are the least likely to get it.

Ⅱ   PAUSE POINT   Can you explain why differences in levels of health and ill health and length of life varies by social group?

    Hint   Close your book and describe different ways of measuring health and ill health.

Extend   Why is the expectation of life in some social groups longer than in others?

Assessment practice 10.3 | C.P5 | C.P6 | C.P7 | C.M3 | C.M4 | C.D2 | C.D3 |

You are a service user at a day centre for people with disabilities. You have been asked to join a team to plan social service provision in your community. In your area, there are high levels of deprivation for all age groups and many people who speak very little English.

In order to assist the team with planning, write an extended essay that addresses the following points. You should:

1   Explain and analyse how social inequalities can affect the health and wellbeing of people in your community.

2   Explain how demographic data can be used to help plan for the provision.

3   Explain the patterns and trends in ill health for different social groups in your community.

4   Analyse how the use of demographic information could impact on, and improve, the planning of provision.

5   You should also evaluate:

   a   the different sociological explanations for the patterns and trends of health and ill health by different groups

   b   how demographic information is used in health and social care settings to reduce inequalities

   c   the importance of sociological perspectives to understand society, reduce social inequalities and improve service provision.

Plan
- Am I clear about what each of the tasks requires?
- I will collect together my notes on inequalities and their impact on health and wellbeing.

Do
- I will organise my notes so that they address each of the tasks.
- I will identify areas that I find difficult and carry out further research to fully address the tasks.

Review
- I can explain what the task was and how I approached the task.
- I can explain how I would approach the difficult elements differently next time, ie what I would do differently.

Further reading and resources

Abbott P, Wallace C and Tyler M – *An Introduction to Sociology: Feminist Perspectives 3rd edition* (Routledge, 2005)

Acheson D – *Independent Inquiry into Inequalities in Health*, (HMSO, 1998)

Blaxter M – *Health and Lifestyles* (Routledge, 1990)

Browne K – *Introducing Sociology for AS Level 2nd ed* (Polity Press, 2006)

Doyal L – *What Makes Women Sick?* (Macmillan, 1999)

Engels F – *The Condition of the Working Class in England* (Oxford University Press, 1845/2009)

Illich I – (1976) *Limits to Medicine* (Marion Boyars, 1976)

Lines C J, Briggs A, Trinder B – *Companion to the Industrial Revolution* (Facts on File Inc., 1991)

Murdock GP – *Social Structure* (Macmillan, 1949)

Oliver M – *The Politics of Disablement*, (Macmillan, 1990)

ONS *Social Trends*, Vol. 36 – (HMSO, 2006)

Parsons T – *The Social System* (The Free Press, 1951)

Popay J and Bartley M – 'Conditions of labour and women's health', in Martin C and McQueen D (eds) *Readings for a New Public Health* (Edinburgh University Press, 1989)

Shakespeare T – *The Disability Reader: Social Science Perspectives* (Cassell, 1998)

Shaw M, Dorling D, Gordon D and Davey-Smith G – *The Widening Gap* (Policy Press, 1999)

Singh J. and Zingg R – *Wolf-children and the Feral Man* (Harper, 1942)

Townroe C and Yates G – *Sociology 3rd edition* (Longman, 1995)

Townsend P, Davidson N and Whitehead M – *Inequalities in Health: The Black Report 2nd edition* (Penguin, 1992)

World Health Organization – *Alma-Ata Declaration* (1978)

Websites

www.ageuk.org.uk
Age UK is a charity dedicated to helping older people.
www.alzheimers.org.uk
Alzheimer's Society is a charity for anyone affected by dementia.
www.equalityhumanrights.com
The *Equality and Human Rights Commission* provides information, news, blogs, advice and support.
www.kingsfund.org.uk
The *King's Fund* is an independent health and health care charity in England, providing information, latest research and publications.
www.ons.gov.uk
The *Office for National Statistics* produces official statistics for the UK.
www.youreable.com
Youreable is a website run by the Disabled Living Foundation that provides and online community of and for disabled people.
www.the trevorproject.org
The website for a national organisation providing crisis intervention and suicide prevention services to the LGBTI community.

THINK ▶▶FUTURE

Joshua Njampa

Care assistant at a day centre for older people

I've been working as a care assistant at a day centre for older people for five years. During this time, I've come across many people who think that what we do is easy and just a matter of common sense. They say it's not hard to organise social activities for service users and make sure they have a good lunch. Many people don't realise the range of skills that are necessary to keep our service users safe, happy and well enough to stay independent at home. Neither do they fully realise that the older people we support are not all the same. We have to address their individual needs. This means understanding their personal circumstances, their links with family and friends, and their ability to carry out daily tasks and manage a budget. When I show people the records we keep, the detail of our policies and procedures and describe the range of our professional duties, they're amazed.

People are also surprised that we don't only work with service users but also support their families and friends. We also work with other professionals including doctors, nurses, occupational therapists, physiotherapists and social workers. This is because we know that an older person's wellbeing is directly related to both their medical condition and their social and economic circumstances.

Focusing your skills

Understanding social and environmental factors

Working in a day centre, it is important to understand the wide range of social and environmental factors that can affect the health and wellbeing of your service users. This will include knowing:

*   who the important people are in the service user's day-to-day life and who to contact in an emergency
*   any medical conditions that may need specific attention at the centre
*   whether the service user can carry out daily routine tasks at home and manage their money
*   whether service users are eating well at home
*   whether they have specific dietary requirements due to their health needs or their cultural background
*   what their interests and hobbies are, the type of music they like and their TV preferences.

Addressing social and environmental concerns

Sociological research has shown that knowing about and addressing social and environmental concerns can be as important to health and wellbeing as treating diagnosed health conditions. Researchers have found that:

*   the people who most need health and care services are the people who find it most difficulty to access services; these service users may need additional support
*   people on low incomes have lower life expectancy and lower healthy life expectancy; it may be necessary to ensure that they are claiming the benefits they are entitled to
*   there is a higher incidence of ill health and premature death if homes are damp or cold; social services departments may be able to help if accommodation is unsuitable
*   older people may not have easy access to friends and family; additional support from care services may be necessary, including warden support, to ensure safety and promote wellbeing.

Getting ready for assessment

Peter is working towards a BTEC National in Health and Social Care. He was given an assignment with the title 'Inequalities, demographic change and patterns of health and illness in different groups within our society' for learning aim C. He has to write a report on:

▶ the sociological explanations for social inequalities, and how these link to patterns of health and ill health in different social groups

▶ how demographic data could be used to reduce inequalities in society, and, specifically, at his work placement (a nursery unit attached to a local infant school)

▶ the importance of sociological perspectives in understanding society and reducing inequality for different social groups

▶ how useful this information is in planning and improving service provision.

Peter shares his experience below.

How I got started

I collected together my notes on this topic and did some further research for the four parts of the report.

1 The *Black Report* and the *Acheson Report* provided important background information on inequalities affecting health and wellbeing in society and explanations for differences between groups, but I also wanted current statistical data. The ONS website was a good source of recent trends.

2 I used the internet to find information from the National Census and the ONS as well as important information on population held by the local authority. I also interviewed the nursery teacher to see how this information is used to reduce inequality at the nursery.

3 I had good class notes about using sociological perspectives to understand society and explain inequalities, but I used some introductory sociology textbooks for additional information and clarification.

4 Finally, I jotted down my thoughts and ideas for evaluating how useful this range of information is for understanding society and reducing inequalities in health and wellbeing and discussed this with my peers.

How I brought it all together

▶ I began by considering each inequality (eg social class, race and ethnicity, and disability) separately and then considered the issues of prejudice, stereotyping, marginalisation and discrimination.

▶ I wrote about how demographic information, especially changes in the birth rate and statistical information about poverty and deprivation, could help with planning. I interviewed the nursery teacher.

▶ I summarised how the sociological perspectives, particularly the conflict perspective and the social model of health, helped to explain society and the inequalities.

▶ The final section was for recording my thoughts on how useful all this information is. I considered the difficulty of getting accurate up-to-date statistics. I also wrote about whether reducing inequality is a high priority for service providers, such as nurseries, and whether they can reduce the inequalities caused by poverty and poor housing.

What I learned from the experience

I realised how important it was to be organised! I needed to decide on the structure of my report and then organise the material according to the main sections.

I should have structured my interview with the nursery teacher in charge of the nursery unit better by planning the questions beforehand and making sure that they related directly to the information I needed for the assignment. I should also have made more detailed notes.

I under-estimated the time I needed to complete the evaluation section. For my next assignment, I'll allow more time to review the material and arrive at a conclusion for my work that is supported by the evidence.

Think about it

▶ Have you written a plan with timings so you can complete your assignment by the submission date?

▶ Have you ensured that your information is current and reliable? Do you have accurate references for the statistical information you are including?

▶ Is your report written in your own words and referenced clearly when you have quoted from books, magazines, journal articles, reports or websites?

Psychological Perspectives 11

Getting to know your unit

Psychology is a science devoted to the study of the human mind and behaviour. There are different 'schools' of psychology, which have grown up around different ways of understanding the mind and behaviour. These are called perspectives. A perspective is a point of view or a way of considering how certain ideas can be linked together, and their relative importance.

In this unit, you will be introduced to several of these psychological perspectives and encouraged not only to understand them but also to apply them to a work setting. Each has its merits, but no single perspective can explain all behaviour. For example, the biological perspective explains behaviour in terms of brain and bodily functions, such as the influence of brain chemicals and hormones. By contrast, the psychodynamic perspective sees behaviour as originating in early childhood experiences and being motivated by unconscious forces. You will, therefore, be encouraged to think critically about the strengths and weaknesses of each one, and to use more than one perspective to explain different types of behaviour in individuals.

How you will be assessed

This unit will be assessed internally. Your tutor will provide you with assessment tasks that enable you to show your understanding of the topic and meet the assessment criteria. You will prepare for your marked assessments by completing a series of assignments as you progress through the material. These will be similar to the final assessment and will give you the opportunity to practise using the concepts, theories and terminology of the subject matter. They will also involve writing essays or reports that will help you to prepare for the final assessment.

When preparing for your assessment, you should become familiar with the Pass grade criteria. Once you have met these criteria, your work will be judged to see whether it meets the criteria for a Merit or Distinction grade. For this reason, early on in your course, you need to develop the skill of checking and re-checking your understanding of what you need to do in order to meet the criteria for the different grades. Do not be afraid to check your understanding with your tutor, who will be more than willing to help you develop your understanding, and give you advice on how to achieve a higher grade. Activities are provided, throughout the unit, to help you develop the higher-level skills required to achieve Merit and Distinction grades.

The final assessment set by your tutor will consist of a number of tasks designed to meet the criteria in the assessment criteria table.

Assessment criteria

This table shows what you must do in order to achieve a **Pass**, **Merit** or **Distinction** grade, and where you can find activities to help you.

Pass	**Merit**	**Distinction**

Learning aim Examine how psychological perspectives contribute to the understanding of human development and behaviour

A.P1

Explain how psychological perspectives are applied to the understanding of human development.
Assessment practice 11.1

A.M1

Analyse the contribution of psychological perspectives to the understanding of human development and behaviours.
Assessment practice 11.1

AB.D1

Evaluate the role of psychological perspectives in the understanding of human development and the management and treatment of service users' behaviours.
Assessment practice 11.2

A.P2

Explain how psychological perspectives contribute to the understanding of specific human behaviours.
 Assessment practice 11.1

Learning aim Examine the contribution of psychological perspectives to the management and treatment of service users' specific behaviours

B.P3

Explain how different factors influence human development and specific behaviours.
Assessment practice 11.2

B.M2

Analyse the value of identifying factors influencing human development and behaviours in the application of psychological perspectives to the management and treatment of different service users' behaviours.
 Assessment practice 11.2

B.P4

Explain the contribution of psychological perspectives to the management and treatment of different service users' behaviours.
Assessment practice 11.2

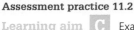 Examine how psychological perspectives are applied in health and social care settings

C.P5

Compare the application of psychological perspectives in local health and social care settings.
Assessment practice 11.3

C.M3

Assess the impact of the use of psychological perspectives in local health and social care settings, in enabling professionals to enhance the social functioning of selected service users.
Assessment practice 11.3

C.D2

Evaluate the importance of the psychological perspectives used in health and social care settings in relation to understanding human development and managing and treating behaviours to enhance the social functioning of service users.
Assessment practice 11.3

C.P6

Explain how professionals use psychological perspectives to improve the social functioning of selected service users.
Assessment practice 11.3

C.D3

Evaluate the application of psychological perspectives in local health and social care settings in enabling professionals to enhance the social functioning of selected service users.
Assessment practice 11.3

Getting started

Ruby, aged three, has a tantrum whenever she is with her father at the supermarket and he refuses to buy her sweets or toys. She does not behave this way with her mother and accepts it when her mother tells her no. In pairs or small groups, discuss why Ruby behaves like this with her father.

A Examine how psychological perspectives contribute to the understanding of human development and behaviour

Principal psychological perspectives as applied to the understanding of development and behaviour

The behaviourist perspective

Perspectives in psychology explain behaviour based on a particular set of beliefs and ideas. The key idea of the behaviourist perspective is that it's possible to understand any type of behaviour by looking at what the person has learned. This will include personality traits such as shyness, confidence, optimism or pessimism, as well as more fleeting behaviours such as offering to help with the washing up.

Behavioural psychologists explain all human behaviour as resulting from experience. Two key thinkers associated with this perspective are Pavlov and Skinner. These theorists believed that different processes were involved but they both explained all types of behaviour as being the result of learning.

Classical conditioning

The first theory of learning you shall investigate is called classical conditioning. This theory was developed by a Russian physiologist called Ivan Pavlov (1849–1936). He experimented with dogs to investigate their digestive systems. The dogs were attached to a harness (see Figure 11.1) and Pavlov attached monitors to their stomachs and mouths so that he could measure the production of saliva. He observed that a dog began to salivate when the laboratory assistant entered the room with a bowl of food, but before it had actually tasted the food. Since salivation is a reflex response (which until then was thought to be produced only as a result of food touching the tongue), this seemed unusual. Pavlov speculated that the dog was salivating because it had learned to associate the laboratory assistant with food.

Since salivation is an automatic (not learned) response, Pavlov called this an **unconditioned response** (UCR). 'Unconditioned' means 'not learned'. As food automatically leads to this response, he called this an **unconditioned stimulus** (UCS). Pavlov then presented food at the same time as ringing a bell (a neutral stimulus), to see if the dog would learn to associate the bell with food. Over several trials, the dog learned that the bell was associated with food and eventually it began to salivate when only the bell was rung and no food was presented. The dog had learned the **conditioned response** (CR) of salivation to the **conditioned stimulus** (CS) of the bell. It has been found that, although humans are more complex than dogs, much behaviour is learned using the principles of classical conditioning.

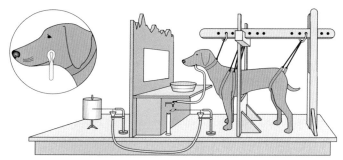

▶ **Figure 11.1:** Classical conditioning: Pavlov's dogs in a harness. How could you apply this type of learning to the development of phobias?

Theory into practice

It has been argued that infants form attachment by associating the caregiver with provision of food. The unconditioned stimulus (UCS) is food, leading to an unconditioned response (UCR) of pleasure (feeling full and comfortable). Over time, the conditioned stimulus (CS) of the caregiver (a neutral object) is associated with the food and the UCR of comfort and satisfaction. Ultimately, the infant associates the caregiver with a pleasant feeling: a conditioned response (CR).

1   Do you think that the principles of classical conditioning 'fit' this explanation?
2   Do you think there might be other factors involved?
3   Are there alternative explanations of how attachments are formed?

Operant conditioning

This type of learning is associated with the theories of Burrhus Frederic Skinner (1904–1990). Skinner was an American psychologist who worked mostly with rats and pigeons, investigating some of the key principles of learning new behaviours. He used a device called a Skinner box (see Figure 11.2). When the animal in the box pressed a lever, a food pellet was released into the box, thus reinforcing lever-pressing behaviour.

When the rat is first placed in the box, it will run around, sniff the various items and, at some point, it will press the lever, releasing a food pellet. After a while, when the rat has repeatedly performed this action, it will learn that pressing the lever (the behaviour) is automatically followed by the release of a food pellet (the consequence). Because the pellet is experienced as **reinforcing** (something the rat would like to have more of), this consequence increases the probability of the behaviour being repeated. There are two types of reinforcement: **positive reinforcement** and **negative reinforcement**.

Key terms

Reinforcing – behaviour that leads to an outcome that is satisfying or desired for whatever reason.

Positive reinforcement – occurs when a particular behaviour is followed by a consequence that is seen as desirable (eg receiving a food pellet).

Negative reinforcement – occurs when a particular behaviour removes something that is unpleasant.

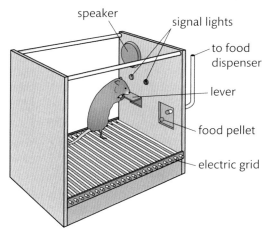

▶ **Figure 11.2:** An example of a Skinner box: the rat presses the lever to release a food pellet

Skinner investigated negative reinforcement by running a very low electrical current on the floor of the Skinner box. The current could be de-activated if the rat pressed the lever. This made the behaviour of lever pressing negatively reinforcing. For humans, this can be demonstrated by the example of using pain relief. For example, if you have a headache and you take a painkiller, which results in the headache going away, you are negatively reinforced for taking a painkiller.

Ⅱ PAUSE POINT

Positive reinforcement can be used to change people's behaviours. For example, children with autism can be reinforced for making eye contact or showing desired behaviours. Do you think this technique will work with other individuals?

    Hint   Think of examples from your work, such as working with people with difficult behaviour. What could you do to positively reinforce them?

    Extend   Research work that has been done with individuals with schizophrenia in hospital to improve their daily functioning.

Social learning

Social learning theory explains behaviour as being the result of learning from people we are exposed to in our environment. We can also learn new behaviours from people we observe, either in real life or in the media. This is known as **observational learning** and this theory was developed by the American psychologist, Albert Bandura (born 1925).

Effects of other individuals

We do not live in a vacuum and there are many influences on our behaviour, including peers, siblings, parents, television, sports personalities and other celebrities. Social learning theory presents role models as being important. We can learn new behaviours from anyone, yet the likelihood of imitating and performing such behaviours is strongly influenced by the way we perceive the person performing the behaviour (the role model).

If we observe someone we admire behaving in a particular way, we are more likely to imitate such behaviour. If, for example, a respected and successful sports personality is shown on television recommending wearing a cycle helmet, we are much more likely to feel motivated to imitate such behaviour ourselves because this will bring us closer to being like this admired role model. On the other hand, if wearing a cycle helmet is associated with a role model we do not respect (for example, someone we regard as a 'geek') then we are much less likely to imitate them. Figure 11.3 illustrates the factors associated with a role model that influence whether we will imitate that individual. In this case, it focuses on the behaviour of deciding whether or not to smoke.

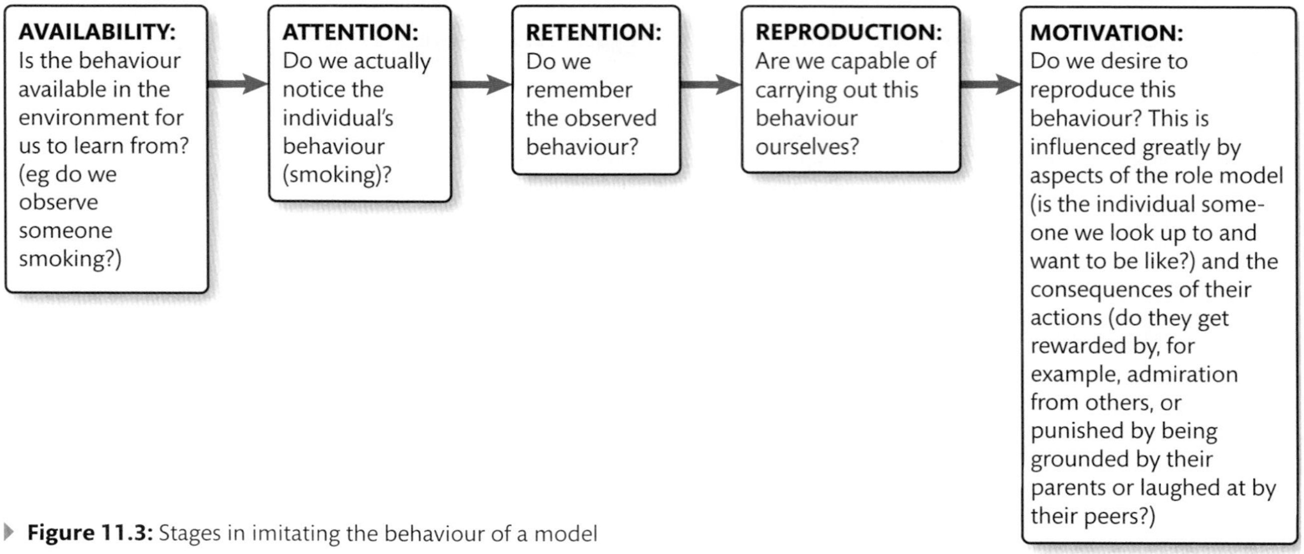

> **Key term**
>
> **Observational learning** – a type of learning in which an individual observes someone behave in a particular way and then later imitates that behaviour.

AVAILABILITY: Is the behaviour available in the environment for us to learn from? (eg do we observe someone smoking?) → **ATTENTION:** Do we actually notice the individual's behaviour (smoking)? → **RETENTION:** Do we remember the observed behaviour? → **REPRODUCTION:** Are we capable of carrying out this behaviour ourselves? → **MOTIVATION:** Do we desire to reproduce this behaviour? This is influenced greatly by aspects of the role model (is the individual someone we look up to and want to be like?) and the consequences of their actions (do they get rewarded by, for example, admiration from others, or punished by being grounded by their parents or laughed at by their peers?)

▶ **Figure 11.3:** Stages in imitating the behaviour of a model

If all these stages are achieved, and we want to be like the model, we are likely to perform the behaviour we have learned from observing them. This can equally apply to behaviour such as being aggressive towards others or to behaving like a saint and giving all our money to charity. A great deal depends on the motivation stage of the process, which is why parents are so concerned about the influence of 'negative' role models who may influence their children to behave in undesirable ways.

The effects of culture and society on the behaviour of individuals

Culture refers to the shared values, norms, language, customs and practices of a group. Although we tend to think of culture as being specific to different countries, it also refers to different subgroups within society. For example, people from different socio-economic groups within the UK will share different aspects of culture, such as the value placed on eating at a table rather than on your lap in front of the television, the way in which money is spent, how to talk to your elders, and so on. It is important to understand how culture affects our behaviour in order to gain a full understanding of the people we encounter and those we work with. Different cultures, for example, have different rules and customs as to the amount of eye contact considered acceptable.

The extent to which we value individualism is also heavily dependent on culture. Generally speaking, in Europe and the USA, self-reliance, assertiveness and individualism are highly-valued traits, and parents see it as part of their duty to enable children to grow up with these characteristics. In contrast, many Asian cultures emphasise collectivism, and children are socialised to put the needs of the group before their own needs. For example, a 40-year-old American male, living at home with his parents, would perhaps be looked down on for not living independently, whereas, in parts of Africa, India and China this would be seen as normal, admirable behaviour and as showing respect for parents.

Role theory

Bandura was an important psychologist in the study of learning (behaviourism) who drew attention to the fact that we are influenced by, and can learn from role models, such as celebrities (see the example of Angelina Jolie Pitt). It appears that, when we admire an individual, we are likely to be influenced by, and try to imitate, their behaviour. Role theory suggests that, because we live within a particular culture, society and social group, we are influenced by other people. This influence leads us to adopt certain roles and try to live up to the expectations that go with these roles. For example, a nurse is expected to be level-headed, empathetic and competent. You might expect a surgeon to be similarly level-headed and competent, but you would not necessarily expect them to be particularly empathetic. Since we all take on many different roles, our behaviour will change according to the role we are currently in. A woman visiting the zoo with her children will take on the role of a mother, whereas, when she goes to work, she may be a colleague, a supervisor or a subordinate, and she will adopt the expectations and behaviour associated with her job role. Later, if she goes out to a party she may adopt the role of a friend.

The self-fulfilling prophecy

The self-fulfilling prophecy is an important concept in psychology that has a big impact on the way we behave towards others and expect them to behave towards us. If we believe ourselves to be worthwhile, pleasant and likeable, then we will almost certainly be polite and cheerful towards those we meet, and thus create a favourable impression. In response, those who come into contact with us perceive us favourably and behave in a positive way towards us, with the result that our positive self-beliefs are confirmed. If, on the other hand, we are angry, full of resentment, and believe the world is against us, then we are likely to behave in a more aggressive, confrontational or argumentative

Discussion

Do you always join the back of queue and wait until you reach the front? Is your language and speech more formal with people in authority than with friends and family? Think of how your upbringing has influenced your behaviour and how much is based on learning. In small groups, discuss your experiences. What are the similarities and differences?

way. In this situation, that is also how we will be responded to, which will confirm our views of ourselves and the world. An example of this is illustrated in Figure 11.4, below.

▶ **Figure 11.4:** The self-fulfilling prophecy. Can you think of examples from your own experience where the self-fulfilling prophecy can explain behaviour and development?

Case study

The self-fulfilling prophecy

Sanjay is a newly qualified nursery nurse. He has just been offered a job in a nursery that has received a Grade 1 from Ofsted. In a meeting about the new intake of children, one of Sanjay's colleagues, Sandra, says: 'You'll have to watch out for Leo – his brother Callum was a real trouble-maker'.

Check your knowledge

1 What sort of expectations do you think Sanjay will have of Leo?
2 Do you think Sandra's negative attitude to Leo may affects his wellbeing, and, if so, how?
3 Do you think it is possible to break the self-fulfilling prophecy?
4 How might you challenge such assumptions about people in your work experience-setting in health and social care so that you see them as individuals rather than 'types of people'?

The psychodynamic perspective

The psychodynamic perspective is associated with the Austrian psychologist Sigmund Freud (1856–1939), who developed the theory of psychodynamic psychology and the treatment known as psychoanalysis. A key follower of Freud was Erik Erikson (1902-1994), who adapted aspects of Freud's approach.

The unconscious mind

Freud was one of the earliest thinkers to bring to public attention the idea that we are not always aware of all aspects of ourselves. He suggested that what we are aware of is represented in our conscious mind but that many of our memories, feelings and past experiences are locked up in a part of our mind he called the **unconscious**.

The contents of our unconscious often 'leak out' in dreams and slips of the tongue. Freud believed that the conscious mind was like the tip of an iceberg – only the small part of the mind that is available to awareness. The part of the unconscious that we can access easily, he called the pre-conscious.

This contains information, not yet in consciousness, but which can be easily retrieved (for example, the name of Aunt Edie's cat). The rest, which is well under the surface, consists of the unconscious.

Key term

Unconscious – processes in the mind that occur automatically, including thought processes, memory and motivation.

⏸ PAUSE POINT A mother, who was unhappy about her daughter's marriage, kept referring to her daughter by her maiden name. What do you think caused the mother to 'forget' that her daughter had taken on her son-in-law's name?

> **Hint** Remember that Freud believed that many of our negative feelings are pushed into the unconscious mind so that we are not aware of them.

> **Extend** Have you made any similar slips of the tongue or noticed anyone else doing so?

The importance of early experiences

The importance of early experience in determining later behaviours is clearly illustrated by Freud's developmental theory of psychosexual stages. He believed that we all go through several stages of psychosexual development. At each stage, the individual's libido (energy) is focused on a part of the body that is particularly relevant at that stage. If the needs of the developing child are met at each stage, it moves on to the next developmental stage. If, however, there is struggle or conflict or some unsatisfactory experience, the individual becomes 'fixated' (stuck) at this stage. This results in certain ways of being, or personality traits, being carried through into adulthood that can explain behaviour later in life.

A second important feature of early experience is the development of **ego** defence mechanisms (see Table 11.1). The use of a defence mechanism allows us to block out from consciousness any events that threaten to overwhelm us. However, the material that has been pushed into the unconscious mind may emerge as unusual behaviour, caused by ego defence mechanisms.

> **Research**
>
> Research Freud's work on psychosexual stages. Make brief notes on the outcomes for development and behaviour in later life which result from fixation at any given stage.

> **Key term**
>
> **Ego** – the part of the mind that develops at around the age of two. Its function is to moderate the demands of the id and prevent the superego being too harsh. It operates on the reality principle.

▷ **Table 11.1:** Examples of ego defence mechanisms

Defence mechanism	Explanation	Example
Repression	The person pushes the event into the unconscious so it seems they have forgotten it.	Forgetting a traumatic event in childhood (eg a car crash in which your sibling dies).
Regression	Reverting to an earlier stage of behaviour.	Wetting the bed when a sibling is born, having previously been dry through the nights.
Denial	Pushing awareness of an event or emotion out of conscious awareness.	Denying that a loved one has died (eg continuing to set a place at the table for someone who has recently died).
Displacement	Redirecting unwanted desires onto a safe object.	Kicking the cat at home because your boss gave you a hard time at work.
Reaction formation	Taking the opposite view to that which you secretly desire.	Showing strong homophobic behaviour and beliefs because you secretly believe yourself to be gay.

A final influence on behaviour is that of the mind. Freud suggested that the mind (which he called the **psyche**) is divided into three dynamic parts. The **id** is a part of the mind which is totally unconscious, and which exists at birth. It is focused on getting what it wants and consists of aggressive, sexual, love and death instincts. It is the part of us that says 'I want it now!' The **superego** is formed as a result of socialisation and consists of all the instructions, morals and values that are repeatedly enforced as we are growing up. It takes on the form of a conscience, and also represents our view of our ideal self. The main role of the superego is to try to subdue the activity of the id. The ego tries to balance the demands of the id and the superego. It is the rational part of the mind, always seeking to do what is most helpful for the individual. Different behaviours can be understood by trying to infer which part of the psyche is dominant at any time.

> **Key terms**
>
> **Psyche** – the structure of the mind, consisting of three dynamic parts: the id, the ego and the superego.
>
> **id** – the part of the psyche we are born with. It operates on the pleasure principle.

Discussion

Elderly people often revert to childlike behaviour in which they can become quarrelsome, difficult, or even soil themselves; they might also show tantrum-like behaviours. Their relatives are often surprised and confused by such behaviour coming from someone who might previously have been very restrained and in control. Can you explain this behaviour using the concepts of the id, ego and superego?

The humanistic perspective

Humanistic psychology looks at human experience from the viewpoint of the individual. It focuses on the idea of free will and the belief that we are all capable of making choices. Two psychologists associated with this approach are Abraham Maslow and Carl Rogers.

Abraham Maslow

Maslow (1908–1970) was an American psychologist who believed that we are all seeking to become the best that we can possibly be – spiritually, physically, emotionally and intellectually. He called this **self-actualisation**. Maslow believed that we are born with a desire to become the best we can possibly be, but that we have to pass through other stages before we reach this height of existence.

Maslow constructed a theory known as the **hierarchy of needs**, in which he explained that every human being requires certain basic needs to be met before they can approach the next level. This hierarchy of needs is shown in Figure 11.5.

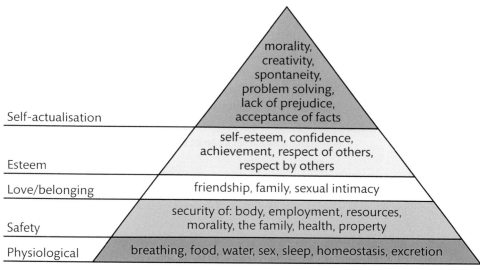

▶ **Figure 11.5:** Maslow's hierarchy of needs. Where do you think the people you work with have reached on this hierarchy?

Maslow believed that, until our basic physiological needs are met, we will focus all our energies on getting them met and are not be able to progress further until this has happened. When we are well-housed, well-fed and comfortable physically, we begin to focus on our emotional needs, such as the need to belong and be loved and to feel **self-esteem**. When our lives are such that these needs are also met, we then strive to self-actualise. The state of self-actualisation might be seen in people who reach the ultimate goals of which they are capable.

Amina – an asylum seeker

Amina is a 16-year-old refugee from Syria. She arrived in the UK, having been given a place on a lorry after both her parents and her two older brothers were killed. When she reached the UK, she applied for asylum. She was housed in temporary accommodation for the first 18 months, and was then granted leave to remain and given a bedsit. She is being supervised by a multi-disciplinary team, including Helen, an outreach worker. Helen is due to visit Amina to assess her needs, and to suggest an educational route that could enable Amina to gain qualifications, so that she can eventually support herself. Helen's supervisor advises Helen to familiarise herself with Maslow's hierarchy of needs before she meets Amina for the first time.

Check your knowledge

1 At what stage of Maslow's hierarchy of needs was Amina when she first arrived in England?

2 What needs may be satisfied if she enters education?

3 Suggest some questions that Helen might ask in order to find out whether or not Amina is ready yet to benefit from further education.

PAUSE POINT

How valuable do you think the hierarchy of needs is in understanding the needs of people you live and work with? Suggest strengths and limitations as you reach your conclusion.

Hint Do you agree that we need to have our physiological needs met before we can begin to think about other needs such as self-esteem, love and belonging?

Extend Imagine that an elderly person you care for used to play jazz piano or paint amazing pictures. Their basic needs have been met; what could you do to promote their self-actualisation?

Carl Rogers

Carl Rogers (1902–1987), a researcher and practitioner in counselling and founder of the concept of person-centred therapy, was particularly interested in the concept of self (see Table 11.2).

▶ **Table 11.2:** Self-concept, self-esteem and incongruence

Concept	Explanation
Self-concept	Self-concept refers to the way we view ourselves. This includes physical and biological attributes such as being male or female, blonde or brunette, tall or short, as well as personality traits such as being kind, humble, assertive or hard-working. The self-concept is formed from an early age and young children internalise other people's judgements of them, which then become part of their self-concept.
	If a child is told they are silly, naughty and will come to no good, part of their self-concept will contain these aspects. If, on the other hand, a child is praised, encouraged to succeed and told they are valued, they will have a positive self-concept, and see themselves as someone who is worthwhile and competent.
	It is worth noting that very young children have no ability to make judgements about the things other people tell them. For example, a five-year-old child will accept being told they are stupid, a waste of space and unwanted just as unquestioningly as they accept being told that a tomato is red, round and can be eaten. So a negative self-concept can be learned from the things people tell us about ourselves.
Self-esteem	Self-esteem refers to how we assign a value to ourselves. It is linked to self-concept but relates more to what we believe we are worth. Children who are loved, treated tenderly and with respect, given positive feedback, love and affection are likely to consider themselves worthwhile, worthy of love and attention and to have a warm glow of self-acceptance. They will approach others with a happy, sunny nature, expecting others to behave towards them in a way that confirms their sense of themselves as worthwhile.
	By contrast, children who have low self-esteem will believe themselves to be unworthy and unlovable. They may be surly and aggressive or shy and withdrawn. They will expect others to treat them in a negative way and will not be surprised if or when they do so.
Incongruence	Rogers believed that we also hold a concept of 'self' called the ideal self. This represents a view of ourselves as we feel we should be and as we would like to be. When there is incongruence (a mismatch) between our actual self and our ideal self we become troubled and unhappy.

The cognitive perspective

This psychological perspective has gained enormous ground since the 1960s, when the influence of behaviourism began to wane. With the development of computers, came the idea that the brain is like the operation of a computer. A huge body of research has gone into understanding cognitive processes such as attention, memory, information processing, problem solving, thought, language, perception and other aspects of cognition. For the purposes of understanding this perspective as it relates to health and social care, however, you shall concentrate on the research of the Swiss psychologist Jean Piaget, who contributed a huge amount to our understanding of cognitive development in young children.

Jean Piaget

Jean Piaget (1896–1980) was a Swiss psychologist who initially worked on measuring intelligence. During his research he noticed that children of the same age made the same mistakes in logic, however intelligent they were. He came to the conclusion that cognition develops through a series of stages, each new stage building on the previous one. The stages and key associated features are described in Table 11.3.

Key term

Egocentric – centred on oneself, selfish.

Link

Piaget's developmental stages and growth of cognitive maturity (conservation) links to *Unit 1: Human Lifespan Development* and *Unit 18: Assessing Children's Development Support Needs*.

Key term

Conservation – the ability to reason logically that a certain quantity will remain the same despite change in its shape or appearance. For example, recognising that as clay is rolled in a sausage shape, it may become longer, but the amount of clay doesn't become larger.

▶ **Table 11.3** Developmental stages described by Jean Piaget

Stage	Age	Key features
Stage 1: Sensorimotor	0–2 years	The world is experienced through motor activity and the senses.
Stage 2: Preoperational	2–7 years	Language develops along with memory. The child is **egocentric** and unable to **conserve**.
Stage 3: Concrete operational	7–11 years	The child can now understand conservation but cannot yet solve problems mentally. For example, they may be able to solve a maths problem by physically adding buttons to other buttons and then counting all the buttons, but they won't be able to add large numbers in their minds without being able to see the concrete objects.
Stage 4: Formal operational	11+	The child/teenager can now use abstract thoughts and represent problems mentally.

Biological perspective

This perspective is concerned with how our biology affects us, such as genes, and the biological environmental influences to which we are exposed (for example, pathogens or influences on the developing foetus).

Maturational theory

The theory of maturation holds that the effects of the environment are minimal. It asserts that the child is born with a set of genetic instructions passed down from its parents and its cognitive, physical and other developmental processes merely unfold over time, rather than being dependent on the environment to mature. It is, in effect, a theory stating that development is due to nature not nurture. This is quite a contrast to the theories where the effects of nurture are considered paramount.

Gesell's theory of maturation

Arnold Gesell (1880–1961) believed that development occurred according to a sequence of **maturational processes.** For example, development in the womb follows a fixed set of stages. The heart begins to form first, along with a rudimentary nervous system. Bones and muscles develop next and, over time, the organism develops into a fully-functioning human being, ready to be born. As the child develops from birth onwards, its genes allow it to develop gradually into the person they are meant to be. The environment should provide support for this unfolding of talents, skills, personality and interests but the main thing driving this development is the maturational process.

> **Key term**
>
> **Maturational processes**
> – a series of developmental changes that occur over time as the organism matures and develops.

Genetic influences on behaviour

Genes can affect behaviour in many ways. Some disorders, such as Huntington's disease, are caused by a single dominant gene, which either parent can pass on to their child. Others, such as cystic fibrosis and sickle cell anaemia, are caused when both parents pass on the gene for the disorder. Certain mental disorders such as schizophrenia, depression, anxiety and phobias have a genetic link. For example, if one of a pair of monozygotic (identical) twins has schizophrenia, there is a 48 per cent chance that the other twin will also develop this disorder (Cardno and Gottesman, 2000). Because the rate of similarity is not 100 per cent, there are clearly environmental factors playing a part, so we tend to talk about individuals having a predisposition to developing a disorder. This will only emerge if the environment is unfavourable.

> **Research**
>
> Investigate the genetic link for one of the following disorders: anxiety, depression or phobia.

The influence of the nervous and endocrine systems on behaviour

The **autonomic nervous system** (ANS) produces its effects through activation of nerve fibres throughout the nervous system, brain and body or by stimulating the release of hormones from glands in the **endocrine system** (such as the adrenal and pineal glands). Hormones are biochemical substances released into the bloodstream that have a profound effect on target organs, and on behaviour. They are present in very small quantities, and individual molecules have a very short life, so their effects quickly disappear if they are not secreted continuously. One good way to investigate the influence of these two systems on behaviour is to look at the stress response (**the fight or flight response**), which activates both the autonomic nervous system and the endocrine system.

> **Key terms**
>
> **Autonomic nervous system** – a division of the nervous system consisting of the sympathetic and parasympathetic branches. Many of its functions occur without conscious awareness.
>
> **Fight or flight response** – a sequence of physiological responses triggered by the perception of danger. These responses prepare the body for either running away from danger (flight) or for defending or attacking the threat (fight).
>
> **Endocrine system** – a collection of glands that produce hormones that regulate body functions such as metabolism.

Link

For more information on the nervous system, see *Unit 3: Anatomy and Physiology for Health and Social Care*.

When someone encounters an event that is threatening in some way, a part of the brain called the hypothalamus sets off activity in the sympathetic branch of the autonomic nervous system and the endocrine system. Figure 11.6 illustrates this activity.

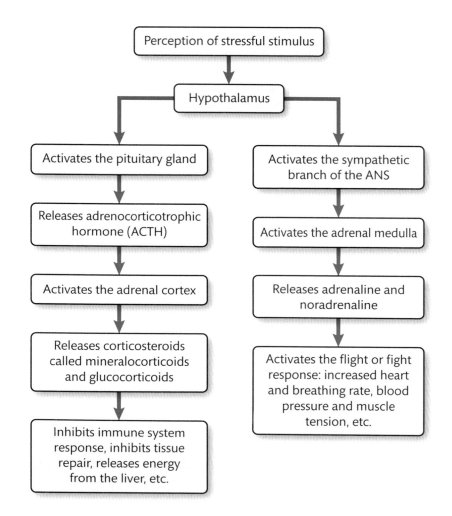

▶ **Figure 11.6:** You may encounter the fight or flight response when working with individuals experiencing the stress response

Theories of human development

In attempting to understand human development, there are a number of approaches that can be taken. Whichever is chosen will often guide research and discussion.

Nature versus nurture

Key terms

Nature – all aspects of a person that are inherited or coded for in their genes.
Nurture – influences from the environment that shape behaviour and development.

This debate centres on the extent to which our personality, development, intelligence and behaviour are genetically inherited (**nature**) or acquired as a result of interaction with the environment (**nurture**). Behavioural psychologists take the view that we are born as 'blank slates' and that our behaviour and personality develop as a result of interactions with the environment (nurture). Biological psychologists believe that many of the influences on our development come from our genes and the influence of biochemistry on our behaviour (nature). Others believe that there is an interaction between the two factors.

▶ **Nature**. This account of development, personality and behaviours focuses on what is innate (what we are born with) such as left-handedness, the genes we have inherited and so on. Issues such as temperament (eg shy and withdrawn or outgoing and confident), intelligence and susceptibility to developing certain illnesses or diseases bring the nature versus nurture debate into focus. There are arguments in favour of the nature perspective that state that someone's inheritance has a very large influence on who they become.

▶ **Nurture**. This refers to everything that happens within the environment (even in the womb) that influences the growing child. It involves the way someone is brought up (socialisation) and the way they are treated by important others such as parents, teachers and peers. All of this influences behaviour and development and goes towards building a personality.

One way of illustrating the nature versus nurture debate is by looking at intelligence. If intelligence is an inborn quality that merely develops, then the influences of the environment should have no effect. This seems unlikely, though, since children exposed to enriching environments seem to do better than those who have less fortunate educational and cultural opportunities.

A second example is the development of gender. While sex refers to the biological characteristics of being male or female, gender is the word used to describe behaviours, beliefs, expectations and attitudes commonly associated with the two genders. A boy might be born with a tendency to be more boisterous than a girl, but if he is brought up in an environment where quietness and restraint are valued and encouraged, these boisterous tendencies may reduce over time.

Continuity versus discontinuity

This debate is about whether development is a smooth process with no distinct changes taking place (**continuity**) or a discontinuous process in which development takes place in stages (**discontinuity**).

▶ **Continuity**. This account of development looks at quantitative rather than qualitative change. Change involves smooth growth, for example, skull size grows, the number of words in a child's vocabulary increases. The analogy of a sponge is sometimes used to explain this, where growth simply drips in just as water soaks into a sponge (which gets heavier and more laden with water but does not change shape).

▶ **Discontinuity**. This explanation of development refers to definite changes in the individual's development. Stage theories are a good example of this type of explanation. For example, Piaget talks about the change from the pre-operational stage to the concrete operational stage.

> **Reflect**
>
> Think about your characteristics and consider whether they are due to nature or nurture. If you choose nurture, what theory of development best explains this? If a combination of the two, how much do you think nature has contributed to your development and behaviour?

> **Key terms**
>
> **Continuity** – a view of development that sees growth and development occurring slowly and continuously, for example growth in height.
>
> **Discontinuity** – this characterisation of development sees the differences between stages as qualitative rather than quantitative. Stages theories, such as those proposed by Freud, Piaget and Erikson, are examples of discontinuity.
>
> **Nomothetic** – this approach is concerned with investigating a group of individuals to see what traits and behaviours they have in common.
>
> **Idiographic** – this approach to development involves the study of all the unique characteristics of one particular individual.

Nomothetic versus idiographic

▶ **Nomothetic**, as applied to psychology, is concerned with the study of features that are common to a group or class of individuals, such as all children aged eight, or all adults who suffer from obsessive compulsive disorder. The cognitive psychologists (for example, Piaget) researched into why all children made similar errors in logic, problem solving and reasoning at a certain age.

▶ **Idiographic** refers to the study of an individual and those unique characteristics that distinguish them from others. Case studies in psychology take an idiographic approach as they are concerned with finding out why a particular individual developed in the way they did.

Application of psychological perspectives to health and social care practice

Behaviourist

Understanding challenging behaviour

The behaviourist perspective is extremely useful in explaining challenging behaviour. It helps you to look at a particular behaviour and trace its origin, using the concepts of association (classical conditioning), reinforcement or punishment (operant conditioning), or modelling (social learning theory). Although a number of different perspectives can be effective in treating behaviour that has been learned, we shall examine, first, how the behaviourist perspective seeks to manage challenging or **maladaptive behaviour**, such as agoraphobia (fear of going out) or uncontrollable anger.

> **Key term**
>
> **Maladaptive behaviour**
> – refers to behaviour that is unhelpful to the individual, getting them into unpleasant situations. For example, being naughty may result in punishment; drinking too much to soothe anxiety can result in financial hardship and even loss of employment or damage to relationships.

> **Case study**
>
> ### Understanding challenging behaviour
>
> Farai is 13 years old. She was recently admitted to a local authority children's home after her foster placement broke down. She has very intense rages, during which she smashes windows and shouts at people. It turns out that Farai used to behave in exactly this way at her foster home and that everyone ran around trying to please her to prevent her having these outbursts.
>
> **Check your knowledge**
>
> 1 Explain, using the terminology of learning theory, how and why Farai may have learned these undesirable behaviours.
>
> 2 Do you think that an explanation that relies entirely on learning is sufficient to explain Farai's behaviour?

Changing behaviour

The basic idea when explaining behaviour using the principles of operant or classical conditioning is that, because maladaptive or challenging behaviour has been learned, it can also be unlearned. The same principles of learning are used when teaching individuals how to change their behaviour. This is sometimes called reconditioning, behaviour modification or behaviour shaping.

For some people, there may be aspects of everyday life that are simply impossible to cope with. A small boy, for example, may be unable to go to the park because he has an overwhelming fear of dogs, which he is likely to encounter in or around the park. An elderly woman may never leave her home because her agoraphobia is so severe that it dominates her life. Fortunately, as well as explaining the development of phobic behaviour, classical conditioning is also useful in changing behaviours.

We can apply the principles of classical conditioning to everyday life in a very practical way. A commonly used method of changing phobic behaviour and treating acquired fears is known as **systematic desensitisation**. It involves first creating a 'hierarchy of fear'. Supposing the feared object is hospitals. The individual would create a list of aspects associated with going to hospital; see, for example, Figure 11.7.

Highest anxiety level — Having an actual procedure (eg chemotherapy)

Settling on the hospital bed

Entering the ward

Going up to the ward in a lift

Entering the hospital

Driving to the hospital

Getting ready to go to the hospital

Lowest anxiety level — Receiving an appointment card

▶ **Figure 11.7:** Hierarchy of fears. The patient begins at the bottom and works their way up. Finally they are able to face the feared object with no signs of anxiety. Do you think this will work? What factors might hinder this process?

The principle of this procedure is to help the person achieve a state of very deep relaxation – on the assumption that relaxation and anxiety are incompatible. The aim is to replace the anxiety and fear with a state of calm and relaxation. An image of the least-feared object or situation is then shown to the individual and they are encouraged to relax until they are able to view this without fear or anxiety. This may take more than one session. When this level of fear has been satisfactorily overcome, the person moves to the object or situation at the next level, again working on relaxing until they are able to contemplate the object or situation without a trace of anxiety. Over a period of time the procedure is repeated until the final, most-feared object or situation can be faced without worry.

With some treatments, the patient is encouraged to practise some of the lower level fear-inducing situations. For example, opening an envelope containing an appointment card or driving as close to the hospital as is possible without arousing too much anxiety. The principles of classical conditioning are also used in a common treatment for alcoholism. Individuals are given a drug which, when mixed with alcohol, leads to extremely unpleasant physiological effects, including nausea and vomiting. The person thus learns to associate alcohol with an unpleasant rather than desired response.

Shaping behaviours

Just as we can learn inappropriate or unhelpful behaviours, so we can use the principles of operant conditioning to create new, more helpful, behaviours and eliminate the unhelpful ones. Using the principles of reinforcement and punishment is a very powerful way to change someone's behaviour: this is sometimes called **behaviour modification**.

This technique has been used with autistic children to help them interact socially. **Target behaviours**, such as making eye contact, are identified. The child is initially reinforced (for example, with a sweet) for looking in the general area of the adult. Once this behaviour is established, more specific behaviours (such as looking at the face) are reinforced, until finally the target behaviour of making eye contact is achieved. This is known as shaping behaviour.

Key term

Systematic desensitisation – a technique in which an individual is trained, over time, to substitute a fear response with a relaxed response. It is often used to 'unlearn' phobic behaviours.

Key terms

Behaviour modification – this is a method of changing behaviour that involves reinforcing desired behaviour and ignoring or punishing undesired behaviour.

Target behaviour – this is the behaviour we want to change.

Reflect

When you are in a relationship with someone (such as a parent, a sibling, or another relationship) do you sometimes find yourself wanting to change aspects of their behaviour? Use behaviourism principles to explain why this is. Do these principles seem adequate?

Social learning

Promotion of anti-discrimination behaviours and practices

In the social learning section, you looked at the way people can learn new behaviours by observing others. You learned that the model's characteristics influence whether someone is likely to imitate their behaviour. An example of a well-known, respected and popular model is the author and actor, Stephen Fry. When he publicly acknowledged that he suffers from bipolar disorder and has attempted suicide, some would argue that it made a difference to public perceptions of mental illness.

Use of positive role models in health education campaigns

Companies use high-profile figures (role models) to endorse and sell their products. Charities and health campaigns use a similar tactic. The actress Angelina Jolie Pitt spoke very publicly about her battle with breast cancer and her decision to have a double mastectomy. She wanted to increase awareness of the risks of breast cancer for those with a family history of the disease. She wrote a series of articles for the *New York Times*, entitled 'Diary of a Surgery' in which she described the experience and processes she went through. Jolie Pitt used the huge media spotlight that was focused on her to raise awareness of breast cancer, and to connect with and empower other women who had been through a similar experience.

Link

This links to *Unit 8: Promoting Public Health* and to *Unit 26: Health Psychology*.

Psychodynamic

Understanding challenging behaviour

To understand challenging behaviour using the psychodynamic perspective, you need to examine the structures of the psyche. If a hospital patient is being difficult (for example, aggressive, hostile, and angrily resisting all attempts to calm them) you could look at the balance of the id, ego and superego. The id is the part of the mind that works on instinct. For example, if you are feeling angry, your id would want you to hit out. The ego and superego are parts of the mind that try to control the behaviour of the id and help restrain negative behaviour. When someone is being difficult, hostile or angry this could be understood as the id not being controlled effectively by the ego and the superego.

Understanding and managing anxiety

To understand anxiety, the psychodynamic perspective would suggest that the superego is very strong and controlling. The individual's ego ideal may consist of a number of requirements that are so close to perfection that they are hard to achieve (for example, 'I must always be patient and calm, no matter how much my daughter has tantrums' or 'if I don't cook a perfect meal my family will love me less'). The methods used to manage anxiety from the psychodynamic perspective involve a treatment known as psychoanalysis. Using this treatment, the analyst would work with the patient to uncover the root of each type of anxiety through a variety of methods, for example dream analysis or free association. The purpose of this is to uncover material that has been buried in the unconscious mind. Once the root of the problem is uncovered (for example, my mother always told me I had to cook perfectly or I would never keep a husband), the patient achieves a state called catharsis, where the symptom (the anxiety) simply melts away and no longer causes problems.

Select and research one of Freud's case studies. Do you agree with his explanations of his patients' symptoms? Famous cases include Anna O, Dora, and the Wolf Man (Sergei Pankejeff).

Humanistic

The importance of empathy and respecting other individuals

One crucial feature of this approach to helping others is to develop empathy. Unlike sympathy, where you feel sorry for someone, empathy requires you to really listen to the other person, to be in tune with their emotions and to respect them for who they are. This is not always easy, as you may not always understand why someone feels so bad about an issue that may feel unimportant or trivial to you. However, if you try to respect the individual you are working with, and understand that the issue is of crucial importance to them, you can come closer to demonstrating empathy. True empathy requires you to put aside judgements about another person and do all you can to 'put yourself in their shoes'.

Case study

Learning empathy

You work with a service user who is terrified that if she does not touch the door handle 25 times every time she closes the door, it will cause her children to suffer some life-threatening event. She also believes that she needs to clean the surface of objects repeatedly in order to remove the germs, which could also cause her children to fall ill. You may know that statistically and logically neither of these beliefs is true and that the service user is thinking irrationally.

Check your knowledge

Conduct a short questionnaire with friends and family, asking them to tell you about things that they fear. These things may seem trivial to you, such as fear of fireworks, or being alone in the house. Ask them how they feel when they experience these situations and what they do to try to manage their fear.

Active listening

Another key feature of the humanistic approach is that of active listening. All too often when interacting with others, what we think of as a conversation is merely two or more people 'queuing up to talk'. One person is just waiting for the other to finish what they are saying before having their own say. This is the opposite of active listening, which involves a very focused approach. You need to avoid daydreaming and distractions and listen sensitively to the meaning and emotions behind the other person's words. Attention must also be paid to the person's body language and facial expressions. The active listener suspends all judgement about what is being said and seeks to use empathic understanding. When the listener does intervene, it is not to pass judgement but to interpret what the other person is saying, or to check understanding.

Cognitive

Supporting individuals with learning difficulties

Individuals with learning difficulties can experience enormous frustration in their daily lives as they seek to make sense of what can be bewildering experiences. The cognitive approach can be used to help people who misread situations. By identifying irrational thoughts, an individual can be guided to change them, with consequent benefits for their emotions and behaviour. Cognitive work of this type can improve self-esteem and reduce outbursts that may be triggered by not understanding the requirements of a given situation (for example, having to wait in turn for a meal). Individuals are encouraged to try out new behaviours which, in turn, lead to more positive responses that can then be reinforced by other service users and staff members.

Supporting individuals with emotional problems

The cognitive perspective is widely used with individuals with a variety of emotional problems. This perspective begins by examining how distorted and irrational negative thoughts influence feelings, which then leads to changes in behaviour.

> **Theory into practice**
>
> Keep a diary of your thoughts for a week and identify whether you have any thoughts that might be considered negative or irrational. For example, you might think 'I did badly on that assignment – I'm going to fail the course', or 'that driver sounded his horn – I must have done something to annoy him'. At the end of the week, look back at your diary and consider how many of these negative thoughts you have had, and how they might have affected your mood.

Depression

The psychologist Aaron Beck (born 1921) has formulated an approach to understanding depression, known initially as cognitive therapy but later reformulated as **cognitive behavioural therapy (CBT)**. The pattern of behaviour common to those suffering from depression is described by Beck as a cognitive triad. To begin with, the individual thinks they are worthless and inadequate. This self-appraisal then leads to the belief that this lack of worth means that the future will be just as bad as the present. This then generalises to a conviction that the world contains problems and difficulties that the individual is powerless to overcome. The goal of cognitive therapy is to challenge these negative thoughts and to encourage the individual to develop alternative, more positive, ways of seeing the world.

Identifying negative/irrational/distorted thinking

Negative, irrational or distorted thinking can be identified by keeping a diary and recording every instance of negative thinking and the feelings that follow. Initially this can be difficult, as these patterns are so automatic that it can be difficult to notice them. However, it will get easier over time. For each example, try to challenge the thinking. Ask yourself these questions.

▸ What is the evidence for such negative thinking?
▸ Are there alternative explanations? It can be helpful to think (or ask) how others would respond.
▸ How does it affect me to think so negatively? (This helps you develop self-awareness.)
▸ What type of thinking errors am I making (for example, magnifying or catastrophising)?

> **Research**
>
> Investigate the following: cognitive errors of selective abstraction; catastrophising; magnification and minimisation; black and white thinking; and over-generalisation. Can you apply these to yourself, a friend or relative, or someone you work with?
>
> Find out how cognitive behavioural therapy works in practice (you could look at leaflets produced by Talking Therapies, or look on their website).

> **Key term**
>
> **Cognitive behavioural therapy (CBT)** – a method used to help people with psychological problems. It involves identifying and challenging negative thoughts. The behavioural aspect involves trying out new behaviours to see whether the outcome can lead to new, more positive thoughts.

Post-traumatic stress disorder (PTSD)

PTSD consists of a set of symptoms outlined in Table 11.4. It is commonly recognised as being experienced by firefighters and members of the armed services, but is also experienced by others who have undergone a traumatic experience (such as rape or a physical assault).

▶ **Table 11.4:** Symptoms of post-traumatic stress disorder

Main symptom	Example
Re-experiencing the traumatic event (intrusion)	<ul><li>Nightmares</li><li>Flashbacks</li><li>Frequent recall of the event</li><li>Intense emotional upset produced by stimuli that symbolise the event (eg a car backfiring may symbolise a gunshot)</li></ul>
Avoidance of stimuli associated with the event (or numbing of responsiveness)	<ul><li>The person tries to avoid thinking about the trauma or encountering stimuli that will bring it to mind</li><li>The person may be unable to remember the event</li><li>There may be decreased interest in, and interaction with, others</li><li>There may be a sense of estrangement</li><li>There may be an inability to feel positive emotions</li></ul>
Increased arousal	<ul><li>Difficulties in falling or staying asleep</li><li>Difficulties concentrating</li><li>Hypervigilance</li><li>An exaggerated startle response</li></ul>

Research

Investigate the incidence of PTSD among paramedics and traffic police.

The treatment of PTSD usually involves a healthcare practitioner (such as a psychiatrist, psychiatric social worker or clinical psychologist) working with an individual to help them reframe their thoughts. The aim is that the individual comes to recognise that the feared events have actually happened and are not recurring, so that eventually constant mulling over these traumas will disappear. There also needs to be some treatment involving behavioural therapy; this might be accomplished by an outreach worker or home carer helping the individual to face feared situations. By confronting their feared situations and learning that they are not going to suffer as they did originally, the physiological effects of fear, panic and anxiety will diminish until the individual is eventually able to lead a normal life.

Link

This links to *Unit 26: Health Psychology*, which investigates stress and the related strategies for managing stress.

The biological perspective

Understanding developmental norms

Arnold Gesell (1880–1961) developed an assessment scale to enable judgements to be made about whether a child's behaviour and understanding matches that of their chronological age (how old the child is). This scale enables the child's scores to be compared against their scores at an earlier age, to determine whether development is proceeding satisfactorily. It also enables a skilled and trained assessor to identify developmental problems that may emerge for an individual. There are three overlapping stages at which development can be measured:

1   between two and a half and six years old
2   between four and six years old
3   between six and nine years old.

At each age, there are various tests to assess different aspects of development. The cubes test, which is used primarily with children aged two to six years old, assesses the ability to follow directions and perform a structured task. Visual perception and fine motor co-ordination skills involved in colouring, cutting and handwriting are assessed against developmental norms. The child's attention span, together with the ability to perceive different shapes accurately, is also measured and, together, these provide information about reading comprehension, spelling and mathematical tasks.

Understanding genetic predisposition to certain illnesses

While it is difficult to determine the extent to which **genetic inheritance** influences illness, there is considerable evidence suggesting that genes do have a role in illness.

One example is **infantile autism**, a rare (but seemingly increasing) disorder, which affects about one child in 2,000. There are psychological explanations for autism (for example, see Bruno Bettelheim, 1972) but these have not been satisfactorily investigated, and current research shows that genetic influences play a more important role in this disorder.

Similarly, schizophrenia shows a genetic link, though not as strongly as in autism. In identical (monozygotic) twins, who share all their genetic material, 50 per cent of schizophrenia cases occur in both twins. This percentage is known as the **concordance rate**.

However, in non-identical (dizygotic) twins who share half as much of their genetic material, schizophrenia only affects both twins in 17 per cent of cases (Cardno and Gottesman, 2000). The concordance rate of 50 per cent tells us that, for monozygotic twins, who share 100 per cent of their DNA, there is a 50:50 chance that both will develop schizophrenia. For dizygotic twins, however, who share only 50 percent of their DNA, the likelihood of both developing schizophrenia is much lower. These findings show that, although there is a genetic component to schizophrenia, this is not the full story. It is generally believed that, although genes can make an individual vulnerable to this disorder, it is only in the event of negative environmental conditions that it is actually triggered, with the risk being higher according to the amount of DNA material shared.

If schizophrenia and asthma are entirely genetically determined (as cystic fibrosis is), then twins who share 100 per cent of their genes should both develop the particular disorder. However, this is not the case, so environmental influences must explain the proportion not accounted for. In schizophrenia, for example, an individual can inherit a vulnerability to this disorder but, if life goes smoothly and is relatively free of stress, this person may live a life free of illness. Similarly with asthma, environmental factors such as stress, pollutants and pollen, can be responsible for the onset of the disorder.

Key terms

Genetic inheritance – qualities transmitted from parents to their offspring through genes. For example, whether their child will be male or female, have blue eyes or brown eyes and whether they will be tall or short.

Infantile autism – a severe disorder appearing in children under two and a half years of age, which includes abnormal behaviour, not communicating with others and developing unusual attachments to objects.

Concordance rate – a statistical expression for the concordance (present in both) of a given genetic trait, in pairs of twins.

Research

Working in groups, select one of the following topics to investigate in terms of genetic inheritance: unipolar (or major) depression; bipolar disorder; anorexia nervosa; bulimia nervosa; anxiety; phobias.

Create a poster with a short summary of your findings.

Health-related behaviours

It is difficult to separate out the effects of nature and nurture in health-related behaviours. Suppose, for example, a child is born with a genetic vulnerability to a disease, such as breast cancer. If, as an adult, she practises regular breast examination, has a healthy lifestyle and has regular screenings, these health-related behaviours may affect the potential outcome. A healthy lifestyle and vigilant health protection measures may reduce the chances of a genetically vulnerable person contracting the disease or allow for prompt action to be taken if she is unfortunate enough to develop breast cancer. Genetic predispositions to illness need to be considered together with health-related behaviours in order to understand fully this aspect of the biological perspective.

Contribution of psychological perspectives to the understanding of specific behaviours

Perspectives

Application of complementary and contrasting psychological theories to the understanding of specific behaviours

Some human behaviour is too complex to be understood using only one perspective, so psychologists often combine perspectives in an attempt to understand particular behaviours. An example is depression. According to the biological perspective, this can be caused by genetic inheritance and/or low levels of the brain chemicals serotonin and noradrenaline. However, as not everyone with a genetic disposition develops depression, other perspectives are also used to explain this disorder. For example, according to the cognitive perspective, the individual has negative thoughts and cognitive biases. The behaviourist perspective would explain this in terms of too much punishment and not enough positive reinforcement.

Specific behaviours

When working within health and social care, you will come across a number of different behaviours, which you will need to recognise and interpret. When deciding which specific behaviours an individual is displaying, it is useful to be aware of the signs and symptoms of that specific behaviour (as shown in Table 11.5).

▶ **Table 11.5:** Signs and symptoms of specific psychological behaviours

Behaviour/problem	Typical behaviours/symptoms
Anxiety	Racing, frightened thoughts. Butterflies in the tummy. Palpitations.
Depression	Slowed or agitated behaviour. Loss of motivation. Negative thoughts. Sadness. Loss of or gain in appetite.
Separation and loss	Searching behaviours; for example, a child looking for a missing loved one where they might previously have been found, or an adult listening out for the sound of a key unlocking the front door. Grief. Feeling the future is hopeless. Disruption to sleep and eating patterns. Depression can result.
Stress and coping	Excessive anxiety caused by activation of the fight or flight response. Ordinary tasks seem impossible to do. Exhaustion.
Self-harm	Hurting oneself physically to relieve mental pain. The relief is only temporary so the individual continues to self-harm.
Prejudice and discrimination	Negative attitudes are shown to members of a group someone is prejudiced against. People may be treated unfairly (eg refused a job) because of who they are.

▶ **Table 11.5:** *– continued*

Behaviour/problem	Typical behaviours/symptoms
Child abuse	This can include physical abuse such as hitting, kicking or inflicting pain using objects. Emotional abuse involves criticism and suggestions that the child is worthless.
Addiction	Addiction involves a compulsion to perform a behaviour that injures you, and often others around you. Examples of addiction include alcoholism, drug addiction and gambling.
Violence and aggression	Violence involves causing harm to another either through bodily contact, such as hitting or kicking, or the use of objects to hurt another person. Aggression can be verbal as well as physical and may consist of insults and deliberately hurtful words or accusations. Physical aggression involves any behaviour that is deliberately performed to cause harm to another person.

Assessment practice 11.1   A.P1   A.P2   A.M1

Sarah has started a job as a childcare assistant in an after-school club. On her induction day, she notices the behaviour of a 7-year-old boy called Troy. Sarah notes the following things:

- Troy's manner with other children is a little forceful
- he snatches toys away from other children and won't share
- he insists on being the leader/main focal point in all games
- he causes a fuss when he doesn't get his own way.

Sara asks her tutor, Unber, for advice on how to understand Troy's behaviour. Unber suggests that Sara re-reads her textbook covering learning theory, looking, in particular, at the section on operant conditioning. Unber explains that Troy may have learned to behave in this particular way and that it would be useful to identify types of reinforcement he might have received in the past for negative behaviour (eg giving in to his behaviour in an attempt to pacify him and keep him quiet).

Task:

1 Why might Troy behave in this manner?

2 Identify types of reinforcement that Troy may have received in the past for negative behaviour.

3 Analyse how useful the principles of operant conditioning are in explaining Troy's development and behaviour.

Plan

- Clarify the task – what am I being asked to do?
- Do I have the necessary textbooks and notes from class?
- How confident am I that I can complete the task? Is there anyone else I could ask for help to discuss my ideas and check my understanding?

Do

- I shall create a list of what I want to achieve.
- I shall look at my notes on operant conditioning and read my textbook on this topic.
- I shall create a list of all possible types of reinforcement of behaviour and form a conclusion about what is motivating Troy's behaviour.

Review

- I can explain what the task was and how I approached it.
- I can explain any shortcomings in the way I approached the task and what I would do differently next time, and why.

Examine the contribution of psychological perspectives to the management and treatment of service users' specific behaviours

Factors that affect human development and specific behaviours

Physical

There are a number of physical processes that influence our behaviour. For example, some people wake early feeling refreshed and ready to start work with enthusiasm, while others find it nearly impossible to drag themselves out of bed in the morning, have problems with alertness and concentration for the first part of the day, but then feel full of energy up until the early hours of the morning. These differences in behaviour are caused by what are known as **circadian rhythms** and can have a serious impact on the functioning of individuals and even be a risk factor for certain shift workers, such as air traffic controllers and health care professionals working on shifts. Circadian rhythms affect our immune system, cognitive processes and aspects to do with the sleep–wake cycle. Other physical influences on development and behaviour include the structure and function of the brain. The brain carries out certain specialised functions, such as memory, concentration, hearing, seeing and judging visuospatial imagery. It also governs aspects of what we would call personality. People with traumatic brain injury, which has damaged the frontal lobes, may show behaviour that is completely different from that which they normally display. Similarly, there may be dramatic behaviour changes in people with dementia.

> **Key term**
>
> **Circadian rhythms** – bodily functions that follow a 24- to 25-hour clock, which include the secretion of hormones and also affects alertness and the sleep-wake cycle.

> **Research**
>
> Investigate the famous case study of Phineas Gage and write a short report on how his brain injury affected his behaviour.

Social, cultural and emotional

We are all social beings who are influenced by the values, norms and behaviours of the society and culture in which we live. For example, we learn table manners from our family; we may learn spiritual values from our family and religious leaders. Societies and cultures vary in what they think is important and it is all too easy for those of us from one culture to see others as being 'different' or 'strange' because their behaviour is not what we would expect of ourselves. Emotionally, also, we are brought up differently. Some people may be brought up to express their feelings and discuss openly issues that are concerning them, including sadness, jealousy and anger. Others may be discouraged from doing this. The ways in which we develop emotionally and within a particular social and cultural setting will greatly influence our development and behaviour.

Economic

The amount of money we have to spend on basic needs will influence our behaviour and health. A person's diet may be poor not because they don't know about healthy eating, but because they cannot afford fresh fruit and vegetables. The ability to access services such as dentists, opticians and chiropodists may also be a problem for people who cannot afford the time or the fares needed to travel to the appointments.

There may be similar problems with screening tests, such as breast screening and cervical smear tests. Psychological and physical well-being are improved when we have the means to do activities such as yoga classes or swimming, which help us to relax and enable us to socialise with others.

Physical environment

The type of environment in which we live will influence our development and behaviour. Someone who has children and lives in an urban area with no nearby safe open spaces for them to play is likely to be more stressed than someone with a large back garden for children to play in. Properties that are damp and overcrowded also contribute to stress and various physical health ailments. Negative conditions can make existing mental disorders worse or cause certain mental disorders, such as anxiety and depression, to develop.

Psychological

The way we are treated as we grow up has a large effect on how we develop and behave. If we are treated with kindness, allowed to express our emotions and given firm but fair boundaries, we are likely to develop into happy individuals with the ability to form good relationships and satisfactory marriages or partnerships. On the other hand, if we experience a great deal of criticism and lack emotional support from those close to us, we may become depressed or anxious in later life. Children with very negative childhood relationships are more likely to become delinquent or alcoholic than those with positive early relationships. For example, in his studies on attachment theory, John Bowlby (1907–1990) found that children who had **insecure attachments** in infancy were more likely to develop negative behaviours in later life than those who had **secure attachments** (Holmes, 2014).

Contribution of psychological perspectives to the management of behaviours

Cognitive behavioural therapy (CBT)

The psychologist Aaron Beck believed that, since thoughts influence feelings and behaviours, it is necessary to identify negative thoughts and to challenge them, so that they can be replaced by more rational and positive thoughts. He also believed that behavioural changes could influence thoughts. Hence the behavioural aspect to this approach.

Beck believed that negative thoughts can be automatic and that a self-critical, hostile and critical commentary can run through our heads in the background so automatically that we are almost never aware of this. He called this **negative automatic thinking**. He also believed that we develop negative cognitive biases. A bias is something that makes us lean towards one explanation rather than towards another.

Cognitive behavioural therapy generally involves working on a one-to-one basis with a client to identify their negative thoughts. Clients will be encouraged to keep a diary of their negative thoughts (see Figure 11.8), including how these thoughts made them feel and what their behaviour was afterwards.

This theory is based on the assumption that replacing negative thoughts with more positive ones will produce a more positive outlook and behaviours. The case study below is an example of how this can work in practice.

Key terms

Insecure attachment – applies to infants whose caregivers are insensitive or inconsistent in the care they provide. These children are said to be anxiously attached.

Secure attachment – refers to the attachment bond between an infant and its primary caregiver when the infant believes the caregiver to be available, sensitive and responsive.

Key term

Negative automatic thoughts – thoughts that appear unconsciously, and which an individual only notices if they pay attention to them. These thoughts tend to be an unfavourably framed interpretation of an individual's experiences, and will usually have an adverse impact on their mood and feelings.

Case study

Social, cultural and emotional development

Henry is the youngest son of Robert, a consultant surgeon, and Millie, a GP. Henry's parents were brought up to believe that any kind of weakness is disgraceful, and that we can achieve anything we want if we just put our minds to it. They set high standards of behaviour, insisting on politeness, good table manners and helping around the house. Religion plays a large part in their lives, and they spend Sunday at church and doing voluntary work in a homeless shelter.

Henry has been brought up to believe that showing emotions is a sign of weakness and whenever he cried as a small boy he was scolded by his parents. He soon learns to keep his emotions to himself. At university, Henry gets a D grade for his first exam and is terrified of the reaction he will get from his parents. He spends

his first holiday in a camp working with underprivileged children so he does not have to go home and face his parents. When he receives another D grade for his second exam, he has a panic attack. From this time on, Henry avoids going to lectures and just lies on his bed staring at the ceiling. Eventually, his tutor visits and suggests that Henry should see his GP. The GP refers Henry to a counsellor for cognitive behavioural therapy.

Check your knowledge

1 How has Henry's social, cultural and emotional development made him who he is?

2 Why was it such a disaster that Henry got a D grade for his exams?

3 Why do you think Henry is behaving in the way he is now?

Day	Event	What I thought and felt	How I behaved	Cognitive biases
Monday	I printed off 50 copies of the wrong document at work.	I'm useless and I'll lose my job. I felt scared.	I avoided my colleagues	catastrophising
Tuesday	I asked Nicola if she wanted to come to the cinema with me tomorrow night. She said she was busy.	She thinks I'm boring and doesn't want to spend any time with me. I felt worthless.	I spent the lunch hour by myself instead of going to the canteen with the others.	Over-generalisation

▶ **Figure 11.8:** An example of a CBT diary

Treatment of phobias

Although phobias are most commonly treated using systematic desensitisation, cognitive behavioural therapy can also help sufferers. Phobias consist of irrational beliefs, and clients can be encouraged to analyse these negative beliefs and discuss whether they are actually realistic. The behavioural part of this therapy would involve the individual testing their beliefs. For example, somebody with a dog phobia might visit a park where dogs have to be kept on leads, and then check whether their beliefs and fears about dogs were realistic.

Mental illnesses

There are a number of mental illnesses that can be treated using CBT, such as anxiety and depression. The basic principles are explained above: identifying negative thoughts, changing behaviour and reflecting on whether the negative thoughts were accurate and true.

Research

Find out about Talking Therapies, an organisation that GPs often refer patients to.

Post-traumatic stress disorder (PTSD)

Since one of the symptoms of PTSD is a belief that something dreadful that happened in the past is going to happen again, CBT is useful in enabling sufferers to reflect on how realistic their beliefs are. The behavioural component might involve an individual placing themselves in a situation that triggers symptoms, such as going to the scene of a car accident. By recognising that this event is not going to happen again, the individual can change their thoughts and the fear can be reduced.

Approaches to challenging behaviour, monitoring and improving behaviour

The use of CBT to manage challenging behaviour would consist of identifying problem behaviours and analysing what those behaviours are meant to achieve. For example, a teenager with aggressive outbursts may be trying to make their feelings known but what they actually achieve is getting punished. A diary could be used to record rising feelings of anger, frustration or hurt, noting the behaviour and consequence that followed. These events could then be analysed with a therapist and the thoughts and feelings discussed, together with suggestions about more appropriate methods of expressing feelings and trying to get their needs met.

Social learning theory

Use of positive role models

We discussed earlier the importance of positive role models, using the example of the talented actress Angelina Jolie Pitt and her message about taking action to minimise a genetic risk of breast cancer. Imitating positive role models can also teach people social skills and ways of dealing with traumatic or difficult situations. Individuals with very severe social phobia can, for example, be exposed to viewing a model with positive social skills. By analysing what it is that the positive role model is doing (for example, body language, use of eye contact, reciprocal interaction and so on), the individual can learn and practise new behaviours to help with overcoming their phobia.

Treatment of eating disorders

Research by Fairburn, Marcus and Wilson (1993) has shown that individuals with eating disorders (particularly anorexia nervosa and bulimia nervosa) can be helped to challenge society's standards of an ideal figure (cited in Davison and Neale, 2001, pp. 237–238). Individuals with these disorders tend to have negative distortions about their physical appearance and shape, believing themselves to be fat when in reality they are dangerously thin. Using social learning theory to treat eating disorders could involve encouraging individuals to look at pictures of women in the public eye who are not excessively thin but are still regarded as desirable and attractive.

Role of the psychodynamic perspective

Psychoanalysis

Psychoanalysis aims to uncover material that has been buried in the unconscious mind because it is too painful to be consciously aware of it. Through analysing dreams, analysis of **transference relationships**, identification of ego defence mechanisms and **free association**, the analyst makes interpretations which, if accepted by the patient, lead to a recognition of the material they have buried and an explanation of why they have done so. This leads to **catharsis**, a state in which the symptom resulting from this denial or repression disappears, and the individual is free to move on.

Link

This links to *Unit 8: Promoting Public Health* and also to *Unit 26: Health Psychology*.

Key terms

Transference relationship – refers to the way in which a patient in therapy transfers feelings, values and beliefs from an important person in their life (eg their father) onto the analyst, believing the analyst to be like this individual.

Free association – involves the patient saying whatever comes into their head, without any internal censoring, and the analyst interpreting what is being said to try to make sense of symptoms.

Catharsis – a sense of release of emotional tension that occurs when something from the unconscious mind has been resolved.

Exploration of factors influencing behaviour

The process of psychoanalysis is long and drawn out, and it takes effort on the part of the patient and analyst. Because our id impulses are unacceptable to the ego and superego, they tend to be buried, but they 'leak out' in other symptoms. It is a painstaking process to unravel all the processes involved in trying to keep this material buried. A useful way of understanding how Freud himself explored factors influencing behaviour is to read some of his case studies.

Humanistic perspective

Person-centred counselling

Person-centred counselling starts with the assumption that we all have the ability to be healthy and live life to the full. Unlike some other perspectives, the therapist in this type of counselling is not seen as an expert. Instead, they work with the client to enable them to recognise aspects of their values, beliefs or behaviours that are getting in the way of their ability to live life to the full, free from stress, worry and depression. The therapist offers **unconditional positive regard**, to enable the client to feel valued and safe in the relationship. It also helps the client to discuss negative feelings or behaviours without the fear of being judged. The client decides what their key issues are and the counsellor does not interpret this, but simply reflects back the client's concerns and needs.

Biological perspective

Drugs

In order to manage behaviours and help individuals to lead a more normal life, a number of drugs can be prescribed by psychiatrists or other trained medical professionals. Drugs are prescribed for a range of symptoms (Table 11.6 shows some examples). For anxiety and stress, anti-anxiety drugs such as the benzodiazepines may be used. These help to induce a state of increased relaxation, which allows the individual to carry on with their everyday life. Such medication is not recommended for long periods of use as it can lead to tolerance (and it becomes less effective) or addiction. It is, however, very helpful when used with a therapy that helps the individual to find coping mechanisms. Depression can be treated very effectively by a range of drugs, the most frequently prescribed being those that increase levels of the neurotransmitter serotonin (a brain chemical). For the condition known as attention deficit hyperactivity disorder (ADHD), an amphetamine-like substance is often used, an example of which is methylphenidate. These are all examples of prescription drugs. Non-prescription drugs, which have an influence on our mood and behaviour, include alcohol, which initially encourages us to feel carefree but ultimately acts as a depressant, and illegal drugs, such as heroin and cocaine, which induce a feeling of euphoria but are highly addictive.

> **Key term**
>
> **Unconditional positive regard** – a non-judgemental acceptance of a client, regardless of what the client thinks or feels, or how they behave.

▶ **Table 11.6** Some examples of medication commonly used

Name/type of medication	Use
Methylphenidate	Calms the behaviour of individuals with attention deficit hyperactivity disorder (ADHD)
Selective serotonin re-uptake inhibitors (SSRIs)	Reduces depression; can be used to help with obsessive compulsive disorder (OCD)
Benzodiazepines	Produces a state of calm and relaxation. Usually only prescribed for a short period of time
Beta blockers	Slows the pumping of the heart and reduces blood pressure. Also sometimes prescribed to relieve anxiety
Antipsychotic medication – such as olanzapine	Reduces the psychotic symptoms of schizophrenia, such as hallucinations and delusions

Biofeedback

Biofeedback is mainly used to treat stress-related disorders and illnesses associated with excessive activity within the brain (for example, epilepsy and ADHD). This technique works on changing the way aspects of our body work. It is thus a biological technique.

Biofeedback involves receiving information (feedback) about physiological aspects of the person's state, such as heart rate, blood pressure and temperature, which show as visual or auditory signals on a monitor. Adrenaline produced by the body causes sweating, which can be measured by placing electrodes on the skin. This shows changes in skin resistance (known as the **galvanic skin response**) which then register as a visual signal or tone. If the signal or tone is high, the level of arousal is similarly high. Initially, by a process of trial and error, the individual attempts various relaxation techniques (deep breathing, visualisation and so on) to reduce the level of signal or tone. As relaxation deepens, blood pressure and heart rate slow down and this is shown (the feedback part of the process) by a lowering of the signal or tone on the monitor. Over time, the individual learns to recognise signs of tension and finds it easier to control physiological functions. This ability to recognise signs of stress (quickened heart rate and so on) gives the user a greater sense of control over their difficulties as they can quickly work to induce relaxation and remove stress symptoms.

Contribution of psychological perspectives to the treatment of behaviours

Interventions

Use of perspectives to inform development of therapeutic practices

Different psychological perspectives are based on different beliefs about what causes particular behaviours, and each perspective, therefore, uses treatments that have been developed according to those beliefs.

For example, in trying to understand and treat depression, psychologists will have different approaches to treatment. The cognitive perspective is that thoughts cause behaviours, including problem behaviours. A cognitive psychologist would look at an individual's thoughts, and how they are influencing behaviour. The behaviourist perspective is that all behaviour is learned. Therefore, a behavioural psychologist would seek to create occasions for the individual to receive increased amounts of positive reinforcement. The psychodynamic perspective assumes that problem behaviours are caused by material stored in the unconscious mind, often dating back to early childhood. Psychologists working within this approach would work on making the contents of the unconscious mind conscious, to find the root source of the depression. The physiological perspective believes difficult behaviour originates from the structure or functioning of the brain or body. A physiological psychologist would only be interested in rebalancing neurotransmitters (brain chemicals) to relieve the symptoms of depression.

Therapeutic practices as relevant to behaviour

Group therapy

Group therapy is based on the idea that we do not live, feel and behave in isolation. We are affected by our relationships (both casual and more permanent) with those around us. Group therapy can work to help individuals develop social skills or self-knowledge. It can also help people recognise how their behaviour may be unhelpful.

There are different types of groups whose members work together for a variety of reasons. In group therapy, the number is usually limited to around six members, with a trained and experienced practitioner in charge of the group. This individual will facilitate interactions between group members and make interpretations, as appropriate. Since we all belong to a variety of groups (the family being an obvious group, and this is why group numbers are often similar to the number of members in a family group), it can be helpful for us to find out what impression we are making on others, how other people perceive us, and how we can change to make our lives easier. An example of a group designed specifically around peer support is Alcoholics Anonymous (AA). Here, alcoholics, who are trying to remain sober, meet on a regular basis, with one member of the group starting the session with their experience of becoming sober. Individuals then speak one at a time, if they choose to, talking about issues or experiences in their life, and maybe relating any recent problems that have threatened their sobriety. In AA, there is no expert leading the group and everyone is considered equal. It is the social support and sense of fellowship that makes this famous organisation so successful.

Case study

Group therapy – working on relationship skills

Munira is a 35-year-old mother of three who has started group therapy to work on her relationship skills. In her day-to-day life she describes herself as a martyr to her family. Her husband and children all treat her like a doormat, and take advantage of her without giving her any thanks or praise. In the group, which consists of other women who are wives and mothers, Munira talks about all the jobs she does. It's not until one of the others points out to her that she is doing this work uncomplainingly that she realises her family may not know that she feels taken for granted. As time goes on in the group therapy sessions, Munira learns that she has been taking on more and more jobs. As her load increased, so did her resentment, but, because she never voiced any of this, the situation got worse not better. She began trying to say 'no' at home to different demands and found, to her surprise, that her elder daughter suggested creating a rota so that the jobs were shared more fairly.

Check your knowledge

1 Suggest why group therapy might have been particularly useful for Munira.

2 What new skills could Munira learn from attending these groups?

Family therapy

Family therapy is based on the idea that we learn to understand ourselves and others through interaction. In family therapy, members of the family attend sessions with a professionally trained family therapist. The purpose of the therapy is to find out how family members relate to one another: the dynamics of the family. It often emerges that such relationships are unhelpful to one or more family member. For example, one member may constantly be blamed by others for causing arguments or problems within the family. The therapist is in a position to analyse these relationships and may note that family members are, in fact, offloading their problems onto this individual. When this information is suggested, it enables members to relate to each other differently and more effectively.

Addiction therapy

Addiction therapy focuses on a range of factors, such as becoming clear about the destructive nature of addictive behaviours. It will also include advice and treatment for physical health, which is usually harmed by addictions. Cognitive therapy is often used to help clients recognise triggers for their addictive behaviours and to look clearly at the consequences. Psychological therapy is often included to deal with underlying issues that may be caught up with the addiction. Some therapies offer support to families as well, in order to help them deal with the addictive member's behaviour and support their recovery.

Behaviour modification programmes

Behaviour modification programmes are based on the techniques of operant conditioning. Positive reinforcers, such as stars on a star chart, or food, are used whenever the patient shows the desired behaviour. Successful use of this technique was reported by Isaacs *et al* in 1960. A woman with schizophrenia, who had not spoken for nineteen years, was reinforced by being given chewing gum whenever she spoke. After a period of just six weeks, she spoke spontaneously and fluently.

Ethical issues

It is very important, when trying to change an individual's behaviour, that this is done ethically. This means that an individual should never be forced to have treatment. Many therapists refuse to treat someone who has been 'brought' to them by a relative or partner. In the past, homosexual individuals were often treated by a technique known as **aversion therapy** to 'cure' them of their homosexuality.

Ethical concerns have changed the way in which people are used as participants in psychological research. It used to be considered acceptable to carry out any kind of experiment or investigation that could cause harm to participants, as long as the findings were useful to science. Examples of research that would not be allowed nowadays are Milgram's obedience experiments and Zimbardo's Stanford Prison simulation study. Today, researchers have to be very careful about how they use their participants. There are certain rules that must be followed, such as obtaining fully **informed consent**. This means that, when the individual agrees to take part in research, they must be genuine volunteers, and that they must have a clear idea of what their part in the experiment entails. Participants must also be given the right to withdraw from the research if they feel uncomfortable at any point, and no pressure should be put on them to remain in the situation. They must be protected from physical or psychological harm. Where public or academic funding is involved for substantial psychological research, an **ethics committee** will be used to examine proposals. If it is considered possible that the proposed research may breach any of the guidelines, the proposal will have to be changed before it is given the go-ahead.

Guidelines on the treatment of patients and on professional codes of ethics for practitioners are published by the British Psychological Society.

Discussion

Do you think that individuals with anorexia nervosa, who are at risk of death if they do not eat, should be given treatment against their will?

How the therapies work

All therapies work by enabling clients to recognise behaviours that are hindering their happiness or wellbeing. This then leads to methods of change, depending on the basic principles of the perspective and the therapy offered.

▶ For behavioural modification, for example, an individual's behaviour can change so that they stop performing behaviours that make them feel sad or lead to punishment.

▶ Cognitive behavioural therapy enables individuals to think differently, which results in more positive feelings and behaviour that will enable them to feel happier, and more at peace with themselves.

A result of all therapies is a change in self-concept and an increase in self-esteem.

Reasons for attending therapy sessions

People attend therapy sessions when they encounter issues in their lives that make it difficult for them to continue to function effectively. For example, they may find it difficult to get out of bed in the mornings; they may be so consumed with anxiety that they cannot go to work and are at risk of losing their job. There are many reasons for attending therapy sessions, including the following:

▶ bereavement

▶ loss of employment

▶ relationship difficulties or relationship break-up

▶ mental disorders.

Assessment practice 11.2 `B.P3` `B.P4` `B.M2` `AB.D1`

Yvonne, a nurse, has recently moved to a new job on a paediatric ward. She is concerned about a three year old, Mathias, who has been admitted for a routine minor operation. He seems very distressed about being in hospital. Despite his mother staying with him, he wet the bed the previous night and he is throwing tantrums, which his mother says he grew out of some time ago. He kicks and screams when Yvonne approaches him to take his temperature, blood pressure and a blood sample.

Task:

1 What factors do psychological perspectives draw on to explain early development, as applied to the specific behaviours shown by Mathias?

2 How can psychological perspectives be used to manage Mathias's behaviour?

3 How have psychological perspectives contributed to the treatment of behaviours such as those shown by Mathias?

4 Evaluate the contribution of psychological perspectives to the understanding of Matthias's development and the management and treatment of Mathias's behaviour.

Plan

• Clarify the task – what am I being asked to do?

• Do I have the necessary textbooks and notes from class? Will I need help from the librarian or my tutor?

• How confident am I that I can complete the task? Is there anyone else I could ask for help to discuss my ideas and check my understanding?

Do

• I shall re-read the section of my textbook and notes that deal with early childhood development and make notes.

• I shall create a table, with columns for different perspectives, so that I can compare more than one perspective. I shall rank each perspective according to how useful it is.

Review

• I can explain how I approached and completed the task.

• I can identify my strengths and limitations and suggest what I would do differently next time.

C Examine how psychological perspectives are applied in health and social care settings

Behaviour of service users in health and social care settings

Concept of role

One concept that has been investigated among researchers looking at service users is that of the sick role. This is when the individual steps outside their other **roles** (eg as employee, father or football coach) and takes on the role of patient. There are certain behaviours that go along with this role and certain expectations from others. For example, nurses and doctors expect the patient to take their medication and follow medical advice. According to Parsons' (1951) concept of the sick role, whilst the

> **Key term**
>
> **Role** – the part played by an individual according to a set of socially constructed beliefs about the behaviour expected of someone holding that role.

individual who is ill is not required to carry out normal day-to-day tasks, such as going to work, in exchange for this they are expected to do everything possible to get well quickly so they can resume their normal duties and fulfill their social and economic obligations.

There are also expectations relating to the role of the medical professionals.

Link

See *Unit 10: Sociological Perspectives*, for more information on the sick role.

Influence

Social influence refers to the finding that, when we are in groups, our behaviour changes. We are all socialised to want to belong to groups and it can be difficult to behave differently from the other members of a group with which we identify. This is the case even if the group is a temporary one, as described in the experiments below.

Conformity to minority influence

We are all influenced by others all the time. People put forward views we may not have heard, or may disagree with. They behave in ways we may be influenced by or react against. When we conform to minority influence, it is because we believe a minority group has superior information or knowledge than we do. In a residential care setting, it may be custom and practice to impose a fairly rigid set of rules on how a unit is run, in the interests of providing an atmosphere of security and stability. Suppose that two care workers go on a training course where they are shown evidence that convinces them that such rigid rules may actually increase insecurity, and lead to residents feeling helpless and lacking control. They may argue at a staff meeting in favour of adapting the rules and routines to include more freedom in specific areas. If the arguments they put forward are well thought out, consistent and reasonable, they may well sway the minds of the majority who become converted to this new way of doing things. This is called minority influence.

Key term

Confederate – an individual who is secretly working on behalf of the experimenter, but appears to be a genuine participant.

An important experiment was carried out in 1969 by a French psychologist, Serge Moscovici (cited in Cardwell and Flanagan, 2008), who showed a group of six individuals a series of blue slides. Everyone in the room stated out loud what colour they thought the slides were. Moscovici arranged for two **confederates** to say they were green, either some of the time (inconsistent group) or all of the time (consistent group). He found that in the consistent group, the real participants were more likely to agree with the confederates that the slides were green. This shows that a minority can be influenced by a majority.

Conformity to majority influence

Conformity to majority influence involves an individual temporarily changing their behaviour or stated views in order to be in line with other group members. Privately, however, their views and beliefs do not change.

Psychologist Solomon Asch (1907–1996) conducted an experiment to investigate majority influence. He used groups of six to nine people, all but one of whom was a confederate. The task involved saying out loud whether a target line matched one of a set of three different length lines, labelled A, B and C (see Figure 11.9).

▶ **Figure 11.9:** Stimulus material used in Asch's task on judging the length of lines in comparison with a target line

Altogether, these two cards were shown eighteen times and Asch asked the confederates to give the wrong answer twelve times. He found that the genuine participants gave the **same** wrong answer as the confederates 37 per cent of the time.

When they were interviewed afterwards, many of the participants were clear that they thought the others were wrong and trusted their own judgement, but they did not feel comfortable about speaking out and 'rocking the boat'.

This is really quite a surprising finding as the people taking part didn't know one another, and there would be no negative consequences if they had simply stated what they believed to be true. It does, however, show how groups have enormous power to shape and change our behaviour.

⏸ **PAUSE POINT**   What light has research into conformity shed on the way our behaviour can change in the presence of others?

> **Hint**   Suppose you were working in a setting where everyone had the same opinion about a client's behaviour and what treatment would be suitable for them, but you thought that they were wrong. Would you speak out?

> **Extend**   You have an ethical obligation to do the best for your client. Identify ethical issues that might apply to this situation.

Conformity to social roles

Philip Zimbardo carried out a very famous study in the basement of Stanford University in 1973, known as the Stanford Prison Simulation Experiment. He wanted to see how behaviour could change according to the roles taken on by individuals. He selected 24 male college students and randomly allocated them to the role of either prisoner or guard. Although the 'prisoners' were initially quite confident and assertive, the behaviour of the 'guards' became increasingly harsh. They would punish the prisoners very unfairly, including putting one prisoner in solitary confinement and making others act out humiliating behaviour. There was even a situation in which prisoners were ordered to clean the toilets with toothbrushes. Although the experiment was intended to run for two weeks, it had to be stopped after just six days because the effects on the psychological health of the 'prisoners' was so extreme that they were deteriorating rapidly. This experiment shows that situational factors have great power.

> **Reflect**
>
> If you had been a guard in Zimbardo's study, do you think you would have behaved with cruelty towards the prisoners? If so, why? If not, what would be the factors that influenced you?

Obedience

Milgram

In social psychological terms, obedience refers to a situation in which an individual follows orders given by someone else. We learn this from a very early age when we are expected to obey our parents, our teachers and other people in authority. Sometimes, however, we are asked to do things that go against our morals.

A very famous experiment in social psychology was undertaken by Stanley Milgram in 1963. Milgram was unhappy with the explanations of the Holocaust. These explanations alleged that there was something unusual, different and cruel about Germans that made them particularly obedient to orders, which led to their actions in exterminating Jews and other individuals in concentration camps. Milgram believed, instead, that there are certain aspects of a situation that can induce any one of us to obey unjust authority and act against our moral code.

To investigate this, he carried out a series of experiments designed to identify the features of a situation that will create obedience. His first experiment was conducted when he was working at Yale University in 1963.

In this experiment, Milgram placed male volunteer participants in front of a shock generator, which they were told would deliver electric shocks from 15 volts to 450 volts. (In fact, this was a fake generator and no electric shocks were ever administered.) The participants were told that the experiment was set up to find out if punishment improved learning. The participants asked questions of a man in a separate room, whom the participant could hear but not see. If the answer was wrong, the participant had to administer an electric shock, increasing by 15 volts each time the answer was wrong. As the voltage of the shocks increased, the man in the other room began shouting and saying he wanted the experiment to stop. When the participant turned to the experimenter for guidance, he was told that he must continue delivering the shocks. Milgram found that 65 per cent of participants continued giving shocks right up to 450 volts (potentially lethal) and all participants gave shocks up to 300 volts.

You will no doubt be relieved to hear that, following the experiment, a full debriefing was held where the 'teacher' met the 'learner' and discovered that no shocks had actually been administered. The participant was reassured that he had caused no harm to anyone and told that he had taken part in an important experiment that could shed light on aspects of human behaviour that it is essential to know about.

The whole set-up of Milgram's experiment was very artificial and unlike normal, everyday settings, so it could be argued that his findings about obedience lacked **ecological validity**.

Research

Research the follow up study by Hofling *et al* (1966) with nurses working in a real-life setting. Do you think this contradicts the idea that Milgram's findings were so artificial that they would not be found in an everyday situation?

Reflect

Have you ever been in a situation where you are driving and you see a police car nearby? We tend to ask ourselves questions such as: 'Have I been speeding?' or 'Was I in the correct lane for that roundabout?' In your career as a health or social care practitioner, what would you do if you were given an instruction by a superior that you felt was wrong? Would you obey? What factors would influence your behaviour?

Attitude change

Attitudes are an important component of behaviour, and can be used to predict behaviour. For example, if I have a positive attitude towards taking exercise, and believe that this will improve my life, my behaviour is likely to mirror this and I am more likely to take exercise. If I have a negative attitude to a particular group within society (for example, travellers or the elderly), it is possible that my behaviour towards these groups may be unfriendly.

Festinger

Leon Festinger (1919–1989) devised a theory known as **cognitive dissonance**. This states that if we believe two contradictory concepts (our cognitions), then this induces a state of discomfort (dissonance) which we are motivated to resolve. This state can occur when our attitudes and our behaviours are contradictory. An example of this may be the attitude that smoking is a disgusting habit that harms health, and yet an individual's behaviour is that they persist in smoking. This contradiction between attitude and behaviour creates an internal state of dissonance. To reduce the discomfort of this feeling, the individual can rationalise their behaviour (and continue smoking) by either changing their attitude ('My father smoked all his adult life and lived to be 90!') or changing their behaviour (they stop smoking).

Factors influencing hostility and aggression

Hostility involves an unfavourable attitude towards others, whereas **aggression** involves unfavourable behaviour towards others. Hostility is often the force that fuels aggressive behaviour. Aggressive behaviour can be verbal (for example, shouting at someone), behavioural (for example, cutting up your ex-partner's clothing when they leave you), physical (for example, hitting someone) or even societal (for example, releasing missiles into another country). Within psychology, there have been a number of theories developed to explain aggression:

▶ social learning theory (see the work of Bandura outlined below)
▶ physiological explanations involving brain processes
▶ social explanations that explain aggression in terms of behaviour that occurs in situations where individuals are anonymous and believe they cannot be identified or held to account for their behaviour.

> **Key term**
>
> **Aggression** – any action that has the express purpose of harming another individual, an animal or an object. This can include verbal or physical harm, or damage to an object.

Social learning theory explains aggression as a learned behaviour. Bandura's famous Bobo doll experiments have shown how young children can learn to behave aggressively by imitating the behaviour of an adult model. In one of his experiments, preschool children were shown footage of an adult model behaving aggressively towards a Bobo doll (a large inflatable doll), hitting it, punching it, lifting it in the air and throwing it. A second group was not exposed to this footage (this is what is known as a control group). The children were then allowed to enter a playroom, in which there were a number of age-appropriate toys and a Bobo doll. Many of those who had seen the model behaving aggressively towards the Bobo doll imitated this behaviour, while none of those in the control group did.

A second explanation of aggression is the **frustration-aggression hypothesis** proposed in 1939 by Dollard *et al*. These researchers believed that aggression results when a goal we have in mind is frustrated. For example, if I want to be discharged from hospital that day to attend a friend's wedding but my consultant says I need to stay in for a further night, my goal of being discharged is frustrated and my behaviour may be aggressive. Aggression can be **displaced**, which means it is targeted at someone other than the cause of the goal-frustration – for example, a junior nurse.

> **Research and discussion**
>
> Working as a group, write a short questionnaire, consisting of no more than five questions, to ask your clients at your next work experience opportunity. Ask them what they find frustrating about their condition and/or the treatment they receive. Bring your findings back to the group and create a tally chart. Discuss whether their feelings of frustration fit one of the above explanations.

> **Key terms**
>
> **Frustration-aggression hypothesis** – the idea that when people are frustrated in having their needs met, this leads to aggressive behaviour.
>
> **Displacement** – a concept from psychodynamic theory that, if an individual is unable to express their frustration and annoyance directly at the source, they will take it out on someone of lower status instead.

Practices in health and social care settings

Promoting independence and empowerment by respecting individual rights

Independence is something that many of us take for granted. We can make decisions for ourselves and choose to behave, think and act in ways that suit our goals. For some people, however, such as the sick or elderly, they find themselves in a state of dependence, and it can be very demoralising. They may find that they have no choice over the food they eat, the times they go to bed, the ability to be alone, and other similar factors. Those working in health and social care need to do all they can, wherever possible, to respect the service user's needs and their right to be independent. In **empowering** individuals, you are helping them to achieve what they want in life, however restricted it might be. So, for example, you might help an individual fulfil their desire to worship in a particular place at a particular time. Alternatively, you could arrange for Braille copies of documents for someone with a visual impairment.

> **Key terms**
>
> **Independence** – the ability to take actions by ourselves in the pursuit of our own goals.
>
> **Empowerment** – actions taken or attitudes towards another individual, enabling them to pursue their goals.

Value base of care

Underlying all work within health and social care is the belief in the importance of dignity. Health professionals should all behave with dignity and also ensure the dignity of service users, whatever their position in life or their capabilities. There are seven core principles of care that every health professional should follow.

1 The promotion of anti-discriminatory practice.
2 The promotion and support of dignity, safety and independence.
3 Respect for, and acknowledgement of, personal beliefs and individual identity.
4 The maintenance of confidentiality.
5 Protection from harm and abuse.
6 The promotion of effective communication and relationships.
7 The provision of personalised (individual) care.

Assessment practice 11.3

C.P5 **C.P6** **C.M3** **C.D2** **C.D3**

Serena is a community psychiatric nurse (CPN) attached to a GP surgery. She is working with 13-year-old Sinitta, who has been self-harming for three years and has recently begun staying out all night smoking marijuana with a group of men in their twenties. Sinitta has diabetes that is not well controlled. She has had a lot of contact with her GP surgery and district nurse. She seldom attends school and, when she does, she is very aggressive with classmates and teachers, and is often isolated from them or sent home. This aggression has started to be seen at home; Sinitta hits and swears at her two younger brothers.

Serena has been asked to attend a case conference with Sinitta's family's social worker and other professionals, to discuss how to help Sinitta on both a social and a health level.

1 a How are psychological perspectives used in health care and in social care?
  b What techniques, derived from psychological perspectives, are used in health care and social care?
  c How effective are psychological perspectives in improving the social functioning of a service user in health care and social care?

2 a Explain similarities and differences in the use of psychological perspectives in a health care setting and a social care setting.
  b Write a short essay on how professionals use psychological perspectives to improve the social functioning of service users.
  c Assess the impact of using psychological perspectives to improve the functioning of service users, using Sinitta's case as an example.

3 a Evaluate how well psychological perspectives could enhance the social functioning of the individual in the case study, Sinitta.
  b Evaluate the importance of psychological perspectives in understanding Sinitta's behaviour, and in managing and treating the problem behaviour to enhance her social functioning.

Plan
- Clarify the task – what am I being asked to do?
- Do I have the necessary textbooks and notes from class? Will I need help from the librarian or my tutor?
- How confident am I that I can complete the task? Is there anyone else I could ask for help to discuss my ideas and check my understanding?

Do
- I shall contact the CPN who spoke in college last term and ask some questions about how this case would be dealt with.
- I shall ring the local social services department and ask for permission to give a questionnaire to a family social worker.
- I shall create a table with two columns, one for health and one for social care, and make notes of the similarities and differences in psychological perspectives used.

Review
- I shall look at how I completed the task and focus, in particular, on the way I chose questions for the CPN and social worker, and whether these should be changed if I were to do this again.
- I shall identify my strengths and limitations and suggest what I would do differently next time.

Further reading and resources

Bettelheim B – *The Empty Fortress: Infantile Autism and the Birth of the Self* (The Free Press, 1972)

Davison G and Neale J – *Abnormal Psychology 8th edition* (John Wiley & Sons, 2001)

Holmes J – *John Bowlby & Attachment Theory 2nd edition* (Routledge, 2014)

Cardno, A and Gottesman, I – *Twin Studies of Schizophrenia: From Bow-and-Arrow Concordances to Star Wars Mx and Functional Genomics* (Wiley-Liss, 2000)

Websites

http://www.nytimes.com/2015/03/24/opinion/angelina-jolie-pitt-diary-of-a-surgery.html?_r=0
Angelina Jolie Pitt's 2015 article raising awareness of breast cancer in the *New York Times*.

https://www.goconqr.com/en/p/768326-the-principles-of-the-care-value-base-mind_maps
This links to a mindmap on *goconqr* showing the principles of the care value base.

http://www.nhs.uk/conditions/counselling/pages/talking-therapies.aspx
The *NHS* website has information and links to different psychological therapies.

http://psychclassics.yorku.ca/
http://www.bps.org.uk/system/files/documents/code_of_ethics_and_conduct.pdf
The British Psychological Society publishes a *Code of Ethics and Conduct* for psychologists.

http://www.nhs.uk/NHSEngland/thenhs/about/Pages/nhscoreprinciples.aspx
This website includes details of the value base of care.

THINK ▶FUTURE

Rajeena Pun

District nurse

As a district nurse, I have a really interesting and varied job that involves meeting members of the public in a variety of settings. Sometimes, this can be in their own homes, or it may be in a residential care environment. I provide advice and guidance to service users and their families or carers on how to meet the service users' needs. Reading situations and knowing how to communicate and interact with people is really important, and so is the ability to explain practical tasks so they can be carried out when I'm not there.

Sometimes I don't have as much time as I'd like with each person, so time management is an essential feature of this job. I also need to be clear and concise when communicating with other members of the multi-disciplinary team and passing on important information. I find the variety of people I work with and the variety of tasks required very stimulating. Nursing, to me, is about life-long learning. I feel passionate and committed and am always excited about new opportunities that come up for me to increase my learning and knowledge base.

Most important of all is to ensure dignity for the service users I work with. I believe in working towards mutual respect and ensuring that they receive the best possible care. If there are aspects I can't provide myself, then I'll work towards empowering them to access support and help as needed. If I can provide help, I will. My goal is to ensure that everyone I work with is treated with respect and dignity and that they receive the best care possible.

Focusing your skills

Independence, working with others and professional practice

I need to be able to work autonomously. I am the only person on the scene and I have to be able to make decisions independently, based on clinical practice principles. I have to have good decision-making skills, but I also need to be able to work well in a team and with the wider multi-disciplinary team. I need to ensure that I follow professional guidelines such as from the Nursing and Midwifery Council (NMC) and the National Institute for Health and Care Excellence (NICE).

Interpersonal skills

It is important to treat service users holistically, which includes paying attention to their psychological needs as well as their physical needs. It is important to take time to listen, and to show empathy. Many times, I have encountered service users who need just a little time and concern shown for them to reveal health anxieties that they don't feel able to discuss with a GP as they are afraid they will be seen as a time waster.

Getting ready for assessment

Isaac is working towards a BTEC National in Health and Social Care. He was given an assignment with the following title 'Examine the contribution of psychological perspectives to the understanding of human development and the management and treatment of two selected service users with different behaviours'. The assignment was for learning aims A and B. Isaac had to:

▶ outline how psychological perspectives explain human development and specific behaviours
▶ describe the contribution of psychological perspectives to the management of behaviours
▶ evaluate the contribution of psychological perspectives to the treatment of behaviours.

Isaac shares his experience below.

How I got started

I began by getting out my files, which had notes, handouts, articles, research and worksheets on each different perspective. I had colour coded these so it made it easier not to get muddled between the perspectives.

As my work experience had been in a nursery and a hospital, I decided to select two service users from these settings. This fitted in well with the assignment requirements.

I then looked at the list of behaviours I'd been compiling throughout the course and decided on which specific behaviours I would focus on for the two service users.

How I brought it all together

To start, I wrote a short introduction to the article. For each service user I did the following:

▶ wrote a summary of how perspectives on human development would apply to the individual
▶ identified a list of behaviours that were helpful to the individual, and those that hindered their adjustment or recovery.

To help me really focus on each service user's perspective, I then did the following:

▶ wrote an advice leaflet for one of the individuals explaining the cause of their behaviour and giving guidance on how to treat and manage their behaviour
▶ wrote a report for the second individual, addressed to the head of the nursery, in which I explained how the child's behaviour could be understood and gave advice and guidance on how to manage it.

I then collated everything and spent some time making sure that all of the work clearly related back to the assessment criteria and that it told a story which was easy to follow.

What I learned from the experience

I found out that just using one perspective alone is not easy. Sometimes, there is more than one that needs to be used in order to understand behaviour. I found that drawing a chart to indicate where there was a crossover made it easier for me to write the report and the advice leaflet.

I struggled a bit getting all the information I needed into the advice leaflet. I think that the report format gave me more flexibility and enabled me to go into more detail about the individual.

Think about it

▶ Have you checked your plan with your tutor to ensure that you are going to be able to stay on track?
▶ Are you clear in your mind about the different perspectives? Are you able to identify the difference between management and treatment?
▶ Have you used other sources to write your assignment? If so, remember to reference them.

Physiological Disorders and their Care 14

Getting to know your unit

Assessment

You will be assessed by a series of assignments set by your tutor.

You will explore different types of physiological disorders, how they are diagnosed by doctors and the types of appropriate treatment and support that service users may encounter. You will explore how the disorders you have chosen to study affect the body's systems and how they function, and the effects on an individual's health and wellbeing. You will learn about some physiological disorders associated with the main body systems. These could be the topics of your assignments or you could choose others. However, before you make your final decisions, discuss it with your tutor. You will also learn about diagnostic tests and treatment options, as well as different support agencies and care settings.

How you will be assessed

This unit is internally assessed through two assignments about the causes, signs and symptoms and effects of two different physiological disorders, chosen, by you. You will consider how the physiological disorders are investigated, diagnosed and treated and the impact they have on the health and wellbeing of service users. You will consider the types of carers and care settings involved as well as the support available for the service users. Choosing one of the service users with a physiological disorder, you will construct a treatment plan to meet his or her identified needs.

Assessment criteria

This table shows what you must do in order to achieve a **Pass**, **Merit** or **Distinction** grade, and where you can find practices to help you.

Pass   **Merit**   **Distinction**

Learning aim **A** Investigate the causes and effects of physiological disorders

A.P1	**A.M1**	**A.D1**
Explain the causes, signs and symptoms of physiological disorders on service users. **Assessment practice 14.1**	Analyse the changes in body systems and functions resulting from different types of physiological disorders on service users. **Assessment practice 14.1**	Evaluate the impact of physiological disorders on the health and wellbeing of service users. **Assessment practice 14.1**

Learning aim **B** Examine the investigation and diagnosis of physiological disorders

B.P2	**B.M2**
Compare investigative and diagnostic procedures for different physiological disorders. **Assessment practice 14.2**	Assess the importance of specific procedures in confirming the diagnosis of physiological disorders. **Assessment practice 14.2**

Learning aim **C** Examine treatment and support for service users with physiological disorders

C.P3	**C.M3**	**BC.D2**
Explain the treatment and support available for service users with different physiological disorders. **Assessment practice 14.3**	Assess the provision of treatment, support and types of care for service users with different types of physiological disorders. **Assessment practice 14.3**	Justify the potential benefits of different investigations and treatment options for service users diagnosed with physiological disorders. **Assessment practice 14.3**
C.P4		
Compare the types of carers and care settings for service users with different types of physiological disorders. **Assessment practice 14.3**		

Learning aim **D** Develop a treatment plan for service users with physiological disorders to meet their needs

D.P5	**D.M4**	**D.D3**
Assess care needs of a selected service user with a physiological disorder. **Assessment practice 14.4**	Plan treatment to meet the needs of a selected service user with a physiological disorder, reviewing, as appropriate, to improve outcomes. **Assessment practice 14.4**	Justify the recommendations of the plan in relation to the needs of the service user and state advantages and disadvantages of the treatment options. **Assessment practice 14.4**
D.P6		
Plan treatment to meet the care needs of a selected service user with a physiological disorder. **Assessment practice 14.4**		
D.P7		
Explain how the plan would improve the health and well-being of a selected service user. **Assessment practice 14.4**		

Getting started

In small groups, come up with ideas for potential topic material and individuals with appropriate disorders. List essential questions to consider before making your choice, and assist each other in solving problems. Examples: Can I get enough time with the subject? Is there a known cause and/or treatment for the disorder? Include the way you interact with your subject.

A Investigate the causes and effects of physiological disorders

A physiological disorder is an illness that interferes with the way that the functions of the body are carried out. As a result of the incorrect functioning, certain effects will be seen in the body. These may be due to several reasons, depending on the body system involved and the functions that are not working properly. For example, there may be too little or too much of a specific substance, deterioration of certain cell types or blockages of pathways.

Types of physiological disorders and effects on body systems and functions

A disorder affecting the functioning of a particular body system usually has several effects on other body systems and how they operate.

Endocrine system disorders

The endocrine system consists of endocrine glands, which secrete chemicals called hormones directly into the bloodstream. Hormones travel via the bloodstream to affect other body systems. The endocrine system is a communication system between different body parts.

Diabetes

Diabetes is a disorder of insulin **metabolism**. There are two distinct types of diabetes. Insulin is a hormone secreted by the **pancreas** (a gland associated with the digestive system) and it regulates blood sugar or glucose metabolism. Type 1 diabetes (full name diabetes mellitus) mostly occurs in children and adolescents; it is also called insulin-dependent diabetes or IDD and juvenile diabetes. The incidence of type 1 diabetes is lower than type 2 diabetes and often runs in families, although a direct genetic link has not been proved. Some types of viral infection can cause the insulin-secreting cells of the pancreas to be damaged and fail to secrete the level of insulin that the body requires. **Blood glucose** becomes exceedingly high and the body becomes dehydrated and uses other substances, such as fat and protein, for energy. Insulin enables glucose from the blood to enter body cells to take part in energy production. Without insulin, the cells are 'glucose-proofed' and starved of the main energy-producing nutrient. Using other substances for energy-producing chemical reactions results in unwanted end products forming, such as ketones and acids, and these become increasingly poisonous to body cells.

Type 2 diabetes used to be more common in older people. It is a result of pancreatic cells failing to produce sufficient insulin for their needs. The more body cells an individual has the more insulin is required to meet the body's need for energy. Type 2 diabetes is associated with being overweight. Increasingly, with rising obesity levels in younger people, there are many younger service users being diagnosed with this type of diabetes. Type 2 diabetes is also called NIDD (non-insulin-dependent diabetes) or mature onset, although, with the changes in service user groups, the latter name can be considered inaccurate.

> **Reflect**
>
> Britain is said to have an obesity epidemic, especially in children.
>
> What consequences will this have for those individuals in 30 to 40 years' time?

Infections are more common in untreated and poorly controlled diabetics and service users frequently present with boils, abscesses and skin and chest infections that are failing to heal. Another effect is on the urinary system, as people with diabetes may drink a lot of fluid (polydipsia) and, therefore, produce greater volumes of dilute urine (polyuria). Consequently, the individual may become **dehydrated**. If left untreated or undiagnosed, diabetes is life-threatening – the individual can become very drowsy and pass into a **coma** before dying.

> **Research**
>
> Find out about the normal range of blood glucose levels and the level that would mean a person has diabetes.

Hypo and Hyperthyroidism

These are disorders associated with the thyroid gland which is an H-shaped gland lying in the neck around the trachea. Hypothyroidism results when insufficient thyroid hormone (known as thyroxine) is produced due to an underactive gland. As thyroxine regulates body metabolism, consequently all activities are slowed down, for example heart rate, respiratory rate, bowel movements, cognitive processes and movement. Less heat is produced from the chemical reactions in the body and an individual with untreated hypothyroidism is always cold and may wear layers of clothes even in warmer months. Hyperthyroidism is caused by an overactive gland and speeds up the metabolism, so that heart and respiratory rates are increased, and bowel movements and chemical reactions are faster. This results in an increased temperature, so that the individual is always hot and may prefer cold weather.

> **Reflect**
>
> Think about hyp**er** being ov**er** and hyp**o** being l**o**w. Make a list of other words using these prefixes (beginnings).

Nervous system disorders

The nervous system comprises the brain, spinal cord and nerves. The nervous system is also a communication system, but via nerves not blood. It is much faster than the endocrine system in linking different parts of the body. Disorders result in reduced communication.

> **Key terms**
>
> **Dehydration** – insufficient water in the body systems. Water is an essential component of chemical reactions so untreated dehydration can be life-threatening.
>
> **Coma** – a state of unconsciousness.

Parkinson's disease

Parkinson's disease is a progressive deterioration of a part of the brain known as the *substantia nigra*, in which the cells slowly die. The exact cause is unknown but is thought to be partly genetic and partly environmental.

The damage causes a chemical called dopamine to decline and there is an interruption in nervous function that leads to an involuntary tremor, or trembling, of part of the body, often an arm or a hand. Muscles are stiff and unyielding, so movement is slow. The individual shuffles when walking and both their head and neck are bent. The individual has problems such as loss of smell and memory, difficulty in sleeping and often depression. The disease is more common in men than women, and the onset is mostly in the later stages of life.

Alzheimer's disease

Alzheimer's disease also affects mainly older people and the risk of developing it increases as a person grows older. It is a progressive disease in which individuals may have memory loss and difficulties in thinking and problem solving, which get worse over time. A protein called amyloid builds up around the individual's brain cells forming plaques (plates) – amyloid plaques – and the brain cells atrophy (slowly deteriorate), with a loss of communication between nerve cells. The exact cause is not known. However, there can be a greater risk of genetic inheritance if there is a family history of someone developing the disease when over 65 years old. There is also a clear genetic link between cardiovascular disease, Down's syndrome and head injuries and developing Alzheimer's disease.

> **Link**
>
> *Unit 3: Anatomy and Physiology for Health and Social Care* will help you with anatomy and physiology.

Musculo-skeletal system disorders

These are disorders affecting the skeleton and the muscles that alter the framework of the body, causing problems with movement and flexibility.

Rheumatoid arthritis

Rheumatoid arthritis is a common disorder that affects the lining of the joints where bones meet. It is an autoimmune disorder, where the body's own immune system produces antibodies that attack some of the body's own cells. Usually, the immune system produces antibodies to attack invading microorganisms that could cause infection. Rheumatoid arthritis tends to affect the small joints such as those of the wrist, hands and feet, causing swelling, redness and stiffness in the joints. The affected joints are very painful. Triggers for autoimmune disorders are largely unknown but it is more likely to affect middle-aged women, those with family histories of the disease and smokers. Eventually, the joints become deformed and both cartilage and bone can be affected. Individuals with rheumatoid arthritis suffer from periods of intense inflammation, often called 'flare-ups', followed by quieter less painful times.

▶ Inflammation and swelling of finger joints in a person with rheumatoid arthritis

Osteoporosis

Osteoporosis is a bone-weakening condition that mainly affects post-menopausal women, although other conditions, including endocrine disorders such as hyperthyroidism, and inflammatory diseases like rheumatoid arthritis, increase the risk of developing it. Individuals with a family history of osteoporosis are also more likely to suffer from it. Bone density starts to decrease in middle adulthood as a normal ageing process, but, in vulnerable people, this process is increased. Usually, the first effect is a fracture. This can happen in most bones but the hip and spinal vertebrae are most commonly affected – often without warning. Depending on the bones involved, the fracture can lead to restricted movement and pain.

Respiratory system disorders

The respiratory system consists of the trachea, lungs, diaphragm and chest wall and enables vital gases to move in and out of the body. Taking in oxygen, to aid the breakdown of glucose to provide energy (a process called respiration), is a vital life function, as is eliminating the waste products of respiration, which are carbon dioxide and water.

Asthma

People with asthma have very sensitive airway linings that can easily become inflamed. The inflammation causes muscle contraction which narrows the two divisions of the trachea, known as the bronchi. This results in the individual wheezing, coughing, becoming breathless and feeling tightness in their chest. Substances that cause these effects are called triggers. The most common triggers are infections, dust, fur, pollen and smoke. Exercise can also trigger an asthmatic attack. Although commonly thought of as a young person's condition, individuals of any age can suffer from asthma and it is more common in adults than in children. Asthma attacks can be life-threatening. Individuals with asthma measure their **peak flow expiration** to help them manage their condition by adjusting medication.

> **Key term**
>
> **Peak flow expiration** – an individual's maximum expiration speed, which is measured using a peak flow meter.

▶ A peak flow meter helps to monitor asthma

Chronic Obstructive Pulmonary Disease (COPD)

Chronic Obstructive Pulmonary Disease is mostly linked to middle-aged adults and older service users. It is more of a collection of diseases like bronchitis and emphysema, nearly always resulting from smoking. Service users have difficulty breathing through their narrowed airways and mucus is brought up with coughing.

The scarring of respiratory organs is permanent and more men than women suffer from it.

Circulatory system disorders

The heart and blood vessels circulate blood around the body. Blood contains nutrients, respiratory gases, hormones, water, blood cells, antibodies and enzymes so is vital to all body systems. Diseases linked to the circulatory system can be life-threatening.

Coronary heart disease

Coronary heart disease is a condition affecting the blood vessels (coronary arteries) that supply the heart muscle itself. These become narrowed and may become blocked by plaques of fatty deposits, known as atheroma. As individuals age, blood vessels become hardened (sclerotic) and this, combined with the atheroma, is called atherosclerosis. As blood vessels narrow, the blood has difficulty passing through. When the individual is under pressure, or carrying out physical exertion, the lack of oxygen-rich blood to the heart muscle causes extreme pain, known as angina. Blood clots more easily on linings of blood vessels roughened by atheroma plaques and, if the vessel becomes blocked, a heart attack occurs. This is called coronary thrombosis. This, in turn, causes the death of heart muscle from lack of oxygen, or myocardial infarction. The effect on the individual is intense chest pain, their face shows a grey pallor and they experience breathlessness. This can be a life-threatening situation depending on the size and location of the blocked artery. Heart attacks can occur without warning. They are more common in middle-aged and older men. Coronary heart disease is mainly caused by lifestyle factors such as smoking, raised blood cholesterol (eg from unhealthy diet), raised blood pressure and diabetes.

Leukaemia

Leukaemia is cancer of the white blood cells. However, there are several types of white blood cells, so different types of leukaemia exist. It is caused by an overproduction of particular cells so that immature cells crowd the blood but do not contribute to immunity. Consequently, the individual becomes susceptible to many infections. They also have the signs and symptoms of anaemia, such as pale skin and mucous membranes, breathlessness and fatigue, as the bone marrow is overproducing white blood cells and the manufacture of red blood cells is decreased. Exposure to radiation or radiotherapy, some chemicals, genetic or blood disorders can lead to leukaemia. The disorder can occur at any age but it is more common in older people.

Cancer

Cancer is the term given to a multitude of different disorders. Generally, they are caused by particular groups of cells multiplying out of control to form invasive growths or tumours. Some tumours are localised and do not spread, but may cause problems because of where they are growing, for example brain tumours. Other growths are invasive and may spread to other organs causing secondary tumours, known as metastases. These are malignant tumours and can be life-threatening. Not all tumours are cancerous – these are referred to as benign tumours.

Bowel cancer

Bowel cancer accounts for 12 per cent of new cases of cancer, mainly in older age groups. The bowel is another name for the intestine. There are several different parts of the intestine, such as the small intestine (cancer is rare here), the colon and the rectum, so alternative names can be colon cancer, rectal cancer or colorectal cancer. Causes are not known, but smoking, alcohol, family history, diet, being overweight, inactivity and other bowel conditions increase the risks of bowel cancer. An individual can have the disease for some time before seeking advice as the signs and symptoms can be mistaken for haemorrhoids (piles) and dietary irregularities. The main effects are blood in the stools (faeces) and sometimes bleeding from the rectum (either directly from the tumour or from the damaged intestinal lining), abdominal pain and changes in bowel habits.

Prostate cancer

Only males have a prostate gland. The prostate gland is at the base of the bladder, surrounding the urethra, and its main function is to help in the production of semen.

The prostate gland slowly increases in size in older men and, due to its position around the urethra, this causes some of the same symptoms as prostate cancer. The individual may feel a need to pass urine more often, called frequency, and feel that the bladder is not fully emptied. No exact cause has been found, but family history, age and ethnicity increase the risks.

> **Reflect**
>
> How many physiological disorders described above are partly attributed to lifestyle choices? How does this make you feel about your own choices and the way in which you live your life?

Impact of disorders on service users' physical, mental, social and emotional health

Physical impact

You have learned about many of the physical effects of the disorders described so far in this unit. However, there are other more general effects of feeling unwell that can make it difficult to be precise about what is wrong. This is known as 'general malaise'. An individual may feel weak and tired, and often describe a lack of energy or being unable to motivate themselves. Their appetite may be diminished and they may frequently complain of losing weight. Their skin and hair may look unhealthy and they may lack care in their appearance. Their energy is expended in fighting illness and, together with the lack of appetite, there is little energy available for activity and normal living.

> **Reflect**
>
> Have you suffered with an illness or had influenza or a severe cold that made you feel physically low? Most people have experienced this at some time. Imagine how this would feel if it happened most of the time.

Mental and emotional impact

Disorders can have psychological effects as well as physiological effects and most of these will be negative, such as bouts of **depression** and anxiety. Individuals who have these disorders will naturally be concerned for themselves but also for their family, and especially for their dependants. Psychological changes resulting from the side effects of treatment should also be considered.

Pain is often associated with worry, depression and fear of the unknown. When a diagnosis has been made, the perception of pain and its effects is often less, especially if the sufferer can be reassured. Individuals have very different **pain thresholds**, especially if they have been incapacitated or ill for a long time and are 'used' to experiencing pain.

In a few disorders, such as multiple sclerosis, the individual may have periods of intense or exaggerated wellbeing (for no apparent reason) interspersed with periods of depression. This state of exaggerated wellbeing is known as **euphoria**.

Some service users become angry about their condition and feel that life has been unfair, while others become compliant and expect doctors and nurses to do everything for them.

> **Key terms**
>
> **Depression** – a mental disorder in which the individual is unable to cope with daily life and experiences feelings of worthlessness.
>
> **Pain threshold** – describes the point at which an individual feels that an unpleasant physical feeling, or pain, is no longer bearable.
>
> **Euphoria** – a feeling of extreme happiness and excitement that can be justified by events or, in some mental health conditions, may be unrelated to events.

When collecting case history material for assignments, consider the mental and emotional impact on your service users. Remember that they are human beings and not just information sources.

Before gathering information, consider the following.

- Are they feeling anxious, frightened, frustrated or angry?
- Are there good days and bad days? How will you manage the meeting on a bad day?
- Would it be thoughtful to contact the service user before the appointment to find out how they are feeling? Would it be useful to you or supportive to them to meet on bad days?
- Other mental and emotional effects on your service user caused by the disorder.

Social impact

A service user can be affected socially by an increase or deterioration in social activity. Regular visits to a GP, hospital or clinic can introduce a service user to other service users – often with the same type of illness, counselling sessions, voluntary groups or local organisations. Having to give up work through illness reduces social circles and friendship groups but these can be replaced by other groups. Some service users may be more or less confined to their homes, but if encouraged, or taught if need be, communication can be maintained through texting, telephone calls, emails and letters. Many service users initially feel embarrassed at the physical changes the disorder has caused, such as loss of weight or hair or disabilities gained, and they may need support and encouragement to leave their house.

▶ Taking time to visit can mean a lot if the person you are visiting rarely leaves the house

In groups of three, carry out three role plays. One individual plays the service user, one the learner carrying out the assignment and one the observer. Play each part once.

Before you begin, as a group, consider the introduction, the interview and the conclusion. Produce a checklist of behaviour and conduct that the observer will record. At the end, the observer will feed back to the group, who will then review the whole interaction. Choose three physiological disorders from those described in this unit.

To gain maximum benefit you must:
- treat the exercise seriously, and consider your responsibility to the service user who is helping you with this activity
- read the sections on the disorders – make notes to help you
- provide constructive feedback
- ask your tutor for advice, if you experience difficulties
- spend significant time discussing the feedback.

PAUSE POINT   Can you explain how physiological disorders are investigated and treated?

Hint   Have you made a decision about at least one physiological disorder to study?

Extend   Research the disorder to find out if it will provide the material required for the grade you want to achieve in the assessment.

Causes of physiological disorders

When recognised, the causes of the disorders described so far have been provided in the text. However, risk factors such as smoking are well known. In this section, you will learn about general causes of disorders and will be able to research and apply these to your chosen disorders.

Inherited traits

Inherited traits include disorders that are directly caused by genetics and those where the disorder runs in the family. The science of genetics was developed in the 20th century and knowledge has greatly accelerated since then. The Human Genome Project commenced in 1990 and took 13 years to complete. Scientists in various countries worked together to map the structure, organisation and functions of the complete set of human genes – called a genome. This is leading to new ways to prevent and sometimes cure disease. There are thought to be about 30,000 genes in the human genome and it seems like every month new information and data is being publicised. There is still much work to do in translating this information into practical treatment and prevention so you will need to research the genetic basis of disorders. Disorders may be genetically inherited from either one or both parents, in which case there may be a clear family history.

Link

You will find more about genetic inheritance in *Unit 3: Anatomy and Physiology for Health and Social Care.*

Sickle cell anaemia

Sickle cell anaemia is an inherited genetic disorder that interferes with the normal production of red blood cells, which carry oxygen in the blood. The genetic defect produces abnormal haemoglobin that makes red blood cells crescent shaped. These abnormal red blood cells are short lived and not replaced as quickly. The abnormal cells are also unable to bend and flex like normal red blood cells and get stuck in small blood vessels, such as capillaries and arterioles, causing damage to body cells and intense pain. This is called a sickle cell crisis.

Sickle cell anaemia is most common in African, Caribbean and Mediterranean populations. The sickle cell allele is recessive. An individual must inherit recessive alleles from both parents to develop the disorder. Inheriting one allele causes sickle cell trait in which some sickle cells are produced, but haemoglobin is normal. An individual with sickle cell trait may pass the allele on to their children. If those children later have offspring with another individual with the sickle cell trait, then any of their children could develop sickle cell anaemia. The effects of sickle cell anaemia are breathlessness, lack of energy and tiredness, all worse after exertion. Individuals have an increased risk of stroke and infections. Pregnant women are offered screening tests for this disorder.

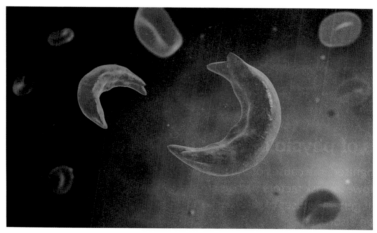

▶ Photomicrograph of red blood cells sickling – the bi-concave red blood cells, adapted for oxygen carriage, have been deformed into sickle or crescent-shaped cells unable to transport enough oxygen for the person's needs

Case study

More children – the dilemma

Stavros and Maria are British born but have Greek grandparents. They were married three years ago and have one child, Niko. Niko has sickle cell anaemia and, after genetic counselling, the parents realise that they are both carriers of the disorder. They would like another child but feel that the predicted risk of having another child with the disorder is too great. They are now looking to adopt another child as they do not believe in terminating a life.

Check your knowledge

1 Niko is often quite poorly. What signs and symptoms would he display?

2 The parents are trying to persuade the adoption agency to have a genetic profile carried out on any child who may be adopted by them. Discuss whether this is a reasonable request from their point of view.

3 Discuss the reasons why the adoption agency might refuse to carry out a genetic profile.

Lifestyle choices

A lifestyle choice is how an individual chooses to live their life. Smoking, overindulging in alcohol, not taking exercise and drug taking are all examples of poor lifestyle choices that might affect an individual's health.

Smoking cigarettes

Smoking cigarettes has long been known to be exceptionally harmful and can lead, in particular, to heart and lung diseases. Smoking is also identified as a risk factor in many other conditions, some of which you have already learned about in this unit, for example coronary heart disease. Cigarette smoke contains a large number of toxic substances such as carbon monoxide, tar, benzene and addictive nicotine. These can affect physical health through hardening of the arteries, causing a rise in blood pressure, lung damage, such as bronchitis and emphysema, increased susceptibility to chest infections and may cause lung, mouth, bladder and other cancers. Smoking interferes with the carriage of oxygen so that smokers become breathless on exertion and, consequently, are likely to be unfit. There are particular dangers for women who smoke when pregnant, with an increase in stillbirths and sudden infant deaths (cot death). Babies are often born smaller than average and are more likely to suffer from infections.

Drug misuse

A single or mixed course of antibiotics or similar drugs can combat infections that might at one time have caused death, disability or chronic illnesses. However, in time, this will no longer be the case, as misuse of antibiotics has led to 'superbugs' developing that are increasingly resistant to standard antibiotic treatment. Scientists have been warning about the sale of antibiotics over the counter in other countries, and their overuse for minor infections in developed countries, including the UK.

In the past, sleeping pills, tranquillisers and other drugs have also been overprescribed long term. Addiction and over reliance on them has caused damage to people's health, particularly liver and kidney damage. The liver clears the blood of drugs by breaking up the chemical groups and the kidneys excrete them in urine, so these organs are vulnerable to damage by overuse. All drugs have side effects and can cause blood disorders, skin rashes and digestive upsets, as well as liver and kidney damage.

Illegal or controlled drugs are taken by some people to achieve a change in mood or behaviour. Some drugs are called recreational or dance drugs and are taken to get a sense of excitement at parties or raves. Taking illegal drugs just once can be dangerous and regular use can become addictive. It is important to know that many of these drugs are manufactured under unsafe circumstances in countries with little or no drug controls, and they are often mixed with other materials such as flour or chalk, to make them go further. The 'dose' of each drug is not calculated accurately and different people may have different reactions to them. The range and mix of drugs is large and varied and extensive side effects are now becoming more widely known.

Table 14.1 shows the health risks associated with some commonly misused drugs.

Table 14.1 The health risks associated with commonly misused drugs

Misused drug	Appearance and method	Possible health risks
Cannabis/hash/weed/marijuana	Dried herbs/brown block/sticky, treacle-like. Usually smoked but may be eaten.	Mental illness, raised blood pressure and pulse, memory loss.
LSD/acid/trips	Impregnated paper, micro-dots. Eaten.	Disorientation, depression, anxiety, flashbacks. User needs to keep increasing the amount taken to get the same effect.
Heroin/H/smack/Henry	White or brown powder. Injected, sniffed or smoked.	Heart and lung disorders. HIV/AIDS, vein thrombosis, septicaemia (blood infection) when injected with shared needles.
Ecstasy/xtc/E/M25s/Adam	White tablets, swallowed.	Heat stroke, collapse, cramps, mental illness.
Cocaine/snow/Charlie/Coke	White powder. Sniffed or injected.	HIV/AIDS, vein thrombosis, septicaemia (blood infection) when injected with shared needles.
Amphetamine/speed/whizz/sulph	White tablets or screws of paper. Swallowed, sniffed or injected.	HIV/AIDS, vein thrombosis, septicaemia (blood infection) when injected with shared needles.

Diet

In 1998, the Acheson Report noted that people in the lowest socio-economic groups consumed cheaper, energy-rich foods high in fat and sugar rather than food high in protective nutrients such as fruit and vegetables. The situation has changed little. With all supermarkets offering microwave-ready meals, the existence of large numbers of fast-food outlets on every high street and a generation of young people with little or no home economics tuition, it is likely to remain static. The government has tried to encourage food manufacturers to reduce salt, fat and sugar content in their foods but this too has made little difference. It was also noted that those on low incomes eat less healthily partly because of cost rather than lack of information, education or concern. This is worrying because it means that vulnerable groups cannot eat more healthily until their income rises. Other troubling features from the report were that people in low socio-economic groups:

▶ consumed more processed food high in salt, fat and sugar – increasing their risk of cardiovascular disease

▶ were less likely to breastfeed their babies, who were more likely to get infections

▶ were more likely to have low birth-weight babies – with a risk of cardiovascular disease

▶ generally had greater health risks through obesity.

Although various research reports have linked types of cancer with diet before, in 2015, the World Health Organization (WHO) produced a further report that classed red meat and processed meat as type A carcinogens, in the same band as smoking and asbestos. The Department of Health recommends that individuals should consume no more than 50–70g of processed/red meat a day, which is roughly equivalent to one sausage or two thin slices of bacon. The association is particularly with colorectal cancer (cancer of the large bowel) – however, the risk of cancer of the pancreas and prostate gland is also increased.

Research

To investigate the WHO report further, go to the WHO website and search for 'processed meat'.

Obesity

Obesity is constantly in the news, yet little progress has been made in eliminating this controllable health risk for both children and adults. The term obesity is used for an individual who is very overweight and whose body carries a lot of fat. One way of identifying whether an individual is obese is to use the body mass index (BMI), which is an individual's body weight in kilograms divided by the square of their height in metres. However, this measure should be used with caution as it is not an accurate measure of body composition (for example, fat and muscle mass).

- ▶ BMI of 25 to 29.9 is overweight.
- ▶ BMI of 30 to 39.9 is considered obese.
- ▶ BMI of over 40 is severely obese.

▶ Being overweight is an increasing problem

Worked Example

Joe is of moderate height at 1.8 m but his weight is 100 kg. Calculate his BMI.

100 divided by 1.8^2 = 30.86

Joe's BMI indicates that he is obese, ie his energy input exceeds his output. He needs to look at his diet, particularly the quantity of food that he eats, as well as the content. He also needs to look at the amount of exercise he takes.

Theory into practice

Work out your own BMI using the method in the worked example above.

Reflect

For some individuals, calculating a BMI is not useful as a measure of weight. This is because they are very muscular through physical training, which will give a false reading.

Another method is to plot your statistics on a height/weight chart or use a waistline measure. Waist measurements over 94 cm for men and 80 cm for women indicate obesity.

Obesity is caused by taking in more calories than you use in physical activity. The potential harmful effects of obesity are developing type 2 diabetes, coronary heart disease, stroke and some types of cancer such as breast and bowel cancer.

Discussion

Working in small groups, consider the contribution to obesity levels made by:

- fast-food outlets
- ready meals
- computer and video games
- television
- cars.

Add any other contributory factors that you can think of.

It is important to remember that extra weight has usually taken years to accumulate. To lose weight sensibly is to do so a little at a time – crash diets will help an individual to lose some excess weight quickly but will not change poor eating habits. The individual usually finds the weight creeps back on when the diet is stopped.

Dietary deficiency

There are many essential components to a diet:

▶ protein, carbohydrates and fat form the bulk of the diet and are the calorie containing foods

▶ vitamins and minerals are needed for correct functions of the body and are only required in small quantities

▶ water is an essential part of all cells and chemical reactions

▶ fibre, or roughage, does not provide nutrients but is important in stimulating bowel movements, and a lack of fibre leads to unpleasant constipation.

Body cells and structures are largely made of protein. Protein deficiency is rare in the UK but common in underdeveloped countries in Africa, Asia and South America. Growth and wound healing are affected by protein deficiency. Carbohydrate and fat supply energy for the body, so too little of these nutrients leads to lethargy (a lack of energy). Table 14.2 shows some of the effects caused by deficiencies of major vitamins and minerals.

▶ **Table 14.2** The effects on health of vitamin and mineral deficiencies

Vitamins	Function	Effect of deficiency
A (carotene, retinol)	Eyesight, skin, body linings, helping immune system.	Night blindness, skin disorders.
B1 (thiamine)	Energy release, growth.	Lack of energy, beri-beri.
B2 (riboflavin)	Energy release, growth.	Lips, tongue and skin disorders.
Nicotinic acid	Energy release, growth.	Nervous and digestive problems.
B12 (cobalamin)	Enzyme systems.	B12 anaemia.
Folic acid	Assists B12.	Anaemia, **spina bifida**.
C (ascorbic acid)	Connective tissues, heals wounds.	Gum bleeding, scurvy, poor healing.
D	Maintains calcium levels.	Tooth decay, soft bones, rickets.
Minerals	**Function**	**Effect of deficiency**
Calcium	Strong bones and teeth.	Tooth decay, soft bones, rickets.
Iron	Part of haemoglobin.	Iron deficiency anaemia.
Iodine	Produces thyroxine.	Hypothyroidism, goitre.
Fluorine	Hardens enamel.	Tooth decay.

> **Key term**
>
> **Spina bifida** – the condition in which some vertebrae (spinal bones) do not develop properly, sometimes leaving the spinal cord exposed and causing mobility impairment.

Environment

Potentially, the environment can have a huge effect on the development of some disorders so you will need to investigate this carefully for your chosen disorders. The environment can be considered as the surroundings in which you live. Environmental influences on health include the quality of air and water, noise and light pollution, housing, crime levels, climate, altitude, natural and man-induced radioactivity levels and many other factors. Fortunately, in the UK, most environmental influences are strictly regulated and their influence on disease is minimised.

Housing conditions

Rented accommodation exists in almost all areas, including many large inner cities and rural communities. When it is of poor quality and overcrowded with tenants (to increase rental income for the landlord), it can cause the spread of tuberculosis, respiratory illnesses and infestations. Additionally, rubbish is now collected less frequently in some areas, attracting vermin and causing infestations. Poorly maintained, dusty premises may have a high level of dust mites, which are a known trigger for asthma and other allergies.

Research has shown that more cases of cancer occur in inhabited areas close to nuclear plants. Mobile phone masts and wind farms have been coming under increasing scrutiny because of concern that they may affect the health of nearby inhabitants, particularly children, in various ways, but as yet no definitive proof has been found.

Air pollution

The poorest in society often live in the most polluted areas and cannot afford to move out. Air pollution, including fumes from traffic, is not believed to cause asthma, but certainly makes attacks more frequent and severe. Carbon dioxide and carbon monoxide are emitted from vehicles, industrial plants and household smokers.

▶ Air pollution can make conditions such as asthma worse – London is considered to have the poorest air quality in the European Union

Signs and symptoms of physiological disorders

A **diagnosis** is usually made by a doctor. When it is based on the **signs** and **symptoms**, it is sometimes called a **clinical diagnosis**. If the signs and symptoms could fit more than one disorder, a **differential diagnosis** is made. A family doctor might need another healthcare professional's opinion and so will make a **referral** to the appropriate professional or professional service.

Physiological disorders are characterised by the signs and symptoms experienced by the individuals suffering from the disorders.

▶ A sign is an objective indication of a disorder noticed by another individual, usually a parent or a spouse, or by a healthcare professional such as a nurse or doctor: for example a rash, pallor or a tremor.

▶ A symptom is a feature that an individual complains of, such as feeling dizzy, nausea, having a headache or a cough. A few characteristics can be both signs and symptoms, for example a lump – the doctor may notice a lump or an individual might complain of a lump. Distinguishing between signs and symptoms is academic and makes no difference to the individual, the clinician or the progress of the disease.

Some of the common signs and symptoms of physiological disorders are given in Table 14.3.

❙❙ PAUSE POINT   Can you explain the causes of physiological disorders?

Hint   Close the book and draw a mind map of causes of physiological disorders, giving one example for each disorder.

Extend   Why is it important to find the causes of physiological disorders?

Observable signs of physiological disorders

Rashes

A rash is an area of red or inflamed skin or groups of spots, sometimes with a raised temperature (fever) or itching. Rashes may be in a localised area or all over the body. The type of spots can be important in diagnosis, for example papular (raised spots like pimples), macular (flat spots of a different colour and texture to the skin) or blistering with clear yellow fluid or serum or be pus filled. Rashes are rarely life threatening. The colour of a rash may be significant. Rashes are common in childhood infections such as measles and chickenpox, and also in allergies, for example eczema and psoriasis.

Swellings

Swellings (lumps/tumours) can occur anywhere in the body, but deep swellings may not be very noticeable. Swellings can be temporary, such as after a knock or an accident, or may be permanent, such as a sebaceous cyst. Unless the cause is accidental and known, all swellings should be investigated. The location, size and nature of the swelling should be noted. Some tumours, such as breast cancer, commonly present as lumps, while a swelling in the neck could be mumps or a sign of hypo or hyperthyroidism. It is useful to obtain full details, such as time of appearance, rate of growth, any discharge and whether it is fluid filled, solid, soft or tense.

Symptoms experienced by the individual

Pain

Pain is a common symptom and its nature, rather like rashes, can be helpful with diagnosis. Find out its characteristics by asking the individual the right questions. Pain can vary from discomfort to absolute agony. It may be at the disorder's location, or some distance from it (known as referred pain). Individuals describe pain in many ways, such as stabbing, throbbing, stinging, intermittent, constant, acute and chronic. This can vary from person to person and it may be that likening it to a pain that the person may already have experienced, such as toothache or childbirth, proves more reliable. One of the worst pains is said to be when a male passes a kidney stone out of the body, as the passageways (ureters and urethra) are very narrow. To confuse matters more, an individual's pain threshold (the level at which the pain becomes unbearable) differs. Past experience may also affect their pain threshold. Some medical establishments have designed scales that service users can use to indicate the severity of their pain. Keeping a record can also be very useful in determining whether the pain is getting more or less severe.

Disorientation

Disorientation can occur when an individual is confused about place, time and/or identity, this confusion can be a sign as well as a symptom. Disorientation is often associated with odd behaviour and speech and the individual is usually unable to respond to simple questions. Their behaviour may be similar to being intoxicated. Mistakes have been made and individuals have been arrested for being drunk and disorderly when they were, in fact, disorientated. The symptom can last for minutes, days or weeks although, in mental illness, such as dementia, there can often be clear (lucid) periods in the early stages. Disorientation may occur with head injuries and in the elderly, if there is an underlying illness.

It is not possible to explain every sign and symptom for all the disorders you might investigate, but some common signs and symptoms could include those shown in Table 14.3.

Common signs	Common symptoms
Pallor/red flush/jaundice	Pain/discomfort/general malaise
Sweating/dehydration (eg increased thirst/dry mouth and swollen tongue)	Thirst
	Palpitations
Trembling/tremors	'Pins and needles'
Smell (breath, body)	Paralysis
Changes in appearance of urine/faeces	Headache
Changes in heart rate	Visual disturbances
Changes in breathing rate/wheezing	Unsteadiness/muscle weakness
Rash/spots	Changes in urination
Changed blood pressure	Changes in bowel habit
Changes in sensation	Loss/gain of weight
Loss/gain of weight	Cough
Changes in consciousness	Seizure or fits
Changes in mobility	Presence of lump/blood
Changes in skin/mucous membranes (eg colour or texture)	Nausea/vomiting
Changes in body temperature	Disorientation
Disorientation	

Assessment practice 14.1

A.P1   A.M1   A.D1

Kieran's mother has taken him to see the GP because he has had several boils (deep local skin infections) and the doctor asked him for a urine sample and a blood sample. Kieran had a severe bout of 'flu' about six months ago and has seemed unhealthy since. His mother thinks he is 'run down'.

The GP believes that Kieran has diabetes.

1 Explain the causes, signs and symptoms of diabetes.

2 Analyse the changes in Kieran's body systems and the way his body would function if he has type 1 diabetes.

3 Evaluate the impact or effect on Kieran's life if type 1 diabetes is diagnosed.

Plan
- How will I approach this task?
- Do I have any existing knowledge about the task at hand?

Do
- Question my own learning approach.
- Set milestones and evaluate my progress and success at these intervals.

Review
- Describe my thought processes.
- Explain which elements I found the hardest.

Reflect

When answering questions, check that you understand the 'command' words.
- **Explain** means give reasons for your answer.
- **Analyse** asks you to identify several relevant facts of a topic, demonstrate how they are linked and explain the importance of each, often in relation to other facts.
- **Evaluate** means bringing all the relevant facts together and judging their success or importance, supported by the facts you have collected.

PAUSE POINT   Can you explain what the learning aim was about? What elements did you find easiest?

> Hint   Consider your choices of physiological disorders carefully. Which will help you? Not all disorders have a known cause and/or treatment. Rare disorders will be more difficult.

> Extend   Are there any prospects that genetic editing will make a substantial difference to service user numbers or future treatments?

B Examine the investigation and diagnosis of physiological disorders

The term diagnosis means to determine the nature of an illness. Sometimes a doctor's experience and knowledge will make this easy. At other times, there may be two or more answers to an individual's problem. In this case, the doctor will start investigative procedures to eliminate the possibilities until a final clinical diagnosis can be made.

Investigative procedures for physiological disorders

When an individual is unwell, medical professionals carry out some general measurements to find out if there are any abnormal readings, and also to get a baseline for reference should the illness progress. Standard measurements taken routinely are body temperature, pulse rate, blood pressure and respiratory rate. These are recorded both numerically and graphically so that you can clearly see any variations.

General measurements that may be undertaken

Many establishments use electronic digital recorders for measuring pulse rate, blood pressure, body temperature and other physiological features.

All items of electrical equipment are potentially hazardous, both to the client and the carer operating them. The major hazards are burns and electric shock. You should be constantly alert for:

▶ equipment malfunction

▶ frayed electric flexes and trapped wires

▶ loose connections, plugs and sockets.

Any fault must be reported immediately – verbally and in writing. Most establishments have standard forms for reporting faults or damaged equipment. The device must be clearly labelled with a notice saying: 'Faulty, Do Not Use', and taken out of use. No one should be asked to use faulty equipment in their job. Only suitably qualified personnel should investigate, modify, repair or scrap equipment belonging to the establishment.

> **Safety tip**
>
> You should be familiar with the manufacturer's instructions for safe practice, potential risks and accuracy levels. In addition, you must be trained by an appropriately qualified person to use this type of equipment. Different pieces of equipment may operate in different ways.

Blood pressure (BP)

The force blood exerts on the walls of the blood vessels it is passing through is known as the blood pressure. It can be measured using a special piece of equipment called a sphygmomanometer, often abbreviated to 'sphyg' (pronounced sfig). Blood pressure should only be measured by a competent operator.

Systolic blood pressure corresponds to the pressure of the blood when the ventricles are contracting. Diastolic blood pressure represents blood pressure when the ventricles are relaxed and filling. Blood pressure is usually written as systolic/diastolic (eg 120/80) and the units are mmHg or millimetres of mercury. A few establishments have converted to SI units or kilopascals (kPa).

120/80 mmHg is taken as standard young healthy adult blood pressure, and in kPa this is 15.99/10.666.

Body temperature

Body temperature must be kept within a narrow range, so that the physiological processes of the body can function at maximum efficiency.

However, body temperature varies between individuals, even when they are in the same environment. Body temperature can vary in the same person at different times of the day, during different activity levels and depending on whether or not they have consumed food and drink. In women, body temperature is affected by the stages of the menstrual cycle – highest at ovulation and lowest during menstruation. Most people experience their lowest temperature at around 3 am and their highest at around 6 pm.

In addition to all these influences, body temperature varies according to where you take the measurement, for example, mouth, axilla (armpit), ear canal and rectum. The latter is only used when the other sites are unavailable and in individuals who are unconscious and/or very seriously ill, as the procedure causes raised anxiety and stress levels. Rectal temperatures are nearer to actual body core temperatures but are slower to change. Mouth or oral temperatures are about 0.5°C higher than axillary temperatures.

Normal body temperatures range from 36.5 to 37.2°C. Most people will quote 37°C as normal body temperature but, given the range of influencing factors, this may be rather too precise.

Temperatures are often taken once or twice daily as a routine, but the frequency will be varied according to need. A person suffering from (or at risk of developing) an infection, or who is recovering from hypothermia or who has had surgery, may have their temperature taken hourly or every four hours.

Several types of thermometer are available. These are:

▶ disposable thermometers
▶ calibrated electronic probes
▶ tympanic (ear canal) thermometers.

> **Reflect**
>
> What do you think is the range of body temperature compatible with life? Although this is not accurately known, experts believe that the upper limit is around 44°C and the lower 27°C. An individual will be seriously ill long before these limits are reached, and will be likely to die.

Many people may still use mercury-filled, clinical thermometers in their own homes, but their use is not allowed in care establishments as they are considered to be dangerous. (Temperatures were once measured in degrees Fahrenheit but now degrees Celsius are used. You should not use a thermometer with a Fahrenheit scale.)

Disposable oral thermometers and oral probe thermometers should be placed under the tongue. There are pouches on either side of the fold of membrane (the frenulum) on the underside of the tongue, and either one of these is a suitable place for the thermometer. This method is not suitable for use with very young children or confused individuals as the individual should not bite or chew on the probe but should close their lips around it for the prescribed length of time. The rest of the procedure is the same as for axillary temperature taking as described in the Step-by-step procedure: Measuring body temperature.

As rectal thermometry should not be carried out by unqualified individuals, it will not be described here.

Step by step: Measuring body temperature

`14 Steps`

You are most likely to take an individual's temperature in the axilla (armpit).

1 Wash your hands first to prevent cross infection.

▼

2 Explain what you are going to do to the individual and obtain their consent and cooperation.

▼

3 Make sure that the individual is sitting or lying comfortably and can hold that position for a few minutes.

▼

4 Respect privacy, and help the individual to remove clothing from one axilla.

▼

5 Dry the axilla with a disposable tissue.

▼

6 Place the temperature probe in the axilla so that it is surrounded by skin.

▼

7 Ask the individual to hold their arm across their chest to hold the probe in position.

▼

8 Stay with the individual to ensure that the position is maintained.

▼

9 Observe the individual throughout the process to check for signs of distress.

▼

10 Leave the thermometer in position for the correct time (as per the manufacturer's instructions).

▼

11 After the appropriate time has elapsed, remove the thermometer, read the measurement and record the individual's temperature, along with the date and time.

▼

12 Safely dispose of, or clean and store, the thermometer, as appropriate for the establishment.

▼

13 Wash your hands again.

▼

14 Check that the individual is still comfortable and, if relevant, compare this reading with previous readings.

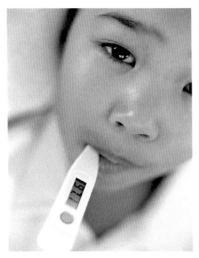

▶ Measuring body temperature using an oral thermometer

▶ Measuring body temperature using an axillary thermometer

▶ Measuring body temperature using a tympanic thermometer

Tympanic thermometers measure the temperature of the eardrum (tympanic membrane), which is very near to the body core temperature. A probe with a disposable cover is inserted into the ear canal, while gently pulling the ear lobe downwards. When the eardrum can no longer be seen (because it is obscured by the probe), hold the thermometer still and take the recording. Remove the probe and dispose of the cover before storing the equipment safely. Otherwise, use the same procedure as for axillary recordings. This is the preferred method for taking temperatures in children, as it is fast and well tolerated.

LCD (liquid crystal display) thermometers are cheap, disposable, safe and easy to use. They are also available in high street pharmacies, and parents of young children are encouraged to keep a supply at home. They are single-use only and the manufacturer's instructions must be followed to obtain correct results.

Investigations as appropriate for each individual

Investigations cost money. For example, transport required, buildings in which they take place, equipment (and maybe chemicals) used for the investigation and staff salaries are a few of the obvious costs. It is reasonable, therefore, to tailor investigations to the service user so that money is not wasted.

Medical history

A medical history is an account of the complaint in the individual's own words but prompted by the medical professional taking the history, so that the full details are obtained. A template is provided so that the history is obtained as soon as possible. Listening to an individual is very, very important. A good history can take half an hour but doctors rarely have that level of time to spare. The doctor is looking for a pattern of signs and symptoms that fit the pattern of a disorder or group of disorders. The next step may be diagnostic tests to confirm the diagnosis.

Blood tests

Blood samples can be obtained in two ways, by venepuncture (inserting a syringe needle into a vein) or by a finger prick, using a small, sterile lancet. Venepuncture is used when several millilitres of blood are required for clinical analysis.

An examination of the blood provides a good indication of an individual's health and wellbeing. Many substances normally present in blood can be analysed and reported on, including:

▶ haemoglobin level (for anaemia)

▶ levels of blood salts, technically known as electrolytes (for renal disorders, diabetes, metabolic bone disorders)

▶ hormone levels (for pregnancy, endocrine disorders)

▶ blood gases, such as oxygen and carbon dioxide (for respiratory disease)

▶ specific enzyme tests (for heart attacks)

▶ plasma proteins (for bleeding disorders)

▶ pH (for renal disorders, diabetes).

A special test known as a blood cell count will reveal whether the different types of blood cells are present in normal quantities and appearance.

The finger-prick test is used when only small quantities of blood are needed to measure the presence of a particular substance. For example, diabetics use small quantities like this, soaked into paper, in a special device for monitoring their blood glucose. Health visitors will use a heel-prick test on newborn babies to collect tiny amounts of blood to test for phenylketonuria (PKU test).

There are also other special blood tests for various purposes – for example, blood culture to determine whether septicaemia or blood poisoning is present.

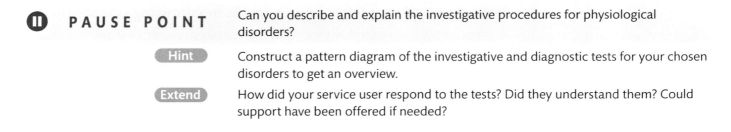

Ⅱ PAUSE POINT   Can you describe and explain the investigative procedures for physiological disorders?

> **Hint**   Construct a pattern diagram of the investigative and diagnostic tests for your chosen disorders to get an overview.

> **Extend**   How did your service user respond to the tests? Did they understand them? Could support have been offered if needed?

Diagnostic procedures for physiological disorders

Some techniques are particularly important when trying to make a diagnosis related to a particular body system. Endoscope (a tube with lenses and a light source for looking into body cavities) examinations are especially effective when investigating the digestive system or the alimentary canal.

Procedures based on specific signs and symptoms

Lumbar puncture

A lumbar puncture is used to take a sample of the cerebrospinal fluid, which bathes both the brain and the spinal cord, for analysis. The procedure is less used now that scanning is available. However, it is still a useful procedure in diagnosing meningitis and brain disorders such as haemorrhages. The spinal cord is shorter than the spinal column so the lower back region (the lumbar area) only contains spinal nerves.

Cerebrospinal fluid is more readily available at this point. With the service user lying on their side, with knees drawn up and head bent, a hollow needle is inserted into the spinal canal to obtain a sample of cerebrospinal fluid for analysis.

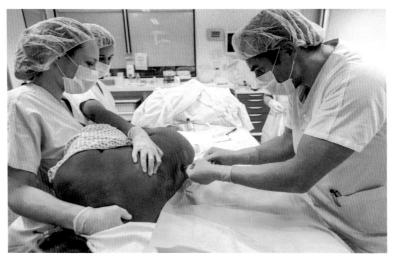

▶ An individual undergoing a lumbar puncture

Biopsy

A biopsy is when tissue or cells are removed for microscopic examination. A biopsy specimen is used for diagnosing many illnesses, including various types of cancer. Tumours, lymph nodes and swellings are the main areas for biopsy. A needle biopsy is often taken from a lump in the breast to determine whether the lump is a cyst or a more solid tumour. A liver or kidney biopsy may be used to determine the disease process and progress. An endoscope can be used to take biopsies from growths in the digestive tract.

Importance of recognising non-specific or confusing symptoms

It is important that an individual should feel they are being listened to as, sometimes, the signs and symptoms they describe are vague, and not necessarily related to a specific disease pattern. Investigations may produce results that make the pattern clearer, and a clinical or differential diagnosis may then be possible. On other occasions, service users can wait months or even years before a clinical diagnosis can be made. Sometimes, a diagnosis is made by eliminating other conditions until there is only one possibility left.

⏸ **PAUSE POINT**   Can you describe the diagnostic and investigative tests for physiological disorders?

Hint   Close the book. Mind map types of diagnostic and investigative tests and the physiological disorder they might be used to diagnose.

Extend   Why are good observation and listening skills so important in diagnosing health disorders?

Myalgic encephalomyelitis or ME

ME is a condition that is difficult to diagnose. The symptoms are non-specific and can be quite debilitating (weakening). An alternative name for it is chronic fatigue syndrome (CFS) as it is characterised by constant exhaustion, often lasting for months, which does not go away with sleep or rest. Sufferers may also have problems sleeping or concentrating. It cannot be explained by any other causes and may improve over time.

Assessment practice 14.2

Maureen is 58 years of age and has come to the GP because she has a pain in her right hand, which now seems to be starting in her left hand too. When the GP examines Maureen's right hand, she finds that the wrist, knuckles and finger joints are red and swollen, but the left hand looks normal. This suggests a form of arthritis, most likely rheumatoid arthritis.

1 Compare the investigative and diagnostic procedures to distinguish between different forms of arthritis.

2 Assess the importance of specific procedures in confirming that Maureen has rheumatoid arthritis.

Plan
- How will I approach the task?
- What resources do I need to complete the task? How can I get access to them?

Do
- I can make connections between what I am reading/ researching and the task, and identify the important information.
- What am I struggling with? Do I know how to overcome this?

Review
- I can explain what I have learned and why it is important.
- I can explain what success looks like.

Reflect

When answering questions, you need to understand the 'command' words.
- **Compare** requires you to supply two or more facts or topics with their differences and similarities, or advantages and disadvantages. You will often use connecting words such as 'whereas' or 'rather than'.
- **Assess** means that you must estimate the nature, ability or quality of something.

C Examine treatment and support for service users with physiological disorders

Individuals with physiological disorders require treatment, support or usually both. Medication may be required and some may need surgery, followed by supportive programmes such as rehabilitation, which is particularly important after cardiovascular disorders. Complementary therapies may be helpful after cancer diagnosis or treatment, and many individuals will need advice on changing lifestyles, especially in regards to stopping smoking, not overindulging in alcohol, and becoming more active.

Provision of treatment and support

Medication

Medication has been used to treat disorders for thousands of years, starting with natural sources such as plants and fungi, and now using synthetic drugs manufactured by chemists and pharmacologists. There are antibiotic drugs to combat infection, antihypertensives to reduce blood pressure, diuretics to increase urine flow and many other types of drugs.

Anti-inflammatory drugs

Anti-inflammatory drugs reduce inflammation.

The characteristics of inflammation are redness, swelling (with fluid), warmth and pain. Most anti-inflammatory drugs work by reducing pain, and brands you may know include aspirin, paracetamol and ibuprofen. Corticosteroids are also useful in reducing inflammation where there is no infection. Drugs must be taken according to their instructions. If there is no response after 48 hours, service users are advised to consult their GP. All drugs have side effects and some drugs can become addictive.

Surgery

Surgery is undertaken for many physiological disorders, for example surgical by-passes may be necessary to relieve angina or coronary thrombosis, and sections of the thyroid gland may be removed to treat hyperthyroidism.

Surgical procedures for cancer

Surgical procedures for cancer can be part of the treatment to remove tumours, such as those in the breast and prostate. Generally, such procedures are undertaken before the cancer has spread to neighbouring lymph nodes or organs, and may be followed by radiotherapy or chemotherapy.

Rehabilitation programmes

This is treatment aimed at allowing service users to regain independent living and can involve physiotherapy, occupational therapy and psychotherapy. Customised programmes are developed, often in special departments or centres that may be associated with hospitals.

Physiotherapy

Physiotherapy treats physiological disorders and injuries using various methods such as exercise, infrared rays, diathermy, hydrotherapy, massage and ultrasound techniques. The main role of a physiotherapist is to improve joint stiffness and muscle strength, although they are also concerned with breathing and post-operative recovery. Exercise programmes can be active or passive – where the physiotherapist moves the affected part to preserve the joint's range of movement.

▶ Physiotherapist helping a service user

Complementary therapies

In conventional medicine, these therapies are used as an accompaniment to more traditional ways of treating disorders. Complementary therapies include acupuncture, aromatherapy, reflexology, reiki, homeopathy and many more. Effectiveness is controversial, but service users are often enthusiastic about them as they may feel good after therapy. Most doctors are sceptical about complementary medicine (also called alternative medicine) and a principal reason is that knowledge, investigative tests and experience leads to a clinical diagnosis, whereas alternative therapists tend to choose treatment based on the complaints an individual describes.

Aromatherapy

Aromatherapy uses sweet-smelling essential oils extracted from plants. These are usually massaged into the skin in tiny quantities, or inhaled. The choice of oils depends on the individual's symptoms.

Acupuncture

Acupuncture is based on ancient Chinese medicine, in which needles are inserted at specifically located points on meridian lines (channels in which the life force, or chi, flows) coursing over the body. It is thought that morphine-like substances, called endorphins, may be released – hence acupuncture's use in anaesthesia for some procedures, such as in childbirth and in pain relief. Another possibility is that acupuncture induces a form of hypnosis. As with aromatherapy, diagnosis is questionable as it relies on pulse examinations. Additionally, practitioners generally lack traditional Western medical qualifications.

Advice on lifestyle changes

There are many sources of advice on making healthy lifestyle choices, ranging from looking at the internet to visiting a general practice and communicating with healthcare professionals. Organisations specialising in specific disorders generally have websites, and most produce newsletters or magazines for their members. Additionally, living healthily is often in the news. The media are helpful, too, with television programmes and newspapers devoting considerable time to these issues. NHS Choices, leaflets in surgeries, libraries and supermarkets have information freely available on all manner of subjects. Well Man and Well Woman clinics, associated with health centres and hospitals, also provide helpful advice for service users.

Smoking cessation

Smoking cessation is a common topic for many of the sources mentioned above, and feedback has shown that people who try to stop smoking with the help of the NHS are more successful than those who try on their own. The government has introduced various pieces of legislation to assist in reducing the number of smokers in the UK and this has been quite successful. There are now several products on the market that individuals can buy to help them stop smoking.

> **Research**
>
> Find out the services and products available locally to help individuals to stop smoking. Produce an annotated diagram of your findings to include in your unit notes.

Types of carers and care settings

You will look at a general range of care settings but it is mainly the people who work in these settings who are fundamental to the caring process. This includes both professional and unqualified, or informal, carers.

Professional carers

General practitioners (GPs)

The GP is likely to be the first (or primary) setting where the individual seeks help for the symptoms they are experiencing. There might already be a long-term relationship between the individual and the GP, which will be advantageous to both. The GP will take a medical history, if it is not already known, and will ask relevant questions about the new symptoms.

As a result of this questioning, the GP will soon come up with a list of possible disorders from which the individual may be suffering. They will carry out a physical examination of the individual to support, or narrow, the differential diagnosis. The physical examination will be enhanced by taking routine measurements such as blood pressure, body temperature, pulse and breathing rates.

The GP may quickly decide that the individual needs to be referred to a hospital specialist, and will write a letter explaining the findings at the initial consultation, requesting an outpatient's appointment with an appropriate specialist or consultant at the earliest opportunity. More usually, however, the GP will arrange to use services allied to the hospital for diagnostic tests such as X-rays, blood tests or other early investigations, and request that the individual returns at a date when these results are likely to be available. After further consultations, the GP might still refer the individual to hospital, or they may decide to treat the individual's condition for a set time and make a referral at a later date if the symptoms do not improve.

Clinical specialists

Clinical specialists have taken further qualifications in their particular field of medicine or surgery to become experts in their field – you may be more familiar with the term consultant.

They are often called by their specialist field with '-ist' on the end, so, for example, a cardiologist specialises in heart disorders, a nephrologist in kidney disorders and a rheumatologist in diseases of the joints, muscles and connective tissues. These types of clinical specialists are usually physicians – people who practise medicine as opposed to surgery.

A doctor who has specialised in heart surgery is a cardiac surgeon, a specialist in kidney surgery is a renal surgeon and a specialist in bone surgery is an orthopaedic surgeon.

There are also specialists for some particular life stages, a paediatrician is an expert in diseases found in children and a geriatrician is concerned with diseases of older people.

An oncologist is a specialist in tumours, especially cancers, and a radiologist studies both the diagnosis and treatment of disease using radiological techniques.

There are clinical specialists in biochemistry, haematology, pathology and cytology, who service users rarely see, but who work behind the scenes in departments that assist other clinical specialists.

The list of clinical specialists is very long and, if you come across an '-ist' name you do not recognise, you can either ask a professional or consult a dictionary. Clinical specialists usually head a team of people including registrars, senior house officers and house officers (in descending order of experience). House officers are now 'foundation year 1 trainees' but are often still called house officers during everyday work. The specialist will often see an individual on their first visit, to make a diagnosis and order investigations, and, on subsequent visits, the individual may be seen by another doctor in the specialist's team.

Nurses

Nurses are expert professionals in individualised client care and make clinical judgements based on sound research and knowledge-based practice.

Like doctors, there are several progression routes for nurses, but all work to a **value-based system**. Nursing education was significantly reformed several years ago and is now a recognised degree programme. Nurses also specialise in different areas. Some key areas are mental health, children, health visiting and midwifery.

Service users rely on nurses to meet their everyday caring needs, as they tend to see doctors infrequently. For this reason, nurses are taking on more and more of the traditional roles of doctors, such as prescribing medicines. Nearly every individual receiving care will have contact with nurses at most levels.

Care assistants

Care assistants undertake most of the care associated with daily living and will, in a hospital setting, be the carers most involved in meeting service users' needs. They undertake more practically based study – National Vocational Qualifications. After achieving these qualifications, many progress to degree programmes in nursing. Care assistants are also employed to carry out similar tasks in social care and domestic settings.

Professions allied to medicine

These professionals all undertake specialist degrees in their fields. They include occupational therapists, physiotherapists, radiographers and chiropodists.

▶ **Occupational therapists** assist people disabled by physical illness or recovering from a serious accident or major surgery to regain their independence in daily living. This may be within the hospital environment or the individual's home.

▶ **Physiotherapists** are concerned with treating and rehabilitating movement, mainly muscles, using heat, light, electricity, massage, remedial exercises and manipulation.

▶ **Radiographers** are professional healthcare workers in either a diagnostic X-ray department or a radiotherapy department. They position an individual for the correct angle of the radiation and manage the radiography or radiotherapy process. (They should not be confused with radiologists, who are clinical specialists in radiology – reading and interpreting X-rays.)

▶ **Chiropodists**, also sometimes known as podiatrists, care for the feet and treat diseases of the feet. The care of feet is particularly important for older diabetic people, as they are prone to gangrene from open cuts.

> **Key term**
>
> **Value-based system** – an approach to care based on standards of conduct such as confidentiality, anti-discrimination, equal opportunities, maintaining personal identity and health and safety.

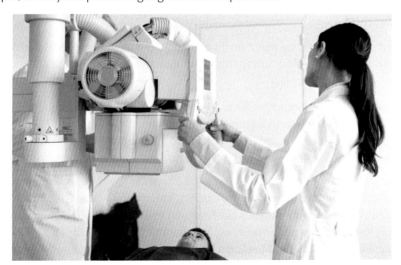

▶ Radiographer working with a service user

PAUSE POINT   Can you explain what the different types of carers are and what they do?

Hint   Close the book and make a list of professional carers and the settings in which they work.

Extend   How do professional carers communicate with each other?

Informal carers

There are estimated to be about 6.5 million informal carers in the UK, with approximately 6000 new carers every day. These carers are friends, neighbours and paid carers such as companions. Above all, they are family members, many of them children. Every day accidents happen, illness strikes, such as strokes and heart attacks, and babies are born with disabilities. Without these informal carers, the NHS and social services would be overwhelmed, and both the economy and society would suffer adverse effects. Some carers live in and work 24 hours a day, while others work for a few hours but may often have to travel long distances to get to the care settings. Many carers manage families, go to work or school, or suffer from poor health themselves. Some become carers virtually overnight following accidents and strokes, while others find themselves in an ongoing situation that gradually becomes more onerous, such as looking after ageing parents who are unable to manage their affairs any more. Many informal carers have financial difficulties, others have given up work to look after relatives and slowly slide into poverty. The care ranges from lighter duties such as paying bills or doing shopping, to more demanding tasks such as bathing, assisting toilet visits and changing dressings. While there is some financial allowance for carers, it is never enough, and life can become very tough.

Private and voluntary carers

There are many private care agencies who, for a fee, will supply carers for sick and disabled service users at home, either as live in, daily or hourly, although this is quite costly. The agencies can be found through the internet or through organisations helping people with their needs. There are also many people who volunteer their services for free to help others. Age UK and similar organisations have websites where people with time to spare to assist others can offer their services in their local area.

Care settings

A care setting is an environment in which service users receive assistance, such as support and treatment.

The level of care provided by these settings will change, as an individual with a disorder is diagnosed, treated and their care is managed.

Home

Most people who are ill would prefer to be cared for in their own homes, especially if they have a loving family around. Older people often have a particular fear of hospitals or going into residential care and would prefer to stay at home, with familiar things around them. They often feel that if they leave home, they will not return.

Individuals with many disorders can usually be cared for at home until the later stages of the illness. If special aids are required, such as **stairlifts**, bath hoists or disabled access, these can be provided after a professional assessment. It is more cost-effective for the NHS for people to continue living independently for as long as possible. Services such as home carers, '**Meals on Wheels**' and chiropody can be arranged to support people in their own homes as part of a **care package** of assistance.

Key terms

Stairlift – mechanical chair that acts as a lift and is fitted to the wall of a staircase. The service user sits on the chair and activates the operating mechanism to move up or down a flight of stairs.

Meals on Wheels – service provided in England and Wales to supply mainly frozen meals to the service user's home. The meals can be heated as and when the service user requires.

Care package – the sum of the types of care provided from the care plan, involving professional carers, organisations, volunteers and informal carers.

Supporting Denis

Anne is 75 and Denis is 82 years of age. They have been married for more than 50 years and do not have any family living nearby. Anne is becoming increasingly forgetful and more remote. The doctors can't find any other physical cause for this and, following memory tests, have diagnosed Alzheimer's disease. Denis has had alarms fitted on all exterior doors because a few weeks ago the police found Anne wandering the streets in the early hours of the morning in her nightgown. Recently, Anne did not recognise her grandson when he visited and became very distressed about this. Denis now does all the cleaning, cooking and shopping, as well as looking after Anne. He is determined that he will care for her at home but is worried about the future, as he has arthritis in both hip joints and walking is quite painful.

Check your knowledge

1 Discuss ways in which Denis could be supported to care for Anne in their home.

2 What points could you put forward for Anne and Denis staying together but moving to a care setting that would be able to provide more support for the couple?

3 Analyse what Denis' feelings might be about the situation.

Residential care settings

People in the late stages of disorders such as Parkinson's disease and Alzheimer's disease, rheumatoid arthritis, stroke and coronary heart disease may have to be cared for in a social care setting, such as a residential care home, because of their increasing disability and the need to keep them safe. Other people may be able to stay at home and attend a day care setting several times a week for specific care, company and relaxation. This can be particularly important if the rest of the family is working during the day or the individual lives alone. Residential care settings may also offer respite care to provide an opportunity for informal carers, particularly family members, to take a holiday or have a rest from caring.

GP surgery

We have already looked at what a GP does in the section on professional carers. A GP usually works in a surgery, which is a place in which primary care is carried out (see care methods below). Service users attend the surgery to consult a GP, usually on an appointment basis, to seek a diagnosis for an illness, access support and medication, and check the progress of their condition.

In addition, practice nurses carry out simple procedures in the surgery, such as ear syringing and monitoring blood pressure. Most surgeries run clinics for special groups of service users, such as individuals with diabetes, mother and baby monitoring and those with high blood pressure. If there are any concerns, the healthcare professionals running the clinic can make a quick referral to a doctor on site.

Some GP surgeries run cryoclinics periodically. At these clinics, a doctor is available to treat certain skin conditions, such as warts and skin tags, by freezing them. Usually, this eliminates the problem, although, occasionally, more than one treatment may be necessary.

Health advice is freely available from doctors and nurses. Many GP surgeries are able to provide facilities for minor surgical procedures and taking blood samples for investigative purposes.

Health centres

GPs are increasingly working together in purpose-built health centres, where extra services and facilities can be offered. Such facilities might include maternity services, counselling, alternative therapy sessions, various specialised clinics, phlebotomists, mobility aid specialists, family planning and health promotion. Such services relieve the pressure on hospitals, serve the local community well and may save service users having to travel long distances to hospitals. They are often located close to pharmacies, or include a pharmacy, so that medication can be more easily obtained.

Hospital care

Individuals may access hospital care as outpatients or inpatients.

People with serious disorders, such as cancer, will be admitted as soon as possible for investigations and treatment. When the condition is less acute, they may make outpatient visits for a long time – for example, for individuals with Parkinson's disease or Alzheimer's disease. Individuals with diabetes may be admitted for a short period to stabilise their condition with appropriate medication, followed by annual checks.

Hospitals have varied facilities and a service user may need to be taken from one hospital to another to access specialist facilities, such as scans. This is usually for a short period only. Smaller hospitals have limited facilities and specialist consultants may visit, for example, for one day every month.

People are likely to be admitted as inpatients for surgery, except in the case of minor complaints.

Rehabilitation settings

Occupational therapists are rehabilitation experts. Although this may involve rehabilitation looking towards gaining employment, or getting back to work, their work is also vital to ensure that people are able to manage at home. For example, an occupational therapist will be involved in the care of an individual who has musculo-skeletal problems before they can transfer from hospital to home. The occupational therapist will assess the individual and, if necessary, visit their home to see which mobility aids will assist them with everyday living.

Rehabilitation settings exist for drug and alcohol addiction, although, because of the often lengthy stays for treatment, there are long waiting lists for free places. Cottage hospitals and nursing homes are regularly used by service users who may need temporary care, for example after surgery, if they live alone.

PAUSE POINT   Can you explain what learning aim C was about? What elements did you find easiest?

Hint   Think about the support available at home, at the health centre, in hospital and, finally, from local or online organisations.

Extend   Why are some service users not willing to use all the support available to them?

Assessment practice 14.3

C.P3   C.P4   C.M3   BC.D2

1 Explain the treatment and support that is available for Kieran who has been diagnosed with diabetes (see assessment practice 14.1).

2 Compare the types of carers and care settings for Kieran and for Maureen (see assessment practice 14.2) who has rheumatoid arthritis.

3 Assess the provision of treatment, support and types of care for Kieran.

4 Justify the potential benefits of different investigations and treatment options for Kieran.

Plan
- Do I need to clarify anything?
- What am I being asked to do?

Do
- What strategies am I employing? Are these right for the task? Are they working? If not, what do I need to do to change?
- I can seek others' opinions.

Review
- I can explain what skills I employed and which new ones I developed.
- I can draw links between this learning and prior learning.

Reflect

When answering questions, it is a good idea to check that you understand what the 'command' words are asking you to do.
Justify – means that you must give reasons to support your point or argument.

Develop a treatment plan for service users with physiological disorders to meet their needs

First, it is important to establish what is meant by service users' needs. These are necessities required to achieve a state of health and wellbeing. Basic needs are for food, water, shelter and so on. Higher needs are to feel valued and loved, and to feel that you have reached your potential in life (self-fulfilment or self-actualisation).

Research

Abraham Maslow was an American psychologist who famously developed a hierarchy grading of needs with the basic needs at the base of a triangle and the higher needs at the apex. Those lower down must be satisfied before the upper ones can be achieved. Research Maslow's hierarchy of needs and add to your notes.

Link

See *Unit 11: Psychological Perspectives* for further information on Maslow.

It is important not to confuse care needs with care 'wants' and this may have to be explained to service users. For example, an elderly service user may decide that her windows need cleaning but be unable to do the task herself. She may expect that the carer who helps her to get up in the morning will stay to clean her windows. However, cleaning windows is not an acceptable need; rather, it is a want. The carer might ask a neighbour to arrange a window cleaner, or contact someone to do this task to stop the service user worrying, but the carer looks after other service users and cleaning windows is not part of a carer's duties.

Care methods and strategies

Care strategies are ways to deliver services or reach goals. For organisations such as social services or the NHS, strategies give guidance and an overall care route.

A care pathway is the way in which services are assembled to meet the service user's needs.

Primary care

This is usually an individual's first point of contact with health services in the community. This might be through a GP, a clinic or after-hours centre, or a community nurse or midwife. This visit may result in referral to secondary or tertiary health care.

Secondary care

This is care that service users receive in acute or general hospitals that usually involves tests, diagnosis and treatment. Secondary care usually follows referral from a primary healthcare practitioner.

Tertiary care

This is care that a service user receives after transfer to units with a special focus, such as a palliative centre (for best care in terminal illness), a spinal unit or an oncology centre (for service users with cancer).

Assessment of care needs

Healthcare professionals work with service users to discover their needs, the results or outcomes the service user wants to get, and the ways in which the service user wants to arrive at the results. A care professional is named as a needs assessor and their role is to contact other people or agencies to get information regarding working with the service user or an advocate. The service user must give permission for these enquiries and contacts and be in control of the needs assessment.

Most assessments now feature person-centred planning, which means that the service user is at the centre of positive planning that focuses on what the service user is able to do, and then examines areas where the service user may need extra support to fill gaps. Customised charts are completed so that all agencies, including the service user, know what care has been decided on and agreed.

Reviewing care needs

Periodically, the care plan needs to be reviewed or reconsidered. A service user's circumstances may have altered. Service users' abilities, for example, may be improved, or reduced, or the service from some agencies may no longer be required (or not be satisfactory). The results or outcomes may have been achieved, or not. Providing services is costly, both in terms of money and time, and there is no point in providing services that are either not required or not effective.

Validity and reliability of sources of information on possible treatments

When you carry out research for your assignments, you will, among other topics, be looking for possible treatments for the conditions you have chosen. Reliability and validity are very important.

Reliability

Reliability is a measure of the methods used to generate information. This means the degree of trust that you have in the source of the information and, if it was experimental, whether you could repeat the experiment and obtain the same results.

Validity

Validity is defined as a measure of the quality of the information and how it is used. This means whether the information is legitimate and true. In experimental terms, whether what you are measuring is accurate or valid.

You may need to challenge (mentally) possible treatments from unreliable sources, for example those found out about from the internet or from popular magazines, as the source may have a financial interest in selling their products, equipment or medication. Some sources predict future treatments, which may never actually happen, or which have rapidly become outdated or superseded because more reliable treatment methods are available. You need to read material carefully to judge its claims. For example, newspapers may run advertisements for solutions to remove 'skin tags' and other skin blemishes common in older people. However, some GP practices will run a cryoclinic to freeze off unwanted blemishes and may not support any other form of removal. Who would you trust?

You can trust authoritative websites such as the NHS, UK government websites or UK national forums like Diabetes UK and the Cystic Fibrosis Trust.

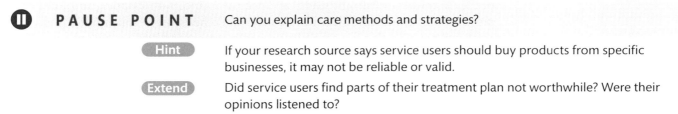

❚❚ PAUSE POINT   Can you explain care methods and strategies?

> **Hint**   If your research source says service users should buy products from specific businesses, it may not be reliable or valid.

> **Extend**   Did service users find parts of their treatment plan not worthwhile? Were their opinions listened to?

Treatment plan processes

When constructing a treatment plan for your service users with physiological disorders, you will need to consider several areas. This section is concerned with assisting you to include the necessary details in your treatment plan, starting with the cycle of planning.

Cycle of planning

A plan is a written record of the stages in arranging treatment or care, and will cover the services that the service user and/or the carer and professionals have chosen. Plans need to conform to a scheme recognised by the needs assessor to ensure that all necessary aspects are included. First, it is necessary to gather all the information required from the service user and the individuals and agencies involved. Once this has been established and made public to all concerned individuals, then the service user's needs can be assessed and the desired outcomes recorded. The care plan can now be implemented, with ongoing monitoring. A time for evaluation and review is set that is appropriate for the service user, and the type of disorder they have, and the agencies involved. The new information from this review is published and the cycle begins again.

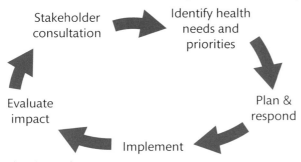

▶ **Figure 14.1** The planning cycle

Individual needs

All human beings are unique and this uniqueness is gathered bit by bit from their background and life experiences, particularly their culture, gender, age, religion and disability. Very few treatment plans will be alike, although most will follow the same general format.

Age

As well as needs arising from a physiological disorder, there may be needs associated with the age of the service user, particularly at the extremes of age such as in infancy, young children and older service users.

Very young people depend on parents and/or siblings to guide them with health issues as they are too young to understand the importance of, for example, taking medication regularly. Carers will have to assess the capabilities of these informal carers in carrying out the support and assistance required. Usually, informal carers will provide the necessary care. However, if this is not the case, then the infant or child may have to be placed in a more reliable setting, such as a hospital, until the situation is resolved.

An older service user may be forgetful and fail to take medication, or take too much, or they may have mobility problems and need assistance with shopping and collecting prescriptions. In addition, older people may have other sensory impairments such as smell, sight and hearing loss that complicates treatment and adds to their care needs. These examples illustrate that every human being is unique and care plans must be tailored to meet individual needs.

Culture

When a group of people share the same values, beliefs, customs, dress, language and behaviour this is known as a culture. A simple example could be that some people are used to eating a midday main meal, while others prefer to eat their main meal in the evening. Another is that some people would not eat a main meal without sitting at a table, whereas others eat in front of the television.

Gender

Gender can be very important. A female service user may be very uncomfortable with male carers, especially if undressing is a necessary part of the care, such as in bathing. Some males prefer male doctors, especially if intimate examinations are required.

Religion

It is vitally important to some groups of people to carry out their religious practices when they are in a care setting, whereas others do not worry. Some religions practise dietary restrictions, such as kosher or halal meat, vegetarianism and abstaining from eating pork or drinking alcohol. You will need to find out about your service user's religious preferences and practices and conduct appropriate research.

Disability

Your service users might have disabilities that may or may not be associated with their particular physiological disorder. Remember that a service user with diabetes or coronary heart disease could also, for example, suffer from painful arthritis that interferes with movement and their ability to exercise.

 **PAUSE POINT**   What is meant by individual needs?

> **Hint**   What needs should you consider for an older male service user with diabetes, who uses a wheelchair? Add to your notes.

> **Extend**   Why is it important to concentrate on what service users can do rather than on what they cannot do?

Purpose and aim of care for the individual

The individual at the centre of the plan is the service user.

When a treatment plan is being constructed, all concerned parties should be fully aware of the reasons why a specified action is being incorporated and carried out. The plan is unsatisfactory if the service user (or an advocate) and/or the carers do not know the purpose of tasks. Although it is accepted that service users with mental or neurological conditions may not remember the reason why a service or means of support is being carried out, the carer must always be able to provide this information and may need to do so several times.

Outcomes to be achieved

A logical reason for defining the purpose of treatment is to identify how those involved will know when they have been successful. End-points or outcomes will determine that success. Just as there is no point in delivering services that are not effective or successful, it is equally futile to continue delivering services when the outcome has been achieved, unless a level of maintenance is required to ensure that there is no slippage. Almost inevitably this may mean a reduction in the level of treatment needed.

Actions to be taken

You will need to detail the actions that must be taken to implement the treatment plan, and to achieve the outcomes identified. The actions must conform to the purpose of the plan, acknowledged after the assessment of needs. Depending on the nature of the service user's physiological disorder, the actions planned may involve medication, regular testing, mobility exercises, surgery and so on.

Overcoming potential barriers

There are many potential barriers and, again, they are dependent on the nature of the service user's physiological disorder. For example, if the service user has difficulties with swallowing tablets or capsules, the prescribed medication may need to be changed to a liquid form. Or, the medication may not agree with the service user, and cause nausea and vomiting. Surgical operations may be repeatedly cancelled. Waiting lists are always a problem, whether for surgery or to see a specialist consultant at a hospital, and transport may become an issue. There may be a bed shortage or wards closed due to staff shortages or infection. The barriers may be slight or complex and the ways to overcome them costly and difficult.

Professional responsibilities

Like all carers involved in the treatment plan, you will need to demonstrate professional responsibilities according to the Care Value Base. These will involve:

▶ maintaining confidentiality of information and discussions on a need-to-know basis

▶ considering the service user's choices and preferences

▶ giving praise, and encouraging independence and support

▶ respecting the service user and their personal worth and dignity

▶ maintaining a positive relationship and showing a sensitive manner

▶ being aware of the service user's needs

▶ using antidiscriminatory practice

▶ respecting individual differences and identity.

Advantages and disadvantages of different types of treatment

These depend on the physiological disorders that you choose. Most will benefit the service user and some will be very costly to the health and social care services.

An example of benefit versus cost is renal dialysis, for service users with chronic renal failure, versus kidney transplant.

The accumulation of products normally excreted by healthy kidneys will make the service user feel unwell, bloated and less able to live a normal life, but dialysis removes most of these products for two to three days, allowing a better quality of life. However, whichever type of dialysis is used, it takes time and haemodialysis usually means travelling to a dialysis unit at least three times every week, which is a disadvantage. Peritoneal dialysis can be carried out at home and, theoretically, the service user can remain in employment, which is an advantage. Either way, dialysis is costly. Successful kidney transplantation is much cheaper, and the service user has only monitoring visits to attend.

Transplantation of any organ means that the service user must take medication for the remainder of their lives to prevent rejection of the transplant. Anti-rejection medication (called immunosuppression) increases the risk that the human body cannot deal with cancer via their immune system and they have a higher risk of, say, skin cancer than people who are not immunosuppressed. You will need to research the benefits and pitfalls for your choice of disorders.

Benefit to service users versus cost to health and social care services

This can often prove a controversial topic, especially when service users are denied treatment, usually medication, on the grounds of the cost to the NHS. Some drugs are very expensive and may benefit only a few individuals, whereas the same amount of money could pay for a much larger group of individuals to have treatment that may increase mobility or independence, or even get some individuals back to work. The decisions are very hard to make. Some health authorities refuse treatment on the grounds of service users being smokers or overweight, both of which make surgical treatment more risky. The media often highlights such issues, particularly when terminal illness or children are involved. The National Institution for Clinical Excellence (NICE) is regularly called on to make such judgements.

> **Discussion**
>
> Is it ethical to prevent surgery, say a knee replacement, if an individual is grossly obese?

Scheduling, including times and locations where treatment will take place

You will discover these details from your service user or their carers and will need to include the information in your treatment plan. For example, Mr Smith might attend the dialysis unit every Monday, Wednesday and Friday morning, from 8 am until 12 noon at the Careful Hospital, Birmingham.

Timescales for achievement

To achieve outcomes in your work, you will need to consider the period of time you have been given for your assignment, as well as what physiological disorders the service users that you have chosen have. Outcomes can be short- or long-term and it will be beneficial to include both types, even though you may have finished your assignment and not be able to monitor long-term outcomes. Outcomes can be small achievements, such as being able to get dressed in the morning without help, assuming that the service user could not accomplish this previously. Or a specific improvement in physical health, such as a reduced blood pressure, or an improved feeling of wellbeing. It is useful to return to the service user's needs when considering the outcomes and to consider the physical, emotional, intellectual or social aspects of the service user's life.

Assessment practice 14.4   D.P5 D.P6 D.P7 D.M4 D.D3

Kieran, Maureen or other service users can be part of this activity.

1 Assess the care needs of your chosen service user.

2 Plan their treatment to meet the needs you have identified in question 1.

3 Explain how the treatment plan would improve the health and wellbeing of your chosen service user.

4 Review the treatment plan, as appropriate, to improve the outcomes.

5 Justify the recommendations in the plan in relation to the service user's needs, and the advantages and disadvantages of treatment options.

Plan
- What am I being asked to do?
- What are the success criteria for the task?

Do
- Have I spent some time planning out my approach to the task at hand?
- I can question my own learning approach.

Review
- I can explain whether I met the task's criteria and succeeded.
- I can make informed choices based on reflection.

Further reading and resources

Leaflets on health and social care topics from health centres, GP surgeries and supermarkets.

Waugh, A. and Grant, A. (2010) *Ross and Wilson Anatomy and Physiology in Health and Illness*, 11th ed, Oxford: Elsevier Health Sciences.

Basset, S. (2011) *Cliffs Notes Anatomy & Physiology Quick Review*, 2nd ed, Oxford: Houghton Mifflin Harcourt.

Patton, K. and Thibodeau, G.A. (2015) *Anatomy and Physiology*, 9th ed, Oxford: Elsevier Health Sciences.

Peate, I. and Nair, M. (2015) *Anatomy and Physiology for Nurses at a Glance*, Oxford: Wiley-Blackwell.

BMA Family Health Encyclopedia: The Essential Reference to over 7,000 Medical Terms Including Symptoms, Diseases, Drugs and Treatments, 5th ed (2008), London: DK Publishing.

Websites

www.nhs.uk

National Health Service website provides information on general health and wellbeing and information on facilities such as doctors and hospitals.

www.cancerresearchuk.org

Cancer Research UK is a charity that raises funds to research ways of fighting cancer.

(Websites *continued*)

www.alzheimers.org.uk
Alzheimer's Society offers advice and support to those with dementia and their families.

www.asthma.org.uk
Asthma UK is a charity raising funds to research and cure asthma.

www.lung.org.uk
Information specifically aimed at helping people maintain healthy lungs and make lifestyle changes.

www.brit-thoracic.org.uk
The *British Thoracic Society* campaigns to support people with respiratory diseases and improve care.

www.bhf.org.uk
The *British Heart Foundation* is a national charity aimed at researching causes of and cures for heart disease.

www.cftrust.org.uk
The *Cystic Fibrosis Trust* campaigns to raise funds to research cystic fibrosis and support sufferers.

www.gig.org.uk
The *Genetic Alliance UK* brings together many organisations to offer support for people suffering from genetic conditions and their families.

www.anthonynolan.org
Anthony Nolan researches blood cancer and matches people willing to donate blood stem cells or bone marrow with those in need of transplants.

www.leukaemiacare.org.uk
Leukaemia Care is a charity aimed at supporting anyone affected by blood cancer.

www.diabetesuk.org.uk
Diabetes UK is a charity that campaigns to support and inform people with diabetes.

www.meassociation.org.uk
The *ME Association* campaigns to raise funds to research ME and support sufferers.

www.nos.org.uk
The *National Osteoporosis Society* raises money to research osteoporosis and provide information, advice and support.

www.parkinsons.org.uk
Parkinson's UK is a charity that works to research Parkinson's and find a cure and provides support and information to sufferers and their families.

www.arthritiscare.org.uk
Arthritis Care campaigns for people suffering with arthritis and offers information and support to those diagnosed.

www.rheumatoid.org.uk
The *National Rheumatoid Arthritis Society* offers information and advice to sufferers and their families.

www.sicklecellsociety.org
The *Sickle Cell Society* raises money to support people affected by sickle cell disease.

THINK ▶▶ FUTURE

Mollie Smith,
Home Care
Assistant

I've been in this job for two years, since my own children grew older. I completed an NVQ training course when I started the job. I care for Mr P, who lives on his own and has prostate cancer; he's desperate to stay at home for as long as he can. My main task is to care for him so that he can remain in the comfort and security of his home for as long as he is able.

I arrive at 8 am and get his breakfast ready before helping him to get up, wash and dress in the clothes he wishes to wear. He takes great pride in his appearance and is able to use his electric shaver himself. I prepare his lunch, either a sandwich or soup, which I leave in a vacuum flask to keep hot. I speak to his neighbour every day to make sure that he's taking in enough food and liquid, and she takes a frozen dinner and cooks it for him for 6 pm. Sometimes I do a bit of 'top-up' shopping and pay his bills, but mostly we plan his meals and the local supermarket delivers every week. I put the washing machine on for bedding and clothes and iron them when dry. On laundry days, I stay much longer. Mr P's daughter comes after work to help him get ready for bed and he watches TV until he is ready to sleep.

Most people don't realise how important it is for sick older people to be able to be cared for at home. Although I go to team meetings and review meetings, I never discuss Mr P's circumstances with anyone else, and I respect him and his wishes every day. I speak to the team manager if I'm worried about Mr P, but I tell him first. He seems content and keeps in good spirits but is always delighted to have visitors. I arrange for his sister to visit once a month, and he loves to chat about football with Andy his neighbour's teenage son, who pops in on Sundays.

Focusing your skills

Two of the main skills I've developed are communication and research. I've developed confidence in my ability to converse easily in a mature way with both service users and carers. I acquired these skills by being fully prepared, by gaining knowledge and understanding through researching the physiological disorders that I chose to study and by practising my interactions in the classroom. It was important to me to read and absorb the professional responsibilities and to maintain confidentiality throughout my collection of information. I made full use of my time with the people I met and wrote up a diary of the issues discussed, straight away, to record important issues.

Getting ready for assessment

Marcus is working towards a BTEC National in Health and Social Care. Part of his assignment is constructing a treatment plan for a service user with a physiological disorder. He has chosen to work with his brother Jon, who has chronic renal failure, and has Jon's permission to study his experiences.

How I got started

I started by reading about the structure and functions of the renal system, with particular attention on the kidneys. I made a list of questions to ask Jon about his history and how he first noticed something was wrong. I followed his journey through the investigations he had, to the diagnosis. As his condition worsened, Jon had surgery to create a fistula (a special connection between blood vessels so that dialysis connections can be made easily and safely) in his arm, ready for renal dialysis later. Jon is now dialysing at a local hospital. He allowed me to accompany him on several visits when he saw the consultant or the registrar, and I have been to the dialysis unit with him twice. The staff were very helpful when I asked questions.

How I brought the information together

To begin with, I told the 'story' of Jon's illness, including the cause, signs, symptoms and effects. I researched the investigative and diagnostic tests that a service user with chronic renal failure would have. I considered the treatment and support from various carers and the care settings that they worked in. I found the next bit difficult – constructing a treatment plan for Jon. This included all his medication and dialysis, special renal diet, hospital visits and admission to be put on the transplant waiting list. Jon gets support from his medical team, other dialysis service users, family and friends and the local branch of the renal network. I made a table to show the treatment planned for him for 10 weeks, with appointments for dialysis and consultant visits as well as the medication routine. I added a support network pattern diagram, typical of one particular busy week, and a food plan for the same week. It is more difficult to go on holiday now as he can only go where there are approved dialysis

units, because of waiting for a transplant. I had no idea so much was involved and my love and admiration for my brother has increased now I understand what he goes through. He can no longer go out to work and is trying to build a small home business using his IT skills, by building websites for small businesses.

What I learned from the experience

I learned a lot about kidney function and how a biopsy can help pathologists make a diagnosis. I learned that people have to be correctly prepared for long-term dialysis and that service users, even young adults like my brother, need a lot of support. I now appreciate the need for good communication between medical teams and how good organisation is important because spaces for dialysis are hard to get. I realise that living as healthily as possible is important as it affects how you feel, and that ignoring dietary advice is not very clever. A transplant could come tomorrow or you could be waiting ten years for one, so take advice and look after your body.

Think about it

- Have you written a plan with timings so that you can complete your assignment by the agreed submission date?
- Do you have notes on all your observations and interactions?
- Is your information written in your own words and referenced clearly to show where you have used quotations or information from a book, journal or website?
- Have you reread the requirements of the assignment and ensured that you have included each one?
- Have you made sure that the command words, such as evaluate, justify and compare, have been addressed if you are working towards a higher grade?
- Have you read your work through before handing it in to meet the deadline?

Glossary

Abbreviation: a shortened form of a word or phrase such as Mon for Monday.

Absorption: taking up the substances to be used by the body cells and tissues.

Abstract logical thinking: the ability to solve problems using imagination without having to be involved practically. This is an advanced form of thinking that does not always need a practical context in order to take place.

Abuse: an action deliberately intended to cause harm or distress.

Accommodation: modifying schemes (concepts) in relation to new information and experiences.

Accountable: has to justify actions.

Acronym: a word made from using initial letters of other words or phrases such as AIDS (acquired immunodeficiency syndrome) or FAST (face, arms, speech, time).

Act of omission: failing to provide something which is needed, such as medication or respect.

Adenosine diphosphate (ADP): a chemical left after ATP has released its stored energy to do work.

Adenosine triphosphate (ATP): a chemical in mitochondria capable of trapping and storing energy to supply the cell when needed.

Adolescence: an important status change following the onset of puberty during which a young person develops from a child into an adult.

Advisory board: a group of people who meet and give advice.

Advocate: a person who speaks for someone else and represents their views and preferences.

Aggression: any action that has the express purpose of harming another individual, an animal or an object. This can include verbal or physical harm or damage to an object.

Agonist/prime mover: the main contracting muscle in a movement.

Allele: half a gene, or the location of a characteristic on one chromosome.

Anabolism: the building up of complex muscles using the energy released in catabolism.

Analyst: someone who studies data to learn something from it, such as a trend or a pattern.

Anonymised: made so that an individual cannot be identified.

Antagonist: the muscle opposite to the agonist, it relaxes to allow the agonist to move the bone.

Antagonistic muscles: one muscle, or a sheet of muscles, contracts while the opposing muscle or sheet relaxes. For example, when the biceps contract the triceps relax.

Antenatal care: care provided for a mother and her baby before the birth of the baby.

Antibody: large protein that recognises antigens and helps remove them. Different antibodies recognise specific antigens.

Anti-discriminatory practice: care practice that ensures that individual and different needs of clients and patients are met regardless of their race, ethnicity, age, disability, sex or sexual orientation and that prejudice and unfair discrimination are challenged.

Antigen: protein found on the surface of microorganisms, specific to that organism.

Arterial blood: flows from the heart and is usually bright red oxygenated blood.

Assistive technology: any tool or strategy used to help people with disabilities complete their studies successfully and reach their potential.

Attachment: the term that describes the strong emotional connection/relationship a child experiences with their significant adult.

Atheroma: weakening of the blood vessel by the deposits of fatty plaques usually leading to thrombosis.

Attitude: assumptions that we use to make sense of our social experience; fixed beliefs or ways of looking at issues.

Autonomic nervous system: part of the nervous system responsible for controlling the internal organs; a division of the nervous system consisting of the sympathetic and parasympathetic branches. Many of its functions occur without conscious awareness.

Autonomy: the freedom to take independent decisions without having to ask anyone else or receive permission.

Aversion therapy: a type of therapy in which the individual learns to associate something desirable with something undesirable. For example, when the drug disulfiram (Antabuse) is taken to treat alcoholism, any intake of alcohol makes the individual feel violently sick and ill.

Behaviour modification: this is a method of changing behaviour that involves reinforcing desired behaviour and ignoring or punishing undesired behaviour.

Beliefs: strongly held opinions stored in the subconscious mind.

Birth rate: the number of births per thousand of the population over a given time period, normally a year.

Biomedical model of health: the identification of health as the 'absence of disease' with a focus on diagnosing and curing individuals with specific illnesses and other medical conditions.

Blood glucose: the volume of a simple sugar dissolved in the liquid part of the blood known as the plasma. It supplies body cells with energy.

Bourgeoisie: the powerful social class who own the factories, land and other capital and are able to organise the economy and other important social institutions to their own advantage.

Braille: system of writing and printing for blind or visually impaired people in which raised dots are used to represent the letters of the alphabet, numbers and punctuation marks.

Capitalist: another word for a member of the bourgeoisie.

Cardiac output: the quantity of blood expelled from the heart in one minute usually expressed in millilitres (ml) per minute.

Cardiovascular problems: any disorder or disease of the heart or blood vessels.

Care package: the sum of the type of care provided from the care plan, involving professional carers, organisations, volunteers and informal carers.

Carer's assessment: assessment of the needs of informal carers providing support for a vulnerable person, such as a person with a physical disability, a person with a mental health need or a frail older person.

Cartilage: the soft tissue that protects the surfaces of the bone.

Catabolism: the breaking down of molecules into smaller units, releasing energy.

Catharsis: a sense of release of emotional tension that occurs when something from the unconscious mind has been resolved.

Cell: the basic unit of living material.

Census: a compulsory, official and detailed count of the population of the UK, held every 10 years. It includes demographic information about households.

Centile lines (percentiles): lines on a graph used to show average measurements of height, weight and head circumference. The lines represent the values of the measurements taking into account age and sex.

Central nervous system: the brain and the spinal cord.

Centrioles: organelles that play an important part in spindle formation during cell division.

Children's centre: a place providing services for young children and their families.

Chromatin network: the dark tangled mass seen in the nucleus of a resting cell.

Chromosomes: long threads of DNA and protein seen in a dividing cell, which contain the genetic material, or genes, responsible for transmitting inherited characteristics.

Chronic (medical) condition: a long-term or recurrent condition or disorder, such as osteoarthritis , arthritis, asthma or diabetes.

Circadian rhythms: bodily functions that follow a 24 to 25-hour clock, which includes the secretion of hormones and also affects the alertness and sleep-wake cycle.

Civil rights: the right to political and social freedom and equality.

Clarification: making something clear and understandable.

Clinical Commissioning Groups (CCGs): groups of general practices (in England) working together to ensure best delivery of local health services: for example, buying health and care services such as hospital care.

Clinical diagnosis: a diagnosis made on the basis of signs and symptoms.

Clinical waste: waste contaminated by blood, urine, saliva or other body fluids which could be infectious.

Clinician: a health care practitioner who has direct contact with service users.

Code of practice: standards of behaviour and professional practice required of health and care practitioners set and monitored by professional bodies such as the GMC, NMC or the HCPC.

Coercive behaviour: manipulation of one person by another, usually through threats.

Cognitive behavioural therapy (CBT): a method used to help people with psychological problems. It involves identifying and challenging negative thoughts. The behavioural aspect involves trying out new behaviours to see whether the outcome can lead to new more positive thoughts.

Cognitive dissonance: a theory that states that we feel uncomfortable if our attitudes and behaviour are not in line with one another.

Cognitive impairment: condition, ranging from mild to more severe, in which an individual has trouble remembering, learning new skills, concentrating or making decisions that affect their everyday life.

Collagen: structural protein in the form of the fibres for extra strength.

Coma: a state of unconsciousness.

Commissioner: someone who contracts a service provider to provide a service.

Commissioning: deciding what services are needed and making sure that they are provided.

Community care assessment: professional assessment of the care needs provided by a local authority adult social services department, which also provides help and advice in accessing services to best meet the service user's need.

Complementary medicine: an approach to improving health and wellbeing not usually prescribed by the medical profession. Complementary medicine is sometimes used as an alternative to, and sometimes alongside, standard treatments as prescribed by the medical profession.

Complementary therapies: a wide range of treatments designed to treat the whole person rather than the symptoms of their disease. For example, acupuncture, aromatherapy and reflexology.

Concordance rate: a statistical expression for the concordance (present in both) of a given genetic trait in pairs of twins.

Concrete logical thinking: the ability to solve problems providing an individual can see or physically handle the issues involved.

Conditioned response: a response produced through learning in specific conditions.

Conditioned stimulus: something that would not produce a response in normal situations. This is called a neutral stimulus.

Confederate: an individual who is secretly working on behalf of the experimenter, but appears to be a genuine participant.

Conflict model: a sociological approach, first associated with Karl Marx, which sees the institutions of society as being organised to meet the interests of the ruling classes.

Conflict of interest: a situation where the concerns or aims of two or more different parties are incompatible.

Congenital: present at birth.

Conservation: the ability to reason logically that a certain quantity will remain the same despite change in its shape or appearance. For example, recognising that as clay is rolled in a sausage shape, it may become longer, but the amount of clay doesn't become larger.

Constrained: restricted, limited or forced to follow a particular course of action.

Constructive criticism: comments made in a qualified manner to change behaviour and develop professional practice.

Consultant: a senior doctor, normally based at a hospital, who provides specialist expert healthcare support in their area of expertise.

Continuity: a view of development that sees growth and development occurring slowly and continuously, for example growth in height.

Controlling behaviour: domination and manipulation of one individual by another.

Conventional medical treatment: also called orthodox treatment. A system of treating an individual's diseases and symptoms by using drugs, radiation or surgery administered by medical doctors and other healthcare professionals (such as nurses, pharmacists and therapists).

Cristae: folds of the inner layer of mitochondrial membrane on which the enzymes responsible for the oxidation of glucose are situated.

Culture: the beliefs, language, styles of dress, ways of cooking, religion, ways of behaving, rituals, customs and rules shared by a particular group of people, or a particular society or social group and is seen as normal.

Cytoplasm: 'cell material', refers to anything inside the cell boundary and outside the nucleus.

DBS check: Disclosure and Barring Service check, carried out on anyone working with or adopting children and anyone working in other areas such as health care, to make sure the individual does not have a criminal record.

Death rate: the number of deaths per thousand of the population over a given period, normally a year.

Defraud: to trick or deceive someone into giving you money.

Dehydration: insufficient water in the body systems. Water is an essential component of chemical reactions so untreated dehydration can be life-threatening.

Demography: term used to describe the study of changes in the size and structure of the population.

Denature: permanent change in the active site (where molecules bind and reaction occurs) of an enzyme. Enzyme functioning is effected by pH and temperature.

Deoxyribonucleic acid (DNA): nucleic acid found only in the chromatin network and chromosomes of the nucleus, which is responsible for the control of the cell, and passing on of inherited characteristics.

Depression: a mental disorder in which the individual is unable to cope with daily life and experiences feelings of worthlessness.

Deprivation: being deprived of a caregiver to whom an attachment already exists.

Development: complex changes including an increase in skills, abilities and capabilities.

Development norms: a description of an average set of expectations with respect to a young child's development. For example, by the age of 12 months a child has the ability to stand alone.

Deviant: an individual who does not conform to the norms of a society or social group.

Diagnosis: the process by which the nature of the disease or disorder is determined or made known.

Diastole: time in heartbeat when the cardiac muscle relaxes.

Diathesis: a predisposition or vulnerability to mental disorder through abnormality of the brain or neuro-transmitters.

Differential diagnosis: recognition of one disease as being distinct from a number of diseases that may present similar signs or symptoms.

Diffusion: the passage of molecules from a high concentration to a low concentration.

Digestion: conversion of food into simple, soluble chemicals capable of being absorbed through the intestinal lining into the blood to be used by body cells.

Diploid: cell that has paired chromosomes, one from each parent.

Disability: restrictions that arise for a person with an impairment because of attitudes and lack of appropriate services and facilities to meet their needs.

Disabling environment: a social context in which adaptations and other necessary facilities are not in place to ensure that people with impairments can take a full part in social life.

Discontinuity: this characterisation of development sees the differences between stages as qualitative rather than quantitative. Stages theories, such as those proposed by Freud, Piaget and Erikson, are example of discontinuity.

Discrimination: treating individuals or a social group in a different way to other individuals or groups, eg treating members of a particular racial group less favourably than other people.

Disempower: make a person or a group less confident or less likely to succeed.

Disequilibrium: a state of cognitive imbalance between experience and what is understood.

Displacement: a concept from psychodynamic theory that, if an individual is unable to express their frustration and annoyance directly at the source, they will take it out on someone of a lower status instead.

Diversity: a variety or range of things.

Domiciliary care: care provided in the service user's own home. This may include district nurses, home care workers and health visitors.

Dominant: the allele that, when present, displays in the individual.

Dysfunctional family: a family that is not providing all of the support and benefits associated with being in a family.

Ecological validity: refers to whether findings obtained in a laboratory setting could be repeated in the real world.

Egestion: process involved in eliminating waste material from the body as faeces.

Ego: the part of the mind that develops at around the age of two. Its function is to moderate the demands of the id and prevent the superego being too harsh. It operates on the reality principle.

Egocentric: centred on oneself, selfish.

Egocentric thinking: not being able to see a situation from another person's point of view. Piaget thought that a young child assumed that other people see, hear and feel exactly the same as the child does.

Electron microscope: a very powerful type of microscope, needed to see inside cells.

Eligible: having the right to obtain or do something.

Emigration: movement of people from their home country to make a permanent home in a different country.

Emotional literacy: the ability to recognise, understand and appropriately express emotions. Emotional literacy is essential for forming positive social relationships.

Emotional vulnerability: a feeling of nervousness and uneasiness that may be caused by an individual thinking that they are in some way inferior to or not as worthy as other people.

Empathy: the ability to identify with, recognise and understand another's situation or feelings, 'walking a mile in someone else's shoes'.

Empowerment: supporting people to take control of their lives and futures by taking a full part in discussions and decisions about their care and treatment; actions taken or attitudes towards another individual enabling them to pursue their goals.

Emulsification: occurs when an emulsifier causes oil or lipids to be suspended as a large number of tiny globules in water.

Enabler: someone who delivers person-centred care in a domiciliary (home) setting which encourages independence.

Endocrine system: a collection of glands that produce hormones that produce hormones that regulate body functions such as metabolism.

Enhance: to improve.

Enzyme: biological catalyst that alters the rates of a chemical reaction (usually speeding them up) but which it itself unchanged at the end of the reaction.

Ethical: dealing with right and wrong behaviour.

Ethics committee: a group of individuals, who may or may not be professionals, that decide whether a research proposal, a procedure or a treatment meets strict guidelines.

Equilibrium: a state of cognitive balance when a child's experience is in line with what they understood.

Euphoria: a feeling of extreme happiness and excitement that can be justified by events or, in some mental health conditions, may be unrelated to events.

Extended family: normally at least three generations who form a close-knit kinship group, and provide support and care for their members.

Extenuating circumstances: conditions beyond your control which delay normal action or reaction time.

False consciousness: lack of awareness by the proletariat that they are supporting the views and beliefs of their class enemy, the bourgeoisie. For example, by working hard, they are serving the interests of the capitalist class much more than their own.

Feminism: the belief that women should have the same rights and opportunities in society as men.

Fight or flight response: a sequence of physiological responses triggered by the perception of danger. These responses prepare the body for either running away from danger (flight) or for defending or attacking the threat (fight).

Fine motor skills: involve smaller movements that require more precise direction (dexterity) and use smaller muscles, for example picking up a pencil.

Fixator: a muscle that holds surrounding bones and joints steady to form a stable base for a movement.

Free association: involves the patient saying whatever comes into their head, without any internal censoring, and the analyst interpreting what is being said to try and make sense of symptoms.

Frustration-aggression hypothesis: the idea that when people are frustrated in having their needs met, this leads to aggressive behaviour.

Functionalism: sees the institutions in a society as working in harmony with each other, making specific and clear contributions to the smooth running of that society.

Galvanic skin response: measurement of increased sweating, which reflects activity in the sympathetic nervous system. It is based on the sweat response to stimuli.

Gamete: reproductive or sex cells, each cell is haploid and carries only one copy of each chromosome.

Gender: refers to the social or cultural expectations of men and women in society as contrasted with the biological, sexual or physical differences between men and women.

Gene: unit of heredity on a pair of chromosomes

General Practitioner: a doctor who does not specialise in a specific branch of medicine but provides ongoing treatment and preventative care in the community for a variety of medical problems that may be experienced by individuals of all ages.

Genetic condition: a condition present at birth, passed on by a defective gene or abnormal chromosome.

Genetic inheritance: qualities transmitted from parents to their offspring through genes. For example, whether their child will be male or female, have blue eyes or brown eyes and whether they will be tall or short.

Genetic predisposition: inherited genes that determine physical growth, development, health and appearance.

Genotype: an individual's genes, which are not outwardly observable, or the identification of alleles an individual inherits for a gene.

Gluten: a protein found in wheat and some other grains. When people with coeliac disease eat gluten they experience an immune response that attacks their small intestine causing symptoms such as abdominal bloating, pain and diarrhoea.

Glycogen: stored form of glucose found in the liver and muscles.

Govern: exercise a controlling influence.

Gross motor skills: large movements that involve using the large muscles of the body which are required for mobility, for example rolling over.

Group values: a common system of beliefs and values shared by all members of a group.

Growth: an increase in some measured quantity such as height or weight.

Halal: an Arabic term meaning 'permissible or allowed'. Used in the context of preparing food according to Islamic law set down in the Quran, for example how animals are killed and meat prepared for consumption.

Haploid: cell with half the usual number of chromosomes, such as a sperm or an ovum.

Hazards: a potential source of harm or adverse health effect on a person or persons, such as climbing stairs, wet floor services, trailing electricity cables, the disposal of waste or bathing a service user.

Hazardous waste: waste containing substances that can cause serious harm to people or equipment including soiled dressings and items contaminated with bodily fluids, explosives, flammable materials and substances that poison or destroy human tissue.

Health screening: the process of checking for the presence of disease in individuals who have no signs or symptoms of the illness. For example screening for the presence of cervical cancer for women or testicular cancer for men before they have any symptom of the disease.

Healthy life expectancy: a statistical measure of the average number of years a person can live in 'full health', unhindered by disease or injury.

Heart rate: the number of heartbeats in one minute.

Heterozygous: having one dominant and one recessive allele.

Hierarchy of needs: a list, in a given order, of an individual's key physiological, psychological, social and intellectual developmental needs. An individual's development progresses through this hierarchy from the bottom to the top as each need is met, with the ultimate need (goal) being self-actualisation.

Holistic approach: an approach to care that address the individual's physical, social, emotional and spiritual health, so addressing the needs of the whole person.

Homeostasis: the process of maintaining a constant internal environment despite changing circumstances. For example, the pH, temperature, concentrations of certain chemicals and the water content in the fluid surrounding body cells (the internal environment) must be kept within a narrow range, even when you are consuming acids (vinegar or lemon juice), are in freezing climate or are doing vigorous exercise.

Homozygous: having two dominant or recessive alleles.

Hormones: chemical substances produced in the body and transported in the blood stream that control or regulate body organs. For example, the sex hormones produced by the ovaries and testes are responsible for the development of secondary sexual characteristics in puberty.

Human rights: the principles of human behaviour expected of everyone regardless of nationality, place of residence, sex, national or ethnic origin, colour or religion.

Hyperthermia: a body temperature above the normal range similar to fever. The heat losing processes are unable to work properly.

Hypothalamus: an important part of the brain lying in the centre of the base of the brain just above the pituitary gland. It controls heart rate, body temperature and breathing rate by the autonomic nerves.

Hypothermia: a body temperature lower than the normal range (below 35 ^{0}C (normal body temperature is 37 ^{0}C)) when heat-conserving processes are unable to cope. Tends to occur in older people and infants as their nervous systems are weak.

id: the part of the psyche we are born with. It operates on the pleasure principle.

Idiographic: this approach to development involves the study of all the unique characteristics of one particular individual.

Imbuing: filling up with, or becoming soaked in, an emotion.

Immigration: arrival in a country of people from their home country who wish to make the new country their permanent home.

Immunity: having adequate body defences to fight infection and disease.

Impairment: physical or mental loss of function, whether permanent or temporary, such as the loss of a limb, loss of hearing or a learning difficulty, such as Down's syndrome, that restricts an individual's ability to perform daily activities independently.

Incidence: the number of new cases, for example of an illness or disability, in a particular population over a given period of time.

Independence: the ability to take actions by ourselves in the pursuit of our own goals.

Independent sector: private sector and not-for-profit organisations together are often referred to as the independent sector because they are not directly managed by the government.

Individualised care: care provision tailored to meet the particular and specific needs of each service user.

Infantile autism: a severe disorder appearing in children under two and a half years of age, which includes abnormal behaviour, not communicating with others and developing unusual attachments to objects.

Infant mortality rate (IMR): the number of deaths of babies under the age of one year per thousand live births over a given time period, usually a year.

Informal care: care and support provided by relatives and friends, normally unpaid and in addition to the care provided by professional health and care providers.

Informed consent: voluntary permission by an individual, once they know all the facts and consequences, to participate in research or to receive medical/surgical treatment. This will usually be in writing and formally documented.

Infringe: to limit, violate or intrude on something.

Ingestion: taking in food, drink and drugs by the mouth.

Insecure attachment: applies to infants whose caregivers are insensitive or inconsistent in the care they provide. These children are said to be anxiously attached.

Interpersonal: between people present in the same place, face-to-face.

Interactionism: a sociological approach that focuses on the influence of small groups on our behaviour rather than the impact of large institutions.

Interactionists: believe that our behaviour is driven by the way we interpret relationships in smaller groups and settings, such as a hospital ward. They suggest that our behaviour is influenced by how we see ourselves in relation to other people in a group and how they see us.

Inverse care law: a situation in which those most in need of health care are the least likely to get it.

Islets of Langerhans: small groups of special hormone-secreting cells scattered throughout the pancreas.

Kosher: means suitable. Used in the context of food preparation and consumption according to Jewish dietary laws. Covers permitted and forbidden foods, for example not cooking or eating milk and meat products together.

Labelling: applying the stereotypical view of a particular group and ignoring individual differences.

Legal guidance: policies or procedures that support the implementation and practice of laws or regulations.

Legal obligation: a legal duty to perform or not perform a particular action.

Legal rights: the rules set by a legal system about what a person is entitled to, such as the protection of property or person.

Life expectancy: a statistical measure of how long a person is expected to live; an estimate of the number of years, on average that a person can expect to live. Sometimes called longevity.

Lifestyle: how a person spends their time and money, a 'style' of living.

Literacy skills: the ability to read and write.

Lone worker's policy: guidance and procedures aimed at ensuring that people working on their own are safe. This is particularly important when providing domiciliary care. Lone workers' policies are in place principally to protect the carer from harm but will also provide additional protection for service users.

Long-term condition: conditions that cannot currently be cured but which can be managed.

Macrophage: large white blood cell that engulfs and destroys invading microorganisms, such as bacteria in the process of phagocytosis.

Maladaptive behaviour: refers to behaviour that is unhelpful to the individual, getting them into unpleasant situations. For example, being naughty may result in punishment, drinking too much to soothe anxiety can result in financial hardship and even loss of employment or damage to relationships.

Malestream sociology: the view that, because sociology has largely been written by men, and from their point of view, there has been insufficient attention paid to the position of women in society.

Marginalisation: when a group of people are discriminated against and prevented from enjoying equal rights or accessing services in society.

Maturation: a genetically programmed sequence of change, for example the onset of the menopause.

Maturational processes: a series of developmental changes that occur over time as the organism matures and develops.

Meals on wheels: service provided in England and Wales to supply mainly frozen meals to the service user's home. The meals can be heated as and when the service user requires.

Median: the middle value in the list of numbers written in numerical order. For example, 5 is the median of 2, 3, 3, 5, 9, 9, 11.

Medicalisation: describes the increased power and influence of the medical profession, extending their role in society.

Meiosis: special kind of cell division that only happens in the ovaries and testes in which the genetic material is duplicated and then divided into four daughter cells, each containing just half of the genetic material.

Menopause: stage in life, usually between 45 and 55, when a woman's menstrual cycle gradually stops and she is no longer able to become pregnant naturally; the ending of female fertility, including the cessation of menstruation and reduction in production of female sex hormones.

Metabolism: the sum of all the chemical reactions occurring in the human physiology that involves using or releasing energy from chemical substances.

Milestone: an ability achieved by most children by a certain age. It can involve physical, social, emotional, cognitive and communication skills, for example walking, sharing with others, expressing emotions, recognising familiar sounds and talking.

Mitochondria: spherical or rod-shaped bodies scattered in the cytoplasm, concerned with energy release.

Mitosis: process in which body cells divide into two daughter cells, each identical to the original and containing all the genetic material.

Morals: views, beliefs and principles of what is right and wrong.

Morbidity: the levels of ill-health in a particular area, in this case the GP practice area.

Morbidity rates: rates of illness or disease in a particular population.

Mortality: the death rate in a particular area.

Motor neuron: nerve cell carrying information from the CNS associated with muscles or glands known as effectors.

Multicultural: many cultures or ethnic groups living in the one area.

Multiculturalism: acceptance and celebration of the different cultural and religious practices in our society.

Multi-cultural society: a population made up of people from a variety of different ethnic backgrounds and cultural traditions.

Multi-disciplinary team: a team in which health and care workers from different professional backgrounds and with different work roles, plan, implement and monitor an individual's care.

Myelin: an insulating sheath around many nerve fibres formed of proteins and phospholipids which increases the speed of nerve conduction.

National eligibility criteria: criteria applied to decide whether a service user is entitled to support from the local authority social services department; a minimum threshold of needs for adult care and support.

Nature: genetic inheritance and other biological factors; all aspects of a person that are inherited or coded for in their genes.

Negative automatic thoughts: thoughts that appear unconsciously, and which an individual only notices if they pay attention to them. These thoughts tend to be an unfavourably framed interpretation of an individual's experiences, and will usually have an adverse impact on their mood and feelings.

Negative reinforcement: the behaviour is not repeated to avoid an adverse experience such as lack of satisfaction or to avoid being told off; occurs when a particular behaviour removes something that is unpleasant.

Neglect: failure to provide proper care.

Nerve: bundles of nerve fibres travelling together and wrapped in connective tissue.

Nerve impulse: wave of electrical discharge passing along a nerve fibre.

Net migration: the difference between the number of immigrants and the number of emigrants in a country over a given time period, normally a year.

Neural tube defects: congenital defects of the brain, spine or spinal cord, such as spina bifida.

Neurotransmitter: chemical substance, such as acetylcholine, which when secreted into the synapse allows the impulse to move across to the next neuron.

NHS Foundation Trusts: health services, largely financed by government that manage the delivery of hospital services, many mental health services and community health services in England.

Node of Ranvier: tiny space between two Schwann cells that allows the nerve impulse to jump to the next node.

Nomothetic: this approach is concerned with investigating a group of individual to see what traits and behaviours they have in common.

Norms: rules or guidelines that govern how we behave in society or in groups within society.

Not-for-profit sector: organisations, such as charities, that are non-profit making care providers, any surplus income is used to improve their provision eg NSPCC.

Nuclear family: normally two generations, consisting of adult carers (who may be the birth parents) and their children.

Nucleus: the central part of the cell which is enclosed in a membrane and is usually darker than the rest of the cell because it contains genetic material.

Nurse practitioner: provides expert consultancy service to patients and their carers. They contribute to the management and development of the care provision. They also undertake research and contribute to the education and training of other members of staff.

Nurture: the influence of external factors after conception such as social and environmental factors; influences from the environment that shape behaviour and development.

Observational learning: a type of learning in which an individual observes someone behave in a particular way and then later imitates that behaviour.

Optometrist: a primary healthcare specialist who examines a person's eyes for signs of defects in vision, injury, ocular diseases and abnormalities. They may also detect problems with general health, such as diabetes or high blood pressure. Where necessary, they issue a prescription for spectacles or contact lenses.

Organ: a collection of tissues joined together to carry out a specific function.

Organelle: a tiny body inside a cell which carries out its own functions.

Orthodox medical practice: a scientific approach to the diagnosis, treatment and prevention of illnesses and disease as practised by the medical profession and other healthcare professionals.

Osmosis: the passage of water molecules from a high concentration (of water molecules) to one of low concentration through a partially permeable membrane, such as a cell membrane of simple epithelial cells.

Pain threshold: describes the point at which an individual feels that unpleasant physical feeling, or pain, is no longer bearable.

Palliative care: specialist care for people with serious illnesses which aims to provide relief from symptoms and to reduce stress for patients and their families.

Pancreas: the leaf-shaped gland beneath the stomach on the left side of the abdomen. It produces digestive juices containing enzymes, which pass down a duct system into the small intestine, and hormones, insulin and glucagon, which pass directly into the blood stream.

Parasympathetic nervous system: the most active part of the autonomic nervous system, which conserves energy by slowing the heart rate, increasing intestinal and gland activity, relaxing sphincter muscles in the gastrointestinal tract.

Parenting styles: a definition of the different strategies/ways that parents use to bring up their children.

Patriarchal society: led and dominated by men.

Peak flow expiration: an individual's maximum expiration speed, which is measured using a peak flow meter.

Perinatal mortality rate: the number of deaths of babies during the first week of life per thousand live births over a given time period, normally a year.

Peristalsis: muscular contraction of the circular and longitudinal muscle in the gut wall which pushes food along the alimentary canal.

Personal attributes: the qualities or characteristics that make an individual who they are: ie their personality.

Personal budget/direct payment: a cash payment made directly to the service user so that they may pay for identified and necessary care services to be provided.

Phenotype: the outward display of a characteristic that is observable.

Philosopher: someone who studies or writes about the meaning of life.

Photomicrograph: a photograph taken of an object magnified using a microscope.

Placebo: chemically inactive substance used in a clinical trial that resembles and is taken in the same way as an active drug but has no effect in the body.

Placenta: a disc like structure attached to the uterine wall and linked to the foetus by the umbilical cord.

Policies: detailed descriptions of the approach, and often the specific procedures that should be followed, in caring for clients.

Policymaker: someone who makes the plans carried out by a government or a business.

Pollutant: a substance that contaminates something such as air or water and may make it unsafe.

Positive reinforcement: the behaviour is repeated because of personal satisfaction (intrinsic reinforcement) or rewards (extrinsic reinforcement); occurs when a particular behaviour is followed by a consequence that is seen as desirable (eg receiving a food pellet).

Post modernism: a view that society is characterised by rapid change, that there is no longer value consensus and that there is fragmentation into many different groups, interests and lifestyles.

Postnatal care: care provided for a mother and her baby after the birth of the baby.

Power of attorney: the legal authority granted to an individual to make decisions on behalf of someone else.

Predictable events: events that are expected to happen at a particular time. While expected they may have a positive or negative effect on a person's health and wellbeing.

Prejudice: an unreasonable feeling against a person or a group of people; preconceived opinions or fixed attitudes about a social group that are not based on reason or evidence. Prejudicial attitudes may lead to active discrimination.

Pressure groups: people who come together to campaign to improve the services offered to their members. They aim to influence public opinion and government decisions.

Prevalence: the total number of cases, for example of an illness or disability, in a particular population over a given period of time.

Preventative care: care and education that aims to ensure people remain healthy, and are aware of the factors that can lead to illness and poor health. It includes screening and vaccination programmes.

Primary health care: care provided by doctors, dentists and opticians for example.

Primary socialisation: the process of a child learning the norms, attitudes and values of the culture and society in which they are growing up; early socialisation that normally takes place within the family.

Private sector: organisations run as commercial, profit making businesses.

Privation: being deprived of an opportunity to form an attachment.

Procedures: written instructions that outline the expected and required routines that care staff must follow in specific situations, for example reporting accidents or administering medicines, in order to implement agreed policies.

Proletariat: the 'working class', they have only their labour to sell. They work for, and are exploited by, the bourgeoisie.

Protocols: procedures following specific guidelines.

Protoplasm: means 'first material', refers to anything inside the cell boundary.

Psyche: the structure of the mind consisting of three dynamic parts: the id, the ego and the superego.

Psychological trauma: a feeling of helplessness and vulnerability following very stressful events.

Psychologist: someone who studies people; how they think, how they act, react and interact.

Psychotherapy: type of therapy used to treat emotional and mental health conditions, usually by talking to a trained therapist one-to-one or in a group.

Puberty: a period of rapid growth during which young people reach sexual maturity and become biologically able to reproduce and secondary sexual characteristics develop.

Public health: organised strategies to prevent disease, promote health and prolong life in a population.

Pulmonary circulation: blood circulation to and from the lungs.

Punnett square: a diagram named after the British geneticist Reginald C. Punnett, used to determine the probability of an offspring having a particular genotype.

Quickening: when a pregnant woman first feels the foetus move.

Recessive: an allele that does not show when a dominant allele is present.

Referral: consulting on, and usually handing over care or treatment of a service user to another professional (usually a specialist) or a type of service, such as physiotherapy.

Registrants: a person who is registered.

Rehabilitation: the process of restoring a person to good health following surgery, an accident or other illness, including recovery from addiction.

Rehabilitative care: aims to restore good health or useful life through therapy and education.

Reinforcing: behaviour that leads to an outcome that is satisfying or desired for whatever reason.

Resilience: the ability to overcome setbacks and disappointments without giving up or being demoralised.

Respiratory disorders: conditions affecting the upper respiratory tract, trachea, bronchi, bronchioles, alveoli, pleura and pleural cavity.

Ribonucleic acid (RNA): nucleic acid found in both the cell and the nucleus, responsible for the manufacture of cell proteins such as pigments, enzymes and hormones.

Risk: the likelihood, high or low, that a person will be harmed by a hazard.

Risk assessment: identifying and evaluating the possible consequences of hazards and the level of risk that the hazard will cause harm.

Role: the part played by an individual according to a set of socially constructed beliefs about the behaviour expected of someone holding that role.

Safeguarding: policies to ensure children and vulnerable adults are protected from harm, abuse and neglect and that their health and wellbeing is promoted.

Safeguarding partners: members of the safeguarding boards such as representatives from the police, the NHS, the local council, appropriate charities and the probation service. The CQC or similar organisations may also be represented.

Schwann cell: manufactures myelin, wraps spirally around a nerve fibre.

Sclerosis: hardening of tissue.

Secondary health care: care which includes most hospital services, normally accessed via a GP or other professional.

Secondary socialisation: the process of learning appropriate behaviour in society. Influences include education, media, government and religion/culture; socialisation that takes place in social settings beyond the family such as nursery, in a friendship groups or in a wide range of other institutions.

Secure attachment: refers to the attachment bond between infant and its primary caregiver when the infant believes the caregiver to be available, sensitive and responsive.

Self-actualisation: having a moral and philosophical view on life. Developing your spiritual capacities. Using your creative abilities to the full. Being accepting of others without judging them.

Self-concept (sense of identity): an awareness formed in early childhood of being an individual, a unique person and different from everyone else.

Self-esteem: the confidence a person feels about themselves, self-worth or pride, sense of self respect and value; the value we give to ourselves based on how we have been treated by others in the past, and how we have performed in various areas of our lives.

Self-funding: a person paying all the costs of their care and support services.

Self-help groups: groups formed by people who share a common issue that they wish to address. The members provide advice, support and care for each other. For example, Alcoholics Anonymous is a self-help group for recovering alcoholics.

Self-image: the way an individual sees themselves, their mental image of themselves.

Sensitive personal data: information about a person's physical or mental health.

Sensory neuron: nerve cell associated with specialist receptors carrying information into the CNS.

Separation anxiety: the fear and apprehension that infants experience when separated from their primary caregiver.

Sick role: the view that illness is a social role and considers the sick where possible to have a duty to resume their active place in society as soon as they are able.

Sign: an objective indication of a disorder noticed by a healthcare professional such as a doctor or a nurse.

Skill: the ability to do something well or to be an expert in something.

Social class: describes a person's social and economic standing in society.

Social dynamics: the study of relationships within a group and how they influence our behaviour.

Social institution: a major building block of society which functions according to widely accepted customs, rules and regulations. The family, the education system, the legal system and social services are all social institutions.

Socialisation: the process of learning the usual ways of behaving in society.

Social mobility: the process of moving from one social stratum (level) to another. Social mobility can be upward or downward.

Social model: an approach that focuses on the social and environmental factors that influence our health and wellbeing, including the impact of poverty, poor housing, diet and pollution.

Social model of disability: focuses on the environmental factors that impact on the health and wellbeing of people with physical or mental impairment. For example, the impact of poverty, of poor or unadapted housing and social isolation.

Social role: expectations about the way an individual behaves that are linked to their position in society, for example being a child, a parent, a lawyer, a nurse or a politician.

Social stratification: a term (borrowed from geology) describing hierarches in society, where some groups have more status and prestige than other groups.

Social vulnerability: the lack of ability to deal with adverse events in life.

Sphincter muscle: circular muscle controlling an aperture (opening). When the muscle contracts the aperture closes and when it relaxes the aperture reopens.

Spina bifida: the condition in which some vertebrae (spinal bones) do not develop properly, sometimes leaving the spinal cord exposed and causing mobility impairment.

Stairlift: mechanical chair that acts a lift and is fitted to the wall of the staircase. The service user sits on the chair and activates the operating mechanism to move up or down a flight of stairs.

Stranger anxiety: when an infant becomes anxious and fearful around strangers.

Stroke volume: the quantity of blood expelled from the left ventricle in one minute, usually expressed in millilitres (ml).

Statutory: required by law and governed by legislation.

Statutory care: care provided as a legal requirement by the NHS, social care services, education and early years services.

Statutory sector: organisations funded and controlled by the government.

Stereotype: a fixed image or view of a social group that ignores individual differences, for example all unemployed people are lazy and do not want to work.

Structuralism: describing and understanding the main institutions in society, how they influence each other and how they mould individual behaviour.

Supported housing: shelter, support and care provided for vulnerable people to help them live as independently as possible in the community.

Supported living services: services that can help a person live in their own home on a long-term basis.

Surface tension: a thin elastic skin of a liquid that allows it to resist an external force, for example it is what causes some objects to float and why some insects can walk on water. Surface tension is caused when similar molecules stick together.

Susceptibility: an increased likelihood of acquiring a disease because of an individual's genetic makeup.

Sympathetic nervous system: part of the autonomic nervous system that acts in opposition to the parasympathetic nervous system, by speeding up the heart rate and causing blood vessels to contract, particularly in times of stress (fight or flight mechanism). It also regulates sweat glands.

Symptom: a feature complained about by the individual.

Synapse: small gap between one neuron and the next.

Synergist: a muscle that cooperates in a movement but is not the agonist, it also stabilises the movement. Synergist comes from synergy 'working together'.

Systemic circulation: blood circulation around the body.

Systematic desensitisation: a technique in which an individual is trained, over time, to substitute a fear response with a relaxed response. It is often used to 'unlearn' phobic behaviours.

Systole: time in heart beat when cardiac muscle contracts.

Target behaviour: this is the behaviour we want to change.

Tendinous cords: fibrous cords that attach the papillary muscle to the atrioventricular valves, preventing the backflow of blood during the cardiac cycle.

Tertiary health care: specialist and often complex care provided in highly specialised units and hospitals, for example spinal injury units.

The superego: roughly equivalent to a conscience, the superego consists of the internalisation of all the values of right and wrong we have been socialised to believe in. It contains an image of our ideal self.

Thrombosis: clotting in part of the circulatory system such as in the coronary arteries: coronary thrombosis.

Tissues: groups of cells joined together to carry out a particular task.

Transference relationship: refers to the way in which a patient in therapy transfers feelings, values and beliefs from an important person in their life (eg their father) onto the analyst, believing the analyst to be like this individual.

Trimester: a period of three months. In pregnancy the first trimester is to 12 weeks, the second from week 13 to 27 and the third trimester is from week 28 till birth.

Unambiguous: clear, no chance of being misunderstood.

Unconditional positive regard: a non-judgemental acceptance of a client, regardless of what the client thinks or feels, or how they behave.

Unconditioned response: an unlearned (natural) response to a given situation (stimulus).

Unconditioned stimulus: something that produces and automatic response without previous learning.

Unconscious: processes in the mind that occur automatically including thought processes, memory and motivation.

Unpredictable events: events that happen unexpectedly and which may have serious physical and psychological effects on the individual. These effects can be positive or negative.

Value based system: an approach to care based on standards of conduct such as confidentiality, anti-discrimination, equal opportunities, maintaining personal identity and health and safety.

Value consensus: general or common agreement about the values and beliefs of a society.

Values: principles and standards that we use to guide our thoughts, our behaviour, and decisions. Values help define our priorities and inform what we think is important in life and society.

Variable: something that changes or is not consistent. In a clinical trial this will include factors such as age, sex and ethnicity.

Vascular dementia: symptoms include problems with language, memory and thought processes caused by problems in the blood supply to the brain, for example through stroke.

Venous blood: flows towards the heart and is usually dark red deoxygenated blood.

Whistleblowing: a situation in which an employee reports poor or dangerous practice at their workplace to the press or to another organisation outside of their work setting, for example the GMC, NMC or the HCPC in order to bring about change for the better; the mechanism by which staff can voice their concerns about the conduct of other members of staff without fear or repercussion.

Zygote: cell produced when the sperm fertilises an ovum, it contains all the genetic material for a new individual – half from the sperm and half from the ovum.

Index